Treasures for Scholars Worldwide

北京大學圖書館　臺灣"中央研究院"近代史研究所胡適紀念館　編纂

胡適藏書目録

Bibliography of the Collection of Hu Shih

·4·

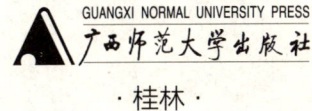
·桂林·

7227　The Histomap of Evolution/by John B. Sparks. —Chicago: Histomap, Inc., 1937

　　附注:

　　　其他:此爲地圖。

7228　The Histomap: Four Thousand Years of History on a Single Page/by John B. Sparks. —Chicago: Histomap, Inc., [n.d.]

　　附注:

　　　其他:此爲地圖。

7229　Histoire de la Religion Chrétienne au Japon Depuis 1458 jusqu'a 1651 Second Partie/par Léon Pagés. —Paris: Charles Douniol, Libraire-Éditeur, 1870

　　352p. ; 22.5cm

　　PKUL（館藏號缺）

　　附注:

　　　其他:本書裝訂破損,缺封底。

7230　Histoire et Doctrines Économiques de L'Angleterre/par W. J. Ashley, traduit par Savinien Bouyssy. —Paris: V. Giard & E. Brière, 1900

　　577p. ; 22.5cm

　　PKUL（館藏號缺）

　　附注:

　　　其他:本書裝訂已散。

7231　Histoire Sociale de l'Epoque Tcheou/par Lou Kan-Jou. —Paris: Librairie L. Rodstein, 1934

　　200p. ; 24cm

　　PKUL（館藏號缺）

　　附注:

題記：扉頁有作者題記："適之先生政，生侃如。"

其他：本書爲作者巴黎大學博士論文。

7232　The Historians' History of the World Volume XII/by Henry Smith Williams. —London：The Times, 1907

　　XIII, 681p. ; 26.9cm

　　PKUL（館藏號缺）

7233　Historical Essays/by Lord MaCaulay. —London & Glasgow：Collins' Clear-Type Press,［n. d.］

　　888p. ; 15.2cm

　　PKUL（館藏號缺）

　　附注：

　　　題記：扉頁有贈書者題記："With very best wish from Da-Tsung Yin, Oxford, June 1939. Nanking, August 1937。"

7234　Historical Evidence/by H. B. George. —Oxford：The Clarendon Press, 1909

　　223p. ; 18.4cm

　　PKUL（館藏號缺）

　　附注：

　　　內附文件：頁28、29間夾有宗錫鈞寫給胡適的借書便條1張。

7235　Historical Illustrations of the Social Effects of Christianity. —London, New York, Toronto, et al：Longmans, Green and Co., 1924

　　XII, 171p. ; 18.4cm

　　PKUL（館藏號缺）

7236　The Historical Nights' Entertainment/by Rafael Sabatini. —New York：Garden City Publishing Co., Inc., 1939

　　XII, 404p. ; 21.6cm

　　PKUL（館藏號缺）

7237 History and Analysis of the Commission and City‑Manager Plans of Municipal Government in the United States/by Tso‑Shuen Chang. —Iowa：[s.n.]，1918

290p. ；23.5cm

PKUL（館藏號缺）

7238 A History of American Political Theories/by C. Edward Merriam. —New York：The Macmillan Company，1903

XV，364p. ；18.5cm

PKUL（館藏號缺）

附注：

題記：扉頁有胡適鋼筆簽名"Suh Hu, October, 1916. New York City"。

7239 A History of Chinese Literature/by Herbert A. Giles. —New York：D. Appleton and Company，1901

VIII，448p. ；19cm

PKUL（館藏號缺）

附注：

題記：扉頁有胡適題記："英人解兒著《中國文學史》。"

批注圈劃：書內76頁有胡適批注圈劃。

夾紙：頁12、13，96、97，116、117，296、297，338、339間夾有書寫內容讀書卡片各1張。

7240 A History of Christian Missions in China/by Kenneth Scott Latourette. —New York：The Macmillan Company，1929

XII，930p. ；24.1cm

PKUL（館藏號缺）

附注：

題記：扉頁有胡適題記："基督教在中國傳教史。"

夾紙：頁366、367間夾有紙條1張。

其他：封內貼有"胡適的書"藏書票。

7241 History of Civilization in England/by Henry Thomas Buckle. ——New York：Hearst's International Library Co. ，1913

    2 Vols.（XXX，677，476p.）；20cm

    PKUL（館藏號缺）

    附注：

    題記：每冊扉頁均有胡適鋼筆簽名"Suh Hu，Oct. 1914"。

    其他：本書每卷分爲 Part I、Part II 2 冊，共 4 冊。

7242 History of Corea：Ancient and Modern/by John Ross. ——Paisley：J. and R. Parlane，［n. d.］

    XII，404p.；21.8cm

    PKUL（館藏號缺）

    附注：

    題記：扉頁内頁有贈書者贈 Robert Lilley 題記，内容不易辨識。

    其他：本書封面、書脊脱落。

7243 A History of Economic Thought/by Eric Roll. ——New York：Prentice-Hall，Inc. ，1942

    XII，585p.；22.9cm

    PKUL（館藏號缺）

    附注：

    題記：扉頁有陳鴻舜等人簽名題記："適之先生五十四壽辰，後學陳鴻舜，尤桐，傅安，朱士嘉，胡敦元，柯德思，王毓銓代表全家，吴光清，王重民，李辛之，丁聲樹，朱壽恒，劉修業，全漢昇，徐伯訏、韓壽萱、馮家昇等敬賀。"

7244 History of England：From the Accession of James II/by Thomas B. Macaulay. ——New York：The Kelmscott Society Publishers，［n. d.］

    4 Vols.；20.5cm

    The Complete Works of Thomas B. Macaulay

PKUL（館藏號缺）

附注：

其他：本書全本5卷，胡適藏書缺第4卷。

7245 History of English Literature/by H. A. Taine. —New York：John Wurtele Lovell，[n. d.]

722p. ；18.7cm

PKUL（館藏號缺）

附注：

題記：扉頁有胡適鋼筆簽名"Suh Hu, June, 1914"。

其他：封內貼有W. Lord Conwell藏書票。

7246 History of European Morals：From Augustus to Charlemagne/by William Edward Hartpole Lecky. —New York, London：D. Appleton and Company，1919

2 Vols. ；18.4cm

PKUL（館藏號缺）

附注：

印章：兩卷題名頁均鈐有"胡適藏書"朱文方印。

7247 A History of Greece/by George Grote. —London：J. M. Dent & Sons Ltd. ；New York：E. P, Dutton & Co. , 1907

12 Vols. ；17.1cm

Everyman's Library：History

PKUL（館藏號缺）

7248 A History of Greece, to the Death of Alexander the Great/by J. B. Bury. —London：Macmillan and Co. , Limited, 1913

XXV, 909p. ；18.8cm

PKUL（館藏號缺）

7249 The History of History Volume I /by James T. Shotwell. —New York：Columbia

University Press, 1939

XII, 407p. ; 22.9cm

PKUL（館藏號缺）

附註：

題記：扉頁有作者題記："To Dr. Hu Shih, friend and colleague, James T. Shotwell."

7250　The History of Japan: From the Earliest Period to the Present Time/by Francis Ottiwell Adams. —London: Henry S. King & Co., 1874

2 Vols.（XVI, 498, 349p.）; 22cm

PKUL（館藏號缺）

附註：

印章：兩卷扉頁均有原書主簽名"R. Lilley"。

其他：本書有破損。

7251　A History of Japanese Literature/by W. G. Aston. —London: William Heinemann, 1908

XI, 410p. ; 19.8cm

PKUL（館藏號缺）

附註：

題記：扉頁有胡適鋼筆簽名"Hu Shih, Tokyo April 29, 1927"。

7252　A History of Kanarese Literature/by Edward P. Rice. —Caltutta: Association Press; London: Oxford University Press, 1921

128p. ; 18.6cm

The Heritage of India Series

PKUL（館藏號缺）

7253　The History of Mr. Polly/by H. G. Wells. —New York: The Press of the Readers Club, 1941

VII, 342p. ; 21.9cm

PKUL（館藏號缺）

7254 A History of Philosophy/by Clement C. J. Webb. —New York: Henry Holt and Company; London: Williams and Norgate, [n. d.]

256p. ;16.7cm

PKUL（館藏號缺）

附注：

題記：扉頁有原書主簽名"Wang Cheng, Oct. 3, 1915"。

7255 A History of Philosophy: With Especial Reference to the Formation and Development of Its Problems and Conceptions/by W. Windelband. —New York: The Macmillan Company; London: Macmillan & Co., Ltd., 1901

XV, 726p. ;23.1cm

PKUL（館藏號缺）

附注：

題記：扉頁有胡適題記："Suh Hu, New York City, May 2, 1917. — the day I completed my dissertation. 德國文代斑著《泰西哲學史》,適。"

批注圈劃：書内 254 頁有胡適批注圈劃。

7256 The History of Psychology/by W. B. Pillsbury. —New York: W. W. Norton & Company, Inc., 1929

X, 326p. ;21.5cm

PKUL（館藏號缺）

附注：

題記：扉頁有胡適簽名"Hu Shih, September 1929"；書末有胡適題記："Murphy: An Historical Introduction to Psychology. (Kegan & Paul), Boring: History of Experimental Psychology (Harvard Univ. Press)。"

7257 The History of Rome/by Theodor Mommsen; translated by W. P. Dickson. —London: J. M. Dent & Sons Ltd.; New York: E. P, Dutton & Co., 1911

4 Vols. ;17.1cm

Everyman's Library: History

PKUL（館藏號缺）

7258　History of Rome: To the Reign of Trajan/by Charles Merivale—London: J. M. Dent & Sons Ltd. ; New York: E. P, Dutton & Co. , 1911

XVI, 560p. ; 17.2cm

Everyman's Library: History

PKUL（館藏號缺）

7259　A History of Sanskrit Literature/by Arthur A. MacDonell. —New York: D. Appleton and Company, 1900

VIII, 472p. ; 19.7cm

Short Histories of the Literature of the World

PKUL（館藏號缺）

7260　History of the Conflict between Religion and Science/by John William Draper. —New York: Vanguard Press, 1926

VII, 116p. ; 17.8cm

PKUL（館藏號缺）

7261　History of the Conflict between Religion and Science/by John William Draper. —New York: D. Appleton and Company, 1896

XXII, 371p. ; 19cm

PKUL（館藏號缺）

7262　The History of the Decline and Fall of the Roman Empire/by Edward Gibbon. —Philadelphia: Porter & Coates, [n. d.]

4 Vols. ; 18.8cm

PKUL（館藏號缺）

附注：

題記：四卷扉頁均有胡適題記："Suh Hu, June, 1914. 吉本《羅馬衰亡史》

共五冊,適之";四卷另均有簽名"W. Lord Conwell, May 16th. 1882"。

夾紙:第3卷頁466、467間夾有英文書信2頁,寄、收人暫無法辨識。

其他:本書全本5卷,胡適藏書缺第1卷。四卷封內均貼有藏書籤"W. Lord Conwell, Reading, Penna- Vol. No. 59"。

7263 A History of the Far East/by G. Nye Steiger. —Boston, New York, Chicago: Ginn and Company, 1936

VII, 928p. ; 20.8cm

PKUL(館藏號缺)

附注:

題記:扉頁有贈書者題記:"To Dr. Hu Shih with the high regard and genuine appreciation of the school for overseas administer at Harvard University while he delivered a brilliant course of lecture. □ Oct. 12, 1943, Anniversary of the 'Columbus Day'。"

7264 The History of the Former Han Dynasty Volume One/by Pan Ku; translated by Homer H. Dubs. —Baltimore: Waverly Press, Inc., 1938

XII, 339p. ; 25.8cm

PKUL(館藏號缺)

7265 A History of the Italian Republics: Being a View of the Origin Progress & Fall of Italian Freedom/by J. C. L. de Sismondi. —London, Toronto: J. M. Dent & Sons, Ltd. ; New York: E. P. Dutton & Co., 1907

X, 338p. ; 17.3cm

Everyman's Library: History

PKUL(館藏號缺)

7266 A History of the Press and Public Opinion in China/by Lin Yutang. —Shanghai, Hong Kong, Singapore: Kelly & Walsh, Limited, 1936

179p. ; 23.5cm

PKUL(館藏號缺)

7267　History of the Rise and Influence of the Spirit of Rationalism in Europe/by William Edward Hartpole Lecky. —London：Watts & Co. , 1910

XVI, 148, IX, 157p. ; 21.4cm

PKUL（館藏號缺）

附注：

題記：扉頁有胡適鋼筆簽名"Hu Shih, Jan, 1924"。

其他：本書爲2卷合訂本。

7268　History of the University of Pennsylvania/by Edward Potts Cheyney. —Philadelphia：University of Pennsylvania Press, 1940

X, 461p. ; 23.5cm

PKUL（館藏號缺）

附注：

題記：扉頁有胡適題記："今年是卞州大學二百年紀念，我參加慶典後，買得此書。胡適，廿九（1940），十一月。"

7269　A History of the Warfare of Science with Theology in Christendom/by Andrew Dickson White. —New York, London：D. Appleton and Company, 1896

2 Vols. ; 22.5cm

PKUL（館藏號缺）

附注：

題記：第1冊封内有鋼筆題記："胡適之先生的書。"

批注圈劃：第1冊書内26頁有胡適批注圈劃。

摺頁：第1冊頁100、115、124、137、156有摺頁。

其他：第2冊内夾購書發票1張。

7270　History, Its Rise and Development/by Harry Elmer Barnes. —[s. l.]：[s. n.], 1934

205-264p. ; 30.5cm

PKUL（館藏號缺）

附注：

其他：書末破損。

7271 Ho Shen and Shu-Ch'un-Yuan: An Episode in the Past of the Yenching Campus/by William Hung. —Peiping: Yenching University, 1934

10p. ;23cm

PKUL（館藏號缺）

附注：

其他：本書爲綫裝。

7272 Hobbes's Leviathan/by Thomas Hobbes. —Oxford: The Clarendon Press, 1909

XXXI, 557p. ;19.3cm

PKUL（館藏號缺）

7273 The Holly Bible, Containing the Old and New Testaments. —New York: Thomas Nelson & Sons, [n. d.]

956, 290, VI, 118, 243, 8p. ;20cm

PKUL（館藏號缺）

附注：

印章：題名頁鈐有"適盦藏書"朱文圓印。

題記：扉頁有胡適題記："'For his word was with power.'—Luke IV. 32. 《舊新約全書》,胡適。"

7274 The Holy Bible: Containing the Old and New Testaments. —New York: American Bible Society, [n. d.]

361, 96p. ;23cm

PKUL（館藏號缺）

附注：

題記：扉頁有胡適題記："民國廿六年十二月,我在紐約,想翻讀《新約》,買了一部《舊新約全書》。後來我的朋友 Edwin C. Loberstine 在我的房裡看見這本子,他去買了一部'The Bible Designed to be Read as Literature'

來送我。這兩本各有長處,應該對照著看。廿七年二月,胡適。"

夾紙:書末貼有剪報"Device for Hiding Bibles—in 1626"1 張。

其他:封內貼有"胡適的書"藏書票。

7275 The Holy Bible：Containing the Old and New Testaments. —London：The British & Foreign Bible Society, 1945

 921p. ；18.5cm

 PKUL（館藏號缺）

附注：

 其他:書末夾有照片1張。

7276 The Home Front/by David Hinshaw. —New York：G. P. Putnam's Sons, 1943

 XII, 352p. ；21.4cm

 PKUL（館藏號缺）

附注：

 題記:書名頁前頁有作者題記:"For Dr. Hu Shih, with regards. David Hinshaw。"

 內附文件:頁48、49間夾有英文書信1封。

7277 Homo Rapiens and Other Verses/by Henry S. Salt. —London：Watts & Co. , 1926

 70p. ；18.6cm

 PKUL（館藏號缺）

7278 The Horse–Stealers and Other Stories/by Anton Tchehov；translated by Constance Garnett. —London：Chatto & Windus, 1921

 312p. ；15.8cm

 The Tales of Tchehov

 PKUL（館藏號缺）

附注：

 題記:扉頁有胡適鋼筆簽名"Hu Shih, December 1924"。

批注圈劃：目錄頁有胡適圈劃。

7279　Hortus Vitate and Limbo/by Vernon Lee. —Leipzig：Bernhard Tauchnitz, 1907

　　　295p. ；16.4cm

　　　Collection of British Authors, Tauchnitz Edition

　　　PKUL（館藏號缺）

7280　Hossfeld's French for the Million/by H. J. Weintz. —London：Hirschfeld Brothers, Limited, [n. d.]

　　　VIII, 160p. ；17.7cm

　　　PKUL（館藏號缺）

　　　附注：

　　　　其他：本書與 Key 在同一盒中。

7281　Houdini：His Life-Story/by Harold Kellock. —New York：Harcourt, Brace & Company, 1928

　　　X, 384p. ；22.4cm

　　　PKUL（館藏號缺）

　　　附注：

　　　　內附文件：書內夾有胡適致仲洽（高夢旦之子）書信 1 頁："仲洽兄：胡帝尼的傳，我看過便丟了，本不預備保藏。貴友譯此書，可見他愛護此書。此書損壞了不足惜，你怎麼買了來送我！我不敢領收，請你把此書轉贈那位譯書的貴友吧！適之，十九，九，二。"

7282　The House of Exile/by Nora Waln. —Boston：Little, Brown, and Company, 1933

　　　337p. ；20.7cm

　　　PKUL（館藏號缺）

　　　附注：

　　　　夾紙：封內夾有卡片，上有胡適手書"Compliments of Dr. Hedwig Kuhn"。

7283　The House of Mitsui/by Oland D. Russell. —Boston：Little, Brown and Company,

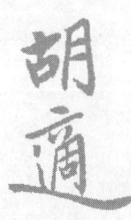

1939

XI, 328p. ; 23.6cm

PKUL（館藏號缺）

附注：

印章：扉頁鈐有"HU SHIH"藍文印。

7284 A House of Pomegranates/by Oscar Wilde. —Leipzig：Bernhard Tauchnitz, 1909

252p. ; 16.2cm

Collection of British Authors, Tauchnitz Edition

PKUL（館藏號缺）

附注：

印章：扉頁有胡適毛筆簽名"Hu Shih"。

7285 A House of Pomegranates/by Oscar Wilde. —Leipzig：Bernhard Tauchnitz, 1909

252p. ; 16.2cm

Collection of British Authors, Tauchnitz Edition

PKUL（館藏號缺）

附注：

印章：扉頁有胡適毛筆簽名"Hu Shih"。

7286 How to Enjoy the Starry Sky/by Marcus Woodward. —London：Hodder and Stoughton Limited, 1928

238p. ; 17.7cm

PKUL（館藏號缺）

7287 How to Cook and Eat in Chinese/by Buwei Yang Zhao. —New York：The John Day Company, 1945

XVIII, 262p. ; 20.3cm

PKUL（館藏號缺）

附注：

　　題記：扉頁有楊步偉題字："送給適之,趙楊步偉。"

7288　How to Fight Nervous Troubles/by James Oppenheim. ——Girard：Haldeman-Julius Company，[n. d.]

　　64p. ；12.6cm

　　Little Blue Book

　　PKUL（館藏號缺）

7289　How to Live Long/by William Lee Howard. ——New York：Edward J. Clode，1916

　　VIII, 210p. ；19.4cm

　　PKUL（館藏號缺）

　　附注：

　　印章：扉頁、扉頁後頁、題名頁鈐有"Ying C. Yang"藍文印。

　　批注圈劃：書內30餘頁有朱筆圈劃。

7290　How to Read Finger Prints/by C. Samuel Campbell. ——Girard：Haldeman-Julius Company，[n. d.]

　　32p. ；12.5cm

　　Little Blue Book

　　PKUL（館藏號缺）

7291　How We Think John Dewey. ——Boston, New York, Chicago：D. C. Heath & Co., 1910

　　VI, 224p. ；18.6cm

　　PKUL（館藏號缺）

　　附注：

　　印章：一冊扉頁有胡適簽名"Hu Shih"；另鈐有"王徵"朱文橢圓印。

　　批注圈劃：一冊書內92頁有胡適批注圈劃。

　　其他：本書有2冊。

7292 How We Think John Dewey. —Boston, New York, Chicago, Atlanta, Dallas, San Francisco, London: D. C. Heath and Company, 1933

X, 301p. ; 19.1cm

PKUL（館藏號缺）

附注：

題記：封內有原書主簽名"Virginia Davis Hartman, 7. 16. 42"。

7293 Hsi Shih: Beauty of Beauties/by Shu Chiung. —Shanghai: Kelly and Walsh Limited, 1931

XVI, 116p. ; 21.2cm

PKUL（館藏號缺）

附注：

題記：扉頁有作者題記："To Dr. Hu Shih, with best wishes, Shu Chiung。"

夾紙：書內夾有作者名片1張，上有作者題字："To Dr. Hu Shih, in grateful appreciation of helpful suggestion and valuable criticisms. Shu Chiung。"

7294 Human Behavior/by Stewart Paton. —New York: Charles Scribner's Sons, 1921

465p. ; 23.3cm

PKUL（館藏號缺）

附注：

題記：扉頁有胡適鋼筆簽名"Hu Shih, Feb. 1924"。

7295 Human Immortality: Two Supposed Objections to the Doctrine/by William James. —Boston and New York: Houghton, Mifflin Company, The Riverside Press Cambridge, 1898

70p. ; 17.8cm

PKUL（館藏號缺）

附注：

題記：扉頁有原書主簽名"Joseph Lilienthal, Harvard '98"。

其他：封內貼有 Joseph Lilienthal 藏書票。

7296 The Human Mind/by Karl A. Menninger. —New York： Alfred A. Knope, 1937

XII, 504, XIIIp. ；23.4cm

PKUL（館藏號缺）

附注：

題記：一冊扉頁有作者題記："For His Excellency Dr. Hu-Shih, ambassador from China to USA (the fellow patient with the author at the Presbyterian Hospital, N. Y. Feb. 1939) Please accept this, Dr. Hu, on behalf of the Chinese People whom I have long regarded as the most mentally healthy, the best adjusted, in the world. with the profound respect. Karl A. Menninger (The Menninger Clinic) Topoka, Kansas, 2.20.39"；另一冊扉頁有作者題記："For the spokesman and intellectual leader of a great people, Dr. Hu Shih, from an admirer of Roth. Karl A. Menninger, Topeka, Kansas, Dec. 31, 1941。"

其他：本書有 2 冊。

7297 Human Nature and Conduct： An Introduction to Social Psychology/by John Dewey. —New York： The Modern Library, 1930

VII, 336p. ；18.3cm

PKUL（館藏號缺）

7298 Human Origins/by Samuel Laing. —London： Watts & Co., 1921

142p. ；21.5cm

PKUL（館藏號缺）

7299 Human Shows Far Phantasies： Songs and Trifles/by Thomas Hardy. —London： Macmillan and Co., Limited, 1927

IX, 279p. ；17.4cm

PKUL（館藏號缺）

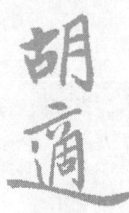

7300 The Human Situation: The Gifford Lectures Delivered in the University of Glasgow, 1935-1937/by W. Macneile Dixon. —New York: Longmans, Green, & Co., [n.d.]

438p. ; 21.2cm

PKUL（館藏號缺）

附注：

題記：書名頁前頁有贈書者題記："To his Excellency Hu Shih, from an amateur philospher to a real one-with great respect and esteem—□,1939。"

其他：書內夾有乾花1枝。

7301 Hume, with Helps to the Study of Berkeley/by Thomas H. Huxley. —New York: D. Appleton and Company, 1897

XV, 319p. ; 18.8cm

Essays by Thomas H. Huxley Vol. VI

PKUL（館藏號缺）

附注：

印章：扉頁有原書主簽名"Benjamin Thaw Jr."。

題記：扉頁有胡適題記："Vol. VI。"

7302 Hundred Altars/by Juliet Bredon. —New York: Dodd, Mead and Company, 1934

VIII, 336p. ; 19.7cm

PKUL（館藏號缺）

附注：

內附文件：頁306、307間夾有英文書信1封,信封1個。

7303 A Hundred and Seventy Chinese Poems/translated by Arthur Waley. —New York: Alfred A. Knofp, 1919

243p. ; 20.4cm

PKUL（館藏號缺）

附注：

    印章：封內有原書主簽名"Singer"。

    批注圈劃：書內有鉛筆批注、繪畫，非胡適所作。

    其他：扉頁貼有"Croline Singer, Cyrus LeRoy Baldridge"藏書票。

7304 A Hundred and Seventy Chinese Poems/translated by Arthur Waley. —New York：Alfred A. Knopf, 1923

    243p. ；17.6cm

    PKUL（館藏號缺）

7305 The Hundred Names/by Henry H. Hart. —Berkeley：University of California Press, 1933

    231p. ；19.8cm

    PKUL（館藏號缺）

附注：

    題記：題名頁前頁有作者題記："To Dr. Hu Shih, in homage and friendship, Henry H. Hart。"

7306 Hunters & Artists/by Harold Peake, Herbert John Fleure. —Oxford：The Clarendon Press, 1927

    VI, 154p. ；20.4cm

    The Corridors of Time

    PKUL（館藏號缺）

7307 Hymns and Tunes in Japanese/by Utato Fuçi. —Yokohama：F. R. Wetmore & Co., 1876

    91, 76p. ；17.2cm

    PKUL（館藏號缺）

7308 I Discover the Orient/by Fletcher S. Brockman. —New York, London：Harper & Brothers Publishers, 1936

XII, 211p. ; 19.1cm

PKUL（館藏號缺）

7309 I Married Adventure: The Lives and Adventure of Matin and Osa Johnson/
by Osa Johnson. —Philadelphia, New York, London, Toronto: J. B. Lippincott
Company, 1944

376p. ; 24cm

PKUL（館藏號缺）

7310 I Paid Hitler/by Fritz Thyssen. —New York, Toronto: Farrar & Rinehart, Inc.,
1941

XXIX, 281p. ; 21.9cm

PKUL（館藏號缺）

附注：

其他：封内貼有"胡適的書"藏書票。

7311 I Promessi Sposi/by Alessandro Manzoni. —New York: P. F. Collier & Son,
1909

668p. ; 19.5cm

The Harvard Classics No. 21

PKUL（館藏號缺）

附注：

印章：扉頁有胡適簽名"Suh Hu"。

7312 I See a New China/by George Hogg. —Boston: Little, Brown and Company,
1944

XV, 211p. ; 20.5cm

PKUL（館藏號缺）

附注：

夾紙：書内夾有出版社贈書卡1張。

7313 I Speak for the Chinese/by Carl Crow. —New York, London: Harper Brothers Publishers, 1937

 VIII, 84p. ; 20.6cm

 PKUL（館藏號缺）

 附注：

  題記：題名頁前頁有作者題記："To Dr. Hu Shih, with best wish, Carl Crow。"

7314 Ibsen：1828-1906/by Ossip-Lourié. —Paris: Bibliothèque Larousse, [n.d.]

 94p. ; 18.6cm

 PKUL（館藏號缺）

 附注：

  印章：封面及題名頁有原書主簽名"Johnson Yuan"；扉頁及書末鈐有"Johnson Yuan, Institut Franco-Chinois, Lyon, France"藍文印。

  批注圈劃：書內有批注圈劃，似非胡適所作。

  其他：本書封面及扉頁脫落。

7315 "Ice Water Pl--"/by Fannie Hurst. —Girard: Haldeman-Julius Company, [n.d.]

 64p. ; 12.7cm

 Little Blue Book

 PKUL（館藏號缺）

7316 Icones Filicum Sinicarum/by Ren-Chang Ching. —Peiping: The Fan Memorial Institute of Biology, 1935

 100p., 圖50；34cm

 PKUL（館藏號缺）

 附注：

  題記：封面有贈書者題記："適之吾兄惠存，弟胡先驌敬贈。"

  其他：本書鈐有"國立北京大學藏書"章，似爲胡適轉贈北京大學圖書館。

7317　Icones Filicum Sinicarum Fascicle 4/by Ren-Chang Ching. —Peiping：Fan Memorial Institute of Biology, 1937

　　100p., 圖 50;34.4cm

　　PKUL（館藏號缺）

　　附注：

　　　題記:封面有贈書者題記:"適之吾兄惠存,弟胡先驌敬贈。"

　　　其他:本書鈐有"國立北京大學藏書"章,似爲胡適轉贈北京大學圖書館。

7318　Icones Plantarum Sinicarum/by Hsen-Hsu Hu, Woon-Young Chun. —Peiping：Fan Memorial Institute of Biology,［n.d.］

　　15p.；44.7cm

　　PKUL（館藏號缺）

　　附注：

　　　題記:封面有贈書者題記:"適之吾兄惠存,弟胡先驌敬贈。"

　　　其他:本書鈐有"國立北京大學藏書"章,似爲胡適轉贈北京大學圖書館。本書破損,裝訂已散。

7319　An Ideal Husband/by Oscar Wilde. —Leipzig：Bernhard Tauchnitz,［n.d.］

　　270p.；16.4cm

　　Collection of British Authors Tauchnitz Edition

　　PKUL（館藏號缺）

7320　The Ideal Life：Addresses Hitherto Unpublished/by Henry Drummond. —New York：Association Press, 1897

　　320p.；18.4cm

　　PKUL（館藏號缺）

　　附注：

　　　題記:扉頁有贈書者題記:"Compliment to Mr. S. Hu, from K. S. Sun。"

7321　The Ideas That Have Influenced Civilization in the Original Documents/by Oliver J. Thatcher. —Boston, Chicago：The Roberts-Manchester Publishing Co.,

[n.d.]

 8 Vols. ;25cm

 PKUL（館藏號缺）

 附注：

  題記：第1卷扉頁有胡適題記："《曾影響文化的思想》共十冊，八年九月，我在美國使館拍賣得來的。價十七元。胡適。"

  其他：本書全本共10卷，胡適藏書現存8卷。

7322 The Iliad of Homer/by Andrew Lang, Walter Leaf, Ernest Myers. —London：Macmillan and Co., Limited, 1914

 504p. ;18.6cm

 PKUL（館藏號缺）

 附注：

  題記：扉頁有胡適鉛筆簽名"Hu Shih, London, Oct. 1926"。

7323 The Iliad of Homer/translated by Alexander Pope. —Humphrey Milford：Oxford University Press, 1902

 XXIX, 502p. ;15cm

 The World's Classics

 PKUL（館藏號缺）

7324 An Illustrated Battle-Account in the History of the Former Han Dynasty/by J. J. L. Duyvendak. —[s.l.]：[s.n.], [n.d.]

 249-264p. ;24.4cm

 PKUL（館藏號缺）

 Reprinted from *T'ong Pao*, Vol. XXXIV-Livr. 4

 附注：

  題記：封面有作者題記："To Dr. Hu Shih, with the author's kind regards。"

  夾紙：書內夾有作者J. J. L. Duyvendak名片1張，上書"Dear Dr. Hu Shih, this is to introduce my stepson Mr. Philip Bagby who is very ancious to meet you. His great grandfather was Young J. Allen(林)，the editor of the 萬

國公報. He is a Harvard graduate and now aspires for the diplomatic service. He is a warm friend of China. Hoping you are well and taking good care of yourself, yours very sincerely, Duyvendak"。

7325 The Illustrated Encyclopedia of American Birds/by Leon Augustus Hausman. —New York: Halcyon House, 1941

XIX, 541p. ; 20.9cm

PKUL（館藏號缺）

附注：

印章：書名頁有作者簽名"Leon Augustus Hausman"。

題記：扉頁有作者題記："To my college classmate and friend, Hu Shih, with my kindest wishes! Leon A. Hausman. March, 1946。"

內附文件：書內夾有作者致胡適英文書信1頁。

7326 Illustrations of China and Its People: A Series of Two Hundred Photographs, with Letterpress Descriptive of the Places and People Represented/by J. Thomson. —London: Sampson Low, Marston, Low and Searte, 1873

3 Vols. ; 47.2cm

PKUL（館藏號缺）

附注：

印章：第1卷扉頁有原書主簽名"R. Lilley"。

夾紙：第3卷書內夾有倫敦、北海道地圖各1張。

7327 Imagina/by Julia Ellsworth Ford. —New York: E. P. Dutton & Company, 1914

178p. ; 24.6cm

PKUL（館藏號缺）

附注：

印章：扉頁有作者之一簽名"by J. Lauren Ford"。

題記：正文前頁有作者題記："To three babies—Big Hu and little Hu, and littler Hu, from a so called baby Ju., a faithful friend in big America to the Hu's in big China. Julia Ellsworth Ford。"

7328 Imagination, Labour, Civilization/by Einar Sundt. —London: William Heinemann, 1920

　　XI, 417p. ; 22.3cm

　　PKUL（館藏號缺）

　　附注：

　　　　題記：扉頁有胡適題記："今天早起，上車站買報紙，見書攤有舊書出賣，其中有此書，書名很使我注意，所以買了回來看看。這是我在英國買的第一本書。十五，八，七，胡適。"

7329 Immanuel Kant's Critique of Pure Reason/by Immanuel Kant; translated by Norman Kemp Smith. —London: Macmillan and Co., Limited, 1929

　　XIII, 681p. ; 22.1cm

　　PKUL（館藏號缺）

7330 Imperial Japan: 1926-1938/by A. Morgan Young. —London: George Allen & Unwin Ltd., 1938

　　328p. ; 21.4cm

　　PKUL（館藏號缺）

　　附注：

　　　　印章：扉頁鈐有"HU SHIH"藍文印。

7331 The Imperial Japanese Mission 1917. —Washington: Carnegie Endowment for International Peace, 1918

　　IV, 125p. ; 25cm

　　PKUL（館藏號缺）

7332 Imperialism, the State and Revolution/by N. Lenin. —New York: Vanguard Press, 1927

　　VIII, 225p. ; 18.2cm

　　PKUL（館藏號缺）

7333 Impressions of Great Naturalists: Darwin, Wallace, Huxley, Leidy, Cope, Balfour, Roosevelt, and Others/by Henry Fairfield Osborn. —New York, London: Charles Scribner's Sons, 1928

X, 294p. ; 19.4cm

PKUL（館藏號缺）

附注：

題記：扉頁有胡適鋼筆簽名"Hu Shih, September 1929"。

夾紙：書内一處有夾紙。

7334 In Aid of Faith/by Lyman Abbott. —New York: E. P. Dutton & Company, 1886

203p. ; 19cm

PKUL（館藏號缺）

附注：

題記：扉頁有著者題記："Mr. S. Hu, with regards of his friend Lyman Abbott, Jan. 1912。"

批注圈劃：書内37頁有胡適批注圈劃。

夾紙：書内夾有讀書卡片1張。

7335 In China Now: China's Need and the Christian Contribution/by J. C. Keyte. —London: United Council for Missionary Education, 1923

160p. ; 18.5cm

PKUL（館藏號缺）

附注：

題記：扉頁有作者題記："To Dr. Hu Shih, with the author's sincere admiration & regards, Peking, 1923。"

7336 In the Days of the Han/by M. Jagendorf. —Los Angeles, New York, San Francisco: Suttonhouse, Ltd., 1936

168p. ; 23cm

PKUL（館藏號缺）

附注：

　　題記：題名頁前頁有贈書者題記："To Dr. Hu Shih, because of my love for China, Julia Ellsworth Jones, Sept. 23, 1936。"

7337　In the Evening of My Thought/by George Lemenceau; translated by Charles Miner Thompson, John Heard. —London：Constable and Company Ltd., 1929

　　2 Vols. ; 24.2cm

　　PKUL（館藏號缺）

　　附注：

　　題記：第1卷封內有贈書者題記："Dear Dr. Hu, I am sending a couple of books to convey my hearty wishes for many many happy returns of the Day, yours Sincerely Sohtsu G. King。"

7338　In the Path of Mahatma Gandhi/by George Catlin. —London：Macdonald & Co., Ltd., 1948

　　332p. ; 22cm

　　PKUL（館藏號缺）

　　附注：

　　夾紙：書內夾有作者贈書函1頁。

7339　Inaugural Address by the Rector Magnificus, Professor W. P. J. Pompe/by W. P. J. Pompe. —[s.l.]：[s.n.], [n.d.]

　　26p. ; 24.8cm

　　PKUL（館藏號缺）

　　附注：

　　題記：扉頁有某人鋼筆題記："At University of Utrecht, March 3, 1947。"

7340　Inauguration of George D. Stoddard, President of the University of the State of New York and Commissioner of Education at the Seventy-eighth Convocation of the University. —New York：[s.n.], 1942

　　79p. ; 23.5cm

PKUL（館藏號缺）

7341 The Increase of God/by A. H. McNeile. —London： Longmans, Green and Co. , 1919

VIII, 130p. ； 19cm

PKUL（館藏號缺）

7342 Independence, Convergence, and Borrowing in Institutions, Thought, and Art/by Presidents and Fellows of Harvard College. —Cambridge： Harvard University Press, 1937

X, 272p. ； 21.4cm

Harvard Tercentenary Publications

PKUL（館藏號缺）

附注：

印章：一冊扉頁有胡適鋼筆簽名"Hu Shih, 胡適"。

其他：一冊封內貼有"胡適的書"藏書票。本書有 2 冊。

7343 Indian Wisdom； Or, Examples of the Religious, Philosophical, and Ethical Doctrines of the Hindus/by Monier Monier-Williams. —London： Luzac & Co. , 1893

575p. ； 22.4cm

PKUL（館藏號缺）

附注：

其他：封內貼有"胡適的書"藏書票。

7344 The Indianization of China： A Case Study in Cultural Borrowing/by Hu Shih. —Cambridge： Harvard University Press, [n. d.]

29p. ； 21cm

PKUL（館藏號缺）

附注：

其他：本書有 2 冊。

7345 Individualism Old and New/by John Dewey. —New York: Minton, Balch & Company, 1930

 171p. ; 19cm

 PKUL（館藏號缺）

附注：

 印章：扉頁有胡適鋼筆簽名"Hu Shih"；另題名頁鈐有"HU SHIH"藍文印。

 批注圈劃：書内數頁有胡適鉛筆圈劃。

7346 Industry, Governments and Labor: Record of the International Labor Organization, 1919-1928. —Boston: World Peace Foundation, 1928

 231p. ; 20cm

 PKUL（館藏號缺）

7347 Industry and Civilisation/by C. Delisle Burns. —London: George Allen & Unwin Ltd., 1925

 278p. ; 21.6cm

 PKUL（館藏號缺）

附注：

 題記：扉頁有作者題記："To my friend professor Hu Shih, from the author C. Delisle Burns, Christmas, 1926。"

7348 Infatuation, and Other Stories of Love's Misfits/by Ben Hecht. —Girard: Haldeman-Julius Company, 1927

 64p. ; 12.6cm

 Little Blue Book

 PKUL（館藏號缺）

附注：

 其他：缺封面、封底。

7349 The Influence of Darwin on Philosophy: And Other Essays in Contemporary

Thought/by John Dewey. —New York：Henry Holt and Company，1910

VI, 309p.；19cm

PKUL（館藏號缺）

附注：

題記：扉頁有胡適簽名"Hu Suh, March 1919"。

批注圈劃：書內53頁有胡適批注圈劃；書末有胡適批注："Read this essay together with his 'The Recovery of Philosophy' in 'Creative Intelligence'。"

7350 The Influence of Emerson/by Edwin D. Mead. —Boston：American Unitarian Association, 1903

304p.；19.1cm

PKUL（館藏號缺）

附注：

題記：扉頁有胡適題記："此為吾友亥叟 C. W. Heizer 之遺物。亥叟死後，其家人以其生平所藏書分贈知交，余得此冊，因記之。民國三年十一月十五日，適。"

7351 The Influence of Invention on Civilization/by M. D. C. Crawford. —Cleveland, New York：The World Publishing Company, 1942

VIII, 449p.；21.8cm

PKUL（館藏號缺）

7352 The Influence of Judge Cardozo on the Common Law/by Irving Lehman. —New York：Doubleday, Doran & Company, Inc., 1942

X, 33p.；16.4cm

PKUL（館藏號缺）

附注：

題記：書名頁前頁有作者題記："To Dr. Hu Shih：An unworthy offering to a man I greatly admire. Irving Lehman。"

7353 Influence of the Great War upon Shipping/by J. Russell Smith. —New York：

Oxford University Press, 1919

VIII, 357p. ; 24.6cm

Preliminary Economic Studies of the War

PKUL（館藏號缺）

7354 Ingersoll's Greatest Lectures/by Robert Green Ingersoll. —New York: The Freethought Press Association, 1944

IV, 419p. ; 21cm

PKUL（館藏號缺）

附注：

題記：扉頁有胡適題記："英格梭爾講演遺集，共收二十三篇。此書題爲一九四四出版，其實是舊版新印的，原版是英氏的講演雜稿，隨時印行的小冊子合訂成的，所以鉛字的小大不一律，篇章的目次不整齊。首頁所謂Original Dresden Edition 即是這些小冊子，而不是一部全集。胡適。一九四五，四，二。"

批注圈劃：目錄頁有胡適標注的講演時間；前 67 頁有胡適批注圈劃 20 餘處；第 65 頁有胡適批注："此可見中國古代自然主義的解放作用"；第 67 頁有胡適批注："Read and greatly enjoyed it,—April 2, 1945. Hu Shih。"

7355 Inland Transport and Communication in Mediaeval India/by Bejoy Kumar Sarkar. —Calcutta: Calcutta University Press, 1925

II, 87p. ; 24.3cm

PKUL（館藏號缺）

7356 Inner Asian Frontiers of China/by Owen Lattimore. —New York: American Geographical Society, 1940

XIII, 585p. ; 21.1cm

American Geographical Society Research Series

PKUL（館藏號缺）

7357 The Inner History of the Chinese Revolution/by T'ang Leang-Li. —London:

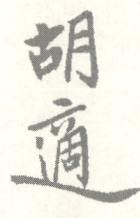

George Routledge & Sons, Ltd., 1930

XII, 391p. ; 22.3cm

PKUL（館藏號缺）

7358 An Inquiry into the Nature and Causes of the Wealth of Nations/by Adam Smith. —New York: P. F. Collier & Son, 1909

500p. ; 19.5cm

The Harvard Classics No. 10

PKUL（館藏號缺）

附注：

　印章：扉頁有胡適簽名"Suh Hu"；題名頁鈐有"適盦藏書"朱文圓印。

　批注圈劃：書內一頁有胡適批注。

7359 An Inquiry into the Nature of Peace and the Terms of Its Perpetuation/by Thorstein Veblen. —New York: B. W. Huebsch, 1919

XIII, 367p. ; 19.6cm

PKUL（館藏號缺）

7360 Insects and Men: Instinct and Reason/by Clarence S. Darrow. —Girard: Haldeman-Julius Company, [n.d.]

64p. ; 12.6cm

Little Blue Book

PKUL（館藏號缺）

7361 Inside Europe/by John Gunther. —New York, London: Harper & Brothers, 1936

XIV, 470p. ; 22.4cm

PKUL（館藏號缺）

7362 Inside Experience: A Naturalistic Philosophy of Life and the Modern World/by Joseph K. Hart. —New York: Longmans, Green and Co., 1927

XXVI, 287p. ; 20.7cm

PKUL（館藏號缺）

7363 Inside Latin America/by John Gunther. —New York, London: Harper & Brothers, 1941

XI, 498p. ; 22.2cm

PKUL（館藏號缺）

7364 Inside the Department of State/by Bertram D. Hulen. —New York, London: McGraw-Hill Book Company, Inc., 1939

XIII, 328p. ; 22.9cm

PKUL（館藏號缺）

附注：

題記：扉頁有胡適題記："崔存璘兄送我的。廿八，九，廿。胡適。"

7365 The Institute of Pacific Relations/by J. Merle Davis. —Worcester: Carnegie Endowment for International Peace, Division of Intercourse and Education, 1926

53p. ; 19.7cm

PKUL（館藏號缺）

7366 Institute of Pacific Relations Yosemite Conference—August 15-29, 1936, Aims and Results of Social and Economic Policies in Pacific Countries/by Institute of Pacific Relations. —[s.l.]: Institute of Pacific Relations, 1936

34p. ; 22.9cm

PKUL（館藏號缺）

附注：

印章：扉頁有胡適鋼筆簽名"Hu Shih"。

7367 Institute of Pacific Relations, Honolulu Session. —Honolulu: Institute of Pacific Relations, 1925

210p. ; 24.3cm

PKUL（館藏號缺）

7368 Intelligence in the Modern World: John Dewey's Philosophy/by Joseph Ratner. —New York: The Modern Library, 1939

XV, 1077p. ; 20.2cm

PKUL（館藏號缺）

附注：

印章：題名頁前頁鈐有"HU SHIH"藍文印。

7369 Intermediate Poetical Selections from Coleridge to Longfellow/by Lewis Chase, P. A. Rashid. —Aligarh: Kays & Co. , [n.d.]

109, 92, 55, 40, 84, 69, 38p. ; 18.2cm

PKUL（館藏號缺）

附注：

印章：扉頁有作者 Lewis Chase 簽名。

7370 International Control of Aviation/by Kenneth W. Colegrove. —Boston: World Peace Foundation, 1930

234p. ; 20cm

PKUL（館藏號缺）

7371 The International Development of China/by Sun Yat-sen. —Chunking: Ministry of Information of the Republic, 1943

XIII, 191p. ; 21.1cm

PKUL（館藏號缺）

附注：

其他：本書有 2 冊。

7372 International Economic Relations in the Pacific: A. Trade Relations/by Secretariat of the Institute of Pacific Relations. —Honolulu: Institute of Pacific Relations, 1931

48p. ;19.8cm

PKUL（館藏號缺）

附注：

印章：一冊封面有胡適鉛筆簽名"Hu"。

其他：本書有2冊。

7373 International Economic Relations: Report of the Commission of Inquiry into National Policy in International Economic Relations/by Robert M. Hutchins. —Minneapolis: The University of Minnesota Press, 1934

IX, 397p. ;23.6cm

PKUL（館藏號缺）

7374 International Financial Stabilization/by Jules I. Bogen, Jacob Viner, Alvin H. Hansen, Ray B. Westerfield, Edwin W. Kemmerer, John H. Williams. —New York: Irving Trust Company, 1944

XVII, 186p. ;23.2cm

PKUL（館藏號缺）

7375 The International Labor Organization: A Study of Labor and Capital in Coöperation/Paul Périgord. —New York, London: D. Appleton and Company, 1926

XXIX, 339p. ;20.9cm

PKUL（館藏號缺）

7376 The International Law of the Future: Postulates, Principles and Proposals. —[s.l.]: [s.n.], [n.d.]

173p. ;21cm

PKUL（館藏號缺）

附注：

內附文件：書內夾有Manley O. Hudson致胡適英文書信1頁；另夾有本書介紹1份。

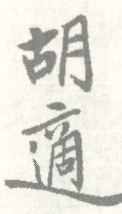

7377 The International Mind: An Argument for the Judical Settlement of International Disputes/by Nicholas Murray Butler. —New York: Charles Scribner's Sons, 1912

 X, 121p. ; 19.2cm

 PKUL（館藏號缺）

7378 International Monetary Fund Financial Statement, Quarter Ended May 31, 1948/by International Monetary Fund. —Washington: [s. n.], [n. d.]

 4p. ; 22.7cm

 PKUL（館藏號缺）

7379 International Relations: Eight Lectures Delivered in the United States in August, 1921/by James Bryce. —New York: The Macmillan Company, 1923

 XII, 275p. ; 20cm

 PKUL（館藏號缺）

 附注：

 題記：扉頁有贈書者題記："送給適之吾兄，鯁生，二九，三，廿六得之於華盛頓舊書肆。"

 其他：封內貼有原書主"Alba Curtis Milgus"藏書票。

7380 The International Relations of Manchuria/by C. Walter Young. —Chicago: The University of Chicago Press, 1929

 XXX, 307p. ; 24cm

 PKUL（館藏號缺）

7381 International Unemployment: A Study of Fluctuations in Employment and Unemployment in Several Countries 1910–1930/by M. L. Fleddérus. —Hague: The Industrial Relations Institute, 1931

 III, 496p. ; 24.3cm

 PKUL（館藏號缺）

7382 The Intimate Papers of Colonel House/by Charles Seymour. ——Boston and New York：Houghton Mifflin Company，1926

  4 Vols. ；24.3cm

  PKUL（館藏號缺）

7383 An Introduction to Mathematics/by A. N. Whitehead. ——New York：Henry Holt and Company；London：Williams and Norgate，1911

  256p. ；16.8cm

  The Home University of Modern Library

  PKUL（館藏號缺）

  附注：

    題記：扉頁有胡適鋼筆簽名"Suh Hu，April，1915"。

7384 An Introduction to Modern Linguistics/by L. R. Palmer. ——[s.l.]：[s.n.]，1936

  XI，216p. ；19.1cm

  PKUL（館藏號缺）

7385 Introduction to Philosophy/by Friedrich Paulsen. ——New York：Henry Holt and Company，1895

  XXII，437p. ；21cm

  PKUL（館藏號缺）

  附注：

    印章：書名頁鈐有"適盦藏書"朱文圓印。

    題記：扉頁有胡適題記："Suh Hu, June, 1914. Bought from Caudee"；另有原書主朱筆簽名"Caudee"；扉頁後頁有胡適題記："鮑而生《哲學入門》，適之。"

    批注圈劃：書内102頁有胡適圈劃。

    夾紙：頁344、345，頁378、379間各有夾紙一。

    摺頁：頁364摺頁。

7386 Introduction to Public Finance/by Carl C. Plehn. —New York：The Macmillan Company, 1909

　　XV, 480p. ; 18.8cm

　　PKUL（館藏號缺）

　　附注：

　　　　印章：扉頁有胡適簽名"S. Hu"。

　　　　題記：扉頁有胡適題記："國家財政。"

7387 Introduction to the Science of Chinese Religion：A Critique of Max Müller and Other Authors/by Ernst Faber. —HongKong：Lane, Crawford & Co.; Shanghai：Kelly & Walsh; Shanghai：Presbyterian Mission Press, [n.d.]

　　XII, 154p. ; 21.2cm

　　PKUL（館藏號缺）

　　附注：

　　　　印章：封面有原書主簽名"R. Lilley"。

　　　　題記：書末有原書主題記。

　　　　其他：封面至題名頁部分脫落。

7388 An Introduction to Statistical Methods/by Horace Secrist. —New York：The Macmillan Company, 1917

　　XXI, 482p. ; 18.9cm

　　PKUL（館藏號缺）

　　附注：

　　　　題記：扉頁有胡適題記："Hu Suh. Nov. 1919.《統計學方法論》,胡適。"

7389 An Introduction to the Experimental Psychology of Beauty/by C. W. Valentine. —London：T. C. & E. C. Jack, [n.d.]

　　94p. ; 16.1cm

　　The People's Books

　　PKUL（館藏號缺）

附注：

　　題記：扉頁有胡適毛筆簽名"Suh Hu, April 1919"。

　　批注圈劃：書內個別頁有圈劃。

7390 An Introduction to the History of Medicine: From the Time of Pharaohs to the End of the XVIIIth Century/by Charles Greene Cumston. —New York: Alfred A. Knopf, 1927

　　XXXII, 390p. ; 23.4cm

　　PKUL（館藏號缺）

附注：

　　印章：扉頁有胡適毛筆簽名"胡適"。

　　題記：書末有胡適鉛筆題記，有一單詞不易辨識。

7391 An Introduction to the Industrial and Social History of England/by Edward P. Cheyney. —New York: The Macmillan Company, 1920

　　XII, 386p. ; 19.5cm

　　PKUL（館藏號缺）

附注：

　　題記：扉頁有胡適題記："在舊書攤上買的此書,送給我自己做生日的禮物。適之,一九三一,十二,十七。"

7392 An Introduction to the Revised Standard Version of the New Testament/by Members of the Revision Committee, Luther A. Weigle. —[s. l.]: The International Council of Religious Education, [n.d.]

　　72p. ; 20.4cm

　　PKUL（館藏號缺）

附注：

　　題記：扉頁有胡適簽名"Hu Shih, 胡適, May 16, 1946"。

7393 Introduction to the Study of the Chinese Characters/by J. Edkins. —London: Trübner & Co., 1876

XVI, 211, 103p. ；24cm

PKUL（館藏號缺）

附注：

　　印章：扉頁有原書主簽名"R. Lilley"。

　　其他：本書缺封面、書脊。

7394　An Introduction to the Study of Organized Labor in America/by George Gorham Groat. —New York：The Macmillan Company, 1919

XV, 494p. ；20.1cm

PKUL（館藏號缺）

附注：

　　其他：書末貼有國立自治學院圖書館書袋及借書日期單，另貼有一條，上書"徐志摩君寄存"。

7395　An Introductory Logic/by James Edwin Creighton. —New York：The Macmillan Company；London：Macmillan & Co., Ltd., 1910

XVI, 520p. ；18.6cm

PKUL（館藏號缺）

附注：

　　印章：扉頁有趙元任英文簽名"Y. R. Chao"。

　　題記：扉頁另有某人題記："胡先生的。"

7396　An Introductory Logic/by James Edwin Creighton. —New York：The Macmillan Company；London：Macmillan & Co., Ltd., 1927

XVI, 502p. ；19.2cm

PKUL（館藏號缺）

附注：

　　題記：扉頁有胡適毛筆簽名"胡適，十七，九，十九"。

7397　The Invention of Printing in China and Its Spread Westward/by Thomas Francis Carter. —New York：Columbia University Press, 1925

XVIII, 282p. ; 23.6cm

PKUL（館藏號缺）

附注：

　　題記：扉頁有贈書者題記："To Dr. Hu Shih with sincere regards. Austin P. Evans。"

7398　Invention：The Master-Key to Progress/by Bradley A. Fiske. —New York：E. P. Dutton & Company, 1921

IX, 356p. ; 21cm

PKUL（館藏號缺）

7399　The Iphigenia in Tauris of Euripides/by Gilbert Murray. —New York：Oxford University Press, 1915

XI, 105p. ; 18.7cm

PKUL（館藏號缺）

附注：

　　題記：題名頁前頁有胡適簽名"Suh Hu, November 1916, New York City"。

7400　Is the Moon a Dead World? /by Maynard Shipley. —Girard：Haldeman-Julius Company, [n.d.]

64p. ; 12.7cm

Little Blue Book

PKUL（館藏號缺）

附注：

　　其他：本書缺封面。

7401　Is There a Substitute for Force in International Relations ? /by Suh Hu. —New York：American Association for International Conciliation, 1916

18p. ; 19.5cm

PKUL（館藏號缺）

附注：

與胡適的關係:本文爲胡適獲獎論文"Prize essay, International Policy Club Competition, Awarded June, 1916"。

7402 Island India Goes to School/by Edwin R. Embree, Margaret Sargent Simon, W. Bryant Mumford. —Chicago: The University of Chicago Press, 1934

120p. ; 22.7cm

PKUL（館藏號缺）

附注:

夾紙:書内夾有該書書評1份,郵寄地址1份。

7403 Isolated America/by Raymond Leslie Buell. —New York and London: Alfred A. Knope, 1940

XIII, 457, XIIIp. ; 21.3cm

PKUL（館藏號缺）

附注:

題記:扉頁有作者題記:"To ambassador Hu Shih, with thanks and regard, Reymond L. Buell。"

夾紙:書内夾有廣告卡片1張。

7404 Italian Self Taught/by Isaac Goldberg. —Girard: Haldeman-Julius Company, [n. d.]

64p. ; 12.7cm

Little Blue Book

PKUL（館藏號缺）

7405 Italy's Financial Policy. —Worcester: Carnegie Endowment for International Peace, Division of Intercourse and Education, 1927

72p. ; 19.6cm

PKUL（館藏號缺）

7406 Ivanhoe/by Walter Scott. —London: J. M. Dent & Sons Ltd. , 1906

XV, 459, 4p. ; 17cm

PKUL（館藏號缺）

附注：

題記：扉頁有胡適題記："五十三歲生日，紐約與華盛頓的朋友們——朱士嘉、王重民、馮家昇、吳光清、韓壽萱、張伯訓、陳鴻舜諸位先生——買了九冊司各德的小說送給我。諸公的盛意可感，我當繼續買'人人叢書'的司各德小說，以作紀念。卅三年十二月十二日，胡適。"

批注圈劃：書末有胡適批注："Dec. 12, 1944. 重讀此書，頗嫌其拖遝。但仍感覺其魔力。我初讀林琴南譯本似在四十年前。今日追憶似林譯底本或是刪節本？當更攷之。胡適。"

7407 The Ivory Mischief/by Arthur Meeker, Jr. . —Boston：Houghton Mifflin Company, 1941

679p. ; 22.1cm

PKUL（館藏號缺）

7408 I've Come a Long Way/by Helena Kuo. —New York, London：D. Appleton-Century Company, 1942

369p. ; 21.3cm

PKUL（館藏號缺）

附注：

題記：扉頁有作者題記："請適之尊先生賜正，後學郭鏡秋，民國卅一年三月。"

7409 Jam Tomorrow/by David Magee. —Boston：Houghton Mifflin Company, 1941

308p. ; 19.1cm

PKUL（館藏號缺）

附注：

題記：扉頁有作者題記："To Dr. Hu Shih, in remembrance of pleasant visits to San Francisco, David Magee, Feb. 1942。"

7410 Jane Eyre/by Charlotte Brontë. ——New York：Random House，1943

　　343p. ；24.8cm

　　PKUL（館藏號缺）

　　附注：

　　　　印章：扉頁鈐有"廷芳長壽"朱文方印。

　　　　題記：扉頁劉廷芳、吳卓生題字："'……天步正艱難，民生為憔悴……吾徒乘願來，爲此一大事……'此任公昔年贈菱生侍御詩也。適之學長兄五十晉三，全力從事學問，完成不朽之作，深慰士林之衆望，因錄陳言爲壽曰：四望雲山，一尊風月。百年事業，千古文章。弟劉廷芳偕室吳卓生敬賀。抗戰第七年冬，時同客紐約。"

7411 Japan Closing the "Open Door" in China/by John Ahleers. ——Shanghai：Kelly & Walsh, Limited, 1940

　　VIII, 140p. ；20.4cm

　　Political and Economic Studies

　　PKUL（館藏號缺）

7412 Japan Fights for Asia/by John Goette. ——New York：Harcourt, Brace and Company, 1943

　　248p. ；20.7cm

　　PKUL（館藏號缺）

　　附注：

　　　　夾紙：書內夾有出版社贈書卡1張。

7413 Japan in American Public Opinion/by Eleanor Tupper, George E. McReynolds. ——New York：The Macmillan Company, 1937

　　XIX, 465p. ；21.9cm

　　PKUL（館藏號缺）

7414 Japan in China/by T. A. Bisson. ——New York：The Macmillan Company, 1938

　　417p. ；21.7cm

PKUL（館藏號缺）

7415 Japan Unmasked/by Hallett Abend. —New York: Ives Washburn, Inc., 1941

322p.；22.5cm

PKUL（館藏號缺）

7416 Japan: A World Problem/by H. J. Timperley. —New York: The John Day Company, 1942

IX, 150p.；19.4cm

PKUL（館藏號缺）

附注：

批注圈劃：書內 3 頁有胡適批注圈劃。

內附文件：頁 34、35,46、47 間各夾有剪報 3 頁。

其他：本書書脊部分脫落。

7417 Japan: An Attempt at Interpretation/by Lafcadio Hearn. —New York: The Macmillan Company, 1924

VII, 549p.；20.1cm

PKUL（館藏號缺）

附注：

題記：扉頁後頁有胡適簽名"Hu Shih, Tokyo, April 29, 1927"。

7418 Japan: Its History, Traditions and Religions: With the Narrative of a Visit in 1879/by Edward J. Reed. —London: John Murray, 1880

2 Vols.；22.1cm

PKUL（館藏號缺）

附注：

印章：兩卷扉頁均有原書主簽名"R. Lilley"。

其他：第 1 卷裝訂散。

7419 Japan: Some Phases of Her Problems and Development/by Inazo Nitobé.

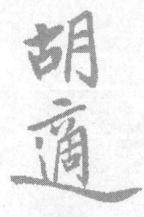

——New York：Charles Scribner's Sons, 1931

398p. ；22.3cm

PKUL（館藏號缺）

7420 Japan：The Hungry Guest/by G. C. Allen. ——London：George Allen & Unwin Ltd. , 1938

261p. ；21.5cm

PKUL（館藏號缺）

附注：

印章：扉頁及題名頁前頁鈐有"HU SHIH"藍文印。

7421 A Japanese Don Juan and Other Poems/by John Pairs. ——London：W. Collins Sons & Co. , Ltd. , 1926

126p. ；22.4cm

PKUL（館藏號缺）

附注：

題記：扉頁有作者題記："Hu Shih, with the good wishes from the China University Committee and a very minor poet. John Paris, Oct. 18th, 1926。"

7422 The Japanese Enemy：His Power and His Vulnerability/by Hugh Byas. ——New York：Alfred A Knopf, 1942

IX, 107p. ；19.1cm

PKUL（館藏號缺）

附注：

題記：扉頁有胡適題記："Hu Shih, March 1942. Gift of Mrs. Blande W. Knopf。"

7423 Japanese Episodes/by Edward H. House. ——Boston：James R. Osgood and Company, 1881

247p. ；14.9cm

PKUL（館藏號缺）

附注：

　　印章：扉頁後頁有"R. Lilley"鉛筆簽名。

7424　Japanese Expansion and American Policies/by James Francis Abbott. —New York：The Macmillan Company，1916

　　VIII，267p. ；19.1cm

　　PKUL（館藏號缺）

　　附注：

　　　　題記：扉頁有胡適題記："Suh Hu, New York, 1916. Gift of American Association for International Conciliation。"

7425　Japanese Expansion on the Asiatic Continent：A Study in the History of Japan with Special Reference to Her International Relations with China，Korea，and Russia/by Yoshi S. Kuno. —Berkeley：University of California Press，1937

　　2 Vols. ；23.4cm

　　PKUL（館藏號缺）

　　附注：

　　　　題記：第1卷扉頁有胡適題記："Gift from the editor, Professor Robert J. Kerner, October, 1937. Hu Shih"；第2卷扉頁有胡適題記："Gift from Proff. Robert J. Kerner and the manager of U. C. Press, Mr. Samuel T. Farquhar. Hu Shih, Sept. 1940。"

　　　　夾紙：第1卷書末夾有 Gold Rail Tavern 菜單1張。

　　　　摺頁：第2卷頁231有摺頁。

7426　Japanese Poetry：An History Essay with Two Hundred and Thirty Translations/by Curtis Hidden Page. —Boston, New York：Houghton Mifflin Company，1923

　　IX，181p. ；21.9cm

　　PKUL（館藏號缺）

　　附注：

　　　　題記：扉頁有贈書者題記："胡適先生惠存，弟大内暢三"。

内附文件：頁 94、95 間夾有 C. Y. Ching 1927 年 6 月 1 日致胡適函 1 封，有信封。

7427　Japanese Pottery：Being a Native Report/by Augustus W. Franks. —London：Chapman and Hall, Limited, 1880

　　VII, 112p. ; 19.4cm

　　PKUL（館藏號缺）

　　附注：

　　　題記：扉頁有贈書者贈送原書主題記："To Miss Clara Wheeler, from "Robert" Xmas 1881。"

7428　Japanese Reading for Beginners Vol. 1/by Arthur Rose-Innes. —Yokohama, Shanghai, Hongkong and Singapore：Kelly & Walsh, Ltd. , [n. d.]

　　246p. ; 21.8cm

　　PKUL（館藏號缺）

　　附注：

　　　題記：扉頁有胡適題記："一九二七，五月，托岩村成允先生代買的。胡適。"

　　　夾紙：頁 6、7 間夾有"貴族院議員海軍中將黑岡帶刀"名片 1 張。

7429　Japanese Trade and Industry：Present and Future/by Mitsubishi Economic Research Bureau. —London：Macmillan and Co. , Limited, 1936

　　XVIII, 663p. ; 23.5cm

　　PKUL（館藏號缺）

7430　Japanese-American Relations/by Iichiro Tokutomi; translated by Sukeshige Yangiwara. —New York：The Macmillan Company, 1922

　　XVI, 207p. ; 19.6cm

　　PKUL（館藏號缺）

　　附注：

　　　題記：題名頁有毛筆標注作者日文名"德富蘇峰"。

7431 Japanese-English and English-Japanese Dictionary/by J. C. Hepburn. —
Shanghai: American Presbyterian Mission Press, 1872

31, 632, 201p. ; 26.5cm

PKUL（館藏號缺）

附注：

印章:封內、題名頁有"R. Lilley"簽名。

夾紙:書內夾有原書主 R. Lilley 讀書筆記 1 頁。

其他:封面脫落,缺書脊。

7432 Japan's Ability to Finance Purchase of War Materials Part I. —[s. l.]:
[s. n.], [n. d.]

17p. ; 28cm

PKUL（館藏號缺）

附注：

題記:封面有作者題記:"適之先生指教,敦元敬贈。"

其他:本書爲油印本。

7433 Japan's Continental Adventure/by Ching-Chun Wang. —London: George
Allen & Unwin Ltd., 1940

224p. ; 20cm

PKUL（館藏號缺）

7434 Japan's Economic Offensive in China/by Lowe Chuan-Hua. —London:
George Allen and Unwin Ltd., 1939

179p. ; 20cm

PKUL（館藏號缺）

7435 Japan's Feet of ClayFreda Utley. —New York: W. W. Norton & Company,
Inc., 1937

393p. ; 22.1cm

PKUL（館藏號缺）

7436 Japan's Fifty-Four Cases/by Shuhsi Hsü. —Peiping：[s. n.]，1932

63p. ；22.6cm

PKUL（館藏號缺）

7437 Japan's Foreign Policy Relating to China/by Tanshowa. —[s. l.]：[s. n.]，[n. d.]

46p. ；27.3cm

PKUL（館藏號缺）

附注：

題記：題名頁有作者題記："儒公大使斧正，招華謹贈，廿六年八月廿六日。"

7438 Japan's Foreign Relations, 1542-1936, a Short History/by Roy Hidemichi Akagi. —Tokyo：The Hokuseido Press, 1936

XIV, 560p. ；22.8cm

PKUL（館藏號缺）

7439 Japan's Public Economy and Finance/by Inazo Nitobé. —Tokyo：The Japan Council of the Institute of Pacific Relations，[n. d.]

42p. ；22.6cm

PKUL（館藏號缺）

7440 Japan's War in China/by Hu Shih. —[s. l.]：[s. n.]，[n. d.]

7p. ；22.9cm

PKUL（館藏號缺）

附注：

其他：本書有9冊。

7441 The Jesuits, 1534-1921：A History of the Society of Jesus from Its

Foundation to the Present Time/by Thomas J. Campbell. —New York: The Encyclopedia Press, 1921

XVI, 937p. ; 21.6cm

PKUL（館藏號缺）

附注：

印章：題名頁鈐有"胡適之印"朱文方印。

題記：扉頁有胡適簽名"Hu Shih, January 9, 1923"。

批注圈劃：書內個別處有胡適批注圈劃。

7442 John Addington Symonds: A Biography/by Horatio F. Brown. —London: Smith, Elder, & Co., 1908

XXIV, 495p. ; 20.8cm

PKUL（館藏號缺）

7443 John Bull's Other Island, in Four Acts/by Bernard Shaw. —London: Constable and Company Ltd., 1914

LIV, 116p. ; 17.5cm

PKUL（館藏號缺）

附注：

題記：扉頁有胡適簽名"Hu Suh, Peking, Oct. 29, 1917"；書名頁前頁有胡適題記："Max O'Rell 曾作'John Bull and His Island'，謂英國也。此書之名本於此。"

批注圈劃：書內7頁有胡適圈劃；書末有胡適注明閱讀日期"Nov. 10, 1917. Hu Suh"。

7444 John Dewey: An Intellectual Portrait/by Sidney Hook. —New York: The John Day Company, 1939

IX, 242p. ; 18.4cm

PKUL（館藏號缺）

附注：

印章：扉頁鈐有"HU SHIH"藍文印。

其他：封內貼有"胡適的書"藏書票。

批注圈劃：書內數頁有胡適批注圈劃。

7445 John Masefield: A Critical Estimate of His Poems and Plays/by Yu Da-yuen. —Peiping: San Yu Press, 1934

109p. ; 18.8cm

PKUL（館藏號缺）

7446 John Webb: A Forgotten Page in the Early History of Sinology in Europe/by Ch'en Shou-Yi. —[s.l.]: [s.n.], [n.d.]

295-330p. ; 24cm

Reprinted from *The Chinese Social and Political Science Review*, Vol. XIX, No. 3

PKUL（館藏號缺）

附註：

題記：封面有作者題記："適之先生教正，受頤敬呈。"

7447 Joint Legislative Committee Report on Education/by The Joint Educational Committee. —Manila: Bureau of Printing, 1926

395p. ; 19.6cm

PKUL（館藏號缺）

附註：

題記：扉頁有贈書者題記："To Dr. Hu Shih, with the compliments of Camilo Osias。"

內附文件：頁 270、271 間夾有 Manuel L. Quezon 致胡適信函 1 封。

7448 Joseph the Provider/by Thomas Mann. —New York: Alfred A. Knopf, 1944

422p. ; 22.2cm

PKUL（館藏號缺）

7449 Journey Among Warriors/by Eve Curie. —Garden City: Doubleday, Doran and

Co., Inc., 1943

501p. ; 23.6cm

PKUL（館藏號缺）

7450 The Journey of Augustus Raymond Margary, from Shanghae to Bhamo, and Back to Manwyne/by Rutherford Alcock. —London: Macmillan and Co., 1876

XXIV, 382p. ; 22cm

PKUL（館藏號缺）

附注：

印章：扉頁有原書主簽名"R. Lilley"。

7451 A Journey to China, or Things Which Are Seen/by Arnold J. Toynbee. —London: Constabel & Co., Ltd., 1931

X, 345p. ; 22.7cm

PKUL（館藏號缺）

附注：

夾紙：書內夾有紙條1張。

7452 Judah P. Benjamin, Confederate Statesman/by Robert Douthat Meade. —New York, London, Toronto: Oxford University Press, 1943

IX, 432p. ; 21.6cm

PKUL（館藏號缺）

7453 The Judas Window/by Carter Dickson. —New York: Pocket Books Inc., 1943

245p. ; 16cm

PKUL（館藏號缺）

附注：

印章：扉頁鈐有"HU SHIH"藍文印。

7454 Junior English Book/by Alfred M. Hitchcock. —New York: Henry Holt and

Company, 1920

XII, 442p. ; 19.2cm

PKUL（館藏號缺）

7455 Junior English Course/by P. H. Deffendall. —Boston: Little, Brown, and Company, 1923

XVI, 384p. ; 19.3cm

PKUL（館藏號缺）

7456 Junior Miss/by Sally Benson. —New York: Random House, 1941

214p. ; 20.8cm

PKUL（館藏號缺）

7457 Juridical Essays and Studies/by John C. H. Wu. —Shanghai: The Commercial Press, Limited, 1928

XVI, 267p. ; 23.5cm

PKUL（館藏號缺）

附注：

題記：扉頁有贈書者題記："With compliments of The Comparative Law School of China。"

7458 The Just and Unjust/by James Gould Cozzens. —New York: Harcourt, Brace and Company, 1942

434p. ; 21.2cm

PKUL（館藏號缺）

7459 Kalle/by Bert G. Anderson. —Stony Creek: [s. n.], 1946

22p. ; 22.9cm

PKUL（館藏號缺）

附注：

印章：書末有作者鋼筆簽名"Bert G. Anderson"。

題記:封內有贈書者題記:"To our very dear friend, Dr. Hu Shih from Pugh and Sucy Ann Moore, of "104"-E-81. This volume is by a friend of yours, whom we saw at New Haven at Christmas。"

7460 Kenil Worth/by Walter Scott. —London: J. M. Dent & Sons Ltd.; New York: E. P. Dutton & Co., Inc., 1906

X, 476p. ; 17.4cm

Everyman's Library: Fiction

PKUL（館藏號缺）

7461 Kenkyusha's New Japanese-English Dictionary/by Takenobu Yoshitaro. — Cambridge: Harvard University Press, 1942

2280p. ; 23.3cm

PKUL（館藏號缺）

7462 Key to Hossfeld's French for the Million/by H. J. Weintz. —London: Hirschfeld Brothers, Limited, [n. d.]

32p. ; 17.9cm

PKUL（館藏號缺）

7463 Key to the Tz? Erh Chi Volume I. —London: Trübner & Co., 1867

IV, 52p. ; 29.2cm

PKUL（館藏號缺）

附注:

題記:扉頁有原書主題記:"Robert Lilley, Chefoo, 20 July, 1869。"

夾紙:書內夾有原書主讀書筆記2頁。

7464 Key to the Tzǔ Erh Chi, Colloquial Series. —London: Trübner & Co., 1867

175, 139, 126, 35, 47p. ; 31.4cm

PKUL（館藏號缺）

附注:

题记：扉页有原书主题记："Robert Lilley, Chefoo, 20 July, 1869, Chefoo, China。"

批注圈劃：书内有原书主批注圈劃甚多。

夹纸：书内夹有原书主读书笔记 18 页，"杨锡蕃"名片 1 张。

其他：本书装订已散。

7465　The Keys of the Kingdom/by A. J. Cronin. —Boston：Little, Brown and Company, 1941

344p. ；20.5cm

PKUL（馆藏号缺）

附注：

题记：扉页有胡适题记："Hu Shih. This work is good in the first half, down to p. 145. The China part is very poor,—very poor in geography, history and sociology. Apparently the author has no real knowledge of China at all. But the first part is as good as his 'Citadel'. This whole work would have been far better if the hero had been allowed to struggle along in some locale well-known to the author, Hu Shih, July 11, 1942"；书名页前页有胡适抄录本书内容："And quite the nicest thing about you, my dear boy, is this—you haven't got that bumptious security which springs from dogma rather than from faith。"

批注圈劃：书中有几处作者蓝笔圈劃。

7466　Kimono/by John Paris. —London：W. Collins Sons & Co., Ltd., 1921

VIII, 345p. ；18.3cm

PKUL（馆藏号缺）

附注：

题记：扉页有胡适题记："John Paris 是英国人 F. Ashton Gankin 的笔名。"

7467　King Lear/by Frank Alanson Lombard. —[s. l.]：[s. n.], [n. d.]

VIII, 385, XVIIp. ；19.3cm

The Students' Shakespeare

PKUL（館藏號缺）

附注：

其他：本書有 21 冊。

7468 The Kingdom of Man/by E. Ray Lankester. —London：Watts & Co.，1912

VIII，114p.；21.3cm

PKUL（館藏號缺）

附注：

印章：題名頁鈐有"胡適"朱文方印。

7469 Kneel to the Prettiest/by Berta Ruck. —Leipzig：Bernhard Tauchnitz，1925

279p.；16.5cm

Collection of British Authors, Tauchnitz Edition

PKUL（館藏號缺）

7470 Know Your Enemy/by T. H. Tetens. —New York：Society for the Prevention of World War III, Inc.，1944

127p.；21.4cm

PKUL（館藏號缺）

7471 Le Kou-Wen Chinois/par Georges Margouliès. —Paris：Librairie Orientaliste，1926

CXXVII, 464p.；25.2cm

PKUL（館藏號缺）

附注：

題記：扉頁有作者題記："胡適之先生教正，俄國馬古烈敬贈，一九廿六。九月廿日。法京巴黎。"

7472 Kuaiwa Hen, Twenty-Five Exercises in the Yedo Colloquial, for the Use of Students/by Ernest Satow. —Yokohama：Lane, Crawford & Co.，1873

2 Vols.；18cm

PKUL（館藏號缺）

附注：

印章：第 1 冊題名頁前頁有 R. Lilley 簽名；第 2 冊扉頁有原書主簽名"R. Lilley"。

其他：第 2 冊封面脫落，書脊破損。

7473 Lady Precious Stream：An Old Chinese Play Done into English According to Its Tradition Style/by S. I. Hsiung. —London：Methuen & Co., Ltd., 1934

XIX, 169p. ；19.4cm

PKUL（館藏號缺）

7474 The Lady with the Dog, and Other Stories/by Anton Tchehov；translated by Constance Garnett. —London：Chatto & Windus, 1917

302p. ；15.7cm

The Tales of Tchehov

PKUL（館藏號缺）

附注：

題記：扉頁有胡適鋼筆簽名"Hu Shih, November 1924"。

夾紙：書內夾有中華郵政快遞郵件收據 1 張。

7475 The Lake/by George Moore. —New York, London：D. Appleton and Company, 1905

309p. ；19cm

PKUL（館藏號缺）

7476 Land and Labour in China/by R. H. Tawney. —London：George Allen & Unwin Ltd., 1932

207p. ；21.9cm

PKUL（館藏號缺）

附注：

題記：扉頁有胡適鋼筆簽名"Hu Shih, Dec. 22, 1932"。

批注圈劃：書內 34 頁有胡適批注圈劃。

7477 Land of the Free/by Herbert Agar. —Boston：Houghton Mifflin Company，1935

VIII，305p. ；21.7cm

PKUL（館藏號缺）

7478 The Land of the Great Image：Being Experiences of Friar Manrique in Arakan/by Maurice Collis. —New York：Alfred Knopf，1943

X，265，Vp. ；21.8cm

PKUL（館藏號缺）

7479 The Land of the Morning：An Account of Japan and Its People, Based on a Four Years' Residence in That Country/by William Gray Dixon. —Edinburgh：James Gemmell，1882

XX，689p. ；19.3cm

PKUL（館藏號缺）

附注：

批注圈劃：書內多頁有鉛筆批注圈劃，非胡適所作。

7480 Land of the Yellow Spring/by Verne Dyson. —New York：Chinese Studies Press，1937

XI，143p. ；19.4cm

PKUL（館藏號缺）

附注：

題記：扉頁有作者題記："Presented by the author to Dr. Hu Shih, a loyal and distinguished son of China, with compliments, and the sincere hope that China may survive disaster as she has done so many times in her long and splended history. Verne Dyson, New York City, November 19, 1937。"

7481 Landmarks in French Literature/by G. L. Strachey. —New York：Henry Holt and Company；London：Williams and Norgate，1912

256p. ;16.8cm

The Home University of Modern Library

PKUL（館藏號缺）

附注：

題記：扉頁有胡適鋼筆簽名"Shu Hu, June 6, 1917"；書末有胡適毛筆題記："此書始終不提 Zola 之名,可謂怪事。"

摺頁：頁 228、230 摺頁。

7482 The Language and Literature of China/by Robert K. Douglas. —London：Trübner & Co., 1875

118p. ;19.1cm

PKUL（館藏號缺）

7483 Language in Action/by S. I. Hayakawa. —New York：Harcourt, Brace and Company, 1940

XIII, 345p. ;20.8cm

PKUL（館藏號缺）

附注：

其他：本書有 2 冊。

7484 Language：A Linguistic Introduction to History/by J. Vendryes; translated by Paul Radin. —New York：Alfred A. Knopf, 1925

XXVIII, 378p. ;23.5cm

The History of Civilization

PKUL（館藏號缺）

附注：

印章：扉頁有胡適毛筆簽名"胡適"。

7485 The Lankavatara Sutra：A Mahayana Text/by Daisetz Teitaro Suzuki. —London：George Routledge and Sons, Ltd., 1932

XLIX, 300p. ;22.2cm

PKUL（館藏號缺）

7486 Laotse Tao Te King, das Buch des Alten vom Sinn und Leben/von Richard Wilhelm. —[s. l.]：Verlag Bei Eugen Diederichs, 1921

XXXII, 118p. ; 21.2cm

PKUL（館藏號缺）

7487 Lao-Tze's Tao-Teh-King/by Paul Carus. —Chicago：The Open Court Publishing Company, 1898

345p. ; 19.9cm

PKUL（館藏號缺）

附注：

題記：扉頁有胡適題記："Hu Shih, Part of the Robert Lilley Library。"

批注圈劃：書內有數處圈劃，似爲原書主所作。

其他：書名頁前幾頁脫落。

7488 Laotzu's Tao and Wu-Wei/by Bhikshu Wai-Tao, Dwight Goddard, Henry Borel, Kiang Kang-hu. —Santa Barbara：[s. n.], 1935

149p. ; 19.2cm

PKUL（館藏號缺）

附注：

夾紙：書內夾有作者 Dwight Goddard 寄書地址。

7489 The Last Puritan：A Memoir in the Form of Novel/by George Santayana. —New York：Charles Scribner's Sons, 1936

602p. ; 20.1cm

PKUL（館藏號缺）

附注：

題記：扉頁有贈書者題記："敬贈適之先生,治,廿五,十,三十,舊金山。"

7490 Latin American Relations with the League of Nations/by Warren H. Kelchner.

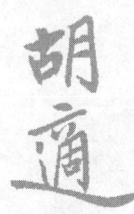

—Boston: World Peace Foundation, 1930

207p. ; 20cm

PKUL（館藏號缺）

7491 Law and Politics: Occasional Papers of Felix Frankfurter, 1913－1938/by Archibald MacLeish, E. F. Prichard, Jr. . —New York: Harcourt, Brace and Company, 1939

XXIV, 352p. ; 22.1cm

PKUL（館藏號缺）

附注：

題記：扉頁有作者題記："For Dr. Hu Shih, humanist, with the highest esteem of Felix Frankfurter, 13 November '39。"

7492 Law and the Administration of Justice/by Roscoe C. Pound. —Nanking: The Sino-American Cultural Service, 1947

113p. ; 18.4cm

PKUL（館藏號缺）

附注：

印章：扉頁有胡適鋼筆簽名"胡適"。

7493 The Law: Business or Prefession? /by Julius Henry Cohen. —New York: The Banks Law Publishing Co. , 1916

XVIII, 415p. ; 18.8cm

PKUL（館藏號缺）

附注：

題記：扉頁有作者題記："To my friend Suh Hu, with very good wishes of Julius Henry Cohen, Nov. 10, 1916。"

夾紙：書內夾有 H. L. Huang 致胡適英文明信片1張。

7494 Lays of Ancient Rome with Ivry and the Armada/by Lord MaCaulay. —London, New York, Toronto: Oxford University Press, [n. d.]

XXVI, 113p. ; 15.4cm

The World's Classics

PKUL（館藏號缺）

附注：

　　印章：扉頁鈐有"適盦藏書"朱文圓印。

　　題記：扉頁胡適題記："戊申十一月陳鍾英贈，適之。"

　　批注圈劃：書內2頁有胡適批注圈劃。

7495 A Leaf in the Storm/by Lin Yutang. —New York：The John Day Company, 1941

368p. ; 21.5cm

PKUL（館藏號缺）

附注：

　　印章：扉頁鈐有"語堂"朱文方印。

　　題記：扉頁林語堂題字："適之兄教正。弟語堂敬贈，卅年十一月十一日於紐約。"

7496 Learning the Ways of Democracy：A Case Book of Civic Education. —Washington：Educational Policies Commission，[n.d.]

486p. ; 23.3cm

PKUL（館藏號缺）

7497 Leaves from My Chinese Scrapbook/by Frederic Henry Balfour. —London：Trübner & Co., 1887

215p. ; 21.8cm

PKUL（館藏號缺）

附注：

　　其他：封面前頁貼有出版社贈書卡："With the Publisher's Compliments。"

7498 Leaves of Grass/by Walt Whitman. —New York：Doubleday, Doran & Co., Inc., 1940

XIII, 316p. ; 27.2cm

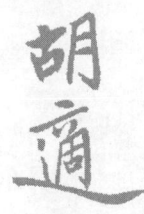

PKUL（館藏號缺）

附注：

其他：封内貼有"胡適的書"藏書票。

7499 Leberecht Hühnchen/von Heinrich Seidel. —Boston：D. C. Heath & Co. , Publishers, 1910

IV, 120p. ; 16.5cm

PKUL（館藏號缺）

附注：

題記：扉頁有胡適題記："此書天趣盎然，短篇小説中不可多得之作也。適之。《虛馨傳》。"

批注圈劃：書内72頁有胡適批注圈劃，以圈劃爲主。文末記有胡適讀書日期"March 6, 1911. S. Hu"。

7500 Lecture and Essays/by William Kingdon Clifford. —London：Watts & Co. , 1918

123p. ; 21.7cm

PKUL（館藏號缺）

7501 Lectures and Essays/by John Tyndall. —London：Watts & Co. , 1920

120p. ; 21.7cm

PKUL（館藏號缺）

7502 Lectures and Essays/by Thomas Henry Huxley. —London：Macmillan and Co. , Limited, 1910

128p. ; 21.6cm

PKUL（館藏號缺）

附注：

題記：題名頁有胡適簽名"Hu Shih, London, (Dec. 29) 1926"。

其他：裝訂破損。

7503 Lectures and Essays/by Colonel R. G. Ingersoll. —London：Watts & Co. ,

1926

160, 160, 160p. ; 21.4cm

PKUL（館藏號缺）

附注：

其他：封面脱落、缺封底。

7504 Lectures on Government/by Edmund J. James. —Urbana: University of Illinois, 1938

62p. ; 23cm

PKUL（館藏號缺）

7505 Lectures on Government Third Series/by Edmund J. James. —Urbana: University of Illinois, 1944

73p. ; 23.4cm

PKUL（館藏號缺）

7506 Lectures on Government Fourth Series/by Edmund J. James. —Urbana: University of Illinois, 1947

93p. ; 23.3cm

PKUL（館藏號缺）

7507 Lectures on Japan: An Outline of the Development of the Japanese People and Their Culture/by Inazo Nitobé. —Tokyo: Kenkyusha, 1936

XII, 393p. ; 19.6cm

PKUL（館藏號缺）

附注：

夾紙：其中一冊夾有明信片1張。

其他：本書有2冊。

7508 The Legal Obligations Arising Out of Treaty Relations between China and Other States/by Min-ch'ien T. Z. Tyau. —Shanghai: Commercial Press,

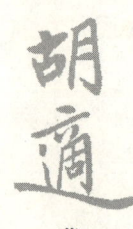

Limited, 1917

XXII, 304p. ; 23.2cm

PKUL（館藏號缺）

7509 The Legend of the Christmas Rose: Five Christmas Paintings and Their Interpretations/by Henry E. Jackson. —New York: George H. Doran Company, 1914

113p. ; 20.1cm

PKUL（館藏號缺）

附注：

印章：獻贈頁有 Robert Jackson 和 Ruth Jackson 簽名。

題記：扉頁有作者題記："Presented to Mr. Suh Hu together with high personal regards and best wishes of his friend the author Henry E. Jackson, Jan 22-1915。"

7510 The Legislative Way of Life/by T. V. Smith. —Chicago: The University of Chicago Press, [n.d.]

XI, 101p. ; 19.1cm

PKUL（館藏號缺）

附注：

題記：扉頁有作者題記："Ambassador Hu Shih, His Excellency, in happy thought of a great tradition celebrated of late in high talk amid gracious hospitality. T. V. Smith, Dec. 25, 1940。"

7511 Leibniz: Discourse on Metaphysics, Correspondence with Arnauld and Monadology/by George R. Montgomery. —Chicago, London: The Open Court Publishing Company, 1902

XXIII, 276p. ; 19.5cm

PKUL（館藏號缺）

附注：

題記：扉頁有胡適毛筆簽名"Hu Suh, March 1919"。

7512 Lessons in the Shanghai Dialect/by F. L. Hawks Pott. —Shanghai: The American Presbyterian Mission Press, 1909

　　VIII, 145p. ; 24.2cm

　　PKUL（館藏號缺）

　　附注：

　　　　題記：扉頁有題記："Mrs. J. C. Clark。"

　　　　其他：本書封面書脊脱落,散頁,缺頁。

7513 Let the People Know/by Norman Angell. —New York: The Viking Press, 1943

　　VIII, 245p. ; 21.8cm

　　PKUL（館藏號缺）

7514 The Letter and the Spirit/by Monroe E. Deutsch. —Berkeley, Los Angeles: University of California Press, 1943

　　VIII, 378p. ; 20.4cm

　　PKUL（館藏號缺）

　　附注：

　　　　題記：扉頁有作者題記："With the friendship and esteem of Monroe E. Deutsch。"

7515 Letters by Baron Richthofen on the Provinces of Chili, Shansi, Shensi, Sz'-Chwan, with Notes on Mongolia, Kansu, Yünnan and Kwei-Chau No. VII/by Baron Richthofen. —Shanghai: Office of the "North China Herald", 1872

　　86p. ; 33.2cm

　　PKUL（館藏號缺）

　　附注：

　　　　其他：本書封面破損,缺封底。

7516 Letters from China and Japan/by John Dewey, Alice Chipman Dewey. —New

York: E. P. Dutton & Company, 1920

VI, 311p. ; 19.2cm

PKUL（館藏號缺）

附注：

題記：扉頁有贈書者題記："With warm regards to Mr. Hu, Peking, 1921。"

摺頁：頁290有摺頁。

7517 Letters Home from Persia with Observation on Palestine and Southern Russia/by Paul D. Cravath. —New York: The Country Life Press, 1936

60p. ; 19.4cm

PKUL（館藏號缺）

附注：

題記：封面有贈書者題記："For Mr. Hu Shih。"

7518 Letters Home from the South Sea Islands, China and Japan, 1934/by Paul D. Cravath. —Garden City: Country Life Press, 1934

VI, 107p. ; 19.4cm

PKUL（館藏號缺）

附注：

題記：題名頁有贈書者填寫"For Mr. Hu Shih"。

7519 Letters of a Chinese Amazon and War-Time Essays/by Lin Yutang. —Shanghai: The Commercial Press, Limited, 1930

XIV, 211p. ; 18.9cm

PKUL（館藏號缺）

附注：

題記：扉頁有作者題記："適之先生，語堂持贈，一九三零，五月十二日於上海。"

7520 The Letters of Bret Harte/by Geoffrey Bret Harte. —Boston, New York: Houghton Mifflin Company, 1926

XVIII, 515p. ; 22.3cm

PKUL（館藏號缺）

7521 The Letters of Disraeli to Lady Chesterfield and Lady Bradford/by The Marquis of Zetland. —New York: D. Appleton and Company, 1929

2 Vols. ; 22.8cm

PKUL（館藏號缺）

附注：

　印章：兩卷扉頁均鈐有"HU SHIH"藍文印。

7522 Letters of Grover Cleveland/by Allan Nevins. —Boston and New York: Houghton Mifflin Company, 1933

XIX, 640p. ; 23.9cm

PKUL（館藏號缺）

附注：

　印章：扉頁鈐有"HU SHIH"藍文印。

7523 The Letters of John Stuart Mill/by Hugh S. R. Elliot, Mary Taylor. —New York, Bombay, Calcutta: Longmans, Green and Co., 1910

2 Vols. (XLVI, 312, 408p.)p. ; 23.2cm

PKUL（館藏號缺）

7524 The Letters of Katherine Mansfield Vol. II/by J. Middleton Murry. —London: Constable & Co., Ltd., 1928

269p. ; 19.1cm

PKUL（館藏號缺）

7525 Letters of Lord Acton to Mary Gladstone/by Herbert Paul. —New York: The Macmillan Company, 1904

353p. ; 20.9cm

PKUL（館藏號缺）

附注：

　　題記：扉頁有胡適朱筆簽名"Suh Hu, Feb. 1917"。

7526　Letters of Marcus Tullius Cicero with His Treatises on Friendship and Old Age, Letters of Gaius Plinius Caecilius Secundus/by Charles W. Eliot. — New York: P. F. Collier & Son, 1909

　　438p. ; 19.5cm

　　The Harvard Classics No. 9

　　PKUL（館藏號缺）

　　附注：

　　　印章：扉頁有胡適簽名"Suh Hu"；題名頁鈐有"適盦藏書"朱文圓印。

7527　Letters to a Missionary/by R. F. Johnston. —London: Watts & Co., 1918

　　XXVI, 158p. ; 18.4cm

　　PKUL（館藏號缺）

　　附注：

　　　題記：扉頁有作者題記："To Dr. Hu Suh, with compliment from R. F. Johnston, Peking, April 24, 1919。"

7528　Leviathan/by Thomas Hobbes. —London: J. M. Dent & Sons Ltd. ; New York: E. P. Dutton & Co., Inc., 1914

　　XXXIV, 392p. ; 17.1cm

　　Everyman's Library: Philosophy and Theology

　　PKUL（館藏號缺）

　　附注：

　　　印章：扉頁鈐有"HU SHIH"藍文印。

7529　Li Hung-Chang: His Korea Policies, 1870–1885/by T. C. Lin. —[s. l.]: [s. n.], [n. d.]

　　202–233p. ; 24.1cm

　　Reprinted from *The Chinese Social and Political Science Review*, Vol. XIX, No.

2, July. 1935

PKUL（館藏號缺）

附注：

 題記：封面有作者題記："適之先生正，林同濟呈。"

7530 Liability in the Law of Aviation/by Lincoln H. Cha. —Shanghai：The Commercial Press, 1935

 VIII, 169p. ; 22.3cm

 PKUL（館藏號缺）

 附注：

  印章：扉頁鈐有作者"查修"朱文方印。

  題記：扉頁有作者題記："適之先生教正，查修敬贈，二四，八，十二。"

7531 Liberal Education Re-examined：Its Role in a Democracy/by Theodore M. Greene. —New York and London：Harper & Brothers Publishers, 1943

 XIV, 134p. ; 22cm

 PKUL（館藏號缺）

 附注：

  夾紙：書內夾有 The American Council of Learned Societies 贈書卡 1 張。

7532 Liberalism and Social Action/by John Dewey. —New York：G. P. Putnam's Sons, 1935

 VIII, 93p. ; 20.2cm

 PKUL（館藏號缺）

 附注：

  印章：一冊書名頁鈐"HU SHIH"藍文印。

  題記：另一冊扉頁有英文簽名，不易辨識；后有"Shanghai, December 1935"字樣。

  批注圈劃：一冊書內 77 頁有胡適批注圈劃。

  其他：本書有 3 冊。

7533 The Liberation of Mankind: The Story of Man's Struggle for the Right to Think/by Hendrik Willem Van Loon. —London, Calcutta, Sydney: George G. Harrap & Company Ltd., 1926

307p. ; 22.6cm

PKUL（館藏號缺）

附注：

印章：扉頁鈐有"上海極司非而路四十九號甲,胡適之"藍文方印。

7534 The Life and Adventure of Nicholas Nickleby/by Charles Dickens. —London: J. M. Dent & Sons Ltd. ; New York: E. P, Dutton & Co., 1907

XXX, 843p. ; 17.2cm

Everyman's Library: Fiction

PKUL（館藏號缺）

7535 The Life and Growth of Language: An Outline of Linguistic Science/by William Dwight Whitney. —New York: D. Appleton and Company, 1896

VII, 326p. ; 19.8cm

PKUL（館藏號缺）

7536 The Life and Letters of Charles Darwin: Including an Autobiographical Chapter/by Francis Darwin. —New York and London: D. Appleton and Company, 1911

2 Vols. ; 19.5cm

PKUL（館藏號缺）

附注：

題記：第1卷扉頁有胡適題記："《達爾文》上,適之"；第2卷扉頁有胡適題記："《達爾文》下,適之。"

內附文件：第1卷頁48、49間夾有翁文灝請柬1份,上書"於十月十日下午二時並潔備茶點,恭請光教。翁文灝謹訂"。

7537 Life and Letters of Thomas Henry Huxley/by Leonard Huxley. —New York and London：D. Appleton and Company，1900

　　2 Vols. ；20.9cm

　　PKUL（館藏號缺）

　　附注：

　　　　題記：第1卷扉頁有胡適題記："《赫胥黎傳》上，適之"；第2卷扉頁有胡適題記："《赫胥黎傳》下，適之。"

7538　The Life and Morals of Jesus of Nazareth/by Thomas Jefferson. —New York：Wilfred Funk，Inc.，1940

　　XI，132p. ；16.6cm

　　PKUL（館藏號缺）

　　附注：

　　　　其他：封內貼有"胡適的書"藏書票。

7539　The Life and Times of William Howard Taft/by Henry F. Pringle. —New York，Toronto：Farrar & Rinehart，Inc.，1939

　　2 Vols.（XII，1106p.）；23cm

　　PKUL（館藏號缺）

　　附注：

　　　　內附文件：書內夾有作者致胡適書信1頁；書內夾有 The Saturday Evening Post 剪報1份。

　　　　其他：兩卷封內均貼有"胡適的書"藏書票。

7540　The Life and Works of Laurence Sterne/by John W. Gunn. —Girard：Haldeman-Julius Company，[n. d.]

　　64p. ；12.6cm

　　Little Blue Book

　　PKUL（館藏號缺）

7541　Life of Christ/by Giovanni Papini；translated by Dorothy Canfield Fisher. —New York：Harcourt，Brace and Company，1923

416p. ；20.8cm

PKUL（館藏號缺）

7542 Life of George Cadbury/by A. G. Gardiner. —London：Cassell and Company, Limited, [n.d.]

XI, 308p. ；18.3cm

PKUL（館藏號缺）

附注：

題記：扉頁有胡適題記："From my friend H. G. Wood, Xmas, 1926。"

7543 The Life of Greece/by Will Durant. —New York：Simon and Schuster, 1939

XVIII, 754p. ；25.3cm

The Story of Civilization

PKUL（館藏號缺）

7544 The Life of Jesus/by Ernest Renan. —London：Watts & Co., 1924

153p. ；21.5cm

PKUL（館藏號缺）

附注：

其他：本書缺封面、封底。

7545 The Life of Lorenzo de' Medici Called the Magnificent/by William Roscoe. —London：George Bell and Sons, 1902

564p. ；18.5cm

PKUL（館藏號缺）

7546 The Life of Pasteur/by René Vallery-Radot. —New York：Doubleday, Page & Company, 1924

XXI, 484p. ；21.5cm

PKUL（館藏號缺）

附注：

题记:扉页有胡适题记:"百年纪念本《巴斯特传》,胡适。"

批注圈劃:書內有20餘處有胡適批注圈劃;書末有胡適注明閱讀日期"Dec. 11, 1925,病中讀完。Hu Shih"。

7547 The Life of the Spider/by J. Henri Fabre; translated by Alexander Teixeira de Mattos. —New York: Dodd, Mead and Company, 1912

404p. ; 19.2cm

PKUL(館藏號缺)

7548 Life of William Booth, the Founder of the Salvation Army/by Harold Begbie. —London: Macmillan and Co., Limited, 1926

2 Vols. ; 18.3cm

PKUL(館藏號缺)

附注:

其他:第2卷頁34、35間夾有名片1張,上印有"救世軍華北區域總指揮,邊衛德,北平王府大街七十一號",背面有英文"Alfred J. Benwell"等字樣。

7549 The Life of William Carey, Shoemaker and Missionary/by George Smith. —London: J. M. Dent & Sons Ltd.; New York: E. P, Dutton & Co., 1909

VIII, 326p. ; 17.1cm

Everyman's Library: Biography

PKUL(館藏號缺)

7550 Life: A Book for Elementary Students/by Arthur E. Shipley. —Cambridge: Cambridge University Press, 1925

XVI, 204p. ; 18cm

PKUL(館藏號缺)

附注:

题记:扉頁有作者題記:"Dr. Hu Shih, from the author, armistice Day 1927。"

7551 The Light of Asia, or the Great Renunciation/by Edwin Arnold. —Boston:
Roberts Brothers, 1880

XI, 238, 23p. ; 17.9cm

PKUL（館藏號缺）

附注：

批注圈劃：書内有多頁鉛筆批注圈劃，非胡適所作。

7552 Limitation of Armament on the Great Lakes. —Washington: The Endowment, 1914

VII, 57p. ; 24.7cm

PKUL（館藏號缺）

附注：

印章：封面有胡適簽名"Suh Hu"。

7553 Lincoln the Unknown/by Dale Carnegie. —New York, London: D. Appleton-Century Company, Incorporated, 1942

X, 305p. ; 20cm

PKUL（館藏號缺）

附注：

題記：扉頁有作者題記："My dear ambassador Shih Hu: Abr. Lincoln used to say: may you pluck a thistle and plant a flower wherever you feel a flower will grow. Dale Carnegie, January 2, 1942。"

7554 List of Embassies and Legations in Washington. —[s. l.]: Department of State, 1942

101p. ; 14.6cm

PKUL（館藏號缺）

7555 Literary and Philosophical Essays: French, German and Italian/by Charles W. Eliot. —New York: P. F. Collier & Son, 1910

419p. ; 19.5cm

The Harvard Classics No. 32

PKUL（館藏號缺）

附注：

　　印章：扉頁有胡適簽名"Suh Hu"。

　　批注圈劃：書內 70 頁有胡適批注圈劃。

　　夾紙：書內夾有"孫洪芬"名片 1 張。

7556　Literary History of Sanskrit Buddhism/by G. K. Nariman. —Bombay：Indian Book Dept, [n. d.]

　　XIII, 393p. ; 24.8cm

　　PKUL（館藏號缺）

　　附注：

　　題記：封面有贈書者題記："Presented to Dr. Hu Shih by his friend □ Peking, January 2nd 1924。"

7557　The Literary Renaissance/by Hu Shih. —Shanghai：China Institute of Pacific Relations, [n. d.]

　　15p. ; 22.3cm

　　Preliminary Paper Prepared for the Fourth Biennial Conference of the Institute of Pacific Relations

　　PKUL（館藏號缺）

　　附注：

　　其他：本書有 21 冊。

7558　The Literary Society in Peace and War/by Thomas M. Spaulding. —Menasha：George Banta Publishing Company, 1947

　　37p. ; 23.7cm

　　PKUL（館藏號缺）

　　附注：

　　題記：扉頁有胡適鋼筆題記："Hu Shih, Presented by the Author,

November, 1947。"

7559 The Little Book of English Composition/by E. A. Cross. —Boston: Little, Brown, and Company, 1926

IX, 175p. ; 18.4cm

PKUL（館藏號缺）

7560 The Little Grammar/by E. A. Cross. —Boston: Little, Brown, and Company, 1927

XVI, 148p. ; 18.5cm

PKUL（館藏號缺）

7561 Little Journeys to the Homes of English Authors Volume VII/by Elbert Hubbard. —New York: The Roycrofters, 1899

161p. ; 19.5cm

PKUL（館藏號缺）

7562 Livelihood in Peking: An Analysis of the Budgets of Sixty Families/by L. K. Tao. —Peking: Social Research Department, China Foundation for the Promotion of Education and Culture, 1928

158, XXIIp. ; 21.2cm

Social Research Publications

PKUL（館藏號缺）

附注：

印章：扉頁鈐有"上海極司非而路四十九號甲,胡適之"藍文長方印。

7563 The Lives, Heroic Deeds & Sayings of Gargantua & His Son Pantagruel Books IV & V/by François Rabelais; translated by Thomas Urquhart, Peter Le Motteux. —London: Chatto & Windus, 1921

XIII, 367p. ; 15.7cm

PKUL（館藏號缺）

附注：

　　印章：扉頁有胡適鋼筆簽名"Hu Shih"。

7564　Living Issues in Religious Thought：From George Fox to Bertrand Russell/
　　by H. G. Wood. —London：George Allen & Unwin Ltd. ; New York：George H.
　　Doran Company，1926

　　　187p. ; 18.5cm

　　　PKUL（館藏號缺）

　　　附注：

　　　　題記：扉頁有胡適題記："From the author H. G. Wood, Woodbrooke, Selly Oak。"

7565　Living Philosophies/by Albert Einstein et al. —New York：Simon and Schuster，1931

　　　334p. ; 23.7cm

　　　PKUL（館藏號缺）

　　　附注：

　　　　印章：一冊扉頁有胡適鉛簽名"Hu Shih"。

　　　　題記：一冊扉頁有編者題記："with the gratitudes of your 'editor' Henry Goddard Leach. Cambridge, March 18, 1945"；另一冊扉頁有胡適藍筆簽名"Hu Shih, July 5, 1931"。

　　　　批注圈劃：另一冊書內個別處有胡適圈劃。

　　　　內附文件：另一冊書末夾有"Book-of-the-Month Club News, June 1931"一份；另書末貼有剪報1份。

　　　　與胡適的關係：本書頁235—263收錄胡適的回憶文章。

　　　　其他：本書有2冊。另一冊封內貼有出版社贈書卡1張。

7566　Living Things/by J. W. N. Sullivan. —London, Edinburgh, Paris, et al：
　　Thomas Nelson & Sons Ltd., 1938

　　　134p. ; 17.2cm

　　　PKUL（館藏號缺）

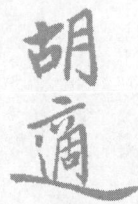

7567 The Living Thoughts of Thomas Jefferson/by John Dewey. —New York, Toronto: Longmans, Green and Co., 1940

173p. ; 18.1cm

PKUL（館藏號缺）

附注：

批注圈劃：書內50頁有胡適批注圈劃。

7568 A Loan Exhibition of the Works of Shepard Alonzo Mount, 1804-1868/by Heckscher Art Museum. —New York: Heckscher Art Museum, 1945

25p. ; 27.8cm

PKUL（館藏號缺）

附注：

題記：扉頁有贈書者題記："To Dr. Hu Shih, from Albert A. Smith。"

7569 Locke/by S. Alexander. —London: Archibald Constable & Co., Ltd., 1908

90p. ; 17.2cm

Philosophies Ancient & Modern

PKUL（館藏號缺）

附注：

題記：扉頁有胡適鉛筆簽名"Suh Hu, March 1919"。

7570 Logic, Inductive and Deductive: An Introduction to Scientific Method/by Adam Leroy Jones. —New York: Henry Holt and Company, 1909

X, 304p. ; 18.7cm

PKUL（館藏號缺）

附注：

印章：扉頁有胡適鉛筆簽名"Hu Shih"。

7571 Logic: In Three Books of Thought, of Investigation and of Knowledge/by Hermann Lotze; translated by Bernard Bosanquet. —Oxford: The Clarendon

Press, 1888

2 Vols. ; 20.2cm

Clarendon Press Series

PKUL（館藏號缺）

附注：

批注圈劃：第1卷書內數頁有鉛筆圈劃。

7572 Logic: The Theory of Inquiry/by John Dewey. —New York: Henry Holt and Company, 1938

VIII, 546p. ; 23.4cm

PKUL（館藏號缺）

附注：

印章：書名頁鈐有"胡適"朱文長方印。

題記：扉頁有胡適題記："一九三八年十月二十日,杜威先生七十九歲生日,他送我這一本新書。胡適。"

7573 London: And Its Environs: Handbook for Travellers/by Karl Baedeker. —Leipzig: Karl Baedeker; London: T. Fisher Unwin; New York: Charles Scribner's Son, 1915

XL, 487p. ; 15.7cm

PKUL（館藏號缺）

附注：

題記：扉頁有贈書者題記："九年十月二十日抵倫敦購閱。這本書是吾到倫敦的第一天在牛津街買的,送給適之。子美,十五,七,十四。"

7574 Looking Forward: What Will the American People Do about It? /by Nicholas Murray Butler. —New York, London: Charles Scribner's Sons, 1932

XIV, 418p. ; 20.8cm

PKUL（館藏號缺）

7575 Lord Jim/by Joseph Conrad. —New York: The Modern Library, 1931

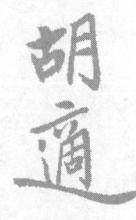

IX, 417p. ; 17.5cm

The Modern Library of the World's Best Books

PKUL（館藏號缺）

7576 Lord Macaulay: Victorian Liberal/by Richmond Croom Beatty. —Norman: University of Oklahoma Press, 1938

XVI, 387p. ; 23.2cm

PKUL（館藏號缺）

附注：

印章：扉頁有胡適藍筆簽名"Hu Shih"。

批注圈劃：書內10餘頁有胡適藍筆批注圈劃。

7577 Lost Horizon/by James Hilton. —New York: William Morrow & Company, 1933

277p. ; 19.5cm

PKUL（館藏號缺）

附注：

夾紙：書內夾有贈書者 Newton D. Baker 名片1張。

7578 Lost Island/by James Norman Hall. —Boston: Little, Brown and Company, 1944

212p. ; 19.6cm

PKUL（館藏號缺）

7579 Lost Visions/by Harry Augustus Garfield. —[s.l.]: Privately Printed, 1944

XI, 277p. ; 20.4cm

PKUL（館藏號缺）

附注：

題記：封內貼有標籤"This volume is sent to you by the children of Mr. and Mrs. Harry A. Garfield as a gift from Mrs. Garfield, in compliance with directions left by her at the time of her death"；扉頁胡適題記："Hu Shih, Dec. 7, 1944. Gift from Estate of Belle M. Garfield, care of Mrs. J. P. Comer, 54 South St., Williams Town, Mass"；書名頁前頁胡適題記："Dr.

Harry A. Garfield 同他的夫人在華府時，常來'雙橡園'看我，常邀我去他們家裏吃飯閒談。此書記他們1934年遊日本、中國的感想，特別留意我的談話與文字，使我讀了很深刻的感覺平時對人說話與發表文字都有很嚴重的意義，都不可不說真話，說負責任的話。這位前輩老友如此注意我的言論（我完全不知道），真使我格外感覺惶恐，格外感覺做一個'公民'的責任嚴重。Dec. 7, 1944. 胡適。"

7580 Louisana Hayride: The American Rehearsal for Dictatorship, 1928·1940/by Harnett T. Kane. —New York: William Morrow & Company, 1941

  VIII, 471p. ; 22.2cm

  PKUL（館藏號缺）

 附注：

  題記：扉頁有作者題記："For Dr. Hu Shih, a gentleman, a scholar, and a good democrat, with all good wishes, Harnett J. Kane。"

7581 Love and Other Stories/by Guy de Maupassant. —Girard: Haldeman-Julius Company, [n. d.]

  63p. ; 12.5cm

  Little Blue Book

  PKUL（館藏號缺）

7582 Lu Hsiang-Shan: A Twelfth Century Chinese Idealist Philosopher/by Siu-Chi Huang. —New Haven: American Oriental Society, 1944

  116p. ; 25.4cm

  American Oriental Series

  PKUL（館藏號缺）

 附注：

  其他：本書缺封底。

7583 Lust for Life: A Novel of Vincent von Gogh/by Irving Stone. —New York: The Heritage Club, 1937

507p. ; 24.4cm

PKUL（館藏號缺）

附注：

夾紙：書內夾有孟治賀年名片1張。

7584 A Lute of Jade: Being Selections from the Classical Poets of China/by L. Cranmer-Byng. —London: John Murray, 1911

116p. ; 16.8cm

The Wisdom of the East Series

PKUL（館藏號缺）

7585 The Lyrical Dramas of Aeschylus/translated by John Stuart Blackie. —London: J. M. Dent & Sons Ltd. ; New York: E. P, Dutton & Co. , 1906

437p. ; 17.2cm

Everyman's Library: Classical

PKUL（館藏號缺）

附注：

題記：扉頁有胡適毛筆簽名"Hu Suh, Peking, Nov. 1917"。

7586 Lyrics from the Chinese/by Helen Waddell. —Boston, New York: Houghton Mifflin Company, 1916

XI, 41p. ; 20cm

PKUL（館藏號缺）

附注：

題記：扉頁有胡適題記："Suh Hu, Gift from Elmer Beller, Sept. 1916. New York."

批注圈劃：書內3頁有胡適批注。

7587 MacArthur and the War against Japan/by Frazier Hunt. —New York: Charles Scribner's Sons, 1944

VIII, 182p. ; 20.8cm

PKUL（館藏號缺）

附注：

題記：扉頁有作者題記："To Mr. Hu Shih—this little book about and the great man. Most sincerely, Frazier Hunt, Sept. 10-1945。"

7588 Mademoiselle Fifi and Other Stories/by Guy de Maupassant. —Girard：Haldeman-Julius Company, [n. d.]

64p. ; 12.6cm

Little Blue Book

PKUL（館藏號缺）

7589 Magic and Fetishism/by Alfred C. Haddon. —London：Constable & Company, 1921

VIII, 99p. ; 17.5cm

PKUL（館藏號缺）

7590 The Magic Casket/by R. Austin Freeman. —London：Hodder and Stoughton Limited, [n. d.]

309p. ; 18.2cm

PKUL（館藏號缺）

7591 Magic Herbs：The Story of Chinese Medicine/by Carlton Kendall. —[s. l.]：[s. n.], [n. d.]

8p. ; 24.7cm

Reprinted from *The China Journal*, Vol. XVI, No. 6

PKUL（館藏號缺）

附注：

題記：首頁有作者題記："To a great scholar with my compliments, Carlton Kendall。"

7592 Main Current in American Thought：An Interpretation of American Literature

from the Beginning to 1920/by Vernon Louis Parrington. —New York: Harcourt, Brace and Company, 1930

XVII, 413; XXII, 493; XXXIX, 429 p. ; 21.7cm

7593 Making International Law Work/by George W. Keeton, George Schwarzenberger. —London: Peace Book Company (London) Ltd., 1939

219p. ; 21.9cm

The New Commonwealth Institute Monographs

PKUL（館藏號缺）

附注：

其他：封內貼有"Sir Montague Burton, Harrogate, England"藏書票 1 張。

7594 The Making of the Modern Mind: A Survey of the Intellectual Background of the Present Age/by John Herman Randall, Jr. . —Boston, New York, Chicago, Dallas, San Francisco: Houghton Mifflin Company, 1926

X, 653p. ; 20.3cm

PKUL（館藏號缺）

附注：

題記：扉頁有胡適題記："H. S from C., 12/IX/33"；封內有鉛筆題記："Ithaca, Sept. '33。"

7595 The Making of Tomorrow/by Raoul de Roussy de Sales. —New York: Reynal & Hitchcock, 1942

340p. ; 21.8cm

PKUL（館藏號缺）

附注：

夾紙：書內夾有本書評論 1 份。

7596 Mammal-like Reptiles from Lufeng, Yunnan, China/by Chung-Chien Young. —[s.l.]: [s.n.], [n.d.]

537-597p. ; 25.5cm

Reprinted from *Proc. Zool. Soc.*, Vol. 117, Parts II & III

PKUL（館藏號缺）

附注：

  題記：封面有作者題記："適之先生賜正,學生楊鍾健贈,廿七,四,十。"

7597 Man and Medicine：An Introduction to Medical Knowledge/by Henry E. Sigerist. —New York：W. W. Norton & Company, Inc.，[n. d.]

  X, 340p. ; 21.5cm

  PKUL（館藏號缺）

  附注：

    題記：扉頁胡適題記："一九三三年一月七日,重到商務印書館發行部,雖有滄海桑田之感,但同時很感覺中興新氣象,故我買了幾部書做紀念,這一冊醫學小史是其中的一部。"

7598 Man and Medicine：An Introduction to Medical Knowledge/by Henry E. Sigerist. —New York：W. W. Norton & Company, Inc., 1932

  X, 340p. ; 22.2cm

  PKUL（館藏號缺）

  附注：

    批注圈劃：書內數頁有胡適批注圈劃。

7599 Man and Society：In an Age of Reconstruction/by Karl Mannheim. —New York：Harcourt, Brace and Company, 1940

  XIX, 469p. ; 22cm

  PKUL（館藏號缺）

  附注：

    內附文件：書內夾有 Lawrence Morris 致胡適英文書信 1 頁。

7600 Man and Superman：A Comedy and a Philosophy/by Bernard Shaw. —Leipzig：Bernhard Tauchnitz, [n. d.]

  326p. ; 16.5cm

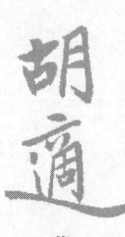

PKUL（館藏號缺）

附注：

題記：書名頁有胡適題記："《人與超人》，一九二五，六，四，病中讀完。適之。"

7601 A Man from the North/by Arnold Bennett. —London：Methuen & Co. , Ltd. , 1912

264p. ; 18.8cm

PKUL（館藏號缺）

7602 Man：The Miracle Maker/by Hendrik Van Loon. —[s. l.]：Horace Liveright Inc. , 1928

252p. ; 24.2cm

PKUL（館藏號缺）

7603 Man, the Unknown/by Alexis Carrel. —New York and London：Harper & Brothers Publishers, 1935

XV, 346p. ; 21.8cm

PKUL（館藏號缺）

附注：

題記：扉頁有贈書者題記："To my good friend Dr. Hu Shih, as a reminder of many visits on the 'Express of Japan' □ to Shanghai。Nov. 14 to Dec. 1, 1936. from Edward H. Hume。"

夾紙：書內夾紙條1張, T. H. Stevenson to Hu Shih。

7604 Man, the Unknown/by Alexis Carrel. —New York, London：Harper & Brothers Publishers, 1939

XXV, 346p. ; 22.5cm

PKUL（館藏號缺）

7605 Manchuria in History/by Li Chi. —Peiping：Peking Union Bookstore, 1932

43p. ; 22.2cm

PKUL（館藏號缺）

7606 Manchuria in the Ming Empire/by T. C. Lin. —[s.l.]: [s.n.], [n.d.]

43p. ; 25.4cm

Reprinted from *Nankai Social and Economic Quarterly* Vol. VIII, No. 1

PKUL（館藏號缺）

附注：

題記：封面有作者題記："適之先生指正，同濟敬呈。"

7607 Manchuria: A Survey of Its Economic Development/by Y. Sakatani. —[s.l.]:[s.n.], [n.d.]

XV, 305p. ; 29.1cm

PKUL（館藏號缺）

附注：

其他：此爲打印件。

7608 Manchuria: Land of Opportunities/by South Manchuria Railway Co. . —New York: Thomas F. Logan, Inc., 1922

IX, 113p. ; 23.5cm

PKUL（館藏號缺）

7609 Manchurian Booty and International Law/by Daniel H. Lew. —[s.l.]: [s.n.],[n.d.]

584-592p. ; 26cm

Reprinted from *The American Journal of International Law* Vol. 40, No. 3

PKUL（館藏號缺）

附注：

題記：封面有作者題記："To Dr. Hu Shih, with highest esteem, from Daniel Lew。"

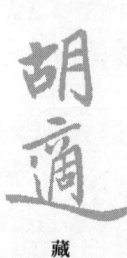

7610 The Manchurian Question/by Shuhsi Hsü. —Peiping：[s. n.]，1931

Ⅲ，120p. ；22.4cm

PKUL（館藏號缺）

附注：

題記：封面有作者題記："To Professor Hu Shih—with the compliements of Shuhsi Hsü。"

7611 The Manchus, or the Reigning Dynasty of China：Their Rise and Progress/by John Ross. —Paisley：J. and Parlane；London：Houlston and Sons，1880

XXXII，496p. ；21.7cm

PKUL（館藏號缺）

附注：

其他：本書缺封面、封底，書末缺頁。

7612 Manhood of Humanity：The Science and Art of Human Engineering/by Alfred Korzybski. —New York：E. P. Dutton and Company，1921

XV，264p. ；20.8cm

PKUL（館藏號缺）

附注：

題記：扉頁有贈書者（疑爲作者）題記："My address is till November 1921, Fifth avenue Bank, New York City. after Wileza 66 Ar., Warsaw Poland。"

7613 Manhood of Humanity：The Science and Art of Human Engineering/by Alfred Korzybski. —New York：E. P. Dutton & Company，1921

XV，263p. ；20.5cm

PKUL（館藏號缺）

附注：

題記：扉頁有贈書者題記："To Hu Shih, my friend and hoping he will like it. Julia Elloworth Ford。"

7614 The Manhood of the MasterHarry/by Emerson Fosdick. —London：Student

Christian Movement, 1918

159p. ; 15.9cm

PKUL（館藏號缺）

附注：

　　題記：書名頁有贈書者題記，不易辨識。

7615　Man's Fate（La Condition Humaine）/by André Malraux; translated by Haakon M. Chevalier. —New York: Harrison Smith and Robert Haas, 1934

VI, 360p. ; 21.2cm

PKUL（館藏號缺）

7616　Man's Place in Nature and Other Anthropological Essays/by Thomas H. Huxley. —New York: D. Appleton and Company, 1896

XII, 328p. ; 18.8cm

Essays by Thomas H. Huxley Vol. VII

PKUL（館藏號缺）

附注：

　　印章：題名頁鈐有"適盦藏書"朱文圓印；目錄頁鈐有"叔璠"朱文方印。
　　題記：扉頁有胡適題記："赫胥黎論文 第七冊。"
　　批注圈劃：書內11頁有胡適批注圈劃。

7617　Man's Supreme Inheritance/by F. Matthias Alexander. —New York: E. P. Dutton & Company, 1918

XVII, 354p. ; 19.5cm

PKUL（館藏號缺）

7618　The Mansion of Philosophy: A Survey of Human Life and Destiny/by Will Durant. —Garden City: Garden City Publishing Co., Inc., 1929

XIX, 704p. ; 25.4cm

PKUL（館藏號缺）

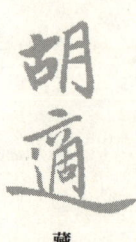

7619 Manual for Teachers, to Accompany the See and Say Series/by Sarah Louise Arnold, Elizabeth C. Bonney, E. F. Southworth. —New York: Iroquois Publishing Company, Inc., 1913-1915

    3 Vols.; 18.8cm

    PKUL（館藏號缺）

7620 A Manual of Budhism, in Its Modern Development/by R. Spence Hardy. —London: Williams and Norgate, 1880

    XII, 566p.; 22.7cm

    PKUL（館藏號缺）

7621 A Manual of Chinese Running-Hand Writing, Especially as It Is Used in Japan/by R. J. de St. Aulaire, W. P. Groeneveldt. —Amsterdam: G. M. Van Gelder, 1861

    IV, 60p.; 30.4cm

    PKUL（館藏號缺）

7622 Manual of Mythology: Greek and Roman Norse and Old German, Hindoo and Egyptian Mythology/by Alexander S. Murray. —Philadelphia: Henry Altemus Co., 1897

    XV, 427p.; 19.4cm

    PKUL（館藏號缺）

    附注：

      題記：扉頁有胡適題記："Suh Hu, Jan. 1915. 今年已去七日，共購二書，其一為英譯本《茶花女》，以贈張熙若，今日購此書，為己有之第一書也。"

7623 Manufacture of Soda, with Special Reference to the Ammonia Process: A Practical Treatise/by Te-Pang Hou. —New York: The Chemical Catalog Company, Inc., 1933

    365p.; 23.4cm

    PKUL（館藏號缺）

7624　Manufacturing the Will of the People/by Suh Hu. —[s. l.]：[s. n.]，[n. d.]

319-328p. ; 23.2cm

Reprinted from *The Journal of Race Development*, Vol. 7, No. 3, January, 1917

PKUL（館藏號缺）

附注：

其他：本抽印本有3冊。

7625　The Manyōshū：One Thousand Poems. —Tokyo：The Iwanami Shoten, 1940

LXXX, 502p. ; 24.8cm

PKUL（館藏號缺）

附注：

題記：扉頁有胡適題記："日本古詩歌《萬葉集》譯本，一九四一年七月十四日在舊書店買得此本。胡適。"

7626　The March of the Barbarians/by Harold Lamb. —New York：Doubleday, Doran & Company, Inc., 1940

VIII, 389p. ; 23.5cm

PKUL（館藏號缺）

7627　Margaret Ogilvy/by J. M. Barrie. —New York：Charles Scribner's Sons, 1896

207p. ; 17.5cm

PKUL（館藏號缺）

附注：

題記：扉頁有贈書者題記："To Mr. Suh Hu, from his friend, Nellie B. Sergent, June 21, 1917。"

7628　Margaret Sanger：An Autobiography/by Margaret Sanger. —New York：W. W. Norton & Company, 1938

504p. ; 20.4cm

PKUL（館藏號缺）

附注：

題記：扉頁有作者題記："New York, Jan. 16, 1939, to Dr. Hu Shih, one of the few great men of today love to help his troubled age, my affectionate regards, Margaret Sanger。"

7629 Maria Chapdelaine：A Tale of the Lake St. John Country/by Louis Hémon；translated by W. H. Blake. ——New York：The Macmillan Company, 1921

288p. ；18.9cm

PKUL（館藏號缺）

7630 Marius The Epicurean：His Sensations and Ideas/by Walter Pater. ——London：Macmillan and Co. , Limited, 1924

VIII, 351p. ；17.4cm

PKUL（館藏號缺）

附注：

題記：扉頁有徐志摩題記："這部著作是裴德七足年勞力的成績。'一字不苟'是他著述的銘言；但他還不止'不苟'；他的字一個個都是他自己'現製的'，像最細心的雕刻匠似的，斲成了最精妙的形象，還得輕輕的把看不見的細屑吹淨了去方才滿意。他是唯一的散文美術家。他的文章是要我們從容的咀嚼，辨味，決不能讓我們胡亂的吞咽。敬呈 適之老夫子大人早晚清玩。志摩，二月二十七日，歐行前布施之二。"

7631 Master Kung：The Story of Confucius/by Carl Crow. ——New York and London：Harpper & Brothers Publishers, 1937

347p. ；23.5cm

PKUL（館藏號缺）

附注：

題記：扉頁後頁有作者題記："To Dr. Hu Shih with best wishes. Carl Crow。"

其他：封內貼有"胡適的書"藏書票。

7632 Masterpieces of Japanese Poetry, Ancient and Modern/by Miyamori Asatarō. —Tōkyō: Maruzen Company Ltd., 1936

2 Vols. (XVII, III, 803 p.); 22.3cm

PKUL（館藏號缺）

附注：

題記：第1卷扉頁有胡適題記："去年在 Ann Arbor, Mich., 住在 Dr. Robert Hall 家裡,我看見他有這部書,託他代買一部。他今年買得此書,寄來送我。胡適。"

其他：本書爲1函2卷。

7633 Matter and Memory/by Henri Bergson; translated by Nancy Margaret Paul, W. Scott Palmer. —London: George Allen & Unwin, Ltd., 1911

XVII, 339p.; 22.6cm

PKUL（館藏號缺）

7634 Matter and Spirit: A Study of Mind and Body in Their Relation to the Spiritual Life/by James Bissett Pratt. —New York: The Macmillan Company, 1922

IX, 232p.; 18.8cm

PKUL（館藏號缺）

附注：

題記：扉頁有作者題記："Professor Hu Shih, with best wishes from his admiring colleague in philosophy, James Bissett Pratt, May 1924。"

7635 McGraw of the Giants/by Frank Graham. —New York: The Council on Books in Wartime, 1944

352p.; 16.2cm

PKUL（館藏號缺）

7636 The Meaning of Atheism/by E. Haldeman-Julius. —Girard: Haldeman-Julius Company, [n.d.]

32p. ; 12.9cm

Little Blue Book

PKUL（館藏號缺）

7637 The Meaning of Faith/by Harry Emerson Fosdick. —New York：Association Press, 1917

IX, 318p. ; 16.5cm

PKUL（館藏號缺）

附注：

題記：扉頁有贈書者題記："To Mr. Suh Hu, from Homin L. Lin, Chiristmas, 1922。"

7638 The Mediaeval Mind：A History of the Development of Thought and Emotion in the Middle Ages/by Henry Osborn Taylor. —New York：The Macmillan Company, 1919

2 Vols. ; 22.2cm

PKUL（館藏號缺）

附注：

印章：第1卷及一冊第2卷題名頁鈐有"王文伯"朱文方印。

批注圈劃：另一冊第2卷書内1頁有胡適鉛筆批注。

其他：本書第2卷有2冊。

7639 Mediaeval Pageant/by John Revell Reinhard. —New York：Harcourt Brace and Company, 1939

XIX, 660p. ; 21.5cm

PKUL（館藏號缺）

附注：

印章：扉頁及題名頁前頁鈐有"HU SHIH"藍文印。

其他：封内貼有關于本書的剪報1份。

7640 Medicine, Magic, and Religion：The Fitz Patrick Lectures Delivered before the Royal College of Physicians of London in 1915 and 1916/by W. H. R. Rivers. —London：Kegan Paul, Trench, Trubner & Co., Ltd., 1924

  Ⅷ, 147p.；21.7cm

  PKUL（館藏號缺）

  附注：

    印章：扉頁有胡適鋼筆簽名"Hu Shih"。

7641 Medieval People/by Eileen Power. —London：Methuen & Co., Ltd., 1925

  Ⅻ, 216p.；18.8cm

  PKUL（館藏號缺）

  附注：

    題記：扉頁有作者題記："Dr. Hu Shih, from Eileen Power, Nov. 1926。"

7642 The Meditations and Selections from the Principles of Réne Descartes/by René Descartes. —Chicago：The Open Court Publishing Company, 1909

  ⅩⅩⅩ, 248p.；19.4cm

  Philosophical Classics

  PKUL（館藏號缺）

  附注：

    題記：扉頁有胡適簽名"Suh Hu, Feb. 1916. New York"。

    批注圈劃：書内53頁有胡適批注圈劃。

7643 Meet the USA：Handbook for Foreign Students in the United States/by Ching-Kun Yang. —New York：Institute of International Education, [n.d.]

  180p.；22.8cm

  PKUL（館藏號缺）

  附注：

    印章：扉頁有胡適鋼筆簽名"Hu Shih, 胡適"；封面有胡適鋼筆簽名"Hu Shih"。

7644 Mei Lan-Fang and Chinese Theatre. —[s.l.]：[s.n.], [n.d.]

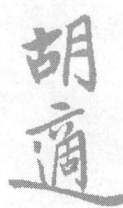

24p. ; 30.8cm

PKUL（館藏號缺）

7645 Mei Lan-Fang: Foremost Actor of China. —Shanghai: The Commercial Press, Limited, 1929

XII, 132p. ; 25.9cm

PKUL（館藏號缺）

附注：

印章：扉頁鈐有"蘭芳之印"朱文方印。

題記：扉頁梅蘭芳題記："適之先生惠存，十九年一月十七日，梅蘭芳謹贈，時將赴美行次滬上。"

7646 Mei Lan-fang: What New York Thinks of Him/by Ernest K. Moy. —[s.l.]: [s.n.], [n.d.]

39p. ; 22.8cm

PKUL（館藏號缺）

7647 Mein Kampf/von Adolf Hitler. —New York: Reynal & Hitchcock, 1939

XXXVI, 1003p. ; 21cm

PKUL（館藏號缺）

附注：

印章：扉頁鈐有"HU SHIH"藍文印。

7648 Mein Leben Als Entdecker/von Sven Hedin. —Leipzig: F. U. Brodhaus, 1928

VIII, 403p. ; 23.3cm

PKUL（館藏號缺）

附注：

題記：扉頁有作者題記："To Dr. Hu Shih, with sincere friendship and gratitude from Sven Hedin, Shanghai, March 30, 1927。"

7649 Membership of the Cosmos Club. —Menasha: George Banta Publishing

Company, 1941

XIV, 66p. ; 23.5cm

PKUL（館藏號缺）

7650 Memoirs of a Midget/by Walter de la Mare. —New York: The Press of the Readers Club, 1941

IX, 379p. ; 21.8cm

PKUL（館藏號缺）

7651 The Memoirs of Jacques Casanova, an Autobiography/by Jacques Casanova. —London and New York: The Venetian Society, 1928

6 Vlos. ; 23.1cm

PKUL（館藏號缺）

附注：

題記：第1卷扉頁有胡適題記："此書向不易得。昨在書店裏見此本，價只十二元美金，當是翻印原十二冊本，用影印法，故能售價如此之廉。胡適，一九四四，一月十八。"

批注圈劃：第1卷末有胡適鉛筆注明閱讀日期"Feb. 17, 1944. H. S."。

其他：本書全本12卷，胡適藏書現存6卷。各卷封內均貼有"胡適的書"藏書票。

7652 Memories and Studies/by William James. —New York, London: Longmans, Green, and Co., 1911

411p. ; 21.7cm

PKUL（館藏號缺）

7653 Men and Ideas: An Informal History of Chinese Political Thought/by Lin Mousheng. —New York: The John Day Company, 1942

XIV, 256p. ; 20.3cm

PKUL（館藏號缺）

附注：

題記：扉頁有作者題記："To Dr. Hu Shih, with the compliments of Lin Mousheng, New Year's Eve, 1942, New York, N. Y.。"

7654 Men and Politics：An Autobiography/by Louis Fischer. —New York：Duell, Sloan and Pearce, 1941

672p. ；23.5cm

PKUL（館藏號缺）

附注：

其他：封內貼有"胡適的書"藏書票。

7655 Men and Women：The World Journey of a Sexologist/by Magnus Hirschfeld. —New York：G. P. Putnam's Sons, 1935

XIX, 325p. ；21.5cm

PKUL（館藏號缺）

附注：

題記：扉頁有贈書者題記："胡適之先生惠存，李紹棠敬贈。"

7656 The Men Around Churchill/by René Kraus. —Philadelphia, New York：J. B. Lippincott Company, 1941

339p. ；22cm

PKUL（館藏號缺）

7657 Men Must Act/by Lewis Mumford. —New York：Harcourt, Brace and Company, 1939

176p. ；20.3cm

PKUL（館藏號缺）

附注：

批注圈劃：書內 12 頁有胡適批注圈劃。

7658 Men of Maryknoll/by James Keller, Meyer Berger. —New York：Grosset & Dunlop Publishers, 1943

191p. ; 19.8cm

PKUL（館藏號缺）

附注：

其他：封內貼有"胡適的書"藏書票。

7659 Men of Science in America: The Role of Science in the Growth of Our Country/by Bernard Jaffe. —New York: Simon and Schuster, 1944

XL, 600p. ; 21.7cm

PKUL（館藏號缺）

附注：

題記：書名頁有胡適題記："五十三歲生日，汪緝齋送我此書。適之，卅三年十二月。"

內附文件：封底內夾有汪緝齋（敬熙）致胡適書信1封2頁，署名敬熙。

7660 Meteorological Records from the Divination Inscriptions of Shang/by Karl August Wittfogel. —[s.l.]: [s.n.], [n.d.]

110-131p. ; 25.4cm

Reprinted from *The Geographical Review*, Vol. XXX, No.1, January, 1940

PKUL（館藏號缺）

附注：

題記：扉頁有作者題記："To Dr. Hu Shih, with the compliments of the author, New York, February 28th, 1940。"

7661 Method and Results/by Thomas H. Huxley. —New York: D. Appleton and Company, 1896

VIII, 430p. ; 18.8cm

Essays by Thomas H. Huxley Vol. I

PKUL（館藏號缺）

附注：

印章：一冊扉頁有原書主簽名"Benjamin Thaw Jr."。

題記：一冊扉頁有胡適題記："Vol. I"，書末有胡適題記："August 25,

1940";另一冊扉頁有胡適題記:"赫胥黎論文,適之。"

批注圈劃:一冊書內 42 頁有胡適批注圈劃;另一冊書內 25 頁有胡適批注圈劃。

夾紙:一冊扉頁貼有黃色紙條 1 張,上有胡適鉛筆書各卷目錄。

其他:本書有 2 冊,一冊出版于 1896 年,一冊出版于 1897 年。

7662 Method for Teaching Modern Languages, English Part First Part/by M. D. Berlitz. —[s. l.]:[s. n.], 1917

111p. ; 19.6cm

PKUL(館藏號缺)

7663 Méthode pour déchiffrer et transcrire les noms sancrits qui se rencontrent dans les livres chinois/by Stanislas Julien. —Paris:L'Imprimerie Impériale, 1861

V, 235p. ; 22.8cm

PKUL(館藏號缺)

附注:

題記:扉頁有作者題記:"A Monsieur Wylie, Hommage de l'auteur. Satanislas Julien。"

7664 Microbe Hunters/by Paul de Kruif. —New York:Harcourt, Brace and Company, 1926

363p. ; 22cm

PKUL(館藏號缺)

附注:

題記:扉頁有胡適題記:"《打倒微菌的英雄》,胡適,一九二六,八,廿一。"

批注圈劃:目錄頁有胡適鉛筆標注的年代;書內 48 頁有胡適圈劃;書末有胡適標注的讀書日期"Sept. 13, 1928"。

夾紙:頁 278、279 間有夾條一。

7665 The Middle Ages/by Edward Maslin Hulme. —New York:Henry Holt and

Company, 1929

XI, 851p. ; 21.5cm

PKUL（館藏號缺）

附注：

印章：扉頁有胡適鉛筆簽名"Hu Shih"。

批注圈劃：書内 168 頁有胡適批注圈劃。

7666 The Middle Kingdom; A Survey of the Geography, Government, Education, Social Life, Arts, Religion, &c., of the Chinese Empire and Its Inhabitants/by S. Wells Williams. —New York: John Wiley & Son, Publishers, 1871

2 Vols. ; 19.9cm

PKUL（館藏號缺）

附注：

題記：兩卷扉頁均有贈書者題記："To Robert Lilley, with kind regards and best wishes of his friend, Ernest L. Holwill, Chefoo, 16th March, 1872。"

其他：本書第 1 卷缺封底、書脊，裝訂有脱落。

7667 The Mikado's Empire/by William Elliot Griffis. —New York: Harper & Brothers Publishers, 1876

625p. ; 22.1cm

PKUL（館藏號缺）

附注：

印章：扉頁有"R. Lilley"鉛筆簽名。

7668 A Military Contact between Chinese and Romans in 36 B. C./by Homer H. Dubs. —[s.l.]：[s.n.]，[n.d.]

64-80p. ; 25cm

Reprinted from *T'oung Pao*, Vol. XXXVI, Livr. 1

PKUL（館藏號缺）

附注：

題記：封面有作者題記："To Ambassador Hu Shih, with the compliments of Homer H. Dubs。"

7669 The Mill on the Floss/by George Eliot. —London：J. M. Dent & Sons Ltd. ; New York：E. P, Dutton & Co. , 1908

XIII, 492p. ; 17.2cm

Everyman's Library：Fiction

PKUL（館藏號缺）

7670 The Mind and Society：Trattato di Sociologia Generale/by Vilfredo Pareto. —New York：Harcourt, Brace and Company, 1935

4 Vols.（2033p.）; 23.6cm

PKUL（館藏號缺）

附注：

印章：四卷扉頁均有"HU SHIH"藍色印章。

題記：扉頁有胡適題記："廿八年八月十四日，我從外面旅行回來，收到此書；同時見報載 Professor James Harvey Rogers 在巴西飛機上慘死的消息，記在這裡，留作紀念。胡適，原價廿元，我用＄9.92 買的。"

7671 Mine Own People/by Rudyard Kipling. —New York：The Regent Press, [n.d.]

338p. ; 18.8cm

The Works of Rudyard Kipling

PKUL（館藏號缺）

附注：

題記：扉頁有胡適鋼筆簽名"Suh Hu, March 1916"。

批注圈劃：目錄頁有胡適圈劃。

7672 Mineral Resources of China/by Vei Chow Juan. —[s. l.]：[s. n.], [n.d.]

399-474p. ; 24.1cm

Reprinted from *Economic Geology*, Vol. XLI, No. 4, Part2, Supplement

PKUL（館藏號缺）

附注：
　　題記：封面有作者題記："適之校長指正,著者敬贈,卅六年十二月。"

7673 Minerva's Progress: Tradition and Dissent in American Culture/by Alfred E. Cohn. —New York: Harcourt, Brace and Company, 1946
　　101p. ; 19.3cm
　　PKUL（館藏號缺）

7674 Ming Printing and Printers/by K. T. Wu. —[s.l.]: [s.n.], [n.d.]
　　203–260p. ; 25.5cm
　　Reprinted from *Harvard Journal of Asiatic Studies* Vol. 7 No. 3
　　PKUL（館藏號缺）
　　附注：
　　　　題記：封面有作者題記："適之先生指正,光清敬呈。"

7675 Minna von Barnhelm/von Gotthold Ephraim Lessing. —New York: Henry Holt and Company, 1906
　　XXX, 212p. ; 16.6cm
　　PKUL（館藏號缺）
　　附注：
　　　　題記：扉頁有胡適題記："德國名劇之一,賴辛著《明娜傳》,一名《軍人福》。適之"；扉頁後頁有胡適題記："此劇爲賴氏名著,德國曲本進化,是劇實其先河。氏蓋以全力經營,故全書無一懈筆,真不朽之作。他日當譯之,以爲吾國戲曲範本云。適之。"
　　　　批注圈劃：書中有胡適批注圈劃80餘處；書末注明時間爲 May 9, 1911, 有 "S. Hu" 簽名。

7676 The Minor Elizabethan Drama (I) Pre-Shakespearean Tragedies. —London: J. M. Dent & Sons Ltd. ; New York: E. P, Dutton & Co. , 1910
　　XVI, 276p. ; 17.3cm
　　Everyman's Library: Poetry and the Drama

PKUL（館藏號缺）

7677 Minor Heresies/by John J. Espey. —New York：Alfred A. Knopf, 1945

202p. ；19cm

PKUL（館藏號缺）

7678 A Miocene Flora from Shantung Province, China/by Hsen Hsu Hu, Ralph W. Chaney . —Peiping：The Geological Survey of China, ［n. d.］

VI, 147p. ；29.2cm

PKUL（館藏號缺）

附注：

題記：扉頁有作者鋼筆題記："To Mr. Hu Shih with the wish that America may become more and more like China, as the fossil forests of the past. Ralph W. Chaney。"

7679 The Misadventure of Sherlock Holmes/by Ellery Queen. —Boston：Little, Brown and Company, 1944

XXII, 363p. ；20.6cm

PKUL（館藏號缺）

附注：

題記：扉頁有胡適鋼筆簽名"Hu Shih, April 26, 1944"。

7680 Misalliance, with a Treatise on Parents and Children/by Bernard Shaw. —Leipzig：Bernhard Tauchnitz, 1921

269p. ；16.4cm

Collection of British Authors, Tauchnitz Edition

PKUL（館藏號缺）

7681 Les Miserables：A Novel by Victor Hugo/by Victor Hugo；translated by Charles E. Wilbour. —London：J. M. Dent & Sons Ltd.；New York：E. P, Dutton & Co. , 1909

2 Vols. ; 17.3cm

Everyman's Library: Fiction

PKUL（館藏號缺）

附注：

　　題記：第1卷書末有胡適鉛筆題記："G. K. Chesterton: Twelve Types: a book of Essays—London, 1902"；第2卷扉頁有胡適鋼筆簽名"Suh Hu, March, 1915"。

7682 Miss Lulu Bett/by Zona Gale. —New York, London: D. Appleton and Company, 1920

V, 264p. ; 19.2cm

PKUL（館藏號缺）

附注：

　　印章：扉頁有"Dewey"鉛筆簽名。

7683 Mission to Moscow/by Joseph E. Davies. —New York: Simon and Schuster, 1941

XXII, 659p. ; 22.1cm

PKUL（館藏號缺）

7684 Modelling for Amateurs/by Clifford and Rosemary Ellis. —New York: The Studio Publications, Inc. ; London: The Studio, Ltd. , [n.d.]

78p. ; 17.5cm

PKUL（館藏號缺）

7685 Modern American Poets/by Conrad Aiken. —New York: The Modern Library, 1927

367p. ; 16.8cm

PKUL（館藏號缺）

7686 Modern and Contemporary European History (1815-1928)/by J. Salwyn

Schapiro. —Boston: Houghton Mifflin Company, 1929

XI, 827, XXV; 20.8cm

PKUL（館藏號缺）

附注：

題記：扉頁有胡夢華、吴淑貞題記："敬獻於我們的證婚人適之博士四十大慶紀念，並祝福壽康寧。夢華，淑貞，十二，十七。"

7687 Modern Art/by Katherine S. Dreier. —New York：[s.n.], 1926

117p.；25.5cm

PKUL（館藏號缺）

附注：

題記：扉頁有作者題記："For Hu Shih, with the warmest regards of Katherine S. Dreier。"

7688 Modern Burma: A Survey of Political and Economic Development/by John Leroy Christian. —Berkeley, Los Angeles: University of California Press, 1942

IX, 381p.；23.4cm

PKUL（館藏號缺）

附注：

題記：扉頁有作者題記："To Dr. Hu Shih, with great respect for China and her ambassador to the United States, John L. Christian, Washington D.C., May 8, 1942。"

7689 Modern Classical Philosophers: Selections Illustrating Modern Philosophy from Bruno to Spencer/by Benjamin Rand. —Boston and New York: Houghton Mifflin Company, 1908

XIII, 740p.；21.8cm

PKUL（館藏號缺）

附注：

題記：扉頁有胡適毛筆簽名"Hu Suh, June 1918"。

批注圈劃：書内 31 頁有胡適圈劃。

7690 A Modern Comedy/by John Galsworthy. —London：William Heinemann Ltd. , 1929

　　　XVII, 1088p. ; 18.8cm

　　　PKUL（館藏號缺）

7691 Modern Democracies/by James Bryce. —New York：The Macmillan Company, 1921

　　　2 vols. (XIV, 508p. , VI, 676p.) ; 22.1cm

　　　PKUL（館藏號缺）

　　　附註：

　　　　　夾紙：Vol. I 書內夾有 The Macmillan Company 書籤 1 枚。

7692 Modern Democracy in China/by Mingchien Joshua Bau. —Shanghai：Commercial Press, Limited, 1923

　　　VII, 467p. ; 19.1cm

　　　PKUL（館藏號缺）

7693 Modern English Drama, Dryden, Sheridan, Goldsmith, Shelley, Browning · Byron/by Charles W. Eliot. —New York：P. F. Collier & Son, 1909

　　　444p. ; 19.5cm

　　　The Harvard Classics No. 18

　　　PKUL（館藏號缺）

　　　附註：

　　　　　內附文件：書內夾有複製英文信件 1 張,紙條 1 張。

7694 Modern English Statesmen/by G. R. Stirling Taylor. —New York：Robert M. McBride & Company, 1921

　　　267p. ; 21.4cm

　　　PKUL（館藏號缺）

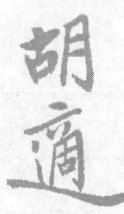

7695 Modern Geography/by Marion I. Newbigin. —London：Williams and Norgate，[n. d.]

256p. ；17cm

Home University Library of Modern Knowledge

PKUL（館藏號缺）

7696 Modern Home Medical Adviser：Your Health and How to Preserve It/by Morris Fishbein. —New York：Garden City Publishing Company, Inc. , 1937

XXXI, 907p. ；22.9cm

PKUL（館藏號缺）

附注：

題記：扉頁有胡適題記："Hu Shih, June 1946. Gift of 朱壽恒。《家庭醫藥顧問》。"

7697 Modern Manchuria/by Henry W. Kinney. —Dairen：[s. n.], 1929

VII, 87p. ；21.1cm

PKUL（館藏號缺）

附注：

題記：扉頁有贈書者題記："胡適先生,Dec. 22, 1929. 坂本義孝。"

內附文件：頁44、45間夾有日本萬朝報社致胡適函1封,各種資料共5頁。

其他：內夾胡適與他人合影照片1張。

7698 Modern Newspaper Chinese/by J. J. Brandt. —Peiping：Henri Vetch, 1935

XII, 321p. ；23.7cm

PKUL（館藏號缺）

7699 The Modern Reader's Bible/by Richard G. Moulton. —New York：The Macmillan Company, 1930

XIV, 1733p. ；19.5cm

PKUL（館藏號缺）

附注：

　　題記：扉頁有贈書者題記："To my good friend Hu Shih, from □"；扉頁另有胡適題記："李觀森先生寄贈的，胡適，一九卅二，十二，廿七。"

7700 The Modern Reader's Bible/by Richard G. Moulton. —New York：The Macmillan Company, 1940

　　XIV, 1733p. ；21.9cm

　　PKUL（館藏號缺）

　　附注：

　　其他：封內貼有"胡適的書"藏書票。

7701 Modern Religious Movements in India/by J. N. Farquhar. —New York：The Macmillan Company, 1915

　　XV, 471p. ；22.4cm

　　PKUL（館藏號缺）

　　附注：

　　題記：題名頁有原書主題記："民國十四年二月十三日，傅彥長。"

7702 Modern Science and Modern Thought/by Samuel Laing. —London：Watts & Co., 1921

　　VI, 121p. ；21.4cm

　　PKUL（館藏號缺）

7703 Modern Scientific Knowledge of Nature, Man, and Society/by Frederick A. Cleveland. —New York：The Ronald Press Company, 1929

　　XVII, 592p. ；21.3cm

　　PKUL（館藏號缺）

　　附注：

　　內附文件：頁238、239間夾有胡適寫給"某卓鏞"未完成書信1頁。

7704 The Modern Temper：A Study and a Confession/by Joseph Wood Krutch. —

New York: Harcourt, Brace and Company, 1929

XVI, 249p. ; 20.7cm

PKUL（館藏號缺）

附注：

夾紙：書內夾有請柬 1 張。

7705 Modern Urology for Nurses/by Sheila Maureen Dwyer, George W. Fish. —Philadelphia: Lea & Febiger, 1945

287p. ; 19.8cm

PKUL（館藏號缺）

附注：

題記：扉頁有作者題記："To Doctor Hu Shih, my friend and erstwhile neighbor with affectionate regard—George Fish, March 3, 1947。"

7706 Modern Wonder Workers: A Popular History of American Invention/by Waldemar Kaempffert. —New York: Blue Ribbon Books, 1924

XVI, 577p. ; 21.3cm

PKUL（館藏號缺）

7707 Modernities/by Horace B. Samuel. —London: Kegen Paul, Trench, Trübner & Co., Ltd., 1914

VIII, 244p. ; 21.7cm

PKUL（館藏號缺）

7708 Molière/by Curtis Hidden Page. —New York and London: G. P. Putnam's Sons, 1908

467p. ; 22cm

French Classics for English Readers

PKUL（館藏號缺）

附注：

題記：扉頁有胡適鋼筆簽名"May, 1915. Suh Hu"。

7709 Das Memorandum des Generalmajor Tada. —[s. l.]：[s. n.]，[n. d.]

 30p. ; 19.1cm

 PKUL（館藏號缺）

 附注：

  題記：封面有贈書者題記："To Dr. Hu Shih, with deepest regards, □。"

7710 The Monetary Problem：Gold and Silver/by Ralph Robey. —New York：Columbia University Press, 1936

 XXVIII, 369p. ; 23.6cm

 PKUL（館藏號缺）

7711 Mongdsi/von Richard Wilhelm. —Jena：Eugen Diederichs Verlag, 1921

 XIX, 206p. ; 21.6cm

 PKUL（館藏號缺）

 附注：

  題記：扉頁作者題字："To my friend Dr. Hu Shih. R. Wilhelm。"

7712 The "Mongol Atlas" of China by Chu Ssu-Pen and the Kuang-Yü-T'u/by Walter Fuchs. —Peiping：Fu Jen University, 1946

 32, 48p. ; 26.4cm

 Reprinted from *Monumenta Serica*, *Journal of Oriental Studies of the Catholic University of Peking*, Monograph VIII

 PKUL（館藏號缺）

 附注：

  題記：題名頁有作者題記："Prof. Hu Shih, with the author's respectful compliments。"

7713 The Mongol Empire：Its Rise and Legacy/by Michael Prawdin; translated by Eden and Cedar Paul. —New York：The Macmillan Company, 1940

 581p. ; 22.2cm

PKUL（館藏號缺）

7714 The Mongol in Our Midst：A Study of Man and His Three Faces/by F. G. Crookshank. —New York：E. P. Dutton & Company, 1924

124p. ；15.4cm

PKUL（館藏號缺）

7715 Monkey/by Arthur Waley. —New York：The John Day Company, 1943

306p. ；21.2cm

PKUL（館藏號缺）

附注：

題記：扉頁有胡適題記："韋來《西遊記》英譯本，適之。卅二，三，三。"

7716 The Moon Is Down/by John Steinbeck. —New York：The Viking Press, 1942

188p. ；18.6cm

PKUL（館藏號缺）

附注：

題記：扉頁有胡適鋼筆簽名"Hu Shih, New York City, April 1, 1942"。

7717 More Fables/by George Ade. —Chicago, New York：Herbert S. Stone & Co., 1900

218p. ；14.9cm

PKUL（館藏號缺）

附注：

印章：封內有 W. K. Gise 簽名；扉頁後頁有簽名"William K. Gise, H. S. N."。

題記：扉頁後頁另有原書主題記："Look Page 151。"

7718 More Translations from the Chinese/by Arthur Waley. —London：George Allen & Unwin Ltd., 1919

109p. ；18.1cm

PKUL（館藏號缺）

附注：

　　題記：扉頁有胡適題記："Hu Shih, from the author。"

7719　Moscow War Diary/by Alexander Werth. —New York：Alfred A. Knopf, 1942

　　297p. ; 21.8cm

　　PKUL（館藏號缺）

7720　A Motley/by John Galsworthy. —Leipzig：Bernhard Tauchnitz, [n.d.]

　　271p. ; 16.5cm

　　Collection of British Authors, Tauchnitz Edition

　　PKUL（館藏號缺）

7721　Motse：The Neglected Rival of Confucius/by Yi-Pao Mei. —London：Arthur Probsthain, 1934

　　XI, 222p. ; 19.2cm

　　Probsthain's Oriental Series

　　PKUL（館藏號缺）

7722　Mourning Becomes Electra：A Trilogy/by Eugene O'Neill. —New York：Horace Liveright, Inc., 1931

　　256p. ; 20.5cm

　　PKUL（館藏號缺）

　　附注：

　　題記：書名頁前頁有胡適題記："一九三三年十月從美洲回去，孟治先生送此書爲我船上的讀物。十月七八兩夜讀完，深受感動。此書可算是現代文學的一部最有氣力的傑作。一九三三，十，八夜一點四十分。胡適。"

　　夾紙：書內夾有"公益捐收據"1張。

7723　Les Mouvements de la Langue Nationale en Chine/par Fu Liu. —Paris：

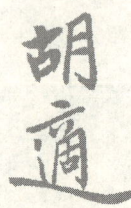

Société d'Édition "Les Belles Lettres"；Pékin：Presses de L'Université Nationale de Pékin，1925

56p.；25.4cm

PKUL（館藏號缺）

附注：

題記：題名頁有作者題記："呈適之兄，復，一九二六。"

7724 Mr. Belloc Objectgs：To "The Outline of History"/by H. G. Wells. —London：Watts & Co.，1926

VII，55p.；18.5cm

The Forum Series

PKUL（館藏號缺）

附注：

題記：扉頁有胡適鋼筆簽名"Hu Shih, London, December 1926"。

7725 Mr. House of Texas/by Arthur D. Howden Smith. —New York，London：Funk & Wagnalls Company，1940

XI，381p.；23.5cm

PKUL（館藏號缺）

7726 Mr. Justice Brandeis：Great American/by Irving Dilliard. —Saint Louis：The Modern View Press，1941

127p.；22.9cm

PKUL（館藏號缺）

附注：

題記：封內有作者題記："To Hu Shih in warmest friendship of EDX fellowship, Irving, Dec. 28, 1941。"

7727 Mr. Pan/by Emily Hahn. —New York：Doubleday, Doran and Company, Inc.，1942

VIII，294p.；20.7cm

PKUL（館藏號缺）

7728 Mr. Skeffington/by Elizabeth. —New York：Doubleday, Doran & Co., Inc., 1940

　　330p. ; 20.6cm

　　PKUL（館藏號缺）

7729 Mr. Tutt Finds a Way/by Arthur Train. —New York：Charles Scribner's Sons, 1945

　　241p. ; 19.5cm

　　PKUL（館藏號缺）

　　附注：

　　　　題記：扉頁有胡適朱筆簽名"Hu Shih, New York, Jan. 1946"。

　　　　批注圈劃：目錄頁有胡適朱筆圈劃。

7730 Mrs. Minver/by Jan Struther. —New York：Harcourt, Brace and Company, 1940

　　VIII, 288p. ; 21cm

　　PKUL（館藏號缺）

7731 The Murder of Roger Ackroyd/by Agatha Christie. —New York：Pocket Books, Inc., 1926

　　249p. ; 16cm

　　PKUL（館藏號缺）

7732 Music at Night & Other Essays/by Aldous Huxley. —London：Chatto & Windus, 1931

　　VI, 269p. ; 19.3cm

　　PKUL（館藏號缺）

7733 My Country and My People/by Lin Yutang. —New York：John Day in

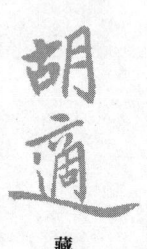

association with Reynal & Hitchcock, 1935

XVIII, 382p. ; 20.5cm

PKUL（館藏號缺）

附注：

印章：一册扉頁鈐有"語堂"朱文方印。

題記：一册扉頁有林語堂毛筆題記："適之兄：我以爲會長稱引你的地方三處，看看引得，美國小姐做的，才知道有九處。謝謝你許多無形中的開導指教。語堂持贈。廿四年九月廿六日於上海"；另一册扉頁有胡適題記："孟治先生給我買的。這一部'初版'（而不是初印）的'玉堂名著'適之 廿九，一月。"

批注圈劃：第 3 册書內 17 頁有胡適批注圈劃。

內附文件：一册封內貼有胡先驌致胡適函 1 頁："適之先生惠鑒：林語堂君大作已讀畢，其文字極佳，惜所見不少淺陋之處，而批評每每過火。然較之一般西人之著作，自遠勝也。原書今賣價奉還，餘不一一。即頌刻安。弟驌頓啓。七日。"

其他：本書有 3 册。

7734 My Country：A Textbook in Civics and Patriotism for Young AmeircansGrace/by A. Turkington. —Boston, New York, Chicago, et al：Ginn and Company, 1923

IV, 418p. ; 18.9cm

PKUL（館藏號缺）

7735 My Credo and Its Evolution/by Hu Shih. —Peiping：The Peiping Chronicle, [n. d.]

23p. ; 19cm

Reprinted from *The Forum*, Jan.–Feb. 1931

PKUL（館藏號缺）

附注：

其他：本抽印本有 62 册。

7736　My Day in Court/by Arthur Train. —New York：Charles Scribner's Sons；London：Charles Scribner's Sons Ltd.，1939

　　　VI，520p. ；23.3cm

　　　PKUL（館藏號缺）

7737　My Friend Flicka/by Mary O'Hara. —Philadelphia，New York：J. B. Lippincott Company，1941

　　　285p. ；20.9cm

　　　PKUL（館藏號缺）

7738　My India, My America/by Krishnalal Shridharani. —New York：Duell, Sloan and Pearce，1941

　　　XII，647p. ；23.5cm

　　　PKUL（館藏號缺）

　附注：

　　　題記：題名頁前頁有贈書者題記："Happy Birthday, Dr. Hu, Pardee Larve, Dec. 25, 1941"；另有作者題記："To Dr. Hu Shih, with deep regards and good-neighborly greetings, from an admirer of his great qualities. Krishnalal Shridharani。"

7739　My Life in China, 1926–1941/by Hallett Abend. —New York：Harcourt, Brace and Company，1943

　　　VIII，396p. ；20.8cm

　　　PKUL（館藏號缺）

7740　My Memoir/by Edith Bolling Wilson. —New York：The Bobbs–Merrill Company，1939

　　　386p. ；24.3cm

　　　PKUL（館藏號缺）

　附注：

　　　印章：扉頁及後頁鈐有"Hu Shih"藍文印。

  題記:扉頁有作者題記:"autographed for Dr. Hu Shih, with high regard, Edith Bolling Wilson, Feb. 11th, 1921。"

7741 My Memoirs/by Von Tirpitz. —London: Hurst & Blackett, Ltd. , [n.d.]

  2 Vols. (XII, 597p.); 22.6cm

  PKUL(館藏號缺)

  附注:

    題記:第1卷扉頁有胡適題記:"Hu Shih, New York City, Dec. 7, 1942. the first Anniversary of Pearl Harbor。"

    內附文件:書內夾有剪報1份。

7742 My Mother's Betrothal/by Hu Shih. —New Haven: Yale University Press, 1946

  13, 33p. ; 21.4cm

  PKUL(館藏號缺)

7743 My Name Is Aram/by William Saroyan. —New York: Harcourt, Brace and Company, 1940

  X, 220p. ; 21.8cm

  PKUL(館藏號缺)

7744 My Philosophy of Industry/by Henry Ford. —New York: Coward-McCann, Inc. , 1929

  107p. ; 19.3cm

  PKUL(館藏號缺)

7745 My Philosophy of the Physical Universe and of Those Who Live in It/by John Benjamin Penniston. —Shanghai: Thomas Chu & Sons, [n.d.]

  XI, 196p. ; 19.3cm

  PKUL(館藏號缺)

7746 My Vision of Canada/by William Arthur Deacon. —Toronto：The Ontario Publishing Company, Limited, 1933

309p. ；21.2cm

PKUL（館藏號缺）

附注：

題記：扉頁有作者題記："To：Dr. Hu Shih, the author begs to use this opportunity of your being on Canadian sail to bring to your attention his strong belief that Canada's hope of future greatness lies in the closest of friendly relations with China. This book was written for the Canadian reader, and may deal with matters in which you are not interested; but the insistent plea for Canada to make China the pivot of her foreign policy is repeated again and again. The author believes that China's goodwill and active help are vital to the success of his own country—Canada. Sincerely—William Arthur Deacon, Toronto, August 9th, 1933。"

7747 My War Memories, 1914–1918/by Erieh Ludendorff. —London：Hutchinson & Co., [n. d.]

2 Vols.（VII, VIII, 793p.）；22.8cm

PKUL（館藏號缺）

附注：

題記：第1卷扉頁有胡適題記："Hu Shih, Dec. 7, 1942, First Anniversary of Pearl Harbor。"

7748 The Mystery of Cloomber/by A. Conan Doyle. —London, New York, Toronto：Hodder and Stoughton, [n. d.]

259p. ；18cm

PKUL（館藏號缺）

7749 Mysticism and Logic and Other Essays/by Bertrand Russell. —New York：Longmans, Green and Co., 1919

VII, 234p. ；22cm

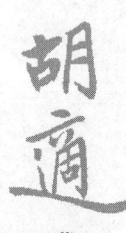

  PKUL（館藏號缺）

  附注：

    題記：扉頁有胡適鋼筆簽名"Hu Suh, Feb, 1921"。

7750 Myth, Magic, and Morals: A Study of Christian Morals/by Fred. Cornwallis Conybeare. —London: Watts & Co. , 1925

  XXVIII, 382p. ; 19.1cm

  PKUL（館藏號缺）

  附注：

    印章：扉頁有胡適朱筆簽名"Hu Shih"。

7751 Myths after Lincoln/by Lloyd Lewis. —New York: The Press of The Readers Club, 1941

  XII, 367p. ; 21.8cm

  PKUL（館藏號缺）

7752 National Institute of Arts and Letters. —New York: [s.n.], [n.d.]

  100p. ; 17.5cm

  PKUL（館藏號缺）

7753 National Socialism: Basic Principles, Their Application by the Nazi Party's Foreign Organization, and the Use of Germans Abroad for Nazi Aims/by Raymond E. Murphy, Francis B. Stevens, Howard Trivers, Joseph M. Roland. —Washington: United States Government Printing Office, 1943

  VI, 510p. ; 24.1cm

  PKUL（館藏號缺）

7754 Nationalism in School Education in China/by Chiu-Sam Tsang. —Hong Kong: The South China Morning Post, Ltd. , 1933

  239p. ; 24.7cm

  PKUL（館藏號缺）

附注：

　　印章：扉頁後頁鈐有"曾昭森印"朱文方印。

　　題記：扉頁有作者題記："適之教授指正，曾昭森敬贈。"

7755　Native Son/by Richard Wright. —New York, London：Harper & Brothers Publishers, 1940

　　XI, 359p. ; 21cm

　　PKUL（館藏號缺）

7756　Naturalist at Large/by Thomas Barbour. —Boston：Little, Brown and Company, 1943

　　XII, 314p. ; 21.6cm

　　PKUL（館藏號缺）

　　附注：

　　題記：扉頁有作者題記："To Dr. Hu Shih：from his unknown admirer. Thomas Barbour. 8/12/43。"

7757　Nature and Mind：Selected Essays of Frederick J. E. Woodbridge/by Frederick J. E. Woodbridge. —New York：Columbia University Press, 1937

　　X, 509p. ; 23.2cm

　　PKUL（館藏號缺）

7758　The Nature of Mathematics/by Philip E. B. Jourdain. —London：T. C. & E. C. Jack；New York：Dodge Publishing Co. , [n.d.]

　　92p. ; 16.4cm

　　PKUL（館藏號缺）

　　附注：

　　題記：扉頁有胡適鋼筆簽名"Suh Hu, Nov. 1914"。

7759　The Nature of the Judicial Process/by Benjamin N. Cardozo. —New Haven：Yale University Press；Humphrey Milford：Oxford University Press, 1921

180p. ；18.6cm

PKUL（館藏號缺）

7760　Nebuchadnezzar/by G. R. Tabouis. —London：George Routledge & Sons, Ltd., 1931

XIV, 402p. ；22.2cm

PKUL（館藏號缺）

7761　The Navy：A History, the Story of a Service in Action/by Fletcher Pratt. —New York：Doubleday, Doran & Company, Inc., 1938

XVI, 496p. ；22.8cm

PKUL（館藏號缺）

附注：

題記：扉頁有胡適題記："此書前幾天剛出版,今天我已在舊書店裡尋著他了。一九三八,四,十二。"

7762　The Nazarene/by Sholem Asch. —New York：G. P. Putnam's Sons, 1939

698p. ；21.5cm

PKUL（館藏號缺）

附注：

印章：扉頁鈐有"HU SHIH"藍文印。

內附文件：書末夾有本書書評1份。

7763　The Need for World Economic Planning/by Lewis L. Lorwin. —[s. l.]：American Council, Institute of Pacific Relations, 1931

16p. ；21.2cm

PKUL（館藏號缺）

附注：

印章：扉頁有胡適鉛筆簽名"Hu Shih"。

7764　Neuf Contes Choisis de Daudet/by Victor E. Francois. —New York：Henry

Holt and Company, 1911

XI, 205p. ; 16.6cm

Everyman's Library: Philosophy and Theology

PKUL（館藏號缺）

附注：

印章：封內有簽名"T. S. chang"。

題記：扉頁有胡適題記："118 Bloomington, 7:00。"

批注圈劃：書內86頁胡適鉛筆、鋼筆批注圈劃。

7765 The New Adventure of Elley Queen/by Ellery Queen. —New York: Pocket Books Inc., 1941

308p. ; 16.4cm

PKUL（館藏號缺）

7766 The New Belief in the Common Man/by Carl J. Friedrich. —Boston: Little, Brown and Company, 1942

XIII, 345p. ; 22.2cm

PKUL（館藏號缺）

附注：

題記：扉頁有作者題記："To Dr. Hu Shih, the forerunner of the movement which recognized the place of the common man in modern China, with high regards, Carl J. Friedrich。"

7767 The New Covenant Commonly Called the New Testament of Our Lord and Savior Jesus Christ. —New York: Thomas Nelson & Sons, 1946

553p. ; 18.9cm

PKUL（館藏號缺）

附注：

題記：扉頁有胡適鋼筆簽名"Hu Shih, 胡適, May 16, 1946, New York"。

7768 The New Culture: An Organic Philosophy of Education/by A. Gordon

Melvin. —New York: Reynal & Hitchcock, 1937

296p. ; 23.5cm

PKUL（館藏號缺）

附注：

題記：扉頁有作者題記："Dr. Hu Shih, with compliment and appreciation. A. Gordon Melvin, Peiping, April 13, 1937。"

7769　The New Decalogue of Science/by Albert Edward Wiggam. —London & Toronto: J. M. Dent and Sons Ltd. , [n. d.]

287p. ; 20.5cm

PKUL（館藏號缺）

附注：

題記：扉頁有胡適題記："此似是王念祖兄的舊書，我在舊書攤上買的。一九三一，十二，十七"；扉頁另有原書主簽名"J. T. Wang"。

7770　A New Date for the Origins of the Forbidden City/by G. N. Kates. —[s. l.]: Harvard-Yenching Institute, 1943

180-202p. ; 25.5cm

Reprinted from *Harvard Journal of Asiatic Studies* Vol. 7, No. 3

PKUL（館藏號缺）

附注：

題記：封面有作者題記："敬呈適之先生教正，學生柯德思贈"；封面另有胡適朱筆書作者英文名"Kates"。

7771　New Developments in Philosophy in the University of Southern California. —[s. l.]:The School of Philosophy, University of Southern California, [n. d.]

15p. ; 24.1cm

PKUL（館藏號缺）

附注：

題記：封面有贈書者題記："To Doctor Hu Shih, with highest esteem, Edwin Diller Starbuck。"

7772 New England: Indian Summer, 1865-1915/by Van Wyck Brooks. —New York: E. P. Dutton & Co., Inc., 1940

557p. ; 22.2cm

PKUL（館藏號缺）

7773 The New Encyclopedia of Social Reform/by William D. P. Bliss, Rudolph M. Binder. —New York, London: Funk & Wagnalls Company, 1908

1321p. ; 25.6cm

PKUL（館藏號缺）

7774 A New Englander in Japan, Daniel Crosby Greene/by Evarts Boutell Greene. —Boston and New York: Houghton Mifflin Company, 1927

X, 374p. ; 22.5cm

PKUL（館藏號缺）

7775 The New Golden Treasury of Songs and Lyrics/by Ernest Rhys. —London: J. M. Dent & Sons Ltd.; New York: E. P, Dutton & Co., 1914

X, 329p. ; 17.3cm

Everyman's Library: Poetry and the Drama

PKUL（館藏號缺）

附註：

印章：一冊扉頁有原書主簽名"John J. Goodhead, July 11, 1916"。

其他：本書有2冊。另一冊封内貼有"洶美的書"藏書票。

7776 The New Idealism/by May Sinclair. —London: Macmillan and Co., Limited, 1922

XVI, 333p. ; 22.5cm

PKUL（館藏號缺）

附註：

題記：扉頁徐志摩題字："適之先生,志摩,十一年冬。"

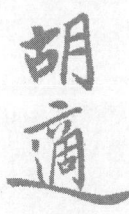

7777 The New Invitation to Learning/by Mark Van Doren. —New York：The New Home Library, 1944

XIII, 436p. ；20.1cm

PKUL（館藏號缺）

附注：

題記：扉頁有胡適題記："Hu Shih, June 1946, Gift of S. A. Chu。"

7778 New Light on Witchcraft/by Joseph McCabe. —Girard：Haldeman‑Julius Company, [n.d.]

62p. ；13cm

Little Blue Book

PKUL（館藏號缺）

附注：

其他：缺封面、題名頁，封底脫落。

7779 A New Mind and Other Essays/by Evan Morgan. —Shanghai：Kelly and Walsh, 1930

244p. ；21.5cm

PKUL（館藏號缺）

附注：

內附文件：書內夾有寄書者英文書信4封4頁；另有書評1頁。

7780 The New Monetary System of China：A Personal Interpretation/by W. Y. Lin. —Shanghai, Hong Kong, Singpore：Kelly & Walsh, Limited, 1936

175p. ；23.5cm

PKUL（館藏號缺）

7781 The New Motherhood/by Margaret Sanger. —London：Jonathan Cape, 1922

243p. ；18.8cm

PKUL（館藏號缺）

附注：

　　夾紙：頁 150、151 間夾有紙條 1 張。

　　內附文件：頁 40、41 間夾有陶孟和致奚湞女士書信 1 頁。

7782　The New Motherhood/by Margaret Sanger. —London：Jonathan Cape，1922

　　243p. ；19.4cm

　　PKUL（館藏號缺）

7783　New Paths for Japan/by Harold Wakefield. —London：Royal Institute of International Affairs，1948

　　VIII，223p. ；21.5cm

　　PKUL（館藏號缺）

　　附注：

　　　　夾紙：書末夾有郵寄地址 1 張。

7784　New Phonetic Pronouncing Dictionary of the English Language. —London：Asprey & Co.，Ltd.，［n. d.］

　　442p. ；15.5cm

　　Reference Library

　　PKUL（館藏號缺）

7785　A New Pocket Dictionary of the English & Italian Languages/by J. E. Wessely. —Leipzig：Bernhard Tauchnitz，1887

　　217p. ；16.1cm

　　PKUL（館藏號缺）

　　附注：

　　　　印章：扉頁有原書主鋼筆簽名，不能辨識。

7786　New Popular Webster Dictionary. —Cleveland，New York：The World Syndicate Publishing Co.，1931

　　380p. ；14cm

PKUL（館藏號缺）

附注：

題記：扉頁後頁有胡適題記："在紐約買的，價十分。胡適，廿二，九，廿七。"

7787 New Practice-Book in English Composition/by Alfred M. Hitchcock. —New York：Henry Holt and Company, 1926

XI, 447p. ; 19.2cm

PKUL（館藏號缺）

7788 The New Realism：Coöperative Studies in Philosophy/by Edwin B. Holt, Walter T. Marvin, William Pepperrell Montague, at al. —New York：The Macmillan Company, 1912

XII, 486p. ; 19.9cm

PKUL（館藏號缺）

附注：

題記：扉頁有胡適毛筆簽名"Hu Suh, June 1918"。

7789 New Schools for Old：The Regeneration of the Porter School/by Evelyn Dewey. —New York：E. P. Dutton & Company, 1919

XI, 337p. ; 19.7cm

PKUL（館藏號缺）

附注：

印章：扉頁後頁鈐有"胡適藏書"朱文方印。

7790 The New Society/by Walther Rathenau. —New York：Harcourt, Brace and Company, 1921

147p. ; 19.1cm

PKUL（館藏號缺）

7791 The New Testament in Basic English. —New York：E. P. Dutton & Co.,

Inc., 1941

548p. ; 20.3cm

PKUL（館藏號缺）

7792 The New Testament in Japanese/by J. C. Hepburn. —Yokohama: Seishi-Bun-Sha, 1886

653p. ; 14.7cm

PKUL（館藏號缺）

7793 The New Testament of Our Lord and Savior Jesus Christ. —Paterson: St. Anthony Guild Press, 1941

VIII, 760p. ; 19.3cm

PKUL（館藏號缺）

附注：

題記：書名頁前頁有田耕莘簽名"+ Thomas Tien S. V. D., Cardinal Archbishop of Peiping"；另有胡適題記："民國卅六年四月廿九日田耕莘樞機大主教來訪,我請他題名在這本書上"；封內藏書票上有胡適題記："此是天主教新修改的'新約',1941年印行的。"

其他：封內貼有"胡適的書"藏書票。

7794 News Is My Job: A Correspondent in War-Torn China/by Edna Lee Booker. —New York: The Macmillan Company, 1940

XII, 375p. ; 21.8cm

PKUL（館藏號缺）

附注：

題記：題名頁有作者題記："To Dr. Hu Shih, with greatest admiration and memories of an interview during Peking days. Edna Lee Booker(Mrs. John S. Potter),Shanghai, Atlanta, Feb. 23, 1940。"

7795 News Is Where You Find It: Forty Years' Reporting at Home and Abroad/by Frederic William Wile. —Indianapolis, New York: The Bobbs-Merrill

Company, 1930

505p. ; 23.2cm

PKUL（館藏號缺）

附注：

印章：扉頁有胡適簽名"Hu Shih, Oct. 30, 1939"。

題記：扉頁有作者題記："To my distinguished friend, Dr. Hu Shih, scholar, diplomat and brother scribe, whose tactful advocacy of his country's cause in the United States has forged new ties of sympathy for China and the gallant people, with the cordial esteem of Frederic William Wile. Washington, November 1, 1939。"

7796 Newspaper Days, 1899-1906/by H. L. Mencken. —New York：Alfred Knopf, 1945

XI, 313p. ; 21.8cm

PKUL（館藏號缺）

7797 The Next Development in Man/by Lancelot Law Whyte. —London：The Cresset Press, 1944

275p. ; 21.5cm

PKUL（館藏號缺）

附注：

題記：扉頁有作者題記："Professor Hu Shih sent at Prof. N. □ suggestion. L. L. W., London, Sept. 1944。"

批注圈劃：書內有圈劃痕迹。

7798 The Next Five Years：An Essay in Political Agreement. —London：Macmillan and Co., Limited, 1935

XVI, 320p. ; 22cm

PKUL（館藏號缺）

7799 The Next Harvard/by Archibald MacLeish. —Cambridge：Harvard University

Press, 1941

50p. ; 18.2cm

PKUL（館藏號缺）

7800 The Nicomachean Ethics of Aristotle/by D. P. Chase. —London：J. M. Dent & Sons Ltd. ; New York：E. P. Dutton & Co. , [n.d.]

XXVIII, 290p. ; 17.3cm

Everyman's Library：Philosophy & Theology

PKUL（館藏號缺）

附注：

印章：一冊扉頁有趙元任簽名"Yuen R. Chao"；另一冊叢書頁鈐有"適盦藏書"朱文圓印。

題記：另一冊扉頁有胡適題記："Suh Hu, Nov. 20, 1913.《阿里士多德之倫理學》,適。"

批注圈劃：一冊書内33頁有鉛筆批注圈劃；另一冊書内159頁有胡適批注圈劃。

夾紙：另一冊書内夾有紙條2張。

其他：本書有2冊。

7801 Night Watches/by W. W. Jacobs. —New York：Charles Scribner's Sons, 1928

247p. ; 19.5cm

PKUL（館藏號缺）

7802 Nine Years in Nipon：Sketches of Japanese Life and Manners/by Henry Faulds. —London：Alexander Gardner, 1885

XII, 304p. ; 20.4cm

PKUL（館藏號缺）

附注：

批注圈劃：書内109頁有鉛筆批注圈劃,以圈劃爲主。

其他：本書裝訂散。

7803 Nipon O Daï Itsi Ran, ou Annales des Empereurs Du Japon/par Isaac Titsingh. —Paris：[s. n.]，1834

XXXVI, 458p. ; 28.5cm

PKUL（館藏號缺）

附注：

印章：扉頁有"R. Lilley"簽名。

其他：本書封面、扉頁脱落。

7804 Nippon：A Charted Survey of Japan, 1936/by Tsuneta Yano, Kyoichi Shirasaki; translated by Z. Tamotsu Iwadô. —Tokyo：Kokusei-Sha, [n. d.]

XXXVI, 487p. ; 22.8cm

PKUL（館藏號缺）

7805 "No Speedier Way".—Shanghai：Christian Literature Society for China, 1938

VII, 143p. ; 22.2cm

PKUL（館藏號缺）

附注：

題記：扉頁有贈書者題記："To Dr. Hu Shih, whose literary revolution brought hope to the illiterate millions in China. From Margaret H. Brown, editor of 'No Speedier Way'."

7806 Northanger Abbey/by Jane Austen. —London：Oxford University Press, 1930

XXII, 274p. ; 15cm

PKUL（館藏號缺）

附注：

印章：題名頁鈐有"盧逮曾印"朱文方印。

7807 A Note on Ch'üan Tsu-Wang, Chao I-Ch'ing and Tai Chên/by Hu Shih. —[s. l.]：American Library of Congress, [n. d.]

970-982p. ; 27.2cm

Reprinted from *The Biographical Dictionary*, *Eminent Chinese of the Ch'ing*

Period, Vol. II

PKUL（館藏號缺）

附注：

 題記：其中一冊封面有胡適鋼筆題記："國會圖書館給我印此單本，共五百份。留此一冊，題作紀念。適之，卅四，五，廿一夜"；另有一冊封面有胡適鋼筆題字："夢鄰。"

 其他：本抽印本有 14 冊。

7808 Note on Direct Stimulation of the Pupillary Dilatator Muscle Fibres in the Iris of the Cat/by Ging-Hsi Wang. —[s. l.]：[s. n.]，[n. d.]

 341–344p.；26.2cm

 Reprinted from *Chinese Journal of Physiology*, Vol. VI, No. 4

 PKUL（館藏號缺）

 附注：

  題記：封面有作者題記："適之先生正之，敬熙。"

7809 Notes on Chinese Alchemy/by A. Waley. —[s. l.]：[s. n.]，[n. d.]

 24p.；24.6cm

 Reprinted from *Bulletin of the School of Oriental Studies*, Vol. VI, Part I, 1930

 PKUL（館藏號缺）

 附注：

  題記：封面有作者題記："To Hu Shih, from the author, with thanks and admiration, Dec. 1930。"

7810 Notes on Chinese Ink/by Wang Chi-Chen. —[s. l.]：[s. n.]，[n. d.]

 114–133p.；31.7cm

 Reprinted from *Metropolitan Museum Studies*, Vol. III, Part I, December, 1930

 PKUL（館藏號缺）

 附注：

  題記：扉頁有作者題記："敬呈適之先生教正，際真上。"

7811 Notes on Chinese Literature: With Introductory Remarks on the Progressive Advancement of the Art/by A. Wylie. —Shanghai: American Presbyterian Mission Press, London: Trübner & Co., 1867

VIII, XXVIII, 260p.; 27cm

PKUL（館藏號缺）

附注：

批注圈劃：書內多處有批注，非胡適所作。

夾紙：書內夾有記錄紙片10餘張，非胡適所記。

其他：本書缺封皮，最後一頁脫落，夾于書中。

7812 Notes on Chinese Materia Medica/by Daniel Hanbury. —London: John E. Taylor, 1862

48p.; 21.4cm

PKUL（館藏號缺）

7813 Notes on the Harvard Tercentenary/by The President and Fellows of Harvard College. —Cambridge: Harvard University Press, 1936

97p.; 21.3cm

PKUL（館藏號缺）

附注：

內附文件：一冊書內貼有剪報1頁。

其他：本書有2冊。

7814 The Notion of Duty in Ethics/by Jen Han. —Strasbourg: Librairie Universitaire d'Alsace, 1931

VII, 168p.; 22.4cm

PKUL（館藏號缺）

附注：

題記：封面有作者題記："胡適之先生指教，學生韓仁，一九三三，六，一四，於北平。"

7815 Nouveaux Mélanges Asiatiques, ou Recueil de Morceaux de Critique et de Mémoires Tome Premier/par Abel-Rémusat. —Paris: Schubart et Heideloff, 1829

    IV, 446p. ; 21.3cm

    PKUL（館藏號缺）

7816 Now I Lay Me Down to Sleep/by Ludwig Bemelmans. —New York: The Viking Press, 1944

    245p. ; 20.3cm

    PKUL（館藏號缺）

7817 The Obliterated Man, and Other Stories/by H. G. Wells. —Girard: Haldeman-Julius Company, [n.d.]

    64p. ; 12.8cm

    Little Blue Book

    PKUL（館藏號缺）

7818 Odd Craft/by W. W. Jacobs. —London: George Newnes, Limited, [n.d.]

    255p. ; 18.5cm

    PKUL（館藏號缺）

    附注：

        題記：扉頁有胡適鋼筆簽名"Hu Shih, March 1942"。

        批注圈劃：目録頁有胡適圈劃。

7819 The Odyssey of Homer/by S. H. Butcher; A. Lang. —New York: P. F. Collier & Son, 1909

    347p. ; 19.5cm

    The Harvard Classics No. 22

    PKUL（館藏號缺）

    附注：

        印章：扉頁有胡適簽名"Suh Hu"。

批注圈劃:書内數處有胡適圈劃;書末有胡適題記:"July 28, 1926, en route to England。"

内附文件:書内夾寫有白話詩紙 1 張:"清無片雲的天上,只有一顆大星,遠遠地伴著圓滿的月亮。望不盡的平原,只有長蛇似的列車,載著行人,蜿蜒地西往。"

夾紙:書内夾有紙條 1 張。

7820 Of Civil Government/by John Locke. —London: J. M. Dent & Sons Ltd. ; New York: E. P, Dutton & Co. , 1924

XX, 242p. ; 17.1cm

Everyman's Library: Philosophy

PKUL (館藏號缺)

附注:

印章:扉頁鈐有"HU SHIH"藍文印。

7821 Official Congressional Directory for the Use of the United States Congress/by R. E. De Sear. —Washington: United States Government Printing Office, 1945

XX, 923p. ; 23.5cm

PKUL (館藏號缺)

7822 The Official Record of the United States' Part in the Great War. —[s. l.]: [s. n.], [n. d.]

310p. ; 23.5cm

PKUL (館藏號缺)

附注:

其他:書内原有帶銅章書籤 1 個。

7823 Oil! /by Upton Sinclair. —New York: Albert & Charles Boni, 1927

527p. ; 19.5cm

PKUL (館藏號缺)

7824 The Oil Vendor and the Sing-Song Girl/by Vincenz Hundhausen. —Peking: The Polar Island Press, 1938

  62, 63-122, 123-164p. ; 14.8cm

  PKUL（館藏號缺）

  附注：

    題記：第1冊扉頁有譯者題記："3/18/39, To his excellency Dr. Hu Shih, with much gratitude, Fritz Ruesch。"

    其他：本書爲綫裝,1函3冊。

7825 Oklahoma: A Guide to the Sooner State. —Norman: University of Oklahoma Press, 1941

  XXVI, 442p. ; 20.9cm

  American Guide Series

  PKUL（館藏號缺）

7826 The Old Fellow/by Herrymon Maurer. —New York: The John Day Company, 1943

  VIII, 296p. ; 20.7cm

  PKUL（館藏號缺）

  附注：

    題記：扉頁有作者題記："To Dr. Hu Shih, with deep respect, Herrymon Maurer。"

7827 On "Inhibition" of the Secretion of Sweat in the Cat by Stimulation of Dorsal Nerve-Roots/by Ging-Hsi Wang, Tze-Wei Lu. —[s.l.]: [s.n.], [n.d.]

  175-181p. ; 26cm

  Reprinted from *Chinese Journal of Physiology*, 1930, Vol. IV, No. 2

  PKUL（館藏號缺）

  附注：

    題記：封面有作者題記："適之先生教正,敬熙,十九,六,十二。"

7828 On a Peking, a St. Petersburg, and a Kyōto Reconstruction of a Sanskrit Stanza Transcribed with Chinese Characters under the Northern Sung Dynasty/by A. von Staël-Holstein. —Peiping：[s. n.]，1932

175-187p. ；26.7cm

Reprinted from Ts'ai Yüan P'ei Anniversary Volume

PKUL（館藏號缺）

附注：

題記：正文首頁有作者題記："To Dr. Hu Shih, with kind regards from AVSH。"

7829 On a Tibetan Text Translated into Sanskrit under Ch'ien Lung (XVIII cent) and into Chinese under Tao Kuang (XIX cent.)/by A. von Staël-Holstein. —[s. l.]：[s. n.]，[n. d.]

20，XVIIp. ；25.9cm

Reprinted from *The Bulletin of the National Library of Peiping*，1932

PKUL（館藏號缺）

附注：

題記：扉頁有作者題記："To Dr. Hu Shih with kind regards from A. S. H。"

7830 On Active Service in Peace and War/by Henry L. Stimson, McGeorge Bundy. —New York：Harper & Brothers，1948

XXII，698p. ；23.4cm

PKUL（館藏號缺）

附注：

題記：扉頁有胡適題記："劉鍇兄寄贈。胡適，卅七，七，卅。"

夾紙：封內貼有劉鍇"With affectionate regard from Liu Chieh"紙條。

7831 On Chinese Poetry/by C. W. Luh. —Peiping：[s. n.]，1935

118p. ；24.1cm

PKUL（館藏號缺）

附注:

    題記:封底有作者題記:"呈適之先生。"(因封底撕毁,僅存上述不完整幾字。)

    其他:本書爲綫裝。

7832 On Compromise/by John Morley. —London: Macmillan and Co., Limited; New York: The Macmillan Company, 1898

    XI, 284p. ; 18cm

    PKUL(館藏號缺)

附注:

    印章:扉頁有原書主簽名"Edward Snell Smith"。

    題記:扉頁有胡適題記:"一九四十年八月廿二日買到這本舊書。胡適。"

7833 On Education, Especially in Early Childhood/by Bertrand Russell. —London: George Allen & Unwin Ltd., 1926

    254p. ; 18.7cm

    PKUL(館藏號缺)

7834 On Liberty/by John Stuart Mill. —London and Felling-on-Tyne, New York and Melbourne: The Walter Scott Publishing Co., Ltd., [n.d.]

    XXVI, 219p. ; 16.6cm

    The Scott Library

    PKUL(館藏號缺)

附注:

    印章:題名頁鈐有"一涵藏書"朱文長方印;扉頁題有"高一涵,一九二〇年,三月"。

    其他:本書散頁,缺1—102頁。

7835 On Oriental Culture and Japan's Mission/by Rabindranath Tagore. —Tokyo: The Indo-Japanese Association, 1931

    28p. ; 21.6cm

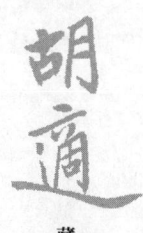

  PKUL（館藏號缺）

  附注：

    題記：封面有贈書者題記："To Prof. Hu Shih。"

7836 On Special Mission to Abyssinia/by Catherine Murray Jacoby. —New York：Argus Graphic Arts Service, [n. d.]

  141p. ; 23cm

  PKUL（館藏號缺）

  附注：

    題記：扉頁有作者題記："To His Excellency ambassador Dr. Hu Shih with kind regards . Catherine Murray-Jacoby。"

7837 On Taste；On the Sublime and Beautiful；Reflection on the French Revolution；A Letter to a Noble Lord/by Edmund Burke. —New York：P. F. Collier & Son, 1909

  443p. ; 19.5cm

  The Harvard Classics No. 24

  PKUL（館藏號缺）

  附注：

    印章：扉頁有胡適簽名"Suh Hu"。

7838 On the Agenda of Democracy/by Charles E. Merriam. —Cambridge：Harvard University Press, 1941

  XIV, 135p. ; 21.2cm

  PKUL（館藏號缺）

  附注：

    其他：封內貼有"胡適的書"藏書票。

7839 On the Magmatic Differentiation of the Tzuchinshan Alkaline Rocks, Linhsien, Shansi/by C. C. Wang. —[s. l.]：[s. n.], [n. d.]

  229-242p. ; 25.7cm

Reprinted from *The Bulletin of Geological Society of China*, 1947

PKUL（館藏號缺）

附注：

題記：封面有作者題記："適之先生教正，弟王竹泉敬贈。"

7840 On the Rim of the Abyss/by James T. Shotwell. —New York：The Macmillan Company, 1936

XIV, 400p. ; 21.1cm

PKUL（館藏號缺）

附注：

題記：一冊扉頁有作者題記："To Dr. Hu Shih, with high regard. James T. Shotwell"；另一冊扉頁有作者題記："To my friend Dr. Hu Shih, with sincere and high regard. James T. Shotwell。"

其他：本書有2冊。

7841 One American and His Attempt at Education/by Frazier Hunt. —New York：Simon and Schuster, 1938

VIII, 405p. ; 24cm

PKUL（館藏號缺）

附注：

題記：扉頁有作者題記："For Dr. Hu Shih—old friend of a quarter century, with gratitude and the greatest respect—Frazier Hunt, Sept. 10-1945。"

7842 One's Company—A Journey to China/by Peter Fleming. —London：Jonathan Cape, 1934

319p. ; 20.7cm

PKUL（館藏號缺）

7843 The Open Door Doctrine：In Relation to China/by Mingchien Joshua Bau. —New York：The Macmillan Company, 1923

XXVIII, 245p. ; 22.4cm

PKUL（館藏號缺）

7844 The Open Door Policy/by En Tsung Yen. —Boston：The Stratford Company，Publishers，1923

191p. ；18.3cm

PKUL（館藏號缺）

附注：

題記：扉頁有作者題記："適之先生惠存，十七年五月廿三，嚴恩椿。"

7845 The Operation of the New Bank Act/by Thomas Conway, Ernest M. Patterson. —Philadelphia, London：J. B. Lippincott Company，1914

VIII, 431p. ；20.3cm

PKUL（館藏號缺）

附注：

印章：扉頁有"Huang Li"鉛筆簽名。

7846 Opinions of Oliver Allston/by Van Wyck Brooks. —New York：E. P. Dutton & Co., Inc., 1941

309p. ；22.1cm

PKUL（館藏號缺）

附注：

題記：扉頁有作者題記："Dr. Hu Shih, with great respect, Van Wyck Brooks, New York, 1943。"

7847 Options/by O. Henry. —[s. l.]：Doubleday, Page & Company, 1909

257p. ；19.3cm

PKUL（館藏號缺）

7848 Organized Banking/by Eugene E. Agger. —New York：Henry Holt and Company, 1918

IX, 385p. ；21cm

PKUL（館藏號缺）

7849 Oriental and Occidental Cultures Contrasted: An Introduction to "Culturology"/by Cheng Che-yu. —Berkeley: The Gillick Press, 1943

 158p. ; 23.2cm

 PKUL（館藏號缺）

 附注：

  印章：題名頁鈐有"鄭啓愚"朱文方印。

7850 Oriental Customs; Or an Illustration of the Sacred Scriptures/by Samuel Burder. —London: Thomas Tegg, [n.d.]

 XII, 500p. ; 21.9cm

 PKUL（館藏號缺）

 附注：

  題記：扉頁有原書主簽名"R. Lilley"；另有簽名"J. H. Hodgson, 5 Chancery Lane"；另有簽名"R. J. Laughton, 1862"。

  其他：本書前後都有散落，缺封皮、書脊。

7851 The Oriental Institute/by James H. Breasted. —Chicago: The University Chicago Press, 1933

 XXIII, 455p. ; 19cm

 The University of Chicago Survey

 PKUL（館藏號缺）

 附注：

  題記：扉頁有胡適鋼筆簽名"Hu Shih, July 27, 1933"。

  內附文件：書內夾有 Haskell Foundation Institute 講座手冊1份。

7852 Oriental Religions and Their Relation to Universal Religion, China/by Samuel Johnson. —Boston: Houghton, Osgood and Company, 1878

 XXIV, 975p. ; 21.8cm

 PKUL（館藏號缺）

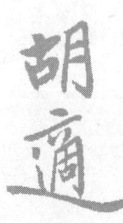

附注：

印章：扉頁有"R. Lilley"簽名。

7853 Oriental Religions and Their Relation to Universal Religion, India/by Samuel Johnson. —Boston：James R. Osgood and Company, 1873

VI, 802p. ；21.7cm

PKUL（館藏號缺）

附注：

印章：扉頁有"R. Lilley"簽名。

7854 Origin and Conclusion of the Paris Pact：The Renunciation of War as an Instrument of National Policy/by Denys P. Myers. —Boston：World Peace Foundation, 1929

196p. ；20.1cm

PKUL（館藏號缺）

7855 The Origin and Nature of Life/by Benjamin Moore. —London：Williams and Norgate,［n.d.］

256p. ；16.6cm

Home University Library of Modern Knowledge

PKUL（館藏號缺）

附注：

印章：扉頁鈐有"北京緞庫後胡同八號,胡適之"藍文長方印。

7856 The Origin of Magic and Religion/by W. J. Perry. —London：Methuen & Co., Ltd., 1923

IX, 212p. ；19.5cm

PKUL（館藏號缺）

7857 The Origin of Parliamentary Sovereignty, or "Mixed" Monarchy/by Yung Chi Hoe. —Shanghai：The Commercial Press, 1935

XIV, 377p. ; 18.4cm

PKUL（館藏號缺）

附注：

　　題記：扉頁有作者題記："適之先生指正，永佶，一九三五，十一，十一。"

7858　The Origin of Religion/by Joseph McCabe. —Girard：Haldeman-Julius Company，[n. d.]

　　64p. ; 12.8cm

　　Little Blue Book

　　PKUL（館藏號缺）

7859　The Origin of Species/by Charles Darwin. —New York：P. F. Collier & Son，1909

　　552p. ; 19.5cm

　　The Harvard Classics No. 11

　　PKUL（館藏號缺）

　　附注：

　　　　印章：扉頁有胡適簽名"Suh Hu"；題名頁鈐有"適盦藏書"朱文圓印。

7860　The Origin of the Chinese/by John Chalmers. —London：Trübner & Co. , 1868

　　78p. ; 20.3cm

　　PKUL（館藏號缺）

　　附注：

　　　　印章：扉頁有原書主簽名"R. Lilley"。

　　　　其他：本書扉頁、題名頁脱落。

7861　L'Origine et le Développement de la Méthode Expérimentale/par Chi-Kai Lin. —Paris：Les Édition Domat-Montchrestien, 1931

　　422p. ; 22.6cm

　　PKUL（館藏號缺）

　　附注：

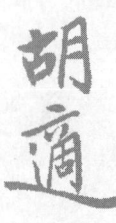

其他：本書缺封面、封底。

7862 Oscar Wilde's Letters to Sarah Bernhardt/by Sylvestre Dorian. —Girard：Haldeman-Julius Company，[n. d.]

64p. ; 12.7cm

Little Blue Book

PKUL（館藏號缺）

7863 Our Age of Unreason：A Study of the Irrational Forces in Social Life/by Franz Alexander. —Philadelphia, New York：J. B. Lippincott Company, 1942

371p. ; 22cm

PKUL（館藏號缺）

7864 Our Cornell/by Hendrik Willem Van Loon, E. B. White, et al. —Ithaca：The Cayuga Press, 1939

82p. ; 17.2cm

PKUL（館藏號缺）

附注：

題記：扉頁有胡適題記："Gift from Dean F. K. Richtmyer of the Graduate School of Cornell University, October, 1939. Dean Richtmyer died early in November before I had time to acknowledge this gift. His death was a lost to Cornell and to Science. Hu Shih。"

7865 Our Enemy/by James R. Young. —Philadelphia：David Mckay Company, 1942

127p. ; 18.3cm

PKUL（館藏號缺）

附注：

題記：扉頁有贈書者題記："Best wishes to Dr. Hu Shih, from □ & Jimmy Young, Oct. 2, 1942。"

7866 Our Enemy Japan/by Wilfrid Fleisher. —[s. l.]：Garden City, Doubleday,

Doran & Company, Inc., 1942

XI, 236p.; 19.5cm

PKUL（館藏號缺）

附注：

題記：題名前頁有胡適鋼筆簽名"Hu Shih, April 1, 1942. N. Y. C."。

7867 Our Heart Were Young and Gay/by Cornelia Otis Skinner, Emily Kimbrough. —New York: Dodd, Mead & Company, 1942

247p.; 20.8cm

PKUL（館藏號缺）

7868 Our Heritage/by Humayun Kabir. —Bombay: The National Information & Publications Ltd., 1946

VIII, 134p.; 18.8cm

PKUL（館藏號缺）

附注：

夾紙：書內夾有"賀燿組"名片1張。

7869 Our Knowledge of the External World: As a Field of Scientific Method in Philosophy/by Bertrand Russell. —Chicago and London: The Open Court Publishing Company, 1915

IX, 245p.; 22.1cm

PKUL（館藏號缺）

附注：

題記：扉頁有胡適簽名"Hu Suh, Feb. 1921"。

7870 Our Short Story Writers/by Blanche Colton Williams. —New York: Dodd, Mead and Company, 1920

384p.; 18.7cm

PKUL（館藏號缺）

附注：

印章：扉頁有胡適朱筆簽名"Hu Shih"。

內附文件：書末夾有剪報1頁。

7871 Our Times：The United States 1900-1925/by Mark Sullivan. —New York，London：Charles Scribner's Sons, 1926-1935

 6 Vols. ;22.8cm

 PKUL（館藏號缺）

附注：

 印章：第1卷扉頁有"S. G. Rosenbaum"簽名；第3卷有一冊扉頁鈐有"HU SHIH"藍文印。

 夾紙：第2卷頁286、287間有夾紙。

 其他：本書第3卷有2冊。各卷主要內容：I. The Turn of the Century; II. American Finding Herself; III. Pre-War America; IV. The War Begins, 1909-1914; V. Over Here, 1914-1918; VI. the Twenties。

7872 Ouroboros：Or the Mechanical Extension of Mankind/by Garet Garrett. —London：Kegan Paul, Trench, Trubner & Co., Ltd. , [n. d.]

 93p. ;15.9cm

 PKUL（館藏號缺）

附注：

 印章：扉頁有胡適鉛筆簽名"Hu Shih"。

7873 Out of This Nettle, Danger…/by Harold W. Dodds. —Princeton：Princeton University Press, 1943

 57p. ;20.2cm

 PKUL（館藏號缺）

7874 An Outline History of China/by Herbert H. Gowen, Josef Washington Hall. —New York, London：D. Appleton and Company, 1926

 XXVIII, 542p. ;22.2cm

 PKUL（館藏號缺）

7875 An Outline History of Japan/by Herbert H. Gowen. —New York, London：D. Appleton and Company, 1927

 XIX, 458p. ；22.1cm

 PKUL（館藏號缺）

 附注：

  批注圈劃：書內 4 頁有胡適批注圈劃。

7876 Outline of the History of Greek Philosophy/by Edward Zeller. —New York：Henry Holt and Company, 1908

 XV, 363p. ；18.6cm

 PKUL（館藏號缺）

 附注：

  印章：書名頁鈐有"適盦藏書"朱文圓印。

  題記：扉頁有胡適題記："《希臘哲學史》,適之。"

  批注圈劃：書內 216 頁有胡適批注圈劃。

  夾紙：頁 136、137,186、187 間各夾有紙條 1 張。

7877 An Outline of the Religious Literature of India/by J. N. Farquhar. —Humphrey Milford：Oxford University Press, 1920

 XXVIII, 451p. ；21.5cm

 PKUL（館藏號缺）

 附注：

  印章：第 1 冊扉頁有胡適毛筆簽名"Hu Shih"。

  題記：第 2 冊扉頁有胡適題記："我本有此書；今年在英國因需用此書,故又買了這一本。胡適"；第 3 冊書名頁有胡適題記："我用此書最久。今年紐約 Orientalia 書店為我買得此本,似是戰時翻印的本子。適之。一九四四,十二月。"

  批注圈劃：第 1 冊書內 54 頁有胡適批注圈劃；第 3 冊書內 26 頁有胡適批注圈劃。

  夾紙：第 3 冊頁 62、63,112、113 間各有夾紙一；第 1 張上有胡適鉛筆書

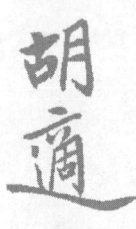

英文。

摺頁:第1冊頁252有摺頁。

其他:本書有3冊。

7878 An Outline of Universal History/by George E. Sokolsky. —Shanghai: The Commercial Press, Limited, 1928

XVI, 889p. ; 22.4cm

PKUL(館藏號缺)

附注:

題記:扉頁有贈書者題記:"To guide and friend Hu Shih, from Jose。"

7879 Outlines of Economics/by Richard T. Ely. —New York: The Macmillan Company, 1908

XIII, 700p. ; 19.5cm

Everyman's Library: Philosophy and Theology

PKUL(館藏號缺)

附注:

題記:扉頁有原藏書者題記:"Willard Judd McKay, Cornell University, March, 1910。"

7880 The Ox-Bow Incident/by Walter Van Tilburg Clark. —New York: The Press of The Readers Club, 1942

XI, 287p. ; 21.8cm

PKUL(館藏號缺)

7881 The Oxford Book of English Verse, 1250-1900/by Arthur Quiller-Couch. —Oxford: The Clarendon Press, 1925

XIX, 1084p. ; 17cm

PKUL(館藏號缺)

附注:

題記:扉頁有胡適鋼筆簽名"胡適,London, Nov. 2, 1926"。

7882 The Oxford Movement/by Wilfrid Ward. —London: T. C. & E. C. Jack, [n. d.]

 92p. ; 16.1cm

 PKUL（館藏號缺）

 附註：

  題記：扉頁有胡適毛筆簽名"Suh Hu, April, 1919"。

7883 Pacific Affairs Dossier, for Pacific Council Meetings, October 12–18, 1931. —[s. l.]: [s. n.], [n. d.]

 62p. ; 27.7cm

 PKUL（館藏號缺）

 附註：

  題記：封面有贈書者朱筆題記："Dr. Hu Shih, Room 500, Cathay。"

  夾紙：書內夾有"Elizabeth Green"名片1張，上書"For your interest—at leisure。"

7884 The Pacific Area: An International Survey/by George H. Blakeslee. —Boston: World Peace Foundation, 1929

 224p. ; 20cm

 World Peace Foundation Pamphlets

 PKUL（館藏號缺）

7885 Pacific Council Minutes, 1936/by Pacific Council. —[s. l.]: [s. n.], 1936

 106p. ; 27.9cm

 PKUL（館藏號缺）

 附註：

  其他：本書爲油印本。

7886 The Pact of Paris as Envisaged by Mr. Stimson: Its Significance in International Law/by Yuen-Li Liang. —[s. l.]: [s. n.], [n. d.]

16p. ; 27.8cm

PKUL（館藏號缺）

附注：

題記：封面有作者題記："To Dr. Hu Shih, with pleasanted recolleticons of happy conversation and in appreciation of his courageous stand in time of storm & stress. Yuen L. Liang。"

其他：此爲打印件。

7887 A Pageant of Asia：A Study of Three Civilizations/by Kenneth Saunders. ——Humphrey Milford：Oxford University Press, 1934

XII, 452p. ; 21.7cm

PKUL（館藏號缺）

附注：

夾紙：書内夾有出版社贈書卡1張。

7888 The Pageant of Chinese History/by Elizabeth Seeger. ——London, New York, Toronto：Longmans, Green and Co. , 1934

XV, 386p. ; 21.2cm

PKUL（館藏號缺）

7889 The Pageant of Greece/by R. W. Livingstone. ——London：Oxford University Press, 1925

240p. ; 18.4cm

PKUL（館藏號缺）

附注：

題記：扉頁有作者題記："Dr. Hu Shih, with best wishes from the author, Καὶ Τύλοθ Χαιροις。"

7890 Palaeogeography and Polar Shift：A Study of Hypothetical Projections/by Davidson Black. ——[s. l.]：[s. n.], [n. d.]

105-157p. ; 25.9cm

Reprinted from *Bulletin of the Geological Society of China*, Vol. X

PKUL（館藏號缺）

附注：

題記：封面有作者題記："To Professor Hu Shih, with kind regards, Davidson Black。"

7891 The Pan American Union Peace Friendship Commerce/by John Barrett. —Washington: Pan American Union, 1911

253p. ; 21.8cm

PKUL（館藏號缺）

附注：

夾紙：書内夾有"Harry O. Sandberg"名片1張,背面寫有"Kindest personal regards and pleasure memories of our acquaintances, Suh Hu"；另封内貼有 Pan American Union 贈書卡1張。

7892 The Panchatantra Reconstructed/by Franklin Edgerton. —London, Edinburgh, Glasgow, Toronto: Oxford University Press, [n. d.]

2 Vols. ; 23.3cm

PKUL（館藏號缺）

附注：

題記：第1卷扉頁有胡適題記："全書兩冊,原價八元。今天我以特價兩元買來。胡適,一九四三,十月十六。"

夾紙：第2卷頁324、325間有夾紙一。

7893 Papers on Religion Delivered at the Formal Opening of Yenching University, October 1930/by J. W. Inglis, Andrew C. Y. Cheng, et al. —Peiping: The School of Religion, Yenching University, 1930

9, 9, 7, 12, 18, 30, 15, 13, 5, 26p. ; 24.6cm

PKUL（館藏號缺）

7894 Papers Relating to the Foreign Relations of the United States, 1924. —

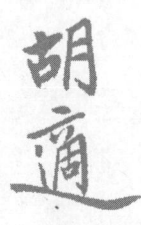

Washington: United States Government Printing Office, 1939

2 Vols. ; 22.9cm

PKUL（館藏號缺）

7895 Papers Relating to the Foreign Relations of the United States, the Lansing Papers 1914-1920. —Washington: United States Government Printing Office, 1939

2 Vols. ; 22.9cm

PKUL（館藏號缺）

7896 Parlez-vous Français? Or Do You Speak French?. —New York: Henry Holt and Company, [n.d.]

111p. ; 15.3cm

PKUL（館藏號缺）

附注：

印章：扉頁有胡適鋼筆簽名"Suh Hu"。

題記：封面有胡適鋼筆題記："Caroline F. Beeke, Suh Hu。"

批注圈劃：書內數頁有胡適批注圈劃。

7897 The Party and Other Stories/by Anton Tchehov; translated by Constance Garnett. —London: Chatto & Windus, 1919

303p. ; 15.6cm

The Tales of Tchehov

PKUL（館藏號缺）

附注：

題記：扉頁有胡適鋼筆簽名"Hu Shih, November 1924"。

批注圈劃：目錄頁有胡適圈劃。

7898 Le Passe de L'Avenir de L'Observatoire Central de Pekin/par Kao Lou. —Pekin: L'Observatoire Central de Pekin, [n.d.]

21, 20, 21p. ; 25.4cm

PKUL（館藏號缺）

7899　Passing through Germany. —Berlin：Terramre Office, [n.d.]

　　207p. ; 19.4cm

　　PKUL（館藏號缺）

7900　The Past and Future of British Relations in China/by Sherard Osborn. — Edingburgh and London：William Blackwood and Sons, 1860

　　184p. ; 19.5cm

　　PKUL（館藏號缺）

7901　Pastoral/by Nevil Shute. —New York：William Morrow & Company, 1944

　　246p. ; 20.9cm

　　PKUL（館藏號缺）

7902　The Pastoral Loves of Daphnis and Chloe/by George Moore. —London：William Heinemann Ltd., 1927

　　161p. ; 17.7cm

　　PKUL（館藏號缺）

　　附注：

　　　　印章：題名頁鈐有"摩曼"朱文方印。

7903　Patents for Hereditary Ranks and Honorary Titles during the Ch'ing Dynasty/by Wolfgang Franke. —Peking：Henri Vetch, [n.d.]

　　38-65p. ; 27.5cm

　　Reprinted from *Monvmenta Serica, Journal of Oriental Studies of the Catholic University of Peking*, Vol. VII, 1942

　　PKUL（館藏號缺）

　　附注：

　　　　題記：封面有作者題記："To Dr. Hu Shih, respectfully presented by Wolfgang Franke。"

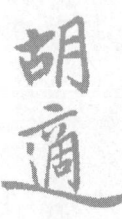

7904 The Path to Peace: Essays and Addresses on Peace and Its Making/by Nicholas Murray Butler. —New York, London: Charles Scribner's Sons, 1930

XIII, 320p. ; 19.1cm

PKUL（館藏號缺）

7905 Pathfinders in Medicine/by Victor Robinson. —New York: Medical Life Press, 1929

XVII, 810p. ; 23.3cm

PKUL（館藏號缺）

附注：

印章：扉頁鈐有"HU SHIH"藍文印。

7906 The Patriot/by Pearl S. Buck. —New York: The John Day Company, 1939

372p. ; 20.5cm

PKUL（館藏號缺）

附注：

印章：扉頁鈐有"HU SHIH"藍文印。

7907 Paul Revere & the World He Lived In/by Esther Forbes. —Boston: Houghton Mifflin Company, 1942

XIII, 498p. ; 22.1cm

PKUL（館藏號缺）

7908 Peace and War: United States Foreign Policy, 1931–1941/by Department of State, United States of America. —Washington: United States Government Printing Office, [n.d.]

XXI, 874p. ; 23.3cm

PKUL（館藏號缺）

附注：

印章：扉頁及書名頁均鈐有"苦撐待變"朱文方印。

題記：扉頁有胡適題記："范旭東先生於民國廿九年底來美國，他問我的外交方針；我對他說，我的主張只有"苦撐待變"四個字。變在人，而苦撐在我，我們只能盡其在我而已。范先生贊成此言，所以他回到重慶就托人刻了這個圖章寄給我。我從來不曾用這圖章；今天讀這本書，第一次用這圖章打在書冊上。胡適，Nov. 15，1943"；扉頁背面有胡適題記："此書所收材料，初看似甚完全，但實有故意隱諱的地方。如 1941 November 21 Secretary Hull 向 A. B. C. D. 四國使節提議的緩和日本辦法，此書全不提及，但有 November 26 的方案而已。又如中國方面的文件，此中一字不載。'信史'談何容易！胡適，June 5，1947。"

內附文件：頁 168、169 間有 1947 年某日《大公報》剪報 1 張，內容爲社評"由東北局面說起"，上有朱筆圈劃痕迹。

夾紙：頁 702、703 間有夾紙 1 張。

7909 Peace and War: United States Foreign Policy, 1931－1941. —Washington: United States Government Printing Office, 1942

  VII, 144p. ; 23.5cm

  PKUL（館藏號缺）

  附注：

  其他：本書有 3 冊。

7910 Peace with the Dictators? A Symposium and Some Conclusions/by Norman Angell. —London: Hamish Hamilton, 1938

  328p. ; 19.9cm

  PKUL（館藏號缺）

  附注：

  印章：扉頁鈐有"HU SHIH"藍文印。

7911 Pearl Harbor Attack: Hearings before the Joint Committee on the Investigation of the Pearl Harbor AttackPart 7. —Washington: United States Government Printing Office, 1946

  XVI, 2921－3378p. ; 23cm

PKUL（館藏號缺）

7912 Pearl Harbor Attack: Hearings before the Joint Committee on the Investigation of the Pearl Harbor Attack Part 8. —Washington: United States Government Printing Office, 1946

XVI, 3379-3927p. ; 23.5cm

PKUL（館藏號缺）

7913 Pearl Harbor Attack: Hearings before the Joint Committee on the Investigation of the Pearl Harbor Attack Part 9. —Washington: United States Government Printing Office, 1946

XVI, 3929-4599p. ; 23cm

PKUL（館藏號缺）

7914 Pearl Harbor Attack: Hearings before the Joint Committee on the Investigation of the Pearl Harbor Attack Part 10. —Washington: United States Government Printing Office, 1946

XVI, 4601-5151p. ; 23.2cm

PKUL（館藏號缺）

7915 Pearl Harbor Attack: Hearings before the Joint Committee on the Investigation of the Pearl Harbor Attack Part 14. —Washington: United States Government Printing Office, 1946

XXIV, 923-1422p. ; 23.2cm

PKUL（館藏號缺）

7916 Pearl Harbor Attack: Hearings before the Joint Committee on the Investigation of the Pearl Harbor Attack Part 17. —Washington: United States Government Printing Office, 1946

XXIV, 2457-2874p. ; 23.1cm

PKUL（館藏號缺）

7917 Pearl Harbor Attack: Hearings before the Joint Committee on the Investigation of the Pearl Harbor Attack Part 21. —Washington: United States Government Printing Office, 1946

 XXIV, 4551-4780p. ; 23cm

 PKUL（館藏號缺）

7918 Pearl Harbor Attack: Hearings before the Joint Committee on the Investigation of the Pearl Harbor Attack Part 30. —Washington: United States Government Printing Office, 1946

 VIII, 2458-3086p. ; 23.2cm

 PKUL（館藏號缺）

7919 Peasant Conditions in Russia, 1925/by Jean Efremoff. —Worcester: Carnegie Endowment for International Peace, Division of Intercourse and Education, 1926

 26p. ; 19.7cm

 PKUL（館藏號缺）

7920 Peasants & Potters/by Harold Peake, Herbert John Fleure. —Oxford: The Clarendon Press, 1927

 V, 152p. ; 20.5cm

 The Corridors of Time

 PKUL（館藏號缺）

7921 Peiping Municipality and the Diplomatic Quarter/by Robert Moore Duncan. —Tientsin-Peiping: Peiyang Press, Ltd., 1933

 V, 146p. ; 23.3cm

 PKUL（館藏號缺）

7922 Peoples and Problems of India/by T. W. Holderness. —London: Williams and Norgate, [n.d.]

256p. ; 16.5cm

Home University Library of Modern Knowledge

PKUL（館藏號缺）

附注：

印章：扉頁鈐有"北京緞庫後胡同八號,胡適之"藍文長方印。

7923 Peoples Speaking to Peoples: A Report on International Mass Communication from the Commission on Freedom of the Press/by Llewellyn White, Robert D. Leigh. —Chicago: The University of Chicago Press, 1946

IX, 122p. ; 19.7cm

PKUL（館藏號缺）

7924 Pepys' Diary/by Charles J. Finger. —Girard: Haldeman-Julius Company, [n.d.]

64p. ; 12.7cm

Little Blue Book

PKUL（館藏號缺）

7925 Performance of Mei Lan-Fang in Soviet Russia. —[s.l.]: [s.n.], [n.d.]

43p. ; 19cm

PKUL（館藏號缺）

附注：

其他：本書爲綫裝。

7926 Personal Reminiscences/by Robert B. Forbes. —Boston: Little, Brown, and Company, 1892

XXXI, 412p. ; 19.5cm

PKUL（館藏號缺）

附注：

題記：扉頁後頁有贈書者題記："To his Excellency Hu Shih, with wishes for a very happy New Year, W. Cameron Forbes. December 31th, 1940。"

夾紙：內夾贈書者地址。

7927 Persons and Places: The Background of My Life/by George Santayana. —
New York: Charles Scribner's Sons, 1944

262p. ; 20.9cm

PKUL（館藏號缺）

附注：

內附文件：書內夾有剪報2份。

7928 Petit Vocabulaire Chinois-Annamite-Français/par Edmond Nordemann. —
Hué: [s. n.], 1905

173p. ; 15cm

PKUL（館藏號缺）

7929 Petition to the Republic Government of China by Koreans in Hawaii. —
[s. l.]: [s. n.], 1931

6p. ; 32.9cm

PKUL（館藏號缺）

7930 Petrarch: The First Modern Scholar and Man of Letters/by James Harvey
Robinson. —New York, London: G. P. Putnam's sons, 1914

XII, 477p. ; 20.5cm

PKUL（館藏號缺）

附注：

印章：扉頁有胡適鉛筆簽名"Suh Hu"。

批注圈劃：Introduction 部分有鉛筆圈劃。

7931 The Phantom 'Rickshaw/by Rudyard Kipling. —New York: The Regent Press,
[n. d.]

225p. ; 19.2cm

PKUL（館藏號缺）

附注：

    題記：扉頁有胡適簽名"Suh Hu, March 1916"。

7932 The Pharisees: The Sociological Background of Their Faith/by Louis Finkelstein. —Philadelphia: The Jewish Publication Society of America, 1938

  2 Vols. (XXVII, V, 793p.) ; 21.6cm

  The Morris Loeb Series

  PKUL（館藏號缺）

  附注：

    題記：第1卷扉頁有贈書者題記："To ambassador Hu, with high regard, □."

    內附文件：第1卷書內夾有剪報2張。

    其他：第1卷封內貼有"胡適的書"藏書票。

7933 Le Phénoménisme de Charles Renouvier/par Wang Tsun-Sheng. —Lyon: BOSC Frères, 1935

  168p. ; 25cm

  PKUL（館藏號缺）

  附注：

    題記：扉頁有作者題記："胡適之先生指正，王駿聲敬贈，民國念五年十二月四日，南京。"

7934 Philology and Ancient China/by Bernhard Karlgren. —Leipzig, Paris, London: H. Aschehoug & Co., 1926

  167p. ; 19.6cm

  PKUL（館藏號缺）

  附注：

    題記：扉頁有作者題記："Professor Hu Shih, with kind regards from the author."

    其他：本書缺封面。

7935 The Philosopher of the Common Man: Essays in Honor of John Dewey to Celebrate His Eightieth Birthday. —New York: G. P. Putmam's Sons, 1940

228p. ; 21.5cm

PKUL（館藏號缺）

附注：

題記：一冊扉頁有胡適題記："去年十月為杜威先生作紀念論文一篇，今年從頭改作，收在此集裏。胡適，廿九，五，一"；另一冊扉頁有胡適題記："杜威先生八十歲生日（一九三六，十月二十日），一班老朋友，老學生，給他做壽，有幾篇論文收在這本小冊子裏。今天我把這小書送給文伯，祝他和杜威先生享同樣的高壽，並且享同樣的健康。適之 卅三，二，十四 紐約，東八一街。"

與胡適的關係：書中頁 205—219 收錄胡適的論文"The Political Philosophy of Instrumentalism"。

內附文件：封底內及前頁貼有 *The Nation* 1940 年 12 月 21 日關於本書的評論介紹。

其他：本書有 3 冊，一冊封內貼有"胡適的書"藏書票。

7936 Philosopher's Holiday/by Irwin Edman. —New York: The Viking Press, 1938

X, 270p. ; 21cm

PKUL（館藏號缺）

7937 Philosophical Essays in Honor of James Edwin Creighton. —New York: The Macmillan Company, 1917

XII, 356p. ; 23.8cm

PKUL（館藏號缺）

附注：

題記：扉頁有胡適題記："Suh Hu, June, 1917. The volume was presented to Prof. Creighton on June 12th, 1917. S. H. 。"

7938 The Philosophical Review, Index Volumes I-XXXV (1892-1926)/by Ernest Albee, William A. Hammond, Frank Thilly. —New York: Longmans, Green, and Company, [n. d.]

IV, 200p. ; 24.3cm

PKUL（館藏號缺）

附注：

題記：封面有胡適題記："Gift from Professor W. A. Hammond, March 7, 1927。"

夾紙：封內夾有贈書條 1 張："With the compliments of The Philosophical Review。"

7940 The Philosophical Works of John Locke/by John Locke; edited by J. A. ST. John. —London: G. Bell and Sons Ltd., 1913

2 Vols. ; 17.9cm

PKUL（館藏號缺）

附注：

題記：兩卷扉頁均有胡適鋼筆簽名"Suh Hu, October, 1914"。

批注圈劃：第 1 卷書內 58 頁有胡適批注圈劃；第 2 卷書內 9 頁有胡適批注圈劃。

夾紙：第 1 卷書內有夾紙一，另夾有類似郵票印刷品 1 枚；第 2 卷書內有夾紙一。

7940 Philosophie de l'Art/par H. Taine. —Paris: Librairie Hachette, [n.d.]

2 Vols. (288, 360p.) ; 19.4cm

PKUL（館藏號缺）

附注：

印章：兩卷題名頁均鈐有"李氏辰冬"朱文方印。

7941 Le Philosophe Meh–Ti et L'Idée de Solidarité/par Alexandra David. —Londres: Luzac et Co., 1907

XVI, 185p. ; 21.2cm

Socialisme Chinois

PKUL（館藏號缺）

附注：

　　批注圈劃：一冊書內 2 頁有胡適批注圈劃。

　　夾紙：一冊正文前夾有"吳振國（榮卿）"名片 1 張，胡適記錄法文單詞紙 1 張。

　　其他：本書有 2 冊。

7942 Philosophies of China/by Wing-tsit Chan. —New York：Philosophical Library，[n. d.]

　　541-571p. ；21cm

　　Reprinted from *Twentieth Century Philosophy*

　　PKUL（館藏號缺）

　　附注：

　　　　題記：封面有作者題記："適之先生教正，陳榮捷贈。"

7943 Philosophy and Civilization/by John Dewey. —New York：Minton, Balch & Company，1931

　　334p. ；24.5cm

　　PKUL（館藏號缺）

7944 Philosophy—East and West/by Charles A. Moore. —New Jersey：Princeton University Press，1944

　　IX, 334p. ；20.4cm

　　PKUL（館藏號缺）

7945 The Philosophy of Courage：Or the Oxford Group Way/by Philip Leon. —London：George Allen & Unwin，1939

　　222p. ；18.4cm

　　PKUL（館藏號缺）

　　附注：

　　　　題記：扉頁有贈書者題記："To His Excellency The Chinese Ambassador at Washington, Dr. Hu Shih, with every good wish from Logan H. Roots,

Bishop. 25 March, 1939。"

7946 Physiology of Development of the Feather III. Growth of the Mesodermal Constituents and Blood Circulation in the Pulp/by Frank R. Lillie. —[s. l.]:[s. n.],[n. d.]

 143-175p. ; 24.1cm

 Reprinted from *Physiological Zoölogy*, Vol. XIII, No. 2

 PKUL（館藏號缺）

 附注：

  題記：封面有贈書者題記："胡適先生惠存,王熙代 Lillie 教授贈。"

7947 Physiology of Development of the Feather V. Experimental Morphogenesis/by Frank R. Lillie, Hsi Wang. —[s. l.]:[s. n.],[n. d.]

 103-133p. ; 24.2cm

 Reprinted from *Physiological Zoölogy*, Vol. XIII, No. 2

 PKUL（館藏號缺）

 附注：

  題記：封面有贈書者題記："胡適先生惠存。"

7948 The Philosophy of Immanuel Kant/by A. D. Lindsay. —London：T. C. & E. C. Jack, Ltd. ; New York：Dodge Publishing Co. ,[n. d.]

 89p. ; 16.4cm

 The People's Books

 PKUL（館藏號缺）

 附注：

  題記：扉頁有胡適毛筆簽名"Hu Suh, April, 1919"。

7949 The Philosophy of John Dewey/by Joseph Ratner. —New York：Henry Holt and Company, 1928

 XII, 560p. ; 21.7cm

 PKUL（館藏號缺）

附注：

　　題記：扉頁有胡適題記："王文伯送給我的。適之。十七，九，廿六。"

7950 The Philosophy of John Dewey/by Paul Arthur Schilpp. —Evanston and Chicago：Northwestern University, 1939

　　XV, 708p. ; 23.3cm

　　The Library of Living Philosophers

　　PKUL（館藏號缺）

　　附注：

　　　　題記：扉頁有胡適鋼筆簽名"Hu Shih, 1940"。

7951 The Philosophy of John Dewey：A Critical Analysis/by W. T. Feldman. —Baltimore：The Johns Hopkins Press, 1934

　　VII, 127p. ; 21.3cm

　　PKUL（館藏號缺）

　　附注：

　　　　題記：扉頁鈐有"HU SHIH"藍文印；另有胡適鋼筆注明："Oct. 20, 1939,— Dr. Dewey's 80th birthday。"

7952 The Philosophy of Mr. B∗rtr∗nd R∗ss∗ll: With an Appendix of Leading Passages from Certain Other Works/by Philip E. B. Jourdain. —London：George Allen & Unwin Ltd., 1918

　　96p. ; 18.5cm

　　PKUL（館藏號缺）

　　附注：

　　　　題記：封面有胡適簽名"Hu Suh, nov. 22, 1920"。

　　　　批注圈劃：書内第3頁有胡適圈劃。

7953 The Philosophy of Nietzsche/by Friedrich Nietzsche. —New York：The Modern Library, 1937

　　X, 340p. ; 20.9cm

PKUL（館藏號缺）

7954　The Philosophy of Religion. —London：Macmillan and Co. , Limited；New York：The Macmillan Company, 1906

　　VIII, 410p. ; 22.4cm

　　PKUL（館藏號缺）

　　附注：

　　　　題記：扉頁有胡適題記："吳弱男女士贈。適。"

7955　The Philosophy of Tai Tung-Yüan/by Mansfield Freeman. —[s. l.]：[s. n.], [n. d.]

　　50–71p. ; 24cm

　　Reprinted from *The Journal of the North China Branch of the Royal Asiatic Society*, Volume LXIV–1933

　　PKUL（館藏號缺）

　　附注：

　　　　印章：封面有胡適簽名"Hu Shih"。

　　　　題記：扉頁有胡適題記："For the word 'Law' in this article, read 'Reason' (Li, 理)。HS. 。"

　　　　批注圈劃：書内5頁有胡適批注圈劃。

7956　The Philosophy of Wang Yang-Ming/by Frederick Goodrich Henke. —London-Chicago：The Open Court Publishing Co. , 1916

　　XVII, 512p. ; 22.8cm

　　PKUL（館藏號缺）

　　附注：

　　　　題記：一冊扉頁有胡適簽名"Hu Suh, April, 1917"。

　　　　批注圈劃：一冊書内19頁有胡適批注圈劃。

　　　　夾紙：一冊頁210、211間夾有抄錄《韓非子・難勢篇》紙條一。

　　　　摺頁：一冊頁177、212、215、227、229、400、422有摺頁。

　　　　其他：本書有2冊。

7957　The Philosophy of William James/by Th. Flournoy. —New York：Henry Holt and Company，1917

　　　Ⅶ，246p. ；18.8cm

　　　PKUL（館藏號缺）

　　　附注：

　　　　印章：一冊扉頁有某人鉛筆簽名"E. P. Allen"。

　　　　題記：一冊扉頁有胡適毛筆簽名"Hu Shih, March, 1921"。

　　　　內附文件：另一冊頁150、151間夾有楊樂公致世界叢書委員會函1頁。

　　　　其他：本書有2冊。

7958　The Philosophy of William James/by Howard V. Knox. —London：Constable and Company Ltd.，1914

　　　Ⅹ，112p. ；17.1cm

　　　Philosophies Ancient & Modern

　　　PKUL（館藏號缺）

　　　附注：

　　　　題記：扉頁有胡適毛筆簽名"Suh Hu, March 1914"。

　　　　批注圈劃：書內頁15有胡適鉛筆圈劃。

7959　The Philosophy of William James, Drawn from His Own Works/by William James. —New York：The Modern Library Publishers，[n. d.]

　　　375p. ；17cm

　　　The Modern Library of the World's Best Books

　　　PKUL（館藏號缺）

　　　附注：

　　　　夾紙：書內一處夾有紙條。

7960　The Pilgrimage of Fa Hian; From the French Edition of the Foe Kuoe KiJ./by W. Laidlay. —Calcutta：J. Thomas Baptist Mission Press, 1848

　　　Ⅵ，373p. ；19.4cm

PKUL（館藏號缺）

附注：

題記：扉頁有原書主簽名"A. Wylie, 1862"。

批注圈劃：書內有多處批注圈劃,非胡適所作。

7961 The Pilgrim's Progress; The Lives of John Donne and George Herbert/by Charles W. Eliot. —New York：P. F. Collier & Son, 1909

424p. ; 19.5cm

The Harvard Classics No. 15

PKUL（館藏號缺）

附注：

印章：扉頁有胡適簽名"Suh Hu"。

7962 Pitman's Complete Mercantile Arithmetic with Elementary Mensuration/by H. P. Green. —London：Sir Isaac Pitman & Sons, Ltd. , [n. d.]

IX, 553p. ; 18cm

PKUL（館藏號缺）

附注：

印章：扉頁有"Wenpole Wang"簽名。

7963 The Pivot of Civilization/by Margaret Sanger. —New York：Brentano's, 1922

XVIII, 284p. ; 18.8cm

PKUL（館藏號缺）

附注：

題記：扉頁有作者題記："To Mr. Hu Shih, with my regards and appreciation. Margaret Sanger, New York City, Oct. 17, 1922。"

7964 Plain Tales from the Hills/by Rudyard Kipling. —Leipzig：Bernhard Tauchnitz, 1890

312p. ; 16.5cm

Collection of British Authors, Tauchnitz Edition

PKUL（館藏號缺）

附注：

　　其他：封面及前面數頁脫落。

7965　Plane Geometry/by George Wentworth, David Eugene Smith. —Boston, New York, Chicago, London：Ginn & Company, 1913

　　VI, 287p. ；18.8cm

　　PKUL（館藏號缺）

附注：

　　印章：扉頁鈐有"ZAO ZUNG KUH"藍文印章。

　　題記：扉頁有鉛筆題記："姚園寺巷四十八號朱。"

7966　Plant Physiology：With Special Reference to Plant Production/by Benjamin M. Duggar. —New York：The Macmillan Company, 1911

　　XV, 516p. ；18.8cm

　　PKUL（館藏號缺）

附注：

　　題記：扉頁有胡適題記："《植物生理學》，適之。"

7967　Platon/von Wilhelm Windelband. —Stuttgart：F. R. Frommanns Verlag, 1910

　　192p. ；20.9cm

　　Frommanns Klassiker der Philosophie

　　PKUL（館藏號缺）

附注：

　　印章：書名頁前頁有胡適簽名"Suh Hu"。

　　題記：扉頁有胡適題記："Suh Hu, Feb. 1914.《柏拉圖》，此万字式紙乃吾國所有，今遽見之于此，如見故人也。適之。"

　　批注圈劃：書内70頁有胡適鉛筆、鋼筆批注圈劃。

7968　The Plattner Story and Others/by H. G. Wells. —Leipzig：Bernhard Tauchnitz, 1900

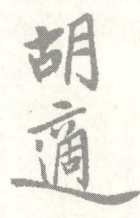

294p. ；16.4cm

Collection of British Authors, Tauchnitz Edition

PKUL（館藏號缺）

7969 The Plays of Euripides in English. —London：J. M. Dent & Sons Ltd. ；New York：E. P, Dutton & Co. , 1906

2 Vols. （XV, 375, 406p. ）；17.2cm

Everyman's Library：Classical

PKUL（館藏號缺）

附注：

題記：兩卷扉頁均有胡適毛筆簽名"Suh Hu, Peking, Oct. 10, 1917"。

批注圈劃：兩卷目錄頁均有胡適朱筆標注。

7970 The Plays of Richard Brinsley Sheridan/by Richard Brinsley Sheridan. —London：J. M. Dent & Co. ；New York：E. P. Dutton & Co. , 1906

411p. ；17.2cm

Everyman's Library：Poetry and the Drama

PKUL（館藏號缺）

附注：

印章：扉頁鈐有"江蘇武進弘士嚴毅"藍文橢圓印。

7971 A Pluralistic Universe/by William James. —London, Toronto, Bombay, Calcutta, Madras：Longmans, Green, and Co. , 1932

405p. ；21.5cm

PKUL（館藏號缺）

7972 Plutarch's Lives/by Edwin Ginn. —Boston, New York, Chicago, London：Ginn and Company, 1886

XIV, 333p. ；17.3cm

PKUL（館藏號缺）

附注：

印章：扉頁鈐有"江蘇武進弘士嚴毅"藍文橢圓印；另有原書主簽名"Yen Yi"。

7973 The Pocket Book of Father Brown/by G. K. Chesterton. —New York：Pocket Books, Inc., 1943
  307p.；16.2cm
  PKUL（館藏號缺）

7974 The Pocket Book of Science-Fiction/by Donald A. Wollheim. —New York：Pocket Books Inc., 1943
  X, 310p.；15.7cm
  PKUL（館藏號缺）

7975 Pocket Dictionary Spanish-English, English-Spanish/by Gaylord Du Bois. —Girard：Haldeman-Julius Company，[n. d.]
  64p.；12.6cm
  Little Blue Book
  PKUL（館藏號缺）

7976 Pocket Guide to Japan. —[s. l.]：The Japanese Government Railways, 1926
  VI, 86p.；18.4cm
  PKUL（館藏號缺）

7977 The Pocket History of the Second World War/by Henry Steele Commager. —New York：Pocket Books, Inc., 1945
  574p.；16.1cm
  PKUL（館藏號缺）

7978 Pocket Manual of Rules of Order for Deliberative Assemblies/by Henry M. Robert. —Chicago, New York：Scott, Foresman and Company, 1904
  218p.；14.5cm

PKUL（館藏號缺）

附注：

印章：書名頁鈐有"適盦藏書"朱文圓印。

題記：扉頁有胡適題記："Suh Hu, Cosmoplitan Club, Ithaca, N. Y.《集會規約》。"

7979 The Pocket Oxford Dictionary of Current English/by F. G. Fowler, H. W. Fowler. —Oxford：The Clarendon Press，1924

XVI, 1000p. ; 17.1cm

PKUL（館藏號缺）

附注：

印章：一冊扉頁有胡適毛筆簽名"Hu Shih"；另一冊扉頁有胡適鉛筆簽名"Hu Shih"。

內附文件：另一冊書內夾有剪報1頁。

其他：本書有2冊，一冊封面脫落，破損。

7980 The Pocket R. L. S./by Stevenson. —New York：Charles Scribner's Sons，[n.d.]

217p. ; 13.6cm

PKUL（館藏號缺）

附注：

印章：一冊題名頁鈐有"適盦藏書"朱文圓印。

題記：扉頁有胡適題記："Gift of N. B. S. 1914。"

批注圈劃：書內10頁有胡適圈劃。

其他：本書裝訂破損。

7981 The Pocket Self-Pronouncing Dictionary and Vocabulary Builder/by W. J. Pelo. —New York：Pocket Books, Inc.，1941

442p. ; 16cm

PKUL（館藏號缺）

7982 The Poems & Plays of Robert Browning, 1833-1844 Volume I/by Robert Browning. —London: J. M. Dent & Sons Ltd. ; New York: E. P, Dutton & Co. , 1906

 XX, 662p. ; 17.3cm

 Everyman's Library: Poetry and the Drama

 PKUL（館藏號缺）

 附注：

  題記：扉頁有胡適鋼筆簽名"Suh Hu, Jan. 1915"。

  批注圈劃：書內3頁有胡適批注圈劃。

7983 The Poems and Songs of Robert Burns/by Robert Burns. —New York: P. F. Collier & Son, 1909

 609p. ; 19.5cm

 The Harvard Classics No. 6

 PKUL（館藏號缺）

 附注：

  印章：扉頁有胡適簽名"Suh Hu"；題名頁鈐有"適盦藏書"朱文圓印。

7984 Poems of Cornell/by Albert W. Smith. —[s.l.]: [s.n.], 1941

 37p. ; 22.8cm

 PKUL（館藏號缺）

 附注：

  題記：扉頁有作者題記："To: Dr. Hu Shih, with kind regards from Albert W. Smith。"

7985 The Poems of John Donne/by John Donne. —London: J. M. Dent & Sons Ltd. ; New York: E. P, Dutton & Co. , 1931

 XXX, 288p. ; 17.3cm

 Everyman's Library: Poetry and the Drama

 PKUL（館藏號缺）

 附注：

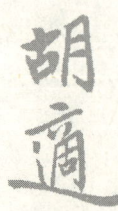

印章：扉頁有鋼筆簽名"C. S."。

其他：書內夾有葉片 1 枚。

7986 Poems of To-Day: An Anthology. —London: Sidgwick & Jackson, Ltd., 1917

XVI, 174p. ; 18.9cm

PKUL（館藏號缺）

7987 Poems of TS'ao Ts'ao/by Diether von den Steinen. —[s. l.]: [s. n.], [n. d.]

125-181p. ; 27.7cm

Reprinted from *Monvmenta Serica*, *Journal of Oriental Studies of the Catholic University of Peking*, Vol. IV, Fasc. 1, 1942

PKUL（館藏號缺）

附注：

題記：封面有作者題記："To Dr. Hu Shih, with the compliments of the translator。"

7988 The Poems of William Morris/by William Morris. —New York: Thomas Y. Crowell Company, 1904

XXXIV, 360p. ; 18.2cm

PKUL（館藏號缺）

附注：

題記：扉頁有胡適題記："Suh Hu, 1913, May, Ithaca, N. Y.《毛力師詩選》。適之。"

批注圈劃：書內 69 頁有胡適批注圈劃。

夾紙：頁 104、105 間夾有胡適在康奈爾大學時填寫的索書條 1 張（Jean J. Rousseau）；頁 184、185 間夾有同樣索書條 2 張（Thomas Hood Works I, IV）；頁 332、333 間有夾紙一。

7989 Poems of Wordsworth/chosen and edited by Matthew Arnold. —[s. l.]: Macmillan and Co., Limited, 1922

XXXI, 331p. ; 15.4cm

PKUL（館藏號缺）

7990 Poems, 1924-1933/by Archibald MacLeish. —Boston and New York: Houghton Mifflin Company, 1933

303p. ; 22.4cm

PKUL（館藏號缺）

附注：

題記：扉頁有作者題記："To Dr. Hu, with the admiration of Archibald MacLeish, New York, Jan. 1938。"

7991 The Poetic and Dramatic Works of Alfred Lord Tennyson/by Alfred Tennyson. —Boston and New York: Houghton Miflin Company; Cambridge: The Riverside Press, 1898

XVII, 882p. ; 20.9cm

PKUL（館藏號缺）

附注：

題記：扉頁有胡適題記："Suh Hu, Feb. 1913.《鄧耐生詩集》。"

批注圈劃：書内309頁有胡適批注圈劃。

夾紙：頁114、115，頁138、139間，書末夾有讀書卡片各1張；頁600、601間夾有讀書卡片2張。

7992 The Poetical Work of Matthew Arnold/by Matthew Arnold. —New York: Thomas Y. Crowell & Co., 1897

XXVII, 502p. ; 18.2cm

PKUL（館藏號缺）

附注：

題記：扉頁有胡適題記："Suh Hu, Ithaca, N. Y., April, 1913.《阿那詩集》。"

批注圈劃：書内125頁有胡適批注圈劃。

7993 The Poetical Works of Jonathan Swift/by Jonathan Swift. —London: William Pickering, 1853

 3 Vols. ; 15.8cm

 PKUL（館藏號缺）

 附注：

  題記：第1卷扉頁有胡思杜題字："祝爸爸五十歲的生日。小三，十二月十日。"

7994 Point Counter Point/by Aldous Huxley. —Leipzig: Bernhard Tauchnitz, 1929

 2 Vols. (294, 295p.) ; 16.3cm

 Collection of British Authors, Tauchnitz Edition

 PKUL（館藏號缺）

7995 The Policeman's Love-Hungry Daughter, and Other Stories of Chicago Life/by Ben Hecht. —Girard: Haldeman-Julius Company, [n.d.]

 63p. ; 12.7cm

 Little Blue Book

 PKUL（館藏號缺）

7996 The Political Conditions of Allied Success: A Plea for the Protective Union of the Democracies/by Norman Angell. —New York and London: G. P. Putnam's Sons, 1918

 XXVIII, 350p. ; 19.1cm

 PKUL（館藏號缺）

7997 The Political Doctrines of Sun Yat-Sen: An Exposition of the San Min Chu I/by Paul Myron Anthony Linebarger. —Baltimore: The Johns Hopkins Press, 1937

 XIV, 278p. ; 21.2cm

 PKUL（館藏號缺）

 附注：

題記:扉頁有作者題記:"To Dr. Hu Shih, with the best wishes of Arthur N. Holcombe and the author, Cambridge, Mass. February 7, 1937。"

夾紙:書內夾有寄書人地址。

7998 Political Thought in England, from Bacon to Halifax/by G. P. Gooch. — London: William and Norgate, 1914

256p. ; 16.9cm

Home University Library of Modern Knowledge

PKUL(館藏號缺)

7999 Popular Science Mechanical Encyclopedia: How It Works/by Ellison Hawks. —New York: Popular Science Publishing Co., Inc., 1941

512p. ; 23.4cm

PKUL(館藏號缺)

8000 A Popular Zoology/by J. Dorman Steele, J. W. P. Jenks. —New York, Cincinnati, Chicago: American Book Company, 1895

XIII, 355p. ; 20.4cm

PKUL(館藏號缺)

附註:

題記:扉頁有作者鋼筆簽名"S. Hu, July 1910. Shanghai"。

8001 The Population of China in 1910/by Walter F. Willcox. —[s. l.]: [s. n.], [n. d.]

18-30p. ; 23.5cm

Reprinted from *The Journal of the American Statistical Association*, March, 1928

PKUL(館藏號缺)

附註:

題記:封面有作者題記:"Prof. Hu Shih, with the compliments of the author。"

夾紙:書內夾有贈書條 1 張:"極司非而路四十九號甲胡適之先生,請留片,陳伯修兄託轉交。"

8002 Portrait of a Chinese Lady and Certain of Her Contemporaries/by Lady Hosie. —London: Hodder and Stoughton Limited, [n. d.]

XV, 404p. ; 23.3cm

PKUL（館藏號缺）

附注：

題記：扉頁有作者題記："To Hu Shih—with the author's best wishes and heartfeel admiration for his courage and live patriotism, Dorothy Hosie, come back soon to Oxford again! Oxford, Christmas, 1929。"

內附文件：書內夾有 G. W. Sheppard 致胡適英文書信 1 頁。

其他：書內夾有"蔣仁裕"名片 1 張。

8003 Portraits in Miniature, and Other Essays/by Lytton Strachey. —London: Chatto & Windus, 1931

218p. ; 20.5cm

PKUL（館藏號缺）

8004 The Position of Woman in Early China/by Albert Richard O'Hara. —Washington: The Catholic University of America Press, 1945

XII, 301p. ; 22.9cm

PKUL（館藏號缺）

附注：

題記：扉頁有作者題記："To Dr. Hu Shih, in admiration of his scholarship and fostering of cultural relation between China and the U. S. Albert R. O'Hara, S. J. 郝繼隆。"

夾紙：書內夾有名片 1 張。

8005 Positive Democracy/by James Feibleman. —Chapel Hill: The University of North Carolina Press, 1940

XV, 256p. ; 21.2cm

PKUL（館藏號缺）

附注：

 題記：扉頁有胡適題記："Hu Shih, gift of the author, Mr. James Feibleman, 1924 Canal Bank Bdg. New Orleans, La。"

8006 The Positive Outcome of Philosophy/by Joseph Dietzgen. —Chicago：Charles H. Herr & Company, [n. d.]

 VI, 444p. ; 18.8cm

 PKUL（館藏號缺）

 附注：

  題記：扉頁有胡適題記："From Alfred Bosch, Jan. 1915。"

8007 The Positive Sciences of the Ancient Hindus/by Brajendranath Seal. —London：Longmans, Green and Co. , 1915

 VII, 295p. ; 21.8cm

 PKUL（館藏號缺）

 附注：

  題記：扉頁有胡適題記："Suh Hu, Feb. 1917, New York, Gift of Professor B. K. Sarkar。"

8008 The Possibilities and Limitations of International Comparisons of Cost of Living and Family Budgets/by The Institute of Pacific Relations. —Honolulu：The Institute of Pacific Relations, 1931

 20p. ; 22.3cm

 PKUL（館藏號缺）

 附注：

  印章：封面有胡適鉛筆簽名"Hu Shih"。

8009 Possible Peace/by W. MacMahon Ball. —Melbourne, London, Edinburgh, et al：Melbourne University Press, 1936

 199p. ; 19.1cm

PKUL（館藏號缺）

8010　The Power of Non‐Violence/by Richard B. Gregg. —Philadelphia：J. B. Lippincott Company, 1934

359, 13p. ; 21.2cm

PKUL（館藏號缺）

8011　The Practical Cogitator or the Thinker's Anthology/by Charles P. Curtis, Jr.; Ferris Greenslet. —Boston：Houghton Mifflin Company, 1945

X, 577p. ; 18.4cm

PKUL（館藏號缺）

附注：

題記：扉頁有胡適鋼筆簽名"Hu Shih, May 7, 1946"。

8012　Practical Fingerprinting/by B. C. Bridges. —New York, London：Funk & Wagnalls Company, 1942

IX, 374p. ; 20cm

PKUL（館藏號缺）

附注：

印章：書名頁有鋼筆書作者名字"B. C. Bridges"，疑爲作者簽名。

內附文件：頁190、191間夾有本書作者B. C. Bridges1942年6月8日致胡適英文函1頁；另有大使館代回作者英文函1頁。

8013　Practical Physic/by Robert Andrews Millikan, Henry Gordon Gale, Wiliard R. Pyle. —Boston, New York, Chicago, London, Atlanta, Dallas, Columbus, San Francisco：Ginn and Company, 1922

X, 472p. ; 19.3cm

PKUL（館藏號缺）

附注：

批注圈劃：書內多處有鉛筆批注圈劃，非胡適所作。

8014 The Practical Working of the League of Nations: A Concrete Example/by Arthur Sweetser. —Worcester: Carnegie Endowment for International Peace, Division of Intercourse and Education, 1929

 29p. ; 19.7cm

 PKUL（館藏號缺）

8015 Pragmatism: A New Name for Some Old Ways of Thinking/by William James. —London, Bomby and Calcutta: Longmans, Green, and Co., 1914.

 XIII, 309p. ; 21.4cm

 PKUL（館藏號缺）

 附注：

  題記：扉頁有贈書者題記："適之兄惠存。弟盧錫榮贈。"

  批注圈劃：書內 90 頁有胡適批注圈劃。

  夾紙：頁 100、101 間夾有英文紙條一；頁 168、169 間夾有中文紙條一；頁 296、297 間夾有空白紙條一。

8016 Preaching from the Audience, Candid Comments on Life/by E. W. Howe. —Girard: Haldeman-Julius Company, [n.d.]

 64p. ; 12.6cm

 Little Blue Book

 PKUL（館藏號缺）

8017 Précis Writing for American Schools/by Samuel Thurber. —Boston: Little, Brown, and Company, 1926

 XI, 150p. ; 18.5cm

 PKUL（館藏號缺）

8018 Predecessors of Adam Smith, the Growth of British Economic Thought/by E. A. J. Johnson. —New York: Prentice-Hall, Inc., 1937

 XII, 426p. ; 22.9cm

 PKUL（館藏號缺）

8019 The Prefaces, Proverbs and Poems of Benjamin Franklin/by Paul Leicester Ford. —New York and London: G. P. Putnam's Sons, [n. d.]

288p. ; 14.1cm

PKUL（館藏號缺）

附注：

印章：扉頁鈐有"藏暉室主人"朱文方印；題名頁鈐有"適盦藏書"朱文圓印。

題記：扉頁有胡適鋼筆題記："窮人李郘之日曆，弗蘭林外集之一，辛亥二月十九日，先人誕辰，購此以為紀念。適，識於美國綺色佳城。"

批注圈劃：書内20餘頁有胡適批注圈劃。

8020 A Preface to Morals/Walter Lippmann. —New York: The Macmillan Company, 1929

VIII, 348p. ; 22.2cm

PKUL（館藏號缺）

附注：

題記：扉頁有贈書者題記："Dr. Hu Shih, from E. C. Williams, 17 Aug. 1929。"

8021 Prefaces to Peace/by Wendell L. Willkie, Herbert Hoover, Hugh Gibson, Henry A. Wallace, Sumner Welles. —[s. l.]: Simon and Schuster; Doubleday, Doran & Company, Inc.; Reynal & Hitchcock, Inc.; Columbia University Press, 1943

XII, 437p. ; 21.8cm

PKUL（館藏號缺）

8022 Prefaces and Prologues to Famous Books/by Charles W. Eliot. —New York: P. F. Collier & Son, 1910

462p. ; 19.5cm

The Harvard Classics No. 39

PKUL（館藏號缺）

附注：

　　印章：扉頁有胡適簽名"Suh Hu"。

8023　Prehistoric Man：A General Outline of Prehistory/by Jacques De Morgan. —New York：Alfred A. Knopf, Inc. , 1925

　　XXIII,304p. ；23.4cm

　　PKUL（館藏號缺）

附注：

　　題記：扉頁有胡適題記："《史前的人》,胡適。一九二八,九月。"

　　批注圈劃：書內有4頁胡適鉛筆圈劃。

　　夾紙：頁70、71間有夾紙1張。

8024　A Preliminary Treatise on Evidence at the Common Law/by James Bradley Thayer. —Boston：Little, Brown, and Company, 1898

　　XXXVI, 636p. ；21.3cm

　　PKUL（館藏號缺）

附注：

　　印章：扉頁有他人簽名"Benjamin Loving Young. B. L. Young"。

　　題記：扉頁有胡適鋼筆簽名"Hu Shih, Cambridge, Mass. , May 23, 1945"。

8025　Prendergast's Mastery System, Applied to the Study of Japanese or English/by S. R. Brown. —Yokohama：F. R. Wetmore & Co. , 1875

　　VIII, 213p. ；18.3cm

　　PKUL（館藏號缺）

附注：

　　印章：扉頁有"R. Lilley"簽名。

8026　The Present Economic Revolution in the United States/by Thomas Nixon Carver. —Boston：Little, Brown, and Company, 1925

VIII, 270p. ; 22.4cm

PKUL（館藏號缺）

8027　President Report, 1928-29/by A. Lawrence Lowell. —[s. l.]: [s. n.], [n. d.]

26p. ; 22.7cm

PKUL（館藏號缺）

8028　President Roosevelt and the Coming of the War 1941: A Study in Appearances and Realities/by Charles A. Beard. —New Haven: Yale University Press, 1948

VI, 614p. ; 23.3cm

PKUL（館藏號缺）

附注：

題記：扉頁有胡適題記："Hu Shih, gift from my friend Liu Chieh 劉鍇。July, 1948。"

內附文件：書末貼有"Beard: History and Fantasy, Basic History of Beard"剪報2張。

8029　Priests & Kings/by Harold Peake, Herbert John Fleure. —Oxford: The Clarendon Press, 1927

208p. ; 20.3cm

The Corridors of Time

PKUL（館藏號缺）

8030　A Primer of Hinduism/by J. N. Farquhar. —London: Oxford University Press, 1912

222p. ; 19.2cm

PKUL（館藏號缺）

8031　A Primer of Phonetics/by Henry Sweet. —Oxford: The Clarendon Press, 1906

VIII, 119p. ; 16.5cm

Clarendon Press Series

PKUL（館藏號缺）

附注：

題記：扉頁有胡適毛筆簽名"Hu Suh, Peking, Oct. 1917"。

8032 The Prince, Utopia, Ninety-Five Theses/by Charles W. Eliot. —New York：P. F. Collier & Son, 1910

397p. ; 19.5cm

The Harvard Classics No. 36

PKUL（館藏號缺）

附注：

印章：扉頁有胡適簽名"Suh Hu"。

8033 The Principle of Individuality and Value：The Gifford Lectures for 1911 Delivered in Edinburgh University/by B. Bosanquet. —London：Macmillan and Co., Limited, 1912

XXXVII, 409p. ; 22.1cm

PKUL（館藏號缺）

附注：

印章：另扉頁、題名頁分別鈐有"適盦藏書"朱文圓印。

題記：扉頁有胡適鋼筆簽名"Suh Hu, June 4, 1915"。

批注圈劃：書內30頁有胡適批注圈劃。

8034 The Principles and Practice of Medicine/by William Osler. —New York, London：D. Appleton and Company, 1914

XIV, 1225p. ; 23.4cm

PKUL（館藏號缺）

附注：

其他：本書有缺頁、散頁。

8035 The Principles of Descartes' Philosophy/by Benedictus de Spinoza. —

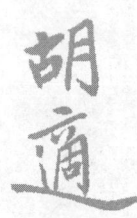

Chicago: The Open Court Publishing Company, 1905

177p. ; 19.7cm

PKUL(館藏號缺)

附注:

題記:扉頁有胡適鋼筆簽名"Suh Hu, Sept. 1915, New York"。

8036 The Principles of Ethics/by Herbert Spencer. —New York: D. Appleton and Company, 1896

2 Vols. ; 19.8cm

PKUL(館藏號缺)

附注:

題記:第1卷扉頁有胡適題記:"哈丁(H. I. Haeding)送我的。"

8037 The Principles of Power: The Great Political Crisis of History/by Guglielmo Ferrero. —New York: G. P. Putnam's Sons, 1942

IX, 333p. ; 21.5cm

PKUL(館藏號缺)

附注:

題記:扉頁有贈書者題記:"適之先生惠存,謝勁□敬贈,卅一,一二,一七,紐約"。

8038 The Principles of Psychology/by Herbert Spencer. —New York: D. Appleton and Company, 1897

2 Vols. ; 19.8cm

PKUL(館藏號缺)

附注:

印章:三冊扉頁均有胡適鋼筆簽名"Suh Hu";目錄頁均鈐有"叔璠"朱文方印。

其他:本書爲2卷本,第2卷又分爲2冊。

8039 The Principles of Psychology/by William James. —New York: Henry Holt and

Company, 1890

2 Vols. ；21.9cm

American Science Series

PKUL（館藏號缺）

附註：

題記：扉頁有胡適鋼筆簽名"Suh Hu, New York, September 1916"。

批注圈劃：書內有胡適鉛筆批注圈劃。

8040 The Principles of Rhetoric/by Adams Sherman Hill. —New York, Cincinnati, Chicago：American Book Company, 1895

X, 431p. ；18.8cm

PKUL（館藏號缺）

8041 The Principles of Social Reconstruction/by Bertrand Russell. —London：George Allen & Unwin Ltd., 1920

252p. ；18.4cm

PKUL（館藏號缺）

附註：

題記：扉頁有胡適簽名"Hu Suh, Feb. 1921"。

8042 The Private Papers of Henry Ryecroft/by George Gissing. —London：Constable & Company Ltd., [n.d.]

124p. ；21.7cm

PKUL（館藏號缺）

附註：

印章：扉頁有胡適鉛筆簽名"Suh Hu"。

8043 The Problem of Federalism：A Study in the History of Political Theory/by Sobei Mogi. —London：George Allen & Unwin Ltd., 1931

2 Vols.（1144p.）；23.9cm

PKUL（館藏號缺）

8044 The Problem of Human Life/by Rudolf Eucken. —New York: Charles Scribner's Sons, 1909

    XXV, 582p. ; 22cm

    PKUL（館藏號缺）

    附注：

    題記:扉頁有胡適毛筆題記:"倭鏗著《人生問題》,吳弱男女士贈。七年七月";另有鉛筆題記:"'Still water runs deep.' Paste。"

    批注圈劃:作者英文版前言中有黑筆圈劃。

    摺頁:頁129 摺頁。

8045 The Problem of Mind and Body/by S. T. Han. —[s.l.]: [s.n.], [n.d.]

    XV, 178p. ; 21.6cm

    PKUL（館藏號缺）

    附注：

    題記:扉頁有作者題記:"適之學長兄教正,弟述組寄贈。"

8046 The Problem of the War & the Peace: A Handbook for Students/by Norman Angell. —London: William Heinemann, [n.d.]

    99p. ; 18.3cm

    PKUL（館藏號缺）

8047 Problems of Journalism: Proceedings Twentieth Annual Convention, American Society of Newspaper Editors, 1942/by American Society of Newspaper Editors. —New York: The Waldorf-Astoria, 1942

    189p. ; 23.3cm

    PKUL（館藏號缺）

8048 Problems of the Pacific, 1931/by Bruno Lasker. —Chicago: The University of Chicago Press, 1932

    XI, 548p. ; 24cm

PKUL（館藏號缺）

8049 Problems of the Pacific, 1931/by Bruno Lasker, W. L. Holland. —Chicago：The University of Chicago Press, 1932

XI, 548p. ; 24cm

PKUL（館藏號缺）

附注：

夾紙：書內夾有"江紹原"名片1張,Institute of Pacific Relations 會議主題2頁。

8050 Proceedings of the Conference on International Relations. —Boston：World Peace Foundation, 1916

IX, 418p. ; 23.2cm

PKUL（館藏號缺）

附注：

題記：扉頁有胡適鋼筆簽名"Suh Hu, March, 1916"。

8051 Proceedings of the General Conference on Foreign Missions Held at the Conference Hall, in Mildmay Park, London, in October, 1878/by The Secretaries to the Conference. —London：John F. Shaw & Co., 1879

VIII, 434p. ; 21.4cm

PKUL（館藏號缺）

附注：

其他：本書封面、書脊脱落,散爲兩部分。

8052 Proceedings of the International Student Assembly, Held at the American University Washington, D. C. 2 - 5 September 1942/by William Allan Neilson. —London, New York, Toronto：Oxford University Press, 1944

XIV, 159p. ; 21cm

PKUL（館藏號缺）

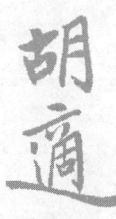

8053 Product Certificate and Distribution According to Labor/by Hsi-Shan Yen, translated by H. C. Yin. —Nanking: The Northwestern Guardian, 1936

92p. ; 18.8cm

PKUL（館藏號缺）

8054 Profiles from the New Yorker/by Clifton Fadiman. —New York: Alfred A. Knopf, [n. d.]

XIII, 400p. ; 21.9cm

PKUL（館藏號缺）"

附注：

印章：扉頁鈐有"HU SHIH"藍文印。

題記：扉頁有胡適鋼筆注明時間"Jan. 1939"。

8055 Progress and Poverty: An Inquiry into the Cause of Industrial Depressions and of Increase of Want with Increase of Wealth; The Remedy/by Henry George. —New York: Robert Schalkenbach Foundation, 1945

XX, 571p. ; 19.4cm

PKUL（館藏號缺）

8056 Project of Law for the Gradual Introduction of a Gold-Standard Currency System in China, Together with a Report in Support Thereof/by National Government of the Republic of China, Commission of Financial Experts. —[s. l.]:[s. n.], 1929

V, 206p. ; 32.2cm

PKUL（館藏號缺）

8057 Prolegomena to Ethics/by Thomas Hill Green. —Oxford: The Clarendon Press, 1906

XXXIX, 470p. ; 19.5cm

PKUL（館藏號缺）

附注：

題記:扉頁有胡適題記:"Suh Hu, October 1914. 葛令著《倫理學》適。"

批注圈劃:書內 158 頁有胡適批注圈劃。

夾紙:頁 56、57 間夾有胡適讀書卡片 1 張。

8058 The Promises Men Live By: A New Approach to Economics/by Harry Scherman. —New York: Random House, 1938

XXVI, 492p. ; 23.8cm

PKUL (館藏號缺)

8059 Propaganda from China and Japan: A Case Study in Propaganda Analysis/by Bruno Lasker, Agnes Roman. —[s. l.]: American Council, Institute of Pacific Relations, 1938

XIV, 120p. ; 22.9cm

PKUL (館藏號缺)

附注:

印章:扉頁鈐有"HU SHIH"藍文印。

內附文件:書末貼有關於本書的書評剪報。

8060 Proudhon's Solution of the Social Problem/by P. J. Proudhon. —New York: Vanguard Press, 1927

XVI, 225p. ; 18.3cm

PKUL (館藏號缺)

8061 Proverbs of Japan. —Girard: Haldeman-Julius Company, [n.d.]

32p. ; 12.7cm

Little Blue Book

PKUL (館藏號缺)

8062 La Psychologie de l'Intelligence chez Renouvier/par Yang Pao-San. —Paris: Les Presses Modernes, 1930

148p. ; 22.7cm

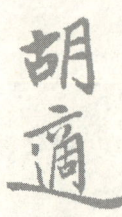

PKUL（館藏號缺）

附注：

題記：扉頁有作者題記："適之先生教正，受業楊寶三謹贈。"

8063 The Psychology of Reasoning/by W. B. Pillsbury. —New York and London：D. Appleton and Company，1910

VIII，306p. ；19.3cm

PKUL（館藏號缺）

附注：

題記：扉頁有胡適簽名"Hu Suh, Peking, Nov. 1918"。

批注圈劃：書內115頁有胡適批注圈劃。

8064 The Psychology of Religion/by Joseph McCabe. —Girard：Haldeman-Julius Company，[n. d.]

64p. ；12.6cm

Little Blue Book

PKUL（館藏號缺）

8065 The Psychology of Tragedy：A Critical Study of Various Theories of Tragic Pleasure/by Chu Kwang-Tsien. —Strasbourg：Librairie Universitaire d'Alsace，[n. d.]

275p. ；25cm

PKUL（館藏號缺）

附注：

題記：扉頁有朱光潛題字："適之先生教正，光潛。"

8066 Psychology：What It Has to Teach You about Yourself and the World You Live In/by Everett Dean Martin. —[s. l.]：The People's Institute Publishing Company, Incorporated，[n. d.]

234p. ；23cm

PKUL（館藏號缺）

8067　The Public and Its Government/by Felix Frankfurter. —New Haven：Yale University Press，1930

　　170p. ；19.2cm

　　PKUL（館藏號缺）

　　附注：

　　　　題記：扉頁有作者題記："To Hu Shi—...□，with the great regard and all good wishes of Felix Frankfurter, Cambridge, December 6, 1937。"

8068　The Public and Its Problems/by John Dewey. —New York：Henry Holt and Company，1927

　　Ⅵ，224p. ；18.8cm

　　PKUL（館藏號缺）

　　附注：

　　　　題記：一冊扉頁有贈書人題記："To Dr. Hu Shih, in remembrance of a memorable afternoon. Joseph Ratner. Oct. 23-24, 1939。"

　　　　批注圈劃：書內90頁有胡適批注圈劃。

　　　　其他：本書有2冊。

8069　Public Faces/by Harold Nicolson. —London：Constable & Co.，Ltd.，1932

　　350p. ；19.4cm

　　PKUL（館藏號缺）

　　附注：

　　　　題記：扉頁有贈書者題記："奉贈適之兄，孟和，廿二年十二月十七日。作者服務美國外交界多年，他的嘲弄外交與政治當然有過火的地方，但去事實並不相遠，記得今年的 Harpers 襍誌也發表與此相似的短篇小説兩篇。孟和誌。"

8070　Public International Unions：Their Work and Organization/by Paul S. Reinsch. —Boston：World Peace Foundation，1916

　　189p. ；24.3cm

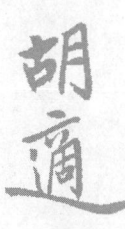

PKUL（館藏號缺）

附注：

題記：扉頁有贈書者題記："To Dr. Sǔh Hǔ, whose life will mean much for the progress of International Polity！Congratulations from Frieda Fligelman, Columbia University, May 1917。"

8071 The Public Papers and Addresses of Franklin D. Roosevelt/by Franklin D. Roosevelt. —New York：Random House, 1933

8 Vols. ；24.5cm

PKUL（館藏號缺）

附注：

題記：1937年卷扉頁有著者題記："To my old friend Dr. Hu Shih with my warm regards, Franklin D. Roosevelt, Dec. 22, 1941。"

8072 The Puppet State of "Manchukuo". —Shanghai：China United Press, 1935

VIII, 272p. ；24.5cm

PKUL（館藏號缺）

附注：

題記：扉頁有編者題記："To Dr. Hu Shih, with the Editor's compliments, Tang Leang-Li, Shanghai, February XXIV。"

8073 Puritan's Progress/by Arthur Train. —New York：Charles Scribner's Sons, 1931

X, 477p. ；22.9cm

PKUL（館藏號缺）

附注：

題記：扉頁有作者題記："To Hu Shih, with admiration and regard from the author. Authur Train, January 14, '43。"

8074 The Purpose of Education in American Democracy/by National Education Association of the United States. —Washington：Educational Policies

Commission, 1938

　　IX, 157p. ; 23.3cm

　　PKUL（館藏號缺）

8075　Quaker Education in the Colony and State of New Jersey/by Thomas Woody. —Philadelphia: University of Pennsylvania, 1923

　　XII, 408p. ; 23.6cm

　　PKUL（館藏號缺）

8076　Quantitative Estimation of Tanning Materials for Vegetable Sole Leather/by Shoo-Tze Leo, Tsing-Nang Shen. —［s. l.］:［s. n.］,［n. d.］

　　120-126p. ; 26.8cm

　　Reprinted from *The Journal of Chemical Engineering* Vol. I, No. 2

　　PKUL（館藏號缺）

　　附註：

　　　　題記：封面有作者題記："適之先生教正,沈青囊上,一九三六年九月於紐約城。"

8077　The Queens of Society/by Grace and Philip Wharton. —Chicago, Philadelphia, Toronto: The John C. Winston Co. ,［n. d.］

　　2 Vols. (451, 439p.) ; 20cm

　　PKUL（館藏號缺）

　　附註：

　　　　題記：扉頁有胡適題記："此書的出版年代及兩篇序的年月都被刪掉了,大概翻印的人還想冒充新書呢！然書中有許多證據可證此書作于1860左右,距今六十多年了。書中見解之舊,與時代大有關係。一九二八,三,十九,胡適。"

8078　The Quest for Certainty: A Study of the Relation of Knowledge and Action/by John Dewey. —New York: Minton, Balch & Company, 1929

　　318p. ; 23.5cm

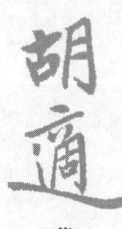

PKUL（館藏號缺）

附注：

　　印章：扉頁鈐有"HU SHIH"藍文印。

8079　The Quest of the Ages/by A. Eustace Haydon. —New York and London：Harper & Brothers Publishers，1929

　　XIII，243p. ；20.7cm

　　PKUL（館藏號缺）

　　附注：

　　　　題記：扉頁有作者題記："To Dr. Hu Shih, with gratitude and admiration, A. Eustace Haydon。"

　　　　內附文件：書內夾"Haskell Foundation Institute on Modern Trends in World Religions, July 25–28, 1933"小冊子3冊。

8080　Quo Vadis/by Henryk Sienkiewicz. —Paris：Idéal-Bibliothèque，[n. d.]

　　96p. ；24.3cm

　　PKUL（館藏號缺）

8081　Racial Intermarriage in the United States：One of the Most Interesting Phenomena in Our National Life/by George S. Schuyler. —Girard：Haldeman-Julius Company，[n. d.]

　　32p. ；12.5cm

　　Little Blue Book

　　PKUL（館藏號缺）

8082　Rain upon Godshill：A Further Chapter of Autobiography/by J. B. Priestley. —New York, London：Harper & Brothers Publishers，1939

　　308p. ；22cm

　　PKUL（館藏號缺）

8083　The Ramayana and the Mahabharata/by Romesh C. Dutt. —London：J. M.

Dent & Sons Ltd. ; New York：E. P. Dutton & Co. , 1910

 XIV, 384p. ; 17.3cm

Everyman's Library：Philosophy and Theology

PKUL（館藏號缺）

附注：

 印章：一册扉頁後頁鈐有"適盦藏書"朱文圓印。

 題記：一册扉頁有贈者題記："To my friend Mr. S. Hu, with best wishes. H. H. Pandya. …Dec. 1913",書名頁前頁有胡適題記："《古印度紀事詩》,印度友人盤地亞贈,胡適";另一册扉頁有贈書者題記："Presented to Dr. S. Hu, with compliments from S. Y. Kiang, Feb. 1919。"

 内附文件：另一册書内夾有江紹原致胡適書信1頁。

8084 Ramparts of the Pacific/by Hallett Abend. —Garden City：Doubleday, Doran and Co. , Inc. , 1942

 XVIII, 332p. ; 23.5cm

PKUL（館藏號缺）

8085 Rand McNally World Atlas. —Chicago, New York, San Francisco：Rand Mcnally & Company, [n.d.]

 271p. ; 36cm

PKUL（館藏號缺）

8086 A Rapid Calculator：How to Make Rapid Arithmetical Calculations/by George Milburn. —Girard：Haldeman-Julius Company, [n.d.]

 63p. ; 12.5cm

Little Blue Book

PKUL（館藏號缺）

8087 The Rational Sex Life for Men/by M. J. Exner. —New York：Association Press, 1914

 XIII, 95p. ; 17cm

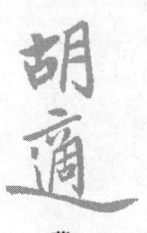

  PKUL（館藏號缺）

  附注：

   題記：扉頁有胡適鋼筆簽名"Suh Hu, May 29, 1915"。

8088 The Rationalist Annual for the Year 1928/by Charles A. Watts. —London：
Watts and Co. ,［n. d.］

  94p. ; 24.4cm

  PKUL（館藏號缺）

  附注：

   印章：封面有胡適鋼筆簽名"Hu Shih"。

8089 The Reader Over Your Shoulder：A Handbook for Writers of English Prose/
by Robert Graves, Alan Hodge. —New York：The Macmillan Company, 1943

  446p. ; 21.3cm

  PKUL（館藏號缺）

  附注：

   題記：扉頁有贈書者題記："適之兄長壽。弟源，三二，十二，十七。"

8090 Reading from English and American Literature/by Walter Taylor Field. —
Boston, New York, Chicago, et al：Ginn and Company, 1919

  X, 612p. ; 20cm

  PKUL（館藏號缺）

8091 Readings in Modern Chinese/by Chi-Chen Wang. —New York：Columbia
University Press, 1944

  219, IXp. ; 22cm

  PKUL（館藏號缺）

8092 Readings in Recent Political Philosophy/by Margaret Spahr. —New York：The
Macmillan Company, 1935

  XV, 776p. ; 21.4cm

PKUL（館藏號缺）

附注：

題記：扉頁有王毓銓等人簽名題記："敬為適之先生五十晉三壽辰紀念。後學王毓銓，劉修業、胡先晉、朱士嘉、傅安、吳光清、王重民、尤桐、韓壽萱、陳鴻舜、胡敦元、馮家昇全祝。卅二年十二月十七日。"

8093 Readings in Traditional Chinese/by Chi-Chen Wang. —New York：Columbia University Press，1944

243，XVp. ；22.1cm

PKUL（館藏號缺）

8094 The Real Diary of a Real Boy/by Henry A. Shute. —Boston：The Everett Press，1902

V，135p. ；15.3cm

PKUL（館藏號缺）

附注：

印章：扉頁有"M. Chiang"簽名。

題記：扉頁有某人1902年題記，不易辨識。

8095 The Real Italians：A Study in European Psychology/by Carlo Sforza. —New York：Columbia University Press，1942

X，156p. ；22.2cm

PKUL（館藏號缺）

8096 Real Persons/by Edwin Diller Starbuck & Staff. —New York：World Book Company，1936

XI，340p. ；20.8cm

Living Through Biography

PKUL（館藏號缺）

8097 Realism in Literature and Art/by Clarence Darrow. —Girard：Haldeman-Julius

Company,［n. d.］

64p. ; 12.7cm

Little Blue Book

PKUL（館藏號缺）

8098 The Realm of Mind: An Essay in Metaphysics/by Frederick J. E. Woodbridge. —New York: Columbia University Press, 1926

VIII, 139p. ; 19.4cm

PKUL（館藏號缺）

8099 Recent Theories of Sovereignty/by Su Ching Chen. —Canton:［s. n.］, 1929

IX, 325p. ; 22.6cm

PKUL（館藏號缺）

8100 Recollections and Letters of General Robert E. Lee/by Robert E. Lee. —New York: Garden City Publishing Co. , Inc. , 1924

XIX, 472p. ; 20.3cm

PKUL（館藏號缺）

附注：

題記:扉頁有贈書者題記:"For Dr. Hu Shih, with the warm regards of Ruth Carter Beckendorff. Nov. 25th, 1930. Shanghai。"

8101 The Reconciliation of Government with Liberty/by John W. Burgess. —New York: Charles Scribner's Sons, 1915

XIX, 394p. ; 21cm

PKUL（館藏號缺）

附注：

題記:扉頁胡適題記:"Hu Shih, Nov. 4, 1939. 我訪求此書,今年才得著這一冊,價美金五元。胡適。孫中山的五權憲法必曾受此書(頁2—8)的影響,故我要尋得一冊,將來帶回國送給國內的圖書館。"

批注圈劃:第3頁有批注:"Burgess必是用一部法文書作根據,故譯名皆是法文，又多錯誤。"

8102 Reconstruction in Philosophy/by John Dewey. —New York：Henry Holt and Company, 1920

  Ⅶ, 224p. ; 18.8cm

  PKUL（館藏號缺）

  附註：

    印章：扉頁鈐有"HU SHIH"藍文長方印。

    批注圈劃：書內49頁有胡適批注圈劃。

    夾紙：書內有夾紙3張，分別在第10、14、26頁。

8103 Reconstruction in Philosophy/by John Dewey. —New York：Henry Holt and Company, 1920

  Ⅶ, 224p. ; 18.6cm

  PKUL（館藏號缺）

  附註：

    題記：一冊扉頁有胡適毛筆簽名"Hu Shih, Hangchow, 1923"。

    夾紙：另一冊書內夾有紙條1張。

    其他：本書有2冊。

8104 A Record of Buddhistic Kingdoms：Being an Account by the Chinese Monk Fâ-Hien of His Travel in India and Ceylon/by James Legge. —Oxford：The Clarendon Press, 1886

  ⅩⅤ, 123, 45p. ; 22.8cm

  PKUL（館藏號缺）

8105 A Record of the Buddhist Religion, as Practised in India and the Malay Archipelago/by I-Tsing; translated by J. Takakusu. —Oxford：The Clarendon Press, 1896

  ⅬⅩⅣ, 240p. ; 22.6cm

  PKUL（館藏號缺）

附注：

題記：扉頁有贈書者題記："Presented to Dr. S. Hu, by his friend and collaborator A. Staël Holstein, Peking, January 1st, 1922。"

8106 Recovery Measures in New Zealand: A Comparison with the New Deal in the United States/by H. Belshaw. —Wellington: New Zealand Institute of Pacific Relations, 1936

　　61p. ; 22.8cm

　　PKUL（館藏號缺）

8107 The Red Decade: The Stalinist Penetration of America/by Eugene Lyons. —Indianapolis, New York: The Bobbs-Merrill Company, 1941

　　423p. ; 22.6cm

　　PKUL（館藏號缺）

8108 Reflections/by Edmund H. Stinnes. —[s. l.]: Privately Printed, 1940

　　64p. ; 22cm

　　PKUL（館藏號缺）

　　附注：

　　　題記：書名頁前頁有贈書者題記："To Dr. Hu Shih, in admiration of China and its great people, □ Washington (DC), August 12th, 1940。"

8109 Reflections on Government/by Ernest Barker. —Oxford: Oxford University Press, 1942

　　XVI, 424p. ; 22cm

　　PKUL（館藏號缺）

　　附注：

　　　印章：扉頁鈐有"廷芳長壽"、"劉吳卓生"朱文方印。

　　　題記：扉頁有劉廷芳夫婦題記："若為此地今重過，得水難留久臥龍。適之吾兄五十晉一壽辰，集長慶集句奉賀。抗戰第六冬，時同客紐約，此二十八年前同留學地也。劉廷芳，劉吳卓生。"

8110 Regionally Planning the Far East/by Elizabeth Green, Craighill Handy. — [s.l.]:[s.n.], [n.d.]

　　394-404p. ; 25.4cm

　　Reprinted from *Social Forces*, Vol. 23, No. 3

　　PKUL（館藏號缺）

　　附注：

　　　　題記：封面有作者題記："To Dr. Hu Shih, compliments of the authors。"

8111 Register of the Department of State, October 1, 1940. —Washington: United States Government Printing Office, 1940

　　VII, 251p. ; 24cm

　　PKUL（館藏號缺）

　　附注：

　　　　印章：扉頁有胡適鋼筆簽名"Hu Shih"。

8112 Relief and Rehabilitation: Implications of the UNRRA Programs for Jewish Needs/by Zorach Warhaftig. —New York: Institute of Jewish Affairs of the American Jewish Congress and World Jewish Congress, 1944

　　223p. ; 22.7cm

　　From War to Peace

　　PKUL（館藏號缺）

8113 The Religion of China: Confucianism and Tâoism Described and Compared with Christianity/by James Legge. —New York: Charles Scribner's Sons, 1881

　　XI, 308p. ; 19.3cm

　　PKUL（館藏號缺）

8114 Religion in China; Containing a Brief Account of the Three Religions of the Chinese/by Joseph Edkins. —London: Trübner & Co., 1878

　　XVI, 260p. ; 21.7cm

PKUL（館藏號缺）

8115 A Religion of Truth, Justice and Peace: A Challenge to Church and Synagogue to Lead in the Realization of the Social and Peace Gospel of the Hebrew Prophets/by Isidor Singer. —New York: The Amos Society, 1924

318p. ; 20.9cm

PKUL（館藏號缺）

8116 The Religious and Social Problems of the Orient/by Masaharu Anesaki. —New York: The Macmillan Company, 1923

XI, 77p. ; 19cm

PKUL（館藏號缺）

附注：

題記：書名頁前頁有作者題記："謹呈胡大人座右,姊崎正治。"

8117 Religious Development between the Old and the New Testaments/by R. H. Charles. —London: Williams and Norgate, 1914

256p. ; 16.7cm

Home University Library of Modern Knowledge

PKUL（館藏號缺）

附注：

印章：扉頁鈐有"北京緞庫後胡同八號,胡適之"藍文長方印。

8118 Remarks on the Korean Language/by G. J. Ramstedt. —[s. l.]: [s. n.], [n. d.]

441–453p. ; 25cm

PKUL（館藏號缺）

附注：

題記：正文首頁有作者題記："To Dr. Hu Shih, with best regards from Dr. G. J. Rt., Tokyo, 29/9 1929。"

8119 Remembrances of Things Past: Cities of Plain; The Captive; The Sweet Cheat Gone; The Past Recaptured/by Marcel Proust; translated by C. K. Scott Moncrieff. —New York: Random House, 1932

 2 Vols. (XV, 1141, 1124p.) ; 21.8cm

 PKUL（館藏號缺）

8120 Reminiscences/by Rabindranath Tagore. —London: Macmillan and Co., Limited, 1917

 XI, 272p. ; 20cm

 PKUL（館藏號缺）

 附注：

  題記：扉頁有胡適題記："Hu Shih. 此書只記泰氏少年時的事蹟，無甚重要。"

  夾紙：頁24、25間夾有廣告書籤一。

8121 Reminiscences/by Huie Kin. —Peiping: San Yu Press, 1932

 115p. ; 20.5cm

 PKUL（館藏號缺）

 附注：

  題記：扉頁有贈書者題記："To Dr. Hu Shih, with compliments of the family, Amos Dorothy, July 28. 1932。"

8122 Reminiscences of Childhood in the Early Days of Modern Japan/by Inazo Nitobé. —Tokyo: Maruzen Company, Ltd., 1934

 II, XIV, 71, VIII, III, VIIp. ; 19.8cm

 PKUL（館藏號缺）

 附注：

  題記：扉頁有贈書者題記："Dr. Hu Shih, with the sincere regards of Marry P. E. Nitobé, Tokyo, March 26th, 1935。"

  內附文件：頁II、III（Introduction）間夾有贈書者致胡適英文書信1頁。

8123 Renaissance in Italy/by John Addington Symonds. —New York: The Modern Library, [n. d.]

2 Vols. ; 20.3cm

PKUL（館藏號缺）

附注：

印章：一套 2 卷扉頁均鈐有"HU SHIH"藍文印。

題記：一冊第 1 卷扉頁有胡適標注的本書綱目；書名頁有胡適標注的年代"（1840-1893）"。

其他：本書有 2 套。

8124 The Renaissance of Asia. —Berkeley and Los Angeles: University of California Press, 1941

XI, 169p. ; 19.4cm

PKUL（館藏號缺）

附注：

題記：扉頁有贈書者題記："Hot off the press to ambassador Hu Shih—with grateful appreciation of his friendship, from Bertwing, Winberta and Lynn, in behalf of Daddy, who is teaching Summer School on Los Angeles, Berkeley, California, July, 1941。"

8125 Renascence and Other Poems/by Edna St. Vincent Millay. —New York: Mitchell Kennerley, 1917

73p. ; 19.5cm

PKUL（館藏號缺）

附注：

題記：扉頁有胡適題記："洪熙送我的。適，十一，一，七。"

8126 Rendezvous and Other Long & Short Stories about Our Navy in Action/by Alec Hudson. —New York: The Press of The Readers Club, 1938

VII, 248p. ; 21.8cm

PKUL（館藏號缺）

8127 Report of the Associate Director of the China Foundation for the Promotion of Education and Culture, on Transactions of the Special Committee in America. —[s. l.]:[s. n.], 1946

 31p. ; 18.7cm

 PKUL（館藏號缺）

8128 Report of the Commission of Enquiry. —Geneva:[s. n.], 1932

 148p. ; 32.7cm

 PKUL（館藏號缺）

 附注：

  印章：封面有胡適簽名"Hu Shih"。

  題記：題名頁有胡適題記："徐淑希先生寄贈。"

8129 Report of the Committee Appointed to Work Out the Details of the Scheme. —Bangalore: The Government Press, 1923

 13, 239p. ; 24.3cm

 PKUL（館藏號缺）

8130 Report of the Henry Street Settlement 1893-1913. —New York: Henry Street Settlement, [n. d.]

 55p. ; 21.5cm

 PKUL（館藏號缺）

 附注：

  題記：題名後頁有作者題記："To my friend Suh Hu, with my complements. A. Davis, Henry St. Settlement。"

8131 Report of the International Commission to Inquire into the Causes and Conduct of the Balkan Wars/by Carnegie Endowment for International Peace, Division of Intercourse and Education. —Washington: Carnegie Endowment for International Peace, 1914

413p. ；24.6cm

PKUL（館藏號缺）

附注：

題記：扉頁有胡適鋼筆簽名"Suh Hu, October, 1914"。

其他：封內貼有 Carnegie Endowment for International Peace 贈書卡。

8132 Report of the Royal Commission Provincial Economic Inquiry/by John Harry Jones, Alexander S. Johnston, Harold A. Innis, G. H. Morrison. —Halifax：King's Printer, 1934

236p. ；25.3cm

PKUL（館藏號缺）

8133 Report of the Survey of the Schools of Tampa, Florida/by George D. Strayer. —New York：Teachers College, Columbia University, 1926

XXV, 308p. ；22.8cm

School Survey Series

PKUL（館藏號缺）

附注：

題記：封面有贈書者題記："To Dr. Hu, From L. K. Yang。"

8134 Report on India/by T. A. Raman. —London, New York, Toronto：Oxford University Press, 1943

231p. ；20.3cm

PKUL（館藏號缺）

8135 Report on the Russians/by W. L. White. —New York：Harcourt, Brace and Company, 1945

309p. ；20.2cm

PKUL（館藏號缺）

附注：

印章：扉頁有胡適鋼筆簽名"Hu Shih"。

8136 Report on the United Nations Conference on International Organization/by Department of External Affairs. —Ottawa: Edmond Cloutier, 1945

 138p. ; 24.1cm

 Conference Series, 1945

 PKUL（館藏號缺）

 附注：

  印章：扉頁有胡適鉛筆簽名"Hu Shih"；題名頁有"John E. □"簽名。

8137 Report to the Trustees/by Eileen Power. —[s. l.] : [s. n.], [n. d.]

 62p. ; 21.5cm

 Albert Kahn Travelling Fellowships

 PKUL（館藏號缺）

 附注：

  題記：題名頁有作者題記："Dr. Hu Shih, from Eileen Power in remembrance of long talks in Peking & London。"

8138 Resistance and Reconstruction: Messages during China's Six Years of War, 1937 – 1943/by Chiang Kai – Shek. —New York, London: Harper & Brothers Publishers, 1943

 XXIV, 322p. ; 22.2cm

 PKUL（館藏號缺）

8139 The Responsibility of Power/by Joseph C. Grew. —Washington: [s. n.], 1945

 16p. ; 20.3cm

 PKUL（館藏號缺）

 附注：

  批注圈劃：書內10頁有胡適朱筆圈劃。

8140 Résumé des Principaux Traités Chinois sur la Culture des Muriers et L'

Éducation des vers a Soie/par Stanislas Julien. —Paris: Imprimerie Royale, 1837

XXII, 224p. ; 23cm

PKUL（館藏號缺）

附注：

其他：本書書脊破損。

8141 Re-Thinking Missions: A Laymen's Inquiry after One Hundred Years/by William Ernest Hocking. —New York, London: Harper & Brothers Publishers, 1932

XV, 349p. ; 21.9cm

PKUL（館藏號缺）

附注：

內附文件：書內夾有 The Christian Century 抽印本及相關評論各 1 份。

8142 Retreat of the West: The White Man's Adventure in Eastern Asia/by No-Yong Park. —Boston, New York: Hale, Cushman & Flint, Inc., 1937

XIV, 336p. ; 22.2cm

PKUL（館藏號缺）

附注：

其他：本書有 2 冊。

8143 The Return of the Native/by Thomas Hardy. —Boston, New York, Chicago: Ginn and Company, 1931

XXII, 506p. ; 18.5cm

Modern Literature Series

PKUL（館藏號缺）

附注：

題記：扉頁有胡適鋼筆簽名"Hu Shih, August 1931"；另書末有胡適題記："秦皇島，廿，八，十四（Aug. 14, 1931）適之閱畢。"

8144 Reveille in Washington, 1860-1865/by Margaret Leech. —New York, London:
Harper & Brothers Publishers, 1941

X, 483p. ; 24.3cm

PKUL（館藏號缺）

8145 The Revolt of Asia: The End of the White Man's World Dominance/by
Upton Close. —New York, London: G. P. Putnam's Sons, 1927

XIII, 325p. ; 22.5cm

PKUL（館藏號缺）

8146 La Révolution/par Louis Madelin. —Paris: Librairie Hachette, 1922

VII, 565p. ; 21.1cm

PKUL（館藏號缺）

附注：

其他：書末裝訂散。

8147 The Revolution of Nihilism/by Hermann Rauschning. —New York: Alliance
Book Corporation, Longmans, Greeen & Co., 1939

XVII, 300p. ; 23.2cm

PKUL（館藏號缺）

附注：

題記：扉頁胡適題記："Hu Shih, June 7, 1940. 今天與鯁生兄出去走路，走到書店裡買的這本書。胡適。"

8148 Rhetoric and the Study of Literature/by Alfred M. Hitchcock. —New York:
Henry Holt and Company, 1927

IV, 410p. ; 19.4cm

PKUL（館藏號缺）

8149 Richard Jones: An Early English Intitutionalist/by Nai-Tuan Chao. —New
York: [s.n.], 1930

2561

169p. ；22.7cm

PKUL（館藏號缺）

附注：

題記：扉頁有作者題記："適之先生指教，弟趙迺摶敬贈，二十，十二，二十三，時得客北平。"

其他：此爲趙迺摶哥倫比亞大學博士論文。

8150　The Riddle of the Universe/by Ernst Haeckel；translated by Joseph McCabe. —London：Watts and Co. , 1913

XXVIII, 324p. ；16.5cm

PKUL（館藏號缺）

8151　The Rights of Man/by Thomas Paine. —London：J. M. Dent & Sons Ltd. ；New York：E. P. Dutton & Co. , Inc. , 1915

XV, 290p. ；17.1cm

Everyman's Library：Philosophy and Theology

PKUL（館藏號缺）

附注：

印章：扉頁鈐有"HU SHIH"藍文印。

批注圈劃：書内75頁有胡適批注圈劃。

内附文件：書内貼有剪報1張。

8152　The Ring and the Book/by Robert Browning. —London：J. M. Dent & Sons Ltd. ；New York：E. P. Dutton & Co. ,［n. d.］

XIX, 534p. ；17cm

PKUL（館藏號缺）

附注：

印章：扉頁后一頁鈐有"適盦藏書"朱文圓印。

題記：扉頁有胡適題記："Suh Hu, 奇獄記。"

夾紙：内夾康奈爾大學圖書館索書條1張。

8153 The Rise and Progress of the Dalton Plan/by A. J. Lynch. —New York: D. Appleton and Company, 1927

　　XII, 164p. ; 20.3cm

　　PKUL（館藏號缺）

8154 The Rise of a Pagan State: Japan's Religious Background/by A. Morgan Young. —London: George Allen & Unwin Ltd, 1939

　　224p. ; 20.1cm

　　PKUL（館藏號缺）

　　附注：

　　　　印章:扉頁鈐有"HU SHIH"藍文印。

　　　　批注圈劃:書內6頁有胡適批注。

8155 The Rise of American Naval Power, 1776–1918/by Harold & Margaret Sprout. —Princeton: Princeton University Press, 1939

　　VII, 398p. ; 22.9cm

　　PKUL（館藏號缺）

　　附注：

　　　　印章:扉頁鈐有"HU SHIH"藍文印。

8156 The Rise of Silas Lapham/by William Dean Howells. —Boston, New York, Chicago: Houghton Mifflin Company, [n.d.]

　　XII, 515p. ; 17.5cm

　　The Riverside Literature Series

　　PKUL（館藏號缺）

8157 Road to War: America 1914–1917/by Walter Millis. —Boston, New York: Houghton Mifflin Company, 1935

　　IX, 466p. ; 21.8cm

　　PKUL（館藏號缺）

8158 Roads of Destiny/by O. Henry. —[s.l.]：Doubleday, Page & Company, 1919

312p. ；19.4cm

PKUL（館藏號缺）

8159 Rob Roy/by Walter Scott. —London：Macmillan and Co., Limited, 1905

CXII, 594p. ；17.4cm

PKUL（館藏號缺）

附注：

印章：扉頁鈐有"Ho Khang Sun, Soochow University"藍文印。

題記：扉頁有贈書者題記："To S. Hu, from C. M. Chen, June 10th, 1910"；另有贈書者題記："From M. Y. Loong to C. M. Chen。"

其他：扉頁貼有贈書者 C. M. Chen 小照片 1 張；書內夾有同樣小照片 5 張。

8160 Roget's International Thesaurus of English Words and Phrases/by C. O. Sylvester Mawson. —New York：Thomas Y. Crowell Company, 1943

XXXVIII, 857p. ；23.6cm

PKUL（館藏號缺）

附注：

印章：封面印有"HU SHIH"燙金字。

8161 Roget's Pocket Thesaurus/by C. O. Sylvester Mawson. —New York：Pocket Books, Inc., 1946

XXVI, 360p. ；15.9cm

PKUL（館藏號缺）

附注：

批注圈劃：書內 4 頁有朱筆圈劃。

8162 Le Roman Chinois/par Ou Itaï. —Paris：Les Éditions Véga, 1933

192p. ；24.5cm

PKUL（館藏號缺）

附注：

    題記：扉頁有作者題記："謹呈適之先生斧正，學生吳益泰謹贈，廿三年六月廿九日。"

8163 The Romance of Scientific Discovery: A Popular and Non-Technical Account of Some of the Most Important Discoveries in Science from the Earliest Historical Times to the Present Day/by Charles R. Gibson. —London: Seeley, Service & Co., Limited, 1922

    318p. ; 19.3cm

    PKUL（館藏號缺）

    附注：

        題記：扉頁有胡適鋼筆簽名"Hu Shih, Jan. 9, 1923"。

8164 The Romance of the Milky Way and Other Studies and Stories/by Lafcadio Hearn. —Leipzig: Bernhard Tauchnitz, 1910

    262p. ; 16.3cm

    Collection of British Authors, Tauchnitz Edition

    PKUL（館藏號缺）

8165 The Romance of the Western Chamber/translated by S. I. Hsiung. —London: Methuen & Co., Ltd., 1935

    XXIII, 281p. ; 19.4cm

    PKUL（館藏號缺）

    附注：

        印章：扉頁鈐有"式一之印"朱文方印。

        題記：扉頁有譯者題記："適之先生教正，熊式一贈。"

        夾紙：書內夾有譯者贈書卡2張。

8166 Romances of Old Japan/by Madame Yukio Ozaki. —Simpkin: [s.n.], [n.d.]

    IX, 278p. ; 25cm

    PKUL（館藏號缺）

附注：

題記：封內有贈書者題記："胡適先生惠存，弟大內暢三。"

8167 Rome and China: A Study of Correlations in Historical Events/by Frederick J. Teggart. —Berkeley: University of California Press, 1939

XVII, 283p. ; 23.4cm

PKUL（館藏號缺）

附注：

題記：扉頁有胡適題記："Hu Shih. Gift of the author Professor Frederick J. Teggart. Nov. 1939。"

8168 Roosevelt Again！/by Joseph F. Guffey. —Franklin：[s. n.]，1940

120p. ; 18.4cm

PKUL（館藏號缺）

8169 Roosevelt's Foreign Policy 1933–1941: Franklin D. Roosevelt's Unedited Speeches and Messages/by Franklin D. Roosevelt. —New York: Wilfred Funk, Inc., 1942

XV, 634p. ; 24cm

PKUL（館藏號缺）

附注：

題記：扉頁有胡適題記："沈允公、郭冲潁贈。適之，卅二，十二，廿五。"

8170 Royal Readers. —London: T. Nelson and Sons, Ltd., 1920

IV, 192p. ; 16.4cm

The Royal School Series, No. III

PKUL（館藏號缺）

附注：

印章：扉頁有原書主簽名"Woo Szu Ching Book"；封底內頁有原書主簽名等，部分不能辨識。

批注圈劃：書內多處有鉛筆標注。

8171 Rubáiyát of Omar Khayyám/by Omar Khayyám; translated by Edward Fitzgerald. y Roy —New York: Pocket Books, Inc., 1941

173p.；16.4cm

PKUL（館藏號缺）

附註：

題記：書末有胡適鉛筆譯詩："XCIX（99）要是偺們倆能和老天爺打成了一氣，好教偺抓住了整個兒天和地，—可不要先摔碎了這不成樣的東西，再從頭改造翻新，好教他真個稱心如意！卅一，二，九夜，牀上改譯，開燈寫下。適之。"（譯詩塗改很多，此為最後定稿。）

批注圈劃：書內4頁有胡適批注圈劃。

8172 Rubáiyát of Omar Khayyám/by Omar Khayyám; translated by Edward Fitzgerald. —New York: Illustrated Editions Company,［n.d.］

191p. 21cm

PKUL（館藏號缺）

8173 Rubáiyát of Omar Khayyám/by Omar Khayyám; translated by Edward Fitzgerald. —Leipzig: Bernhard Tauchinitz, 1910

245p.；16.6cm

Colletion of Britishi Authors

PKUL（館藏號缺）

附註：

題記：叢書頁有胡適題記："志摩送我的。在西湖。十二月十日"；書末有鉛筆書《滬杭道上》詩草稿，另有詩句兩行，似不是胡適筆迹。

內夾文件：頁42、43間夾有胡適毛筆書第73首詩譯稿2頁。

8174 Runyon a la Carte/par Damon Runyon. —Philadelphia, New York: J. B. Lippincott Company, 1944

192p.；18.7cm

PKUL（館藏號缺）

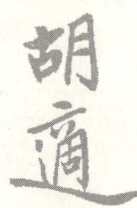

附注：

题记：扉页有胡适钢笔签名"Hu Shih, July 6, 1944"。

批注圈划：目录页有胡适圈划。

8175　The Russian Adventure：Perspectives and Realities/by Robert J. Kerner. —Berkeley, Los Angeles：University of California Press, 1943

　　45p. ; 18.8cm

　　PKUL（馆藏号缺）

8176　A Russian Gentleman/by Sergei Aksakov; translated by F. D. Duff. —New York：The Press of The Readers Club, 1943

　　VIII, 242p. ; 21.8cm

　　PKUL（馆藏号缺）

8177　The Rye Is the Sea：A Book of Poems/by Paul Southworth Bliss. —Bismarck：The Cirrus Company, 1936

　　61p. ; 25.5cm

　　PKUL（馆藏号缺）

　　附注：

　　题记：扉页有作者题记："To Dr. Hu Shih, Chinese ambassador to the United States from Paul Southworth Bliss, Federal Joint Security Bureau, 414 Dierks Bldg., Kansas City Mo. 10/7/40 See page 41 line 10。"

8178　The Sacred Books of China：The Texts of Confucianism：Vol. XVI Part II, the Yî King/by James Legge. —Oxford：The Clarendon Press, 1882

　　XXI, 448p. ; 22.1cm

　　The Sacred Books of the East

　　PKUL（馆藏号缺）

　　附注：

　　印章：扉页有原书主签名"R. Lilley"。

　　批注圈划：书内多处有原书主 R. Lilley 批注圈划。

8179 The Sacred Books of the East/by F. Max Müller. —Oxford：The Clarendon Press，1899

    4 Vols. ；22.7cm

    PKUL（館藏號缺）

  附注：

    印章：第3卷題名頁鈐有"狄堅"朱文方印。

    批注圈劃：第40卷目録頁有胡適鋼筆批注；第28卷目録頁有胡適鋼筆批注。

    其他：本書全本卷數不詳，胡適藏書僅存第3、28、39、40卷，各卷包括内容：Volume III, Shu King, Shih King, Hsiao King; Volume XXVIII, The Li Ki Books XI–XLVI; Volume XXXIX, The Texts of Taoism, Part I; Volume XL, The Texts of Taoism, Part II。

8180 Sacred Books of the East/by Timothy Dwight, et al. —New York：The Colonial Press，1900

    457p. ；23.9cm

    The World's Great Classics

    PKUL（館藏號缺）

8181 The Sacred Tree：Being the Second Part of "The Tale of Genji"/by Arthur Waley. —London：George Allen & Unwin Ltd. , 1926

    394p. ；20.4cm

    PKUL（館藏號缺）

  附注：

    題記：扉頁有胡適題記："Hu Shih, from the translator Arthur Waley, Dec. 1926。"

8182 Sacred Writings：Volume I, Confucian, Hebrew Christian（Part I）/by Charles W. Eliot. —New York：P. F. Collier & Son, 1910

    495p. ；19.5cm

The Harvard Classics No. 44

PKUL（館藏號缺）

附注：

印章：扉頁有胡適簽名"Suh Hu"。

批注圈劃：書內 20 頁有胡適批注圈劃。

夾紙：書內夾有胡適讀書卡片 1 張。

8183 Secret Agent of Japan/by Amleto Vespa. —Boston：Little, Brown and Company, 1938

XIV, 301p. ; 22.5cm

PKUL（館藏號缺）

8184 Sādhanā/by Rabindranath Tagore. —New York：The Macmillan Company, 1913

XI, 164p. ; 18.6cm

PKUL（館藏號缺）

附注：

題記：扉頁有胡適題記："Suh Hu, February, 1915. 昨日吾友鄭秉書來極稱道此書，今日偶過書肆，見此冊，購之以歸。適，民國四年二月六日。"

批注圈劃：本書第五部分 Realisation in Love 有胡適朱筆圈劃多處。

8185 Saito's Idiomological English-Japanese Dictionary/by H. Saito. —Tokyo：S. E. G. Publishing Department, 1915

2 Vols.（10, 1594p.）; 18.9cm

PKUL（館藏號缺）

附注：

印章：兩卷題名頁均鈐有"一涵之章"；第 1 卷題名頁前頁有原書主簽名"M. B. Kao"（高夢弼，即高一涵）。

其他：本書第 1 卷正文前部分頁脫落。

8186 Salthaven/by W. W. Jacobs. —New York：Charles Scribener's Sons, 1908

VIII, 316p. ; 19.4cm

PKUL（館藏號缺）

8187 San Kokf Tsou Ran To Sets, ou Aperçu Général des Trois Royaumes/par J. Klaproth. —Paris：[s. n.]，1832

  VI, 288p. ; 25.3cm

  PKUL（館藏號缺）

  附注：

    其他：本書缺封面。

8188 San Min Chu I：The Three Principles of The People/by Sun Yat-Sen；translated by Frank W. Price. —Shanghai：China Committee, Institute of Pacific Relations, 1927

  XVII, 514p. ; 20.7cm

  PKUL（館藏號缺）

  附注：

    內附文件：書內夾有贈書者劉湛恩（Herman Chan-En Liu）名片、Book Post 各1張，名片上書"吉士斐爾路49A，胡適之先生，敬請指正並賜言介紹"。

8189 San Min Chu I：The Three Principles of The People/by Sun Yat-Sen；translated by Frank W. Price；edited by L. T. Chen. —Chunking：Ministry of Information of the Republic, 1943

  XVII, 514p. ; 20.4cm

  International Understanding Series

  PKUL（館藏號缺）

8190 The Sanctity of Law：Wherein Does It Consist? /by John W. Burgess. —Boston, New York, Chicago, et al：Ginn and Company, 1927

  IX, 335p. ; 21.3cm

  PKUL（館藏號缺）

  附注：

夾紙：書内夾有鉛筆書寫書目1張。

8191 A Sanskrit Grammar, Including Both the Classical Language, and the Older Dialects, of Veda and Brahmana/by William Dwight Whitney. —Leipzig: Breitkopf and Härtel; Boston: Ginn & Company, 1891

XXV, 551p. ; 22.7cm

PKUL（館藏號缺）

附注：

題記：扉頁有胡適鋼筆簽名"Hu Shih, New York City, July, 1944"。

8192 A Sanskrit-Chinese Dictionary. —[s. l.]: [s. n.], [n. d.]

20.8cm

PKUL（館藏號缺）

附注：

其他：本書缺封面及正文之前部分，裝訂已散。頁數不詳。

8193 Sapphira and the Slave Girl/by Willa Cather. —New York: Alfred A. Knopf, 1940

295p. ; 19.6cm

PKUL（館藏號缺）

8194 Sappho: Pris Morals and Manners/by Alphonse Daudet. —St. Islingtou: The Camden Publishing Co., [n. d.]

204p. ; 18.3cm

PKUL（館藏號缺）

8195 Sartor Resartus: The Life and Opinions of Herr Teufelsdröckh/by Thomas Carlyle. —London, New York, Toronto: Oxford University Press, [n. d.]

VI, 264p. ; 15cm

The World's Classics

PKUL（館藏號缺）

附注：

　　題記：扉頁有胡適題記："Suh Hu, March, 1916. 張亦農贈。適之。"

8196　The Satsuma Rebellion：An Episode of Modern Japanese HistoryAugustus/by H. Mounsey. —London：John Murray，1879

　　　IX，294p. ；18.8cm

　　　PKUL（館藏號缺）

　　　附注：

　　　　印章：扉頁有原書主簽名"R. Lilley"。

8197　Savage Survivals：The Story of the Race Told in Simple Language/by J. Howard Moore. —London：Watts & Co.，1919

　　　XI，148p. ；18.3cm

　　　PKUL（館藏號缺）

　　　附注：

　　　　題記：封面有胡適鋼筆簽名"Hu Shih, Dec., 1926"。

8198　The Sayings of Confucius/by Leonard A. Lyall. —London, New York, Toronto：Longmans, Green and Co.，1935

　　　XIII，117p. ；22.7cm

　　　PKUL（館藏號缺）

　　　附注：

　　　　題記：扉頁有作者題記："Hu Shih, with kind regards from Leonard A. Lyall。"

8199　Scapegoats/by Julian Sherrod. —New York：Brewer, Warren & Putnam，1931

　　　XI，127p. ；19.4cm

　　　PKUL（館藏號缺）

　　　附注：

　　　　題記：扉頁有鋼筆題記："Shanghai, June 6, 1932。"

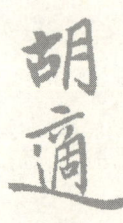

8200 Scholasticism/by Joseph Rickaby. —London：Constable & Company Ltd.，1911

121p.；17.3cm

PKUL（館藏號缺）

附注：

題記：扉頁有胡適毛筆簽名"Hu Suh, June 1918"。

8201 The School and Society/by John Dewey. —Chicago：The University of Chicago Press, 1915

XV, 164p.；18.9cm

PKUL（館藏號缺）

附注：

題記：扉頁有胡適鋼筆簽名"Hu Suh, Feb. 1921"。

8202 School for Overseas Administration, Harvard University ASTP Program—Far Eastern Area Chinese Language Lessons. —[s.l.]：[s.n.]，[n.d.]

38,13,11,13,9,11,7,11,4,12,11,14,12,12,9,109,5,8p.；27.9cm

PKUL（館藏號缺）

附注：

其他：本書爲油印本。

8203 School Histories at War/by Arthur Walworth. —Cambridge：Harvard University Press，1938

XX, 92p.；21cm

PKUL（館藏號缺）

附注：

題記：扉頁有作者題記："To Dr. Hu Shih, with the admiration of Arthur Walworth。"

8204 The Schoolmaster and Other Stories/by Anton Tchehov；translated by Constance Garnett. —London：Chatto & Windus, 1921

312p. ; 15.8cm

The Tales of Tchehov

PKUL（館藏號缺）

附注：

 題記：扉頁有胡適鋼筆簽名"Hu Shih, November 1924"。

 批注圈劃：目録頁有胡適圈劃；頁 159 有胡適鉛筆批注："絶妙。"

8205 The Schoolmistress and Other Stories/by Anton Tchehov; translated by Constance Garnett. —London：Chatto & Windus, 1920

309p. ; 15.8cm

The Tales of Tchehov

PKUL（館藏號缺）

附注：

 題記：扉頁有胡適鋼筆簽名"Hu Shih, November 1924"。

 批注圈劃：目録頁有胡適圈劃；書内四篇小説后有胡適批注。

8206 Schools of To-Morrow/by John Dewey, Evelyn Dewey. —New York：E. P. Dutton & Company, 1915

316p. ; 19.2cm

PKUL（館藏號缺）

附注：

 題記：一冊扉頁有胡適鋼筆簽名"Suh Hu, Dec. 1, 1915, New York"。

 批注圈劃：一冊書内數頁有胡適朱筆圈劃。

 其他：本書有 2 冊。

8207 Science and Christian Tradition/by Thomas H. Huxley. —New York：D. Appleton and Company, 1896

XXXIV, 419p. ; 18.8cm

Essays by Thomas H. Huxley Vol. V

PKUL（館藏號缺）

附注：

印章：扉頁有原書主簽名"Benjamin Thaw Jr."。

題記：扉頁有胡適題記："Vol. V."。

8208 Science and Education/by Thomas H. Huxley. —New York：D. Appleton and Company，1896

  Ⅸ，451p. ；18.8cm

  Essays by Thomas H. Huxley Vol. Ⅲ

  PKUL（館藏號缺）

  附注：

  印章：一冊扉頁有原書主簽名"Benjamin Thaw Jr."。

  題記：另一冊扉頁有胡適題記："赫胥黎論文，適之。"

  批注圈劃：另一冊書内42頁有胡適批注圈劃。

  夾紙：另一冊頁144、145間夾有讀書卡片1張。

  其他：本書有2冊，另一冊印於1897年。

8209 Science and Hebrew Tradition/by Thomas H. Huxley. —New York：D. Appleton and Company，1897

  ⅩⅣ，372p. ；18.8cm

  Essays by Thomas H. Huxley Vol. Ⅳ

  PKUL（館藏號缺）

  附注：

  印章：扉頁有原書主簽名"Benjamin Thaw Jr."。

8210 Science and Human Progress：Halley Stewart Lectures，1926/by Oliver Lodge. —New York：George Doran Company，1927

  243p. ；20.9cm

  PKUL（館藏號缺）

8211 Science and the Modern World：Lowell Lecture，1925/by Alfred North Whitehead. —New York：The Macmillan Company，1925

  Ⅻ，304p. ；18.8cm

PKUL(館藏號缺)

附注：

題記：扉頁有贈書者題記："適之先生：賽恩斯女士托我寄信，說謝謝你在中國爲她努力介紹，祝你康健，因爲以後她有好多好多的事情要請你爲她介紹給中華國民。我也附筆祝你四十壽辰，願你康彊多福。劉吳卓生。十九，十二，十七。"

8212 Science and the New Civilization/by Robert A. Millikan. ——New York, London：Charles Scribner's Sons, 1930

194p. ; 18.7cm

PKUL(館藏號缺)

附注：

印章：扉頁有胡適簽名"Hu Shih"。

題記：扉頁有贈書者題記："From Charles R. Crane, Peking, October 14/30。"

8213 Science for a New World：The Scientific Outlook on World Problems Explained by Leading Exponents of Modern Scientific Thought/by J. Arthur Thomson. ——New York：Harper & Brothers, Publishers, [n.d.]

398p. ; 22.3cm

PKUL(館藏號缺)

8214 The Science of Love：A Study in the Teachings of Therese of Lisieux/by John C. H. Wu. ——Huntington：Our Sunday Visitor Press, 1944

59p. ; 19.2cm

PKUL(館藏號缺)

附注：

題記：扉頁有贈書者題記："敬贈適之先生，熊，三十四年，七．七。"

8215 Science Philosophy and Religion, Second Symposium/by The Conference on Science, Philosophy and Religion in Their Relation to the Democratic Way of Life.

—New York: The Conference on Science, Philosophy and Religion in Their Relation to the Democratic Way of Life, Inc., 1942

XV, 559p. ; 21.3cm

PKUL（館藏號缺）

8216　Science Philosophy and Religion, Third Symposium/by The Conference on Science, Philosophy and Religion in Their Relation to the Democratic Way of Life.
—New York: The Conference on Science, Philosophy and Religion in Their Relation to the Democratic Way of Life, Inc., 1943

XIX, 438p. ; 20.8cm

PKUL（館藏號缺）

8217　Science: The False Messiah/by C. E. Ayres. —Indiannapolis: The Bobbs-Merrill Company, 1927

296p. ; 21.9cm

PKUL（館藏號缺）

附注：

題記：扉頁有胡適題記："Gift of Dr. John Dewey, March 15, 1927. New York City. Hu Shih。"

批注圈劃：書內41頁有胡適批注圈劃；書末有胡適注明的閱讀日期"Jan. 2, 1928"。

8218　Scientific Method in Aesthetics/by Thomas Munro. —New York: W. W. Norton & Company, Inc., 1928

XI, 101p. ; 19cm

PKUL（館藏號缺）

附注：

題記：扉頁有作者題記："For Hu Shih, with greetings from Thomas Munro。"

8219　Scientific Papers: Physics, Chemistry, Astronomy, Geology/by Charles W. Eliot. —New York: P. F. Collier & Son, 1910

367p. ；19.5cm

The Harvard Classics No. 30

PKUL（館藏號缺）

附注：

  印章：扉頁有胡適簽名"Suh Hu"。

  題記：目錄頁有胡適標注。

8220 Scientific Papers：Physiology, Medicine, Surgery, Geology/by Charles W. Eliot. —New York：P. F. Collier & Son, 1910

440p. ；19.5cm

The Harvard Classics No. 40

PKUL（館藏號缺）

附注：

  印章：扉頁有胡適簽名"Suh Hu"。

8221 Scientists Are Human/by David Lindsay Watson. —London：Watts & Co. , 1938

XX, 249p. ；20.3cm

PKUL（館藏號缺）

8222 Scum of the Earth/by Arthur Koestler. —New York：The Macmillan Company, 1941

287p. ；21.8cm

PKUL（館藏號缺）

附注：

  其他：封內貼有"胡適的書"藏書票。

8223 Sea Urchins/by W. W. Jacobs. —London：Lawrence and Bullen, Ltd. , 1898

243p. ；18.7cm

PKUL（館藏號缺）

附注：

題記：扉頁有胡適鋼筆簽名"Hu Shih, March 1942"。

8224 The Second Jungle Book/by Rudyard Kipling. —Leipzig：Bernhard Tauchnitz, 1897

    286p. ; 16.4cm

    Collection of British Authors, Tauchnitz Edition

    PKUL（館藏號缺）

8225 The Secret Agent, a Simple Tale/by Joseph Conrad. —Leipzig：Bernhard Tauchnitz, 1907

    312p. ; 16.5cm

    Collection of British Authors, Tauchnitz Edition

    PKUL（館藏號缺）

8226 The Secret City：A Novel in Three Parts/by Hugh Walpole. —New York：George H. Doran Company, 1919

    386p. ; 20.1cm

    PKUL（館藏號缺）

8227 The See and Say Series/by Sarah Louise Arnold, Elizabeth C. Bonney, E. F. Southworth. —Syracuse, Iroquois Publishing Company, Inc., 1920

    160p. ; 19cm

    PKUL（館藏號缺）

附注：

    其他：本書全本冊數不詳，胡適藏書存第2、3冊。

8228 See Here, Private Hargrove/by Marion Hargrove. —New York：Pocket Book Inc., [n. d.]

    XII, 166p. ; 16.2cm

    PKUL（館藏號缺）

8229 Selected Czech Tales/by Marie Busch, Otto Pick. —Humphrey Milford: Oxford University Press, 1925

　　XI, 258p. ; 14.9cm

　　The World's Classics: CCLXXXVIII

　　PKUL（館藏號缺）

　　附注：

　　　印章：扉頁鈐有"胡適"朱文方印；另題名頁鈐有"胡適"朱文方印。兩章大小不一。

　　　夾紙：書內夾有紙片1張。

8230 Selected English Short Stories: Nineteenth Century/by Hugh Walker. —Humphrey Milford: Oxford University Press, [n.d.]

　　XXXV, 486p. ; 15cm

　　The World's Classics

　　PKUL（館藏號缺）

　　附注：

　　　印章：扉頁鈐有"上海極司非而路四十九號甲,胡適之"藍文長方印。

8231 Selected English Short Stories: XIX & XX Centuries. —Humphrey Milford: Oxford University Press, 1927

　　507p. ; 15cm

　　The World's Classics: CCCXV, Selected English Short Stories

　　PKUL（館藏號缺）

　　附注：

　　　印章：扉頁鈐有"上海極司非而路四十九號甲,胡適之"紫文長方印；另題名頁鈐有"胡適之印"朱文方印。

8232 Selected English Short Stories: XIX & XX Centuries. —Humphrey Milford: Oxford University Press, [n.d.]

　　IX, 483p. ; 15cm

　　The World's Classics: CCXXVIII: Selected English Short Stories

PKUL（館藏號缺）

附注：

印章：扉頁鈐有"上海極司非而路四十九號甲，胡適之"藍文長方印。

批注圈劃：書內數處有圈劃。

8233 Selected Papers on Philosophy/by William James. —London：J. M. Dent & Sons Ltd. ; New York：E. P, Dutton & Co. , ［n. d.］

XVII, 273p. ; 17.3cm

Everyman's Library：Philosophy and Theology

PKUL（館藏號缺）

附注：

題記：扉頁有胡適鉛筆簽名"Suh Hu, March, 1914"。

8234 Selected Poems by Witter Bynner/by Robert Hunt. —New York, London：Alfred A. Knopf, 1936

LXXVI, 259, VIIp. ; 19.2cm

PKUL（館藏號缺）

附注：

題記：扉頁有作者題記："To Hu Shih, with the admiration of Witter Bynner, Santa Fe, New Mexico, April 4, 1939。"

其他：書內夾有作者照片1張。

8235 Selected Stories by Guy de Maupassant Vol. III/by Guy de Maupassant. —New York：The Leslie-Judge Company, 1912

390p. ; 18.3cm

PKUL（館藏號缺）

附注：

題記：扉頁有胡適題記："《穆白桑集》1850—1893"；扉頁後頁有胡適題記："Hanbert（傅羅貝），Zola（索納）。"

批注圈劃：書內4頁有胡適批注。

內附文件：頁204、205間夾有北大哲學系一年級學生包鷟賓1922年10

月29日寫給胡適的信2頁；另有信封1個。

夾紙：書內夾"聶澄澤"名片1張。

8236 Selected Works of Stephen Vincent Benét/by Stephen Vincent Benét. —New York：Farrar & Rinehart, Inc. , 1942

2 Vols. (XIV, 487, 487p.) ; 21.3cm

PKUL（館藏號缺）

附注：

其他：兩卷主要內容：Volume One, Poetry; Volume Two, Prose。

8237 Selections from John Milton/by Martin W. Sampson. —New York：F. S. Crofts & Co. , 1925

LVI, 318p. ; 17.2cm

PKUL（館藏號缺）

附注：

題記：扉頁有作者題記："To my dear friend Hu Shih with happy recollections of his student life at Cornell, from Martin Sampson, 24 March 1927。"

8238 Selections from Lenin Volume Two/by V. I. Lenin. —London：Martin Lawrence Limited, 1929

VII, 398p. ; 18.4cm

PKUL（館藏號缺）

附注：

其他：本書破損，缺封面、封底。

8239 Selections from the Greek Anthology/by Graham R. Tomson. —London and Felling-on-Tyne, New York and Melbourne：The Walter Scott Publishing Co. , Ltd. , [n. d.]

XL, 277p. ; 13.4cm

PKUL（館藏號缺）

附注：

题记:扉页有赠书者题记:"To Dr. Hu Shih, from Josyline B. Crane, 1942, March."

8240 Semantics: Studies in the Science of Meaning/by Michel Breal. —New York: Henry Holt & Company, 1900

LIX, 341p. ; 19.7cm

PKUL(馆藏号缺)

附注:

题记:扉页有胡适题记:"Suh Hu, May 31, 1917. 伯里亞爾著《字義學》(訓詁學)。適。"

批注圈划:书内69页有胡适批注圈划。

8241 The Senate and the League of Nations/by Henry Cabot Lodge. —New York, London: Charles Scribner's Sons, 1925

424p. ; 22.8cm

PKUL(馆藏号缺)

附注:

题记:扉页有胡适铅笔签名"Hu Shih, march, 1938";扉页有胡适钢笔题记。

其他:封内贴有"胡适的书"藏书票。

8242 Senate Manual Containing the Standing Rules and Orders of the United States Senate/by The Senate Committee on Rules Seventy-Fifth Congress. —Washington: United States Government Printing Office, [n. d.]

756p. ; 22.9cm

PKUL(馆藏号缺)

附注:

印章:扉页钤有"HU SHIH"蓝文印。

8243 Series Praelectionum in Regia Scientiarum Universitate Hungariaca Budapestinensi, Pro Semestri Secundo.—Budapestini: Typis Regiae

Universitatis Scientiarum, 1917

 48p. ；22cm

 PKUL（館藏號缺）

8244 Seven Ages/by Harold Begbie. —London：Mills & Boon, Limited, 1923

 188p. ；19cm

 PKUL（館藏號缺）

 附注：

  印章：扉頁有胡適簽名"Hu Shih"。

  批注圈劃：書內 21 頁有胡適批注圈劃。

  內附文件：書內夾有 Adleide W. Anderson1926 年 10 月 8 日致胡適函 1 頁。

8245 The Seven Seas/by Rudyard Kipling. —Leipzig：Bernhard Tauchnitz, 1897

 256p. ；16.5cm

 Collection of British Authors, Tauchnitz Edition

 PKUL（館藏號缺）

8246 Shakespeare's Comedy of the Merchant of Venice/by William J. Rolfe. —Washington：National Home Library Foundation, 1932

 134p. ；16.7cm

 PKUL（館藏號缺）

8247 Shakespeare's Henry IV. Part First/by Henry N. Hudson. —Boston, New York, Chicago et al：Ginn and Company, 1908

 205p. ；16.3cm

 PKUL（館藏號缺）

8248 Shanghi Bund/by Kung Tai. —[s. l.]：[s. n.], [n. d.]

 23cm

 PKUL（館藏號缺）

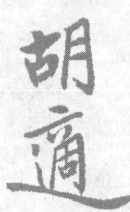

附注:

其他:本書裝訂破損。

8249 The Shape of Things to Come/by H. G. Wells. —New York: The Macmillan Company, 1933

IX, 431p. ; 21.6cm

PKUL（館藏號缺）

附注:

題記:扉頁有贈書者題記:"Aloha！'一路好！'October 13, 1933. 送給適之兄,彭春。"

批注圈劃:書內多處有鉛筆圈劃。

8250 Shaw and Galsworthy: A Contrast/by Jolin Huang. —[s. l.]: [s. n.], [n. d.]

37p. ; 19.2cm

PKUL（館藏號缺）

附注:

印章:兩冊題名頁鈐有"小自然堂"朱文方印。

題記:一冊扉頁有作者題記:"送給胡適先生,黃作霖,十四,六,三二。"

夾紙:一冊書內夾有作者題贈卡1張。

其他:本書有2冊。

8251 Shelley/by Newman Ivey White. —New York: Alfred A. Knopf, 1940

2 Vols. ; 24.2cm

PKUL（館藏號缺）

8252 Shinto: The Ancient Religion of Japan/by W. G. Aston. —London: Constable & Company Ltd., 1921

83p. ; 17.5cm

Religions Ancient and Modern

PKUL（館藏號缺）

8253 Ship's Company/by W. W. Jacobs. —London, New York, Toronto：Hodder and Stoughton,［n. d.］

 XII, 272p. ；19.5cm

 PKUL（館藏號缺）

 附註：

  題記：扉頁有胡適鋼筆簽名"Hu Shih, March 1942"。

8254 Shopping in Oxford/by John Masefield. —London：William Heinemann Ltd., 1941

 14p. ；21.6cm

 PKUL（館藏號缺）

 附註：

  印章：書名頁前頁有作者簽名,爲限量發行本第289本。

  題記：扉頁有贈書者題記："Margaret Thomas to Dr. Hu Shih（'The Happy Warrior'）, London, 1945"；書名頁前頁有贈書者題記,不易辨識。

  內附文件：書內夾有剪報1份。

8255 A Short History of Chinese Civilization/by Tsui Chi. —New York：G. P. Putnam's Sons, 1943

 XIX, 388p. ；22.2cm

 PKUL（館藏號缺）

8256 A Short History of Christianity/by J. M. Robertson. —London：Watts & Co., 1913

 XX, 352p. ；21.8cm

 PKUL（館藏號缺）

 附註：

  題記：扉頁有胡適鉛筆簽名"Hu Shih, December, 1926, London"。

8257 A Short History of Civilization/by Lynn Thorndike. —New York：F. S. Crofts &

Co., 1926

XIV, 619p.；22.8cm

PKUL（館藏號缺）

附注：

題記：扉頁有胡適題記："桑代克著《文化略史》,胡適"；書末空白頁有胡適關於本書的中文綱目。

批注圈劃：書内184頁有胡適批注圈劃,主要爲圈劃。

夾紙：頁347前有夾條一。

8258 A Short History of Freethought：Ancient and Modern Vol. I/by John M. Robertson. —London：Watts & Co., 1914

XII, 484p.；22.1cm

PKUL（館藏號缺）

附注：

印章：扉頁鈐有"適之"朱文橢圓印。

内附文件：書内夾有某書刊左明徹作《從軍》1頁。

8259 A Short History of Science/by W. T. Stedgwick, H. W. Tyler. —New York：The Macmillan Company, 1917

XV, 474p.；21.7cm

PKUL（館藏號缺）

附注：

印章：扉頁鈐有王雲五藏書章："Private Library of Y. W. Wong, Shanghai. 岫盧藏書。"

題記：扉頁有贈書者題記："適之同學,雲,十,九,十五。"

批注圈劃：書内有多處批注。

内附文件：書内夾有"某叔蘭"致胡適書信1頁。

8260 A Short History of the Chinese People/by L. Carrington Goodrich. —New York, London：Harper & Brothers Publishers, 1943

XV, 260p.；20.1cm

PKUL（館藏號缺）

附注：

　　批注圈劃：書内84頁有胡適批注圈劃。

8261　A Short History of the English People/by John Richard Green. —London, Toronto：J. M. Dent & Sons Ltd. ; New York：E. P. Dutton & Co., 1915

　　XLIII, 874p. ; 17cm

　　Everyman's Library

　　PKUL（館藏號缺）

附注：

　　題記：扉頁有胡適朱筆題記："Macmillan Co. Mr. Green 改本。"

8262　Short Stories of To-day & Yesterday/by Bret Harte. —London, Bomby, Sydney：George G. Harrap & Co., Ltd., 1928

　　VII, 218p. ; 17.3cm

　　PKUL（館藏號缺）

附注：

　　題記：扉頁有胡適簽名"Hu Shih, March 1931"。

　　批注圈劃：目録頁有胡適批注圈劃；書末有胡適批注："此篇很不好，不應入選。Jan. 3, 1932。"

　　内附文件：扉頁夾有信封一，上書"敬煩李辰冬兄面陳米糧庫四號胡適之先生，侃如敬上"。

8263　Short Story Classics：Volume One, Russian/by William Patten. —New York：P. F. Collier & Son, 1907

　　X, 326p. ; 19.4cm

　　PKUL（館藏號缺）

附注：

　　題記：扉頁有胡適題記："《短篇小説彙刻》俄國之部第一。"

　　批注圈劃：書内26頁有胡適批注圈劃；多篇小説後有評語。

　　其他：本書書前有散頁。

8264 Short Story Classics：Volume Two, Italian and Scandinavian/by William Patten. —New York：P. F. Collier & Son，1907

329–660p. ；19.4cm

PKUL（館藏號缺）

附注：

題記：扉頁有胡適題記："《短篇小説彙刻》意大利、瑞典、那威之部第二。"

批注圈劃：書內 16 頁有胡適批注圈劃；多篇小説後有評語。

夾紙：頁 342、343 間夾有日曆紙 1 張，有胡適鉛筆字迹；頁 478、479 間夾有紙條 1 張。

其他：本書書前有散頁。

8265 Short Story Classics：Volume Three, German/by William Patten. —New York：P. F. Collier & Son，1907

XII, 1004p. ；19.4cm

PKUL（館藏號缺）

附注：

題記：扉頁有胡適題記："《短篇小説彙刻》德國之部第三。"

批注圈劃：書內 23 頁有胡適批注圈劃；多篇小説後有評語。

8266 Short Story Classics：Volume Four, French/by William Patten. —New York：P. F. Collier & Son，1907

1007–1410p. ；19.5cm

PKUL（館藏號缺）

附注：

題記：扉頁有胡適題記："《短篇小説彙刻》法國之部,第四。"

批注圈劃：目錄頁有胡適圈劃；頁 1064 "The Price of Life"篇後有胡適批注："此篇極詼詭（詼字前有圈掉的謔字），然氣勢貫注有突如其來之神"；頁 1146"The Vendean Marriage"篇後有胡適批注："此則頗似吾國小説所記戰士受擒結婚之事,然何等磊落大方也"；頁 1182 "The Marquise"篇後有胡適批注："讀此篇令人有知己之感,江州司馬青衫之淚,猶是自傷淪落若此。公爵夫人則真是憐才俠意，無一毫私見存乎其中也。中有情書甚動人。"

8267 A Shorter French Course/by W. H. Fraser, J. Squair. —Boston, New York, Chicago：D. C. Heath & Co., 1913

XXVII, 316p.；17.7cm

PKUL（館藏號缺）

附注：

題記：扉頁有胡適簽名"Suh Hu, June, 1915"。

批注圈劃：書內 5 頁有胡適批注圈劃。

夾紙：頁 60、61 間夾有讀書卡片 1 張。

8268 The Shorter Oxford English Dictionary on Historical Principles/by William Little, H. W. Fowler, J. Coulson, C. T. Onions. —Oxford：The Clarendon Press, 1933

2 Vols.（XXI, VII, 2475p.）；28.2cm

PKUL（館藏號缺）

8269 Siècle de Louis XIV/par Voltaire. —Paris：Ernest Flammarion, Éditeur,［n. d.］

2 Vols.（368, 359p.）；18.7cm

PKUL（館藏號缺）

8270 The Signature of All Things, with Other Writings/by Jacob Boehme. —London：J. M. Dent & Sons Ltd.；New York：E. P. Dutton & Co.,［n. d.］

XIV, 295p.；17.6cm

Everyman's Library：Philosophy and Theology

PKUL（館藏號缺）

附注：

題記：扉頁有胡適毛筆簽名"Suh Hu, Sept. 1919"。

8271 The Signpost/by E. Arnot Robertson. —New York：The Macmillan Company,

1944

240p. ; 21.7cm

PKUL（館藏號缺）

8272 The Silk Road/by Sven Hedin; translated by F. H. Lyon. —New York: E. P. Dutton & Company, Inc., 1938

VIII, 322p. ; 24cm

PKUL（館藏號缺）

8273 Since Lenin Died/by Max Eastman. —London: The Labour Publishing Company Limited , 1925

158p. ; 18.2cm

PKUL（館藏號缺）

附注：

題記：扉頁有胡適鋼筆簽名"Hu Shih, April 23, 1926"。

8274 The Singing Bone/by R. Austin Freeman. —London: Hodder and Stoughton Limited, [n. d.]

255p. ; 18.2cm

PKUL（館藏號缺）

附注：

批注圈劃：目錄頁有胡適鉛筆圈劃。

8275 Sino-European Cultural Contacts Since the Discovery of the Sea Route: A Bibliographical Note/by Ch'ên Shou-yi. —[s. l.]: [s. n.], [n. d.]

44–74p. ; 25.3cm

Reprinted from *Nankai Social and Economic Quarterly* Vol. VIII, No. 1

PKUL（館藏號缺）

附注：

題記：封面有作者題記："適之先生教正，受頤敬呈。"

8276 The Sino-Japanese Controversy and the League of Nations/by Westel W. Willoughby. —Baltimore: The Johns Hopkins Press, 1935

XXV, 733p. ; 22.8cm

PKUL（館藏號缺）

8277 Sino-Japanese Problems/by Yasunosuke Sato. —Tokyo: Japan Council of the Institute of Pacific Relations, 1931

48p. ; 22.5cm

PKUL（館藏號缺）

附注：

印章：扉頁有胡適鉛筆簽名"Hu Shih"。

內附文件：書內夾有作者說明打印條1張。

8278 Six Contes : Tiré des Souvenirs d'Enfant et des contes de Bonne Perrete par René Bazin/par G. H. Clarke. —London, Edinburgh, Glasgow, et al: Henry Frowde, Oxford University Press, 1912

143p. ; 16.9cm

Oxford Junior French Series

PKUL（館藏號缺）

附注：

批注圈劃：書內60餘頁有鉛筆批注圈劃。

夾紙：頁32、33間夾有讀書卡片1張。

8279 The Six Systems of Indian Philosophy/by Max Müller. —London: Longmans, Green and Co. , 1903

XIX, 478p. ; 19.2cm

PKUL（館藏號缺）

附注：

題記：扉頁有胡適鋼筆簽名"Hu Suh, September 1918"。

8280 Sixes and Sevens/by O. Henry. —[s. l.]: Doubleday, Page & Company,

1919

283p. ; 19.3cm

PKUL（館藏號缺）

附注：

批注圈劃：目錄頁有胡適鉛筆圈劃。

8281 The Sixth Colum: Inside the Nazi-Occupied Countries. —New York: Alliance Book Corporation, 1942

XI, 313p. ; 20.9cm

PKUL（館藏號缺）

8282 The Sixth International Conference of American Sates/by James Brown Scott. —Worcester: Carnegie Endowment for International Peace, Division of Intercourse and Education, 1928

81p. ; 19.7cm

PKUL（館藏號缺）

8283 A Sketch of Chinese History, Ancient and Modern Volume I/by Charles Gutzlaff. —New York: John P. Haven, 1834

2 Vols. ; 19.5cm

PKUL（館藏號缺）

8284 Slave of the Gods/by Katherine Mayo. —London: Jonathan Cape, 1929

VI, 249p. ; 19.2cm

PKUL（館藏號缺）

附注：

題記：扉頁有胡適題記："《神的奴隸》,胡適,一九二九,五,十四。"

8285 Slaves Need no Leaders: An Answer to the Fascist Challenge to Education/ by Walter M. Kotschnig. —New York, London, Toronto: Oxford University Press, 1943

XV, 284p. ; 22.1cm

PKUL（館藏號缺）

附注：

其他：書內夾有出版社贈書卡1張。

8286 A Smaller Classical Dictionary.—London：J. M. Dent & Sons Ltd.；New York：E. P. Dutton & Co., Inc., 1937

XXII, 584p. ; 17cm

Everyman's Library：Reference

PKUL（館藏號缺）

附注：

題記：扉頁有胡適鋼筆簽名"Hu Shih, New York, Dec. 3, 1942"。

8287 Snickerty Nick/by Julia Ellsworth Ford. —New York：Moffat, Yard & Co., 1919

78p. ; 24cm

PKUL（館藏號缺）

附注：

題記：扉頁後頁有作者題記："To Dr. Hu Shih's little children hoping they will like my little friend Snickerty Nick, affectionately Julia Ellsworth Ford, N 3 West 74' St., N. Y.。"此外，第9頁有作者題記。

8288 So Big/by Edna Ferber. —New York：Grosset & Dunlap Publishers, 1924

372p. ; 19.4cm

PKUL（館藏號缺）

8289 So Little Time/by John P. Marquand. —Boston：Little, Brown and Company, 1943

595p. ; 20.8cm

PKUL（館藏號缺）

8290 So This Is Science/by H. F. Ellis. —London：Methuen & Co., Ltd., 1932

XI, 109p. ; 19cm

PKUL（館藏號缺）

附注：

題記：扉頁有胡適題記："叔初送在君，在君送適之。"

8291 The Social Interpretation of History：A Refutation of the Marxian Economic Interpretation of History/by Maurice William. ——New York：Sotery Publishing Company，1921

XXXI, 397p. ; 20.1cm

PKUL（館藏號缺）

附注：

題記：扉頁有作者題記："To Dr. Hu Shih, Philosopher – Statesman – Humanitarian 'Explorer', with warm appreciation of Maurice William, November 1938。"

內附文件：封底內頁貼有 John Dewey 致本書作者書信 1 頁，打印件。

8292 Social Life of the Chinese/by Justus Doolittle. ——New York：Harper & Brothers Publishers，1865

2 Vols. ; 18.6cm

PKUL（館藏號缺）

附注：

印章：兩卷扉頁均有"R. Lilley"簽名。

8293 Social Organization/by W. H. R. Rivers. ——London：Kegan Paul, Trench, Trubner & Co., Ltd., 1924

X, 226p. ; 23.7cm

PKUL（館藏號缺）

附注：

印章：扉頁有胡適鋼筆簽名"Hu Shih"。

8294 Social Problems/by Serafin E. Macaraig. ——Manila：The Educational Supply

　　　　Co., 1929

　　　　　431p. ;22.4cm

　　　　　PKUL（館藏號缺）

　　　　　附注：

　　　　　　題記：封內有作者題記："To Amb. Hu Shih, with the compliments of Serafin E. Macaraig, Bauff, August 24 1933。"

8295　Social Theory/by G. D. H. Cole. —London: Methuen & Co., Ltd., 1920

　　　　　219p. ;19cm

　　　　　PKUL（館藏號缺）

　　　　　附注：

　　　　　　題記：扉頁有贈書者題記："適之先生，崧年奉贈。"

8296　The Society of Nations: Its Organization and Constitutional Development/by Felix Morley. —Washington: The Brookings Institution, 1932

　　　　　XXII, 678p. ;22.6cm

　　　　　PKUL（館藏號缺）

　　　　　附注：

　　　　　　題記：扉頁有胡適朱筆簽名"Hu Shih, New York, Nov. 22, 1942"。

　　　　　　批注圈劃：書內個別處有鉛筆圈劃。

8297　Socratic Discourses/by Plato, Xenophon. —London: J. M. Dent & Sons, Ltd.; New York: E. P. Dutton & Co., 1910

　　　　　XXIII, 364p. ;17.3cm

　　　　　Everyman's Library: Classical

　　　　　PKUL（館藏號缺）

　　　　　附注：

　　　　　　題記：扉頁有胡適簽名"Suh Hu, Nov. 1915. New York"。

8298　Socratic Discourses/by Plato & Xenophon. —London: J. M. Dent & Sons Ltd.; New York: E. P. Dutton & Co., Inc., 1910

XXIII, 364p. ; 17.1cm

Everyman's Library: Classical

PKUL（館藏號缺）

附注：

　　印章：扉頁鈐有"HU SHIH"藍文印。

8299 Soil Erosion in China/by T. Min Tieh. —[s.l.]：[s.n.]，[n.d.]

570-590p. ; 25.5cm

Reprinted from *The Geographical Review*, Vol. XXXI, No. 4, October, 1941

PKUL（館藏號缺）

附注：

　　印章：封面鈐有"適"朱文方印。

8300 Some Aspects of Chinese Civilization. —[s.l.]：[s.n.]，[n.d.]

10, 23, 8, 12, 12, 25, 19, 13, 17, 16p. ; 22.5cm

PKUL（館藏號缺）

附注：

　　其他：本書爲非正式出版物，A Souvenir。

8301 Some Aspects of Chinese Life and Thought: Being Lectures Delivered under the Auspices of Peking Language School, 1917-1918. —Shanghai, Peking: Kwang Hsueh Publishing House, [n.d.]

II, 186p. ; 18.6cm

PKUL（館藏號缺）

8302 Some Aspects of Japanese Expansionism/by H. J. Timperley. —[s.l.]：[s.n.]，[n.d.]

18-34p. ; 24.6cm

Reprinted from *T'ien Hsia Monthly*, January, 1937

PKUL（館藏號缺）

附注：

題記:封面有作者題記:"To Dr. Hu Shih, with the author's compliments, H. J. Timperley。"

8303 Some Elements in the Chinese Renaissance/by De Vargas. —[s. l.]: [s. n.],[n. d.]

 26p. ; 25.1cm

 Reprinted from *The New China Review*

 PKUL（館藏號缺）

 附注：

  批注圈劃:書內 2 頁有胡適批注圈劃。

8304 Some Fecundity Symbols in Ancient China/by Bernhard Karlgren. —[s. l.]: [s. n.],[n. d.]

 54p. ; 26.5cm

 Reprinted from *The Bulletin of the Museum of Far Eastern Antiquities*, 1930

 PKUL（館藏號缺）

 附注：

  題記:封面有作者題記:"Professor Hu Shih, with kind regards from the author。"

8305 Some General Hints on Self-Improvement/by Lloyd E. Smith. —Girard: Haldeman-Julius Company,[n. d.]

 64p. ; 12.6cm

 Little Blue Book

 PKUL（館藏號缺）

8306 Some Mistakes of Moses/by Robert G. Ingersoll. —New York: Freethought Press Association,[n. d.]

 270p. ; 19.2cm

 PKUL（館藏號缺）

8307 Some Recent Contributions to Chinese Historical Studies/by Ch'en Shou-Yi. —[s. l.]：[s. n.]，[n. d.]

121-135p. ; 25.5cm

PKUL（館藏號缺）

附注：

題記：封面有作者題記："適之先生教正，受頤敬呈。"

8308 Some Types of Modern Educational Theory/by Ella Flagg Young. —Chicago：The University of Chicago Press, 1909

70p. ; 18.7cm

Contributions to Education

PKUL（館藏號缺）

8309 A Son of China/by Sheng-Cheng. —New York：W. W. Norton & Company, Inc., 1930

VIII, 286p. ; 20.6cm

PKUL（館藏號缺）

附注：

題記：扉頁有作者題記："適之先生教正，盛成敬贈，一九三三，一，二七，北平。"

8310 Son of Han/by Richard La Piere. —New York, London：Harper & Brothers, 1937

314p. ; 20.3cm

PKUL（館藏號缺）

附注：

題記：題名頁有作者題記："Berkeley, California, Sept. 26, 1937. To master Hu Shih, with sincere good wishes from the author, Richard La Piere, and his assistant, Oasdee Laive。"

8311 The Son of Man/by Emil Ludwig. —London：Ernest Benn Limited, 1928

319p. ; 21.5cm

PKUL（館藏號缺）

附注：

　　印章：扉頁有"洵侯"簽名。

　　題記：扉頁有鉛筆題記："John Said to Eddi…（Bishop）."

　　批注圈劃：書內多處有鉛筆批注，非胡適所作。

8312 The Song of Bernadette/by Franz Werfel; translated by Ludwig Lewisohn. — New York：The Viking Press, 1942

575p. ; 20.9cm

PKUL（館藏號缺）

8313 Sonnets, Passionate Pilgrim, Etc./by William Shakespeare. —Philadelphia：Henry Altemus Company,［n. d.］

170, 21p. ; 13.7cm

PKUL（館藏號缺）

附注：

　　題記：扉頁有胡適題記："My Birthday Present. S. Hu, December, 1910."

8314 A Soul's Faring/by Muriel Strode. —New York：Boni and Liveright, 1921

167p. ; 20.6cm

PKUL（館藏號缺）

附注：

　　題記：扉頁有贈書者題記："To：Dr. Hu Shih：Chinese Philosopher-friend of all aspiring humanity! May his wish for cosmic unity be realized! Mabel Leslie Fleischer（…Mch. 17'27）."

　　其他：書內夾有 Mrs. Mabel Leslie Fleischer 名片1張。

8315 Sound & Symbol in Chinese/by Bernhard Karlgren. —London：Oxford University Press, 1923

112p. ; 18.4cm

Language and Literature Series

PKUL（館藏號缺）

附注：

印章：一册扉頁有胡適鋼筆簽名"Hu Shih"。

題記：另一册扉頁有作者題記："Professor Hu Shih, with the compliments of the author。"

8316 Source Book in Ancient Philosophy/by Charles M. Bakewell. —New York, Chicago, Boston, Atlanta, San Francisco, Dallas：Charles Scribner's Sons, 1939

XIV, 423p. ; 20.2cm

PKUL（館藏號缺）

附注：

題記：扉頁有作者題記："Hu Shih, with cordial regard of Charles M. Bakewell。"

8317 A Source Book of American Political Theory/by Benjamin Fletcher Wright, Jr. . —New York：The Macmillan Company, 1929

XI, 644p. ; 21.5cm

PKUL（館藏號缺）

附注：

題記：扉頁有吴光清等人題記："敬爲適之先生五十晉三壽辰紀念。後學吴光清、尤桐、傅安、胡敦元、王毓銓、陳鴻舜、朱士嘉、劉修業、韓壽萱、王重民、胡先晉、馮家昇全祝。卅二年十二月十七日。"

其他：胡適藏書中還發現有在美朋友爲胡適祝壽的紀念册一本，最早爲民國二十九年十二月十七日，首頁祝壽人爲朱士嘉、吴光清、王重民、房兆楹。第3、4頁有52位祝壽人簽名，此後有1942、1943、1945年生日祝壽簽名。

8318 Source Records of the Great War/by Charles F. Horne, Walter F. Austin. —[s.l.]：National Alumni, 1923

7 Vols. ; 24cm

PKUL（館藏號缺）

8319 Southern California Panama Expositions Commission. —[s. l.]: Southern California Panama Expositions Commission, 1914

263p. ; 26.5cm

PKUL（館藏號缺）

8320 Speaking Frankly/by James F. Byrnes. —New York and London: Harper & Brothers Publishers, 1947

XII, 324p. ; 21.2cm

PKUL（館藏號缺）

附注：

題記：扉頁有胡適題記："錫予兄寄贈的。胡適。卅六，十一，廿七"；另有湯用彤題記："Merry Xmas. From Y. T. Tang。"

批注圈劃：書內151頁有胡適批注圈劃。

內附文件：書末貼有剪報"Molotov's Tactics"。

8321 Special Plays and Scenes to Be Presented by Mei Lan-fang on His American Tour/by George Kin Leung. —Peking: [s.n.], 1929

116p. ; 18.8cm

PKUL（館藏號缺）

8322 Specimens of the Pre-Shakespearean Drama Vol. II/by John Matthews Manly. —Boston, New York, Chicago, London: Ginn & Company, 1897

VII, 590p. ; 18.3cm

PKUL（館藏號缺）

附注：

印章：扉頁鈐有"柯樂文"朱文方印；另扉頁有胡適簽名"Suh Hu"。

批注圈劃：書內101頁有胡適鉛筆、鋼筆批注圈劃。

8323 The Spectator Vol. 1/by Joseph Addison, Richard Steele. —London: J. M.

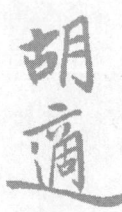

Dent & Co. ; New York: E. P. Dutton & Co. , 1907

X, 377p. ; 17.3cm

PKUL（館藏號缺）

附注：

題記：扉頁有胡適題記："世界第一流行最久之報紙《旁觀報》, 適之。"

其他：本書缺封面、封底。

8324　The Speculations on Metaphysics, Polity and Morality, of "the Old Philosopher", Lau-Tsze/by John Chalmers. —London: Trübner & Co. , 1868

XIX, 62p. ; 18.9cm

PKUL（館藏號缺）

附注：

印章：扉頁有原書主簽名"R. Lilley"。

8325　Speeches and Documents on International Affairs, 1918 – 1937/by Arthur Berriedale Keith. —London: Oxford University Press, 1938

LV, 290p. ; 15cm

The World's Classics

PKUL（館藏號缺）

附注：

題記：兩卷扉頁均有贈書者題記："敬贈適之兄, 鯁生, 二八, 十二, 十七。"

批注圈劃：第1卷書末有朱筆圈劃；第2卷書內13頁有胡適朱筆圈劃。

其他：兩卷封內均貼有"胡適的書"藏書票。

8326　Spelling Self Taught/by Lloyd E. Smith. —Girard: Haldeman-Julius Company, [n. d.]

64p. ; 12.6cm

Little Blue Book

PKUL（館藏號缺）

8327　The Spinners of Silk/by Hsiao Ch'ien. —London: George Allen & Unwin Ltd. ,

1944

 102p. ；18.6cm

 PKUL（館藏號缺）

 附注：

  題記：扉頁後頁有作者題記："敬送給適之先生指正，蕭乾拜贈，一九四五年，四月，於舊金山。"

  內附文件：書內夾有蕭乾致胡適書信1封。

8328 Spinoza's Ethics and "De Intellectus Emendatione"/by Spinoza. —London：J. M. Dent & Sons Ltd. ; New York：E. P, Dutton & Co. , 1910

 XLVIII, 263p. ；17.2cm

 Everyman's Library：Philosophy and Theology

 PKUL（館藏號缺）

 附注：

  題記：扉頁有胡適鋼筆簽名"Suh Hu, March 1916, New York"。

  批注圈劃：書內49頁有胡適批注圈劃。

  摺頁：頁25、41、63、64、81有摺頁。

8329 The Spirit of English History/by A. L. Rowse. —London, New York, Toronto：Longmans Green & Co. , 1943

 150p. ；18.5cm

 PKUL（館藏號缺）

8330 The Spirit of Language in Civilization/by Karl Vossler; translated by Oscar Oeser. —New York：Harcourt, Brace and Company; London：Kegan Paul, Trench, Trubner & Co. , Ltd. , 1932

 VII, 247p. ；21.7cm

 International Library of Psychology Philosophy and Scientific Method

 PKUL（館藏號缺）

 附注：

  印章：扉頁鈐有"HU SHIH"藍文印。

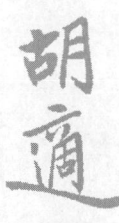

8331 The Spirit of Laws/by Baron De Montesquieu; translated by Thomas Nugent. —New York: P. F. Collier & Son, 1900

2 Vols. ; 20.8cm

The World's Greatest Literature

PKUL（館藏號缺）

附注：

題記：兩卷扉頁均有胡適鋼筆簽名"Suh Hu, April 1916"。

批注圈劃：第1卷書內3頁有胡適批注。

8332 The Spirit of the Chinese People/by Ku Hung‐Ming. —Peking: The Commercial Press, Work Ltd. , 1922

X, 160p. ; 19.9cm

PKUL（館藏號缺）

8333 Sprechen Sie Deutsch? Or, Do You Speak German?. —New York: Henry Holt and Company, [n. d.]

147p. ; 15.3cm

PKUL（館藏號缺）

附注：

題記：扉頁有胡適鋼筆簽名"Suh Hu, July, 1914"。

8334 St. Francis of Assisi G. K. Chesterton. —London, Toronto: Hodder and Stoughton Ltd. , [n. d.]

185p. ; 17.1cm

PKUL（館藏號缺）

附注：

題記：扉頁有胡適鉛筆簽名"Hu Shih, Oct. 1926, London"。

8335 Stakes of the War: Summary of the Various Problems, Claims of Interests of the Nations at the Peace Table/by Lothrop Stoddard, Glenn Frank. —New

York: The Century Co. , 1918

XII, 377p. ; 20.7cm

PKUL（館藏號缺）

8336 The Statesman's Year-Book: Statistical and Historical Annual of the States of the World for the Year 1923/by John Scott Keltie, M. Epstein. —London: Macmillan and Co. , Limited, 1923

XXXII, 1583p. ; 18.1cm

PKUL（館藏號缺）

8337 The Steep Places/by Norman Angell. —New York and London: Harper & Brothers, 1947

247p. ; 20.3cm

PKUL（館藏號缺）

附注：

題記:扉頁有贈書者題記:"To Dr. Hu Shih—with kindest regards from Juliet B. Rublee。"

夾紙:書內夾有贈書者便條1張。

8338 The Steppe & the Sown/by Harold Peake, Herbert John Fleure. —Oxford: The Clarendon Press, 1928

160p. ; 20.5cm

PKUL（館藏號缺）

8339 StoneHenge: Today & Yesterday/by Frank Stevens. —London: His Majesty's Stationary Office, 1936

94p. ; 18.1cm

PKUL（館藏號缺）

8340 Stories from China/by T. K. Ch'u. —London: Kegan Paul, Trench Trubner & Co. , Ltd. , 1937

84p. ; 15.6cm

PKUL（館藏號缺）

8341 Stories from the Arabian Nights, with Chinese Notes/by Tseu Yih Zan. —Shanghai: The Commercial Press, Limited, 1924

194, 56p. ; 19.1cm

PKUL（館藏號缺）

8342 Stories from the Thousand and One Nights/by Edward William Lane. —New York: P. F. Collier & Son, 1909

460p. ; 19.5cm

The Harvard Classics No. 16

PKUL（館藏號缺）

附注：

印章：扉頁有胡適簽名"Suh Hu"；題名頁鈐有"適盦藏書"朱文圓印。

8343 Storm/by George R. Stewart. —New York: Random House, 1941

349p. ; 20.9cm

PKUL（館藏號缺）

8344 Story of a Secret State/by Jan Karski. —Boston: Houghton Mifflin Company, 1944

VI, 391p. ; 20cm

PKUL（館藏號缺）

8345 The Story of Chung Mei/by Charles R. shepherd. —Philadelphia: The Judson Press, 1938

264p. ; 19.5cm

PKUL（館藏號缺）

附注：

題記：扉頁有作者題記："To His Excellency Dr. Hu Shih, Compliments of

Charles R. Shepherd。"

8346 The Story of Dragon Seed/by Pearl S. Buck. —New York：The John Day Company, 1944

  9-15p. ；19.2cm

  PKUL（館藏號缺）

8347 The Story of Philosophy：The Lives and Opinions of the Great Philosophers/ by Will Durant. —New York：Simon and Schuster, 1926

  XIII, 589p. ；23.5cm

  PKUL（館藏號缺）

 附注：

  題記：扉頁有胡適題記："Hu Shih, Jan. 12, 1927. New York. 前年在英國,杜威先生來信稱贊此書。去年一月十一日到紐約,席上與洛司爾院長同坐,他又對我盛稱此書,故次日便買了此冊。適之。"

  批注圈劃：書內 60 頁有胡適批注圈劃。

8348 The Story of Surgery/by Harvey Graham. —New York：Doubleday, Doran & Company, Inc. , 1939

  425p. ；23.5cm

  PKUL（館藏號缺）

8349 The Story of The Bible/by Hendrik Willem Van Loon. —New York：Boni & Liveright, Inc. , 1923

  XXV, 452p. ；23.1cm

  PKUL（館藏號缺）

 附注：

  題記：扉頁有胡適簽名"Hu Shih, February, 1924"。

8350 The Story of the Chinese Eastern Railway/by George E. Sokolsky. —Shanghai：North-China Daily News & Herald Ltd. , [n.d.]

68p. ; 21.7cm

PKUL（館藏號缺）

附注：

題記：扉頁有作者題記："To my preface writer Hu Shih, another volume which bear our joint names—may neither of us be deported for it. Sok, Shanghai, Oct. 23, 1929。"

8351 The Story of the Democratic Party/by Henry Minor. —New York：The Macmillan Company, 1928

X, 501p. ; 21.6cm

PKUL（館藏號缺）

附注：

其他：封內貼有"胡適的書"藏書票。

8352 The Story of the Political Philosophers/by George Catlin. —New York, London：Whittlesey House, 1939

802p. ; 23.6cm

PKUL（館藏號缺）

附注：

印章：扉頁鈐有"HU SHIH"藍文印。

批注圈劃：書內 159 頁有胡適批注圈劃。

8353 The Story of the United States by Those Who Made It/by Ernest Carroll Moore. —Los Angeles：U. S. Library Association, Inc., 1933

95p. ; 18.5cm

PKUL（館藏號缺）

附注：

夾紙：書內夾有 Carnegie Endowment for International Peace 卡片 1 張。

8354 Strange Fruit/by Lillian Smith. —New York：Reynal & Hitchcock Publishers, 1944

314p. ; 19.7cm

PKUL（館藏號缺）

8355 Strong Man of China: The Story of Chiang Kai-Shek/by Robert Berkov. —
Boston: Houghton Mifflin Company, 1938

XV, 288p. ; 21.4cm

PKUL（館藏號缺）

8356 Structural Features of the Stone-Built T'ing-Pagoda/by Gustav Ecke. —
Peiping: Henri Vetch, [n.d.]

253-276, XVp. ; 27.9cm

PKUL（館藏號缺）

Reprinted from *Monvmenta Serica, Journal of Oriental Studies of the Catholic University of Peking*, Vol. I, Fasc. 2, 1935

附注：

　題記：封面有作者題記："To Dr. Hu Shih, as a token of admiration of the author G. E.。"

8357 A Structural Key to Han Mural Art/by Wilma Fairbank. —[s. l.]: [s. n.], [n. d.]

52-88p. ; 25.7cm

PKUL（館藏號缺）

Reprinted from *Harvard Journal of Asiatic Studies*, Volume &, No. 1

附注：

　題記：封面有作者題記："For Hu Shih, with the compliments of Wilma Fairbank。"

8358 The Structure and Administration of Education in American Democracy/by National Education Association of the United States. —Washington: Educational Policies Commission, 1938

128p. ; 23.4cm

PKUL（館藏號缺）

8359 The Struggle between Science and Superstition/by Arthur M. Lewis. —
Chicago: Charles H. Kerr & Company, [n.d.]
188p. ; 17cm
PKUL（館藏號缺）

8360 The Student's Four Thousand 字 and General Pocket Dictionary/by W. E.
Soothill. —[s.l.]: Kwang Hsueh Publishing House, 1932
XXXI, 428p. ; 13.5cm
PKUL（館藏號缺）

8361 Students' Logic/by Dhirendra Nath Roy. —Manila: The Educatinal Supply,
1933
XII, 310p. ; 21.7cm
PKUL（館藏號缺）

8362 Studies in Early Chinese Culture/by Herrlee Glessner Creel. —Baltimore:
Waverly Press, Inc., 1937
XXII, 266p. ; 25.8cm
PKUL（館藏號缺）

8363 Studies in Grammar/by Mabel C. Hermans. —New York: Henry Holt and
Company, 1926
XI, 464p. ; 19.3cm
PKUL（館藏號缺）

8364 Studies in Humanism/by F. C. S. Schiller. —London: Macmillan and Co.,
Limited, 1912
XIX, 492p. ; 22.7cm
PKUL（館藏號缺）

8365 Studies in Political Science and Sociology/by Hu Shih, Newton Edwards, et al. —Philadelphia: University of Pennsylvania Press, 1941

194p. ; 22.9cm

University of Pennsylvania Bicentennial Conference

PKUL（館藏號缺）

附注：

 其他：封內貼有"胡適的書"藏書票。

 與胡適的關係：胡適論文"Instrumentalism as a Political Concept"作爲第 1 篇收入本書。

8366 Studies in the History of Culture: The Disciplines of the Humanities. — Menasha: George Banta Publishing Company, 1942

331p. ; 25.9cm

PKUL（館藏號缺）

8367 Studies in the History of Ideas Vol. I/by The Department of Philosophy of Columbia University. —New York: Columbia University Press, 1918

272p. ; 20.6cm

PKUL（館藏號缺）

附注：

 印章：扉頁鈐有"胡適之印"朱文方印。

 題記：扉頁有胡適毛筆簽名"Hu Suh, Peking, March 1919"。

8368 A Study of Hobson's Welfare Economics/by William Tien–Chen Liu. — Peiping: Kwang Yuen Press, 1934

X, 228p. ; 23.4cm

PKUL（館藏號缺）

附注：

 題記：扉頁有贈書者題記："適之學長指正，劉甸忱謹贈。"

8369 The Study of Sociology/by Herbert Spencer. —New York and London：D. Appleton and Company，1910

　　X，411p.；19.7cm

　　PKUL（館藏號缺）

　　附注：

　　　題記：扉頁有胡適題記："Suh Hu，斯賓塞爾《群學肄言》，適之讀。"

8370 A Study of the Principles of Politics：Being an Essay towards Political Rationalization/by George E. G. Catlin. —New York：The Macmillan Company，1930

　　469p.；23.8cm

　　PKUL（館藏號缺）

　　附注：

　　　題記：扉頁有贈書者題記："To Hu Shih—for steamer reading，from Elle，1930。"

8371 A Study on the Lolo Manuscript Sii-zeu-bo-p'a "The Origin of the Gods" from the Taliang Mountains/by Fu Mao-Chi. —［s. l.］：［s. n.］，1945

　　38p.；25.6cm

　　PKUL（館藏號缺）

　　附注：

　　　題記：封面有作者題記："適之先生教正，受業傅懋勣敬贈。"

8372 A Study on the Lolo Proverbs，in and near the Taliang Mountains/by Fu Mao-Chi. —［s. l.］：［s. n.］，1945

　　15p.；26cm

　　PKUL（館藏號缺）

　　附注：

　　　題記：封面有作者題記："適之先生教正，受業傅懋勣敬贈。"

8373 Style of Chinese Bronze/by Ch'en Meng-Chia. —［s. l.］：［s. n.］，［n. d.］

26-52p. ; 30.4cm

PKUL（館藏號缺）

附注：

　　題記：封面有作者題記："適之先生教正，陳夢家寄自芝加哥。"

8374 A Subtreasury of American Humor/by E. B. White, Katharine S. White. —New York：Tudor Publishing Co. , 1945

XXXII, 814p. ; 21.2cm

PKUL（館藏號缺）

附注：

　　題記：扉頁有胡適題記："Hu Shih, Gift of S. H. Chu, June, 1946。"
　　摺頁：頁583摺頁。

8375 Suggestions for a Quantitative Mineralogical Classification of Sedimentary Rocks/by Vei Chow Juan. —[s.l.]：[s.n.]，[n.d.]

205-228p. ; 25.8cm

Reprinted from *The Bulletin of Geological Society of China*, 1947

PKUL（館藏號缺）

附注：

　　題記：封面有作者題記："適之校長指正，著者敬贈，卅六年十二月。"

8376 The Sun Also Rises/by Ernest Hemingway. —New York：The Modern Library, 1926

IX, 259p. ; 18.3cm

PKUL（館藏號缺）

8377 Sun Yat Sen and the Chinese Republic/by Paul Linebarger. —New York, London：The Century Co. , 1925

XVIII, 371p. ; 20.5cm

PKUL（館藏號缺）

附注：

题记：扉頁有作者题记："To Dr. Hu Shih, to China's greatest modern poet and foremost philosopher, whose poetic genius and philosophic wisdoms □ with the □ of a Chinese Patriotism which ever is thus, to world progress. Cordially the author, Sept. XXVII, 1933, Wash. D. C.。"

8378 Sun Yat-sen Versus Communism/by Maurice William. —Baltimore：The Williams & Wilkins Company, 1932

XX, 232p. ; 22.8cm

PKUL（館藏號缺）

附注：

题记：一冊扉頁有作者题记："To Dr. Hu Shih, with the warm appreciation of his friend, Maurice William, April 20-1939"；另一冊扉頁有作者题记："To Dr. Hu Shih, with the sincere appreciation of Maurice William, March 1933。"

8379 The Sunpapers of Baltimore/by Gerald W. Johnson, Frank R. Kent, H. L. Mencken, Hamilton Owens. —New York：Alfred A. Knopf, 1937

XII, 430, XVIp. ; 24cm

PKUL（館藏號缺）

8380 Suppressing Communist-Banditry in China. —Shanghai：China United Press, 1934

VII, 110p. ; 24.9cm

PKUL（館藏號缺）

附注：

题记：扉頁有贈書者题记："To Dr. Hu Shih, to whom the editor is greatly indebted. Tang Leang-li, Peiping, June 3, 1934。"

8381 Sur L'Authenticité du Ta Tch'eng K'I Sin Louen/par Paul Demiéville. —Tokyo：[s.n.], 1929

78p. ; 22cm

Extrait du *Bulletin de la Maison Franco-Japonaise*, tome II, n0 2

PKUL（館藏號缺）

附注：

題記：正文首頁有作者題記："胡適之先生惠正，戴密微。"

8382 A Survey of Indian History/by K. M. Panikkar. —Bombay：The National Information & Publications Ltd. ，1947

338p. ；19.1cm

PKUL（館藏號缺）

8383 The Survival of Man：A Study in Unrecognised Human Faculty/by Oliver Lodge. —London：Methuen & Co. ，Ltd. ，1926

239p. ；16.7cm

PKUL（館藏號缺）

附注：

題記：扉頁有胡適鉛筆簽名："Hu Shih, Dec. 21, 1926"；前言前頁有胡適鋼筆題記："Dec. 22, 1926. 見Dickinson，他説，他現在沒有這種希冀靈魂不滅的想頭了。今年他六十五歲了，越老，反越不作此种妄想了。我很高興。Hu Shih。"

8384 Suspense/by Joseph Conrad. —Leipzig：Bernhard Tauchnitz, 1925

286p. ；16.5cm

Collection of British Authors, Tauchnitz Edition

PKUL（館藏號缺）

8385 The Sutra of Wei Lang (or Hui Neng)/by Wong Mou-Lam, Christmas Humphreys. —London：Luzac & Co. ，1944

128p. ；16.4cm

PKUL（館藏號缺）

8386 Sutra Spoken by the Sixth Patriarch, Wei Lang, on the High Seat of the

Gem of Law. —[s. l.]：[s. n.]，[n. d.]

　　76p. ; 26.3cm

　　PKUL（館藏號缺）

8387　Swann's Way/by Marcel Proust. —London：Chatto and Windus, 1922

　　2 Vols.（303, 288p.）; 17.5cm

　　The Phoenix Libray

　　PKUL（館藏號缺）

　　附注：

　　　題記：第1卷扉頁有胡適鋼筆簽名"Hu Shih, Nov, 1933"。

8388　Switzerland：Together with Chamonix and the Italian Lakes/by Karl Baedeker. —Leipzig：Karl Baedeker, Publisher; London：George Allen & Unwin Ltd. ; New York：Chas. Scribner's Sons, 1938

　　LVIII, 600p. ; 16cm

　　Baedeker's Guide Books

　　PKUL（館藏號缺）

8389　Switzerland：With Chamonix and the Italian Lakes/by Findlay Muirhead. —London：Macmillan & Co., Ltd. ; Paris：Librairie Hachette & Cie., 1923

　　LVIII, 512p. ; 15.8cm

　　The Blue Guides

　　PKUL（館藏號缺）

8390　The Symbols of Government/by Thurman W. Arnold. —New Haven：Yale University Press, 1935

　　VI, 278p. ; 20.3cm

　　PKUL（館藏號缺）

　　附注：

　　　題記：扉頁有胡適鋼筆簽名"Hu Shih, Dec. 22, 1937"。

8391 The Symbols of Yi King, or the Symbols of the Chinese Logic of Changes/ by Z. D. Sung. —Shanghai: The China Modern Education Co., 1934

  VIII, 159p. ; 18.3cm

  PKUL（館藏號缺）

  附注：

   題記:題名頁有胡適標注作者中文名字"沈仲濤"。

8392 La Symphonie des Ombres chinoises/par S. Horose. —Paris: Édition de la Madeleine, 1932

  XIX, 267p. ; 19.1cm

  PKUL（館藏號缺）

  附注：

   題記:扉頁後頁有作者題記。（作者題贈胡適,法文不易辨識。）

   其他:內夾雷峰塔照片1張。

8393 Symposium on Chinese Culture/by Sophia H. Chen Zen. —Shanghai: China Institute of Pacific Relations, 1931

  316p. ; 23.3cm

  PKUL（館藏號缺）

  附注：

   題記:一冊扉頁有作者題記,貼于印製名片上:"To Dr. Hu Shi, 104 E. 81 St. N. Y. This is the last copy in stock! W. L. H.。"

   夾紙:另有一冊書內夾有名片1張。

   其他:本書有4冊。

8394 Syntaxe Nouvelle de la Langue Chinoise Fondé sur la Position des Mots Confirmée par L'Analyse d'un Texte Ancien Second Volume/par Stanislas Julien. —Paris: Librairie de Maisonneuve & Cie, 1870

  438p. ; 24.5cm

  PKUL（館藏號缺）

  附注：

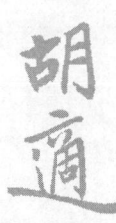

其他:本書裝訂破損。

8395 The System of Basic English/by C. K. Ogden. —New York: Harcourt, Brace and Company, 1934

  IX, 322p. ; 20.8cm

  PKUL（館藏號缺）

8396 A Systematical Digest of the Doctrines of Confucius/by Ernst Faber; translated by P. G. von Moellendorff. —Hongkong: China Mail Office, 1875

  VIII, 131p. ; 24.5cm

  PKUL（館藏號缺）

8397 The Ta-Ming Shih-Lu/by A. C. Moule, Chung Kei-Won. —[s.l.]: [s.n.], [n.d.]

  289–328p. ; 24.3cm

  Reprinted from *T'oung Pao*, Vol. XXXV, Livr. 4

  PKUL（館藏號缺）

  附注：

    題記:封面有贈書者題記:"To Dr. Hu Shih。"

8398 The Tagore Birthday Book/by C. F. Andrews. —London: Macmillan and Co., Limited, 1928

  XIX,[314]p. ; 18.4cm

  PKUL（館藏號缺）

  附注：

    題記:扉頁有泰戈爾題記:"To may and mou, with love and blessings, Rabindranath Tagore, 1st January, 1929。"

8399 T'ai-Shang Kan-Ying P'ien: Treatise of the Exalted One on Response and Retribution/by Teitaro Suzuki, Paul Carus. —Chicago: The Open Court Publishing Co., 1906

139p. ；20.5cm

PKUL（館藏號缺）

附注：

 其他：扉頁貼有作者贈書卡。

8400 Tales from Henryk Sienkiewicz/by Henryk Sienkiewicz. —London：J. M. Dent & Sons Ltd. ; New York：E. P, Dutton & Co. , 1931

 XIII, 332p. ；17.1cm

 Everyman's Library：Fiction

 PKUL（館藏號缺）

8401 Tales of a Chinese Grandmother/by Frances Carpenter. —Garden City：Doubleday, Doran & Co. , Inc. , 1938

 XII, 261p. ；23.5cm

 PKUL（館藏號缺）

 附注：

  內附文件：書末貼有作者 Frances Carpenter Huntington 致胡適英文書信1封。

8402 The Tales of a Grandfather/by Walter Scot. —London：Adam & Charles Black, 1893

 470p. ；23.5cm

 PKUL（館藏號缺）

 附注：

  印章：扉頁鈐有"儀徵張氏珍藏"朱文方印。

8403 Tales of Edgar Allan Poe/by Edgar Allan Poe. —New York：Random House, 1944

 XII, 562p. ；21cm

 PKUL（館藏號缺）

8404 Tales of Mean Streets/by Arthur Morrison. —New York: Boni and Liveright Publishers, 1921

XXVII, 251p. ; 16.9cm

The Modern Library of the World's Best Books

PKUL（館藏號缺）

附注：

印章：題名頁鈐有"胡適之印"朱文方印。

8405 Tales of Old Japan/by A. B. Mitford. —London: Macmillan and Co., 1876

VII, 383p. ; 18.4cm

PKUL（館藏號缺）

附注：

夾紙：書內夾有胡適便箋1張。

其他：本書書脊脫落，裝訂已散。

8406 Talks in China/by Rabindranath Tagore. —Calcutta: Karunabindu Biswas, 1924

157, IIIp. ; 21.8cm

PKUL（館藏號缺）

附注：

題記：扉頁有泰戈爾簽名"Rabindranath Tagore"；另有徐志摩題字："適之存念，志摩，十七年十一月。"

8407 Tantrism in China/by Chou Yi-Liang. —[s.l.]: Harvard-Yenching Institute, 1944-45

241-332p. ; 25.3cm

Reprinted from *Harvard Journal of Asiatic Studies*, Volume 8, Number 3 and 4, March, 1945

PKUL（館藏號缺）

附注：

題記：封面有作者題記："唐代密宗三僧攷，適之先生誨正，晚一良謹贈。"

批注圈劃：書內6頁有胡適批注圈劃。

8408 The Tâo Teh King/by James Legge. —[s. l.]：[s. n.], 1883

  36p. ; 21.2cm

  Reprinted from *The British Quarterly Review*, July, 1883

  PKUL（館藏號缺）

  附注：

    題記：封面有作者題記："To the Rev. Dr. Jowitt, master of Balliol college, and the chancellor, with kind regard of J. Legge。"

8409 Taps for Private Tussie/by Jesse Stuart. —New York：E. P. Dutton & Company, Inc., 1943

  300p. ; 21.8cm

  PKUL（館藏號缺）

8410 Tariff Retaliation：Repercussions of the Hawley-Smoot Bill/by Joseph M. Jones, Jr.. —Philadelphia：University of Pennsylvania Press, 1934

  X, 352p. ; 23.5cm

  PKUL（館藏號缺）

8411 Tea Time：A Selection from the Writings of Lady Adams/by Lady Adams. —Los Angeles：Times-Mirror, 1942

  XVIII, 283p. ; 19.8cm

  PKUL（館藏號缺）

  附注：

    其他：內夾胡適照片1張。

8412 Tea Trade in Central China/by T. H. Chu. —Shanghai, Hong Kong, Singpore：Kelly & Walsh, Limited, 1936

  259p. ; 23.1cm

  PKUL（館藏號缺）

8413 The Teacher's Guide to the Little Book of English Composition/by E. A., Cross. —Boston: Little, Brown, and Company, 1927

88p. ; 18.1cm

PKUL（館藏號缺）

8414 Teaching of History: In Elementary and Secondary Schools/by Henry Johnson. —New York: The Macmillan Company, 1921

XVII, 497p. ; 19.7cm

PKUL（館藏號缺）

8415 The Teaching of Science to the Chinese/by L. G. Morgan. —Hong Kong: Kelly and Walsh, Limited, 1933

XXI, 150p. ; 23cm

PKUL（館藏號缺）

附注：

題記：扉頁有作者題記："Dr. Hu Shih, with the author's Compliments, 5. 1. 35。"

內附文件：書內夾有作者致胡適書信3頁。

8416 The Temple and Other Poems/by Arthur Waley. —London: George Allen & Unwin Ltd., 1923

151p. ; 19.1cm

PKUL（館藏號缺）

附注：

題記：扉頁有胡適題記："Hu Shih, from the author。"

8417 The Temple of the Warriors/by Earl H. Morris. —New York, London: Charles Scribner's Sons, 1931

XII, 245p. ; 23.3cm

PKUL（館藏號缺）

8418 Ten Years in Japan/by Joseph C. Crew. —New York: Simon and Schuster, 1944

    XII, 554p. ; 21.8cm

    PKUL（館藏號缺）

8419 Tentative Course of Study for the Core Curriculum of Virginia Secondary Schools: Grade VIII/by Sidney B. Hall, D. W. Peters, H. L. Caswell. —[s.l.]:[s.n.], [n.d.]

    XIII, 319p. ; 27.3cm

    PKUL（館藏號缺）

8420 Tentative Course of Study for Virginia Elementary Schools: Grade I–VII/by Sidney B. Hall, D. W. Peters, Helen Ruth Henderson, H. L. Caswell. —[s.l.]:[s.n.], [n.d.]

    XIII, 560p. ; 27.2cm

    PKUL（館藏號缺）

8421 The Tercentenary of Harvard College: A Chronicle of the Tercentenary Year, 1935–1936/by Presidents and Fellows of Harvard College. —Cambridge: Harvard University Press, 1937

    XIV, 492p. ; 24.6cm

    Harvard Tercentenary Publications

    PKUL（館藏號缺）

    附注：

      夾紙：一冊書內夾有編者贈書卡1張。

      其他：本書有2冊。

8422 Terrorisme et Communisme/par L. Trotsky. —Pétrograd: L'Internationale Communiste, 1920

    241p. ; 20.2cm

    PKUL（館藏號缺）

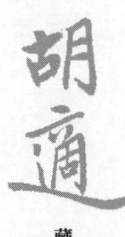

8423 Test Tubes and Dragon Scales/by George C. Basil. ——Chicago, Philadelphia, Toronto: The John C. Winston Company, 1940

XI, 316p. ; 23.2cm

PKUL（館藏號缺）

8424 Tests for Studies in Grammar/by Mabel C. Hermans. ——Boston, New York, Chicago, San Francisco: Henry Holt and Company, [n.d.]

[42]p. ; 19.4cm

PKUL（館藏號缺）

8425 The Text of Yi King/by Z. D. Sung. ——Shanghai: The China Modern Education Co., 1935

XVI, 369p. ; 18.7cm

PKUL（館藏號缺）

附注：

題記：題名頁有胡適鋼筆題記："沈仲濤。"

8426 Textbook of Biochemistry/by Pan Yuan-King. ——Peiping: The Commercial Press, Ltd., 1935

XVIII, 443p. ; 22.3cm

PKUL（館藏號缺）

附注：

題記：題名頁有贈書者題記："適之先生惠存,元耿敬贈。"

8427 Texts from the Buddhist Canon, Commonly Known as Dhammapada, with Accompanying Narratives/by Samuel Beal. ——London: Trübner & Co., 1878

VIII, 176p. ; 21.7cm

Trübner's Oriental Series

PKUL（館藏號缺）

8428 Le Théatre Chinois/by Tchou-Kia-Kien. —Pékin：Albert Nachbaur, 1927

21p. ; 32.7cm

PKUL（館藏號缺）

附注：

題記：題名頁後頁有作者題記："適之先生斧正,朱家健敬贈。"

8429 Theory of History/by Frederick J. Teggart. —New Haven：Yale University Press, 1925

XIX, 231p. ; 23.4cm

PKUL（館藏號缺）

附注：

題記：扉頁有作者題記："Dr. Hu Shih, with the cordial regards of Frederick J. Teggart. April 5, 1927。"

8430 The Theory of Legal Science/by Huntington Cairns. —Chapel Hill：The University of North Carolina Press, 1941

VIII, 155p. ; 21.3cm

PKUL（館藏號缺）

附注：

題記：扉頁有作者題記："For Dr. Hu Shih, in the sincest of the deluge with damiration and regards, Huntington Cairns, July 4, 1941。"

8431 The Theory of the Leisure Class：An Economic Study of Institutions/by Thorstein Veblen. —New York：Vanguard Press, 1926

VIII, 404p. ; 18.2cm

PKUL（館藏號缺）

8432 Theosophy, the Path of the Mystic/by Katherine Tingley. —Point Loma：Woman's International Theosophical League, 1922

185p. ; 17.3cm

PKUL（館藏號缺）

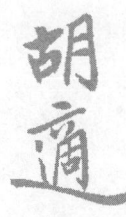

8433 There Is a Nip in the Air and Other Southwest Pacific Rhymes/by Harold Riegelman. —[s. l.]:[s. n.], 1945

61p. ; 24cm

PKUL（館藏號缺）

附注：

题記：扉頁有作者題記："To my classmate and friend Hu Shih, from Harold Riegelman, Xmas 1945。"

8434 They Wanted War/by Otto D. Tolischus. —New York：Reynal & Hitchcock, 1940

VIII, 340p. ; 22cm

PKUL（館藏號缺）

8435 Things Chinese：Being Notes on Various Subjects Connected with China/by J. Dyer Ball. —New York：Charles Scribner's Sons, 1893

497, XIVp. ; 21.7cm

PKUL（館藏號缺）

8436 Things Japanese：Being Notes on Various Subjects Connected with Japan/by Basil Hall Chamberlain. —London：Kegan Paul, Trench, Trübner & Co. , Ltd. , 1891

503p. ; 21.7cm

PKUL（館藏號缺）

8437 Third Class World：A Roving Philosopher Observes the Common Man/by Marion J. Bradshaw. —[s. l.]：Alliance, The Bradshaw Printing Company, [n. d.]

266p. ; 24.4cm

PKUL（館藏號缺）

附注：

題記:封內貼有作者題記:"Oct. 29, 1938, Dear Dr. Hu Shih: I send you herewith a copy of a book which grew out of a year in the East, during which you kindly gave me time from your busy life. Chapter 14 deals largely with yourself, in an appreciative way. Please accept the book as an acknowledgement of your kindness, and with hopes of great success in your present high mission. M. J. Bradshaw, 319 union, Bango, Me。"

8438 Thirty Seconds Over Tokyo/by Ted W. Lawson. —New York: Random House, 1943

221p. ; 18.6cm

PKUL（館藏號缺）

8439 This Is My Story/by Louis Francis Budenz. —New York, London: McGraw-Hill Book Company, Inc., 1947

XV, 379p. ; 20.2cm

PKUL（館藏號缺）

附注：

印章:扉頁有傅斯年簽名"Fu SSn-nien, 1947"。

8440 This Is Our World/by Paul B. Sears. —Norman: University of Oklahoma Press, 1937

XI, 292p. ; 19.8cm

PKUL（館藏號缺）

8441 This Troubled World/by Eleanor Roosevelt. —New York: H. C. Kinsey & Company, Inc., 1938

47p. ; 18.8cm

PKUL（館藏號缺）

附注：

題記:扉頁有胡適鋼筆簽名"Hu Shih, Jan. 4, 1938"。

8442 Thomas Hobbes/by A. E. Taylor. —London：Archibald Constable & Co.，Ltd.，1908

　　VII，129p. ；17.5cm

　　PKUL（館藏號缺）

　　附註：

　　　題記：扉頁有胡適鉛筆簽名"Suh Hu, March 1919"。

8443 Thomas Jefferson：World Citizen/by Elbert D. Thomas. —New York：Modern Age Books，1942

　　VIII，280p. ；21.5cm

　　PKUL（館藏號缺）

　　附註：

　　　題記：扉頁有作者題記："To Dr. Hu Shih, Elbert Thomas, March 3/43。"

8444 Thomas Jefferson's Garden Book，1766-1824/by Thomas Jefferson. —Philadelphia：The American Philosophical Society，1944

　　XIV，704p. ；24.1cm

　　PKUL（館藏號缺）

8445 Thomas Percy and His Chinese Studies/by Ch'ên Shou-yi. —[s. l.]：[s. n.]，[n. d.]

　　202-230p. ；23.6cm

　　Repinted from *The Chinese Social & Political Science Review*

　　PKUL（館藏號缺）

　　附註：

　　　題記：封面有作者題記："適之先生教正，受頤敬呈。"

8446 The Thought and Character of William James：As revealed in Unpublished Correspondence and Notes，Together with His Published Writings/by Ralph Barton Perry. —Boston：Little，Brown，and Company，1936

　　2 Vols.（XXXVIII，826，XXII，786p.）；24.2cm

PKUL（館藏號缺）

8447 Thought and Expression in the Sixteenth Century Vol. II/by Henry Osborn Taylor. —New York：The Macmillan Company, 1920

　　432p. ；22.5cm

　　PKUL（館藏號缺）

8448 Thoughts; Letters; Minor Works/by Blaise Pascal. —New York：P. F. Collier & Son, 1910

　　451p. ；19.5cm

　　The Harvard Classics No. 48

　　PKUL（館藏號缺）

　　附注：

　　　印章：扉頁有胡適簽名"Suh Hu"。

8449 A Thousand Shall Fall/by Hans Habe. —New York：Harcourt, Brace and Company, 1941

　　442p. ；21.5cm

　　PKUL（館藏號缺）

　　附注：

　　　其他：封內貼有"胡適的書"藏書票。

8450 The Three Musketeers/by Alexandre Dumas. —London, Calcutta, Sydney：George G. Harrap & Co. , Ltd. , 1920

　　554p. ；22.5cm

　　PKUL（館藏號缺）

　　附注：

　　　題記：扉頁有胡適題記："英譯插圖本《俠隱記》,胡適,十三,五,卅。"

8451 Three Plays for Puritans/by Bernard Shaw. —New York：Brentano's, 1906

　　XLI, 301p. ；19.5cm

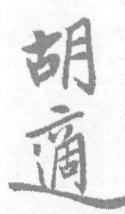

PKUL（館藏號缺）

附注：

印章：封内有"E. P. Allen"鋼筆簽名。

題記：扉頁有胡適毛筆簽名"Hu Shih, March 1921"；扉頁另有某人鉛筆題贈"Edgar"。

8452 Three Plays for Puritans/by Bernard Shaw. —Leipzig：Bernhard Tauchnitz, 1919

384p. ; 16.4cm

Collection of British Authors, Tauchnitz Edition

PKUL（館藏號缺）

8453 Three Tales/by Gustave Falubert. —New York：Alfred A. Knopf, Inc. , 1924

178p. ; 17.1cm

PKUL（館藏號缺）

附注：

題記：扉頁有胡適題記："Hu Shih. Peking, 1925. 三篇皆不甚佳。適之。十四,八,十二。"

8454 Thunder on the Left/by Christopher Morley. —London：Penguin Books, 1937

255p. ; 17.8cm

PKUL（館藏號缺）

8455 Thunderhead/by Mary O'Hara. —Philadelphia, New York：J. B. Lippincott Company, 1943

353p. ; 20.9cm

PKUL（館藏號缺）

8456 Tibet and the Origin of Man/by A. W. Grabau. —[s. l.]：[s. n.], [n. d.]

317-325p. ; 24.5cm

Reprinted from *Geografiska Annaler* 1935

PKUL（館藏號缺）

附注：

題記：封面有作者題記："Dr. Hu Shih, with the regard, A. W. Grabau。"

8457 Tibet：A Geographical, Ethnographical, and Historical Sketch, Derived from Chinese Sources/by W. Woodville Rockhill. —Peking：[s. n.], 1939

288p. ; 23.4cm

Extract from the Journal of the Royal Asiatic Society of Great Britain and Ireland

PKUL（館藏號缺）

附注：

其他：本書封面脫落，缺封底。

8458 Time and Free Will/by Henri Bergson; translated by F. L. Pogson. —London：George Allen & Unwin, Ltd., 1913

XXIII, 252p. ; 22.8cm

PKUL（館藏號缺）

8459 The Time for Decision/by Summer Welles. —New York, London：Harper & Brothers Publishers, 1944

VII, 431p. ; 22.2cm

PKUL（館藏號缺）

8460 The Time Is Now! /by Pierre Van Paassen. —New York：The Dial Press, 1941

80p. ; 20.3cm

PKUL（館藏號缺）

附注：

題記：扉頁有贈書者題記："In fond remembrance to Dr. Hu Shih, a rare and gentle gentleman. Gerhard Herman。"

8461 The Timeless Land/by Eleanor Dark. —New York：The Macmillan Company, 1941

IX, 499p. ; 21.7cm

PKUL（館藏號缺）

8462 The Tinder Box of Asia/by George E. Sokolsky. —New York：Doubleday, Doran & Company, Inc., 1933

XII, 453p. ; 20cm

PKUL（館藏號缺）

附注：

題記：扉頁內頁有作者題記："To my oldest friend in China, Hu Shih, from George E. Sokolsky, New York, Sept. 16, 1933。"

8463 To the Finland Station：A Study in the Writing and Acting of History/by Edmund Wilson. —New York：Harcourt, Brace and Company, 1940

509p. ; 21.5cm

PKUL（館藏號缺）

附注：

印章：扉頁有胡適簽名"Hu Shih"。

8464 To the Lighthouse/by Virginia Woolf. —London：The Hogarth Press, 1927

320p. ; 19.1cm

PKUL（館藏號缺）

附注：

印章：題名頁鈐有"摩曼"朱文方印；書末鈐有"志摩"朱文方印，並有建築畫一幅，有某人鋼筆題記："by James Wood, from 8 King's Parade。"

8465 Tōjūrō's Love and Four Other Plays/by Kikuchi Kwan; translated by Glenn W. Shaw. —Tokyo：The Hokuseido, 1925

V, 138p. ; 18.6cm

PKUL（館藏號缺）

附注：

題記：扉頁有胡適簽名"Hu Shih, Tokyo, May 2, 1927"。

8466 Tom Bryan: First Warden of Fircroft/by H. G. Wood, Arthur E. Ball. —London: George Allen & Unwin Ltd., 1922

 156p. ; 18.3cm

 PKUL（館藏號缺）

8467 The Touch of Nutmeg and More Unlikely Stories/by John Collier. —New York: The Press of the Readers Club, 1943

 VIII, 247p. ; 22cm

 PKUL（館藏號缺）

8468 Tourist's Vade Mecum of French Colloquial Conversation: With Vocabularies, Tables, and Imitated Pronunciation of Every Word. —London: Sir Isaac Pitman & Sons, Ltd., 1931

 VIII, 95p. ; 16.8cm

 PKUL（館藏號缺）

8469 Towards an Enduring Peace: A Symposium of Peace Proposals and Programs, 1914 – 1916/by Randolph S. Bourne. —New York: American Association for International Conciliation, [n. d.]

 XV, 336p. ; 18.8cm

 PKUL（館藏號缺）

 附注：

  題記：扉頁有胡適題記："Suh Hu, Gift of the American Association for International Conciliation, N. Y. C., September, 1916。"

  內附文件：頁166、167間夾有"某經"1916年8月24日給胡適的明信片1張。

8470 Trade and Tariffs of Certain Pacific Countries/by Philip G. Wright. —Honolulu: The Institute of Pacific Relations, 1933

 279p. ; 22.8cm

PKUL（館藏號缺）

附注：

印章：封面有胡適鋼筆簽名"Hu Shih"。

8471 The Tragedy of Hamlet, Prince of Denmark/by William Shakespeare. —Boston：D. C. Heath & Co., Publishers, [n. d.]

224p.；16.3cm

PKUL（館藏號缺）

附注：

印章：扉頁有陳鍾英簽名"C. S. Stephenson Cheng"。

題記：扉頁有胡適題記："此吾友陳鍾英之書也，庚戌將出都，向鍾英假得是書，舟中讀之。七月匆匆去國，遂攜之東行。辛亥用作校課，細細校讀，並加丹黃，是冊遂不能歸趙矣。書此以志吾故人之思。適之"；另扉頁內頁有胡適題記："蕭氏哀劇之一《漢納特》，適之。"

批注圈劃：書中有胡適批注圈劃116頁，正文部分幾乎全部都有。

8472 The Tragedy of Hamlet, Prince of Denmark/by William Shakespeare. —Washington：National Home Library Foundation, 1935

177p.；16.3cm

PKUL（館藏號缺）

8473 The Tragedy of Romeo and Juliet/by Henry Norman Hudson, Ebenezer Charlton Black. —Boston, New York, Chicago, London, Atlanta, Dallas, Columbus, San Francisco：Ginn and Company, 1916

LV, 150p.；17.2cm

The New Hudson Shakespeare

PKUL（館藏號缺）

8474 The Tragic Fallacy：A Study of America's War Policies/by Mauritz A. Hallgren. —New York, London：Alfred A. Knopf, 1937

VIII, 474p., XIV；21.6cm

PKUL（館藏號缺）

附注：

　　印章：扉頁鈐有"HU SHIH"藍文印。

8475 The Tragic Sense of Life: In Men and in Peoples/by Miguel de Unamuno; translated by J. E. Crawford Litch. —London: Macmillan and Co., Limited, 1921

　　XXXV, 332p. ; 22.2cm

　　PKUL（館藏號缺）

　　附注：

　　　　題記：扉頁有某人題記，不能辨識。

　　　　批注圈劃：書内數頁有胡適批注圈劃。

　　　　夾紙：書内夾有火車票1張。

8476 Translations and Reprints from the Original Sources of European History Vol. I. —Philadelphia: The Department of History of the University of Pennsylvania, 1910

　　24, 24, 42, 36, 36p. ; 20.9cm

　　PKUL（館藏號缺）

8477 The Travels of an Alchemist: The Journey of the Taoist Ch'ang Ch'un from China to the Hindukush at the Summons of Chingiz Khan/by Arthur Waley. —London: George Routledge & Sons, Ltd., 1931

　　XI, 166p. ; 21.7cm

　　PKUL（館藏號缺）

　　附注：

　　　　題記：扉頁有胡適題記："魏萊譯《長春真人西遊記》，適之，在紐約買的。卅五，四，卅。"

8478 The Travels of Marco Polo, the Venetian. —London: J. M. Dent & Sons, Ltd.; New York: E. P. Dutton & Co., 1911

XVI, 461p. ; 17.3cm

Everyman's Library: Travel and Topography

PKUL（館藏號缺）

附註：

印章：扉頁後頁鈐有"適盫藏書"朱文圓印。

題記：扉頁有胡適題記："S. Hu, Feb. 1913.《馬可頗羅遊記》,適之。"

8479 Treasure Island/by Robert Louis Stevenson. —Washington: National Home Library Foundation, 1932

194p. ; 16.7cm

PKUL（館藏號缺）

8480 Treasure Island/by Robert Louis Stevenson. —New York: The Macmillan Company; London: Macmillan & Co., Ltd., 1919

XXIX, 229p. ; 14.3cm

PKUL（館藏號缺）

8481 A Treasury of Science/by Harlow Shapley, Samuel Rapport, Helen Wright. —New York: Harper & Brothers Publishers, 1943

XI, 716p. ; 21.4cm

PKUL（館藏號缺）

附註：

題記：扉頁有題記："適之兄大壽。三二,十二,十七。源。"（按：似應爲陳源,胡適生日簽名簿1943年簽名中似有陳源。）

8482 Treaties and Agreements with and Concerning China, 1894–1919 Vol. II/by John V. A. MacMurray. —New York: Oxford University Press, 1921

929–1729p. ; 25.9cm

PKUL（館藏號缺）

8483 Treaty of Peace with Germany. —New York: American Association for

International Conciliation, 1919

265p. ; 19.7cm

PKUL（館藏號缺）

8484 The Treaty of Peace with Germany in the United States Senate: An Exposition and a Review/by George A. Finch. —Greenwichi: American Association for International Conciliation, 1920

65p. ; 19.1cm

PKUL（館藏號缺）

8485 A Treatise of Human Nature/by David Hume. —Oxford: The Clarendon Press, 1896

XXIII, 709p. ; 19.1cm

PKUL（館藏號缺）

附注：

題記：扉頁有胡適簽名"Suh Hu, November 1914"。

批注圈劃：書内209頁有胡適批注圈劃。

夾紙：頁16、17、80、81,532、533、588、589間各夾有讀書卡片1張,頁494、495間夾有讀書卡片2張。另有胡適鉛筆字迹。頁478、479間夾有紙條1張。另有九處夾有紙條。

8486 Treaty-Making Power under the Constitution of Japan/by Tsunejiro Miyaoka. —Worcester: Carnegie Endowment for International Peace, Division of Intercourse and Education, 1926

17p. ; 19.6cm

PKUL（館藏號缺）

8487 Trois Pieces de Ting Sy-ling/traduites par Tchang Tien-Ya. —Pekin: La Politique de Pékin, 1932

46p. ; 26.3cm

Colletion de la "Politique de Pekin"

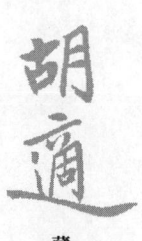

PKUL(館藏號缺)

附注:

題記:一冊封面有譯者題記:"西材著《一隻馬蜂》,適之先生指教,生奠亞,一九三二,七月。"

其他:本書爲綫裝,有2冊。

8488 The Trojan Women of Euripides/by Gilbert Murray. —New York: Oxford University Press, 1915

93p. ; 18.4cm

PKUL(館藏號缺)

附注:

題記:扉頁有胡適題記:"Suh Hu, Feb. 1916. New York. 此書有二特色,一為世界最早之亡國哀劇,一為世界最早之'非攻文'之一。適。"書名頁後頁有鉛筆題記:" OF EURIPIDES. TRANSLATED BY GILBERT MURRAY",似不是胡適筆迹;此頁右上角有鉛筆書"起"字。

8489 The True Facts about the Expropriation of the Oil Companies' Properties in Mexico. —Mexico City: Government of Mexico, 1940

271p. ; 22cm

PKUL(館藏號缺)

8490 The Trumpet-Major/by Thomas Hardy. —Leipzig: Bernhard Tauchnitz, 1881

2 Vols. (287, 272p.) ; 16.3cm

Collection of British Authors, Tauchnitz Edition

PKUL(館藏號缺)

8491 The Truth about Galileo and Medieval Science/by Joseph McCabe. —Girard: Haldeman-Julius Company, [n.d.]

64p. ; 12.8cm

Little Blue Book

PKUL(館藏號缺)

8492 Truth and Reality: An Introduction to the Theory of Knowledge/by John Elof Boodin. —New York: The Macmillan Company, 1911

 IX, 334p. ; 19.8cm

 PKUL（館藏號缺）

 附注：

  題記:扉頁有胡適鉛筆簽名"Suh Hu, 1917"。

8493 Tseng Kuo-Fan, Pioneer, Promoter of the Steamship in China/by Gideon Chen. —Peiping: Department of Economics, Yenching University, 1935

 98p. ; 21.5cm

 PKUL（館藏號缺）

8494 Twenty Years After/by Alexandre Dumas. —London: J. M. Dent & Sons Ltd. ; New York: E. P, Dutton & Co. , [n.d.]

 751p. ; 17.3cm

 Everyman's Library: Fiction

 PKUL（館藏號缺）

 附注：

  題記:扉頁有胡適毛筆簽名"Hu Shih, May, 1924"。

8495 The Twenty-Fifth Anniversary of the Founding of the Cosmos Club of Washington D. C./by The Cosmos Club. —Washington: The Cosmos Club, 1904

 351p. ; 20.9cm

 PKUL（館藏號缺）

8496 Twenty-Five Years, 1892-1916/by Viscount Grey. —New York: Frederick A. Stokes Company, 1925

 2 vols. ; 23.8cm

 PKUL（館藏號缺）

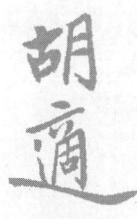

附注：

　　題記：第1卷扉頁有胡適題記："葛雷自傳，周鯁生兄送我的。適之。卅一年八月。"

8497　Twin Stars of China: A Behind-the-Scenes Story of China's Valiant Struggle for Existence by a U. S. Marine Who Lived & Moved With the People/by Evans Fordyce Carlson. —New York: Dodd, Mead & Company, 1940

　　XIV, 331p. ; 22cm

　　PKUL（館藏號缺）

8498　'Twixt Land and Sea Tales/by Joseph Conrad. —Leipzig: Bernhard Tauchnitz, 1912

　　271p. ; 16.8cm

　　Collection of British Authors, Tauchnitz Edition

　　PKUL（館藏號缺）

8499　Two Leaders of Asia/by K. M. Panikkar. —University of Calcutta: [s. n.], [n. d.]

　　4p. ; 24.7cm

　　Reprinted from *The Calcuta Review*, July, 1943

　　PKUL（館藏號缺）

　　附注：

　　題記：封面有作者題記："To His Excellency Prof. Hu Shih, with the compliments of K. M. Panikkar。"

8500　Two Survived: The Story of Tapscott and Widdicombe, Who Were Torpedoed in Mid-Atlantic and Survived Seventy Days in an Open Boat/by Guy Pearce Jones. —New York: Random House, 1941

　　XVII, 192p. ; 18.6cm

　　PKUL（館藏號缺）

　　附注：

题记:扉页有作者题记:"To His Excellency, Dr. Hu Shih, in memory of a pleasant and edifying meeting, Guy Pearce Jones。"

8501　Two Too Many/by Cecilia Sieu-Ling Zung. —London: Samuel French, Ltd. , 1939

　　106p. ; 18.7cm

　　PKUL(館藏號缺)

　　附注:

　　　　印章:題名頁有作者簽名"Cecilia Sieu-Ling Zung"。

8502　Two Treatises on Civil Government/by John Locke. —London: George Routledge and Sons Limited; New York: E. P. Dutton and Co. , [n.d.]

　　320p. ; 18.1cm

　　PKUL(館藏號缺)

　　附注:

　　　　題記:扉頁有胡適鋼筆簽名"Suh Hu, Dec. 1915, New York"。

　　　　夾紙:頁190、191間夾有帶字紙條1張。

8503　Two Years before the Mast, and Twenty-Four Years After/by R. H. Dana Jr. . —New York: P. F. Collier & Son, 1909

　　424p. ; 19.5cm

　　The Harvard Classics No. 23

　　PKUL(館藏號缺)

　　附注:

　　　　印章:扉頁有胡適簽名"Suh Hu"。

8504　Types of Cultural Response/by Hu Shih. —[s.l.]: [s.n.], 1934

　　529-552p. ; 23.1cm

　　Reprinted from *The Chinese Social & Political Science Review* Vol. XVII, No. 4, 1934

　　PKUL(館藏號缺)

8505 Types of Philosophy/by William Ernest Hocking. —New York, Chicago, Boston, Atlanta, San Francisco, Dallas: Charles Scribner's Sons, 1929

　　XV, 462p. ; 21.5cm

　　PKUL（館藏號缺）

　　附注：

　　　　題記：封套有某人鋼筆題記："這是從胡適之先生處借來的書。"

8506 U. S. Foreign Policy: Shield of the Republic/by Walter Lippmann. —Boston: Little, Brown and Company, 1943

　　XVII, 177p. ; 19.7cm

　　PKUL（館藏號缺）

8507 U. S. War Aims/by Walter Lippmann. —Boston: Little, Brown and Company, 1944

　　XII, 235p. ; 19.7cm

　　PKUL（館藏號缺）

8508 Unbeaten Tracks in Japan/by Isabella L. Bird. —London: John Murray, 1880

　　2 vols. ; 20.3cm

　　PKUL（館藏號缺）

　　附注：

　　　　印章：第1卷扉頁有原書主簽名"R. Lilley"。

8509 Under the Greenwood Tree/by Thomas Hardy. —Washington: National Home Library Foundation, 1932

　　166p. ; 16.6cm

　　PKUL（館藏號缺）

8510 Union Now with Britain/by Clarence K. Streit. —New York, London: Harper & Brothers Publishers, [n.d.]

XV, 234p. ; 19.1cm

PKUL（館藏號缺）

附注：

題記：封面有作者題記："For Dr. Hu Shih, Ambassador of China and a pioneer works in this field, with the warmest admiration for your people and yourself, sincerely, Clarence Streit, March 8, 41。"

8511 The Union Prayerbook for Jewish Worship Part I. —Cincinnati：The General Conference of American Rabbis, 1941

395p. ; 16.5cm

PKUL（館藏號缺）

附注：

題記：題名頁前頁有贈書者題記："To a righteous man as a token of our friendship of the heart in the milding of a world of justice and peace, Hanna Justinford, May '42。"

8512 The Unique Function of Education in American Democracy/by National Education Association of the United States. —Washington：Educational Policies Commission, [n.d.]

129p. ; 23.4cm

PKUL（館藏號缺）

8513 United Nations Conference for the Establishment of an Educational, Scientific and Cultural Organisation. —Washington：The American Council of Learned Societies, [n.d.]

16p. ; 28cm

PKUL（館藏號缺）

8514 The United Nations Conference on International Organization：Provisional List of Members of the Delegations and Officers of the Secretariat. —San Francisco：[s.n.], 1945

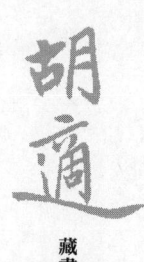

70p. ; 14.5cm

PKUL（館藏號缺）

附注：

印章：扉頁有胡適鉛筆簽名"Hu Shih"。

8515 The United States and Japan's New Order/by William C. Johnstone. —London, New York, Toronto: Oxford University Press, 1941

XII, 392p. ; 21.8cm

PKUL（館藏號缺）

附注：

夾紙：書內夾有出版社請寫書評卡 1 張。

8516 The United States in the Mediterranean/by William Reitzel. —New Haven: [s.n.], 1947

31p. ; 28.4cm

Yale Institute of International Studies

PKUL（館藏號缺）

8517 The United States in World Affairs: An Account of American Foreign Relations, 1934-1935/by Whitney H. Shepardson, William O. Scroggs. —New York, London: Harper & Brothers, 1935

XIII, 357p. ; 22cm

PKUL（館藏號缺）

8518 The United States of Europe/by Alfred M. Bingham. —New York: Duell, Sloan and Pearce, 1940

IX, 336p. ; 19.3cm

PKUL（館藏號缺）

8519 United States Policy Toward China: Diplomatic and Public Documents, 1839-1939/by Paul Hibbert Clyde. —Duham: Duke University Press, 1940

XV, 321p. ; 23.4cm

PKUL（館藏號缺）

附注：

 題記：題獻頁有作者題記："With the author's grateful appreciation of your scholarship and your personal generosity. Paul H. Clyde, June 28/40"；此外，題獻頁印有"Dedicated to His Excellency Dr. Hu Shih, father of the modern Chinese Written Language educational leader and reformer, historian, essayist, poet and diplomat"。

 批注圈劃：目錄頁兩處有胡適批注圈劃。

 與胡適的關係：題名頁前頁印有胡適題寫本書中文題名："美國對華政策百年來要件選讀，胡適題"；另印有"胡適"朱文長方印。

8520 The Unity of India: Collected Writings, 1937–1940/by Jawaharlal Nehru. —［s. l.］: Lindsay Drummond, 1941

 VIII, 432p. ; 21.4cm

 PKUL（館藏號缺）

附注：

 夾紙：書內夾有名片1張，郵寄圖書信封1個。

8521 L'Université de Caen, son Passé- son Présent/par M. Guerrin. —［s. l.］: Imprimerie Artistique Malherbe de Caen,［n. d.］

 296p. ; 25.1cm

 PKUL（館藏號缺）

8522 The University of Chicago Press Catalogue of Books and Journals, 1891–1941. —Chicago: The University of Chicago Press, 1941

 XXXI, 432p. ; 23.5cm

 PKUL（館藏號缺）

8523 University of London, the Calendar for the Year 1926–1927. —London: University of London Press, Ltd., 1926

839, 24p. ; 21.4cm

PKUL（館藏號缺）

8524 The University of Pennsylvania Today: Its Buildings Departments & Work/ by Cornell M. Dowlin. —Philadelphia: University of Pennsylvania, 1940

X, 209p. ; 22.1cm

PKUL（館藏號缺）

8525 The Unknown Guest/by Maurice Maeterlinck. —New York: Dodd, Mead and Company, 1914

410p. ; 19.1cm

PKUL（館藏號缺）

附注：

題記：扉頁有胡適題記："Christmas gift from M. & Mrs. L. E. Patterson, December, 1914。"

夾紙：頁186、187間夾有藏書標籤1張。

8526 Der Ursprung Der Ju und Ihre Beziehung zu Konfuzius und Lau-Dsï/von Hu Schï. —[s.l.]: [s.n.], [n.d.]

141-171p. ; 27.2cm

PKUL（館藏號缺）

8527 Urvaçī, Een Oud-Indisch Tooneelstuk Vankālidāsa/by R. H. Van Gulik. —S-Gravenhage: N. V. Adī Poestāka, 1932

84p. ; 24.1cm

PKUL（館藏號缺）

附注：

題記：扉頁有作者題記："To Prof. Hu Shih, with the author's compliments。"

夾紙：書內夾有贈書者寄贈包裹地址1張。

8528 The Use of the Self: Its Conscious Direction in Relation to Diagnosis, Functioning and the Control of Reaction/by F. Matthias Alexander. —New York: E. P. Dutton and Co., Inc., 1932

 XIX, 143p. ; 19.3cm

 PKUL（館藏號缺）

 附注：

  夾紙:書內夾有贈書卡 1 張,上書"with Seasons Greetings and Best wishes from J. H. Tsui"。

8529 Utilitarianism, Liberty, and Representative Government/by John Stuart Mill. —London: J. M. Dent & Sons Ltd. ; New York: E. P. Dutton & Co., Inc., 1910

 XXVI, 393p. ; 17.4cm

 Everyman's Library: Philosophy & Theology

 PKUL（館藏號缺）

 附注：

  批注圈劃:書內 32 頁有胡適批注圈劃。

8530 The Valor of Ignorance/by Homer Lea. —New York, London: Harper & Brothers Publishers, 1942

 343p. ; 21.1cm

 PKUL（館藏號缺）

 附注：

  批注圈劃:書內 69 頁有胡適批注圈劃。

8531 The Value and Destiny of Individual: The Gifford Lectures for 1912, Delivered in Edinburgh University/by B. Bosanquet. —London: Macmillan and Co., Limited, 1913

 XXXII, 331p. ; 22cm

 PKUL（館藏號缺）

 附注：

印章：題名頁鈐有"適盦藏書"朱文圓印。

題記：扉頁有胡適鋼筆簽名"Suh Hu, May, 1915"。

批注圈劃：書內 105 頁有胡適批注圈劃。

8532 Vanity Fair：A Novel without a Hero/by William Makepeace Thackeray. —London：J. M. Dent & Sons Ltd. ; New York：E. P, Dutton & Co. , 1908

XV, 699p. ; 17.1cm

Everyman's Library：Fiction

PKUL（館藏號缺）

8533 The Vicomete de Bragelonne/by Alexandre Dumas. —London：J. M. Dent & Sons Ltd. ; New York：E. P, Dutton & Co. , 1912

3 Vols.（VIII, 542, 566, 568p.）; 17.1cm

Everyman's Library：Fiction

PKUL（館藏號缺）

附注：

題記：第 3 卷書末有胡適鉛筆題記："Finished May 10, 1924, Hu Shih."

8534 Victor Hugo：A Realistic Biography of the Great Romantic/by Matthew Josephson. —Garden City：Doubleday, Doran & Co. , Inc. , 1942

XII, 514p. ; 23.5cm

PKUL（館藏號缺）

8535 Victorian Prose Masters/by W. C. Brownell. —New York：Charles Scribner's Sons, 1901

VIII, 289p. ; 20.3cm

PKUL（館藏號缺）

附注：

題記：扉頁有贈書者題記："贈適之哥，弟致遠。"

8536 Une Vie/par Guy de Maupassant. —New York：Boni and Liveright, Inc. ,

[n. d.]

VI, 188p. ; 17cm

The Modern Library of the World's Best Books

PKUL（館藏號缺）

附注：

其他:本書有 23 冊。

8537 La Vie Affective Livre II. —[s. l.]：[s. n.]，[n. d.]

336p. ; 22.2cm

PKUL（館藏號缺）

附注：

其他:本書缺封面。

8538 The Vigil of a Nation/by Lin Yutang. —New York：The John Day Company, 1945

VII, 262p. ; 20.5cm

PKUL（館藏號缺）

附注：

題記:扉頁有作者題記："適之兄，弟語堂，卅四年春。"

8539 Virgil's Aeneid/by Charles W. Eliot. —New York：P. F. Collier & Son, 1909

432p. ; 19.5cm

The Harvard Classics No. 13

PKUL（館藏號缺）

附注：

印章:扉頁有胡適簽名"Suh Hu"；題名頁鈐有"適盦藏書"朱文圓印。

8540 Virgin Soil/by Ivan S. Turgenev. —London：J. M. Dent & Sons Ltd. ; New York：E. P. Dutton & Co. , [n. d.]

IX, 317p. ; 17.3cm

Everyman's Library：Fiction

PKUL（館藏號缺）

附注：

題記：扉頁有胡適題記："Suh Hu, Feb. 22, 1915.《新土》適"；扉頁內頁有胡適題記："In an introduction to Constance Garnett's version (London: Wm. Heinemann, 1901), Edward Garnett wrote: 'In drawing Solomin, Turgenev did not achieve an artistic success. ... By temperament Turgenev was antagonistic to it, and accordingly Solomin is a little too doubtful, a little too undetermined, a little too wooden.' It seems to me that the contrary is true. The characterization of Solomin is a great 'artistic success'. The author could not possibly be antagonistic to this type of man. Indeed, he worshipped it, longed for its coming, and dreamed of it。"

批注圈劃：書內82頁有胡適批注圈劃。

8541 Visva-Bharati. —[s. l.]: Santiniketan and the Educational Institutions, 1929

[II,19]p.；25cm

Bulletin No. 12

PKUL（館藏號缺）

附注：

題記：題名頁有作者題記："Visva-Bharati represents India where she has her wealth of mind which is for all. Visva-Bharati acknowledges India's obligation to offer to others the hospitality of her best culture and India's right to accept from others their best. Rabindranath Tagore"；封面有贈書者題記："To Prof. Hu Shih。"

8542 Vocabulaires Garnier: Russian-English. —Paris: Librairie Garnier Frères, [n. d.]

VIII, 377p.；13.3cm

PKUL（館藏號缺）

8543 A Vocabulary and Hand-Book of the Chinese Language/by Justus Doolittle. —Foochow: Rozario, Marcal, and Company, 1872

2 Vols. ; 21.8cm

PKUL（館藏號缺）

附注：

 印章:第 2 冊封內及扉頁有原書主簽名"Robert Lilley"。

 其他:第 1 冊缺封面至前言部分。

8544 The Voice of Fighting Russia/by Lucien Zacharoff. —New York: Alliance Book Corporation, 1942

 XIX, 336p. ; 24.2cm

 PKUL（館藏號缺）

8545 The Voice of the City: Further Stories of the Four Million/by O. Henry. —Doubleday, Page & Company, 1908

 244p. ; 19.4cm

 PKUL（館藏號缺）

8546 The Voice of the City: Further Stories of the Four Million/by O. Henry. —New York: Doubleday, Page & Company, 1911

 243p. ; 19.4cm

 PKUL（館藏號缺）

 附注：

  題記:扉頁有胡適題記:"Suh Hu, May 31, 1917。倭亨利之短篇,二十五種。"

8547 The Voice of the Silence/by H. P. B. . —Point Loma: The Aryan Theosophical Press, 1909

 XIII, 123p. ; 14.1cm

 PKUL（館藏號缺）

8548 La Voix de la Chine/par S. E. Wang King KY. —Bruxelles: Office de Publicité, 1929

241p. ；18.4cm

PKUL（館藏號缺）

8549 Volcanic Isle/by Wilfrid Fleisher. —Garden City，New York：Doubleday，Doran & Company, Inc. , 1941

IX, 345p. ；21.2cm

PKUL（館藏號缺）

附注：

其他：封内貼有"胡適的書"藏書票。

8550 Voltaires the Age of Louis XIV/by Voltaire；translated by Martyn P. Pollack. —London：J. M. Dent & Sons Ltd. ；New York：E. P, Dutton & Co. ，［n. d.］

XIV, 475p. ；17.3cm

Everyman's Library：History

PKUL（館藏號缺）

8551 Le Voyage de Monsieur Perrichon/par Labiche，Martin. —Boston：D. C. Heath & Co. , 1909

VIII, 126p. ；16.5cm

PKUL（館藏號缺）

附注：

題記：扉頁有胡適題記："法國喜劇之一《滑稽旅行》，適之。"

批注圈劃：書内49頁有胡適批注圈劃；書末有胡適鉛筆字迹。

8552 The Voyage of the Beagle/by Charles Darwin. —New York：P. F. Collier & Son, 1909

547p. ；19.5cm

The Harvard Classics No. 29

PKUL（館藏號缺）

附注：

印章：扉頁有胡適簽名"Suh Hu"。

8553 Voyages and Travels: Ancient and Modern/by Charles W. Eliot. —New York: P. F. Collier & Son, 1910

　　394p. ; 19.5cm

　　The Harvard Classics No. 33

　　PKUL（館藏號缺）

　　附注：

　　　　印章：扉頁有胡適簽名"Suh Hu"。

8554 Waifs and Strays from the Far East; Being a Series of Disconnected Essays on Matters Relating to China/by Frederic Henry Balfour. —London: Trübner & Co. ; Shanghai: Kelly & Walsh, 1876

　　223p. ; 24.1cm

　　PKUL（館藏號缺）

8555 The Wallet of Kai Lung/by Ernest Bramah. —London: [s. n.], 1900

　　286p. ; 17.3cm

　　PKUL（館藏號缺）

　　附注：

　　　　題記：扉頁有贈書者題記："To a singleman of the autochthonous, Dr. Hu Shih, with warmest regards, □, Shanghai, Jun 28, 1930。"

8556 Wang Li, Chung-kuo yü-fa li-lun/by Lien-sheng Yang. —[s. l.] : [s. n.], [n. d.]

　　62-75p. ; 25cm

　　Reprinted from *Harvard Journal of Asiatic Studies*, Volume 10, Number 1, June, 1947

　　PKUL（館藏號缺）

　　附注：

　　　　題記：封面有作者題記："適之先生教正，學生聯陞敬呈。"

8557 Wang Wei, le Poète/par Liou Kin-Ling. —Paris: Jouve & Cie, Éditeurs, 1941

165p. ; 25.3cm

PKUL（館藏號缺）

附注：

題記：扉頁有作者題記："au Dr. Hoo She en □ de respectueure et profonde admiration, V. Liou Kin Ling, Washington, le 5 juillet 1941。"

8558 War/by Ludwig Renn. —New York: A. L. Burt Company, 1929

342p. ; 19.4cm

PKUL（館藏號缺）

8559 War and Diplomacy in the Japanese Empire/by Tatsuji Takeuchi. —London: George Allen & Unwin, Ltd. , [n. d.]

505p. ; 23.5cm

PKUL（館藏號缺）

8560 War and the Ideal of Peace/by Henry Rutgers Marshall. —New York: Duffield & Co. , 1915

234p. ; 18.8cm

PKUL（館藏號缺）

附注：

題記：扉頁有胡適題記："Suh Hu, March 1916. Gift of the Am. Association for International Conciliation。"

8561 War Memoirs of David Lloyd George, 1914-1915/by David Lloyd George. —Boston: Little, Brown, and Company, 1933

VII, 469p. ; 24.3cm

PKUL（館藏號缺）

附注：

題記：扉頁有胡適鋼筆簽名"Hu Shih, August 1942"。

8562 War Memoirs of David Lloyd George, 1915-1916/by David Lloyd George. —
Boston: Little, Brown, and Company, 1933
449p. ; 24.2cm
PKUL（館藏號缺）

8563 War Memoirs of David Lloyd George, 1916-1917/by David Lloyd George. —
Boston: Little, Brown, and Company, 1934
X, 597p. ; 23.5cm
PKUL（館藏號缺）

8564 War Memoirs of David Lloyd George, 1917/by David Lloyd George. —Boston:
Little, Brown, and Company, 1934
603p. ; 23.5cm
PKUL（館藏號缺）

8565 War Memoirs of David Lloyd George, 1917-1918/by David Lloyd George. —
Boston: Little, Brown, and Company, 1934
464p. ; 23.5cm
PKUL（館藏號缺）

8566 War Memoirs of David Lloyd George, 1918/by David Lloyd George. —Boston:
Little, Brown, and Company, 1934
XII, 406p. ; 23.5cm
PKUL（館藏號缺）

8567 War Notes of a Casual/by Harold Riegelman. —New York: The Ballou Press,
1931
191p. ; 21.6cm
PKUL（館藏號缺）
附注：
題記：扉頁有作者題記："With affectionate regards to my classmate and

friend Hu Shih. From Harold Riegelman. 6/7/'39"；扉頁另有胡適題記：
"吾友 Riegelman 的從軍日記，他只印了六十本，這是第五十九本。
適之。"

8568 Warning to the West/by Shridharani. —New York：Duell, Sloan and Pearce,
1942

　　IX, 274p. ; 20.2cm

　　PKUL（館藏號缺）

　　附注：

　　　　題記：扉頁有作者題記："To Dr. Hu Shih, in profound respect, and in
　　　　common devotion to the future of the two great and good neighbors-China and
　　　　India-Krishnalal Shridharani。"

8569 Washington Is Like That/by W. M. Kiplinger. —New York, London：Harper &
Brothers Publishers, 1942

　　VI, 522p. ; 21.5cm

　　PKUL（館藏號缺）

　　附注：

　　　　印章：扉頁有胡適紅筆簽名"Hu Shih"。

8570 Washington Waltz：Diplomatic People and Policies/by Helen Lombard. —
New York：Alfred A. Knopf, 1941

　　271, VIp. ; 20.2cm

　　PKUL（館藏號缺）

8571 The Way and Its Power：A Study of the Tao Tê Ching, and Its Place in
Chinese Thought/by Arthur Waley. —London：George Allen & Unwin Ltd.,
1934

　　262p. ; 19.8cm

　　PKUL（館藏號缺）

　　附注：

印章：扉頁有胡適朱筆簽名"Hu Shih"。

批注圈劃：書內 14 頁有胡適批注圈劃。

夾紙：書內夾有紙條 1 張。

8572 The Way of Contentment/by Ken Hoshino. —London：John Murray, 1913

124p. ; 16.9cm

The Wisdom of the East Series

PKUL（館藏號缺）

8573 The Way of Life：According to Laotzu/by Witter Bynner. —New York：The John Day Company, 1944

76p. ; 18.2cm

PKUL（館藏號缺）

8574 The Ways of Knowing, or the Methods of Philosophy/by Wm. Pepperell Montague. —New York：The Macmillan Company, 1925

427p. ; 21.4cm

PKUL（館藏號缺）

附注：

題記：扉頁有作者題記："To My Friend Professor Hu Shih, from Wm. Pepperell Montague。"

8575 We Would Know Jesus/by John A. Scott. —New York, Cincinati, Chicago：The Abingdon Press, 1936

176p. ; 19.3cm

PKUL（館藏號缺）

附注：

夾紙：書內夾有"Robert McDougal"名片 1 張。

8576 Wealth & Culture/by Eduard C. Lindeman. —New York：Harcourt Brace and Company, 1936

IX, 135p. ; 28cm

PKUL（館藏號缺）

8577 Webster's New International Dictionary of the English Language/by W. T. Harris, F. Sturges Allen. —Springfield：G. & C. Merriam Company, 1910

LXXX, 2620p. ; 31cm

PKUL（館藏號缺）

附注：

印章：封面鈐有"適盦藏書"朱文圓印、"藏暉室主人"朱文方印。

其他：本書有破損，封面脫落。

8578 Wei Shih Er Shih Lun/by Vasubandhu; translated by Clarence H. Hamilton. —New Haven：American Oriental Society, 1938

82p. ; 25.9cm

PKUL（館藏號缺）

附注：

夾紙：書內夾有譯者贈書名片1張。

8579 The Well of Loneliness/by Radclyffe Hall. —New York：Blue Ribbon Books, 1928

506p. ; 20.7cm

PKUL（館藏號缺）

附注：

印章：扉頁鈐有"HU SHIH"藍文印。

8580 The Wellsprings of Liberty/by Edouard Herriot; translated by Richard Duffy. —New York, London：Funk & Wagnalls Company, 1939

VIII, 279p. ; 20.7cm

PKUL（館藏號缺）

附注：

印章：扉頁後頁鈐有"HU SHIH"藍文印。

8581 Wên-Chien Tzǔ-erh Chī/by Thomas Francis Wade. —London: Trübner & Co., 1867

    XII, 453p. ; 29.5cm

    PKUL（館藏號缺）

    附注：

        題記：扉頁有原書主簽名"Robert Lilley, Chefoo, 20 July, 1867"。

        夾紙：書内夾有讀書便箋2頁。

8582 Werden und Wirken der Büchergilde Gutenberg/von Helmut Dressler. —Zurichi: Büchergilde Gutenberg, [n.d.]

    218p. ; 23.3cm

    PKUL（館藏號缺）

    附注：

        内附文件：頁78、79間夾有Walter Bosshard 1947年10月27日致胡適函1頁。

8583 Westering/by Thomas Hornsby Ferril. —New Haven: Yale University Press, 1934

    90p. ; 20.3cm

    PKUL（館藏號缺）

    附注：

        題記：扉頁有贈書者題記："with deepest appreciation and affection for Dr. Hu Shih from Edith and Ben Cherington, Ouser, Colorado, May 3, 1942。"

8584 Western Literature: Vol. 2, Specimens of Literature with Introductions Embodying the Chief Tradition of Europeans and Americans/by A. E. Zucker. —Shanghai: Commercial Press, Ltd., 1922

    XIX, 509p. ; 20.4cm

    PKUL（館藏號缺）

    附注：

題記:扉頁有胡適題記:"Hu Shih. At the cave of Mist and Twilight, Hangchow. June, 1923。"

8585 Western Literature: Volume III, the Renaissance/by A. E. Zucker. — Shanghai: The Commercial Press, Limited, 1928

XII, 526p. ; 20.4cm

PKUL（館藏號缺）

附注:

印章:一冊扉頁有原書主簽名"Yin Yu Sung";另有胡適鉛筆書寫原書主姓名"殷玉松"。

批注圈劃:一冊書内批注處甚多,似爲原書主所作。

夾紙:一冊書内夾有數頁讀書筆記紙片。

其他:本書有2冊。

8586 Western Star/by Stephen Vincent Benét. —New York, Toronto: Farrar & Rinehart, Inc., 1943

VIII, 181p. ; 20.5cm

PKUL（館藏號缺）

附注:

内附文件:書内夾有本書書評1份。

8587 Western Stories/by Gene Autry. —New York: Dell Publishing Company, [n. d.]

191p. ; 16.1cm

PKUL（館藏號缺）

8588 What Are We to Do with Our Lives/by H. G. Wells. —London: William Heinemann Limited, 1931

148p. ; 18.9cm

PKUL（館藏號缺）

8589 What Does Gandhi Want? /by T. A. Raman. —New York, London, Toronto:

Oxford University Press, 1942

X, 117p. ; 20.3cm

PKUL（館藏號缺）

附注：

印章:扉頁有胡適簽名"Hu Shih"。

8590 What Every Girl Should Know/by Margaret Sanger. —London: Jonathan Cape, 1922

109p. ; 19.4cm

PKUL（館藏號缺）

8591 What Germany Forgot/by James T. Shotwell. —New York: The Macmillan Company, 1940

VI, 152p. ; 20.4cm

PKUL（館藏號缺）

附注：

題記:一冊扉頁有胡適題記:"Gift of the author, Dr. James T. Shotwell, Hu Shih";一冊扉頁有作者題記:"To Dr. Hu Shih, with high regard, James T. Shotwell。"

其他:本書有2冊。

8592 What I Believe/by Bertrand Russell. —London: Kegan Paul, Trench, Trubner & Co., Ltd., 1925

95p. ; 15.7cm

PKUL（館藏號缺）

附注：

題記:扉頁有作者題記:"Dr. Hu Shih, from the author, Bertrand Russell。"

8593 What War Means: The Japanese Terror in China/by H. J. Timperley. —London: Victor Gollancz Ltd., 1938

288p. ; 18.4cm

PKUL（館藏號缺）

附注：

題記：扉頁有作者題記："To Dr. Hu Shih, with the author's warmest regards, H. J. Timperley, Paris, July, 1935。"

8594 "What You Want to Say and How to Say It" in German/by W. J. Hernan. —London: George Newnes, Limited, 1930

95p. ; 13.1cm

PKUL（館藏號缺）

附注：

批注圈劃：書內有鉛筆圈劃。

8595 The Wheels of Chance/by H. G. Wells. —London: J. M. Dent & Sons Ltd., [n.d.]

VI, 297p. ; 17.5cm

The Wayfarer's Library

PKUL（館藏號缺）

8596 When Peacocks Called/by Hilda Seligman. —London: John Lane The Bodley Head, 1940

296p. ; 19cm

PKUL（館藏號缺）

附注：

印章：題名頁前頁鈐有"曾經滄海"藍文方印。

題記：題名頁前頁有作者題記："Lincoln House, Wimbledon Common, it has been a great pleasure to meet some of the wise men of China-War huan-Shee jien nidi mien! My I claim one moment more of your precious time to glance at pages 187-188, Hilda Seligman, 1945"；另扉頁後頁有作者題記："Hilda Seligman, Lincoln House, Wimbledon Common, 1945。"

內附文件：書內夾有明信片1張。

8597 When There Is No Peace/by Hamilton Fish Armstrong. —New York：The Macmillan Company, 1939

　　236p. ; 20.4cm

　　PKUL（館藏號缺）

　　附注：

　　　　題記：扉頁有贈書者題記："Dr. Hu Shih, from E. C. Carter, January 30 1939."

　　　　內附文件：封內貼有贈書者致胡適書信1封。

8598 Where Do We Go from Here? /by Harold F. Laski. —New York：The Viking Press, 1940

　　192p. ; 21.2cm

　　PKUL（館藏號缺）

　　附注：

　　　　其他：封內貼有"胡適的書"藏書票；另貼有贈書卡片1張，上書"Dr. Hu, with best wishes & greeting, Mr. & Mrs. Tsech'ang Kent Chang"。

8599 Whirligigs/by O. Henry. —[s.l.]：Doubleday, Page & Company, 1910

　　314p. ; 19.4cm

　　PKUL（館藏號缺）

　　附注：

　　　　批注圈劃：目錄頁有胡適鉛筆圈劃。

8600 White China：An Austral-Asian Sensation/by John H. C. Sleeman. —Sydney：Published by the author, [n.d.]

　　VIII, 343p. ; 19.3cm

　　PKUL（館藏號缺）

8601 Whither Asia? A Study of Three Leaders/by Kenneth Saunders. —New York：The Macmillan Company, 1933

　　221p. ; 19cm

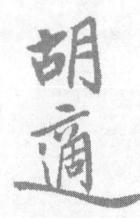

PKUL（館藏號缺）

附注：

題記：扉頁有胡適鉛筆題記："Hu Shih, Dec. 1933. From the Publisher。"

8602 The Whole World & Company/by Gretchen Green. —New York：Reynal & Hitchcock, 1936

313p. ；20.6cm

PKUL（館藏號缺）

附注：

題記：扉頁有作者題記："For Dr. Hu Shih, Gretchen Green。"

8603 Why I Am an Infidel/by Luther Burbank. —Girard：Haldeman-Julius Company, [n.d.]

32p. ；12.5cm

Little Blue Book

PKUL（館藏號缺）

8604 Why I Do Not Fear Death/by E. Haldeman-Julius. —Girard：Haldeman-Julius Company, [n.d.]

Little Blue Book

32p. ；12.7cm

PKUL（館藏號缺）

8605 Why War? Essays and Addresses on War and Peace/by Nicholas Murray Butler. —New York：Charles Scribner's Sons；London：Charles Scribner's Sons Ltd. , 1940

XII, 323p. ；18.2cm

PKUL（館藏號缺）

8606 Wickford Point/by John P. Marquand. —Boston：Little, Brown and Company, 1939

458p. ；20.8cm

PKUL（館藏號缺）

附注：

　　印章:扉頁鈐有"HU SHIH"藍文印。

　　題記:扉頁有胡適題記:"孟治先生送給我的。"

　　批注圈劃:書末有胡適注明閱讀日期"May 9，1939. Hu Shih"。

8607　The Widening Stain/by Bolingbroke Johnson. —New York：Alfred A. Knopf, Inc.，1942

242p. ；19cm

PKUL（館藏號缺）

附注：

　　題記:扉頁有贈書者題記:"To Hu Shih, with the warmest regards of Morris Bishop. 'If he who reads a mystery story wastes time, god's most precious gift, how shall we term him who writes one?' —Confucius。"

8608　William/by E. H. Young. —New York：The Press of the Readers Club, 1926

VII, 312p. ；21.9cm

PKUL（館藏號缺）

8609　William Allen White of Emporia/by Frank C. Clough. —New York, London：Whittlesey House, 1941

XIV, 264p. ；21.6cm

PKUL（館藏號缺）

附注：

　　其他:封內貼有"胡適的書"藏書票。

8610　William Henry Welch and the Heroic Age of American Medicine/by Simon Flexner, James Thomas Flexner. —New York：The Viking Press, 1941

X, 539p. ；24.2cm

PKUL（館藏號缺）

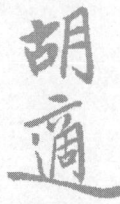

附註：

　　批注圈劃：書內多處有胡適圈劃；書末有胡適鋼筆注明閱讀日期"June 27, 1947, Hu Shih"。

　　其他：封內貼有"胡適的書"藏書票。

8611　William James: The Man and the Thinker/by Max C. Otto, Dickinson S. Miller, et al. —Madison: The University of Wisconsin Press, 1942

　　147p. ; 22cm

　　PKUL（館藏號缺）

8612　Wills: How to Make and How to Break Them/by Harry Hibschman. —Girard: Haldeman-Julius Company, [n. d.]

　　64p. ; 12.6cm

　　Little Blue Book

　　PKUL（館藏號缺）

8613　Wind, Sand and Stars/by Antoine de Saint Exupéry; translated by Lewis Galantière. —New York: Reynal & Hitchcock, 1939

　　306p. ; 22cm

　　PKUL（館藏號缺）

附註：

　　批注圈劃：書內130餘頁有鉛筆圈劃。

8614　Winnie-the-Pooh/by A. A. Milne. —[s. l.]: E. P. Dutton & Company, 1926

　　VIII, 158p. ; 19.2cm

　　PKUL（館藏號缺）

附註：

　　題記：扉頁後頁有胡適題記："Gift from N. B. S. 。"

8615　The Winning of the Far East: A Study of the Christian Movement in China,

Korea and Japan/by Sidney L. Gulick. —New York: George H. Doran Company, 1923

 IX, 185p. ; 19.4cm

 PKUL（館藏號缺）

8616 Winning the Peace in the Pacific: A Chinese View of Far Eastern Postwar Plans and Requirements for a Stable Security System in the Pacific Area/by S. R. Chow. —New York: The Macmillan Company, 1944

 XI, 98p. ; 20.8cm

 PKUL（館藏號缺）

 附註：

  題記：題名頁前頁有作者題記："適之老兄指正，鯁生，卅三年元旦，於紐約。"

8617 Winter's Tales/by Isak Dinesen. —New York: Random House, 1942

 313p. ; 20.2cm

 PKUL（館藏號缺）

8618 Wisdom of the East Taoist Teachings/by Lionel Giles. —New York: E. P. Dutton and Company, 1912

 121p. ; 16.7cm

 PKUL（館藏號缺）

 附註：

  印章：書名頁鈐有"適盦藏書"朱文圓印。

  題記：扉頁有胡適題記："Suh Hu, August, 1914.《列子》七篇，其第七篇他譯。"

8619 With Japan's Leaders: An Intimate Record of Fourteen Years as Counsellor to the Japanese Government, Ending December 7, 1941/by Frederick Moore. —New York: Charles Scribner's Sons, 1942

 365p. ; 20.2cm

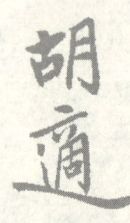

PKUL（館藏號缺）

附注：

題記：扉頁有胡適鋼筆簽名"Hu Shih, December 1942, New York City"。

8620 With Malice Toward Some/by Margaret Halsey. —New York：Simon and Schuster, 1938

278p. ；20.7cm

PKUL（館藏號缺）

附注：

題記：扉頁有贈書者題記："To Hu Shih, with love from Robby Lowitz and John Dewey。"

8621 Within a Budding Grove /by Marcel Proust. —New York：The Modern Library, 1944

356p. ；16.6cm

PKUL（館藏號缺）

附注：

題記：扉頁有贈書者題記："To Dr. Hu Shih, from Yi Ying。"

8622 Within a Budding Grove/by Marcel Proust；translated by C. K. Scott Moncrieff. —London：Chatto and Windus, 1929

2 vols.（396, 356p. ）；17.7cm

The Phoenix Libray

PKUL（館藏號缺）

8623 Wives/by Gamaliel Bradford. —New York, London：Harper & Brothers Publishers, 1925

XIII, 298p. ；22.3cm

PKUL（館藏號缺）

8624 Woman and the New Race/by Havelock Ellis. —Girard：Haldeman-Julius

Company, [n. d.]

 64p. ; 12.7cm

 Little Blue Book

 PKUL（館藏號缺）

8625 A Woman's Heart, and Other Stories/by H. G. Wells. —Girard：Haldeman-Julius Company, [n. d.]

 64p. ; 12.6cm

 Little Blue Book

 PKUL（館藏號缺）

8626 Woman's Place in Chinese History/by Hu Shih. —New York：Trans-Pacific News Service, Inc. , [n. d.]

 15p. ; 22.9cm

 PKUL（館藏號缺）

8627 Women at the Hague：The International Congress of Women and Its Results/by Jane Addams, Emily G. Balch, Alice Hamilton. —New York：The Macmillan Company, 1915

 Ⅶ, 171p. ; 17.3cm

 PKUL（館藏號缺）

 附注：

  題記：扉頁有胡適題記："Suh Hu, March 1916. Gift of the Am. Asso. for International Conciliation。"

8628 Women in the Factory：An Administrative Adventure, 1893 to 1921/by Adelaide Mary Anderson. —London：John Murray, 1922

 XIII, 316p. ; 19.4cm

 PKUL（館藏號缺）

8629 The Wonder of Words：An Introduction to Language for Everyman/by Isaac

Goldberg. —New York, London: D. Appleton-Century Company Incorporated, 1938

 XII, 485p. ; 22.6cm

 The World's Classics

 PKUL（館藏號缺）

 附注：

  印章：扉頁鈐有"HU SHIH"藍文印。

8630 The Wonders of Life: A Popular Study of Biological Philosophy/by Ernst Haeckel; translated by Joseph McCabe. —London: Watts & Co., 1916

 160p. ; 21.4cm

 PKUL（館藏號缺）

8631 Wong's System to Chinese Lexicography/by Y. W. Wong. —Shanghai: The Commercial Press, Limited, 1926

 48p. ; 22.7cm

 PKUL（館藏號缺）

 附注：

  題記：封面有作者題記："適之先生教正，雲五"；另扉頁有胡適題記："一橫刁，二三竪。撇四，叉撇五。點捺同是六，有叉變成七。左勾右勾八九畢。十五，四，二三，戲作歌訣。適之。"

8632 Woodbrooke: Its History and Aims/by Arnold S. Rowntree. —Selly Oak: Robert Davis, Woodbrooke, 1923

 87p. ; 18.9cm

 PKUL（館藏號缺）

8633 Woodrow Wilson and World Settlement: Written from His Unpublished and Personal Material/by Ray Stannard Baker. —Garden City, New York: Doubleday, Page & Company, 1922

 3 vols. ; 24.2cm

PKUL（館藏號缺）

8634 Woodrow Wilson as I Know Him/by Joseph P. Tumulty. —Garden City：
Doubleday, Page & Co., 1921

XVI, 553p. ; 23.4cm

PKUL（館藏號缺）

附注：

印章：封內鈐有"Dr. E. S. Bishop"藍文印。

批注圈劃：書內 302 頁有胡適圈劃。

8635 Woodrow Wilson：Life and Letters, Youth 1856–1890/by Ray Stannard
Baker. —Garden City：Doubleday, Page & Co., 1927

XXXIV, 335p. ; 24.5cm

PKUL（館藏號缺）

8636 Woodrow Wilson：Life and Letters, Princeton 1890–1910/by Ray Stannard
Baker. —Garden City：Doubleday, Page & Co., 1927

VI, 373p. ; 24.5cm

PKUL（館藏號缺）

8637 Woodrow Wilson：Life and Letters, Governor, 1910–1913/by Ray Stannard
Baker. —Garden City：Doubleday, Doran & Company, Inc., 1931

XII, 483p. ; 24.4cm

PKUL（館藏號缺）

8638 Woodrow Wilson：Life and Letters, President, 1913–1914/by Ray Stannard
Baker. —Garden City：Doubleday, Doran & Company, Inc., 1931

VI, 518p. ; 24.5cm

PKUL（館藏號缺）

8639 Woodrow Wilson：Life and Letters, Facing War, 1915–1917/by Ray Stannard

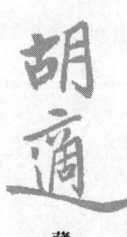

Baker. —Garden City: Doubleday, Doran & Company, Inc., 1937

XI, 543p.；24.5cm

PKUL（館藏號缺）

附注：

題記：書末有鉛筆題記："H. M. Hon. Wagner, Lake Station, Ruxton, Md.。"

8640 Woodrow Wilson: Life and Letters, War Leader, April 6, 1917 – February 28, 1918/by Ray Stannard Baker. —New York: Doubleday, Doran & Company, Inc., 1939

XIX, 604p.；23.8cm

PKUL（館藏號缺）

附注：

印章：扉頁有胡適鋼筆簽名"Hu Shih, 胡適"。

批注圈劃：書內數頁有胡適圈劃。

夾紙：書內五處夾有紙條。

8641 Woodrow Wilson's Principles of Democracy/by Robert R. Gailey. —Shanghai: The Commercial Press, Limited, [n.d.]

VIII, 205p.；19cm

PKUL（館藏號缺）

8642 The Woodrow Wilsons/by Eleanor Wilson McAdoo, Margaret Y. Gaffey. —New York: The Macmillan Company, 1937

X, 301p.；21.9cm

PKUL（館藏號缺）

8643 Word Families in Chinese/by Bernhard Karlgren. —Stockholm: [s.n.], 1934

9–120p.；26.5cm

reprinted from *The Bulletin of the Museum of Far Eastern Antiquities*, No. 5

PKUL（館藏號缺）

附注：

  題記：封面有作者題記："With the author's compliments"；另有胡適題記："高本漢古韵部論,胡適,廿三,十一,廿二寄到。"

8644 The Word "One" in Chinese Poetry/by Lin Tung-Chi. —[s. l.]：[s. n.],[n. d.]

  50-55p. ；24.4cm

  Reprinted from *The Journal of the North China Branch of the Royal Asiatic Society* Vol. LXVI

  PKUL（館藏號缺）

附注：

  題記：封面有作者題記："適之先生,林同濟呈。"

8645 The Work of the Open Court Publishing Co. .—Chicago：The Open Court Publishing Company, 1908

  208p. ；23.4cm

  PKUL（館藏號缺）

8646 Works of Art Silver and Furniture Belonging to the Century Association/by Charles Downing Lay, Theodore Bolton. —New York：The Century Association, 1943

  78p. ；21.6cm

  PKUL（館藏號缺）

8647 The Works of Li Po, the Chinese Poet/by Shigeyoshi Obata. —New York：E. P. Dutton & Co. , 1922

  XVIII, 236p. ；21.3cm

  PKUL（館藏號缺）

附注：

  題記：扉頁後頁有作者題記："胡適先生哂正,小畑熏良敬贈。"

8648 The Works of Rabelais/by François Rabelais. —[s. l.]：The Bibliophilist Society, [n. d.]

XX, 640p. ; 24.8cm

PKUL（館藏號缺）

8649 The World Almanac and Book of Facts for 1929/by Robert Hunt Lyman. —New York：The New York World, [n. d.]

925p. ; 20.6cm

PKUL（館藏號缺）

8650 The World Almanac and Book of Facts for 1944/by E. Eastman Irvine. —New York：New York World-Telegram, [n. d.]

912p. ; 21.4cm

PKUL（館藏號缺）

附注：

其他：書內夾有"秦子青"名片1張。

8651 The World Almanac and Book of Facts for 1946/by E. Eastman Irvine. —New York：The New York World-Telegram, 1946

816p. ; 20.9cm

PKUL（館藏號缺）

附注：

其他：本書缺封底。

8652 The World Almanac and Encyclopedia, 1917.—New York：The Press Publishing Co., [n. d.]

908p. ; 19.5cm

PKUL（館藏號缺）

附注：

其他：本書破損，缺封面、封底。

8653 The World-Conception of the Chinese: Their Astronomical, Cosmological, and Physico-Philosophical Speculations/by Alfred Forke. —London: Arthur Probsthain, 1925

XIV, 300p. ; 19.3cm

Probsthain's Oriental Series

PKUL（館藏號缺）

8654 The World Crisis, 1915/by Winston S. Churchill. —New York: Charles Scribner's Sons, 1923

XII, 578p. ; 22.8cm

PKUL（館藏號缺）

8655 The World Crisis: 1911-1914/by Winston S. Churchill. —New York: Charles Scribner's Sons, 1923

XII, 588p. ; 22.2cm

PKUL（館藏號缺）

附註：

印章：扉頁有胡適鋼筆簽名"Hu Shih"。

8656 World English: A Suggestion That We Simplify English as the International Language for the World/by J. W. Hamilton. —St. Paul: [s.n.], [n.d.]

9p. ; 22.8cm

PKUL（館藏號缺）

附註：

題記：扉頁有作者題記："To Dr. Shih-Chih, with the compliments of J. W. Hamilton。"

8657 A World in Ferment: Interpretations of the War for a New World/by Nicholas Murray Butler. —New York: Charles Scribner's Sons, 1919

VIII, 254p. ; 19.6cm

PKUL（館藏號缺）

8658 The World of Action/by Valentine Williams. —London: Hamish Hamilton, 1938

479p. ; 22cm

PKUL（館藏號缺）

附注：

題記：扉頁後頁有胡適題記："Gift of General and Mrs. William Crozier, September 1938, Hu Shih。"

8659 World Order in Historical Perspective/by Hans Kohn. —Cambridge: Harvard University Press, 1942

XIV, 352p. ; 19.3cm

PKUL（館藏號缺）

附注：

批注圈劃：書内 12 頁有胡適批注圈劃。

8660 A World to Live In/by Leland D. Case. —Chicago: Rotary International, [n.d.]

95p. ; 19.2cm

PKUL（館藏號缺）

8661 World's Great Short Stories/by M. E. Speare. —Cleveland, New York: The World Publishing Company, 1942

334p. ; 20.9cm

PKUL（館藏號缺）

8662 The World's Destiny and the United States: A Conference of Experts in International Relations. —Chicago: World Citizens Association, 1941

XX, 309p. ; 20.3cm

PKUL（館藏號缺）

8663 The World's Greatest War/by Holland Thompson. —New York: The Grolier

Society, 1921

2 Vols.（876 p.）; 24.2cm

The Book of History Volume XVI- XVII

PKUL（館藏號缺）

附注：

　　印章：兩卷扉頁均鈐有"HU SHIH"藍文印。

8664　A Wreath of Cloud: Being the Third Part of "The Tale of Genji"/by Lady Murasaki. —Boston and New York: Houghton Mifflin Company, The Riverside Press Cambridge, 1927

312p.; 22cm

PKUL（館藏號缺）

附注：

　　題記：扉頁有胡適簽名"Hu Shih, Tokyo, April 25, 1927"; 扉頁後頁有胡適題記："For the title, see p.53。"

　　批注圈劃：書內一頁有胡適圈劃；書末有胡適鉛筆注明閱讀日期"June 22, 1927. Hu Shih"。

8665　Written English/by Edwin C. Wooley. —Shanghai: The Commercial Press, Limited, 1918

XIII, 322p.; 18.4cm

PKUL（館藏號缺）

附注：

　　印章：扉頁鈐有"盧逮曾印"朱文方印；另有"Tai-tseng Lu"英文鉛筆簽名。

　　批注圈劃：書內有多處標注，但非胡適本人所寫。

8666　Written English: A Course of Lessons in the Main Things to Known in Order to Write English Correctly/by Edwin C. Wooley. —Boston, New York, Chicago: D. C. Heath & Co., Publishers, 1915

XIII, 317p.; 18.4cm

PKUL（館藏號缺）

附註：

夾紙：頁 60、61 間夾有書籤 1 枚。

8667 Wu Lien-Teh—A Short Autobiography/by Wu Lien-Teh. —［s. l.］：［s. n.］,［n. d.］

10p. ; 25cm

PKUL（館藏號缺）

附註：

題記：封面有作者題記："To Dr. Hu Shih, with compliments of Wu Lien-Teh。"

8668 Wuthering Heights/by Emily Brontë. —New York：Random House Publishers, 1943

XIV, 212p. ; 24.8cm

PKUL（館藏號缺）

附註：

印章：扉頁鈐有"廷芳長壽"朱文方印。

題記：扉頁有贈書者題記："適之吾兄五十三壽辰。廷芳，卓生敬贈。"

8669 Wuthering Heights/by Emily Bronte. —New York：Pocket Books, Inc., 1939

364p. ; 16.1cm

PKUL（館藏號缺）

附註：

題記：書末有胡適題記："Ludwig Renn：War, Dodd-Mead & Co., N. Y.（1929）。"

8670 Yang Koui Fei/par Ho Ju. —Paris：Albert Messein, Éditeur, 1935

43p. ; 19.3cm

PKUL（館藏號缺）

附註：

題記:扉頁有作者題記:"適之先生指正,何如郵贈,廿四年四月,巴黎。"

8671 Yankee Lawyer: The Autobiography of Ephraim Tutt/by Arthur C. Train. —
New York: Charles Scribner's Sons, 1943

XIII, 464p. ; 20.3cm

PKUL(館藏號缺)

附注:

題記:扉頁有胡適題記:"這是作者 Arthur Train 給我題的,他用的是書名主人名字。適之";另有作者題贈:"To my very dear and esteemed friend Dr. Hu Shih, with best wishes and sincere regards from the author. Ephraim Tutt。"

內附文件:書末貼有關于作者去世的剪報。

8672 Yarns of Valour/by McEwan Lawson. —London: The Livingstone Press, 1936

64p. ; 18.4cm

PKUL(館藏號缺)

8673 Yen Hsi Chai, a 17th Century Philosopher/by Mansfield Freeman. —[s. l.]: [s. n.], [n. d.]

70-91p. ; 24.2cm

Reprinted from *The Journal of the North China Branch of the Royal Asiatic Society*, Vol. LVII

PKUL(館藏號缺)

附注:

印章:封面有胡適鋼筆簽名"Hu Shih"。

8674 Yenching Windows. —Peiping: Yenching University, 1935

145p. ; 22.8cm

PKUL(館藏號缺)

附注:

內附文件:書內夾有 A. Douglas Rugh 致胡適英文書信1頁。

8675 Yin Chin Wen: The Tract of the Quiet Way with Extracts from the Chinese Commentary/by Teitaro Suzuki, Paul Carus. —Chicago: The Open Court Publishing Company, 1906

　　48p. ; 19.8cm

　　PKUL（館藏號缺）

8676 "Yin-Yang"/by Hardy Wilson. —Tasmania: J. Walch & Sons Pty. Ltd., [n.d.]

　　213p. ; 19.6cm

　　PKUL（館藏號缺）

8677 Yorkshire from the Air. —[s.l.]: The Yorkshire Post, [n.d.]

　　64p. ; 30.9cm

　　PKUL（館藏號缺）

8678 You Are Younger than You Think/by Martin Gumpert. —New York: Duell, Sloan and Pearce, 1944

　　IX, 244p. ; 20.9cm

　　PKUL（館藏號缺）

8679 Young Man with a Horn/by Dorothy Baker. —New York: The Press of the Readers Club, 1943

　　IX, 243p. ; 21.7cm

　　PKUL（館藏號缺）

8680 The Young Jefferson: 1743-1789/by Claude G. Bowers. —Boston: Houghton Mifflin Company, 1945

　　XXX, 544p. ; 19.4cm

　　PKUL（館藏號缺）

　　附注：

題記:扉頁有贈書者題記:"To Dr. Hu Shih with great admiration from Jane Yelle. Cambridge, June 4, 1945。"

8681 Your Career in Business/by Walter Hoving. —New York: Duell, Sloan & Pearce, 1940

211p. ; 18.7cm

PKUL (館藏號缺)

附注:

題記:扉頁有作者題記:"To Dr. Hu Shih, with my compliment, Walter Hoving。"

8682 Youth and Heredity/by Amram Scheinfeld, Morton D. Schweitzer. —New York: Frederick A. Stokes Company, 1939

XVII, 434p. ; 21.6cm

PKUL (館藏號缺)

8683 Yü Ch'ien, Staatsmann und Kriegsminister, 1398-1457/by Wolfgang Franke. —[s.l.]: [s.n.], [n.d.]

87-122p. ; 26cm

Reprinted from *Monumenta Serica, Journal of Oriental Studies of the Catholic University of Peking*, Vol. XI, fasc. 1, 1946

PKUL (館藏號缺)

附注:

題記:封面有作者題記:"□ Prof. Dr. Hu Shih, □□□, von Wolfgang Franke。"

8684 Yung-Ho-Kung, an Iconography of the Lamaist Cathedral in Peking Volume One/by Ferdinand Diederich Lessing. —Stockholm: [s.n.], 1942

XX, 179p. ; 29.1cm

Reports from the Science Expedition to the North-Western Provinces of China under the Leadership of Dr. Sven Hedin

PKUL（館藏號缺）

附注：

題記：扉頁有作者題記："To my dear friend Hu Shih in commemoration of happy days and in recognition of never-failing encouragement. Ferdinand D. Lessing, New York, December 1945。"

8685 Zen Buddhism and Its Influence on Japanese Culture/by Daisetz Teitaro Suzuki. —Kyoto：The Eastern Buddhist Society，[n. d.]

XII, 288p. ; 21.7cm

PKUL（館藏號缺）

附注：

題記：扉頁有胡適題記："To Dr. Hu Hsi, with the regards of the author Daisetz Teitaro Suzuki, Kawahara- Ward; Showa XVI (1941)。"

內附文件：頁6、7間夾有陳榮捷1941年4月26日致胡適函1封。

8686 Zur Rekonstruktion der Altchinesischen Endkonsonanten/by Walter Simon. —Berlin, Leipzig：Verlag von Walter de Gruyter & Co., 1928

21p. ; 24.1cm

Sonderabdruck aus den Mitteilungen des *Seminars für Orientalische Sprachen* Bd. XXX, Abteilung I

PKUL（館藏號缺）

附注：

題記：封面有作者德文題記。

（二）胡適紀念館館藏目錄

2766 101 Questions about Taiwan. —Taipei, Taiwan：Government Information Office, [n. d.]

36 p. ; 22.5 cm

HSMH(HS-N20F2-072)

2767 1984/by George Orwell. —New York: The American Library, 1959

256 p. ; 18 cm

HSMH(HS-N04F1-026)

附注:

印章:内封面頁鈐有"胡適的書"朱文方印。

2768 7 Years' Solitary: The Story of a Remarkable Woman Who Triumphed over Her Captors/by Edith Bone. —New York: Harcourt, Brace and Company, 1957

256 p. ; 21 cm

HSMH(HS-N04F1-036)

附注:

印章:内封面頁鈐有"胡適的書"朱文方印。

題記:扉頁有贈書者題贈:"To Dr Hu Shih W. K. G. P.。"

2769 Accent on Form: An Anticipation of the Science of Tomorrow/by Lancelot Law Whyte. —New York : Harper & Brothers Publishers, 1954

xi, 198 p. ; 19.5 cm

World Perspectives, Vol. 2

HSMH(HS-N19F4-026)

附注:

印章:内封面頁鈐有"胡適的書"朱文方印。

2770 Accents of the World's Philosophies/by Huston Smith. —Honolulu, Hawaii: The University of Hawaii Press, 1957

7-19 p. ; 25.5 cm

Philosophy East and West: A Journal of Oriental and Comparative Thought, Vol. 7, Nos. 1 & 2, April, July 1957

HSMH(HS-N20F1-037)

附注:

批注圈劃:其中一冊的封面裏在 Lily Pao-hu Chong 旁有藍筆記"(鄭寶滬)"。

與胡適的關係:胡適是顧問編輯(Advisory Editors)之一。

其他:抽印本,館藏 2 冊。

2771 Addresses Made in Honor of Henry L. Stimson at the Club House, April 6, 1950/addressed by Paul Manship, et al. —New York: MCML Printed for the Century Association, 1950

43 p.; 21.7 cm

HSMH(HS-N04F1-037)

附註:

印章:內封面頁鈐有"胡適的書"朱文方印。

2772 Adenovirus Infections in Chinese Army Recruits on Taiwan/by F. H. Tai, J. T. Grayston, P. B. Johnston, R. L. Woolridge, C. H. Lee and T. J. Wu. —Taipei, Taiwan: United States Naval Medical Research No. 2, 1959

11 p.; 26.5 cm

NAMRU TWO, October 12, 1959 (NM 52 05 02. 10. 3)

HSMH(HS-N19F5-017)

附註:

其他:(1)釘書針裝訂。(2)館藏 2 冊。

2773 The Adventure of Chess/by Edward Lasker. —Garden City, New York: Doubleday & Company, 1950

xxiv, 296 p., illus., viii plates; 21.6 cm

HSMH(HS-N20F1-024)

附註:

印章:扉頁有胡適簽名"Hu Shih New York City March 28, 1951";內封面頁鈐有"胡適的書"朱文方印。

夾紙:書中有夾紙 1 張。

2774 Adventures in Time and Space: An Anthology of Modern Science-Fiction Stories/edited by Raymond J. Healy and J. Francis McComas. —New York: Random House, 1946

    xv, 997 p.; 20.9 cm

    HSMH (HS-N19F4-019)

    附注:

        印章:扉頁鈐有"胡適的書"朱文方印。

        題記:另一扉頁有題記:"…Please return to Ely Culbertson。"

        批注圈劃:書中有鉛筆注記數處。

2775 The Aeneid of Virgil/translated by C. Day Lewis. —Garden City, New York: Doubleday & Company, Inc., 1953

    320 p.; 18.2 cm

    HSMH (HS-N04F5-038)

    附注:

        印章:內封面頁鈐有"胡適的書"朱文方印。

        批注圈劃:書中有鉛筆批注劃綫數處。

        夾紙:頁40、41間有夾紙1張。

2776 The Age of Enlightenment: The 18th Century Philosophers/selected, with an introduction and interpretive commentary by Isaiah Berlin. —New York: The New American Library, 1956

    282 p.; 18.2 cm

    HSMH (HS-N04F5-032)

    附注:

        印章:內封面頁鈐有"胡適的書"朱文方印。

2777 The Age of Faith: A History of Medieval Civilization—Christian, Islamic, and Judaic—from Constantine to Dante: A.D. 325-1300/by Will Durant. —New York: Simon and Schuster, 1950

    xviii, 1196 p.; 25 cm

The Story of Civilization, Part IV

HSMH（HS-N12F4-030）

附注：

印章：內封面頁鈐有"胡適的書"朱文方印。

2778 Agricultural Planning and Production/by T. H. Shen. —Taipei, Taiwan：Committee D., Economic Stabilization Board, Executive Yuan, 1958

42 p.；26 cm

HSMH（HS-N19F5-027）

附注：

印章：內封面頁鈐有"胡適的書"朱文方印。

批注圈劃：頁 22 有校改兩處。

其他：作者爲沈宗瀚。

2779 Agricultural Resources of China/by T. H. Shen（沈宗瀚）. —Ithaca, New York：Cornell University Press, 1951

xviii, 407 p.；24.1 cm

HSMH（HS-N03F3-018）

附注：

印章：內封面頁鈐有"胡適的書"朱文方印。

2780 An Album of Crayon and Water-color Sketches by an Unknown Artist/bought by Eugene Delafield. —［s. l.］：［s. n.］, ［n. d.］

［22］p., illus.；31 cm

HSMH（HS-N21F2-020）

附注：

印章：扉頁鈐有"胡適的書"朱文方印。

題記：附泛黃紙套 1 個，紙套上有胡適黑筆題記："An album of crayon and water-color sketches by an unknown artist, of Chinese boats & peasant life in a coastal area. Bought of Mr. Eugene Delafield, July 15, 1954. Hu Shih。"

批注圈劃：封面內頁有鉛筆注記。

其他：書名依胡適題記訂定。

2781 Alexander Hamilton：Selections Representing His Life, His Thought and His Style/edited by Bower Aly. ——New York：The Liberal Arts Press, 1957

xxvi, 261 p. ; 18.5 cm

Forum Books, No. 14

HSMH（HS-N04F3-033）

附注：

印章：内封面頁鈐有"胡適的書"朱文方印。

2782 All Man Are Brothers（Shui Hu Chuan）/translated from the Chinese by Pearl S. Buck; with an introduction by Lin Yutang and illustrations by Miguel Covarrubias. ——New York：For the Members of the Limited Editions Club, 1948

2 Vols.（688 p.）; 31 cm

HSMH（HS-N20F1-050, HS-N20F1-51）

附注：

印章：兩冊内封面頁均鈐有"胡適的書"朱文方印；第2冊版權頁有繪圖者簽名"Miguel Covarrubias"，並注記"H. S."。

夾紙：第1冊頁94、95間夾有書目登錄卡1張。

其他：(1)封面有中文書名"水滸傳"。(2)譯者中文名爲"賽珍珠"。

2783 Allegory and Courtesy in Spenser：A Chinese View/by Hsin-Chang Chang. ——Edinburgh：Edinburgh University Press, 1955

227 p. ; 22.7 cm

Edinburgh University Publications：Language & Literature, No. 8

HSMH（HS-N04F5-040）

附注：

題記：扉頁有作者題贈："謹贈胡適先生並請多多指正 張心滄 一九六一年九月於英國劍橋。"

夾紙：頁106、107間有夾紙2張，一張記"2 Publications To Dr. Hu Shih Academia Sinica Taipei Formosa"；另一張記"From H. C. Chang University

2689

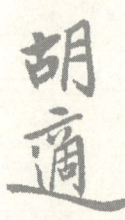

of Cambridge 16 Brooklands Avenue Cambridge England"。

2784 An Almanac for Moderns/by Donald Culross Peattie; with drawings by Lynd Ward. —New York: G. P. Putnam's Sons, 1935

396 p. ; 20.9 cm

HSMH（HS-N19F6-018）

附注：

印章：內封面頁鈐有"胡適的書"朱文方印。

題記：扉頁有鉛筆題記："Chi-Chen Wang My 4th or 5th copy 1957（?）"，鋼筆題記："To Hu Shih for whiling away the Bath Room minutes With Best Regards Chi-Chen Wang August 1960。"

批注圈劃：書中有批注劃綫數十處。

摺頁：頁 121 右下有摺角。

其他：本書爲第 2 次印刷。

2785 Always the Young Strangers/by Carl Sandburg. —New York: Harcourt, Brace and Company, 1953

445 p. ; 22 cm

HSMH（HS-N04F3-006）

附注：

印章：扉頁鈐有"胡適的書"朱文方印。

題記：扉頁有胡適題記："山保格的自傳 孟治送我的 胡適 一九五三,三,廿四。"

2786 America's Arts and Skills/by the editors of *Life*; with an introduction by Charles F. Montgomery. —New York: E. P. Dutton & Co., Inc., 1957

172p., illus. ; 36 cm

HSMH（HS-N13F1-013）

附注：

其他：內封面頁有"Presented by the UNITED STATES INFORMATION SERVICE Taipei 台北 美國大使館新聞處敬贈"的藍色戳印。

2787 America's Retreat from Victory: The Story of George Catlett Marshall/by
Joseph R. McCarthy. —New York: The Devin-Adair Company, 1951

187 p.; 18.7 cm

HSMH（HS-N04F2-004）

附註：

　　印章：扉頁鈐有"胡適的書"朱文方印。

　　夾紙：扉頁夾有書籍訂購單2張。

　　內附文件：書中夾有1951年12月11日Alfred Kohlberg致讀者函1張，信函上有紅筆劃綫。

　　相關記載：陳之邁致胡適函，告知受友人Forrest Davis之托，寄上1951年6月14日Joe McCarthy參議員的演講紀錄"America's Retreat from Victory"，參見館藏號：HS-US01-036-001。

2788 The American College Dictionary/edited by Clarence L. Barnhart. —New York: Rondom House, 1947

xl, 1432 p.; 25.2 cm

HSMH（HS-N19F1-045）

附註：

　　印章：內封面頁鈐有"胡適的書"朱文方印。

　　題記：扉頁有V. D. Hartman題贈："Father's Day 1950 Rily。"

2789 American Diplomacy during the World War/by Charles Seymour. —Baltimore: The Johns Hopkins Press, 1934

xii, 417 p.; 19.8 cm

HSMH（HS-N04F3-001）

附註：

　　印章：內封面頁鈐有"胡適的書"朱文方印。

　　題記：扉頁有贈書者題贈："Mrs. Virginia Hartman With—my good wishes, □ 1934-。"

2790 American Government and Politics/by Charles A. Beard. —New York：The Macmillan Company，1939

viii，814 p.；24.2 cm

HSMH（HS-N04F4-028）

附註：

印章：內封面頁鈐有"胡適的書"朱文方印；扉頁鈐有"HU SHIH"藍色戳印。

批注圈劃：書中有胡適的劃綫數處。

其他：第8版。

2791 The American Historical Association's Guide to Historical Literature/edited by George Frederick Howe, et al. —New York：The Macmillan Company，1961

xxxv，962 p.；24 cm

HSMH（HS-N20F1-049）

附註：

印章：內封面頁鈐有"胡適的書"朱文方印。

夾紙：頁360、361間夾有贈書單1張，上記"Compliments of American Historical Association Boyd C. Shafer Executive Secretary"。

與胡適的關係：頁116的G202條提及胡適著作"Chung-kuo che-hsueh Shih ta-kang"；頁270的O289條提及胡適著作"Wang Mang, the socialist emperor of nineteen centuries ago"；頁272的O347條提胡適著作"The development of Zen Buddhism in China"；頁282的O700條提及胡適著作"The Chinese Renaissance"。

2792 American Historical Documents 1000-1904/edited by Charles W. Eliot. —New York：P. F. Collier & Son Corporation，1910

462 p.，[1] plate；21 cm

Harvard Classics：The Five-Foot Shelf of Books，Vol. 43

HSMH（HS-N12F5-013）

附註：

印章：內封面頁鈐有"胡適的書"朱文方印。

批注圈劃：書中有胡適的批注劃綫數十處，其中頁 425 有批注："檢 Basler Text p.793，句讀與我校改的相合。適之 Jan. 27，1959。"

2793　The American：The Making of a New Man/by James Truslow Adams. ——New York：Charles Scribner's Sons, 1943

　　ix, 404 p. ; 21.5 cm

　　HSMH（HS-N04F4-030）

　　附注：

　　　　印章：扉頁鈐有"胡適的書"朱文方印。

　　　　題記：扉頁有胡適題記："小三愛讀歷史，我盼望他愛看這本新式的歷史。適之 卅二，十二，廿五。"

2794　The American Mind：An Interpretation of American Thought and Character Since the 1880's/by Henry Steele Commager. ——New Haven：Yale University Press, 1955

　　ix, 476 p. ; 24 cm

　　HSMH（HS-N04F4-029）

　　附注：

　　　　印章：內封面頁鈐有"胡適的書"朱文方印。

2795　American Philosophical Society：Year Book 1959. ——Philadelphia：The American Philosophical Society, 1960

　　779 p. ; 22.9 cm

　　HSMH（HS-N19F1-002）

　　附注：

　　　　印章：內封面鈐有"胡適的書"朱文方印。

　　　　夾紙：頁 280、281 間夾有 American Philosophical Society 寄給胡適的地址片 1 張。

　　　　與胡適的關係：頁 713 的會員表，列有胡適在 1936 年獲選入 American Philosophical Society 及通訊地址。

2796 The Analects of Confucius/translated from the Chinese, with an introduction and notes by Lionel Giles. —Shanghai: Printed for the Members of the Limited Editions Club by the Commercial Press, 1933

114 p., plates; 28 cm

HSMH（HS-N02F3-015）

附注：

批注圈劃：書中有鉛筆劃綫數十處。

其他：(1)封底有中文簽題："論語 中國上海商務印書館署檢"。(2)綫裝書。

2797 The Analects of Confucius/translated by Arthur Waley. —New York: Random House, 1938

257 p.; 18.5 cm

HSMH（HS-N03F5-003）

附注：

印章：內封面頁鈐有"胡適的書"朱文方印。

與胡適的關係：內容提及《胡適文存》(*Hu Shih Wen Ts'un*)。

其他：封面有中文書名"論語"。

2798 The Ancient City: A Study on the Religion, Laws, and Institutions of Greece and Rome/by Fustel De Coulanges. —Garden City, New York: Doubleday & Company, Inc., 1956

396 p.; 18 cm

Doubleday Anchor Books

HSMH（HS-N19F6-023）

附注：

印章：內封面頁鈐有"胡適的書"朱文方印。

2799 The Ancient Civilizations of Peru/by John Alden Mason. —Harmondsworth, Middlesex: Penguin Books, 1957

xx, 330 p., 64 plates; 18.1 cm

HSMH（HS-N19F6-026）

附注：

印章：内封面頁鈐有"胡適的書"朱文方印。

2800 Ancient Religions：A Symposium/edited by Vergilius Ferm. —New York：Philosophical Library, 1950

xv, 392 p.；22.2 cm

HSMH（HS-N03F6-016）

附注：

印章：内封面頁鈐有"胡適的書"朱文方印。

2801 And Quiet Flows the Don/by Mikhail Sholokhov. —New York：The New American Library, 1959

512 p.；17.8 cm

HSMH（HS-N04F5-009）

附注：

印章：内封面頁鈐有"胡適的書"朱文方印。

2802 Annual Report of the Council on Economic and Cultural Affairs 1959/by Arthur T. Mosher. —New York：The Council on Economic and Cultural Affairs, Inc., 1959

32 p.；22.9 cm

HSMH（HS-N19F5-036）

附注：

印章：内封面頁鈐有"胡適的書"朱文方印。

2803 Annual Report of the Librarian of Congress for the Fiscal Year Ending June 30, 1956. —Washington：The Library of Congress, 1957

x, 151 p.；26.6 cm

HSMH（HS-N19F4-001）

附注：

印章：内封面頁鈐有"胡適的書"朱文方印。

批注圈劃：書中有胡適的批注劃綫數處。

2804 The Apology, Phaedo and Crito of Plato; The Golden Sayings of Epictetus; the Meditations of Marcus Aurelius/edited by Charles W. Eliot. —New York: P. F. Collier & Son Corporation, 1909

345 p., [1] plate; 21 cm

Harvard Classics: The Five-Foot Shelf of Books, Vol. 2

HSMH（HS-N12F6-002）

附注：

印章：内封面頁鈐有"胡適的書"朱文方印。

内附文件：書末夾有剪報 1 張，標題爲"Making Money: Some Businesses Seem to Profit from Patriotic Appeals"。

2805 Approaches to the Oriental Classics: Asian Literature and Thought in General Education/edited by Wm. Theodore De Bary. —New York: Columbia University Press, 1959

xvi, 262 p.; 22.1 cm

HSMH（HS-N03F5-016）

附注：

印章：内封面頁鈐有"胡適的書"朱文方印。

題記：扉頁有作者題贈："To Dr. Hu Shih In appreciation of his contribution to the conference. W. T. de Bary June 1, 1960。"

2806 April Snow/by Lillian Budd. —New York: Pocket Books, Inc., 1954

311 p.; 16.3 cm

HSMH（HS-N19F5-080）

附注：

印章：扉頁鈐有"胡適的書"朱文方印。

題記：内封面頁有作者題贈："To Dr. Hu, in admiration, Lillian Budd Madison, Wisconsin Sept. 2, 1956。"

夾紙:頁 22、23 間夾有本書的廣告單 1 張;頁 50、51 間夾有 Pocket Books 的書籤 1 張。

2807 The Arabs:A Short History/by Philip K. Hitti. —Chicago:Gateway Editions, Inc., 1949

 256 p. ; 17.8 cm

 HSMH(HS-N19F6-030)

附注:

 印章:內封面頁鈐有"胡適的書"朱文方印。

2808 The Architecture of Humanism:A Study in the History of Taste/by Geoffrey Scott. —Garden City, New York:Doubleday & Company, Inc., 1954

 197 p. ; 18 cm

 Doubleday Anchor Books

 HSMH(HS-N19F6-020)

附注:

 印章:內封面頁鈐有"胡適的書"朱文方印。

2809 Arrows in the Gale/by Arturo Giovannitti. —Riverside, Connecticut:Hillacre Bookhouse, 1914

 108 p. ; 20.7 cm

 HSMH(HS-N04F6-008)

附注:

 印章:扉頁有英文簽名"Walter B. Kahn";內封面頁鈐有"胡適的書"及"胡適之"朱文方印。

 題記:扉頁有胡適題記:"About 1914 or 1915, a copy of this book was given to me by Will Edgerton. From that copy I quoted the 4 lines on page 18 (Whither Mankind). Mr. Eugene Delafield was kind enough to find this copy for me in June, 1949. Hu Shih July 4, 1949。"

 批注圈劃:頁 18 有鉛筆劃綫。

2810 Art and Reality: Ways of the Creative Process/by Joyce Cary. —New York: Harper & Brothers, 1958

xv, 175 p. ; 19.5 cm

World Perspectives, Vol. 20

HSMH（HS-N20F1-015）

附注：

印章：内封面頁鈐有"胡適的書"朱文方印。

2811 The Art of Letters: Lu Chi's "Wen Fu," A. D. 302/translated by E. R. Hughes. —New York: Pantheon Books, 1951

xviii, 261 p. ; 23.5 cm

The Bollingen Series, XXIX

HSMH（HS-N03F4-026）

附注：

印章：内封面頁鈐有"胡適的書"朱文方印。

與胡適的關係：内容提及胡適。

2812 Art Treasures from the Vienna Collections, 1949-1950. —[s. l.]：[s. n.]，[n. d.]

67 p. , xliii plates; 22.9 cm

HSMH（HS-N20F1-014）

附注：

印章：内封面頁鈐有"胡適的書"朱文方印。

内附文件：本書之補遺"A supplement to the catalogue listing a group of objects sent specially from Vienna for their first showing in the United States at the Metropolitan Museum of Art, February twenty-third through May twenty-first, 1950"。

2813 Asia and the Humanities: Papers Presented at the Second Conference on Oriental-Western Literary and Cultural Relations Held at Indiana University/edited by Horst Frenz. —Bloomington, Indiana: Comparative Literature

Committee, Indiana University, 1959

232 p. ; 23 cm

HSMH (HS-N03F1-009)

附注：

印章：兩冊的內封面頁均鈐有"胡適的書"朱文方印。

夾紙：其中一冊夾有本書的內容簡介暨訂購單 1 張。另一冊有夾紙 2 張，一張是本書的內容簡介暨訂購單；另一張是信封地址殘片，上寫"Box 70, Philosophy Indiana University Bloomington, Indiana"。

2814 Asian Influenza in Taiwan 1958/by J. Thomas Grayston, San-Pin Wang and Paul B. Johnston. —Taipei, Taiwan: United States Naval Medical Research No. 2, 1959

17 p. ; 26.5 cm

NAMRU TWO, February 17, 1959 (NM 52 05 02. 4. 4)

HSMH (HS-N19F5-009)

附注：

其他：(1)釘書針裝訂。(2)館藏 2 冊。

2815 At Sunwich Port/by W. W. Jacobs. —London: George Newnes, Limited, 1902

viii, 292 p. ; 19.7 cm

HSMH (HS-N19F5-075)

附注：

印章：封面裏有簽名"Stanfords"；內封面頁鈐有"胡適的書"朱文方印。

題記：扉頁有贈書者題贈："To Dr. Hu Shih one of his favorite authors, from his friend Eugene L. Delafield Mar. 15, 1958."

摺頁：頁 243、244 間有摺角的痕迹。

2816 Atomic Power and Moral Faith/by T. V. Smith. —Claremont, California: Claremont College, 1946

vii, 56 p. ; 21.3 cm

HSMH (HS-N19F3-029)

附注：

  印章：内封面頁鈐有"胡適的書"朱文方印。

2817 Australian Accent/by John Douglas Pringle；illustrated by George Molnar. —London：Chatto and Windus, 1958

  204 p. ; 22.2 cm

  HSMH（HS-N19F6-016）

  附注：

    印章：扉頁有簽名"P. C. Ma Sydney, Australia March, 1959 馬保之"；内封面頁鈐有"胡適的書"朱文方印。

    批注圈劃：書中有批注劃綫數十處。

2818 Authority and the Individual/by Bertrand Russell. —New York：Simon and Schuster, 1949

  79 p. ; 21 cm

  HSMH（HS-N04F5-017）

  附注：

    印章：館藏 2 冊，其中一冊扉頁有胡適簽名"Hu Shih 8 April, 1953"；另一冊扉頁亦有胡適簽名"Hu Shih"。兩冊的内封面頁均鈐有"胡適的書"朱文方印。

    批注圈劃：其中一冊（簽名"Hu Shih 8 April, 1953"）有胡適的批注劃綫數處。

    其他：本書爲第 2 次印刷。

2819 The Autobiography of Alice B. Toklas/by Gertrude Stein. —New York：Random House, 1933

  252 p. ; 18.5 cm

  HSMH（HS-N04F5-025）

  附注：

    印章：扉頁鈐有"胡適的書"朱文方印。

2820 The Autobiography of Benjamin Franklin; The Journal of John Woolman; Fruits of Solitude/by William Penn; edited by Charles W. Eliot. —New York: P. F. Collier & Son Corporation, 1909

 397 p., [1] plate; 21 cm

 Harvard Classics: The Five-Foot Shelf of Books, Vol. 1

 HSMH（HS-N12F6-001）

 附注：

  印章：内封面頁鈐有"胡適的書"朱文方印。

  題記：扉頁有胡適朱筆題記："趙元任同楊韵卿贈送這部五尺叢書給胡適。一九四九年。"

2821 The Autobiography of Benvenuto Cellini/translated by John Addington Symonds. —New York: P. F. Collier & Son Corporation, 1910

 436 p., [1] plate; 21 cm

 Harvard Classics: The Five-Foot Shelf of Books, Vol. 31

 HSMH（HS-N12F5-001）

 附注：

  印章：内封面頁鈐有"胡適的書"朱文方印。

2822 The Autobiography of Michel de Montaigne/edited by Marvin Lowenthal. —New York: Vintage Books, 1956

 xlvii, 292, vi p.; 18.5 cm

 HSMH（HS-N04F6-003）

 附注：

  印章：内封面頁鈐有"胡適的書"朱文方印。

2823 Autumn Leaves/by E. T. C. Werner. —Shanghai: Kelly & Walsh Limited, 1928

 747 p.; 22.5 cm

 HSMH（HS-N03F2-042）

 附注：

印章：內封面頁鈐有"胡適的書"朱文方印；目錄後一頁鈐有"適之"朱文方印。

題記：扉頁有胡適題記："This volume was obtained for me by my friend Mr. Eugene Delafield. It is valuable because it contains, among other things, nearly 200 pages of the author's autobiography. Hu Shih Oct. 22, 1950. 秋葉集 His translation of my article on 'Reform in Mourning Rites' appears on pages 70-95。"

批注圈劃：書中有胡適的批注圈劃數處。

夾紙：書中有夾紙6張。

與胡適的關係：書中"Reform in Chinese Mourning Rites"翻譯胡適的《我對於喪禮的改革》一文。

其他：封面有中文書名"秋葉"及作者譯名"文仁亭"。

2824 The Awakening of a New Consciousness in Zen/by Daisetz Teitaro Suzuki. — Zürich：Rhein-Verlag, 1955

275-304 p., x plates; 20.7 cm

Eranos-Jahrbuch, XXIII

HSMH（HS-N19F2-063）

附注：

印章：頁275鈐有"胡適的書"朱文方印。

題記：封面有作者題記："呈 胡適先生 惠存 大拙拜。"

其他：(1)作者爲鈴木大拙。(2)抽印本。

2825 The Beginnings of Chinese Civilization：Three Lectures Illustrated with Finds at Anyang/by Li Chi. —Seattle：University of Washington Press, 1957

xvii, 123 p.; 24.8 cm

HSMH（HS-N03F5-031）

附注：

印章：內封面頁鈐有"胡適的書"朱文方印。

題記：扉頁有作者題贈："Compliments of Li Chi。"

其他：封面印有"李濟著 中國文明的開始 三個講演用安陽發掘資料的圖

片說明 勞榦謹題"。

2826 Belphagor/by Niccolo Machiavelli. —Emmaus, Penna.：Rodale Press, 1954

32 p. ; 20.7 cm

HSMH（HS-N04F6-005）

附注：

印章：內封面頁鈐有"胡適的書"朱文方印。

2827 Benjamin Franklin：The Autobiography and Selections from His Other Writings/edited by Herbert W. Schneider. —New York：The Liberal Arts Press, 1952

xx, 218 p. ; 18.5 cm

Forum Books, No. 1

HSMH（HS-N04F3-034）

附注：

印章：內封面頁鈐有"胡適的書"朱文方印。

2828 The Best of Damon Runyon/by Damon Runyon. —New York：Pocket Books, Inc. , 1941

xxiii, 318, [10] p. ; 16.5 cm

HSMH（HS-N19F5-060）

附注：

印章：內封面頁有胡適簽名"Hu"，並鈐有"胡適的書"朱文方印。

題記：扉頁有胡適鉛筆題記："For Ginny on her return trip. S. 。"

批注圈劃：書中有胡適的圈劃數處。

2829 The Betrayal of the Intellectuals（La Trahison des Clercs）/by Julien Benda. —Boston：The Beacon Press, 1955

xxxii, 188 p. ; 20.3 cm

HSMH（HS-N04F5-031）

附注：

印章：内封面頁鈐有"胡適的書"朱文方印。

2830 Between War and Peace: The Potsdam Conference/by Herbert Feis. — Princeton, New Jersey: Princeton University Press, 1960

viii, 367 p. ; 24.2 cm

HSMH（HS-N04F2-023）

附注：

印章：扉頁有胡適簽名"Hu Shih New York, October, 1960"；内封面頁鈐有"胡適的書"朱文方印。

2831 Beyond Theology: The Autobiography of Edward Scribner Ames/edited by Van Meter Ames. —Chicago: The University of Chicago Press, 1959

x, 223 p. ; 22.1 cm

HSMH（HS-N04F3-014）

附注：

印章：扉頁有胡適簽名"Hu Shih Sept. 14, 1959"；另一扉頁鈐有"胡適的書"朱文方印。

夾紙：扉頁粘貼卡片1張，印有"With the Compliments of the Author"。

2832 Bibliography of Korean Studies: A Bibliographical Guide to Korean Publications on Korean Studies Appearing from 1945 to 1958. —Seoul, Korea: Asiatic Research Center, Korea University, 1961

vii, 410 p. ; 24 cm

HSMH（HS-N19F6-005）

附注：

印章：内封面頁鈐有"胡適的書"朱文方印。

2833 The Big Change: America Transforms Itself 1900-1950/by Frederick Lewis Allen. —New York: Harper & Brothers Publishers, 1952

xi, 308 p. ; 21.7 cm

HSMH（HS-N04F4-025）

附注:

　　印章:扉頁有胡適簽名"Hu Shih";內封面頁鈐有"胡適的書"朱文方印。

　　批注圈劃:書中有胡適的批注劃綫數十處,其中頁293 記"Read the second time, Oct. 31, 1953. Hu Shih"。

2834　Blaise Pascal: Thoughts, Letters, Minor Works/translated by W. F. Trotter, M. L. Booth and O. W. Wight; edited by Charles W. Eliot. —New York: P. F. Collier & Son Corporation, 1910

　　444 p., [1] plate; 21 cm

　　Harvard Classics: The Five-Foot Shelf of Books, Vol. 48

　　HSMH(HS-N12F5-018)

附注:

　　印章:內封面頁鈐有"胡適的書"朱文方印。

2835　Blueprint for World Conquest: As Outlined by the Communist International/with an introduction by William Henry Chamberlin. —Washington, Chicago: Human Events, 1946

　　264 p.; 23.8 cm

　　HSMH(HS-N04F1-035)

附注:

　　印章:扉頁鈐有"胡適的書"朱文方印。

　　批注圈劃:書中有胡適的批注劃綫數十處。

　　夾紙:書中有夾紙5張。

　　內附文件:封底裏粘貼打字索引表1張,標題爲"Communism's Official Policy on following issues may be found on the pages of Blueprint for World Conquest as follows",並有胡適手寫的主題索引頁次。

　　相關記載:館藏有此書的書訊"Communist Guidebook",參見館藏號:HS-JDSHSE-0508-114。

2836　The Book of Mencius (abridged)/translated by Lionel Giles. —New York: E. P. Dutton & Company Inc., 1942

128 p.; 17.3 cm

HSMH（HS-N03F4-038）

附注：

　　印章：內封面頁鈐有"胡適的書"朱文方印。

　　批注圈劃：書中有胡適的劃綫數處。

　　夾紙：書中有夾紙1張。

2837　The Book of Odes: Chinese Text, Transcription and Translation/by Bernhard Karlgren. —Stockholm: The Museum of Far Eastern Antiquities, 1950

270 p.; 24.5 cm

HSMH（HS-N03F5-014）

附注：

　　印章：內封面頁鈐有"胡適的書"朱文方印。

2838　Boule de Suif and Other Stories/by Guy de Maupassant; translated by H. N. P. Sloman. —Harmondsworth, Middlesex: Penguin Books, 1951

240 p.; 18 cm

The Penguin Classics

HSMH（HS-N04F6-004）

附注：

　　印章：封面有胡適簽名"Hu Shih"；內封面頁鈐有"胡適的書"朱文方印。

　　批注圈劃：頁189有胡適批注："這是Maupassant的最好、最寫實的一篇。參攷Maugham選的'無用的嘴'。適之 3 August, 1960。"

2839　Brain-Washing in Red China/by Edward Hunter. —New York: Vanguard Press, Inc., 1951

311 p.; 21 cm

HSMH（HS-N03F2-023）

附注：

　　印章：扉頁鈐有"胡適的書"朱文方印。

　　批注圈劃：書中有胡適的批注劃綫數十處。

摺頁：書中有摺頁兩處。

相關記載：(1)1951 年 11 月 8 日 Deotsude R. Vogt 致胡適函,提及胡適爲此書撰寫書評事,並寄贈書,參見館藏號：HS-US01-081-001。(2)1952 年 3 月 11 日 John Chamberlain 致胡適函,爲轉告本書作者 Edward Hunter 之歉意,有關第 1 版打字不清之處,已在第 2 版時作修正。參見館藏號：HS-US01-092-009。

其他：封面有中文書名"洗腦"。

2840 A Brief Study of Some Facts and Many Not-Facts Regarding "China" and United States " China Policy "/by Stanley K. Hornbeck. —New York： American-Asian Educational Exchange, Inc. , 1961

56 p. ; 19.5 cm

HSMH（HS-N20F2-067）

附注：

題記：館藏 3 冊,其中一冊的封面有題記："July 1961。"

夾紙：其中一冊的封面夾有贈書卡片 1 張,上有作者題贈："To Hu Shih with the compliments & all best wishes of SKH"；另一冊的內封面頁夾有卡片 1 張,上印"American-Asian Educational Exchange Incorporated Marvin Liebman Executive Vice-chairman 79 Madison Avenue New York 16, N. Y. MUrray Hill 5-0190"。

其他：其中一冊的封面有"Complimentary copy"的紅色戳印。

2841 Brill's News/with an introduction by E. J. Brill. —Leiden, Netherlands： E. J. Brill, 1961

127 p. ; 18.5 cm

HSMH（HS-N03F2-007）

附注：

夾紙：書中夾有 E. J. Brill 書店的書籍訂購單 1 張,以及給 E. J. Brill 書店的回郵信封(未貼郵票)1 個。

2842 Buddhism/by Christmas Humphreys. —Harmondsworth, Middlesex： Penguin

Books, 1951

256 p., plates; 18 cm

Pelican books

HSMH（HS-N06F1-013）

附注：

　　印章：鈐有"胡適的書"朱文方印。

　　批注圈劃："Introduction"有胡適的紅筆劃綫。

2843 Buddhism in Translations/selected and translated by Henry Clarke Warren. ——Cambridge, Mass.：Havard University Press, 1947

xxvi, 496 p., plates; 26 cm

Harvard Oriental Series, Vol. 3

HSMH（HS-N06F1-005）

附注：

　　印章：內封面頁鈐有"胡適的書"朱文方印及"胡適"紫色戳印。

　　批注圈劃：偶有胡適的鉛筆注記與劃綫。

　　夾紙：書中有夾紙 5 張。

　　其他：書末附有 Harvard Oriental Series 簡介及"Henry Clarke Warren：A Brief Memorial", by C. R. Lanman。

2844 Buddhist Texts through the Ages/edited by Edward Conze. ——New York：Philosophical Library, 1954

322 p.; 21 cm

HSMH（HS-N06F1-009）

附注：

　　印章：內封面頁有胡適簽名"Hu Shih"，並鈐有"胡適的書"朱文方印。

　　批注圈劃：書衣摺頁處有胡適的紅筆劃綫與注記；"Introduction"有胡適的紅筆劃綫。

2845 Building the Constitution/by Irving Dilliard. ——St. Louis：St. Louis Post-Dispatch, [n.d.]

33 p.;21.7 cm

St. Louis Post-Dispatch

HSMH(HS-N19F2-042)

附注：

　　印章:封面裏鈐有"胡適的書"朱文方印。

　　批注圈劃:封面裏有胡適注記印刷冊數。

2846 Butterfield 8/by John O'Hara. —New York：Bantam Books, 1960

280 p.;17.8 cm

HSMH（HS-N19F5-064）

附注：

　　印章:內封面頁鈐有"胡適的書"朱文方印。

2847 Can People Learn to Learn? How to Know Each Other/by Brock Chisholm.
—New York：Harper & Brothers Publishers, 1958

xiv, 143 p.;19.6 cm

World Perspectives, Vol. 8

HSMH（HS-N19F4-038）

附注：

　　印章:扉頁鈐有"胡適的書"朱文方印。

　　批注圈劃:書中有胡適的劃綫數處。

2848 Canadians in the Making：A Social History of Canada/by Arthur R. M. Lower. —Toronto：Longmans, Green and Company, 1958

xxiv, 475 p.;23.5 cm

HSMH（HS-N19F6-013）

2849 The Canon of Reason and Virtue：Chinese and English = 老子道德經/by Paul Carus. —Chicago：The Open Court Publishing Co., 1945

209 p.;16.5 cm

HSMH（HS-N03F5-010）

附注：

印章：內封面頁鈐有"胡適的書"朱文方印及"胡適"紫色戳印。

批注圈劃：書中有胡適的圈劃數十處。

2850 Captain Dreyfus：The Story of a Mass Hysteria/by Nicholas Halasz. —New York：Grove Press，1955

274 p.；20.3 cm

HSMH（HS-N19F3-007）

附注：

印章：內封面頁有胡適簽名"Hu Shih July 1958"，並鈐有"胡適的書"朱文方印。

批注圈劃：書中有胡適的批注劃綫數十處。

內附文件：頁 90、91 間夾有剪報 2 張，標題分別為"Two Presidents Re-elected"、"2 Judges Say U.S. Intervened For Chiang Relative, a Speeder"，前者有胡適注記："March 22, 1960。"

2851 The Case Against Adolf Eichmann/edited and with a Commentary by Henry A. Zeiger；with a Forword by Harry Golden. —New York：The New American Library，1960

192 p., plates；18 cm

HSMH（HS-N19F3-013）

附注：

印章：內封面頁鈐有"胡適的書"朱文方印。

2852 A Catalogue of Books in the Library of the College of New Jersey，January 29，1760/published by order of the Trustees at Woodbridge, New Jersey, by James Parker, 1760；reprinted by the Friends of the Library. —Princeton：Princeton University Library，1949

[8], 36 p.；22.2 cm

HSMH（HS-N19F2-026）

附注：

印章：扉頁鈐有"胡適的書"朱文方印。

2853 Cause of Change in Sea Level in the Western Pacific/by Ting Ying H. MA. —Taipei, Taiwan：Ting Ying H. MA, 1957

6 p.；26.2 cm

Oceanographia Sinica, Vol. IV, No. 2, October 1957

HSMH（HS-N20F1-090）

附注：

其他：中文封底：中國海洋誌 第四卷第二號 馬廷英著 西太平洋海水面變動之原因 中華民國四十六年十月。"

2854 Caves of Biak：An American Officer's Experiences in the Southwest Pacific/by Harold Riegelman. —New York：The Dial Press, 1955

xii, 278 p., illus., maps；23.6 cm

HSMH（HS-N04F2-002）

附注：

印章：內封面頁鈐有"胡適的書"朱文方印。

題記：扉頁有作者題贈："Classmate and friend Hu Shih with grateful and affectionate regards Harold Riegelman 2/28/55。"

與胡適的關係："Another Prefatory Note"爲胡適所撰寫。

2855 The Century Association Year-Book, 1958. —New York：The Century Association, 1958

287 p.；17.7 cm

HSMH（HS-N19F1-029）

附注：

印章：內封面頁鈐有"胡適的書"朱文方印。

與胡適的關係：頁 97 的"Members"，記有 1943 年胡適成爲 The Century Association 的會員。

2856 Champlain：The Life of Fortitude/by Morris Bishop. —New York：Alfred A.

Knopf, Inc., 1948

364, vii p., map; 22 cm

HSMH（HS-N19F6-010）

附注：

印章：内封面頁鈐有"胡適的書"朱文方印。

題記：扉頁有胡適題記："Hu Shih Gift from Liu Chieh。"

2857 Character Text for Mandarin Primer/by Yuen-ren Chao. —Cambridge, Mass.：Harvard University Press, 1948

142 p.；23.5 cm

HSMH（HS-N03F1-026）

附注：

印章：扉頁有胡適的英文簽名"Hu Shih"；内封面頁鈐有"胡適的書"朱文方印。

其他：(1)書末有題籤："國語入門 趙元任。"(2)本書爲中文内容。

2858 The Chemical Arts of Old China = 中國古代之化學工藝/by Ch'iao-p'ing Li. —Easton, Pennsylvania：Journal of Chemical Education, 1948

viii, 215 p.；23.5 cm

HSMH（HS-N03F1-017）

附注：

印章：内封面頁鈐有"胡適的書"朱文方印；扉頁鈐有"胡適之印章"白文方印。

與胡適的關係：扉頁有胡適毛筆題籤："李喬苹著 中國古代之化學工藝 胡適題。"

2859 Chiang Kai-Shek：A Pictorial Biography of the President of the Republic of China. —Taipei, Taiwan："China Publishing Company", 1957

180 p.；30.1 cm

HSMH（HS-N20F1-105）

附注：

夾紙：書中有夾紙1張。

與胡適的關係：頁84有蔣介石自胡適手中接受"總統當選證書"的照片1張；頁125有蔣介石、胡適與Henry R. Luce三人的合照1張。

其他：照片集。

2860 The Child and the Curriculum and the School and Society/by John Dewey. —Chicago：The University of Chicago Press, 1943

xii, 159 p.；20.4 cm

HSMH（HS-N04F4-016）

附注：

印章：內封面頁有胡適簽名"Hu Shih April 1956"，並鈐有"胡適的書"朱文方印。

批注圈劃：頁iii、iv有劃綫。

2861 China：A Model for Europe/by Lewis A. Maverick. —San Antonio, Texas：Paul Anderson Company, 1946

xi, 334 p.；24 cm

HSMH（HS-N03F6-013）

附注：

印章：扉頁有胡適簽名"Hu Shih 胡適 Dec. 7, 1951"；內封面頁鈐有"胡適的書"朱文方印。

2862 China：Its People, Its Society, Its Culture/by Chang-tu Hu, et al.；edited by Hsiao Hsia. —New Haven：Hraf Press, 1960

611 p.；21.5 cm

Survey of World Cultures

HSMH（HS-N03F5-033）

附注：

印章：內封面頁鈐有"胡適的書"朱文方印。

批注圈劃：書中有胡適的批注劃綫數十處。

與胡適的關係：內容提及胡適。

2863 China in Stalin's Grand Strategy/by Hu Shih. —New York：Council on Foreign Relations, Inc. , 1950

　　11-40 p. ; 25 cm

　　Foreign Affairs：An American Quarterly Review, October 1950

　　HSMH（HS-N19F2-022）

　　附註：

　　　印章：頁11鈐有"胡適的書"朱文方印。

　　　相關記載：此文即《史達林策略下的中國》，胡適紀念館藏有多筆相關檔案。

　　　其他：抽印本。

2864 China in the Sixteenth Century：The Journals of Matthew Ricci 1583-1610/ translated from the Latin by Louis J. Gallagher; with a foreward by Richard J. Cushing. —New York：Random House, 1953

　　xxii, 616 p. ; 24 cm

　　HSMH（HS-N03F4-018）

　　附註：

　　　印章：内封面頁鈐有"胡適的書"朱文方印及"胡適之印"白文方印。

　　　批注圈劃：書中有胡適的批注劃綫數處。

2865 China in Western Literature：A Continuation of Cordier's Bibliotheca Sinica/complied by Tung-li Yuan（袁同禮）. —New Haven：Far Eastern Publications, Yale University, 1958

　　xix, 802 p. ; 26.2 cm

　　HSMH（HS-N03F6-001）

　　附註：

　　　印章：内封面頁鈐有"胡適的書"朱文方印。

　　　與胡適的關係：内容提及胡適及其著作"China's own critics"、"The Chinese Renaissance"、"A note on Chuan Tsu-wang, Chao I-ching and Tai Chen"、"Two papers on post-war China"、"The issues behind the Far Eastern conflict"、"The development of the logical method in ancient China"、"Ch'an (Zen) Buddhism in China, its history and method"。

相關記載：館藏有"Final Report of Supplement to Cordier's Bibliotheca Sinica",參見館藏號:HS-US01-026-014。

2866 China Mainland Today, Vol. 1: Communist-Controlled China as Foreign Visitors See It/by Russell Spurr, et al. —Taipei, Taiwan: "Free China Review", 1957

58 p. ; 19 cm

HSMH（HS-N03F2-004）

2867 China Mainland Today, Vol. 2: Communist-Controlled China as Foreign Residents See It/by Lucian Taire, et al. —Taipei, Taiwan: "Free China Review", 1957

94 p. ; 19 cm

HSMH（HS-N03F2-005）

2868 China Mainland Today, Vol. 3: Communist-Controlled China as Foreign Missionaries See It/by Henry R. Lieberman, et al. —Taipei, Taiwan: "Free China Review", 1957

108 p. ; 19 cm

HSMH（HS-N03F2-006）

2869 The China Story/by Freda Utley. —Chicago: Henry Regnery Company, 1951

xiii, 274 p. ; 21.5 cm

HSMH（HS-N03F2-030）

附注：

印章：扉頁有胡適簽名"Hu Shih June 3, 1951";內封面頁鈐有"胡適的書"朱文方印。

題記：書末有作者題贈:"With affection, esteem and warmest best wishes Freda Utley. June 1951";封底扉頁亦有鉛筆題記:"Freda 1717 20th N. W.

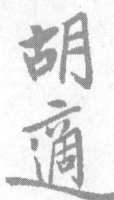

Washington 9. D. C. Hobart 6893。"

批注圈劃:書中有胡適的批注劃綫數處。

相關記載:館藏有 1951 年 5 月 9 日 Alfred Kohlberg 對本書的書評"Book Review of Freda Utley, The China Story",參見館藏號:HS-US01-094-023。

2870 The China Tangle: The American Effort in China from Pearl Harbor to the Marshall Mission/by Herbert Feis. —Princeton, New Jersey: Princeton University Press, 1953

x, 445 p. ; 24.6 cm

HSMH(HS-N04F2-022)

附注:

印章:扉頁有胡適簽名"Hu Shih";內封面頁鈐有"胡適的書"朱文方印。

題記:書末有胡適題記:"1529 29th St. Washington D. C.。"

批注圈劃:書中有胡適的批注劃綫數十處。

夾紙:書中夾有胡適手記紙片 2 張,一張記"Herbert Feis 1529 29th St. Washington, D. C."及"Call 以忠 to return 自由中國";另一張記關於王文成全書。

2871 China Yearbook 1957-1958/compiled by the China Yearbook Editorial Board. —Taipei, Taiwan: "China Publishing Co.", 1958

[10], 768 p. ; 21.2 cm

HSMH(HS-N12F3-037)

附注:

印章:內封面頁鈐有"胡適的書"朱文方印及"行政院新聞局 敬贈 With the Compliments of Government Information Office The Republic of China"藍色戳印。

與胡適的關係:書中有胡適的英文簡介。

其他:封面有中文書名"中華民國英文年鑑"。

2872 China Yearbook 1958-1959/compiled by the China Yearbook Editorial Board.

—Taipei, Taiwan："China Publishing Co.", 1959

[13], 858 p.; 21.2 cm

HSMH（HS-N12F3-038）

附註：

　　印章：內封面頁鈐有"胡適的書"朱文方印。

　　與胡適的關係：書中有胡適的英文簡介。

　　相關記載：1958年7月7日英文"中華民國年鑑編輯委員會"致"中央研究院"函，參見館藏號：HS-NK01-298-001。

　　其他：封面有中文書名"中華民國英文年鑑"。

2873 China Yearbook 1959-1960/compiled by the China Yearbook Editorial Board.

—Taipei, Taiwan："China Publishing Co.", 1960

1016 p.; 21.2 cm

HSMH（HS-N12F5-023）

附註：

　　印章：內封面頁鈐有"胡適的書"朱文方印。

　　與胡適的關係：頁732有胡適的英文簡介。

　　相關記載：1959年8月8日英文"中華民國年鑑編輯委員會"致胡適函，參見館藏號：HS-NK01-298-003。

　　其他：封面有中文書名"中華民國英文年鑑"。

2874 China Yearbook 1960-1961/compiled by the China Yearbook Editorial Board.

—Taipei, Taiwan："China Publishing Co.", 1961

1059 p.; 21.2 cm

HSMH（HS-N12F5-024）

附註：

　　印章：內封面頁鈐有"胡適的書"朱文方印。

　　夾紙：書中有夾紙2張，其中一張夾於序（Foreword）中，上印"請指教批評 行政院新聞局敬贈 臺北市中正路一七〇九號"。

　　與胡適的關係：頁784有胡適的英文簡介。

　　相關記載：1960年9月"中華民國英文年鑑編輯委員會"致胡適函，參見館藏號：HS-NK01-298-007。

其他：封面有中文書名"中華民國英文年鑑"。

2875 China's Entrance into the Family of Nations: The Diplomatic Phase 1858-1880/by Immanuel C. Y. Hsu. —Cambridge, Mass.: Harvard University Press, 1960

xi, 255, xxxvi p.; 24.1 cm

HSMH（HS-N03F3-023）

附注：

夾紙：內封面頁夾有贈書卡片1張，內容爲"With the Compliments of the Asia Foundation at the Request of J. K. Fairbank"。

2876 China's First Hundred/by Thomas E. La Fargue. —Pullman: State College of Washington, 1942

xiv, 176 p.; 23.5 cm

HSMH（HS-N03F3-026）

附注：

印章：內封面頁鈐有"胡適的書"朱文方印。

題記：扉頁有贈書者題贈："'借花獻佛'送給適之 湘眉 一九五四年六月，紐約。"

批注圈劃：書中有胡適的批注圈劃數處。

2877 China's Response to the West: A Documentary Survey, 1839-1923/by Ssu-yü Teng and John K. Fairbank. —Cambridge: Harvard University Press, 1954

vii, 296 p.; 24.2 cm

HSMH（HS-N03F6-028）

附注：

印章：內封面頁鈐有"胡適的書"朱文方印。

題記：扉頁有作者題贈："For Dr. Hu Shih with the thanks and cordial regards of the authors SYT JKF May '54。"

批注圈劃:書中有胡適的批注劃綫數十處。

夾紙:頁128、129間夾有地址殘片1張,印有"友聯出版社 The Union Press 香港九龍窩打老道——〇號 110, Waterloo Road, Kowloon, Hong Kong"。

與胡適的關係:內容提及胡適。

其他:John K. Fairbank 即費正清。

2878 The Chinese and Their Rebellions, Viewed in Connection with Their National Philosophy, Ethics, Legislation, and Administration/by Thomas Taylor Meadows. —London: Smith, Elder & Co., 1856

lx, 656 p.; 22.3 cm

HSMH(HS-N03F5-034)

附注:

印章:扉頁鈐有"胡適之印"白文方印。

2879 A Chinese Biographical Dictionary = 古今姓氏族譜/by Herbert A. Giles. —London: Bernard Quaritch; Shanghai: Kelly & Walsh, Ltd., 1897

2 Vols. (vii, 1022 p.); 24.4 cm

HSMH(HS-N03F1-027, HS-N03F1-028)

附注:

印章:兩冊內封面頁均鈐有"胡適的書"朱文方印。

2880 Chinese Characteristics/by Arthur H. Smith. —New York: Fleming H. Revell Company, 1894

342 p.; 21 cm

HSMH(HS-N03F3-024)

附注:

印章:扉頁有簽名"K. Sugimoto 1917";內封面頁鈐有"胡適的書"朱文方印。

批注圈劃:書中有批注劃綫數處。

2881 Chinese Civilization: A Political, Social, and Religious History of Ancient China/by Marcel Granet; translated by Kathleen E. Innes and Mabel R. Brailsford. —New York: Meridian Books, Inc., 1958

xxiii, 444 p.; 20.4 cm

HSMH（HS-N03F5-030）

附注：

　　印章：內封面頁鈐有"胡適的書"朱文方印。

　　與胡適的關係：內容提及胡適。

2882 Chinese Civilization in Liberal Education: Proceedings of a Conference Held at the University of Chicago, November 28-29, 1958/edited by H. G. Creel. —Chicago, Illinois: The University of Chicago Press, 1959

viii, 222 p.; 22.9 cm

HSMH（HS-N03F6-012）

附注：

　　印章：內封面頁鈐有"胡適的書"朱文方印。

2883 The Chinese Classics, Vol. I: Confucian Analects, the Great Learning, and the Doctrine of the Mean/with a translation, critical and exegetical notes, prolegomena, and copious indexes by James Legge. —Oxford: At the Clarendon Press, 1893

xv, 503 p.; 25.9 cm

The Chinese Classics

HSMH（HS-N12F4-001）

附注：

　　印章：內封面頁鈐有"胡適的書"朱文方印。

　　題記：內封面背面有胡適題記："Legge 原來的計畫，此書共七篇（7 Volumes），後來只譯完了五篇，共八冊，其目如下：Vol. I.《論語》,《大學》,《中庸》。Vol. II.《孟子》。Vol. III.《書經》分兩冊。Vol. IV.《詩經》分兩冊。Vol. V.《春秋左傳》分兩冊。今日我買到的是 Vols. I, II+IV，共四冊。若能得《左傳》譯本，當收存。胡適 Oct. 21, 1953, in New

York City."

其他:修訂 2 版(Second Edition, Revised)。

2884 The Chinese Classics, Vol. II: The Works of Mencius/with a translation, critical and exegetical notes, prolegomena, and copious indexes by James Legge. —Oxford: At the Clarendon Press, 1895

viii, 587 p. ; 25.9 cm

The Chinese Classics

HSMH (HS-N12F4-002)

附注:

印章:內封面頁鈐有"胡適的書"朱文方印。

批注圈劃:頁 474 有鉛筆校改一字"change"。

其他:修訂 2 版。

2885 The Chinese Classics, Vol. IV-Part 1: The First Part of the She-King, or the Lessons from the States; and the Prolegomena/with a translation, critical and exegetical notes, prolegomena, and copious indexes by James Legge. —London: Henry Frowde, Oxford University Press Warehouse, Amen Corner, E. C., [n.d.]

xii, 182, 243 p., fold. map; 25.9 cm

The Chinese Classics

HSMH (HS-N12F4-003)

附注:

印章:內封面頁鈐有"胡適的書"朱文方印。

題記:扉頁有鉛筆注記:"Vol. IV. Pts 1 & 2。"

批注圈劃:前半部"The Prolegomena"頁 126、127 之間的"The Kingdom of Chow"地圖,有胡適的紅筆圈劃。

2886 The Chinese Classics, Vol. IV-Part 2: The Second, Third and Fourth Parts of the She-King, or the Minor Odes of the kingdom, the Greater Odes of the Kingdom, the Sacrificial Odes and Praise-songs ; And the

Indexes/with a translation, critical and exegetical notes, prolegomena, and copious indexes by James Legge. —London：Henry Frowde, Oxford University Press Warehouse, Amen Corner, E. C., [n. d.]

245-785 p.；25.9 cm

The Chinese Classics

HSMH（HS-N12F4-004）

附註：

印章：内封面頁鈐有"胡適的書"朱文方印。

2887 The Chinese Classics, Vol. V-Part 1：Dukes Yin, Hwan, Chwang, Min, He, Wan, Seuen and Ching; And the Prolegomena/with a translation, critical and exegetical notes, prolegomena, and copious indexes by James Legge. —London：Henry Frowde, Oxford University Press Warehouse, Amen Corner, E. C., [n. d]

x, 147, 410 p., fold. map；25.9 cm

The Chinese Classics

HSMH（HS-N12F4-005）

附註：

印章：内封面頁鈐有"胡適的書"朱文方印。

題記：内封面頁背面有胡適題記："今天又買得《春秋左傳》兩冊，是為全書的第五篇。（Vol. V）原譯成的五篇八冊，我已收得四篇六冊了。此篇兩冊皆很新，未割葉，很可愛。胡適 Nov. 10, 1953, in New York。"

批注圈劃：前半部"The Prolegomena"頁134、135之間的地圖，有胡適的圈劃。

2888 The Chinese Classics, Vol. V-Part 2：Dukes Seang, Ch'aou, Ting, and Gae, with Tso's Appendix; And the Indexes/with a translation, critical and exegetical notes, prolegomena, and copious indexes by James Legge. —London：Henry Frowde, Oxford University Press Warehouse, Amen Corner, E. C., [n. d.]

411-933 p.；25.9 cm

The Chinese Classics

HSMH（HS-N12F4-006）

附注：

印章：内封面頁鈐有"胡適的書"朱文方印。

2889 Chinese Communism and the Rise of Mao/by Benjamin I. Schwartz. — Cambridge, Mass.：Harvard University Press, 1951

258 p.；21.5 cm

HSMH（HS-N03F2-034）

附注：

印章：内封面頁鈐有"胡適的書"朱文方印。

題記：扉頁有贈書者題記："To Dr. Hu Shih Many thanks for your sage advice and counsel. Rolph L. Powell。"

批注圈劃：書中有胡適的批注劃綫數十處。

夾紙：書中有夾紙1張。

2890 Chinese Culture as a Bulwark Against Communism/by Chi-yun Chang. — Taipei, Taiwan："Institute of Chinese Culture in Cooperation with Free Pacific Association, the Republic of China", 1959

68 p.；21 cm

HSMH（HS-N03F2-009）

附注：

印章：内封面頁鈐有"胡適的書"朱文方印。

題記：内封面頁有作者題贈："適之先生 賜正 後學 張其昀敬贈。"

2891 A Chinese "Divina Commedia"/by J. J. L. Duyvendak. —Leiden, Netherlands：E. J. Brill, 1952

62 p.；24.2 cm

HSMH（HS-N19F5-022）

附注：

印章：内封面頁鈐有"胡適的書"朱文方印。

題記：封面有作者題贈："Professor Hu Shih with the author's kind regards to mind。"

2892 A Chinese Garden of Serenity/translated by Chao Tze‑chiang. —Mount Vernon, New York：The Peter Pauper Press, 1959

60 p.；19 cm

HSMH（HS‑N03F4‑007）

附註：

印章：內封面頁鈐有"胡適的書"朱文方印。

題記：扉頁有譯者題贈："適之先生斧正 晚趙自強敬贈 一九五九年九月十三日。"

批注圈劃：書中有胡適的校改數處。

相關記載：1959年9月13日趙自強致胡適函,贈送自譯的《菜根譚》,參見館藏號：HS‑NK05‑118‑006。

2893 Chinese Humanism：A Study of Chinese Mentality and Temperament/by Chai Ch'u. —New York：Graduate Faculty of Political and Social Science, New School for Social Research, 1959

31–46 p.；24 cm

Social Research, Vol. 26, No. 1, Spring, 1959

HSMH（HS‑N19F5‑023）

附註：

印章：頁31鈐有"胡適的書"朱文方印。

題記：封面有作者題贈："適之先生指正 後學 崔誉敬贈。"

其他：抽印本。

2894 Chinese Literature：A Historical Introduction/by Ch'ên Shou‑yi. —New York：The Ronald Press Company, 1961

xii, 665 p.；23.7 cm

HSMH（HS‑N03F5‑018）

附註：

印章：內封面頁鈐有"胡適的書"朱文方印。

題記:扉頁有作者題贈:"適之先生教正 受頤敬呈。"

與胡適的關係:內容提及胡適。

其他:封面有中文書名"中國文學史略"及作者"陳受頤"。

2895 Chinese Love Songs: Famous Poems from the Time of Confucius to the Present/translated by Mabel Lorenz Ives. —New Jersey: B. L. Hutchinson, 1949

　91 p. ; 18.4 cm

　HSMH (HS-N03F4-014)

附注:

印章:館藏2冊,內封面頁均鈐有"胡適的書"朱文方印,其中一冊封面裏有譯者簽名"Mabel Lorenz Ives"。

題記:其中一冊的封面裏有譯者題贈:"For Dr. Hu Shih Mabel Lorenz Ives VII-6-1949";封底有鉛筆題記:"Mrs. Frank L. Hough China Society of America 570 Lexington Ave. N. Y. 22 Tel: 5-9268";另一冊的封面裏,在譯者簽名之下有胡適的題贈:"To Ginny with love H. S. Sept. 16, 1949。"

相關記載:可參考1949年胡適與Mrs. Herbert E. Ives (Mabel Lorenz Ives)的往來函,館藏號:HS-NK02-006-005～007。

2896 Chinese Miscellanies (China 1846-1854). —[s. l.]: [s. n.], [n. d.]

　1 Vol. ; 24.5 cm

　HSMH (HS-N03F3-027)

附注:

印章:內封面頁鈐有"胡適的書"朱文方印。

夾紙:書中有夾紙9張。

2897 Chinese Painting/with an introduction and notes by Chiang Yee. —London: Faber and Faber Limited, [n. d.]

　24 p., illus. ; 31 cm

　The Faber Gallery of Oriental Art

　HSMH (HS-N13F1-020)

附注：

印章：内封面頁鈐有"胡適的書"朱文方印。

題記：扉頁有作者題贈："適之先生教正 蔣彝 寄自波斯頓。"

2898　Chinese Philosophy in Classical Times/edited and translated by E. R. Hughes. —London：J. M. Dent；New York：E. P. Dutton, 1944

xliii, 336 p.；17.5 cm

HSMH（HS-N03F5-015）

附注：

印章：内封面頁鈐有"胡適的書"朱文方印及"胡適"紫色戳印。

2899　A Chinese Printing Manual/translated from the Chinese with notes and introduction by Richard C. Rudolph. —Los Angeles：The Ward Ritchie Press for members of the Zamorano Club, 1954

xxvi, 20 p., 16 plates；18.3 cm

HSMH（HS-N03F1-023）

附注：

印章：内封面頁鈐有"胡適的書"朱文方印。

題記：扉頁有譯者題贈："To Dr. Hu Shih in appreciation, R. C. Rudolph 22 February 1960。"

2900　The Chinese Renaissance：The Haskell Lectures · 1933/by Hu Shih. —Chicago, Illinois：The University of Chicago Press, 1934

110 p.；22.1 cm

HSMH（HS-N03F6-026）

附注：

印章：館藏3冊，其中一冊的内封面頁鈐有"胡適的書"朱文方印。

題記：有鈐印的一冊扉頁有胡適題記："To Virginia Hartman Hu Shih January 1939 Harkness Pavillion New York City"；另一冊的扉頁有胡適題記："送給孟真 適之 一九三四，七，六"；再另一冊有鉛筆注記："31-V-34。"

批注圈劃:有鈐印的一冊有胡適的批注圈劃數十處;另一冊(題"送給孟真"的)有胡適的批注劃綫數處。

夾紙:題"送給孟真"的一冊扉頁夾有台灣大學白德蓀的名片 1 張。再另一冊的頁 44、45 間夾有卡片及紙張各 1 張,卡片印有"With the Compliments of the Author",紙張上有韋蓮司(Edith Clifford Williams)鉛筆筆迹;頁 80、81 之間夾有小紙片 2 張,上面亦有韋蓮司鉛筆筆迹。

內附文件:再另一冊頁 68、69 間夾有韋蓮司手寫札記 2 張,標題爲"'Blue Monday!' 5 Nov. 62"。

與胡適的關係:本書爲 1933 年胡適在芝加哥大學演講"中國文化的趨勢"(Cultural Trends in Presentday China)六講的演説詞,彙成一本書,名爲"中國的文藝復興",由芝加哥大學出版部出版。

其他:再另一冊爲韋蓮司奉還胡適所贈之書。

2901　The Chinese Student Movement/by Wen-han Kiang. —New York: King's Crown Press, 1948

x, 176 p. ; 20.9 cm

HSMH(HS-N03F3-020)

附注:

印章:內封面頁鈐有"胡適的書"朱文方印。

與胡適的關係:注釋提及胡適的著作"Tsan Tung Ti Hui I Yu Fan Sheng(Tragic Memory and Repentance)"(《慘痛的回憶與反省》)、"Chin Jih Chiao Hui Chiao Yu Ti Nan Kuan(The Difficulties Confronting Mission Education Today)"(《今日教會教育的難關》)、"Living Philosophies"、"K'o Hsueh Yu Jen Sheng Kuan Hsu(A Preface to "Science and the Philosophy of Life")"(《〈科學與人生觀〉序》)、*Pou Hsiu*(*Immortality*)(《不朽》)、*The Chinese Renaissance*、"The Civilizations of the East and the West"、*Hu Shih Lun Hsueh Chin Chu*(《胡適論學近著》)、*Hu Shih Wen Tsun*(《胡適文存》)。

2902　The Chinese Theater/by A. E. Zucker. —Boston: Little, Brown, and Company, 1925 xvi, 234 p.；24.9 cm

HSMH（HS-N03F5-017）

附注：

批注圈劃：頁165有劃綫一處。

與胡適的關係：書中有胡適圖片1張,內容及注釋均提及胡適。

2903 Chinese Thought and Institutions/edited by John K. Fairbank. —Chicago：The University of Chicago Press,1957

xiii, 438 p.；24.8 cm

HSMH（HS-N03F5-025）

附注：

印章：內封面頁鈐有"胡適的書"朱文方印。

與胡適的關係：注釋提及《胡適文存二集》(*Hu Shih Wen-tsun Erhchi*)。

其他：John K. Fairbank 即費正清。

2904 Chinese Thought：From Confucius to Mao Tse-tung/by H. G. Creel. —Chicago：The University of Chicago Press,1953

ix, 293 p.；21.5 cm

HSMH（HS-N03F5-026）

附注：

印章：內封面頁鈐有"胡適的書"朱文方印。

題記：扉頁有作者題贈："To Dr. Hu Shih with thanks for all that I have learned from his many works that I have used in writing this book Herrlee Creel。"

批注圈劃：書中有胡適的批注劃綫數十處。

夾紙：書中有夾紙1張。

與胡適的關係：內容提及胡適及其著作《中國哲學史大綱》、"Confucianism"、"Development of Zen Buddhism in China"、"The Establishment of Confucianism as a State Religion during the Han Dynasty"、《戴東原的哲學》。

2905 The Chinese View of Life: The Philosophy of Comprehensive Harmony/by Thomé H. Fang. —Hong Kong: The Union Press, 1957

 v, 274 p. ; 21.1 cm

 HSMH（HS-N03F3-013）

 附注：

  印章：內封面頁鈐有"胡適的書"朱文方印。

  其他：作者：方東美。

2906 Chronicle and Romance: Froissart, Malory, Holinshed/edited by Charles W. Eliot. —New York: P. F. Collier & Son Corporation, 1910

 383 p., [1] plate; 21 cm

 Harvard Classics: The Five-Foot Shelf of Books, Vol. 35

 HSMH（HS-N12F5-005）

 附注：

  印章：內封面頁鈐有"胡適的書"朱文方印。

2907 Churchill, Roosevelt, Stalin: The War They Waged and the Peace They Sought/by Herbert Feis. —Princeton, New Jersey: Princeton University Press, 1957

 xi, 692 p. ; 24.3 cm

 HSMH（HS-N04F2-021）

 附注：

  印章：內封面頁鈐有"胡適的書"朱文方印。

  題記：扉頁有題字，似爲"Drumright"。

  夾紙：書中夾有白色棉紙1張。

2908 Classic Art: An Introduction to the Italian Renaissance/by Heinrich Wölfflin. —London: Phaidon Press, 1953

 xviii, 296 p., illus. (some col.) ; 25.5 cm

 HSMH（HS-N20F1-011）

 附注：

印章：内封面頁鈐有"胡適的書"朱文方印。

其他：本書爲再版（Second Edition）。

2909 The Cold War: A Study in U. S. Foreign Policy/by Walter Lippmann. —New York: Harper & Brothers, 1947

　　62 p.; 19.5 cm

　　HSMH（HS-N04F2-018）

附注：

　　印章：内封面頁鈐有"胡適的書"朱文方印。

　　相關記載：館藏有本書之書訊，參見館藏號：HS-JDSHSE-0508-029。

2910 A Collection of Essays/by George Orwell. —Garden City, New York: Doubleday & Company, Inc., 1953

　　320 p.; 18.2 cm

　　HSMH（HS-N04F1-027）

附注：

　　印章：扉頁有胡適簽名"Hu Shih, August 1960. New York"，並鈐有"胡適的書"朱文方印。

　　批注圈劃：書中作者簡介有胡適的批注劃綫。

2911 The College at Princetown, May 1784/by Gijsbert Karel van Hogendorp; with an introduction by Howard C. Rice. —Princeton, New Jersey: Princeton University Library, 1949

　　xii, 7 p.; 22.9 cm

　　HSMH（HS-N19F2-034）

附注：

　　印章：内封面頁鈐有"胡適的書"朱文方印。

　　内附文件：封底夾有英文手稿影本2張。

2912 Collision of East and West/by Herrymon Maurer. —Chicago: Henry Regnery Company, 1951 xvi, 352 p.; 21.8 cm

HSMH（HS-N03F6-020）

附注：

印章：館藏2冊，內封面頁均鈐有"胡適的書"朱文方印，其中一冊鈐有"胡適"紫色戳印。

題記：其中一冊的扉頁有作者1951年的題贈："To my friend and teacher, Dr. Hu Shih, with very warm thanks and esteem, Herrymon Maurer June 6, 1951"；另一冊（無紫色戳印）扉頁則有作者1959年的題贈："Taipei, Taiwan To Dr Hu Shih with high esteem and warmest thanks. Herrymon Maurer January 14, 1959。"

批注圈劃：其中一冊（無紫色戳印）的頁xvi，有胡適的校改一處。

夾紙：其中一冊夾有卡片1張。

與胡適的關係："Introduction"由胡適撰寫，內容提及胡適的著作"The Chinese Renaissance"、"A Criticism of Some Recent Method of Dating Lao Tzu"、"The Development of the Logical Method in Ancient China"、"China in Stalin's Grand Strategy"。

相關記載：本書作者Herrymon Maurer請胡適寫序的記載，可參考《胡適日記》1951年3月26日條；胡適寫的序，參見館藏號：HS-US01-030-015。

2913 The Coming of Ulysses: A Play in Four Acts/by Philip Dorf. —New York: Oxford Book Company, 1949

73 p.; 19.6 cm

HSMH（HS-N04F5-030）

附注：

印章：內封面頁鈐有"胡適的書"朱文方印。

題記：扉頁有作者題贈："To Dr. Hu Shih A memento of a very pleasant visit. Philip Dorf Ithaca N.Y. July 15, 1953。"

2914 Common Sense and Nuclear Warfare/by Bertrand Russell. —New York: Simon and Schuster, 1959

92 p.; 20.5 cm

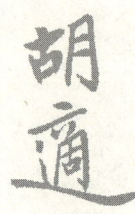

HSMH（HS-N04F5-016）

附注：

印章：內封面頁鈐有"胡適的書"朱文方印。

2915　Communism in China/by Union Research Institute. —Kowloon, Hong Kong：Union Research Institute, 1959

xiv, 254 p. ; 23 cm

HSMH（HS-N03F2-027）

附注：

印章：內封面頁鈐有"胡適的書"朱文方印。

題記：封面有贈書者題贈："適之先生指正　史誠之敬贈　於美國華盛頓　一九六〇　七月。"

2916　Communism in Our World/by John C. Caldwell. —New York：The John Day Company, 1956

126 p. ; 21.9 cm

HSMH（HS-N04F1-034）

附注：

印章：內封面頁鈐有"胡適的書"朱文方印。

2917　Communist China 1956/by Ti Chin, et al. —Kowloon, Hong Kong：Union Research Institute, 1957

xl, 236 p. ; 25.1 cm

Communist China Problem Research Series

HSMH（HS-N03F2-012）

附注：

印章：內封面頁鈐有"胡適的書"朱文方印。

批注圈劃：書中有胡適的批注劃綫數處。

2918　Communist China 1949-1959, Vol. I/by Chin Szu-k'ai, et al. —Kowloon, Hong Kong：Union Research Institute, 1961 iv, 264 p. ; 25.9 cm

Communist China Problem Research Series

HSMH（HS-N13F1-025）

附注：

夾紙:書中夾有信封地址殘片 1 張。

其他:封面有"Complimentary Copy"的藍色戳印。

2919 Communist China 1949-1959, Vol. II/by Ling Ch'i, et al. —Kowloon, Hong Kong: Union Research Institute, 1961

219 p. ; 25.8 cm

Communist China Problem Research Series

HSMH（HS-N03F2-013）

附注：

夾紙:書中夾有信封地址殘片 1 張。

其他:封面有"Complimentary Copy"的藍色戳印。

2920 Communist China Power & Prospects/by Richard L. Walker. —East Stroudsbury, Pa. : The American Labor Conference on International Affairs, Inc., 1958

31 p. ; 27.8 cm

The New Leader, Special Issue, October 20, 1958

HSMH（HS-N20F2-008）

2921 Communist China Power & Prospects/by Richard L. Walker. —New York: American-Asian Educational Exchange, Inc., [n. d.]

31 p. ; 27.8 cm

The New Leader, Special Issue, October 20, 1958

HSMH（HS-N19F2-068）

附注：

其他:此爲再印本,封面下方印有"Reprinted by American - Asian Educational Exchange, Inc."。

2922 The Communist Movement in China/an essay written in 1924 by Ch'en Kung-po; edited with an introduction by C. Martin Wilbur. —New York：East Asian Institute of Columbia University, 1960

 148 p. ; 28 cm

 HSMH（HS-N13F1-022）

 附注：

  夾紙：頁43 有夾紙1 張。

2923 Communist Policies toward the Intellectual Class：Freedom of Thought & Expression in China/by Chalmers A. Johnson. —Kowloon, Hong Kong：Union Research Institute, 1959

 130 p. ; 25.2 cm

 Communist China Problem Research Series

 HSMH（HS-N03F2-016）

 附注：

  印章：內封面頁鈐有"胡適的書"朱文方印。

  與胡適的關係：內容有"'Hu Shih Ideology' and the Dream of the Red Chamber Case"一文。

  其他：扉頁與目次頁有"Complimentary Copy"的藍色戳印。

2924 Communist Propaganda and the Fall of China/by Hu Shih. —New York：the Trustees of Columbia Law Review, 1954

 780-786 p. ; 25.3 cm

 Columbia Law Review, Vol. 54（May 1954）, pp. 780-786

 HSMH（HS-N19F2-023）

 附注：

  其他：抽印本2 冊。

2925 Communitas：Ways of Livelihood and Means of Life/by Percival Goodman and Paul Goodman. —New York：Vintage Books, 1960

 248 p. ; 18.4 cm

HSMH（HS-N04F1-033）

附注：

　　印章：内封面頁鈐有"胡適的書"朱文方印。

　　題記：扉頁有作者題贈："For Dr. Hu Shih Percival Goodman Nov. 1960。"

　　夾紙：書中夾有紙條 1 張，上記"這是秋華轉來古德曼教授（秋華的先生）Percival Goodman 託寄的一部書 古先生和秋華的事務所地址如下 1860 Broadway, N. Y. C. 業生附榮"。

2926 The Comparative Philosophy of Comparative Law/by F. S. C. Northrop. —Ithaca, New York：Cornell University, 1960

　　617-658 p. ; 25 cm

　　Cornell Law Quarterly, Vol. XLV, No. 4, Summer, 1960

　　HSMH（HS-N19F3-027）

附注：

　　題記：封面作者下有胡適題記："Yale Law School New Haven, Conn. 。"

　　批注圈劃：書中有數處劃綫。

2927 The Complete Poems of John Milton/edited by Charles W. Eliot. —New York：P. F. Collier & Son Corporation, 1909

　　459 p., [1] plate; 21 cm

　　Harvard Classics：The Five-Foot Shelf of Books, Vol. 4

　　HSMH（HS-N12F6-004）

附注：

　　印章：内封面頁鈐有"胡適的書"朱文方印。

2928 The Complete Works of O. Henry/by O. Henry; with a foreword by Harry Hansen. —Garden City, New York：Doubleday & Company, Inc., 1953

　　2 Vols. (1692 p.); 21.5 cm

　　HSMH（HS-N19F5-061, HS-N19F5-062）

附注：

　　印章：第 1 册扉頁鈐有"胡適的書" 朱文方印及"適之"朱文方印。第 2 册內封面頁鈐有"胡適的書"朱文方印；扉頁鈐有"適之"朱文方印。

題記：第 1 冊扉頁有胡適題記："六十九歲生日前三天，此書寄到，是我給自己的生日紀念物。適之 四九，十二，十四。"

批注圈劃：第 2 冊有胡適的圈劃數處。

2929 The Concise Biographical Dictionary of Famous Men & Women/by Harriet Lloyd Fitzhugh and Percy K. Fitzhugh. —New York：Grosset & Dunlap, 1949

xiii, 830 p. ; 21.7 cm

HSMH（HS-N04F6-038）

附注：

印章：內封面頁鈐有"胡適的書"朱文方印。

題記：扉頁有胡適題記："Hu Shih New York Sept. 1950. This book has Thomas E. Dewey but not John Dewey! It has Henry James, but not William James!"

批注圈劃：書中有胡適的批注劃綫數處。

夾紙：頁 760 有夾紙 1 張。

2930 Concise Dictionary of Spoken Chinese = 國語字典/by Yuen-Ren Chao and Lien-Sheng Yang(趙元任楊聯陞合編). —Cambridge, Mass. : Published for the Harvard-Yenching Institute by Harvard University Press, 1947

xxxix, 292 p. ; 23.5 cm

HSMH（HS-N20F1-003）

附注：

印章：扉頁有胡適簽名"Hu Shih"；內封面頁鈐有"胡適的書"朱文方印。

批注圈劃：頁 292 有胡適的校改一處。

2931 The Confessions of St. Augustine; The Imitation of Christ/edited by Charles W. Eliot. —New York：P. F. Collier & Son Corporation, 1909

364 p. , [1] plate; 21 cm

Harvard Classics：The Five-Foot Shelf of Books, Vol. 7

HSMH（HS-N12F6-007）

附注：

    印章：內封面頁鈐有"胡適的書"朱文方印。

    批注圈劃：頁3有鉛筆注記"卅三"。

2932 Conflict and Conciliation of Cultures/by Ralph Tyler Flewelling. —Stockton, California: College of the Pacific Press, 1951

    x, 106 p. ; 23.6 cm

    HSMH（HS-N03F6-014）

    附注：

        印章：內封面頁鈐有"胡適的書"朱文方印。

        題記：內封面頁有作者題贈："Dr. Hu Shih with appreciation and esteem Ralph Tyler Flewelling。"

2933 Conflict in Marriage: The Unhappy Undivorced/by Edmund Bergler. —New York: Harper & Brothers, 1949

    viii, 216 p. ; 20.9 cm

    HSMH（HS-N19F4-034）

    附注：

        印章：內封面頁鈐有"胡適的書"朱文方印。

2934 Confucius: His Life and Time/by Liu Wu-chi. —New York: Philosophical Library, 1955

    xv, 189 p. ; 22.3 cm

    HSMH（HS-N03F4-036）

    附注：

        印章：內封面頁鈐有"胡適的書"朱文方印。

        題記：扉頁有作者題贈："適之先生指教 柳無忌謹贈 一九五六，新港"，其下有胡適題記："Wu-Chi Liu 3 Woodbine St. Hamden 17, Conn.。"

        批注圈劃：書中有胡適的劃綫數處。

        其他：封面有中文書名"孔子"。

2935 Confucius: The Man and the Myth/by H. G. Creel. —New York: The John Day Company, 1949

xi, 363 p.; 22 cm

HSMH（HS-N03F5-001）

附注：

印章：内封面頁鈐有"胡適的書"朱文方印。

與胡適的關係：内容提及胡適。

2936 Conservatism in America/by Clinton Rossiter. —New York: Alfred A. Knopf, 1955

326, xii p.; 22 cm

HSMH（HS-N04F3-017）

附注：

印章：扉頁有胡適簽名"Hu Shih April 22, 1955"；内封面頁鈐有"胡適的書"朱文方印。

2937 The Constitution and What It Means Today/by Edward S. Corwin. —Princeton, New Jersey: Princeton University, 1948

xiii, 273 p.; 20.8 cm

HSMH（HS-N04F3-035）

附注：

印章：内封面頁鈐有"胡適的書"朱文方印。

題記：扉頁有作者題贈："4/30/52 To my highly esteemed friend, Dr. Hu Shih, with sincere admiration and regard, Edward S. Corwin。"

批注圈劃：書中有胡適的批注劃綫數處。

其他：此爲完全修訂的第10版（Tenth Edition, Completely Revised）。

2938 The Constitution of the Republic of China（with Chinese Text）= 中華民國憲法/by "China Culture Publishing Foundation"（"中華文化出版事業委員會"）. —Taipei, Taiwan: "China Culture Publishing Foundation", 1954

46 p.; 21.8 cm

Pamphlets on Chinese Affairs(國事叢刊)

HSMH(HS-N19F2-065)

附注：

夾紙：書中有夾紙1張。

其他：内容爲中英文對照。

2939 Constitution of the Republic of China and Organic Laws/adopted by the National Assembly on December 25, 1946. —Taipei, Taiwan："Government Information Office", 1957

51 p.；21.2 cm

HSMH(HS-N03F2-008)

附注：

印章：内封面頁鈐有"胡適的書"朱文方印。

2940 Contemporary China and the Chinese/edited by Howard L. Boorman. —Philadelphia：The American Academy of Political and Social Science, 1959

x, 220 p.；23.5 cm

The Annals of the American Academy of Political and Social Science, January, 1959

HSMH(HS-N19F5-053)

附注：

印章：内封面頁鈐有"胡適的書"朱文方印。

與胡適的關係：書中"Thought Reform of Intellectuals"的頁85，"Continuity and Change in Modern Chinese Literature"的頁91、92、99，以及"Taiwan's Development as Free China"的頁132均提及胡適。

2941 Contemporary China II. 1956-57：Economic and Social Studies Documents・Chronology・Bibliography = 當代中國/edited by E. Stuart Kirby. —Hong Kong：Hong Kong University Press, 1958

xi, 352 p.；22.8 cm

HSMH(HS-N03F2-026)

附注：

　　印章：內封面頁與頁1鈐有"胡適的書"朱文方印。

　　與胡適的關係：書中列有金達凱的《中共批判胡適思想研究》及石放的《胡適的政治思想和反革命的罪行》等書。

　　其他：編者譯名"葛壁"。

2942　Continental Drama: Calderon, Corneille, Racine, Molière, Lessing, Schiller/edited by Charles W. Eliot. —New York: P. F. Collier & Son Corporation, 1910

489 p., [1] plate; 21 cm

Harvard Classics: The Five-Foot Shelf of Books, Vol. 26

HSMH（HS-N12F6-026）

附注：

　　印章：內封面頁鈐有"胡適的書"朱文方印。

2943　Continental Drift and the Present Velocity of Shift of the Continental Margin of Eastern Asia/by Ting Ying H. MA. —Taipei, Taiwan: Ting Ying H. MA, 1957

22 p.; 26.2 cm

Research on the Past Climate and Continental Drift, Vol. XII, October 1957

HSMH（HS-N20F1-093）

附注：

　　其他：中文封底："古氣候與大陸漂移之研究 第十二號 馬廷英著 大陸漂移及亞洲東緣現在的漂移速度 中華民國四十六年十月出版。"

2944　Control of Radiation Hazards in the Atomic Energy Program/by United States Atomic Energy Commission. —Washington: U. S. Government Printing Office, 1950

230 p., illus.; 23.3 cm

HSMH（HS-N19F5-051）

附注：

印章：內封面頁鈐有"胡適的書"朱文方印。

夾紙：內封面頁有夾紙1張。

2945 Cornell University: Founders and the Founding/by Carl L. Becker. —Ithaca, New York: Cornell University Press, 1943

viii, 240 p., illus. (facsim.) plates, ports.; 24 cm

HSMH（HS-N19F3-019）

附注：

印章：扉頁有胡適簽名"Hu Shih 胡適"；內封面頁鈐有"胡適的書"朱文方印。

批注圈劃：書中有胡適的批注劃綫數處。

夾紙：扉頁夾有名片1張，上有江冬秀用綠筆記"這本書，是陳樹人先生二月廿四日親自送來交還給我。並告訴我，是他六年前，向適之借的。他現以〔已〕退修〔休〕了，找著這本書來奉還"。

相關記載：胡適提及閱讀此書的心得，參見《胡適日記》1953年7月21日條。

2946 Cornell University Announcements: College of Arts & Sciences, 1959-1960/by Cornell University. —Ithaca, New York: Cornell University, 1959

144 p.; 22.9 cm

HSMH（HS-N19F5-037）

附注：

印章：內封面頁鈐有"胡適的書"朱文方印。

內附文件：頁70、71間夾有文件1張，內容爲"China and Southeast Asia"各課程的師資。

2947 Court Is in Session/compiled by Isaac D. Levy and Bernard J. Smolens; with an Introduction by Owen D. Roberts. —New York: Crown Publishers, 1950

xi, 241 p.; 21.3 cm

HSMH（HS-N19F3-023）

附注：

印章：扉頁有胡適簽名"Hu Shih"；內封面頁鈐有"胡適的書"朱文方印。

2948 Courtroom/by Quentin Reynolds. —New York：Popular Library, 1957

400 p.；17.5 cm

HSMH（HS-N19F3-009）

附注：

印章：內封面頁鈐有"胡適的書"朱文方印。

2949 Cracks in the Kremlin Wall/by Edward Crankshaw. —New York：The Viking Press, 1951

vi, 279 p.；21.5 cm

HSMH（HS-N04F1-021）

附注：

印章：內封面頁鈐有"胡適的書"朱文方印。

2950 The Creation of the Universe/by George Gamow. —New York：The Viking Press, 1956

xii, 147 p.；19.6 cm

HSMH（HS-N19F4-014）

附注：

印章：內封面頁鈐有"胡適的書"朱文方印。

2951 The Crimes of the Stalin Era：Special Report to the 20th Congress of the Communist Party of the Soviet Union/by Nikita S. Khrushchev；annotated especially for this edition by Boris I. Nicolaevsky. —New York：The New Leader, 1956

67 p.；21.8 cm

The New Leader, Section Two, July 16, 1956

HSMH（HS-N19F2-066）

附注：

批注圈劃：書中有胡適的批注劃綫數處。

2952 The Criminal Law/by F. T. Giles. —Harmondsworth, Middlesex: Penguin Books, 1954

271 p. ; 18.2 cm

HSMH (HS-N19F3-024)

附注：

印章：封面有胡適簽名"Hu Shih"；内封面頁鈐有"胡適的書"朱文方印。

批注圈劃：書中有胡適的批注劃綫數十處。

2953 The Crisis Decade: A History of the Foreign Missionary Work of the Presbyterian Church in the U. S. A. 1937-1947/edited by W. Reginald Wheeler. —New York: The Board of Foreign Missions of the Presbyterian Church in the U. S. A., 1950

xiii, 369 p. ; 23.5 cm

HSMH (HS-N04F2-027)

附注：

印章：扉頁鈐有"胡適的書"朱文方印。

與胡適的關係：内容提及胡適。

夾紙：封底裏夾有"W. Reginald Wheeler"名片1張。

2954 Critics & Crusaders/by Charles A. Madison. —New York: Henry Holt and Company, Inc., 1948

534 p. ; 21 cm

HSMH (HS-N04F3-036)

附注：

印章：扉頁有胡適簽名"Hu Shih Chantangua, N. Y. August 15, 1951"，並鈐有"胡適的書"朱文方印。

批注圈劃：書中有胡適的批注劃綫數十處，其中頁366記"I first came to know Altgeld's life through reading Clarence Darrow's 'The story of my Life.' H. S."；頁419記"I met Bourne at an 'at home' in John Dewey's home on Rivenide Dr. & W. 116th St. Probably in 1915-16. H. S."。

2955 The Delight of Great Books/by John Erskine. —Indianapolis: The Bobbs-Merrill Company, 1928

314 p. ; 19.8 cm

HSMH（HS-N04F6-039）

附注：

印章：内封面頁鈐有"胡適的書"朱文方印。

2956 Democracy in America/by Alexis de Tocqueville; the Henry Reeve text as revised by Francis Bowen now further corrected and edited with a historical essay, editorial notes, and bibliographies by Phillips Bradley. —New York: Vintage Books, 1954

2 Vols. ; 18.5 cm

HSMH（HS-N04F4-023, HS-N04F4-024）

附注：

印章：兩冊扉頁均鈐有"胡適之印章"白文方印；内封面頁亦均鈐有"胡適的書"朱文方印。

2957 Democracy Versus Communism/by Kenneth Colegrove. —Princeton, New Jersey: The Institute of Fiscal and Political Education, 1957

vii, 424 p. ; 23.6 cm

HSMH（HS-N04F1-025）

附注：

印章：内封面頁鈐有"胡適的書"朱文方印。

2958 The Democratic Way of Life: An American Interpretation/by T. V. Smith and Eduard C. Lindeman. —New York: The New American Library, 1953

160 p. ; 18.1 cm

HSMH（HS-N19F3-018）

附注：

印章：扉頁有胡適簽名"Hu Shih October, 1954"；内封面頁鈐有"胡適的書"朱文方印。

題記:扉頁有胡適題記:"此書中 T. V. Smith 所極力主張的 sportsmanship 最不容易翻譯。'逢場作戲'的精神,則太輕率。似可譯作'角技道德'。孔子似深曉此意:'君子無所争,必也射乎,揖讓而升,下而飲。'此真可以表現所謂'角技道德'了。適之 Oct. 23, 1954。"

批注圈劃:書中有胡適的批注劃綫數十處。

2959 Department of Far Eastern Studies 1958–1959 and 1959–1960. —Ithaca, New York: Cornell University, 1958

 20 p.; 22.9 cm

 Cornell University Announcements, Vol. 50, No. 10, October 8, 1958

 HSMH（HS-N19F2-038）

 附注:

  印章:内封面頁鈐有"胡適的書"朱文方印。

  批注圈劃:頁 18 有鉛筆注記。

2960 The Development of China/by Kenneth Scott Latourette. —Boston; New York: Houghton Mifflin Company, 1946

 xi, 343 p.; 21.2 cm

 HSMH（HS-N03F2-036）

 附注:

  印章:内封面頁鈐有"胡適的書"朱文方印。

  批注圈劃:書中有胡適的批注劃綫數十處。

  夾紙:書中有夾紙 1 張。

  與胡適的關係:内文提及胡適及其文章"The Development of the Logical Method in Ancient China"。

  其他:修訂第 6 版(Sixth Edition, Revised)。

2961 The Development of Chinese Zen: After the Sixth Patriarch in the Light of Mumonkan/by Heinrich Dumoulin. —New York: The First Zen Institute of America, Inc., 1953 xxii, 146 p. ; 26 cm

HSMH（HS-N03F4-008）

附注：

印章：内封面頁鈐有"胡適的書"朱文方印。

批注圈劃：書中有胡適的批注劃綫數處。

與胡適的關係：注釋提及胡適；内容提及胡適的《神會和尚遺集》及胡適日文拼音"Ko Teki"。

2962 The Development of the Logical Method in Ancient China = 先秦名學史/by Hu Shih (Suh Hu). —Shanghai：The Oriental Book Company, 1928

187 p. ; 23.5 cm

HSMH（HS-N03F6-030）

附注：

印章：館藏 3 册，其中兩册内封面頁鈐有"胡適的書"朱文方印。

題記：其中一册的扉頁有胡適題記："Hu Shih's own copy"；另一册扉頁有胡適題記："This copy is from the library of my sinological friend, the late Roswell S. Britton, who died in 1951. Hu Shih May 1951."

批注圈劃：其中一册（Hu Shih's own copy）有胡適的劃綫校改數處；另一册（扉頁有題記的）有胡適的批注劃綫數十處；又一册有胡適的劃綫數處。

與胡適的關係：本書爲上海亞東圖書館 1928 年出版的胡適哥倫比亞大學哲學博士論文。

相關記載：《胡適日記》1922 年 7 月 11 日記事："英文論文《先秦名學史》印成，校改序文寄去。"

其他：本書爲 1958 年胡適自紐約寓所運回臺灣的藏書之一，參見館藏號：HS-NK05-215-005。

2963 Development of Volcanic Belts Together with Zones of Defficient Gravity along the Margin of Crustal Masses/by Ting Ying H. MA and Chia-Lin Pan. —Taipei, Taiwan：Ting Ying H. MA, 1957

4 p. ; 26.2 cm

Oceanographia Sinica, Vol. IV, No. 3, October 1957

HSMH（HS-N20F1-091）

附注：

其他：中文封底："中國海洋誌 第四卷第三號 馬廷英潘家驊共著 火山帶與重力不足帶之形成 中華民國四十六年十月。"

2964　Dialogue on John Dewey/edited by Corliss Lamont. —New York：Horizon Press, 1959

155 p. ; 20.6 cm

HSMH（HS-N04F4-007）

附注：

印章：館藏2冊，內封面頁均鈐有"胡適的書"朱文方印。

題記：其中一冊的扉頁有贈書者題贈："適之先生惠存 桂中樞 敬贈 十月三十日。"

夾紙：其中一冊夾有Womrath's Book Shop & Library 寄給胡適的信封地址殘片1張。

2965　Dialogues of Plato：Apology, Crito, Phaedo, Symposium, Republic/edited by J. D. Kaplan. —New York：Pocket Books, Inc., 1950

xi, 388 p. ; 17 cm

HSMH（HS-N04F6-029）

附注：

印章：內封面頁鈐有"胡適的書"朱文方印及"胡適"紫色戳印。

夾紙：頁4夾有"Collector's Editions：Fine Books for Everyman-With-A-Dollar"簡介1張。

2966　A Dictionary of Chinese Buddhist Terms：With Sanskrit and English Equivalents and a Sanskrit-Pali Index/compiled by William Edward Soothill and Lewis Hodous. —London：Kegan Paul, Trench, Trubner & Co., Ltd., 1937

xix, 510 p. ; 29cm

HSMH（HS-N06F1-007）

附注：

印章：扉頁有胡適藍筆簽名"Hu Shih October, 1953"；內封面頁鈐有"胡適的書"朱文方印。

批注圈劃：偶有胡適的綠、紅、藍筆注記與校改。

其他：William Edward Soothill 的中文名爲"蘇慧廉"。

2967 The Dictionary of Philosophy/edited by Dagobert D. Runes. —New York：Philosophical Library, [n.d.]

343 p.；23.5 cm

HSMH（HS-N04F6-037）

附注：

印章：內封面頁鈐有"胡適的書"朱文方印及"胡適"紫色戳印。

批注圈劃：頁 30、245 有胡適的劃綫及打勾。

2968 Diderot：Rameau's Nephew and Other Works/translated by Jacques Barzun and Ralph H. Bowen. —Garden City, New York：Doubleday & Company, Inc., 1956

xviii, 333 p.；18.1 cm

HSMH（HS-N04F6-011）

附注：

印章：扉頁鈐有"胡適的書"朱文方印。

2969 Directory of American Scholars：A Biographical Directory/edited by Jaques Cattell. —Lancaster, PA.：The Science Press, 1951

1072 p.；25.4 cm

HSMH（HS-N19F1-037）

附注：

印章：扉頁有胡適簽名"Hu Shih 胡適 1952"；內封面頁鈐有"胡適的書"朱文方印。

相關記載：館藏有 Directory of American Scholars 第 2 版的出版通知，參見

館藏號:HS-US01-009-034。

其他:本書爲第 2 版。

2970 Directory of Princeton University, 1958–1959. —Princeton: Bureau of Student Aid, 1960

　　192 p. ; 15 cm

　　HSMH (HS-N18F3-016)

　　附注:

　　　夾紙:書中夾有信封地址殘片 1 張。

2971 Directory of the Class of 1914/by Cornell University. —Ithaca, New York: Cornell University, 1954

　　50 p. ; 14.3 cm

　　HSMH (HS-N19F3-016)

　　附注:

　　　印章:内封面頁鈐有"胡適的書"朱文方印。

　　　其他:小冊子。

2972 A Diversity of States, Each Growing in Accord with Its Own Traditions: An Address by Robert F. Kennedy, United States Attorney General, February 6, 1962/by Robert F. Kennedy. —[s. l.]: United States Information Service, 1962

　　9 p. ; 17.9 cm

　　United States Policy Statement Series-1962

　　HSMH (HS-N19F2-016)

2973 The Divine Comedy of Dante Alighieri: Hell, Purgatory, Paradise/translated by Henry F. Cary. —New York: P. F. Collier & Son Corporation, 1909

　　428 p. , [1] plate; 21 cm

　　Harvard Classics: The Five-Foot Shelf of Books, Vol. 20

　　HSMH (HS-N12F6-020)

附注：

　　印章：内封面頁鈐有"胡適的書"朱文方印。

2974 Doctors East Doctors West: An American Physician's Life in China = 道一風向/by Edward H. Hume. —New York: W. W. Norton & Company, Inc., 1946

　　278 p. ; 21.8 cm

　　HSMH（HS-N03F3-003）

　　附注：

　　　　印章：扉頁鈐有"胡適的書"朱文方印。

　　　　與胡適的關係："Acknowledgment"提及感謝胡適。

2975 Documents on Communism, Nationalism, and Soviet Advisers in China 1918-1927/edited by C. Martin Wilbur and Julie Lien-ying How. —New York: Columbia University Press, 1956

　　xviii, 617 p. ; 24.1 cm

　　HSMH（HS-N03F2-033）

　　附注：

　　　　印章：内封面頁鈐有"胡適的書"朱文方印。

　　　　批注圈劃：書中有胡適的批注劃綫數處。

　　　　夾紙：書中有夾紙1張。

　　　　與胡適的關係：内文提及胡適。

2976 The Double: A poem of St. Petersburg/by F. M. Dostoyevsky. —Bloomington: Indiana University Press, 1958

　　254 p. ; 20 cm

　　HSMH（HS-N04F5-010）

　　附注：

　　　　印章：扉頁有陳之藩簽名"C. F. Chen Oct. 2 '58 Memphis, Tenn."；内封面頁鈐有"胡適的書"朱文方印。

2977 The Dreyfus Case: A Reassessment/by Guy Chapman. —New York: Reynal & Company, 1955

   400 p., plates; 21.8 cm

   HSMH（HS-N19F3-008）

   附注：

   　印章：内封面頁鈐有"胡適的書"朱文方印。

   　批注圈劃：書中有胡適的批注劃綫數十處。

   　内附文件：(1)封面裏貼有作者 Guy Chapman 的簡介。(2)封底裏及扉頁貼有本書書評剪報2張，一爲 Herbert Kupferberg 所寫，胡適在此剪報上批注："A very good review! H. S."；另一爲 Walter Millis 所寫。

2978 The Dynamics of Soviet Society/by W. W. Rostow. —New York: The New American Library, 1954

   264 p.; 18.3 cm

   HSMH（HS-N04F1-017）

   附注：

   　印章：内封面頁鈐有"胡適的書"朱文方印。

2979 East and West: Episodes in a Sixty Years' Journey/by F. T. Cheng. —London: Hutchinson & Co. (Publishers) Ltd., 1951

   247 p.; 22 cm

   HSMH（HS-N03F6-011）

   附注：

   　印章：扉頁鈐有"胡適的書"朱文方印。

   　題記：扉頁有作者題贈："To my old and good friend Dr. Hu Shih with kindest remembrances & best wishes F. T. Cheng 1953."

   　批注圈劃：頁164、165 有胡適的劃綫兩處。

2980 Eastern Science: An Outline of Its Scope and Contribution/by H. J. J. Winter. — London: John Murray Ltd., 1952

   114 p.; 17.3 cm

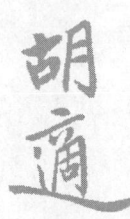

HSMH（HS-N03F1-016）

附注：

印章:内封面頁鈐有"胡適的書"朱文方印。

2981 Economic Development of Communist China: An Appraisal of the First Five Years of Industrialization/by Choh-ming Li. —Berkeley: University of California Press, 1959

xvi, 284 p. ; 24.2 cm

HSMH（HS-N03F2-018）

附注：

印章:内封面頁鈐有"胡適的書"朱文方印。

題記:扉頁有作者題贈:"To Dr. Hu Shih with warmest regards C. M. Li 1/1/59。"

夾紙:頁76、77間夾有地址殘片1張,上寫"From C. M. Li University of California Berkeley, California"。

其他:作者爲李卓敏。

2982 The Editor's Introduction Reader's Guide Index to the First Lines of Poems, Songs & Choruses, Hymns & Psalms/edited by Charles W. Eliot. —New York: P. F. Collier & Son Corporation, 1910

474 p., [1] plate; 21 cm

Harvard Classics: The Five-Foot Shelf of Books, Vol. 50

HSMH（HS-N12F5-020）

附注：

印章:内封面頁鈐有"胡適的書"朱文方印。

批注圈劃:書中有胡適的批注劃綫數處。

2983 Editorials and Cartoons on the 1952 Republican and Democratic Conventions. — St. Louis: St. Louis Post-Dispatch, 1952

40 p. ; 28 cm

HSMH（HS-N19F5-045）

附注：

　　印章：頁1鈐有"胡適的書"朱文方印。

2984　Edmund Burke: On Taste, on the Sublime and Beautiful, Reflections on the French Revolution, a Letter to a Noble Lord/edited by Charles W. Eliot. —New York: P. F. Collier & Son Corporation, 1909

　　421 p., [1] plate; 21 cm

　　Harvard Classics: The Five-Foot Shelf of Books, Vol. 24

　　HSMH（HS-N12F6-024）

　　附注：

　　印章：內封面頁鈐有"胡適的書"朱文方印。

2985　Edmund J. James Lectures on Government: Sixth Series. —Urbana, Illinois: University of Illinois Press, 1954

　　88 p.; 23.6 cm

　　HSMH（HS-N19F3-030）

　　附注：

　　印章：內封面頁鈐有"胡適的書"朱文方印。

　　夾紙：扉頁夾有 The Edmund J. James Lectures Committee 的贈書卡片1張。

2986　Education, Bricks and Mortar: Harvard Buildings and Their Contribution to the Advancement of Learning. —Cambridge, Mass.: Harvard University, 1949

　　100 p., illus.; 27.4 cm

　　HSMH（HS-N19F5-046）

　　附注：

　　印章：內封面鈐有"胡適的書"朱文方印。

　　夾紙：目次頁夾有贈書卡1張，印有"With the Compliments of the President Harvard University"。

2987　Education in China/by K. E. Priestley. —Hong Kong: The Green Pagoda Press

Ltd., 1961

viii, 72 p.; 18.4 cm

HSMH（HS-N03F2-025）

附注：

印章：内封面頁鈐有"胡適的書"朱文方印。

2988 The Education of Henry Adams/by Henry Adams. —New York：The Modern Library, 1931

x, 517 p.; 18.2 cm

HSMH（HS-N04F3-018）

附注：

印章：内封面頁鈐有"胡適的書"朱文方印。

題記：扉頁有題記："Ginny Hartman Blue Ridge Summit September 21-22 1940。"

相關記載：胡適購買此書事，參見《胡適日記》1936年8月5日條。

2989 The Effect of Warm and Cold Currents in the Southwestern Pacific on the Growth Rate of Reef Corals/by Ting Ying H. MA. —Taipei, Taiwan：Ting Ying H. MA, 1957

34 p.; 26.2 cm

Oceanographia Sinica, Vol. 5, No. 1, November 1957

HSMH（HS-N20F1-092）

附注：

批注圈劃：書中有校改一處。

其他：中文封底："中國海洋誌 第五卷第一號 馬廷英著 西南太平洋寒暖流對於造礁珊瑚長成之影響 中華民國四十六年十一月。"

2990 Eichmann：The Man and His Crimes/by Comer Clarke. —New York：Ballantine Books, 1960

153 p., plates; 18 cm

HSMH（HS-N19F3-014）

附注：

　　印章：内封面頁鈐有"胡適的書"朱文方印。

2991　Eleven Centuries of Chinese Printing: An Exhibition of Books from the Gest Oriental Library, Princeton University Library, February 20-April 20, 1952/ by Hu Shih and Shih-kang Tung. —Princeton: Princeton University Library, 1952

　　[3] p. ; 21.8 cm

　　HSMH（HS-N19F2-011）

　　附注：

　　　　與胡適的關係：此爲胡適與童世綱爲葛思德東方圖書館（Gest Oriental Library）作的特展簡介。

　　　　相關記載：館藏檔案亦有此小冊，參見館藏號：HS-US01-041-003。

2992　Elizabethan Drama, Vol. I: Marlowe, Shakespeare/edited by Charles W. Eliot. —New York: P. F. Collier & Son Corporation, 1910

　　463 p. , [1] plate; 21 cm

　　Harvard Classics: The Five-Foot Shelf of Books, Vol. 46

　　HSMH（HS-N12F5-016）

　　附注：

　　　　印章：内封面頁鈐有"胡適的書"朱文方印。

2993　Elizabethan Drama, Vol. II: Dekker, Jonson, Beaumont and Fletcher, Webster, Massinger/edited by Charles W. Eliot. —New York: P. F. Collier & Son Corporation, 1910

　　469-943 p. , [1] plate; 21 cm

　　Harvard Classics: The Five-Foot Shelf of Books, Vol. 47

　　HSMH（HS-N12F5-017）

　　附注：

　　　　印章：内封面頁鈐有"胡適的書"朱文方印。

　　　　夾紙：書中有夾紙5張。

2994 Eminent Chinese of the Ch'ing Period（1644-1912）/edited by Arthur W. Hummel. —Washington：United States Government Printing Office, 1943

  2 Vols.（1103 p.）; 28 cm

  HSMH（HS-N20F1-001, HS-N20F1-002）

  附註：

    印章：兩冊内封面頁均鈐有"胡適的書"朱文方印。

    批注圈劃：兩冊均有胡適的批注劃綫數十處。

    與胡適的關係：（1）頁 iii—vii 收錄胡適所寫的前言"Preface"。（2）頁 970—982 收錄胡適的文章"A Note on Ch'uan Tsu-wang, Chao I-ch'ing and Tai Ch'en: A study of independent convergence in research as illustrated in their works on the Shui-ching Chu"。（3）頁 40、136、629、722、738、776、867 等提及胡適及其著作。

    相關記載：館藏有多件相關資料，參見胡適紀念館胡適檔案檢索系統。

    其他：編者中文名爲"恆慕義"。

2995 Encyclopedia of American History/edited by Richard B. Morris. —New York：Harper & Brothers, 1953

  xv, 776 p. ; 21.7 cm

  HSMH（HS-N04F5-002）

  附註：

    印章：内封面頁鈐有"胡適的書"朱文方印。

    題記：扉頁有胡適題記："Hu Shih Dec. 24, 1956,—A Christmas Present to myself. 。"

    批注圈劃：書中有胡適的批注劃綫數十處。

    夾紙：書中有夾紙 1 張。

    内附文件：書中夾有 C. Wang 致胡適便箋 1 張。

2996 An Encyclopedia of World History: Ancient, Medieval, and Modern, Chronologically Arranged/compiled and edited by William L. Langer. —Boston：Houghton Mifflin Company, 1948 xlvi, 1270 p., maps, geneal. tables; 21.5 cm

HSMH（HS-N19F6-040）

附注：

 印章：扉頁有胡適簽名"Hu Shih July, 1949"；内封面頁鈐有"胡適的書"朱文方印。

 批注圈劃：書中有胡適的批注劃綫數處。

 夾紙：書中有夾紙1張。

2997 English Essays from Sir Philip Sidney to Macaulay/edited by Charles W. Eliot. —New York: P. F. Collier & Son Corporation, 1910

401 p., [1] plate; 21 cm

Harvard Classics: The Five-Foot Shelf of Books, Vol. 27

HSMH（HS-N12F6-027）

附注：

 印章：内封面頁鈐有"胡適的書"朱文方印。

2998 English Index to Mathews' Chinese-English Dictionary/by R. H. Mathews. —Cambridge, Mass.: Harvard University Press, 1947

186 p.; 26.1 cm

HSMH（HS-N19F1-042）

附注：

 印章：内封面頁鈐有"胡適的書"朱文方印及"胡適"紫色戳印。

2999 The English Philosophers from Bacon to Mill: The Golden Age of English Philosophy/edited by Edwin A. Burtt. —New York: The Modern Library, 1939

xxiv, 1041 p.; 21 cm

HSMH（HS-N04F6-021）

附注：

 印章：扉頁有胡適簽名"Hu Shih New York, N. Y. May 28, 1949"；内封面頁鈐有"胡適的書"朱文方印。

3000 English Philosophers of the Seventeenth and Eighteenth Centuries: Locke, Berkeley, Hume/edited by Charles W. Eliot. —New York: P. F. Collier & Son Corporation, 1910

420 p., [1] plate; 21 cm

Harvard Classics: The Five-Foot Shelf of Books, Vol. 37

HSMH (HS-N12F5-007)

附注:

印章:内封面頁鈐有"胡適的書"朱文方印。

3001 English Poetry, Vol. 1: From Chaucer to Gray/edited by Charles W. Eliot. —New York: P. F. Collier & Son Corporation, 1910

464 p., [1] plate; 21 cm

Harvard Classics: The Five-Foot Shelf of Books, Vol. 40

HSMH (HS-N12F5-010)

附注:

印章:内封面頁鈐有"胡適的書"朱文方印。

3002 English Poetry, Vol. 2: From Collins to Fitzgerald/edited by Charles W. Eliot. —New York: P. F. Collier & Son Corporation, 1910

465-958 p., [1] plate; 21 cm

Harvard Classics: The Five-Foot Shelf of Books, Vol. 41

HSMH (HS-N12F5-011)

附注:

印章:内封面頁鈐有"胡適的書"朱文方印。

3003 English Poetry, Vol. 3: From Tennyson to Whitman/edited by Charles W. Eliot. —New York: P. F. Collier & Son Corporation, 1910

959-1422 p., [1] plate; 21 cm

Harvard Classics: The Five-Foot Shelf of Books, Vol. 42

HSMH (HS-N12F5-012)

附注:

印章：内封面頁鈐有"胡適的書"朱文方印。

批注圈劃：書中有胡適的批注劃綫數處。

3004 Ennin's Diary：The Record of a Pilgrimage to China in Search of the Law/translated from the Chinese by Edwin O. Reischauer. —New York：The Ronald Press Company, 1955

 xvi, 454 p.；24.2 cm

 HSMH（HS-N03F4-022）

 附注：

 印章：内封面頁鈐有"胡適的書"朱文方印。

 題記：扉頁有作者題贈："Respectfully dedicated to a great scholar Edwin O. Reischauer。"

 批注圈劃：頁357有胡適的批注一處。

 夾紙：書中有夾紙1張，上記"Lent by Dr. Hu Shih"。

3005 Ennin's Travels in T'ang China/by Edwin O. Reischauer. —New York：The Ronald Press Company, 1955

 xii, 341 p.；24.2 cm

 HSMH（HS-N03F4-024）

 附注：

 印章：内封面頁鈐有"胡適的書"朱文方印。

 題記：扉頁有作者題贈："Respectfully dedicated to a great scholar Edwin O. Reischauer。"

 夾紙：扉頁有夾紙1張，上記"Lent by Dr. Hu Shih"。

3006 Entretiens du maître de dhyâna Chen-houei du Ho-tsö（668-760）/by Jacques Gernet. —Hanoi, [s. n.], 1949

 x, 126 p.；27 cm

 HSMH（HS-N07F5-051）

 附注：

 印章：内封面頁鈐有"胡適的書"朱文方印。

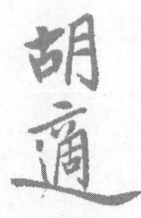

題記：(1)扉頁有贈書者題贈："To my teacher Richard De Martino。"(2)封面有胡適題記："神會語錄 四殘卷的法文譯本。"

批注圈劃：書中有胡適的紅筆注記與劃綫。

3007 Epic and Saga: Beowulf, the Song of Roland, the Destruction of Dá Derga's Hostel, the Story of the Volsungs and Niblungs/edited by Charles W. Eliot. —New York: P. F. Collier & Son Corporation, 1910

438 p., [1] plate; 21 cm

Harvard Classics: The Five-Foot Shelf of Books, Vol. 49

HSMH（HS-N12F5-019）

附注：

印章：内封面頁鈐有"胡適的書"朱文方印。

3008 Epid Emic Keratoconjunctivitis (E. K. C.) Part III Adenovirus isolation from E. K. C./by Yen-Fei Yang, Liang-Shi Ko, Paul B. Johnston and J. Thomas Grayston. —Taipei, Taiwan: United States Naval Medical Research No. 2, 1959

7 p.; 26.5 cm

NAMRU TWO, June 4, 1959（NM 52 05 02. 1. 0. 2）

HSMH（HS-N19F5-015）

附注：

其他：(1)釘書針裝訂。(2)館藏2冊,其中一冊封面將"NM 52 05 02. 1. 0. 2"删改爲"NM 52 05 02. 10. 2"。

3009 Epid Emic Rubella in Taiwan 1957-1958: III. Gamma Globulin in the Prevention of Rubella/by J. Thomas Grayston and Raymond H. Watten. —Taipei, Taiwan: United States Naval Medical Research No. 2, 1959

12 p.; 26.5 cm

NAMRU TWO, May 20, 1959（NM 52 05 02. 1. 2）

HSMH（HS-N19F5-013）

附注：

其他:(1)釘書針裝訂。(2)館藏2冊。

3010 Epid Emiologic Studies of the 1958 Cholera Epidemic in Bangkok, Thailand/ by Pradith Siddhichai and J. Thomas Grayston. —Taipei, Taiwan: United States Naval Medical Research No. 2, 1959

 18 p. ; 26.5 cm

 NAMRU TWO, April 21, 1959 (NM 52 11 02. 3. 3)

 HSMH (HS-N19F5-012)

 附注:

  其他:(1)釘書針裝訂。(2)館藏2冊。

3011 Erasmus of Rotterdam/by Stefan Zweig. —New York: The Viking Press, 1956

 247 p. ; 19.7 cm

 HSMH (HS-N04F6-010)

 附注:

  印章:扉頁有胡適簽名"Hu Shih Dec. 10, 1957"。

  批注圈劃:書中有胡適的批注劃綫數十處。

3012 An Essay for Our Times/by H. Stuart Hughes. —New York: Alfred A. Knopf, 1950

 196 p. ; 19.5 cm

 HSMH (HS-N03F6-006)

 附注:

  印章:內封面頁鈐有"胡適的書"朱文方印。

  批注圈劃:書中有胡適的批注劃綫數十處。

  夾紙:封面裏夾有名片1張,印有" Y. C. Koo Deputy Treasurer International Monetary Fund Washington D. C. "。

3013 Essay on Literature Written by the Third-Century Chinese Poet Lu Chi/ translated by Shih-Hsiang Chen. —Portland, Maine: The Anthoensen Press, 1953 xxxv p. ; 28.4 cm

HSMH（HS-N03F4-027）

附註：

印章：内封面頁鈐有"胡適的書"朱文方印。

題記：扉頁有陳世驤題贈："適之師賜正 世驤 一九五四 二月。"

批注圈劃：頁 xix 有胡適的批注一處。

夾紙：内封面頁有夾紙 1 張。

相關記載：陳世驤致胡適函"奉寄所譯《陸機文賦》散文詩並請指正"，參見館藏號：HS-US01-080-015。

其他：(1) 扉頁夾有抽印本 1 冊："In Search of the Beginnings of Chinese Literary Criticism", in *Semitic & Oriental Studies*, Vol. XI (1951)，頁 45—63。(2) 此爲《陸機文賦》英譯本，陳世驤譯。

3014 Essays：Darwiniana/by Thomas H. Huxley. —New York：D. Appleton and Company, 1904

x, 475 p. ; 19.7 cm

HSMH（HS-N12F4-022）

附註：

印章：内封面頁鈐有"胡適的書"朱文方印。

相關記載：胡適購買赫胥黎《文集》共 9 冊的記載，參見《胡適日記》1952 年 1 月 15 日條。

其他：此書爲審定版。

3015 Essays：Discourses：Biological and Geological/by Thomas H. Huxley. —New York：D. Appleton and Company, 1904

xv, 388 p. ; 19.7 cm

HSMH（HS-N12F4-028）

附註：

印章：内封面頁鈐有"胡適的書"朱文方印。

相關記載：胡適購買赫胥黎《文集》共 9 冊的記載，參見《胡適日記》1952 年 1 月 15 日條。

其他:此書爲審定版。

3016 Essays：Evolution and Ethics, and Other Essays/by Thomas H. Huxley. — New York：D. Appleton and Company, 1904

xv, 334 p.；19.7 cm

HSMH（HS-N12F4-029）

附注:

　印章:內封面頁鈐有"胡適的書"朱文方印。

　批注圈劃:書中有胡適的劃綫數處。

　相關記載:胡適購買赫胥黎《文集》共9冊的記載,參見《胡適日記》1952年1月15日條。

　其他:此書爲審定版。

3017 Essays：Hume, with Helps to the Study of Berkeley/by Thomas H. Huxley. —New York：D. Appleton and Company, 1904

xiv, 321 p.；19.7 cm

HSMH（HS-N12F4-026）

附注:

　印章:內封面頁鈐有"胡適的書"朱文方印。

　夾紙:扉頁夾有胡適的筆記小紙片9張。

　相關記載:胡適購買赫胥黎《文集》共9冊的記載,參見《胡適日記》1952年1月15日條。

　其他:此書爲審定版。

3018 Essays：Man's Place in Nature and Other Anthropological Essays/by Thomas H. Huxley. —New York：D. Appleton and Company, 1904

xv, 329 p.；19.7 cm

HSMH（HS-N12F4-027）

附注:

　印章:內封面頁鈐有"胡適的書"朱文方印。

　相關記載:胡適購買赫胥黎《文集》共9冊的記載,參見《胡適日記》1952

年1月15日條。

其他：此書爲審定版。

3019 Essays：Method and Results/by Thomas H. Huxley. —New York：D. Appleton and Company, 1904

viii, 430 p.；19.7 cm

HSMH（HS-N12F4-021）

附註：

印章：内封面頁鈐有"胡適的書"朱文方印。

題記：扉頁有胡適題記："赫胥黎論文集 共九冊 胡適"。

批注圈劃：書中有胡適的批注劃綫數十處。

相關記載：胡適購買赫胥黎《文集》共9冊的記載，參見《胡適日記》1952年1月15日條。

其他：此書爲審定版。

3020 Essays：Science and Christian Tradition/by Thomas H. Huxley. —New York：D. Appleton and Company, 1904

xxxiv, 419 p.；19.7 cm

HSMH（HS-N12F4-025）

附註：

印章：内封面頁鈐有"胡適的書"朱文方印。

批注圈劃：書中有胡適的批注劃綫數十處。

夾紙：書中有夾紙4張，其中頁58、59間的夾紙有胡適記"This 'Prologue' was originally written as Preface to his 'Controverted Questions,' 1892, which volume is not included in the 9 volumes of 'Essays.' So the 'Essays' unforced to in the 'Prologue' on pp. 33, 34, & 36, are not in this volume. H. S."。

相關記載：胡適購買赫胥黎《文集》共9冊的記載，參見《胡適日記》1952年1月15日條。

其他：此書爲審定版。

3021 Essays: Science and Education/by Thomas H. Huxley. —New York: D. Appleton and Company, 1904

ix, 451 p.; 19.7 cm

HSMH（HS-N12F4-023）

附註：

印章：內封面頁鈐有"胡適的書"朱文方印。

夾紙：書中有夾紙1張。

相關記載：胡適購買赫胥黎《文集》共9冊的記載，參見《胡適日記》1952年1月15日條。

其他：此書爲審定版。

3022 Essays: Science and Hebrew Tradition/by Thomas H. Huxley. —New York: D. Appleton and Company, 1904

xvi, 372 p.; 19.7 cm

HSMH（HS-N12F4-024）

附註：

印章：內封面頁鈐有"胡適的書"朱文方印。

批注圈劃：書中有胡適的批注劃綫數十處。

相關記載：胡適購買赫胥黎《文集》共9冊的記載，參見《胡適日記》1952年1月15日條。

其他：此書爲審定版。

3023 Essays and English Traits/by Ralph Waldo Emerson. —New York: P. F. Collier & Son Corporation, 1909

474 p., [1] plate; 21 cm

Harvard Classics: The Five-Foot Shelf of Books, Vol. 5

HSMH（HS-N12F6-005）

附註：

印章：內封面頁鈐有"胡適的書"朱文方印。

3024 Essays, Civil and Moral, and the New Atlantis; Areopagitica and Tractate on Education; Religio Medici/edited by Charles W. Eliot. —New York: P. F. Collier & Son Corporation, 1909

 332 p., [1] plate; 21 cm

 Harvard Classics: The Five-Foot Shelf of Books, Vol. 3

 HSMH（HS-N12F6-003）

 附註：

  印章：內封面頁鈐有"胡適的書"朱文方印。

3025 Essays, English and American/edited by Charles W. Eliot. —New York: P. F. Collier & Son Corporation, 1910

 470 p., [1] plate; 21 cm

 Harvard Classics: The Five-Foot Shelf of Books, Vol. 28

 HSMH（HS-N12F6-028）

 附註：

  印章：內封面頁鈐有"胡適的書"朱文方印。

3026 Essays in East-West Philosophy: An Attempt at World Philosophical Synthesis/edited by Charles A. Moore. —Honolulu, Hawaii: University of Hawaii Press, 1951

 ix, 467 p.; 23.4 cm

 HSMH（HS-N03F6-010）

 附註：

  印章：內封面頁鈐有"胡適的書"朱文方印。

  批注圈劃：書中有胡適的劃綫數處。

  夾紙：書中有夾紙1張。

3027 Essays in Experimental Logic/by John Dewey. —New York: Dover Publications, Inc., 1953

 444 p.; 20.5 cm

 HSMH（HS-N04F4-018）

 附註：

印章：内封面頁鈐有"胡適的書"朱文方印。

批注圈劃：書中有胡適的批注劃綫數十處。

夾紙：書中有夾紙4張。

3028 Essays in Medieval Life and Thought: Presented in Honor of Austin Patterson Evans/edited by John H. Mundy, Richard W. Emery and Benjamin N. Nelson. —New York: Columbia University Press, 1955

xviii, 258 p. ; 22.3 cm

HSMH（HS-N04F6-022）

附注：

印章：内封面頁鈐有"胡適的書"朱文方印。

3029 Essays in Zen Buddhism, First Series/by Daisetz Teitaro Suzuki. —London: Published for the Buddhist Society by Rider and Company, [n. d.]

383 p. , plates; 19 cm

HSMH（HS-N06F1-016）

附注：

印章：内封面頁鈐有"胡適的書"朱文方印及"胡適"紫色戳印。

批注圈劃：扉頁有胡適的黑、鉛筆注記，其中一句是"'October 1926' —date of his Preface"；内文有胡適的紅、藍、鉛筆注記與劃綫。

夾紙：偶有夾紙。

3030 Essays in Zen Buddhism, Second Series/by Daisetz Teitaro Suzuki. —London: Published for the Buddhist Society by Rider and Company, 1950

348 p. , illus. ; 19 cm

HSMH（HS-N06F1-017）

附注：

印章：内封面頁鈐有"胡適的書"朱文方印及"胡適"紫色戳印。

批注圈劃：扉頁有胡適的注記："'Febrary 1933' — date of Preface"；内文有胡適的藍、鉛筆注記劃綫數十處。

3031 The Essays of Ralph Waldo Emerson/by Ralph Waldo Emerson. —New York：The Illustrated Modern Library，1944

    557 p. ; 19 cm

    HSMH（HS-N04F3-023）

    附注：

        印章：書的外盒有胡適簽名"Hu Shih"；扉頁鈐有"胡適的書"朱文方印。

3032 Essays on Church and State/by Lord Acton; edited and introduced by Douglas Woodruff. —New York：The Viking Press，1953

    518 p. ; 22.3 cm

    HSMH（HS-N04F6-018）

    附注：

        印章：扉頁有胡適簽名"Hu Shih Jan. 28，1953"；內封面頁鈐有"胡適的書"朱文方印。

        批注圈劃：頁 v 目錄頁有胡適的注記。

3033 Ethics in a Business Society/by Marquis W. Childs and Douglass Cater. —New York：The New American Library，1954

    192 p. ; 18 cm

    HSMH（HS-N19F4-033）

    附注：

        印章：內封面頁鈐有"胡適的書"朱文方印。

        與胡適的關係：內容提及胡適。

3034 Europe Today：A Report on the European Economic Community. —New York：The First National City Bank of New York，[n. d.]

    39 p. ; 25.3 cm

    HSMH（HS-N20F2-015）

    附注：

        印章：目次頁鈐有"胡適的書"朱文方印。

3035 Evolution and the Founders of Pragmatism/by Philip P. Wiener. —Cambridge：Harvard University Press，1949

xiv, 288 p.；24.4 cm

HSMH（HS-N04F4-002）

附注：

印章：扉頁有胡適簽名"Hu Shih December 4，1949"；內封面頁鈐有"胡適的書"朱文方印。

批注圈劃：書中有胡適的批注劃綫數處。

3036 Exploring the Child's World/by Helen Parkhurst. —New York：Appleton-Century-Crofts, Inc.，1951

xxx, 290 p., plates；21 cm

HSMH（HS-N19F4-037）

附注：

印章：扉頁鈐有"胡適的書"朱文方印。

夾紙：頁 xiii 夾有紙卡 2 張，一張爲出版商的贈書卡，另一張爲書籍出版資料卡。

內附文件：頁 150、151 間夾有 1951 年 5 月 6 日作者 Helen Parkhurst 致胡適函 1 張。

3037 Facts on Communism, Vol. 2：The Soviet Union, from Lenin to Khrushchev/by Committee on Un-American Activities. —Washington, D. C.：United States Government Printing Office, 1960

367, xix p.；23.3 cm

HSMH（HS-N04F1-024）

附注：

印章：內封面頁鈐有"胡適的書"朱文方印。

3038 The Family of Man：The Preatest Photographic Exhibition of All Time—503 Pictures from 68 Countries—Created by Edward Steichen for the Museum of Modern Art/by Edward Steichen. —New York：Museum of Modern Art, 1955

192 p. ; 28.6 cm

HSMH（HS-N19F4-005）

3039 Farmington/by Clarence Darrow. —New York：Charles Scribner's Sons, 1932

255 p. ; 20.8 cm

HSMH（HS-N19F5-078）

附注：

印章：内封面頁鈐有"胡適的書"朱文方印。

3040 Faust, Part I：Egmont, Hermann and Dorothea; Doctor Faustus/edited by Charles W. Eliot. —New York：P. F. Collier & Son Corporation, 1909

410 p., [1] plate; 21 cm

Harvard Classics：The Five-Foot Shelf of Books, Vol. 19

HSMH（HS-N12F6-019）

附注：

印章：内封面頁鈐有"胡適的書"朱文方印。

3041 The FBI Story：A Report to the People/by Don Whitehead. —New York：Random House, 1956

368 p. ; 23.6 cm

HSMH（HS-N04F2-026）

附注：

印章：内封面頁鈐有"胡適的書"朱文方印。

批注圈劃：書中有鉛筆劃綫數十處。

3042 Fifteen Minutes a Day：The Reading Guide/by Charles W. Eliot. —New York：P. F. Collier & Son Corporation, 1930

95 p., [1] plate; 21 cm

Harvard Classics：The Five-Foot Shelf of Books

HSMH（HS-N12F5-022）

附注：

印章:内封面頁鈐有"胡適的書"朱文方印。

3043 Fifty Major Documents of the Twentieth Century/by Louis L. Snyder. —Princeton, New Jersey: D. Van Nostrand Company, Inc., 1955

185 p.; 18.1 cm

HSMH(HS-N04F2-013)

附注:

印章:内封面頁鈐有"胡適的書"朱文方印。

夾紙:書中夾有 Pan American 航空公司空白明信片 2 張。

3044 Fifty Years of Chinese Philosophy 1898-1950/by O. Briere. —London: George Allen & Unwin Ltd., 1956

159 p.; 22.1 cm

HSMH(HS-N03F3-016)

附注:

印章:内封面頁鈐有"胡適的書"朱文方印。

批注圈劃:頁 142 有校改一處。

夾紙:書中有夾紙 1 張。

與胡適的關係:內容有"Hu Shih and the Pragmatism of Dewey"一文,其他篇章亦有提及胡適著作《四十自述》、《胡適文存》一集、《胡適文存》二集、The Chinese Renaissance、"Intellectual China in 1919"、"The Literary Revolution in China"。

相關記載:1953 年 4 月 10 日 Miriam Brokaw 致胡適函,爲諮詢對於此書的意見,參見館藏號:HS-US01-064-034。

3045 Fighting Editors/edited by Walter Howey. —Washington Square, Philadelphia: David McKay Company, 1948

viii, 163 p.; 24 cm

HSMH(HS-N19F3-006)

附注:

印章:内封面頁鈐有"胡適的書"朱文方印。

3046 The Figure of the Earth from Measurement in China/by Mo Tsao. —Taipei, Taiwan：Tsao Mo, 1955

  3 p.；21.9 cm

  HSMH（HS-N03F2-010）

  附注：

    題記：封面有作者題贈："適之先生指正 曹謨敬贈。"

    其他：此爲會議論文"Presented to the United Nations Regional Cartographic Conference for Asia and the Far East, Mussoorie, India, February, 1955"。

3047 The Fire's Center/by Henry Goddard Leach. —New York：The Fire Editions Press, 1950

  55 p.；19.6 cm

  HSMH（HS-N19F5-056）

  附注：

    印章：内封面頁鈐有"胡適的書"朱文方印。

    其他：本書是詩集。

3048 The First Part of the Delightful History of the Most Ingenious Knight：Don Quixote of the Mancha/by Miguel de Cervantes. —New York：P. F. Collier & Son Corporation, 1909

  519 p., [1] plate；21 cm

  Harvard Classics：The Five-Foot Shelf of Books, Vol. 14

  HSMH（HS-N12F6-014）

  附注：

    印章：内封面頁鈐有"胡適的書"朱文方印。

3049 Fitzpatrick Cartoons/by D. R. Fitzpatrick. —St. Louis：The Pulitzer Publishing Company, 1947

  240 p.：illus.；31 cm

  HSMH（HS-N13F1-018）

附注:

  印章:扉頁鈐有"胡適之印"白文方印;另一扉頁鈐有"胡適之鉨"白文方印及"胡適的書"朱文方印。

  題記:封面裏有作者題贈:"For Dr. Hu Shih the greatest authority on American Editorial Cartoons, with respect and affection. D. R. Fitzpatrick。"

  夾紙:書中有夾紙8張。

  其他:附紙盒1個。

3050 The Five Thousand Dictionary: A Chinese-English Pocket Dictionary and Index to the Character Cards of the College of Chinese Studies/originally compiled by Courtenay H. Fenn; fifth edition with additions and revisions by George D. Wilder and Chin Hsien Tseng. —Peking: Union Press, 1940

  xxxviii, 697 p.; 16.8 cm

  HSMH (HS-N19F1-038)

  附注:

  印章:扉頁有胡適簽名"Hu Shih 胡適";内封面頁鈐有"胡適的書"朱文方印。

  題記:扉頁有題記:"'物歸原主' 晚 黃漢新拜上 紐約 一九四五年。"

  批注圈劃:書中有劃綫數十處。

  其他:此爲第5版。

3051 Flight to Cathay: An Aerial Journey to Yale-in-China/by W. Reginald Wheeler; with a Foreword by Henry Sloane Coffin. —New Haven, Connecticut: Yale University Press, 1949

  81 p.; 23.5 cm

  HSMH (HS-N19F2-060)

  附注:

  印章:内封面頁鈐有"胡適的書"朱文方印。

  題記:扉頁有作者題贈:"For Dr. Hu Shih The Leader and Pioneer in the Renaissance in China With □ respect and admiration. From W. Reginald Wheeler Dec 1, 49。"

批注圈劃：書中有劃綫數處。

3052 Flight to Destiny: An Interpretation for Youth of the Life of Theodore Carswell Hume/edited by Ruth Isabel Seabury. —New York: Association Press, 1945

124 p. ; 19.4 cm

HSMH（HS-N19F3-032）

附注：

印章：內封面頁鈐有"胡適的書"朱文方印。

題記：扉頁有贈書者題贈："To my good friend Doctor Hu Shih with affection from Edward H. Hume Cambridge 9th April 1945。"

3053 Fluctuating Exchange Rates in Countries with Relatively Stable Economies: Some European Experiences after World War I/by S. C. Tsiang. —Washington: International Monetary Fund, 1959

244-273 p. ; 22.9 cm

The October 1959 Issue of the International Monetary Fund Staff Papers

HSMH（HS-N19F5-028）

附注：

題記：封面有作者題贈："適之院長教正 後學 蔣碩傑敬呈。"

其他：抽印本。

3054 The Fo-Sho-Hing-Tsan-King: A Life of Buddha/by Asvaghosha Bodhisattva; translated from Sanskrit into Chinese by Dharmaraksha, A. D. 420 and from Chinese into English by Samuel Beal. —Oxford: The Clarendon Press, 1883

xxxvii, 376 p. ; 22.6 cm

HSMH（HS-N12F4-016）

附注：

印章：內封面頁鈐有"胡適"紫色戳印。

批注圈劃：頁376有鉛筆注記："Finis。"

3055 Folk-Lore and Fable: Aesop, Grimm, Andersen/edited by Charles W. Eliot. —New York: P. F. Collier & Son Corporation, 1909

   361 p., [1] plate; 21 cm

   Harvard Classics: The Five-Foot Shelf of Books, Vol. 17

   HSMH (HS-N12F6-017)

   附註：

   印章：內封面頁鈐有"胡適的書"朱文方印。

3056 Food and Money in Acient China: The Earliest Economic History of China to A. D. 25/translated and annotated by Nancy Lee Swann. —Princeton: Princeton University Press, 1950

   xiii, 482, [79] p.; 25cm

   HSMH (HS-N03F4-032)

   附註：

   印章：扉頁鈐有"胡適的書"朱文方印。

   夾紙：內封面頁夾有小卡片1張，印有"With the Compliments of Princeton University Press"。

   與胡適的關係：頁107有胡適題籤："美國孫念禮譯註 漢書食貨志 附史記漢書貨殖傳 胡適題"；頁483有胡適題簽書名"漢書食貨志"。內容與注釋均提及胡適。

   相關記載：1944年9月11日楊聯陞致胡適函，參見館藏號：HS-LS01-001-029，HS-JDSHSC-1205-003。

3057 Fool in the Reeds/by Chen Chi-ying. —Hong Kong: Rainbow Press, 1959

   295 p.; 18.8 cm

   HSMH (HS-N03F3-006)

   附註：

   印章：扉頁鈐有"胡適的書"朱文方印。

   題記：另一扉頁有作者題贈："適之先生存正 後學陳紀瀅拜贈 四八、十二、廿七日。"

夾紙:版權頁夾有重光文藝出版社的信封地址殘片 1 張,上有藍筆記"已復 四八、十二、卅一"。

其他:(1)封面有中文書名"荻村傳"及作者"陳紀瀅"。(2)本書的內封面頁裝訂顛倒。

3058 Forbidden Area/by Pat Frank. —Philadelphia: J. B. Lippincott Company, 1956

221 p. ; 21.8 cm

HSMH (HS-N19F5-077)

附注:

印章:內封面頁鈐有"胡適的書"朱文方印。

其他:扉頁右下角有藍色鉛筆記"Mayer"。

3059 Foreign Reviews of President Chiang's Book: Soviet Russia in China, Vol. 2/by M. Veynbaum, et al. —Taipei, Taiwan: "Free China Review", 1958

60 p. ; 18.8 cm

HSMH (HS-N03F2-003)

3060 Formosa (Taiwan)/by W. G. Goddard. —Taipei, Taiwan: "China Post Printing Shop", 1958

161 p. ; 18.7 cm

HSMH (HS-N03F2-002)

3061 Formosa and Free World Policy/by Herrymon Maurer. —New York: The New Leader, 1955

15 p. ; 28 cm

The New Leader, April 4, 1955

HSMH (HS-N19F2-067)

3062 The Forrestal Diaries/edited by Walter Millis. —New York: The Viking Press, 1951

xxiv, 581 p. ; 21.9 cm

HSMH（HS-N04F2-008）

附注：

　　印章：内封面頁鈐有"胡適的書"朱文方印。

　　批注圈劃：書中有胡適的批注劃綫數十處。

　　夾紙：書中有夾紙5張。

　　與胡適的關係：内容提及胡適。

3063　The Four Books: Confucian Analects, the Great Learning, the Doctrine of the Mean, and the Works of Mencius = 中英對照四書/translated by James Legge. —Shanghai, China: The Chinese Book Company, 1933

　　1014 p. ; 19 cm

　　HSMH（HS-N03F5-005）

　　附注：

　　　　印章：内封面頁鈐有"胡適的書"朱文方印。

　　　　題記：扉頁有胡適題記："To Ginny Rily March 31, 1946. 胡適從舊金山買來的。一九四二年冬季。"

　　　　批注圈劃：書中有胡適的批注劃綫數處。

　　　　夾紙：書中有夾紙11張。

　　　　其他：扉頁粘貼一紙張，印有"中英對照 四書 The Four Books With English Translation and Notes 商務印書館印行 The Commercial Press, Ltd."。

3064　Fourth Advanced Management Program in the Far East: A Program for the Development of Asian Management Manpower, June-August, 1959. —Manila, Philippines: National Printing Co., Inc., 1959

　　32 p. ; 23 cm

　　HSMH（HS-N20F1-046）

3065　Free Admission/by Ilka Chase. —Garden City, New York: Doubleday & Company, Inc., 1948

　　319 p. ; 20.8 cm

　　HSMH（HS-N19F5-079）

附注：

　　印章：内封面貞鈐有"胡適的書"朱文方印。

　　其他：扉頁有"Fennell's News Room 380 Broadway"黑色戳印。

3066 Freedom：Its Meaning/edited by Ruth Nanda Anshen. —New York：Harcourt, Brace and Company, 1940

　　xii, 686 p.；22.4 cm

　　HSMH（HS-N03F6-022）

　　附注：

　　印章：扉頁鈐有"胡適的書"朱文方印。

　　題記：扉頁有胡適題記："Hu Shih 胡適 See pp. 114-122。"

　　夾紙：書中有夾紙 1 張。

　　與胡適的關係：頁 114—122 收錄胡適的文章"The Modernization of China and Japan：a Comparative Study in Cultural Conflict and a Consideration of Freedom"。

3067 Freedom and Culture/by John Dewey. —New York：G. P. Putnam's Sons, 1939

　　176 p.；21.2 cm

　　HSMH（HS-N04F4-017）

　　附注：

　　印章：内封面頁鈐有"胡適的書"朱文方印。

3068 Freedom and Responsibility in the American Way of Life/by Carl L. Becker. —New York：Vintage Books, 1955

　　xlviii, 135, iv p.；18.5 cm

　　HSMH（HS-N04F4-022）

　　附注：

　　印章：内封面頁鈐有"胡適的書"朱文方印。

　　批注圈劃：書中有胡適的批注劃綫數十處。

3069 French and English Philosophers: Descartes, Rousseau, Voltaire, Hobbes/ edited by Charles W. Eliot. —New York: P. F. Collier & Son Corporation, 1910

 417 p., [1] plate; 21 cm

 Harvard Classics: The Five-Foot Shelf of Books, Vol. 34

 HSMH（HS-N12F5-004）

附注：

 印章：內封面頁鈐有"胡適的書"朱文方印。

 批注圈劃：書中有胡適的批注劃綫數十處。

3070 From the Declaration of Independence to the Constitution/edited by Carl J. Friedrich and Robert G. McCloskey. —New York: The Liberal Arts Press, 1954

 lxviii, 71 p.; 18.5 cm

 Forum Books, No. 3

 HSMH（HS-N04F3-030）

附注：

 印章：內封面頁鈐有"胡適的書"朱文方印。

3071 The Gabbroic Rocks of Hutoushan and Kuanshan, East Taiwan/by V. C. Juan, F. H. Chang, and L. C. Hsu. —Taipei, Taiwan: Geological Society of China, 1959

 5-31 p.; 26.4 cm

 The Proceedings of the Geological Society of China, No. 2, March, 1959

 HSMH（HS-N19F5-031）

附注：

 題記：封面有作者題贈："適之學長指正　著者敬贈。"

 其他：(1) 抽印本。(2) 中文篇名"台灣台東虎頭山及關山輝長岩類之研究"；作者爲阮維周、王源、孫獻祥。

3072 Genetics and Animal and Plant Breeding/by C. C. Li. —Washington: American Association for the Advancement of Science, 1961

 297-321 p.; 23 cm

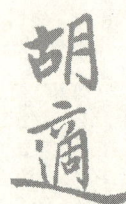

Sciences in Communist China, 1961

HSMH（HS-N20F1-045）

附注：

批注圈劃:書中有注記數處。

其他:抽印本。

3073 Geological and Geophysical Development of the Structures along the Continental Slopes of the Circum-pacific Coasts and the True Concept of a Geosyncline/by Ting Ying H. MA. —Taipei, Taiwan: Ting Ying H. MA, 1957

8 p.; 26.2 cm

Oceanographia Sinica, Vol. IV, No. 1, October 1957

HSMH（HS-N20F1-089）

附注：

其他:中文封底:"中國海洋誌 第四卷第一號 馬廷英著 太平洋周邊構造之地質與地球物理之研究 中華民國四十六年十月。"

3074 Goat Red Blood Cells in the Agglutination Test for Infectious Mononucleosis/by San-Pin Wang and J. Thomas Grayston. —Taipei, Taiwan: United States Naval Medical Research No. 2, 1959

7 p.; 26.5 cm

NAMRU TWO, February 25, 1959（NM 52 11 02. 4. 2）

HSMH（HS-N19F5-010）

附注：

其他:(1)釘書針裝訂。(2)館藏2冊。

3075 The God That Failed/edited by Richard Crossman. —New York: Harper & Brothers, 1949

273 p.; 21.2 cm

HSMH（HS-N04F1-030）

附注：

印章:内封面頁鈐有"胡適的書"朱文方印。

題記:扉頁有胡適題記:"Hu Shih April 26, 1950 失敗了的上帝(神)。"

批注圈劃:書中有胡適的批注劃綫數十處。

相關記載:董時進在紐約時曾向胡適借閱此書,已閱過歸還,參見董時進致胡適函,館藏號:HS-US01-091-015。

3076 God's Men/by Pearl S. Buck. —New York: Pocket Books, Inc., 1953

452 p.; 16.3 cm

HSMH(HS-N19F5-081)

附注:

印章:扉頁鈐有"胡適的書"朱文方印。

批注圈劃:頁 133 有批注劃綫一處。

其他:作者中文名爲"賽珍珠"。

3077 Goetterdaemmerung (the dusk of the Gods): A Music Drama in Three Acts and a Prelude/by Richard Wagner. —New York: Fred Rullman Inc., [n.d.]

56 p.; 25.4 cm

Metropolitan Opera House Grand Opera

HSMH(HS-N19F5-038)

附注:

印章:内封面頁鈐有"胡適的書"朱文方印。

3078 The Golden Year of Fan Cheng-ta/translated by Gerald Bullett. —Cambridge: Cambridge University Press, 1946

44 p.; 19.3 cm

HSMH(HS-N03F4-029)

附注:

印章:内封面頁鈐有"胡適的書"朱文方印。

其他:扉頁有題籤:"范成大四時田園雜興六十首。"

3079　Grammata Serica: Script and Phonetics in Chinese and Sino-Japanese/by Bernhard Karlgren. —Stockholm: Museum of Far Eastern Antiquities, 1940

　　471 p.；27.9 cm

　　The Bulletin on the Museum of Far Eastern Antiquities, No. 12, 1940

　　HSMH（HS-N03F1-029）

　　附注：

　　　印章：內封面頁鈐有"胡適的書"朱文方印。

　　　題記：扉頁有贈書者題贈："To Dr. Hu Shih on his 60th birthday with compliments of Yen Wen-yu & Tung Shih-kang 嚴文郁 童世綱"，胡適補記："December 17, 1951。"

　　　批注圈劃：書中有胡適的批注圈劃數處。

3080　The Great Cultural Traditions: The Foundations of Civilization, Vol. I: The Ancient Cities/by Ralph Turner. —New York: McGraw-Hill Book Company, Inc., 1941

　　xviii, 1-601, xxiv p., illus., maps（part fold.）；23.5 cm

　　HSMH（HS-N19F6-031）

　　附注：

　　　印章：內封面頁鈐有"胡適的書"朱文方印。

　　　題記：扉頁有作者題贈："Aug. 16, 1953 To Dr. Hu Shih, with sincere regards. Ralph E. Turner。"

　　　批注圈劃：書中有胡適的批注劃綫數百處，其中頁 370 記"這樣的 Zoroastrian 背景，故這一帶的民族不能接受佛教而能接受回教 適之"。

　　　夾紙：另一扉頁夾有胡適的筆記紙片 3 張；書中另有夾紙 6 張。

　　　其他：此爲第 1 版第 3 次印刷。

3081　The Great Cultural Traditions: The Foundations of Civilization, Vol. II: The Classical Empires/by Ralph Turner. —New York: McGraw-Hill Book Company, Inc., 1941

　　xv, 602-1333, xxxii p., illus., maps（part fold.）；23.5 cm

　　HSMH（HS-N19F6-032）

附注：

　　印章：内封面頁鈐有"胡適的書"朱文方印。

　　批注圈劃：書中有胡適的批注劃綫數十處。

　　夾紙：頁1120、1121間夾有Hotel Dupont Plaza的空白便條紙1張。

　　其他：此爲第1版第3次印刷。

3082　The Great EB：The Story of the Encyclopædia Britannica/by Herman Kogan. —Chicago：The University of Chicago Press，1958

　　vii，339 p.；24 cm

　　HSMH（HS-N19F6-015）

　　附注：

　　　印章：内封面頁鈐有"胡適的書"朱文方印。

　　　相關記載：1958年5月23日William Benton致胡適函，提及寄贈此書事，參見館藏號：HS-US01-087-009。

3083　The Great Enterprise：Relating Ourselves to Our World/by H. A. Overstreet. — New York：W. W. Norton & Company，Inc.，1952

　　332 p.；21.5 cm

　　HSMH（HS-N19F4-040）

　　附注：

　　　印章：内封面頁鈐有"胡適的書"朱文方印。

　　　夾紙：頁252、253間夾有出版社贈書卡1張。

3084　Great Essays in Science/edited by Martin Gardner. —New York：Pocket Books，Inc.，1957

　　xx，408 p.；16.15 cm

　　HSMH（HS-N19F4-028）

　　附注：

　　　印章：内封面頁鈐有"胡適的書"朱文方印。

3085　The Great Globe Itself：A Preface to World Affairs/by William C. Bullitt. —

New York: Charles Scribner's Sons, 1946

vii, 310 p. ; 20 cm

HSMH（HS-N04F2-014）

附注：

印章：扉頁鈐有"胡適的書"朱文方印。

題記：扉頁背面有贈書者題贈："For Dr Hu Shih From W. R. W. April 1, 50。"胡適在"W. R. W."旁註"（Wheeler）"。

批注圈劃：書中有胡適的批注劃綫數十處。

夾紙：書中有夾紙12張。

3086 Great Mistakes of the War/by Hanson W. Baldwin. —New York: Harper & Brothers, 1950

114 p. ; 19.9 cm

HSMH（HS-N04F5-006）

附注：

印章：扉頁有胡適簽名"Hu Shih May 1950"；内封面頁鈐有"胡適的書"朱文方印。

批注圈劃：書中有胡適的批注劃綫數十處。

3087 Great Reading from Life/edited by Edward K. Thompson. —New York: Harper & Brothers, 1960

xii, 775 p. ; 26 cm

HSMH（HS-N19F5-084）

附注：

印章：館藏2册,其中一册的内封面頁鈐有"胡適的書"朱文方印。

夾紙：其中一册的頁86、87間夾有 Mr. and Mrs. Henry R. Luce 名片1張。

3088 Growth and Structure of the English Language/by Otto Jespersen. —Garden City, New York: Doubleday & Company, Inc., 1955

v, 274 p. ; 18.1 cm

Doubleday Anchor Books

HSMH（HS-N19F5-054）

附注：

　　印章：内封面頁鈐有"胡適的書"朱文方印。

　　其他：本書爲第9版。

3089 Growth and Structure of the English Language/by Otto Jespersen. —Garden City, New York: Doubleday & Company, Inc., 1956

　　v, 274 p.; 18.1 cm

　　Doubleday Anchor Books

　　HSMH（HS-N19F5-055）

附注：

　　印章：内封面頁鈐有"胡適的書"朱文方印。

　　其他：本書爲第9版。

3090 The Growth of Philosophic Radicalism/by Elie Halevy. —Boston: The Beacon Press, 1955

　　xix, 554 p.; 20.4 cm

　　HSMH（HS-N04F6-019）

附注：

　　印章：内封面頁鈐有"胡適的書"朱文方印。

3091 H L Mencken: A Portrait from Memory/by Charles Angoff. —New York: Thomas Yoseloff, Inc., 1956

　　240 p.; 21.8 cm

　　HSMH（HS-N04F3-008）

附注：

　　印章：内封面頁鈐有"胡適的書"朱文方印。

3092 The Hall of Light: A Study of Early Chinese Kingship/by William Edward Soothill(蘇慧廉). —London: Lutterworth Press, 1951

　　xxii, 289 p.; 22.1 cm

Lutterworth Library Vol. xxxviii, Missionary Research Series, No. 18

HSMH（HS-N03F4-031）

附註：

　　印章：內封面頁鈐有"胡適的書"朱文方印。

　　夾紙：書中有夾紙2張，一張是此書簡介，另一張是小卡片，印有"With the Compliments of Lady Hosie and Lutterworth Press"。

　　相關記載：1952年2月15日 Amy S. Eppenheim 致胡適函，代 Lady Hosie 詢問是否收到此書，參見館藏號：HS-US01-092-008。

3093　Hamilton, Madison and Jay on the Constitution/edited by Ralph H. Gabriel. —New York: The Liberal Arts Press, 1954

xviii, 231 p. ; 18.5 cm

Forum Books, No. 4

HSMH（HS-N04F3-032）

附註：

　　印章：內封面頁鈐有"胡適的書"朱文方印。

3094　A Handbook of Greek Mythology/by H. J. Rose. —New York: E. P. Dutton & Co., 1959

ix, 363 p. ; 18.4 cm

HSMH（HS-N04F6-034）

附註：

　　印章：扉頁有胡適簽名"Hu Shih"；內封面頁鈐有"胡適的書"朱文方印。

3095　Handy Dictionary of the French and English Languages with Phonetic Transcription of Every French Vocabulary Word/by J. O. Kettridge. —Washington Square, Philadelphia: David McKay Company, 1947

xiv, 526 p. ; 17.1 cm

HSMH（HS-N19F1-039）

附註：

　　印章：扉頁有胡適簽名"Hu Shih 胡適 July14, 1950"；內封面頁鈐有"胡適的書"朱文方印。

3096 Handy Dictionary of the German and English Languages/by K. Wichmann with rules as to pronunciation. —Philadelphia: David McKay Company, 1950

xv, 736 p. ; 17.3 cm

HSMH（HS-N19F1-040）

附注：

印章：扉頁有胡適簽名"Hu Shih 胡適 July14, 1950"；内封面頁鈐有"胡適的書"朱文方印。

3097 Harem Favorities of an Illustrious Celestial ＝ 漢宫專寵/by Howard S. Levy. —Taichung, Taiwan: Lin Yun-peng, 1958

viii, 198 p. ; 26.6 cm

HSMH（HS-N03F4-028）

附注：

題記：扉頁有作者題贈："Taichung, Taiwan June 14, 1959 To Doctor Hu Shih, with admiration and respectful regards, Howard S. Levy。"

其他：版權頁作者名"李豪偉"。

3098 The Harvard Reading List in American History/edited by John Merriman Gaus, et al. —Cambridge, Mass.: Harvard University Press, 1949

22 p. ; 21.2 cm

HSMH（HS-N19F2-036, HS-N20F1-044）

附注：

印章：館藏2册，内封面頁均鈐有"胡適的書"朱文方印。

3099 Harvard - Yenching Institute Chinese - English Dictionary Project. —Cambridge, Mass.: Harvard University Press, 1953

［3］, 68, 27 p. ; 26.7 cm

HSMH（HS-N19F2-061）

附注：

印章：内封面頁鈐有"胡適的書"朱文方印。

夾紙：内封面頁夾有贈書卡片 1 張，印有"With the Compliments of the Harvard- Yenching Institute"。

3100 Heaven's My Destination/by Thornton Wilder；with an introduction by John Henry Raleigh. —Garden City，New York：Doubleday & Company, Inc.，1960

viii, 186 p.；18.2 cm

Anchor Books

HSMH（HS-N19F5-057）

附注：

印章：扉頁鈐有"胡適的書"朱文方印。

3101 Heavenly Humor. —St. Louis, Missouri：Rationalist Association, 1958

149 p.，illus.；16.15 cm

HSMH（HS-N19F3-039）

附注：

印章：内封面頁有胡適簽名"Hu Shih"，並鈐有"胡適的書"朱文方印。

3102 Henry D. Thoreau：Selected Writings on Nature and Liberty/edited by Oscar Cargill. —New York：The Liberal Arts Press，1952

xx, 163 p.；18.7 cm

HSMH（HS-N04F3-022）

附注：

印章：内封面頁鈐有"胡適的書"朱文方印。

3103 Helps to the Study of the Bible. —London：Humphrey Milford，Oxford University Press，[n. d.]

xxiii, 464 p.；14 cm

HSMH（HS-N07F2-057）

附注：

印章：扉頁有傅斯年簽名"Fu Szenien Canton 1927"；内封面鈐有"斯年"朱

文方印。

3104 The Herald Wind: Translations of Sung Dynasty Poems, Lyrics and Songs/by Clara M. Candlin. —London: John Murray, 1947

113 p.; 17.3 cm

HSMH（HS-N03F6-024）

附注：

印章：內封面頁鈐有"胡適的書"朱文方印。

與胡適的關係："Foreword"爲胡適所撰寫。

3105 The Heritage of Asia/by Kenneth Saunders. —New York: The Macmillan Company, 1932

224 p.; 19.4 cm

HSMH（HS-N03F1-011）

附注：

印章：內封面頁鈐有"胡適的書"朱文方印。

與胡適的關係：本書第 2 章節介紹胡適，篇名爲"（b）Hu Shih: The Father of the Chinese Renaissance"。

3106 Hinduism: Its Meaning for the Liberation of the Spirit/by Swami Nikhilananda. —New York: Harper & Brothers Publishers, 1958

xxii, 196 p.; 19.5 cm

World Perspectives, Vol. 17

HSMH（HS-N03F1-002）

附注：

印章：內封面頁鈐有"胡適的書"朱文方印。

與胡適的關係：胡適是 World Perspectives 的編輯委員會成員之一。

3107 Hinduism and Buddhism: An Historical Sketch/by Charles Eliot. —London: Routledge & Kegan Paul Ltd., 1954

3 Vols.; 22 cm

HSMH（HS-N06F1-008）

附註：

印章：三冊內封面均鈐有"胡適的書"朱文方印。

批注圈劃：第 2 冊有胡適的鉛筆注記與劃綫。

3108 The Histories/by Herodotus; newly translated and with an introduction by Aubrey de Selincourt. —Harmondsworth, Middlesex：Penguin Books, 1955

599 p., maps; 18.2 cm

The Penguin Classics

HSMH（HS-N04F6-032）

附註：

印章：內封面頁鈐有"胡適的書"朱文方印。

3109 History in the Writing by the Foreign Correspondents of Time, Life & Fortune/selected and edited by Gordon Carroll. —New York：Duell, Sloan and Pearce, 1945

xii, 401 p.; 23.8 cm

HSMH（HS-N04F2-025）

附註：

印章：內封面頁鈐有"胡適的書"朱文方印。

批注圈劃：書中有胡適的劃綫數處。

3110 A History of Chinese Philosophy, Vol. 1：The Period of the Philosophers/by Fung Yu-lan; edited and translated by Derk Bodde. —Princeton：Princeton University Press, 1952

xxxiv, 455 p.; 24.3 cm

HSMH（HS-N03F5-023）

附註：

印章：內封面頁鈐有"胡適的書"朱文方印。

批注圈劃：頁 170 有胡適的劃綫及校改。

夾紙：書中有夾紙 15 張。

與胡適的關係:內文提及胡適。

相關記載:(1)胡適寫作此書書評及對此書之看法,參見《胡適日記》1955年1月24日條。(2)1955年7月胡適對此書的書評,參見館藏號:HS-US01-023-002。(3)1954年12月楊聯陞對此書的書評,參見館藏號:HS-US01-029-007。

其他:內封面頁左側印有"中國哲學史 馮友蘭"。

3111 A History of Chinese Philosophy, Vol. 2: The Period of Classical Learning/ by Fung Yu-lan; edited and translated by Derk Bodde. —Princeton: Princeton University Press, 1953

xxv, 783 p.; 24 cm

HSMH(HS-N03F5-024)

附注:

印章:內封面頁鈐有"胡適的書"朱文方印。

批注圈劃:書中有胡適的批注圈劃數百處。

夾紙:書中有夾紙6張。

相關記載:(1)胡適寫作此書書評及對此書之看法,參見胡適日記1955年1月24日條。(2)1955年7月胡適對此書的書評,參見館藏號:HS-US01-023-002。(3)1954年12月楊聯陞對此書的書評,參見館藏號:HS-US01-029-007。

其他:內封面頁左側印有"中國哲學史 馮友蘭"。

3112 History of England/by W. E. Lunt. —New York: Harper& Brothers, 1950

xvi, 954 p.; 21.5 cm

HSMH(HS-N19F6-014)

附注:

印章:內封面頁鈐有"胡適的書"朱文方印。

批注圈劃:書中有胡適的批注劃綫數十處。

其他:本書爲第3版。

3113 A History of Greece: To the Death of Alexander the Great/by J. B. Bury.

——New York: The Modern Library, 1937

xi, 885 p.; 21 cm

HSMH（HS-N19F6-025）

附注：

印章：内封面頁鈐有"胡適的書"朱文方印。

3114 A History of Modern China/by Kenneth Scott Latourette. ——Melbourne; London; Baltimore: Penguin Books, 1954

233 p.; 18 cm

Pelican Books, A302

HSMH（HS-N03F3-029）

附注：

印章：内封面頁鈐有"胡適的書"朱文方印。

與胡適的關係：内容提及胡適。

3115 A History of Modern Chinese Fiction 1917-1957 = 近代中國小説史/by C. T. Hsia(夏志清). ——New Haven: Yale University Press, 1961

xii, 662 p.; 22.1 cm

HSMH（HS-N03F3-011）

附注：

印章：扉頁鈐有"胡適的書"朱文方印。

與胡適的關係：内容提及胡適及其 The Chinese Renaissance 一書。

3116 A History of Science: Ancient Science through the Golden Age of Greece/by George Sarton. ——Cambridge: Harvard University Press, 1952

xxvi, 646 p.; 24.8 cm

HSMH（HS-N19F4-032）

附注：

印章：扉頁有胡適簽名"Hu Shih New York Feb. 4, 1952"；内封面頁鈐有"胡適的書"朱文方印。

3117 A History of Sino-Russian Relations/by Tien-fong Cheng. —Washington, D. C.: Public Affairs Press, 1957

　　viii, 389 p.; 23.8 cm

　　HSMH（HS-N03F3-022）

　　附注：

　　　　印章：內封面頁鈐有"胡適的書"朱文方印。

　　　　題記：扉頁有作者題贈："適之先生教正　程天放敬贈　四十九年一月於台北。"

3118 The History of the Former Han Dynasty, Translation, Vol. I/by Ku Pan; a critical translation with annotations by Homer H. Dubs, with the collaboration of Jen T'ai and P'an Lo-chi. —Baltimore: Waverly Press, Inc., 1938

　　xiii, 339 p., fold. map; 26 cm

　　HSMH（HS-N12F4-010）

　　附注：

　　　　印章：內封面頁鈐有"胡適的書"朱文方印。

　　　　其他：《前漢書》英譯本。

3119 The History of the Former Han Dynasty, Translation, Vol. II/by Ku Pan; a critical translation with annotations by Homer H. Dubs, with the collaboration of P'an Lo-chi and Jen T'ai. —[s. l.]: The American Council of Learned Societies, 1954

　　ix, 426 p.; 26 cm

　　HSMH（HS-N12F4-011）

　　附注：

　　　　印章：內封面頁鈐有"胡適的書"朱文方印。

　　　　其他：(1)《前漢書》英譯本。(2)再印本。

3120 The History of the Former Han Dynasty, Translation, Vol. III/by Ku Pan; a critical translation with annotations by Homer H. Dubs, with the collaboration of P'an Lo-chi. —Baltimore: Waverly Press, Inc., 1955 xiv, 563 p. ; 26 cm

HSMH（HS-N12F4-012）

附注：

印章：内封面頁鈐有"胡適的書"朱文方印。

其他：《前漢書》英譯本。

3121 History of the Hebrews: Their Political, Social and Religious Development and Their Contribution to World Betterment/by Frank Knight Sanders. —New York: Charles Scribner's Sons, 1914

xiii, 367 p., illus. (plan), maps (part fold.) ; 20 cm

HSMH（HS-N19F6-027）

附注：

印章：内封面頁鈐有"胡適的書"朱文方印。

題記：扉頁有鉛筆題記："A phrase is a group of closely related words that does not contain a subject and a predicate。"

批注圈劃：頁89 注記："Nov. 3。"

3122 A History of Western Philosophy/by Bertrand Russell. —New York: Simon and Schuster, 1945

xxiii, 895 p. ; 22 cm

HSMH（HS-N04F5-024）

附注：

印章：内封面頁鈐有"胡適的書"朱文方印。

相關記載：1946 年 5 月 28 日 M. Lincoln Schuster 致胡適，詢問是否收到羅素（Bertrand Russell）的近作《西方哲學史》（*A History of Western Philosophy*），參見館藏號：HS-JDSHSE-0337-014。

3123 The History Of Zadig; Or, Destiny/by M. de Voltaire. —Paris: For the members of the Limited Editions Club, 1952

171 p. ; 22.1 cm

HSMH（HS-N04F5-035）

附注：

　　印章:封底裏有胡適簽名"H. S.";內封面頁鈐有"胡適的書"朱文方印。

　　其他:外裝紙匣。

3124　How the Soviet System Works/by Raymond A. Bauer, et al. —New York：
Vintage Books, 1960

　　xiii, 312, xii p.；18.4 cm

　　HSMH（HS-N04F1-018）

　　附注：

　　　印章:扉頁及內封面頁均鈐有"胡適的書"朱文方印。

3125　The Hsiao Ching = 孝經/edited by Paul K. T. Sih. —New York：St. John's
University Press, 1961

　　xiv, 67 p.；23.7 cm

　　HSMH（HS-N03F4-035）

　　附注：

　　　印章:內封面頁鈐有"胡適的書"朱文方印。

　　　夾紙:扉頁夾有出版社贈書卡片1張。

3126　Hsün Tze 荀子：The Moulder of Ancient Confucianism/by Homer H. Dubs.
—London：Arthur Probsthain, 1927

　　xxix, 308 p.；19.3 cm

　　Probsthain's Oriental Series, Vol. XV

　　HSMH（HS-N03F4-037）

　　附注：

　　　印章:內封面頁鈐有"胡適的書"朱文方印。

　　　題記:封面裏有贈書者題贈:"To a dear Friend who always was so kind So we with the best wishes for a Happy New Year 1955 □□ New York December 29, 1954。"

3127　Huang Hsing and the Chinese Revolution/by Chün-tu Hsüeh. —Stanford,

California：Stanford University Press，1961

ix，260 p.；22.3 cm

Stanford Studies in History，Economics，and Political Science，xx

HSMH（HS-N03F3-021）

附注：

題記：扉頁有贈書者題贈："適之老先生七十晉一華誕 晚 呂光 呂古伊德 敬祝 辛丑十一月初十日台灣。"

與胡適的關係：內容提及《胡適留學日記》（*Hu Shih Liu hsueh jih-chi*）。

3128 Huang Ti Nei Ching Su Wên：The Yellow Emperor's Classic of Internal Medicine/chapters 1-34 translated from the Chinese with an introductory study by Ilza Veith. —Baltimore：The Williams & Wilkins Company，1949

xix，253 p.，illus.；26 cm

HSMH（HS-N12F4-007）

附注：

印章：內封面頁鈐有"胡適的書"朱文方印。

夾紙：(1)內封面頁夾有空白紙卡 1 張。(2)頁 16、17 間夾有卡片 1 張，上記"Many happy returns of the Day! Best wishes N. S. Cheng"。

其他：封面印有"內經 京口文成堂摹刻宋本"。

3129 The Hundred Flowers/edited by Roderick MacFarquhar. —London：Stevens & Sons Limited，1960

xii，324 p.；24.5 cm

HSMH（HS-N03F2-021）

附注：

夾紙：扉頁有夾紙 2 張，一張是 Congres pour la Liberte de la Culture 由巴黎寄給胡適的信封地址殘片；另一張是贈書卡片。

與胡適的關係：書中的"Biographical Notes"提及胡適。

其他：封面有中文書名"百花齊放"。

3130 Hunter's Horn/by Harriette Arnow. —New York：The Macmillan Company，

1949

508 p.；21.5 cm

HSMH（HS-N19F5-082）

附注：

印章：扉頁有 V. D. Hartman 簽名"Rily Chinese New Year 1950"；內封面頁鈐有"胡適的書"朱文方印。

3131 Hydrothermal, Alteration of Dacite at the Chinkuashih Mine, Taipeihsien, Taiwan/by V. C. Juan, Y. Wang and S. S. Sun. ——Taipei, Taiwan："Geological Society of China", 1959

73-92 p.；26.4 cm

The Proceedings of the "Geological Society of China", No. 2, March, 1959

HSMH（HS-N19F5-032）

附注：

題記：封面有作者阮維周題贈："適之學長指正 著者敬贈。"

其他：(1)抽印本。(2)末頁有本文的中文節要。標題為"台北縣金瓜石礦山石英安山岩之熱水變質"；作者爲阮維周、王源、孫獻祥。

3132 The I Ching or Book of Changes, Vol. I/the Richard Wilhelm translation rendered into English by Cary F. Baynes；foreword by C. G. Jung. ——New York：Pantheon Books, 1950

xliii, 395 p.；23.3 cm

The Bollingen Series XIX

HSMH（HS-N12F4-013）

附注：

印章：內封面頁鈐有"胡適的書"朱文方印。

相關記載：胡適提及尉禮賢（Richard Wilhelm）演講《易經》的哲學事，參見《胡適日記》1922 年 6 月 28 日條。

其他：扉頁有董作賓題簽："衛禮賢譯解 周易 董作賓題。"

3133 The I Ching or Book of Changes, Vol. II/The Richard Wilhelm translation rendered into English by Cary F. Baynes; foreword by C. G. Jung. —New York: Pantheon Books, 1950

376 p. ; 23.3 cm

The Bollingen Series XIX

HSMH（HS-N12F4-014）

附注：

　　印章：内封面頁鈐有"胡適的書"朱文方印。

　　夾紙：扉頁夾有贈書卡片1張。

　　内附文件：頁186、187間夾有信封1個，郵戳日期爲1950年，收件人爲"Mrs. A. Virginia Hartman 104 East 81 Street New York 28 New York"；信封内有小紙張12張及黃色空白紙7張。

　　相關記載：胡適提及尉禮賢演講《易經》哲學的事，參見《胡適日記》1922年6月28日條。

3134 I Promessi Sposi (the Betrothed)/by Alessandro Manzoni. —New York: P. F. Collier & Son Corporation, 1909

643 p., ［1］plate; 21 cm

Harvard Classics: The Five-Foot Shelf of Books, Vol. 21

HSMH（HS-N12F6-021）

附注：

　　印章：内封面頁鈐有"胡適的書"朱文方印。

　　内附文件：書末粘貼書評剪報二則，一則爲"Return of a Classic Italian Novel", by Thomas G. Bergin, in Herald Tribune Book Review, October 28, 1951；另一則爲"A Novel Poe Liked", by Paolo Milano。

3135 I Was There/by William D. Leahy. —New York: Whittlesey House, 1950

527 p. ; 23.4 cm

HSMH（HS-N04F2-005）

附注：

　　印章：内封面頁鈐有"胡適的書"朱文方印。

　　批注圈劃：書中有胡適的批注劃綫數十處。

夾紙:書中有夾紙1張。

3136 The Idea of History/by R. G. Collingwood. —New York：Oxford University Press, 1956

xxiv, 339 p.；20.4 cm

HSMH（HS-N04F5-019）

附注:

印章:內封面頁鈐有"胡適的書"朱文方印。

3137 Ideological Purge of Professors in Peiping and Tientsin/by Hsiao Tso-liang. —[s. l.]：[s. n.], [n. d.]

9 p.；26.5 cm

The Free China Review, May 1952

HSMH（HS-N19F2-018）

附注:

其他:抽印本。

3138 The Illusion of Immortality/by Corliss Lamont. —New York：Philosophical Library, 1950

xvii, 316 p., plates；22.4 cm

HSMH（HS-N19F4-041）

附注:

印章:扉頁有胡適簽名"Hu Shih 1953 New York City",並鈐有"胡適的書"朱文方印。

夾紙:頁60、61間夾有Harkness Pavilion的空白便條紙2張。

3139 The Imam's Story/by Kao Hao-jan. —Hong Kong：The Green Pagoda Press Ltd., 1960

106 p.；18.3 cm

HSMH（HS-N03F2-040）

附注:

印章:内封面頁鈐有"胡適的書"朱文方印。

題記:扉頁有作者題贈:"胡院長適之賜正 高浩然敬贈 四九,五,廿六 永和鎮永和路文化街94巷20弄3號。"

夾紙:頁55夾有信封地址殘片1張。

內附文件:扉頁夾有1960年5月31日高浩然致胡適函1張。

3140 The Impact of Science on Society/by Bertrand Russell. ——New York: Simon and Schuster, 1953

114 p. ; 20.4 cm

HSMH(HS-N04F5-023)

附注:

印章:内封面頁鈐有"胡適的書"朱文方印。

3141 Imperialism and Social Classes/by Joseph A. Schumpeter; translated by Heinz Horden; edited with an introduction by Paul M. Sweezy. ——New York: Augustus M. Kelley, Inc., 1951

xxv, 221 p. ; 19.3 cm

HSMH(HS-N04F5-026)

附注:

印章:内封面頁鈐有"胡適的書"朱文方印。

題記:扉頁有贈書者題贈:"To Hu Shih from Elizabeth Schumpeter Taconic August 8, 1951。"

3142 Impressions of Lincoln and the Civil War: A Foreigner's Account/by Marquis Adolphe De Chambrun. ——New York: Random House, 1952

x, 174 p. ; 20.8 cm

HSMH(HS-N04F3-004)

附注:

印章:扉頁鈐有"胡適的書"朱文方印。

3143 In Our Town: Twenty Seven Slices of Life/by Damon Runyon. ——New York:

Creative Age Press, 1946

vi, 120 p.; 22.4 cm

HSMH (HS-N19F5-059)

附注：

印章：扉頁有胡適簽名"Hu Shih"；内封面頁鈐有"胡適的書"朱文方印。

題記：扉頁有胡適題記："倫寧小品 胡適 卅五，五，五。"

批注圈劃：書中有胡適的批注劃綫數處，其中頁33記"此篇意義深長，但多數人不會了解。適之"。

3144 In the Minds of Men: The Study of Human Behavior and Social Tensions, Conducted at the Request of the Government of India/by Gardner Murphy. —New York: Basic Books, Inc., 1953

306 p.; 21.1 cm

HSMH (HS-N19F6-008)

附注：

印章：内封面頁鈐有"胡適的書"朱文方印。

3145 Inauguration of George D. Stoddard, President of the University of the State of New York and Commissioner of Education at the Seventy-eighth Convocation of the University, October 16, 1942/by Thomas J. Mangan, et al. —New York: The University of the State of New York, 1942

79 p.; 22.6 cm

HSMH (HS-N03F6-021)

附注：

題記：封面有贈者題記："Hu Shih pp. 44, 76-78 Hon. Deg.: Doctor of Letters Univ. State of N. Y. 1942。"

批注圈劃：目次頁及頁75、76有鉛筆劃勾。

與胡適的關係：書中有胡適接受美國紐約州立大學(University of the State of New York)榮譽博士學位的照片，以及George D. Stoddard校長的致詞與胡適的答詞。

相關記載：館藏有"Inauguration of George D. Stoddard at the Seven-Eighth

Convocation of the University, October Sixteenth, 1942"節目單,參見館藏號:HS-JDSHSE-0466-015。

3146 Independence, Convergence and Borrowing in Institutions, Thought and Art/by V. Gordon Childe, et al. —Cambridge, Mass.: Harvard University Press, 1937

272 p.; 22.3 cm

HSMH(HS-N03F6-023)

附注:

印章:内封面頁鈐有"胡適的書"朱文方印。

批注圈劃:書中有胡適的批注劃綫數處。

夾紙:書中有夾紙1張。

與胡適的關係:收録胡適的文章"The Indianization of China: A Case Study in Cultural Borrowing"。

3147 Index to the Material on Communist China Held by the Union Research Institute/translated by the staff of the Union Research Institute. —Kowloon, Hong Kong: Union Research Institute, 1957

xii, 250 p.; 26 cm

HSMH(HS-N03F2-011)

附注:

印章:内封面頁鈐有"胡適的書"朱文方印。

3148 India. —New York: The First National City Bank of New York, [n.d.]

24 p., illus.; 22.9 cm

HSMH(HS-N19F2-009)

附注:

印章:頁1鈐有"胡適的書"朱文方印。

3149 India: A Short Cultural History/by H. G. Rawlinson. —London: The Cresset Press, 1948 xiv, 454 p., illus., xxiii plates, fold. map; 22.4 cm

HSMH（HS-N03F1-005）

附注：

  印章：內封面頁鈐有"胡適的書"朱文方印。

  批注圈劃：書中有胡適的批注劃綫數十處。

  夾紙：書中有夾紙1張。

3150 India and China: A Thousand Years of Cultural Relations/by Prabodh Chandra Bagchi. —New York: The Philosophical Library, Inc., 1951

  vi, 234 p.; 19 cm

HSMH（HS-N03F1-006）

附注：

  印章：館藏2冊，其中一冊的封面及扉頁有胡適簽名"Hu Shih"；兩冊的內封面頁均鈐有"胡適的書"朱文方印。

  批注圈劃：其中一冊有胡適的批注劃綫數十處；另一冊有胡適的批注劃綫數處。

  夾紙：其中一冊夾有筆記1張，上寫"Wei（Toba）381-534"等朝代世系。

  其他：封面有中文書名"中印千年史"及作者譯名"師覺月"。

3151 An Inquiry into the Nature and Causes of the Wealth of Nations/by Adam Smith. —New York: P. F. Collier & Son Corporation, 1909

  564 p., [1] plate; 21 cm

New York: P. F. Collier & Son Corporation, 1909

HSMH（HS-N12F6-010）

附注：

  印章：內封面頁鈐有"胡適的書"朱文方印。

3152 The Inquisition of the Middle Ages: Its Organization and Operation/by Henry Charles Lea. —New York: The Citadel Press, 1954

  xi, 260 p.; 22.1 cm

HSMH（HS-N19F3-038）

附注：

印章：内封面頁鈐有"胡適的書"朱文方印。

3153 The Inscription of the Sino-Tibetan Treaty of 821-822/by Fang-kuei Li(李方桂). —Leiden, Netherlands：E. J. Brill, 1956

99 p. ; 23.9 cm

T'oung Pao, Vol. XLIV, LIVR. 1-3

HSMH（HS-N19F5-024）

附注：

印章：頁1鈐有"胡適的書"朱文方印。

題記：封面有作者題贈："適之先生賜正 方桂謹贈。"

其他：中文篇名"唐蕃會盟碑的研究"（參考丁邦新編《李方桂先生著作目錄》）。

3154 Inscriptions Juives de K'ai-Fong-Fou/by Le P. J'erome Tobar. —Chang-Hai：Imprimerie De La Mission Catholique, 1912

v, 111 p. ; 25.3 cm

HSMH（HS-N03F4-012）

附注：

印章：内封面頁鈐有"胡適的書"朱文方印。

3155 Institutes of the Christian Religion/by John Calvin. —Chicago, Illinois：Henry Regnery Company for the Great Books Foundation, 1949

91 p. ; 18.2 cm

HSMH（HS-N04F6-016）

附注：

印章：内封面頁鈐有"胡適的書"朱文方印。

3156 Intelligence in the Modern World：John Dewey's Philosophy/edited by Joseph Ratner. —New York：The Modern Library, 1939

xv, 1077 p. ; 21 cm

HSMH（HS-N04F4-008）

附注：

印章：扉頁有胡適簽名"Hu Shih August 1949"；內封面頁鈐有"胡適的書"朱文方印。

批注圈劃：書中有胡適的批注劃綫數處。

3157 International Conflict in the Twentieth Century: A Christian View/by Herbert Butterfield. —New York: Harper & Brothers, 1960

123 p.; 21.2 cm

Religious Perspectives, Vol. 2

HSMH（HS-N04F2-012）

附注：

印章：扉頁鈐有"胡適的書"朱文方印。

題記：扉頁有 Religious Perspectives 叢書編者題贈："To Dr. Hu Shih with admiration and esteem Ruth Nanda Anshen August 1960。"

3158 The International Development of China/by Sun Yat-sen. —Chungking: Ministry of Information of the Republic of China, 1943

xiii, 191 p.; 21.2 cm

HSMH（HS-N03F3-012）

附注：

印章：內封面頁鈐有"胡適的書"朱文方印。

其他：(1)作者爲孫逸仙。(2)此爲2版再印本。

3159 Intestinal Protozoans and Helminths in U.S. Military and Allied Personnel, Naval Hospital, Bethesda, Maryland/by Robert E. Kuntz. —Taipei, Taiwan: United States Naval Medical Research No. 2, 1959

10 p.; 26.5 cm

NAMRU TWO, May 27, 1959（NM 52 11 02. 1. 3）

HSMH（HS-N19F5-014）

附注：

其他：(1)釘書針裝訂。(2)館藏 2 冊。

3160 Introduction to Anglo-American Law/selected and Compiled by Andrew Lee. —Taipei, Taiwan：Soochow University，1961

387 p.；20.9 cm

HSMH（HS-N19F3-025）

附注：

題記：扉頁有作者題贈："適之老先生尊鑒：奉獻這本書給您，事前未徵得您的同意，非常冒昧，還請原諒。晚 呂光拜 五十年十月 台灣。"

與胡適的關係："Preface"前一頁印有"To Dr. Hu Shih A Liberal Scholar, A True Patriot and A Noble Man This Book Is Respectfully Dedicated"。

相關記載：1961 年 10 月 5 日胡適覆呂曉光函，答謝贈書及在獻詞中的褒獎。

其他：封面有中文書名"英美法導論"及編者中文姓名"呂光"。

3161 An Introduction to the Study of Robert Browning's Poetry/by Hiram Corson. —Boston：D. C. Heath & Co.，1888

x, 338 p.；18.8 cm

HSMH（HS-N04F6-017）

附注：

印章：內封面頁有韋蓮司夫人簽名"Mrs. H. S. Williams Edgewood Jan 1889"，並鈐有"胡適的書"朱文方印。

題記：(1)內封面頁有注記："91 & 93 Fifth Ave New York。"(2)內封面頁背面有胡適題記："Prof. Corson 是專治 Robert Browning 的詩的學人。他死後，他收藏的有關 Browning 夫婦的詩的書籍全歸 Cornell 大學。Cornell 大學每年設的 Corson Prize on the Poetry of Browning 即是紀念他的。1914 年，我得了那年的 Corson Prize。這本小書是 Prof. Corson 選註的 Browning 的詩，和他的論文。原是老朋友 Mrs. Henry S. Williams 的書，前年 Clifford Williams 贈送給我，作為紀念。胡適。"

批注圈劃：(1)頁 267、270 有原持有此書者注記："Prof. Corson read this to us June 5th 1905。"(2)書中另有非胡適筆跡的注記數處。

內附文件：(1) 扉頁粘貼剪報一則："Professor Corson。"(2) 扉頁夾有 Robert Browning 像 1 張。(3) 頁 98、99 間夾有關於作者 Corson 的剪報一則："Personal Notes。"(4) 頁 126、127 間夾有 3 張關於 Robert Browning 的文章"An Interpreter of Browning", by Ella B. Nallock, *in Methodist Review*, July 1910, 頁 610—614。

3162　An Introduction to Zen Buddhism/by Daisetz Teitaro Suzuki; edited by Christmas Humphreys; with a foreword by C. G. Jung. —London：Published for the Buddhist Society by Rider and Company, [n.d.]

　　136 p.；19cm

　　HSMH（HS-N06F1-018）

　　附注：

　　印章：內封面頁鈐有"胡適的書"朱文方印及"胡適"紫色戳印。

　　題記：扉頁有胡適題記："August 1934" — date of Preface. But much of the material in this volume goes back to the years before 1926。"

　　批注圈劃：書中有胡適的藍、黑、鉛筆注記與劃綫。

　　其他：編者序的時間為 1948 年。

3163　Introductory Circuit Theory/by Ernst A. Guillemin. —New York：John Wiley & Sons, Inc., 1953

　　xxv, 550 p.；23.7 cm

　　HSMH（HS-N19F4-018）

　　附注：

　　印章：扉頁鈐有"胡適的書"朱文方印；致謝頁有陳之藩簽名"C. F. Chen Memphis 4, Tenn. March 21, '59"。

　　題記：扉頁有陳之藩題贈："適之先生,您那本神會和尚小冊中,有幾句話,'以不見性,故言深遠',您還特別加小註,說是見解高明。我送給您此書,請看序上的罵街,如出神會和尚之口,好玩,好玩。之藩 Sept 14, 1959 Memphis 4, Tenn. 。"

　　批注圈劃：書中有胡適的劃綫數處。

　　其他：書中有些劃綫處疑是出自陳之藩。

3164 The Invention of Printing in China and Its Spread Westward/by Thomas Francis Carter. —New York：Columbia University Press，1931

 xxvi, 282 p. ; 23.1 cm

 HSMH（HS-N03F1-022）

 附注：

  印章：内封面頁鈐有"胡適的書"朱文方印。

  題記：封面裹粘貼的名片上有胡適題記："From Mrs. Dagny Carter Hu Shih June 14, 1950。"

  批注圈劃：書中有胡適的批注圈劃數十處。

  夾紙：書中有夾紙4張。

3165 The Invention of Printing in China and Its Spread Westward/by Thomas Francis Carter; revised by L. Carrington Goodrich. —New York：The Ronald Press Company, 1955

 xxiv, 293 p. ; 23.6 cm

 HSMH（HS-N03F1-021）

 附注：

  印章：内封面頁鈐有"胡適的書"朱文方印。

  題記：粘貼於扉頁的名片有 Mr. Luther Carrington Goodrich 的題贈："To my good friend Dr. Hu with homage C.。"

  批注圈劃：書中有胡適的批注圈劃數十處。

  夾紙：書中有夾紙2張。

  與胡適的關係：注釋提及胡適。

3166 The Irreverent Mr. Mencken：An Informal History of the Man and His Era/by Edgar Kemler. —Boston：Little, Brown and Company, 1950

 x, 317 p. ; 21 cm

 HSMH（HS-N04F3-007）

 附注：

  印章：内封面頁鈐有"胡適的書"朱文方印。

題記：扉頁有胡適題記："Hu Shih Feb. 12, 1951,— Lincoln's birthday。"

批注圈劃：頁 26 有鉛筆劃叉。

3167 Issues of Freedom: Paradoxes and Promises/by Herbert J. Muller. —New York: Harper & Brothers Publishers, 1960

xv, 170 p. ; 19.6 cm

World Perspectives, Vol. 23

HSMH（HS-N19F3-034）

附注：

印章：館藏 2 冊，其中一冊內封面頁鈐有"胡適的書"朱文方印；另一冊扉頁亦鈐有"胡適的書"朱文方印。

夾紙：其中一冊的頁 36、37 間，夾有 Womrath's Book Shop & Library 寄給胡適的信封地址殘片 1 張。

3168 Japan in World History/by G. B. Sansom. —New York: International Secretariat, Institute of Pacific Relations, 1951

94 p. ; 21.6 cm

HSMH（HS-N19F6-007）

附注：

印章：內封面頁鈐有"胡適的書"朱文方印。

夾紙：扉頁夾有記橋川時雄住址的紙條 1 張。

其他：書末貼有日本太平洋問題調查會發行此書的版權頁 1 張。

3169 Japanese Art in the Seattle Art Museum/by Richard E. Fuller. —Seattle: Seattle Art Museum, 1960

210 p., illus. ; 28.1 cm

HSMH（HS-N20F1-012）

附注：

印章：內封面頁鈐有"胡適的書"朱文方印。

題記：封面有作者題贈："To Dr. Hu Shih as a smile taken of my admiration Richard E. Fuller。"

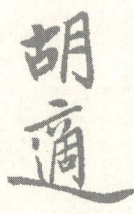

3170 Japanese Studies of Modern China: A Bibliographical Guide to Historical and Social-Science Research on the 19th and 20th Centuries/by John King Fairbank and Masataka Banno. —Rutland, Vermont, Tokyo: Published for the Harvard-Yenching Institute by Charles E. Tuttle Company, 1955

xviii, 331 p.; 26.2 cm

HSMH（HS-N03F3-031）

附注：

印章：内封面頁鈐有"胡適的書"朱文方印。

夾紙：内封面頁夾有贈書卡片1張。

與胡適的關係：書中的宇野精一、竹内好、福井康順、中村忠行、青木正兒、内藤虎次郎、瀧川政次郎、近藤春雄的著作都提及胡適。

其他：John King Fairbank 即費正清。

3171 Jefferson Selleck/by Carl Jonas. —Boston: Little, Brown and Company, 1952

xiii, 303 p.; 20.5 cm

HSMH（HS-N19F5-071）

附注：

印章：内封面頁鈐有"胡適的書"朱文方印。

批注圈劃：書中有鉛筆劃綫數十處。

3172 Jim Farley's Story: The Roosevelt Years/by James A. Farley. —New York: McGraw-Hill Book Company, Inc., 1948

388 p.; 23.5 cm

HSMH（HS-N04F2-031）

附注：

印章：内封面頁鈐有"胡適的書"朱文方印。

其他：本書爲第2次印刷。

3173 John Dewey's Challenge to Education/by Oscar Handlin. —New York: Harper & Brothers, 1959

59 p.；20.8 cm

HSMH（HS-N04F4-009）

附注：

印章：内封面頁鈐有"胡適的書"及"適之"朱文方印。

内附文件：書末夾有1961年4月25日美國新聞處（United States Information Service）的Charles A. McGinley, Jr.致胡適函1張。

其他：内封面頁有"Presented by the UNITED STATES INFORMATION SERVICE Taipei 台北 美國大使館新聞處敬贈"的藍色戳印。

3174 John Dickinson, 1894-1952/by George L. Haskins. —Philadelphia：University of Pennsylvania Law Review, 1952

25 p.；26 cm

University of Pennsylvania Law Review, Vol. 101, No. 1, October, 1952

HSMH（HS-N19F5-026）

附注：

印章：内封面頁鈐有"胡適的書"朱文方印。

其他：抽印本。

3175 John Kennedy：A Political Profile/by James MacGregor Burns. —New York：Harcourt, Brace and Company, 1960

x, 309 p.；21 cm

HSMH（HS-N04F2-030）

附注：

印章：内封面頁鈐有"胡適的書"朱文方印。

内附文件：扉頁夾有1941年3月6日Richard M. McCarthy致胡適函1張。

3176 John Stuart Mill/by Karl Britton. —Melbourne；London；Baltimore：Penguin Books, 1953

224 p.；18 cm

Pelican Books, A274

HSMH（HS-N04F5-018）

附注：

印章：封面有胡適簽名"Hu Shih"；内封面頁鈐有"胡適的書"朱文方印。

3177 John Stuart Mill：Autobiography, Essay on Liberty；Thomas Carlyle：Characteristics, Inaugural Address, Essay on Scott/edited by Charles W. Eliot. —New York：P. F. Collier & Son Corporation, 1909

451 p., [1] plate；21 cm

Harvard Classics：The Five-Foot Shelf of Books, Vol. 25

HSMH（HS-N12F6-025）

附注：

印章：内封面頁鈐有"胡適的書"朱文方印。

批注圈劃：書中有胡適的批注劃綫數十處。

3178 The Journals of André Gide, Vol. III：1928-1939/translated from the French and annotated by Justin O'Brien. —New York：Alfred A. Knopf, 1949

450, xx p.；24.4 cm

HSMH（HS-N04F5-021）

附注：

印章：扉頁鈐有"胡適的書"朱文方印。

3179 The Judas Time/by Isidor Schneider. —New York：The Dial Press, 1946

xiv, 361 p.；20.7 cm

HSMH（HS-N19F5-058）

附注：

印章：内封面頁鈐有"胡適的書"朱文方印。

批注圈劃：書中有鉛筆劃綫數十處。

3180 The Justice Holmes Reader/selected and edited by Julius J. Marke. —New York：Oceana Publications, 1955

v, 282 p.；17.5 cm

Docket Series

HSMH（HS-N19F3-010）

附注：

 印章：館藏2冊，内封面頁均鈐有"胡適的書"朱文方印。

 題記：其中一冊的内封面頁有贈書者題贈："適之老先生 賜存 晚 呂光敬贈 五十年六月 台灣 Holmes letters to Pollock on page 161。"

 其他：另一冊裝訂已散，以棉綫固定綁住，無法檢視内容。

3181 Karlgren's Glottal Stop Initial in Ancient Chinese/by E. R. Hope. —Ottawa：E. R. Hope, 1953

 88 p. ; 27 cm

 HSMH（HS-N13F1-024）

 附注：

  題記：封面右上處有黑筆題注："謹呈。"

3182 The Lakes Country/by Arch Merrill. —Rochester, New York：The Democrat and Chronicle, 1944

 154 p. ; 19.7 cm

 HSMH（HS-N19F5-065）

 附注：

  印章：内封面頁鈐有"胡適的書"朱文方印。

  題記：内封面頁有題記："E. T. B. S. M.。"

3183 The Lankavatara Sutra：A Mahayana Text/translated by Daisetz Teitaro Suzuki. —London：Routledge & Kegan Paul Ltd., 1956

 xlix, 300 p. ; 22.3 cm

 HSMH（HS-N03F4-006）

 附注：

  印章：内封面頁鈐有"胡適的書"朱文方印。

  夾紙：書中夾有此書出版社的讀者回函1張，以及1956年9月19日 Paragon Book Gallery 開立給胡適購買此書的收據1張。

與胡適的關係：內容提及胡適。

其他：譯者爲鈴木大拙。

3184 The Law of Civilization and Decay/by Brooks Adams. —New York：Vintage Books, 1955

lxii, 308, xi p.；18.5 cm

HSMH（HS-N04F3-025）

附注：

印章：內封面頁鈐有"胡適的書"朱文方印。

3185 Leaders of Twentieth-Century China：An Annotated Bibliography of Selected Chinese Biographical Works in the Hoover Library/by Eugene Wu. —Stanford, California：Stanford University Press, 1956

vii, 106 p.；25.5 cm

HSMH（HS-N03F2-038）

附注：

印章：內封面頁鈐有"胡適的書"朱文方印。

批注圈劃：書中有胡適的批注圈劃數處。

夾紙：內封面頁夾有卡片1張，印有"This Review Copy is sent you With Our Compliments We shall appreciate receiving clippings of notices as they appear Standford University Press Stanford, California"。

內附文件：書中夾有1956年10月1日 The Journal of Asian Studies 的 Joseph R. Levenson 致胡適的信函1張。

與胡適的關係：內容提及胡適及其《中國哲學史大綱》。

其他：作者爲吳文津。

3186 A Letter from Benjamin Franklin to Benjamin Vaughan/with an introduction by Carl Van Doren. —Princeton, New Jersey：The Friends of the Princeton Library, 1949

[5, 9 p.]；28.8 cm

HSMH（HS-N04F3-037）

附注：

　　印章：内封面頁鈐有"胡適的書"朱文方印。

3187　The Letters of Robert G. Ingersoll/edited by Eva Ingersoll Wakefield. —New York：Philosophical Library, 1951

　　xii, 747 p. ; 23.5 cm

　　HSMH（HS-N04F5-029）

　　附注：

　　　印章：内封面頁鈐有"胡適的書"朱文方印。

　　　題記：扉頁有胡適題記："Hu Shih, Gift of Mr. Dagobert D. Runes, Editor of the Philosophical Library, New York。"

　　　批注圈劃：頁61有胡適的批注劃綫一處。

　　　内附文件：書中夾有胡適悼念友人Edman逝世的函稿2張。

3188　The Life and Morals of Jesus of Nazareth/by Thomas Jefferson. —Boston：The Beacon Press, 1951

　　151 p. ; 18.3 cm

　　HSMH（HS-N04F3-021）

　　附注：

　　　印章：内封面頁鈐有"胡適的書"朱文方印。

　　　題記：扉頁有胡適題記："Gift from Dr. Julian Boyd Oct. 5, 1951. Hu Shih。"

　　　相關記載：胡適閱讀此書之心得，參見《胡適日記》1940年12月26日條。

3189　The Life of Andrew Jackson/by Marquis James. —New York：The Bobbs-Merrill Company, 1938

　　972 p. ; 24 cm

　　HSMH（HS-N04F3-028）

　　附注：

　　　印章：内封面頁鈐有"胡適的書"朱文方印；扉頁鈐有"HU SHIH"的藍色戳印。

批注圈劃：頁 48 有胡適的批注。

3190 The Life of Jesus/by Ernest Renan. —New York：The Modern Library，1927

　　ix，15-393 p.；18.4 cm

　　HSMH（HS-N04F6-023）

　　附注：

　　　印章：內封面頁鈐有"胡適的書"朱文方印。

3191 The Life of John Birch：In the Story of One American Boy，the Ordeal of His Age/by Robert H. W. Welch，Jr.. —Chicago：Henry Regnery Company，1954

　　118 p.；19.9 cm

　　HSMH（HS-N04F3-013）

　　附注：

　　　印章：內封面頁鈐有"胡適的書"朱文方印。

　　　題記：扉頁有作者藍筆題贈："For The Honorable Hu Shih with all good wishes Robert H. W. Welch, jr. November 14, 1954"，其下有胡適的鉛筆注記："810 Main St. Cambridge, Mass.。"

　　　批注圈劃：頁 47、50 有胡適的批注劃綫。

3192 The Limited Editions Club：The Twenty-Eighth Series，1959-1960. —New York：The Limited Editions Club，[n.d.]

　　14 p.；23.5 cm

　　HSMH（HS-N19F2-033）

　　附注：

　　　印章：封面鈐有"胡適的書"朱文方印。

3193 A Linguistic Study of the Shih Ming：Initials and Consonant Clusters = 釋名/by Nicholas Cleaveland Bodman. —Cambridge, Mass.：Harvard University Press，1954

　　xi，146 p.；25.5 cm

Harvard-Yenching Institute Studies, XI

HSMH（HS-N03F1-025）

附注：

印章：内封面頁鈐有"胡適的書"朱文方印。

3194 Living by Zen/by Daisetz Teitaro Suzuki. —London：Rider & Company, 1950

187 p.；19 cm

HSMH（HS-N03F4-005）

附注：

印章：内封面頁鈐有"胡適的書"朱文方印及"胡適"紫色戳印。

題記：扉頁有胡適題記："1950— Editor's date. The author's preface give, no date, but he refers to 'since the end of the war.' It is probably the most recent of his works. H. S. In his preface, the author says that 'he has reconsidered to some extent his understanding of Zen in accordance with later experience and reflection.' See also the Editor's note about 'certain passages which seemed to be so at variance with the rest of the author's views.' I am sorry that those passages have been omitted by the Editor. H. S. 。"

批注圈劃：書中有胡適的批注劃綫數處。

其他：作者爲鈴木大拙。

3195 The Living Stage：A History of the World Theater/by Kenneth Macgowan and William Melnitz. —Englewood Cliffs, New Jersey：Prentice-Hall, Inc. , 1955

xii, 543 p., illus.；25 cm

HSMH（HS-N20F1-010）

附注：

印章：内封面頁鈐有"胡適的書"朱文方印。

3196 The Living Thoughts of Clausewitz/presented by Joseph I. Greene. —Washington Square, Philadelphia：David McKay Company, 1943

185 p.；18.6 cm

The Living Thoughts Library

HSMH（HS-N04F5-003）

附注：

印章：内封面頁鈐有"胡適的書"朱文方印。

3197 The Living Thoughts of Darwin/presented by Julian Huxley. —Washington Square, Philadelphia：David McKay Company, 1939

151 p. ; 18.8 cm

The Living Thoughts Library

HSMH（HS-N04F6-013）

附注：

印章：内封面頁鈐有"胡適的書"朱文方印。

3198 The Living Thoughts of Thomas Jefferson/presented by John Dewey. —Washington Square, Philadelphia：David McKay Company, 1940

173 p. ; 19 cm

The Living Thoughts Library

HSMH（HS-N04F4-015）

附注：

印章：扉頁後的 Jefferson 圖版背面與内封面頁均有胡適簽名"Hu Shih"；内封面頁鈐有"胡適的書"朱文方印。

3199 The Living Thoughts of Tom Paine/presented by John Dos Passos. —Washington Square, Philadelphia：David McKay Company, 1940

184 p. ; 18.7 cm

The Living Thoughts Library

HSMH（HS-N04F3-020）

附注：

印章：内封面頁鈐有"胡適的書"朱文方印。

批注圈劃：封底書衣摺頁有胡適的藍筆圈劃和打勾。

3200 Lost Peace in China/by George Moorad. —New York: E. P. Dutton & Co., Inc., 1949

　　262 p.; 21.2 cm

　　HSMH（HS-N03F2-037）

　　附註：

　　　印章：扉頁有胡適簽名"Hu Shih July 1949"；內封面頁鈐有"胡適的書"朱文方印。

　　　批注圈劃：書中有胡適的批注劃綫數十處。

　　　夾紙：書中有夾紙4張。

　　　與胡適的關係：內文提及胡適。

　　　相關記載：1949年9月30日胡適致William M. Doerflinger函,答謝他推薦此書,參見館藏號：HS-NK02-004-009。

3201 The Lunatic Fringe/by Gerald W. Johnson. —Philadelphia, New York: J. B. Lippincott Company, 1957

　　248 p.; 21.9 cm

　　HSMH（HS-N19F3-036）

　　附註：

　　　印章：內封面頁鈐有"胡適的書"朱文方印。

　　　批注圈劃：頁105的"Phryne"之下有胡適注記："Greek courtesan of the 4th century B. C. See Eney. Brit. Her story is more fantastic than that of the Claflin sisters. Hu Shih。"

3202 Jonah: Fact or Fiction? /by M. R. De Haan. —Grand Rapids, Michigan: Zondervan Publishing House, 1957

　　168 p.; 20.2 cm

　　HSMH（HS-N04F6-024）

　　附註：

　　　印章：內封面頁鈐有"胡適的書"朱文方印。

3203 Julian P. Boyd: A Bibliographical Record/compiled and offered by his friends on the occasion of his tenth anniversary as Librarian of Princeton University. — Princeton, New Jersey: Princeton University Press, 1950

62 p. ; 19.7 cm

HSMH（HS-N19F5-049）

附注：

印章：扉頁鈐有"胡適的書"朱文方印。

夾紙：另一扉頁有夾紙 2 張，一張印有"Hu Shih, Dr. Gest Oriental Library Princeton University Princeton, N. J."；另一張印有"With the compliments of Mr. Boyd's Friends and Princeton University Press"。

3204 Knowing and the Known/by John Dewey and Arthur F. Bentley. —Boston: The Beacon Press, 1949

xiii, 334 p. ; 22.3 cm

HSMH（HS-N04F4-012）

附注：

印章：内封面頁鈐有"胡適的書"朱文方印。

題記：扉頁有贈書者題贈："To Dr. Hu Shih with warm regards and high esteem, Sidney Ratner May 25, 1951。"

批注圈劃：頁 xi 有劃綫。

3205 La Traviata（the Lost one）: A Grand Opera in Three Acts/music by Giuseppe Verdi; book by F. M. Piave. —New York: Fred Rullman Inc. , [n. d.]

25 p. ; 25.4 cm

Metropolitan Opera House Grand Opera

HSMH（HS-N19F5-042）

附注：

印章：内封面頁鈐有"胡適的書"朱文方印。

3206 Lao Tzu/Tao Teh Ching = 道德經/translated by John C. H. Wu; edited by Paul K. T. Sih. —New York: St. John's University Press, 1961 xiv, 115 p.；23.6 cm

HSMH（HS-N03F5-008）

附注：

　　印章：内封面頁鈐有"胡適的書"朱文方印。

　　夾紙：封面裏夾有出版社贈書卡片1張；扉頁夾有St. John's University寄給胡適的信封地址殘片1張。

3207　The Lattimore Story/by John T. Flynn. —New York：The Devin-Adair Company, 1953

118 p.；20 cm

HSMH（HS-N03F2-031）

附注：

　　印章：内封面頁鈐有"胡適的書"朱文方印。

3208　Laws of Republic of China：First Series-Major Laws/translated by Law Revision Planning Group CUSA, The Executive Yuan of The Republic of China. —Taipei, Taiwan："Law Revision Planning Group CUSA, The Executive Yuan of The Republic of China", 1961

xxix, 1479 p.；21.3 cm

HSMH（HS-N12F5-025）

附注：

　　題記：扉頁有"行政院美援運用委員會敬贈"的藍色戳印。

　　内附文件：頁xiv—xv間夾有1962年1月26日李國鼎致胡適函1張。

3209　Lectures on the Harvard Classics/by William Allan Neilson. —New York：P. F. Collier & Son Corporation, 1914

466 p.,［1］plate；21 cm

Harvard Classics：The Five-Foot Shelf of Books

HSMH（HS-N12F5-021）

附注：

　　印章：内封面頁鈐有"胡適的書"朱文方印。

3210 Leonardo Da Vinci：Military Engineer/by Bern Dibner. —New York：The Burndy Library, Inc. , 1946

viii, 27 p. , plates；23.5 cm

HSMH（HS-N19F5-035）

附注：

印章：致謝頁鈐有"胡適的書"朱文方印。

3211 Let a Hundred Flowers Bloom/by Tse-tung Mao；with notes and an introduction by G. F. Hudson. —New York：The New Leader, 1957

58 p. ; 21.6 cm

The New Leader, Section 2, September 9, 1957

HSMH（HS-N19F2-062）

附注：

印章：封面有胡適簽名"Hu Shih"；頁3鈐有"胡適的書"朱文方印。

批注圈劃：書中有胡適的批注圈劃數處，其中頁13記"He seems to have ignored the Chinese students entirely. HS."。

其他：本書爲毛澤東《關於正確處理人民内部矛盾的問題》之英譯本。

3212 Letters of English Authors from the Collection of Robert H. Taylor：A Catalogue of an Exhibition in the Princeton University Library, May 13 to September 30, 1960. —[s. l.]：[s. n.], [n. d.]

35 p. ; 23.4 cm

The Princeton University Library Chronicle, Vol. XXI, No. 4, Summer, 1960

HSMH（HS-N19F2-032）

附注：

其他：抽印本。

3213 Letters of Marcus Tullius Cicero：With His Treatises on Friendship and Old Age；Letters of Gaius Plinius Caecilius Secundus/edited by Charles W. Eliot. —New York：P. F. Collier & Son Corporation, 1909

416 p., [1] plate; 21 cm

Harvard Classics: The Five-Foot Shelf of Books, Vol. 9

HSMH（HS-N12F6-009）

附注：

　　印章：内封面頁鈐有"胡適的書"朱文方印。

3214 Leviathan and Natural Law/by F. Lyman Windolph. —Princeton, New Jersey: Princeton University Press, 1951

ix, 147 p.; 20.5 cm

HSMH（HS-N19F3-026）

附注：

　　印章：扉頁鈐有"胡適的書"朱文方印。

　　批注圈劃：書中有胡適的批注劃綫數十處。

3215 Library of Congress Sesquicentennial Exhibit, April 24, 1950: Catalog of the Exhibit Commemorating the 150th Anniversary of Its Establishment/with an introduction by David C. Mearns. —Washington: United States Government Printing Office, 1950

xi, 38p.; 26.7 cm

HSMH（HS-N19F5-047）

附注：

　　印章：内封面頁鈐有"胡適的書"朱文方印。

3216 Life: Its Dimensions and Its Bounds/by Robert M. MacIver. —New York: Harper & Brothers Publishers, 1960

xv, 144 p.; 19.5 cm

World Perspectives, Vol. 25

HSMH（HS-N19F4-048）

附注：

　　印章：内封面頁鈐有"胡適的書"朱文方印。

　　題記：扉頁有 World Perspectives 編者題記："Qui Facit per alium Facit per

se. Ruth Nanda Anshen August－1960。"

與胡適的關係：胡適爲 World Perspectives 的編輯委員會成員之一。

3217 The Life Treasury of American Folklore/by the editors of Life; with paintings by James Lewicki. —New York: Time, Inc., 1961

348 p., illus. (part col.); 29 cm

HSMH（HS-N13F1-015）

附注：

夾紙：內封面頁夾有 American Folklore 訂購單 1 張。

3218 Literary and Philosophical Essays: French, German and Italian/edited by Charles W. Eliot. —New York: P. F. Collier & Son Corporation, 1910

396 p., [1] plate; 21 cm

Harvard Classics: The Five-Foot Shelf of Books, Vol. 32

HSMH（HS-N12F5-002）

附注：

印章：內封面頁鈐有"胡適的書"朱文方印。

3219 The Literary Mind and the Carving of Dragons/by Liu Hsieh; translated with an introduction and notes by Vincent Yu-chung Shih. —New York: Columbia University Press, 1959

xlvi, 298 p.; 23.8 cm

Number LVIII of the Records of Civilization: Sources and Studies

HSMH（HS-N03F4-025）

附注：

印章：內封面頁鈐有"胡適的書"朱文方印。

夾紙：書中夾有卡片 1 張，印有"This book is a gift from the Asian Book Fund Far Eastern Institute University of Washington Seattle 5, Washington U. S. A."。

相關記載：館藏有此書的廣告，參見館藏號：HS-NK05-339-007。

其他：劉勰《文心雕龍》英譯本。

3220 Live without Fear/by T. V. Smith. —New York: The New American Library, 1956

 192 p. ; 18.2 cm

 HSMH（HS-N19F3-028）

 附註：

  印章：内封面頁後鈐有"胡適的書"朱文方印。

  題記：内封面頁有作者題贈："Hu Shih International □ or courage □ □ T. V. Smith。"

  內附文件：頁104、105間夾有剪報1張："The People Speak: Danger Seen in China Story。"

3221 Living Biographies of Great Scientists/by Henry Thomas and Dana Lee Thomas ; illustrations by Gordon Ross. —Garden City, New York: Blue Ribbon Books, 1946

 viii, 314 p. , plates ; 20.8 cm

 HSMH（HS-N19F4-025）

 附註：

  印章：扉頁有胡適簽名"Hu Shih"；内封面頁鈐有"胡適的書"朱文方印。

  批注圈劃：書中有胡適的批注劃綫數處。

3222 The Living Thoughts of Karl Marx Based on Capital: A Critique of Political Economy/presented by Leon Trotsky. —Washington Square, Philadelphia: David McKay Company, 1939

 184 p. ; 18.7 cm

 The Living Thoughts Library

 HSMH（HS-N04F1-032）

 附註：

  印章：扉頁有胡適簽名"Hu Shih Sept. 1949"；内封面頁鈐有"胡適的書"朱文方印。

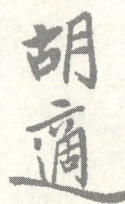

3223 Logic: The Theory of Inquiry/by John Dewey. —New York: Henry Holt and Company, Inc., 1951

viii, 546 p.; 21.6 cm

HSMH(HS-N04F4-013)

附注:

印章:内封面页钤有"胡适的书"朱文方印。

3224 Long-Range Aid Programs for Long-Range Progress: United States Policy Statement Series 1962/by Dean Rusk. —Manila: United States Information Service, 1962

14 p.; 17.9 cm

HSMH(HS-N04F2-017)

3225 The Lost Art/by Augusto Iturralde. —Manila: Aurora Publications, 1959

34 p.; 16.5 cm

HSMH(HS-N03F1-014)

附注:

题记:扉页有作者题赠:"Nov. 2 / 59 To Dr. Hu Shih with the sincere admiration of Augusto Iturralde。"

3226 The Loyalty of Free Men/by Alan Barth. —New York: Pocket Books, Inc., 1952

xxxii, 266 p.; 16.4 cm

HSMH(HS-N04F1-031)

附注:

印章:内封面页钤有"胡适的书"朱文方印。

3227 Lun-Hêng, Part I: Philosophical Essays of Wang Ch'ung/translated from the Chinese and annotated by Alfred Forke. —Berlin: The Imperial German Printing Office, 1907

iv, 577 p.; 24.5 cm

HSMH（HS-N12F4-008）

附注：

印章：扉頁有胡適簽名"胡適 Hu Shih June 6, 1956 New York, n. y."；内封面頁鈐有"胡適的書"朱文方印。

批注圈劃：書中有胡適的批注劃綫數十處。

相關記載：1956 年 8 月 13 日胡適致楊聯陞夫婦函，提及買得"Forke's Lun Heng"，有兩大冊，把《論衡》84 篇全譯出了，參見館藏號：HS-LS01-006-030。

3228 Lun-Hêng, Part II: Miscellaneous Essays of Wang Ch'ung/translated from the Chinese and annotated by Alfred Forke. —Berlin: Georg Reimer, 1911

vi, 536 p. ; 24.5 cm

HSMH（HS-N12F4-009）

附注：

印章：内封面頁鈐有"胡適的書"朱文方印。

批注圈劃：書中有胡適的批注劃綫數十處。

内附文件：封面夾有 H. H. Frankel 寄給胡適的信封 1 個，内裝信紙 3 張，内容爲 Alfred Forke 的傳記資料，包括"Alfred Forke（1867-1944）"、"Some Works by Alfred Forke"及"Additional Notes on Alfred Forke"。信封上有胡適注記："Biographical Data on Forke。"

相關記載：1956 年 8 月 13 日胡適致楊聯陞夫婦函，提及買得"Forke's Lun Heng"，有兩大冊，把《論衡》84 篇全譯出了，參見館藏號：HS-LS01-006-030。

3229 Lyrical Ballads with a Few Other Poems/by William Wordsworth and Samuel Taylor Coleridge. —Garden City, New York: Doubleday & Company, Inc., [n. d.]

117 p. ; 18.2 cm

HSMH（HS-N04F5-034）

附注：

印章：内封面頁鈐有"胡適的書"朱文方印。

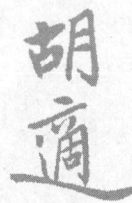

3230 Mackenzie King of Canada/by H. Reginald Hardy. —London：Oxford University Press, 1949

xii, 390 p. ; 23.7 cm

HSMH（HS-N19F6-012）

附注：

印章：內封面頁鈐有"胡適的書"朱文方印。

3231 The Mādhyamika in Korea/by Richard A. Grad. —Tokyo：Journal of Indian and Buddhist Studies, 1959

773-755 p. ; 21 cm

HSMH（HS-N17F5-026）

附注：

批注圈劃：封面有胡適的紅筆英文注記。

內附文件：夾有"Zen and Intuited Knowledge"短文1篇，有作者的英文藍筆題贈："To Dr. Hu Shih with the compliments of Shunzo Sakamaki 1-20-59。"

其他：抽印本。

3232 Magic Lotus：A Romantic Fantasy/by Prem Chaya. —Bangkok：Prachandra Printing Press, 1949

110 p. ; 19 cm

HSMH（HS-N19F2-045）

附注：

其他：本書爲大學版（University Edition）。

3233 The Mainspring of Human Progress/by Henry Grady Weaver. —Irvington-on-Hudson, New York：The Foundation for Economic Education, Inc. , 1953

279 p. ; 19.2 cm

HSMH（HS-N19F6-037）

附注：

印章：内封面頁鈐有"胡適的書"朱文方印。

其他：此書與 HS-N19F6-038 同,此爲平裝本,彼爲精裝本。

3234 The Mainspring of Human Progress/by Henry Grady Weaver. —Irvington-on-Hudson, New York: The Foundation for Economic Education, Inc., 1953

279 p.；19.9 cm

HSMH（HS-N19F6-38）

附注：

印章：内封面頁鈐有"胡適的書"朱文方印。

題記：扉頁粘貼贈書小紙片 1 張："This history of human progress in given as an Enduring Memorial to Dr. Edward H. Hume 1876 - 1957 who contributed so wholesomely to the cause of individual freedom From Dagny and James Clise To Hu Shih"；紙片下有胡適題記："2107 North 34 St. Seattle, Wash。"

其他：此書與 HS-N19F6-037 同,此爲精裝本,彼爲平裝本。

3235 The Man from Nazareth/by Harry Emerson Fosdick. —New York: Harper & Brothers, 1949

282 p.；21.5 cm

HSMH（HS-N04F6-025）

附注：

印章：内封面頁鈐有"胡適的書"朱文方印。

題記：扉頁有贈書者題贈："To my dear friend Dr. Hu Shih. This book interests me. I am confident it will interest you also. It meets a very real present need, namely the need to Ruoro, as far as is possible, 'what manner of man the historic Jesus was, what he thought and did, and how he felt.' In attempting to show this, Harry Fosdick has used the indirect approach 'by way of the response whim of man and women who saw and heard him, before their thoughts about him because 'set in inherited patterns of theology.' With affectionate greetings Ed Lobenstine。"

批注圈劃：書中有胡適的批注劃綫數十處。

3236 Mandarin Primer: An Intensive Course in Spoken Chinese/by Yuen-ren Chao. —Cambridge, Mass.: Harvard University Press, 1948

　　viii, 336 p.; 23.5 cm

　　HSMH（HS-N20F1-004）

　　附註：

　　　　印章：扉頁有胡適簽名"Hu Shih"；內封面頁鈐有"胡適的書"朱文方印。

　　　　夾紙：書中有夾紙1張。

　　　　其他：封面有中文書名"國語入門"及作者"趙元任"。

3237 Manual of Zen Buddhism/by Daisetz Teitaro Suzuki; edited by Christmas Humphreys. —London: Published for the Buddhist Society by Rider and Company,［n. d.］

　　192 p., plates; 19 cm

　　HSMH（HS-N06F1-019）

　　附註：

　　　　印章：內封面頁鈐有"胡適的書"朱文方印及"胡適"紫色戳印。

　　　　題記：扉頁有胡適題記："'August 1935' — date of Preface to First Edition。"

　　　　批注圈劃：目錄與內文有胡適的朱、藍、鉛筆注記與劃綫。

　　　　夾紙：書中有夾紙1張。

　　　　其他：編者序的時間爲1950年。

3238 Marx and America: A Study of the Doctrine of Impoverishment/by Earl Browder. —New York: Duell, Sloan and Pearce, 1958

　　xiii, 146 p.; 21 cm

　　HSMH（HS-N04F3-016）

　　附註：

　　　　印章：內封面頁鈐有"胡適的書"朱文方印。

3239 Mathematician's Delight/by W. W. Sawyer. —Harmondsworth, Middlesex:

Penguin Books, 1956

238 p. ; 18.1 cm

HSMH（HS-N19F4-013）

附注：

印章：内封面頁鈐有"胡適的書"朱文方印。

3240 Mathews' Chinese-English Dictionary/by R. H. Mathews. —Cambridge, Mass. : Harvard University Press, 1950

xxiv, 1226 p. ; 26 cm

HSMH（HS-N19F1-041）

附注：

印章：内封面頁（American Edition）鈐有"胡適"紫色戳印；另一内封面頁（Shanghai, 1931）鈐有"胡適的書"朱文方印與"胡適"紫色戳印。

其他：此書爲修訂版（Revised, American Edition, Fifth Printing），1931年出版的原書名爲"A Chinese-English Dictionary: Compiled for the China Inland Mission"。

3241 Matter, Mind and Man: The Biology of Human Nature/by Edmund W. Sinnott. —New York: Harper & Brothers Publishers, 1957

xvii, 225 p. ; 19.6 cm

World Perspectives, Vol. 11

HSMH（HS-N19F4-047）

附注：

印章：内封面頁鈐有"胡適的書"朱文方印。

與胡適的關係：胡適爲 World Perspectives 的編輯委員會成員之一。

3242 The May Fourth Movement: Intellectual Revolution in Modern China = 五四運動史/by Chow Tse-tsung（周策縱）. —Cambridge, Mass. : Harvard University Press, 1960

xi, 486 p. ; 24 cm

HSMH（HS-N03F3-014）

附注：

　　題記：扉頁有作者題贈："適之先生指正　周策縱敬贈　一九六〇年五月　于哈佛。"

　　批注圈劃：書中有胡適的批注劃綫數處。

　　與胡適的關係：內容提及胡適。

　　相關記載：1964 年 5 月 20 日王志維致周策縱函，告知當年 4 月間費正清見到胡適在此書中的補正後之建議，參見館藏號：HS-NK05-356-002。

3243　McGraw-Hill Books，1958. —New York：McGraw-Hill International Corporation，1958

　　550 p. ; 21.5 cm

　　HSMH（HS-N19F1-034）

　　附注：

　　　其他：封面有"秀鶴行 H. C. Ling Book Store"的戳印。

3244　McGraw-Hill Export Subscription Catalogue，1958-1959. —New York：McGraw-Hill Export Subscription Agency，1958

　　480 p. ; 23.2 cm

　　HSMH（HS-N19F1-035）

　　附注：

　　　夾紙：頁 226、227 間夾有"秀鶴行 李葆蓀"名片 1 張。

　　　其他：內封面頁有"秀鶴行 H. C. Ling Book Store"的戳印。

3245　The Meaning of a Liberal Education/by Everett Dean Martin. —Garden City，New York：Garden City Publishing Company，Inc.，1926

　　ix, 319 p. ; 20.9 cm

　　HSMH（HS-N19F3-031）

　　附注：

　　　印章：扉頁鈐有"胡適的書"朱文方印。

　　　批注圈劃：書中有鉛筆劃綫數十處。

3246 The Meaning of Evolution/by George Gaylord Simpson. —New York: The New American Library, 1954

　　192 p. ; 18 cm

　　HSMH（HS-N04F6-012）

　　附注：

　　　　印章：內封面頁鈐有"胡適的書"朱文方印。

　　　　其他：本書爲特別修訂及刪節的版本的第 4 次印刷。

3247 Medieval and Early Modern Science, Volume I: Science in the Middle Ages/by A. C. Crombie. —Garden City, New York: Doubleday & Company, Inc. , 1959

　　xxii, 296 p. , xxxix plates; 18.1 cm

　　HSMH（HS-N19F4-029）

　　附注：

　　　　印章：內封面頁鈐有"胡適的書"朱文方印。

　　　　批注圈劃：版權頁有胡適的劃綫一處。

　　　　其他：本書爲修訂版。

3248 Medieval Cities/by Henri Pirenne; translated from the French by Frank D. Halsey. —Garden City, N. Y. : Doubleday & Company, Inc. , 1956

　　185 p. ; 18 cm

　　HSMH（HS-N19F2-070）

　　附注：

　　　　印章：內封面頁鈐有"胡適的書"朱文方印。

3249 Meeting of Convocation, May 9th, 1961. —Hong Kong: Hong Kong University, 1961

　　19 p. ; 21.6 cm

　　HSMH（HS-N19F2-043）

3250 The Meeting of East and West: An Inquiry Concerning World Understanding/

by F. S. C. Northrop. —New York：The MacMillan Company，1958

xxii，531 p.；21.5 cm

HSMH（HS-N03F6-008）

附注：

印章：内封面頁鈐有"胡適的書"朱文方印。

批注圈劃：書中有胡適的批注劃綫數處。

夾紙：書中有夾紙3張。

與胡適的關係：内容提及胡適及其著作"Development of the Logical Method in Ancient China"。

3251 A Memoir of William Edward Hartpole Lecky/by his wife, Elisabeth Lecky. —New York：Longmans, Green, and Co.，1909

xvii，432 p.；20cm

HSMH（HS-N07F2-055）

附注：

印章：内封面頁鈐有"胡適的書"朱文方印。

3252 The Memoirs of Cordell Hull/by Cordell Hull. —New York：The Macmillan Company，1948

2 Vols.（xii，1804 p.）；21.6 cm

HSMH（HS-N04F2-006，HS-N04F2-007）

附注：

印章：第1冊的感謝頁鈐有"胡適的書"朱文方印；第2冊的扉頁亦鈐有"胡適的書"朱文方印。

與胡適的關係：第2冊内容提及胡適。

3253 A Memorandum to School Boards：Recommendations for Education in the Junior High School Years/by James Bryant Conant. —Princeton, New Jersey：Educational Testing Service，1960

46 p.；21.7 cm

HSMH（HS-N19F2-035）

3254 Men and Ideas: An Informal History of Chinese Political Thought/by Lin Mousheng. —New York: The John Day Company, 1942

 xiv, 256 p. ; 21 cm

 HSMH（HS-N03F5-020）

 附注：

  印章：内封面頁鈐有"胡適的書"朱文方印。

  題記：封面裹粘貼名片1張，有作者題贈："To Dr. Hu Shih with the compliments of Lin Mousheng。"

  批注圈劃：書中有胡適的劃綫數處。

  與胡適的關係：書中提及胡適的文章"Chungkuo Chehsueh Shih Takang（History of Chinese Philosophy）"（《中國哲學史大綱》）、"The Origin of the Confucian School"、"Historical Foundations for a Democratic China"。

  相關記載：1945年1月17日胡適致Edwin R. Walker函，館藏號：HS-JDSHSE-0113-002。

3255 A Mencken Chrestomathy/by H. L. Mencken. —New York: Alfred A Knopf, 1949

 xvi, 627 p. ; 21.9 cm

 HSMH（HS-N04F3-010）

 附注：

  印章：扉頁有胡適簽名"Hu Shih"；内封面頁鈐有"胡適的書"朱文方印。

  題記：扉頁有V. D. Hartman題記："To my Valentine Rily ± 1950。"

  其他：此書爲第3次印刷。

3256 The Mid-Century Challenge to U. S. Foreign Policy. —Garden City, New York: Doubleday & Company, Inc., 1959

 xii, 74 p. ; 22.8 cm

 America at Mid-century Series

 HSMH（HS-N20F1-029）

 附注：

批注圈劃：書中有胡適的批注劃綫數處。

其他：封面有"DEC 11 1959"的戳印。

3257 The Miraculous Birth of Language/by Richard A. Wilson. —New York：Philosophical Library, 1948

256 p. ; 21 cm

HSMH（HS-N19F4-039）

附註：

印章：內封面頁鈐有"胡適的書"朱文方印。

題記：扉頁有贈書者題贈："Dear Dr. Hu：I think you may find this interesting — Your good and affectionate friend Josephine B. Crow May 24-1950。"

3258 A Miscellany on the Shin Teaching of Buddhism/by Daisetz Teitaro Suzuki. —Kyoto：Shinshu Otaniha Shumusho, 1949

151 p. ; 18.7 cm

HSMH（HS-N03F4-002）

附註：

印章：內封面頁鈐有"胡適的書"朱文方印。

其他：版權頁有中文書名"真宗要録"及作者"鈴木大拙"。

3259 Modern China：A Brief History/by David Nelson Rowe. —Princeton, New Jersey：D. Van Nostrand Company, Inc., 1959

192 p. ; 18.2 cm

HSMH（HS-N03F3-028）

附註：

印章：內封面頁鈐有"胡適的書"朱文方印。

夾紙：書中夾有名片1張，印有"With the compliments of American-Asian Educational Exchange Incorporated Marvin Liebman Executive Vice-Chairman"。

與胡適的關係：內容有"Dr. Hu Shih on The Chinese Renaissance, 1933"—

文;另書目提及胡適的著作"The Chinese Renaissance"。

3260 Modern Education and Human Values/by Mildred McAfee Horton, et al. —Pittsburgh: University of Pittsburgh Press, 1954

   86 p.; 21.5 cm

   Pitcairn-Crabbe Foundation Lecture Series, Vol. V

   HSMH(HS-N03F6-019)

   附注:

   　印章:內封面頁鈐有"胡適的書"朱文方印。

   　夾紙:書中夾有出版社贈書卡片1張。

   　與胡適的關係:收錄1953年11月5日胡適的演講文"An Oriental Looks at the Modern Western Civilization"。

3261 Modern English Drama: Dryden, Sheridan, Goldsmith, Shelly, Browning, Byron/edited by Charles W. Eliot. —New York: P. F. Collier & Son Corporation, 1909

   450 p., [1] plate; 21 cm

   Harvard Classics: The Five-Foot Shelf of Books, Vol. 18

   HSMH(HS-N12F6-018)

   附注:

   　印章:內封面頁鈐有"胡適的書"朱文方印。

3262 Modern Science and Modern Man/by James B. Conant. —New York: Doubleday Anchor Books, 1953

   187 p.; 18.1 cm

   HSMH(HS-N19F4-023)

   附注:

   　印章:扉頁鈐有"胡適的書"朱文方印。

   　批注圈劃:書中有胡適的批注劃綫數處。

3263 Money and Credit in China: A Short History/by Lien-sheng Yang. —Cambridge,

Mass.：Harvard University Press，1952

143 p.；24.2 cm

HSMH（HS-N03F5-028）

附注：

印章：內封面頁鈐有"胡適的書"朱文方印。

題記：扉頁有作者題贈："適之先生教正 學生聯陞敬呈 一九五二年九月二十三日。"

批注圈劃：頁55 有胡適的批注劃綫。

與胡適的關係：書中提及《胡適文存》。

相關記載：胡適與楊聯陞的來往函，參見館藏號：HS-LS01-003-028，HS-LS01-003-029。

3264 Moral Principles of Action/edited by Ruth Nanda Anshen. —New York：Harper & Brothers，1952

xii，720 p.；24 cm

Science of Culture Series，Vol. VI

HSMH（HS-N04F5-033）

附注：

印章：內封面頁鈐有"胡適的書"朱文方印。

題記：扉頁有編者題贈："To Dr. Hu Shih with every wish of friendship, Ruth Nanda Anshen June, 1953。"

批注圈劃：頁600、602 有胡適的批注劃綫。

3265 Mothers and Daughters/by Evan Hunter. —New York：Simon and Schuster, Inc. ，1961

605 p.；22 cm

HSMH（HS-N11F1-021）

附注：

題記：扉頁有陳香梅紅筆題贈："To Dr. Hu, with best wish Anna Chennault, 1961, Summer Taipei, Taiwan。"

3266 Mount Sinai and the Monastery of St. Catherine/by Howard C. Rice, Jr.. — Princeton, New Jersey: Princeton University Library, 1960

　　8 p.; 21.5 cm

　　HSMH（HS-N19F2-056）

　　附注：

　　　其他：展覽小冊子。

3267 Mouse Adaptation of the Asian Influenza Virus/by Hsi-Shan Wen and San-Pin Wang. —Taipei, Taiwan: United States Naval Medical Research No. 2, 1958

　　14 p.; 26.5 cm

　　NAMRU TWO, November 1, 1958（NM 52 05 02. 4. 3）

　　HSMH（HS-N19F5-006）

　　附注：

　　　其他：釘書針裝訂。

3268 Moving the Obelisks/by Bern Dibner. —New York: Burndy Library, 1950

　　61 p.; 27.6 cm

　　HSMH（HS-N19F4-002）

　　附注：

　　　印章：内封面頁鈐有"胡適的書"朱文方印。

3269 The Multi-State System of Ancient China/by Richard Louis Walker. — Hamden, Conn.: The Shoe String press, 1953

　　xii, 135 p.; 22.3 cm

　　HSMH（HS-N20F1-008）

　　附注：

　　　印章：扉頁鈐有"胡適的書"朱文方印。

　　　題記：扉頁有作者題贈："For Hu Shih, a respected scholar and statesman and a good friend and teacher. Dick Walker 19 April 1954。"

　　　批注圈劃：書中有胡適的批注圈劃數十處。

　　　其他：扉頁後印有李田意題簽之中文書名"吴克著 春秋時代之國際制度

李田意題"。

3270 Music Appreciation: Outlines of Study Book Two—Instrumental/by John L. Geiger. —Bloomington, Indiana: Indiana University Bookstore, 1931

103 p. ; 22.8 cm

HSMH（HS-N19F2-028）

附注:

印章:内封面頁鈐有"胡適的書"朱文方印。

其他:此爲修訂第 2 版（Second Revised Edition）。

3271 The Music Lover's Handbook/edited by Elie Siegmeister. —New York: William Morrow and Company, 1943

xiii, 817 p. ; 21.8 cm

HSMH（HS-N20F1-023）

附注:

印章:内封面頁鈐有"胡適的書"朱文方印。

3272 Musings of a Chinese Gourmet: Food has Its Place in Culture=食論/by F. T. Cheng. —London: Hutchinson & Co., Ltd., 1954

156 p. ; 19 cm

HSMH（HS-N20F1-009）

附注:

印章:内封面頁鈐有"胡適的書"朱文方印。

題記:扉頁有作者題贈:"To my old friend Dr. Hu Shih with kindest remembrances & best wishes F. T. Cheng the author 3rd Nov. 1954。"

批注圈劃:頁 11 有校改一處。

其他:封面印有李國欽題的中文書名"食論"。

3273 Musings of a Chinese Mystic: Selections from the Philosophy of Chuang Tzǔ/with an introduction by Lionel Giles. —New York: E. P. Dutton and Company, 1910

112 p. ; 17 cm

The Wisdom of the East Series

HSMH（HS-N03F5-007）

附注：

　　印章：扉頁有胡適簽名"Suh Hu October, 1914"；簽名下鈐有"嗣糜藏書"朱文圓印。另一扉頁（印有書名）鈐有"胡適的書"朱文方印。

　　題記：扉頁有胡適題記："Miss Clifford Williams returns this volume to me on August 8, 1960. H. S. 。"

　　批注圈劃：書中有胡適的批注劃綫數十處。

　　夾紙：頁82、83間夾有胡適的札記1張，上記"J. Legge：'In his attracting and uniting them to himself in such a way, there must have been that which made them involuntarily express then words (of condolence), and involuntarily wail, as they were doing.' 適按 involuntarily 近是矣。下文不無為諸家謬註所誤"。

3274 My Life in China, 1926-1941/by Hallett Abend. —New York：Harcourt, Brace and Company, 1943

　　396 p. ; 20.9 cm

HSMH（HS-N03F3-004）

附注：

　　印章：內封面頁及頁3均鈐有"胡適的書"朱文方印。

　　題記：扉頁有胡適題記："Many untruths are contained in this volume. For instance, Abend's story of me on p. 141-145 is full of untruths. I was never 'arrested', never 'secretly condemned to death', etc. (all on p. 145). Hu Shih Oct. 11, 1960。"

　　批注圈劃：書中有胡適的批注劃綫數十處。

　　夾紙：書中有夾紙2張。

　　與胡適的關係：內文提及胡適。

　　其他：作者譯名"安培德"。

3275 My Mission in Israel/by James G. McDonald. —New York：Simon and

2841

Schuster, 1951

xiv, 303 p.; 22 cm

HSMH（HS-N04F2-003）

附注：

印章：内封面頁鈐有"胡適的書"朱文方印。

題記：扉頁有作者題贈："My good friend Dr. Hu Shih with high admirations & warm personal greeting in memory of old days cordially James G. McDonald 3/7/53。"

夾紙：封底夾有記 James G. McDonald 地址的紙條 1 張。

3276 My Mother's Betrothal/by Hu Shih; edited by Mary Rouse. —New Haven： Yale University Press, 1946

vi, 13, 33 p.; 21.6 cm

Mirror Series C, No. 3

HSMH（HS-N19F2-041）

附注：

内附文件：封面裏粘貼贈書小紙條 1 張，内容爲"Presented to The Library of Dr. Hu Shih's Memorial Hall in honor of the Late Dr. Hu Shih C. H. Kwock Aug., 1967"。

與胡適的關係：此書内容即是胡適《四十自述》的"我的母親的訂婚"。

其他：(1)書中前 13 頁爲英文内容，後 33 頁爲中文内容。(2)此書爲 C. H. Kwock 在胡適身後贈給胡適紀念館的書。

3277 Mysticism: Christian and Buddhist/by Daisetz Teitaro Suzuki. —New York： Harper & Brothers Publishers, 1957

xix, 214 p.; 18 cm

World Perspectives, Vol. 12

HSMH（HS-N06F1-020）

附注：

印章：内封面頁鈐有"胡適的書"朱文方印。

夾紙：書中夾有出版社箋紙 1 張。

3278 The Myth of the Good and Bad Nations/by René Wormser. —Chicago：Henry Regnery Company, 1954

   ix, 180 p.；21.7 cm

   HSMH（HS-N04F2-016）

   附注：

   印章：內封面頁鈐有"胡適的書"朱文方印。

   題記：扉頁有作者題贈："To Dr. Hu Shih with respects and best wishes René A. Wormser。"

   夾紙：扉頁夾有卡片1張。

   相關記載：1955年10月20日René A. Wormser致函胡適,並寄贈此書,參見HS-US01-008-003。

3279 NAMRU TWO/by C. E. Knight, et al. —Taipei, Taiwan：United States Naval Medical Research No. 2, 1956

   40 p.；26.5 cm

   HSMH（HS-N19F5-005）

3280 The Natural History of Nonsense/by Bergen Evans. —New York：Vintage Books, 1959

   262, xiii p.；18.5 cm

   HSMH（HS-N19F4-042）

   附注：

   印章：內封面頁鈐有"胡適的書"朱文方印。

   題記：扉頁有題記："S. Z. Y. from〔以人物卡通畫像代表〕。"

3281 Nature and Mind/by Frederick J. E. Woodbridge. —New York：Columbia University Press, 1937

   509 p.；23.4 cm

   HSMH（HS-N04F4-020）

   附注：

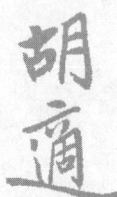

印章：内封面頁鈐有"胡適的書"朱文方印。

題記：扉頁有作者題贈："To Virginia Hartman: Some say this is a weighty book. I could wish it were heavier, if that would help me when I try to weigh my indebtedness to you. Sincerely yours, Frederick J. E. Woodbridge April 14, 1937."

批注圈劃：書中有胡適的劃綫數處。

3282 Nazi-Soviet Relations, 1939–1941/edited by Ramond James Sontag and James Stuart Beddie. —Washington: Department of State, 1948

xxxvii, 362 p.; 23.2 cm

HSMH（HS-N04F1-022）

附注：

印章：内封面頁有胡適簽名"Hu Shih"。

題記：目次頁背面有吳相湘題記："此書爲適之師撰'史達林大戰略下的中國'重要參考資料，民國四十年蒙寄贈相湘，今謹奉陳紀念館珍存 吳相湘謹誌 六十三年十一月廿七日。"

批注圈劃：書中有胡適的批注劃綫數十處。

夾紙：書中有夾紙1張。

相關記載：1951年12月4日吳相湘致胡適，借閱此書（胡適逝世後，歸還給紀念館保存），參見館藏號 HS-US01-063-028。

3283 Neo-Confucianism and Chinese Scientific Thought/by Wing-Tsit Chan. — Honolulu, Hawaii: The University of Hawaii Press, 1957

309-332 p.; 25.5 cm

Philosophy East and West: A Journal of Oriental and Comparative Thought, Vol. 6, No. 4, January, 1957

HSMH（HS-N20F1-036）

附注：

與胡適的關係：(1)胡適爲顧問編輯之一。(2)頁328的内文及注脚71、74，頁329的内文及注脚75，以及頁332的内文及注脚80均提及胡適。

其他：抽印本。

3284 New Art in America/by John I. H. Baur, editor [and others]. —Greenwich, Conn.：New York Graphic Society in cooperation with Frederick A. Praeger, Inc, New York, 1957

  280 p., illus. (part col.)；31 cm

  HSMH（HS-N13F1-014）

3285 New Bottles for New Wine/by Julian Huxley. —New York：Harper & Brothers Publishers, 1957

  318 p.；22 cm

  HSMH（HS-N04F6-007）

  附注：

   印章：内封面頁鈐有"胡適的書"朱文方印。

3286 New Chinese Poetry/edited and translated by Yu Kwang-chung(余光中). —Taipei, Taiwan：Heritage Press, 1960

  xvi, 94 p.；19 cm

  HSMH（HS-N03F3-009）

  附注：

   印章：内封面頁鈐有"胡適的書"朱文方印。

   題記：扉頁的一面有本書的幾位作者題贈："適之先生賜正：余光中、紀弦、鍾鼎文、覃子豪、周夢蝶、夏菁、葉珊"；扉頁的另一面有 Dave Phillips 的簽名。

   相關記載：館藏剪報"Ambassador, Mrs. Drumright Honor Chinese Poets At Tea"（載 *China Post*, January 11, 1961），描述 1961 年 1 月 10 日莊萊德夫婦舉行茶會，慶祝余光中等所作新詩集的英譯本（即本書）的出版，會中並邀請胡適講述中國新詩的發展，參見館藏號：HS-NK05-337-003。

3287 New Chinese Stories：Twelve Short Stories by Contemporary Chinese Writers/edited and translated by Lucian Wu. —Taipei, Taiwan：Heritage Press, 1961 viii, 309 p. ; 18.6 cm

HSMH（HS-N03F3-008）

附注：

　　印章：館藏 2 冊，内封面頁均鈐有"胡適的書"朱文方印。

　　批注圈劃：其中一冊的目次頁有胡適的批注數處。

3288　A New Dictionary of Quotations on Historical Principles from Ancient and Modern Sources/selected and edited by H. L. Mencken. —New York：Alfred A. Knopf, 1952

　　xiii, 1347 p. ; 24.1 cm

HSMH（HS-N19F1-043）

附注：

　　印章：内封面頁鈐有"胡適的書"朱文方印。

3289　New Dimensions of Learning in a Free Society：Seminar Addresses, Discussions, Public Lectures, Inaugural Address Delivered on the Occasion of the Inauguration of Edward Harold Litchfield, Twelfth Chancellor, University of Pittsburgh, May 9, 10, 11, 1957/by John W. Dodds, et al. —Pittsburgh：University of Pittsburgh Press, 1958

　　ix, 289 p. ; 23.6 cm

HSMH（HS-N12F4-015）

附注：

　　印章：内封面頁鈐有"胡適的書"朱文方印。

3290　The New English Bible：New Testament. —Cambridge：Oxford University Press, 1961

　　xiii, 446 p. ; 19.5 cm

HSMH（HS-N04F6-028）

附注：

　　印章：内封面頁鈐有"胡適的書"朱文方印。

　　題記：内封面頁有胡適題記："Hu Shih March 30, 1961, at The NTU

Hospital。"

内附文件:书末粘贴剪报 1 张,标题爲"英文新譯聖經的問世"(《聯合報》,4 月 15 日)。

3291 The New Physics: Talks on Aspects of Science/by Sir C. V. Raman. —New York: Philosophical Library, 1951

[4], 144 p.; 21 cm

HSMH(HS-N19F4-011)

附注:

印章:内封面頁鈐有"胡適的書"朱文方印。

3292 The New Testament of Our Lord and Saviour Jesus Christ & The Book of Psalms. —Philadelphia: National Bible Press, 1941

512,[123] p.; 11.8 cm

HSMH(HS-N04F6-027)

附注:

題記:扉頁有題記:"To Beloed [Beloved] Shuming from Yours Fangkuen Date 16-9-48, Nanking。"

批注圈劃:書中有紅、藍、鉛筆劃綫數十處。

夾紙:頁 302、303 間有夾紙 1 張。

其他:這是美國軍方用袖珍本《聖經》。

3293 Newnes National Trade Press Heywood: 1958 Technical Books. —London: George Newnes Limited, 1958

64 p.; 20.7 cm

HSMH(HS-N19F1-033)

附注:

批注圈劃:書中有胡適的劃綫數處。

其他:出版頁有"秀鶴行 H. C. Ling Book Store"的戳印。

3294 The Next Development in Man/by Lancelot Law Whyte. —New York: The New

American Library, 1950

255 p. ; 18 cm

HSMH（HS-N19F6-035）

附注：

印章：内封面頁鈐有"胡適的書"朱文方印。

3295 The Night-Watchman and Other Longshoremen/by W. W. Jacobs. — London：Hodder and Stoughton, 1932

viii, 1024 p. ; 19.3 cm

HSMH（HS-N19F5-074）

附注：

印章：内封面頁鈐有"胡適的書"朱文方印。

題記：扉頁有贈書者題贈："For Dr. Hu Shih from I think now one of his old friends. Eugene L. Delafield Oct. 15, 1960。"

夾紙：書中有夾紙1張。

3296 Nine Greek dramas/by Aeschylus, Sophocles, Euripides and Aristophanes; translated by E. D. A. Morshead, E. H. Plumptre, Gilbert Murray and B. B. Rogers. —New York：P. F. Collier & Son Corporation, 1909

487 p., [1] plate; 21 cm

Harvard Classics：The Five-Foot Shelf of Books, Vol. 8

HSMH（HS-N12F6-008）

附注：

印章：内封面頁鈐有"胡適的書"朱文方印。

夾紙：目次頁夾有胡適的筆記紙片1張。

3297 Ninety Three Drawings/by Boardman Robinson; with an introduction by George Biddle. —Colorado：Colorado Springs Fine Arts Center, 1937

93 plates; 29.5 cm

HSMH（HS-N20F1-025）

附注：

印章：扉頁有胡適簽名"Hu Shih Jan. 14, 1952"；內封面頁鈐有"胡適的書"及"胡適"朱文方印。

3298 Northern India According to the Shui-Ching-Chu/by L. Petech. —Roma：Istituto Italiano Per Il Medio Ed Estremo Oriente, 1950

viii, 89 p.；24.5 cm

HSMH（HS-N03F4-015）

附注：

印章：內封面頁鈐有"胡適的書"朱文方印。

相關記載：1951 年 1 月 18 日楊聯陞寫信給胡適，提及此書及作者 L. Petech，參見館藏號：HS-LS01-003-006。

3299 Not Guilty/by Judge Jerome Frank and Barbara Frank in Association with Harold M. Hoffman. —New York：Doubleday & Company, 1957

261 p.；21.8 cm

HSMH（HS-N19F3-012）

附注：

印章：內封面頁鈐有"胡適的書"朱文方印。

題記：扉頁有胡適題記："冤獄三十六案 胡適 一九五七，七，十八（出版之日）。"

批注圈劃：書中有胡適的批注劃綫數十處。

內附文件：（1）頁 254、255 間夾有剪報一則："Convict 10 Years Pleads Mistake：Seeking Freedom, He Says Another Admits Hold-Up in Brooklyn in 1947", in *New York Times*, Nov. 12, 1957。（2）書末貼有剪報三則，第一則爲本書的書評："Book Review", by Herbert Kupferberg, in *Herald Tribune*, July 18, 1957；第二則爲"Innocent Man Freed after Year in Prison：Cautions Robbery Victims, Jury：'I Could Have Gotten 30 Years'", by Francis Sugrue, in *New York Herald-Tribune*, Aug. 9, 1957；第三則爲"Youth in Jail, Another Confesses in Rape Case", Aug. 4, 1957。

3300 A Notice of the Chinese Calendar and a Concordance with the European

Calendar/by Peter Hoang. —Shanghai：The Catholic Mission Press, 1904

384 p. ; 23.8 cm

HSMH（HS-N20F1-005）

附注：

 印章：中文内封面頁鈐有"胡適的書"朱文方印及"胡適"紫色戳印。

 批注圈劃：書中有胡適的批注圈劃數十處。

 其他：西文内封面頁前，有1885年上海徐滙書坊的中文内封面頁："海門黃伯祿斐默甫輯譯 中西歷日合璧 光緒甲辰仲秋滬西徐滙書坊重印。"

3301 Odd Craft/by W. W. Jacobs. —London：George Newnes, Limited, 1903

255 p., illus. ; 19 cm

HSMH（HS-N19F5-073）

附注：

 印章：内封面頁鈐有"胡適的書"朱文方印。

 題記：扉頁有贈書者題贈："To Dr. Hu Shih from his friend Eugene L. Delafield Mar. 15, 1958。"

3302 Odyssey of a Santo Domingan Creole：A Sprightly Account of American Manners by a Refugee from Haiti/edited and translated by Edward Larocque Tinker. —Worcester, Mass. : American Antiquarian Society, 1957

18 p. ; 25 cm

The Proceedings of the American Antiquarian Society, April 1957

HSMH（HS-N04F4-026）

附注：

 題記：扉頁粘貼編譯者名片1張，上有題贈："I hope this account of the quaint American mores of the 19th century may amuse you. Cordially ELT。"

3303 The Odyssey of Homer/by S. H. Butcher and A. Lang. —New York：P. F. Collier & Son Corporation, 1909

334 p., [1] plate; 21 cm

Harvard Classics：The Five-Foot Shelf of Books, Vol. 22

HSMH（HS-N12F6-022）

附注：

印章：内封面頁鈐有"胡適的書"朱文方印。

3304 The Odyssey of Homer/translated by T. E. Shaw. —New York：Oxford University Press, 1956

327 p.；21 cm

HSMH（HS-N04F6-031）

附注：

印章：内封面頁鈐有"胡適的書"朱文方印。

3305 Of Civil Government：Second Essay/by John Locke. —Chicago：Henry Regnery Company for Great Books Foundation，[n.d.]

150 p.；17.4 cm

HSMH（HS-N04F6-006）

附注：

印章：内封面頁鈐有"胡適的書"朱文方印。

批注圈劃：書中有胡適的批注劃綫數處。

夾紙：頁76、77間有夾紙1張。

3306 Of God, the Devil and the Jews/by Dagobert D. Runes. —New York：Philosophical Library, 1952

186 p.；22 cm

HSMH（HS-N19F6-028）

附注：

印章：内封面頁鈐有"胡適的書"朱文方印。

夾紙：頁10、11間夾有作者贈書卡片1張。

3307 Old China/by Charles Lamb. —Westport, Connecticut：The Redcoat Press, 1940

viii, 30 p.；17 cm

HSMH（HS-N03F5-032）

附注：

印章：内封面頁鈐有"胡適的書"朱文方印。

3308 On Active Service in Peace and War/by Henry L. Stimson and McGeorge Bundy. —New York：Harper & Brothers, 1948

xxii, 698 p.；24.3 cm

HSMH（HS-N04F2-001）

附注：

印章：扉頁有胡適簽名"Hu Shih December 28, 1949"；内封面頁鈐有"胡適的書"朱文方印。

批注圈劃：書中有胡適的批注劃綫數十處，其中頁258記"This view was comfirmed by Jamas G. Rogers in Conversation to me in 1940 or 1941. Hu Shih"。

夾紙：書中有夾紙3張。

3309 On Being Canadian/by Vincent Massey. —Toronto：J. M. Dent & Sons, 1948

xiv, 198 p.；22.3 cm

HSMH（HS-N19F6-011）

附注：

印章：扉頁鈐有"胡適的書"朱文方印。

題記：另一扉頁有胡適題記："Hu Shih August 1949 Gift of Ambassador Liu Chieh。"

3310 On Experience, Nature, and Freedom：Representative Selections/by John Dewey. —New York：The Liberal Arts Press, 1960

xlvii, 293 p.；20.4 cm

HSMH（HS-N04F4-014）

附注：

印章：内封面頁鈐有"胡適的書"及"適之"朱文方印。

其他：内封面頁有"Presented by the UNITED STATES INFORMATION SERVICE Taipei 台北 美國大使館新聞處敬贈"的藍色戳印。

3311 On Some Problems of Statistical Analysis of Fractions (or Percentages)/by Chueh-ming Wang(汪厥明). —Ottawa Canada: Queen's Printer and Controller of Stationery, 1958

25 p. ; 24.2 cm

Abstracts and Papers to be presented before the Fourth International Biometric Conference and Symposium on Biometrical Genetics, August 28 to September 2, 1958, Ottawa, Canada

HSMH (HS-N19F2-053)

附注:

題記:封面有作者題贈:"胡適之先生指正 著者敬贈。"

夾紙:頁 16、17 間有夾紙 1 張,印有"國立臺灣大學農學院生物統計研究室。"

其他:抽印本。

3312 On the Analytic and the Synthetic/by Shih-chao Liu. —Taipei, Taiwan: Taiwan University, 1956

218-228 p. ; 23 cm

The Philosophical Review, Vol. LXV, No. 2, April 1956

HSMH (HS-N19F2-020)

附注:

題記:封面有作者題贈:"適之先生指正 劉世超敬贈。"

其他:抽印本。

3313 On the Analytic Properties of the 4-Point Function in Perturbation Theory/by Alfred Chi-tai Wu. —Denmark: Bianco Lunos Bogtrykkeri A-S, 1961

88 p. ; 23.3 cm

Mat. Fys. Medd. Dan. Vid. Selsk. 33, No. 3, 1961

HSMH (HS-N20F1-088)

附注:

夾紙:封面裏有夾紙 1 張,內容爲"To 中央研究院 From: Alfred Chi-tai

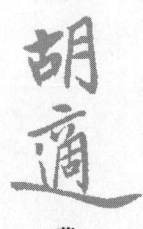

Wu, PH. D. 吳期泰 The Institute for Advanced Study Princeton, N. J., U. S. A."。

其他：抽印本。

3314 On the Nature of Man: An Essay in Primitive Philosophy/by Dagobert D. Runes. —New York: Philosophical Library, 1956

105 p.；22.2 cm

HSMH（HS-N19F4-045）

附注：

印章：內封面頁鈐有"胡適的書"朱文方印。

3315 On Understanding Science: An Historical Approach/by James B. Conant. —New York: The New American Library, 1952

144 p.；18 cm

HSMH（HS-N19F4-022）

附注：

印章：扉頁有胡適簽名"Hu Shih"。

批注圈劃：書中有胡適的批注劃綫數處。

其他：此書爲第2次印刷。

3316 On War/by Raymond Aron. —Garden City, New York: Doubleday & Company, Inc., 1959

143 p.；18.2 cm

HSMH（HS-N04F5-007）

附注：

印章：內封面頁鈐有"胡適的書"朱文方印。

批注圈劃："Preface"及扉頁有胡適的劃綫注記。

3317 Once in a Lifetime: A Comedy in Three Acts/by George S. Kaufman and Moss Hart；edited with an introduction and notes by Y. Z. Chang. —Taipei, Taiwan: Hwa Kuo Publishing Company, 1959 xii, 152 p. ; 18.9 cm

HSMH（HS-N19F5-070）

附注：

 印章：內封面頁鈐有"胡適的書"朱文方印。

 題記：內封面頁有贈書者題贈："請適之先生指正 張沅長敬贈 四九年十一月三日。"

3318 One Great Society：Humane Learning in the United States/by Howard Mumford Jones. —New York：Harcourt, Brace & Company, 1959

ix, 241 p. ; 21 cm

HSMH（HS-N19F3-020）

附注：

 印章：內封面頁鈐有"胡適的書"朱文方印。

 相關記載：1960 年 1 月 6 日 Charles A. McGinley Jr. 致胡適函，告知美國新聞處（United States Information Agency）贈此書給胡適，參見館藏號：HS-NK05-160-019。

 其他：內封面頁印有"台北美國大使館新聞處敬贈"藍色方印。

3319 One Increasing Purpose：The Life of Henry Winters Luce/by B. A. Garside. —New York：Fleming H. Revell Company, [n. d.]

271 p. ; 21 cm

HSMH（HS-N04F3-011）

附注：

 印章：感謝頁鈐有"胡適的書"朱文方印。

 題記：扉頁有作者題贈："To Hu Shih, from whom Henry Winters Luce learned much of Chinese ancient and modern wisdom, and for whom he had great admiration and affection. B. A. Garside 3/27/49。"

 批注圈劃：頁 225 有胡適的鉛筆劃綫；頁 224 有胡適批注："Strange imagination! Mr. Luce was never a house guest of mine! H. S. 。"

 與胡適的關係：內容提及胡適。

3320 One Mind, Common to All/by Earl D. Bond. —New York：The MacMillan Company, 1958

vii, 200 p.；21.7 cm

HSMH（HS-N19F4-044）

附注：

印章：內封面頁鈐有"胡適的書"朱文方印。

夾紙：頁 78、79 間夾有小卡片 1 張，有贈書者記"Compliments of K. Nimick"。

3321 Only Yesterday：An Informal History of the Nineteen-Twenties/by Frederick Lewis Allen. —New York：Bantam Books, 1952

viii, 338 p.；16.4 cm

HSMH（HS-N04F3-015）

附注：

印章：內封面頁鈐有"胡適的書"朱文方印。

批注圈劃：書中有胡適的批注劃綫數處。

3322 The Orient Analyzed = 東方分析/by Orient Lee. —Taipei, Taiwan：The Tsoh Ping Monthly, 1960

89 p.；18.8 cm

HSMH（HS-N03F1-007）

附注：

印章：內封面頁鈐有"胡適的書"朱文方印。

其他：著作人爲黎東方。

3323 Oriental Alchemy/by Masumi Chikashige. —Tokyo：Rokakuho Uchida, 1936

vii, 102 p.；19.5 cm

HSMH（HS-N03F1-015）

附注：

印章：扉頁有胡適中文簽名；內封面頁鈐有"胡適的書"朱文方印。

其他：封面有中文書名"東洋鍊金術"。

3324 Oriental Despotism: A Comparative Study of Total Power/by Karl A. Wittfogel. —New Haven: Yale University Press, 1957

xix, 556 p.; 24 cm

HSMH (HS-N03F5-027)

附注:

印章:内封面頁鈐有"胡適的書"朱文方印。

夾紙:書中有夾紙1張。

內附文件:扉頁夾有 Edwin O. Reischauer 對此書之書評剪報一則。

3325 The Origin of Species/by Charles Darwin. —New York: P. F. Collier & Son Corporation, 1909

530 p., [1] plate; 21 cm

Harvard Classics: The Five-Foot Shelf of Books, Vol. 11

HSMH (HS-N12F6-011)

附注:

印章:内封面頁鈐有"胡適的書"朱文方印。

3326 The Origin of Species: Chapters 1-6, 15/by Charles Darwin. —Chicago, Illinois: Henry Regnery Company for The Great Books Foundation, 1949

270 p.; 18.1 cm

HSMH (HS-N04F6-014)

附注:

印章:内封面頁鈐有"胡適的書"朱文方印。

3327 Out of My Later Years/by Albert Einstein. —New York: Philosophical Library, 1950

282 p.; 22.1 cm

HSMH (HS-N04F5-015)

附注:

印章:内封面頁鈐有"胡適的書"朱文方印。

批注圈劃：書中有胡適的劃綫數處。

3328 Out of Red China/by Shaw-tong Liu. ——New York：Duell, Sloan and Pearce, 1953

xvi, 269 p.；21 cm

HSMH（HS-N03F2-022）

附注：

印章：內封面頁鈐有"胡適的書"朱文方印。

夾紙：書中夾有名片 3 張：一張是羅家倫的名片，上寫"歡欣轉呈 胡先生 羅家倫敬呈 上台中荔園新標下荔支一小筐 敬祈 惠嚐 敬頌 適之師座 晨安 學生家倫拜上"；另一張是朱家驊的名片；第三張是堀內謙介的名片，上寫"適之先生"。

與胡適的關係："Introduction"爲胡適所作。

相關記載："'Introduction' to Liu Shaw-tong's Out of Red China"（劉紹唐《〈紅色中國的叛徒〉序》）一文，約作於 1952 年下半年，係胡適爲劉紹唐《紅色中國的叛徒》（*Out of Red China*）一書的英譯本寫的導言，參見館藏號：HS-NK05-201-006，或周質平主編《胡適英文文存》第 3 冊，頁 1343—1348。

3329 Outer Mongolia：A Study in Soviet Colonialism/by Jeanne Nickell Knutson. ——Kowloon, Hong Kong：Union Research Institute, 1959

174 p.；25.9 cm

Communist China Problem Research Series

HSMH（HS-N03F2-014）

附注：

印章：內封面頁鈐有"胡適的書"朱文方印。

其他：封面有"Complimentary Copy"的藍色戳印。

3330 An Outline and an Annotated Bibliography of Chinese Philosophy/by Wing-tsit Chan（陳榮捷）. ——New Haven：Far Eastern Publications, Yale University, 1959 vi, 127 p. ; 21.7 cm

HSMH（HS-N20F1-026）

附注：

> 批注圈劃：頁 96 有胡適注記："1. Indianization of China: a Harvard Tercentenary Paper. 2. The Establishment of Confucianism as a state Religion under [during] the Han Empire. 3. Wang Mang: the Socialist-Emperor。"

3331 An Outline of the Religious Literature of India/by J. N. Farquhar. —London: Oxford University Press, 1920

xxviii, 451 p. ; 22.1 cm

The Religious Quest of India

HSMH（HS-N03F1-003）

附注：

> 印章：內封面頁鈐有"胡適的書"朱文方印。
>
> 題記：扉頁有胡適題記："Hu Shih July 19, 1955, in New York 此書出版在 1920, 久已絕版, 今日我從 Paragon Book Gallery 買得, 甚高興！胡適。"
>
> 批注圈劃：書中有非胡適筆迹的鉛筆批注劃綫數處。
>
> 相關記載：胡適閱讀本書的記事，參見《胡適日記》1922 年 5 月 10 日條。

3332 An Outline Plan for Long-Range National Development of Science; The Constitution and Operation Rules of the National Council on Science Development. —Taipei, Taiwan: "National Council on Science Development", 1959

11 p. ; 21.2 cm

HSMH（HS-N19F2-039）

附注：

> 其他：此即"國家長期發展科學計劃綱領"的英文版, 有 2 冊。

3333 Outlines of the History of Dogma/by Adolf Harnack; translated by Edwin Knox Mitchell; with an Introduction by Philip Rieff. —Boston: Beacon Press, 1957

xii, [23], 567 p. ; 20.3 cm

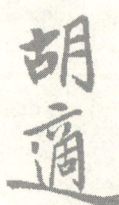

HSMH（HS-N19F3-040）

附注：

印章：内封面頁有胡適簽名"Hu Shih 胡適 August 13，1957"，並鈐有"胡適的書"朱文方印。

批注圈劃：書中有胡適的批注劃綫數處。

3334 Pakistan.—New York：The First National City Bank of New York，[n.d.]

16 p.，illus.；22.9 cm

HSMH（HS-N19F2-010）

附注：

印章：頁1鈐有"胡適的書"朱文方印。

3335 Papermaking：The History & Technique of an Ancient Craft／by Dard Hunter.—New York：Alfred A. Knopf，Inc.，1947

xxiv，611，xxxvii p.，illus.，fold. map；23.5 cm

HSMH（HS-N03F1-013）

附注：

印章：扉頁鈐有"胡適之鉢"白文方印；内封面頁鈐有"胡適之印章"白文方印及"胡適的書"朱文方印。

題記：扉頁有胡適的親筆題字："大德·亨脱著 造紙的歷史 胡適 一九五二，二，廿一。"

3336 Parsifal：A Festival-Drama／by Richard Wagner；translated into English in exact accordance with the original by H. L. and F. Corder. —New York：Fred Rullman Inc.，[n.d.]

43 p.；25.4 cm

Metropolitan Opera House Grand Opera

HSMH（HS-N19F5-039）

附注：

印章：内封面頁鈐有"胡適的書"朱文方印。

3337 Patterns of Progress：Matchette Foundation Lectures Delivered at Columbia University，1949/by Horace M. Kallen. —New York：Columbia University Press，1950

ⅸ，87 p.；20.8 cm

HSMH（HS-N19F6-036）

附注：

印章：扉頁鈐有"胡適的書"朱文方印。

批注圈劃："Foreword"有鉛筆劃綫。

夾紙：頁72、73 間夾有"Committee of the Conference of Methods in Philosophy and Science"的贈書紙條1張。

3338 Peace Can Be Won/by Paul G. Hoffman. —Garden City, New York：Doubleday & Company, 1951

93 p.；25.1 cm

HSMH（HS-N04F2-019）

附注：

印章：封面有胡適簽名"Hu Shih April 24, 1951"；内封面頁鈐有"胡適的書"朱文方印。

3339 Peacetime Uses of Atomic Energy/by Martin Mann. —New York：The Studio Publications, Inc., 1957

175 p., illus.；22.8 cm

HSMH（HS-N19F4-016）

3340 Peirce and Pragmatism/by W. B. Gallie. —Harmondsworth, Middlesex：Penguin Books, 1952

247 p.；18 cm

Pelican Books, A254

HSMH（HS-N04F4-003）

附注：

印章：内封面頁鈐有"胡適的書"朱文方印。

3341 Pentastomida from Reptiles of Lan Yü Island (Taiwan), with a Description of Raillietiella Hebitihamata N. SP./by J. Teague Self and Robert E. Kuntz. —[s.l.]: [s.n.], [n.d.]

 885-888 p.; 26.1 cm

 The Journal of Parasitology, Vol. 46, No. 6, December, 1960

 HSMH（HS-N19F5-030）

 附注：

  相關記載：館藏另有此文，參見館藏號：HS-NK05-302-016。

3342 The People's Communes/by Chu-yuan Cheng. —Hong Kong: The Union Press, 1959

 139 p.; 17.3 cm

 HSMH（HS-N03F2-024）

 附注：

  印章：内封面頁鈐有"胡適的書"朱文方印。

3343 Peoples and Policies: A World Travelogue/by Frank L. Howley. —Chicago: Henry Regnery Company, 1959

 211 p.; 20.9 cm

 HSMH（HS-N19F6-017）

 附注：

  印章：内封面頁鈐有"胡適的書"朱文方印。

  題記：扉頁有贈書者題贈："Dear Dr. Hu I hope you enjoy reading this book by our good friend, General Howley. Sincerely Nattei Ditwars。"

  夾紙：頁84、85間夾有Taylor-Carlisle's Book Store, Inc.致胡適的信封地址殘片1張。

3344 The Person or the Significance of Man/by Ralph Tyler Flewelling. —Los Angeles: The Ward Ritchie Press, 1952

 xii, 339 p.; 24.1 cm

HSMH（HS-N19F3-033）

附注：

印章：内封面頁鈐有"胡適的書"朱文方印。

題記：内封面頁有胡適題記："Gift of the author, Prof. Ralph T. Flewelling, to Hu Shih, April 1952。"

3345 The Petrov Story/by Michael Bialoguski. —Melbourne: William Heinemann Ltd., 1955

xvi, 247 p.; 22.2 cm

HSMH（HS-N04F1-015）

附注：

印章：内封面頁鈐有"胡適的書"朱文方印。

3346 Pharyngoconjunctival Fever in Taiwan: A Report of Four Cases Caused by Adenovirus Type 3/by C. Y. Lee, P. B. Johnston, Y. F. Yang, L. S. Ko and J. T. Grayston. —Taipei, Taiwan: United States Naval Medical Research No. 2, 1959

13 p.; 26.5 cm

NAMRU TWO, January 20, 1959（NM 52 05 02. 1. 0. 1）

HSMH（HS-N19F5-008）

附注：

其他：釘書針裝訂。

3347 The Philosopher of the Common Man: Essays in Honor of John Dewey to Celebrate His Eightieth Birthday/by Sidney Ratner, et al. —New York: G. P. Putnam's Sons, 1940

228 p.; 22.2 cm

HSMH（HS-N04F4-010）

附注：

印章：内封面頁鈐有"胡適的書"朱文方印。

題記：扉頁有胡適題記："一九三九年十月二十日是杜威先生八十壽辰。我在紐約的慶祝會上曾有演講,我的全文載在此冊裏,是我用心寫的。今年我的朋友 Eugene Delafield 替我尋回這一冊早已絕版的書，我很高興。胡適 一九五〇、一、二十，杜威先生九十生辰之後三個月。"

批注圈劃：書中有胡適的批注劃綫數十處。

與胡適的關係：收錄胡適的文章"The Political Philosophy of Instrumentalism"。

相關記載：館藏有多筆"The Political Philosophy of Instrumentalism"的資料，參見館藏號：HS-JDSHSE-0017-008，HS-JDSHSE-0017-011，HS-NK05-200-003。

3348 Philosophies of India/by Heinrich Zimmer；edited by Joseph Campbell. —New York：Pantheon Books, Inc., 1953

xvii, 687 p. ; 23.4 cm

HSMH（HS-N03F1-004）

附注：

印章：內封面頁鈐有"胡適的書"朱文方印。

題記：扉頁粘貼 Philip S. Broughton 的贈書小卡片 1 張。

3349 Philosophy and Culture—East and West：East-West Philosophy in Practical Perspective/edited by Charles A. Moore. —Honolulu, Hawaii：The University of Hawaii Press, 1962

viii, 832 p. ; 25.5 cm

HSMH（HS-N03F6-017）

附注：

印章：扉頁鈐有"胡適的書"朱文方印。

夾紙：書中有夾紙 1 張及出版社贈書卡片 1 張。

內附文件：書中夾有 1963 年 1 月 16 日胡適夫人致 Charles A. Moore 函副本 1 張。

與胡適的關係：收錄胡適的文章"The Scientific Spirit and Method in Chinese Philosophy"及"John Dewey in China"；內容與注釋亦提及胡適。

3350 Philosophy East and West/edited by Charles A. Moore. —Princeton：Princeton

University Press, 1946

ix, 334 p.; 20.3 cm

HSMH（HS-N03F6-009）

附注：

印章：館藏 2 冊，內封面頁均鈐有"胡適的書"朱文方印。

題記：其中一冊的扉頁有胡適題記："Hu Shih, Gift of President G. M. Sinclair and Professor Charles A. Moore, of the University of Hawaii, April 16, 1949。"

批注圈劃：其中一冊有胡適的批注劃綫數十處。

夾紙：其中一冊有夾紙 4 張。

與胡適的關係：內容與注釋均提及胡適。

相關記載：胡適紀念館館藏有多封胡適與 Charles A. Moore 的來往信函。

3351 A Philosophy for Our Time/by Bernard M. Baruch. —New York：Simon and Schuster, Inc., 1954

xi, 49 p.; 20.4 cm

HSMH（HS-N03F6-003）

3352 The Philosophy of Wang Yang-Ming/translated from the Chinese by Frederick Goodrich Henke. —London; Chicago：The Open Court Publishing Co., 1916

xvii, 512 p.; 23.7 cm

HSMH（HS-N03F4-019）

附注：

印章：內封面頁鈐有"胡適的書"朱文方印。

題記：扉頁有胡適題記："I read this work when it first appeared about 1917. It is a great pleasure to own this copy of the first edition and to re-read it with much more appreciation of the pains - taking effort required in this undertaking. Hu Shih Nov. 7, 1950 New York。"

批注圈劃：書中有胡適的批注劃綫數處。

相關記載：館藏有胡適評 Frederick Goodrich Henke 譯"The Philosophy of Wang Yang Ming"的書評稿，參見館藏號：HS-JDSHSE-0086-031。

其他：《王陽明哲學》英譯本。

3353 Philosophy Today: Conflicting Tendencies in Contemporary Thought/by
José Ferrater Mora. —New York: Columbia University Press, 1960
x, 193 p. ; 23.5 cm
HSMH（HS-N03F6-002）
附注：
印章：内封面頁鈐有"胡適的書"朱文方印。

3354 Physics and Philosophy: The Revolution in Modern Science/by Werner
Heisenberg. —New York: Harper & Brothers Publishers, 1958
xv, 206 p. ; 19.6 cm
World Perspectives, Vol. 19
HSMH（HS-N19F4-012）
附注：
印章：扉頁有胡適簽名"Hu Shih August, 1959"；另一扉頁鈐有"胡適的書"朱文方印。
批注圈劃：書中有胡適的批注劃綫數處。
與胡適的關係：胡適爲 World Perspectives 的編輯委員會成員之一。

3355 The Pilgrim's Progress; The Lives of John Donne and George Herbert/
edited by Charles W. Eliot. —New York: P. F. Collier & Son Corporation, 1909
418 p. , [1] plate; 21 cm
Harvard Classics: The Five-Foot Shelf of Books, Vol. 15
HSMH（HS-N12F6-015）
附注：
印章：内封面頁鈐有"胡適的書"朱文方印。

3356 The Piltdown Forgery/by J. S. Weiner. —Oxford: Oxford University Press, 1955
xii, 214 p. ; 20 cm
HSMH（HS-N19F6-033）

附注：

印章：内封面頁鈐有"胡適的書"朱文方印。

批注圈劃：書中有胡適的批注劃綫數處。

內附文件：書末夾有剪報 1 張，標題爲"Letters to Pearl Harbor", in *The New York Times Book Review*, May 26, 1957。

3357 Pine Knots and Bark Peelers: The Story of Five Generations of American Lumbermen/by W. Reginald Wheeler. —California: La Jolla, 1960

252 p.; 20.8 cm

HSMH（HS-N04F3-005）

附注：

印章：内封面頁鈐有"胡適的書"朱文方印。

夾紙：扉頁夾有"W. Reginald Wheeler"名片 1 張。

3358 The Plague and I/by Betty MacDonald. —Philadelphia: J. B. Lippincott Company, 1948

254 p.; 20.8 cm

HSMH（HS-N19F5-069）

附注：

印章：内封面頁鈐有"胡適的書"朱文方印。

3359 Plague Fighter: The Autobiography of a Modern Chinese Physician/by Wu Lien-Teh. —Cambridge: W. Heffer and Sons Ltd., 1959

x, 667 p.; 23 cm

HSMH（HS-N03F2-039）

附注：

印章：内封面頁鈐有"胡適的書"朱文方印。

題記：扉頁有作者題贈："With Compliment of the Author。"

夾紙：書中有夾紙 1 張。

與胡適的關係：内容提及胡適。

其他：作者爲伍連德。

3360 Plutarch's Lives of Themistocles, Pericles, Aristides, Alcibiades and Coriolanus, Demosthenes and Cicero, Cæsar and Antony/edited by Charles W. Eliot. —New York：P. F. Collier & Son Corporation，1909

389 p.，[1] plate；21 cm

Harvard Classics：The Five-Foot Shelf of Books，Vol. 12

HSMH（HS-N12F6-012）

附注：

　　印章：内封面頁鈐有"胡適的書"朱文方印。

　　批注圈劃：頁4有胡適的朱筆劃綫。

3361 Po Hu T'ung =白虎通：The Comprehensive Discussions in the White Tiger Hall，Vol. 1/by Tjoe-som Tjan（曾珠森）. —Leiden：E. J. Brill，1949

ix，367 p.；25.3 cm

Sinica Leidensia Edidit Institutum Sinologicum Lugduno Batavum，Vol. VI

HSMH（HS-N03F4-030）

附注：

　　印章：内封面頁鈐有"胡適的書"朱文方印。

　　題記：扉頁有作者題贈："To Dr. Hu Shih with Compliments of the author"；封底裏粘貼一紙張題記："From：Dr. TjAN TjOE SOM SiNOLOGiSCH INSTiTUUT Le BiNNENVESTGRACHT LEiDEN—HOLLAND。"

　　與胡適的關係：内容提及胡適的著作"The Establishment of Confucianism as a State Religion during the Han Dynasty"。

3362 The Pocket Book of Old Masters/edited by Herman J. Wechsler. —New York：Pocket Books，Inc.，1949

xiv，112 p.；16.4 cm

HSMH（HS-N04F6-020）

附注：

　　印章：内封面頁鈐有"胡適的書"朱文方印。

3363 The Poems and Songs of Robert Burns/edited by Charles W. Eliot. —New York: P. F. Collier & Son Corporation, 1909

574 p., [1] plate; 21 cm

Harvard Classics: The Five-Foot Shelf of Books, Vol. 6

HSMH(HS-N12F6-006)

附注:

印章:内封面頁鈐有"胡適的書"朱文方印。

3364 The Poems of Alfred Lord Tennyson/by Alfred Tennyson; with an introduction and notes by Eugene Parsons. —New York: Thomas Y. Crowell Company, 1928

xxi, 725 p.; 17.5 cm

HSMH(HS-N04F5-012)

附注:

印章:内封面頁鈐有"胡適的書"朱文方印。

批注圈劃:頁94—97 有胡適的批注劃綫數處。

夾紙:頁386、387 間有夾紙1 張。

摺頁:頁669 有摺角。

3365 Poems of Five Decades/by Max Eastman. —New York: Harper & Brothers, 1954

xv, 249 p.; 21.3 cm

HSMH(HS-N04F3-024)

附注:

批注圈劃:頁33、34 間有胡適的藍筆注記。

夾紙:頁32、33 間夾有胡適英文筆記2 張。

3366 Point of No Return/by John P. Marquand. —Boston: Little, Brown and Company, 1949

ix, 559 p.; 20.6 cm

HSMH(HS-N19F5-068)

附注:

印章：扉頁鈐有"胡適的書"朱文方印。

題記：另一扉頁有胡適題記："In Celebration of Ginny's Recovery — Jan. 23, 1950 H. S. 。"

夾紙：頁 204、205 間夾有破裂書衣 2 張，一張是本書簡介，另一張是作者簡介。

3367　Political and Social Growth of the American People 1492–1865/by Homer Carey Hockett. —New York：The Macmillan Company, 1943

xxi, 861 p. ; 21.1 cm

HSMH（HS-N04F4-032）

附注：

印章：扉頁有丁聲樹簽名"Ting Sheng-Shu Cambridge, Mass. March 3, 1945"；内封面頁亦有簽名"Ting Sheng-Shu March 3, 1945"。

題記：扉頁有丁聲樹題記："一九四五年三月購於哈佛合作社 聲樹。"

其他：本書爲第 3 版第 4 次印刷。

3368　Political and Social Growth of the American People 1865–1940/by Arthur Meier Schlesinger. —New York：The Macmillan Company, 1943

xxi, 783 p. ; 21 cm

HSMH（HS-N04F4-031）

附注：

印章：扉頁有丁聲樹簽名"Ting Sheng-Shu Cambridge, Mass. March 3, 1945"；内封面頁亦有簽名"Ting Sheng-Shu March 3, 1945"。

題記：扉頁有丁聲樹題記："一九四五年三月購於哈佛合作社 聲樹。"

其他：本書爲第 3 版第 4 次印刷。

3369　Political Power and Personal Freedom/by Sidney Hook. —New York：Criterion Books, Inc., 1959

xviii, 462 p. ; 21.6 cm

HSMH（HS-N04F4-019）

附注：

题记：扉页有作者题赠："To Hu Shih a worker in the same vineyards from Sidney Hook 1959。"

批注圈劃：书中有胡适的批注劃綫数十处。

3370 The Political Writings of John Adams/edited by George A. Peek. —New York：The Liberal Arts Press，1954

xxxii, 223 p. ; 18.5 cm

Forum Books, No. 5

HSMH（HS-N04F3-029）

附注：

印章：内封面頁鈐有"胡適的書"朱文方印。

3371 The Political Writings of Thomas Jefferson/edited by Edward Dumbauld. —New York：The Liberal Arts Press，1955

xlii, 204 p. ; 18.5 cm

Forum Books, No. 6

HSMH（HS-N04F3-031）

附注：

印章：内封面頁鈐有"胡適的書"朱文方印。

3372 The Portable Cervantes/edited and translated by Samuel Putnam. —New York：The Viking Press，1951

854 p. ; 17 cm

HSMH（HS-N04F6-015）

附注：

印章：内封面頁鈐有"胡適的書"朱文方印。

3373 The Portable Chekhov/by Anton Pavlovich Chekhov. —New York：The Viking Press，1947

631 p. ; 17.1 cm

HSMH（HS-N04F5-011）

附注：

印章：内封面頁鈐有"胡適的書"朱文方印。

批注圈劃：頁 34 有鉛筆注記劃綫一處。

夾紙：書中夾有"Hunt Foods"的小卡 1 張。

3374 The Portable Gibbon：The Decline and Fall of the Roman Empire/edited by Dero A. Saunders. —New York：The Viking Press，1955

691 p.；18.1 cm

HSMH（HS-N04F6-009）

附注：

印章：内封面頁有胡適簽名"Hu Shih Sept. 10，1955"，並鈐有"胡適的書"朱文方印。

批注圈劃：書中有胡適的批注劃綫數十處。

3375 The Portable Rabelais/by François Rabelais. —New York：The Viking Press，1946

623 p.；17.2 cm

HSMH（HS-N04F6-002）

附注：

印章：内封面頁鈐有"胡適的書"朱文方印。

3376 The Portable Voltaire/edited and with an introduction by Ben Ray Redman. —New York：The Viking Press，1949

569 p.；17 cm

HSMH（HS-N04F5-036）

附注：

印章：内封面頁鈐有"胡適的書"朱文方印。

批注圈劃：書中有胡適的批注劃綫數處。

夾紙：頁 328、329 間有夾紙 1 張。

摺頁：頁 187 右上有摺角。

3377 The Position of Woman in Early China = 列女傳/by Albert O'Hara. —Hong Kong: Orient Publishing Company, 1946

   xii, 302 p. ; 21.6 cm

   HSMH（HS-N03F4-033）

   附注：

   　印章：感謝頁鈐有"胡適的書"朱文方印。

   　題記：內封面頁有作者題贈："To Dr. Hu Shih With admiration for your work and best wishes, Albert R. O'Hara, SJ 郝繼隆〈印章〉。"

3378 Power and Politics: The Price of Security in the Atomic Age/by Hanson W. Baldwin; preface by David P. Barrows. —Pasadena, California: Claremont College, 1950

   xv, 117 p. ; 21.3 cm

   HSMH（HS-N04F5-005）

   附注：

   　印章：內封面頁鈐有"胡適的書"朱文方印。

   　題記：扉頁粘貼卡片 1 張，有題記："To Dr. Hu Shih with highest esteem and appreciation Dec. 5, 1950. David P. Barrows。"

3379 The Practice of Zen = 禪道修習/by Chang Chen-chi. —New York: Harper & Brothers, 1959

   199 p. ; 21 cm

   HSMH（HS-N03F4-004）

   附注：

   　印章：內封面頁鈐有"胡適的書"朱文方印。

   　夾紙：扉頁夾有購此書憑據 1 張，以及 Boyd R. Compton（The Rockefeller Foundation）的名片 1 張。

   　與胡適的關係：內容提及胡適的文章"Ch'an (Zen) Buddhism in China"。

3380 Prefaces and Prologues: To Famous Books/edited by Charles W. Eliot. —New York: P. F. Collier & Son Corporation, 1910

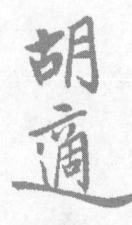

437 p., [1] plate; 21 cm

Harvard Classics: The Five-Foot Shelf of Books, Vol. 39

HSMH (HS-N12F5-009)

附注:

印章:内封面頁鈐有"胡適的書"朱文方印。

3381 President Chiang Kai-Shek Selected Speeches and Messages in 1957/by Kai-Shek Chiang. —Taipei, Taiwan: "Govt. Information Office, Republic of China", etc., [n.d.]

53 p.; 21.3 cm

HSMH (HS-N20F2-013)

附注:

其他:頁49—52的頁數順序裝訂錯誤。

3382 The President's Review including a Quarter Century in the Natural Sciences from the Rockefeller Foundation Annual Report 1958/by Warren Weaver. —New York: Rockefeller Foundation, 1958

viii, 168 p., illus., plates (incl. ports.); 21.8 cm

HSMH (HS-N20F1-047)

附注:

印章:目錄頁後一頁鈐有"胡適的書"朱文方印。

3383 Presidents Who Have Known Me/by George E. Allen. —New York: Simon and Schuster, 1950

x, 254 p.; 20.8 cm

HSMH (HS-N04F2-015)

附注:

印章:内封面頁鈐有"胡適的書"朱文方印。

3384 The Prince, Utopia & Ninety-Five Theses (Address to the German Nobility Concerning Christian Liberty)/by Niccolo Machiavelli, Sir Thomas More and

Martin Luther; edited by Charles W. Eliot. —New York: P. F. Collier & Son Corporation, 1910

378 p., [1] plate; 21 cm

Harvard Classics: The Five-Foot Shelf of Books, Vol. 36

HSMH (HS-N12F5-006)

附注：

印章：內封面頁鈐有"胡適的書"朱文方印。

批注圈劃：書中有胡適的批注劃綫數處。

3385 Princeton University Catalogue: Undergraduate Issue, Two Hundred and Twelfth Year 1958-1959.—Princeton, New Jersey: Princeton University, 1958

596 p.; 21.6 cm

HSMH (HS-N19F1-031)

附注：

印章：內封面頁鈐有"胡適的書"朱文方印。

與胡適的關係：頁 40 的"Officers of Instruction"有"Hu Shih, PH. D., Honorary Curator of the Gest Oriental Library with rank of Professor"及通訊處。

3386 Principles of War/by Carl von. Clausewitz. —Harrisburg Pennsylvania: The Military Service Publishing Company, 1942

82 p.; 19.7 cm

HSMH (HS-N04F5-004)

附注：

印章：內封面頁鈐有"胡適的書"朱文方印。

3387 Prisna/translated into English by Tulachandra. —Bangkok: Chatra Books, 1961

392 p.; 19 cm

HSMH (HS-N19F2-049)

3388 Prophets and Peoples: Studies in Nineteenth Century Nationalism/by Hans

Kohn. —New York: The Macmillan Company, 1946

213 p.; 20.9 cm

HSMH（HS-N03F6-004）

附注：

印章：扉頁有胡適簽名"Hu Shih October, 1949"；内封面頁鈐有"胡適的書"朱文方印。

批注圈劃：書中有胡適的劃綫數處。

3389 The Psychology of Invention in the Mathematical Field/by Jacques Hadamard. —Princeton: Princeton University Press, 1949

xiii, 145 p.; 20.1 cm

HSMH（HS-N19F4-035）

附注：

印章：内封面頁鈐有"胡適的書"朱文方印。

3390 Public Health and Demography in the Far East: Report of a Survey Trip, September 13-December 13, 1948/by Marshall C. Balfour, Roger F. Evans, Frank W. Notestein and Irene B. Taeuber. —New York: The Rockefeller Foundation, 1950

ii, 132 p., illus., maps; 28 cm

HSMH（HS-N13F1-023）

附注：

印章：鈐有"胡適的書"朱文方印。

批注圈劃：書中有胡適的紅筆批注劃綫數處。

3391 Public Policy in a World at War/edited by Dwight L. Dumond. —Philadelphia: The American Academy of Political And Social Science, 1941

vii, 260 p.; 23.3 cm

The Annals of the American Academy of Political and Social Science, Vol. 218, November 1941

HSMH（HS-N20F1-048）

附注：

  印章：扉頁有胡適簽名"Hu Shih 1941"；書末鈐有"胡適的書"朱文方印。

  批注圈劃：書中有胡適的批注劃綫數十處。

  夾紙：書中有夾紙 1 張。

  與胡適的關係：頁 26—35 收錄胡適的文章"The Conflict of Ideologies"。

3392 The Pyramids of Egypt/by I. E. S. Edwards. —Harmondsworth, Middlesex：Penguin Books, 1952

  256 p. ; 18.1 cm

  HSMH（HS-N19F6-029）

  附注：

    印章：內封面頁鈐有"胡適的書"朱文方印。

3393 Quelques mots sur la politesse chinoise/by Le P. Simon Kiong（龔古愚）. —Chang-Hai：Imprimerie De La Mission Catholique, 1906

  119 p. ; 26.5 cm

  HSMH（HS-N03F4-013）

  附注：

    印章：內封面頁鈐有"胡適的書"朱文方印。

    其他：(1) 內封面後有中文書名"中華儀注"。(2) 書中有 2 張粉紅色名片樣例；書末粘貼 1 個桃紅色的信封，內有紅帖子樣例 1 件。

3394 Ran In-Ting's Taiwan/by Ran In-Ting. —Taipei, Taiwan：Heritage Press, 1961

  1 Vol. : plates. ; 37 cm

  HSMH（HS-N13F1-019）

  附注：

    其他：作者爲藍蔭鼎。

3395 Readings in Contemporary Chinese Literature, Vol. 1: Plays and Poems =

現代中國文學讀本/edited by Wu-chi Liu and Tien-yi Li. —New Haven：The Institute of Far Eastern Languages, Yale University, 1953

xxxv, 110 p.；23.6 cm

Mirror Series C, No. 7

HSMH（HS-N03F3-010）

附注：

印章：内封面頁鈐有"胡適的書"朱文方印。

題記：内封面頁有編者題贈："適之先生指正 田意敬贈 一九五三，六,二。"

與胡適的關係：收錄胡適的戲劇文章《終身大事》（Life's Great Affair）及詩《一笑》（A Smile）；其他篇章亦提及胡適。

其他：（1）封底内封面頁題簽："現代中國文學讀本第一册：戲劇與詩歌 柳無忌、李田意合編。"（2）内文爲中文。

3396 Rebel at Large：Recollections of Fifty Crowded Years/by George Creel. —New York：G. P. Putnam's Sons, 1947

viii, 384 p.；21.8 cm

HSMH（HS-N04F2-010）

附注：

印章：内封面頁鈐有"胡適的書"朱文方印。

夾紙：書中夾有粘貼郵票的報紙碎片3張。

3397 Reconstruction in China：A Record of Progress and Achievement in Facts and Figures with Illustrations and Maps/edited by T'ang Leang-li. —Shanghai：China United Press, 1935

xiv, 401 p., plates, ports., maps（part fold.）；25.1 cm

HSMH（HS-N03F3-017）

附注：

印章：内封面頁鈐有"胡適的書"朱文方印。

題記：扉頁有題記："The New York Times Mch/5/36 Nanking。"

批注圈劃：書中有胡適的劃綫數處。

與胡適的關係：內容提及胡適，並刊載胡適照片 1 張，照片說明是 "Hu Shih Father of the Chinese Renaissance and Editor of the 'Independent Critic'"（獨立評論）"。

相關記載：關於胡適閱讀本書的記事，可參考《胡適日記》1936 年 7 月 23 日條。

其他：編者爲湯良禮。

3398 Reconstruction in Philosophy/by John Dewey. —New York：The New American Library, 1950

168 p.；18.1 cm

HSMH（HS-N04F4-011）

附注：

印章：內封面頁鈐有"胡適的書"朱文方印及"胡適"紫色戳印。

批注圈劃：書中有胡適的批注劃綫數十處。

3399 Red Star over China/by Edgar Snow. —New York：Random House, 1944

xiii, 529 p.；18.3 cm

HSMH（HS-N03F2-032）

附注：

印章：內封面頁鈐有"胡適的書"朱文方印。

批注圈劃：書中有胡適的批注劃綫數十處，其中頁 157 記"中文本此節改正最多（似譯本根據初版，後來版本有脫落？適之）"。

夾紙：書中有夾紙 2 張。

與胡適的關係：內文提及胡適。

3400 Reflections at Fifty/by James T. Farrell. —New York：The Vanguard Press, Inc., 1954

223 p.；21.3 cm

HSMH（HS-N04F3-012）

附注：

印章：內封面頁鈐有"胡適的書"朱文方印。

題記：扉頁有作者題贈："To Dr. Hu Shih With my very best wishes James T Farrell"，其下有胡適題記："150 E. 39th St. New York 16, N. Y.。"

批注圈劃：書中有胡適的批注劃綫數十處。

相關記載：1955 年 1 月 25 日 James T. Farrell 致胡適函提及此書，參見館藏號：HS-US01-032-013。

3401 Reflections of a Physicist/by Percy Williams Bridgman. —New York：Philosophical Library, 1950

ix, 392 p. ; 22.2 cm

HSMH（HS-N19F4-024）

附注：

印章：内封面頁鈐有"胡適的書"朱文方印。

3402 Reflections on the Failure of Socialism/by Max Eastman. —New York：The Devin-Adair Company, 1955

127 p. ; 21 cm

HSMH（HS-N04F1-029）

附注：

印章：内封面頁鈐有"胡適的書"朱文方印。

批注圈劃：書中有胡適的批注劃綫數十處。

3403 The Reformation：A History of European Civilization from Wyclif to Calvin：1300-1564/by Will Durant. —New York：Simon And Schuster, 1957

xviii, 1025 p. , plates; 25 cm

The Story of Civilization, Part VI

HSMH（HS-N12F5-026）

附注：

印章：内封面頁鈐有"胡適的書"朱文方印及"胡適校書記"朱文長方印。

題記：書末有胡適題記："題杜鸞特先生'文化史'第六冊後 此君與我同時在哥侖比亞大學（1915—1917），他比我大六歲，今年七十二歲了。他的'文化史'已出了六大冊。他的勤勞而有恒，博聞而能專力，故能有此過人的絕大成就。我題此短跋,很誠懇的感覺慚愧。胡適 一九五七,十,十三夜。"

批注圈劃:書中有胡適的批注劃綫數十處。

夾紙:書中有夾紙4張。

3404 The Relation of Growth Rate of Reef Corals to Surface Temperature of Sea Water as Basis for Study of Causes of Diastrophisms Instigating Evolution of Life/by Ting Ying H. MA. —Taipei, Taiwan: Ting Ying H. MA, 1958

60 p. , illus. , xxiv plates; 34.4 cm

Research on the Past Climate and Continental Drift, Vol. XIV, June 1958

HSMH（HS-N20F1-087）

附注:

批注圈劃:書中有校改數處。

其他:中文封底:"古氣候與大陸漂移之研究 第十四號 馬廷英著 造礁珊瑚成長率與海水溫度的關係 中華民國四十七年七月。"

3405 The Religion of the Samurai: A Study of Zen Philosophy and Discipline in China and Japan/by Kaiten Nukariya. —London: Luzac & Co. , 1913

xxii, 253 p. ; 24.2 cm

HSMH（HS-N03F4-001）

附注:

印章:扉頁有簽名:"Sunahoritch";内封面頁鈐有"胡適的書"朱文方印及"胡適"紫色戳印。

題記:扉頁有胡適題記:"忽活谷快天早年的作品還是很幼稚的。後來他有兩大冊《中國禪學史》,就很不同了。胡適 一九五二,七,十。"

批注圈劃:書中有胡適的批注劃綫數十處。

夾紙:書中有夾紙1張。

相關記載:胡適閱讀忽活谷快天之《中國禪學史》上、下兩冊的記事,可參考《胡適日記》1951年9月7日條。

其他:作者爲忽滑谷快天。(胡適稱之爲"忽活谷快天")

3406 Religious Trends in Modern China/by Wing-tsit Chan. —New York: Columbia University Press, 1953

　　xiii, 327 p.; 22.3 cm

　　HSMH（HS-N03F3-015）

　　附註：

　　　印章：扉頁有胡適簽名"Hu Shih"；內封面頁鈐有"胡適的書"朱文方印。

　　　批注圈劃：書中有胡適的批注劃綫數處。

　　　夾紙：扉頁夾有卡片1張。

　　　與胡適的關係：內容提及胡適及其著作"The Chinese Renaissance"、"The Establishment of Confucianism as a State Religion during the Han Dynasty"、"My Credo and Its Evolution"、*Hu Shih lun-hsueh chin-chu*（《胡適論學近著》）。

3407 Remnants of Han Law, Vol. 1/by A. F. P. Hulsewé. —Leiden: E. J. Brill, 1955

　　455 p.; 24.1 cm

　　Sinica Leidensia Edidit Institutum Sinologicum Lugduno Batavum, Vol. IX

　　HSMH（HS-N03F4-034）

　　附註：

　　　印章：內封面頁鈐有"胡適的書"朱文方印。

　　　相關記載：館藏有1956年12月瞿同祖對此書的書評，參見館藏號：HS-NK05-299-031。

3408 The Renaissance Philosophy of Man/by Ernst Cassirer, Paul Oskar Kristeller and John Herman Randall. —Chicago: The University of Chicago Press, 1948

　　vi, 405 p.; 20.5 cm

　　HSMH（HS-N04F5-020）

　　附註：

　　　印章：內封面頁有胡適簽名"Hu Shih"，並鈐有"胡適的書"朱文方印。

3409 Report: Royal Commission on National Development in the Arts, Letters &

Sciences, 1949-1951. —Ottawa: Printer to the King's Most Excellent Majesty, 1951

xxi, 517 p. ; 24.8 cm

HSMH (HS-N19F4-006)

附注：

　　印章:内封面頁鈐有"胡適的書"朱文方印。

　　批注圈劃:書中有胡適的批注劃綫數處。

　　夾紙:書中夾有計算紙1張,空白紙1張。

3410 Report of the A. W. Mellon Educational and Charitable Trust 1951-1960. —Pittsburgh, Pa. : Price Waterhouse & Co. , 1961

108 p. , illus. ; 23.4 cm

HSMH (HS-N20F2-011)

附注：

　　相關記載:1961年10月13日 P. S. Broughton致胡適函,提及此書,參見館藏號:HS-NK05-145-058。

3411 Report on Mao's China/by Frank Moraes. —New York: The Macmillan Company, 1953

212 p. ; 21.5 cm

HSMH (HS-N19F2-069)

附注：

　　印章:内封面頁有胡適簽名"Hu Shih 1953";封底裏亦有胡適簽名"Hu Shih 35"。

　　批注圈劃:書中有胡適的批注劃綫數十處。

　　夾紙:書中有夾紙2張。

　　內附文件:(1)扉頁與内封面頁之間夾有剪報1張:"Frank Moraes, 66 Indian Journalist", by Paul L. Montgomery, in the *New York Times*。(2)封底裏粘貼"Universit Ati Sancti Joannis Dono Dedit Prof. C. M. Chang"影印畫像1張。

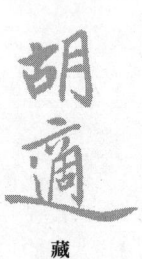

3412 Report on Trematodes from Turkey with Descriptions of New Species in the Genera Creptotrema and Phagicola/by William H. Coil and Robert E. Kuntz. —Taipei, Taiwan: United States Naval Medical Research No. 2, 1959

 10 p.; 26.5 cm
 NAMRU TWO, June 4, 1959（NM 52 15 02. 1. 5）
 HSMH（HS-N19F5-016）
 附注:
  其他:(1)釘書針裝訂。(2)館藏2冊。

3413 Reports, Speeches and Proceedings of the First Inter-Council Conference of the Research Councils for East Asian Studies of China, Japan and Korea=東亞學術研究委員會中日韓第一次會際會議報告/by the China Council for East Asian Studies. —Taipei, Taiwan:"National Taiwan University", March, 1961

 221 p. front., plates; 26.6 cm
 HSMH（HS-N19F3-004）
 附注:
  印章:內封面頁鈐有"胡適的書"朱文方印。
  與胡適的關係:(1)頁15—22 收錄《胡適博士歡迎詞》一文。(2)"東亞學術研究委員會中日韓第一次會際會議開幕式後合影"、"開幕式後三會首席代表與來賓合影"及"胡適博士致歡迎詞"等圖片,均有胡適。
  其他:內容含中英文。

3414 Reprisal/by Arthur Gordon. —New York: Simon and Schuster, 1950

 310 p.; 21.6 cm
 HSMH（HS-N19F5-076）
 附注:
  印章:內封面頁鈐有"胡適的書"朱文方印。

3415 The Return of Germany: A Tale of Two Countries/by Norbert Muhlen. —Chicago: Henry Regnery Company, 1953

310 p. ; 21.5 cm

HSMH（HS-N19F6-009）

附注：

  印章：内封面頁鈐有"胡適的書"朱文方印。

3416 Das Rheingold（the Rhinegold）：A Music Drama in Four Scenes/by Richard Wagner; English version by Charles Henry Meltzer. —New York：Fred Rullman Inc., [n. d.]

  51 p. ; 25.4 cm

  Metropolitan Opera House Grand Opera

  HSMH（HS-N19F5-041）

附注：

  印章：封面鈐有"胡適的書"朱文方印。

3417 The Rice-Sprout Song/by Eileen Chang. —New York：Charles Scribner's Sons, 1955

  vi, 182 p. ; 19.2 cm

  HSMH（HS-N03F3-007）

附注：

  印章：内封面頁鈐有"胡適的書"朱文方印。

  題記：扉頁有作者題贈："To dear Dr. Hu Shih, with sincerest regards and gratitude, Eileen Chang。"

3418 The Right to Heresy：Castellio against Calvin/by Stefan Zweig. —Boston：The Beacon Press, 1951

  238 p., illus.（facsim.）plates; 21.7 cm

  HSMH（HS-N19F3-037）

附注：

  印章：内封面頁鈐有"胡適的書"朱文方印 。

  題記：扉頁有胡適題記："Hu Shih 胡適 August 5, 1957. This remarkable book came as a present or 'dividend' from the Rationalist Press of St. Louis,

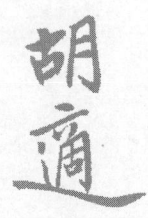

　　　Mo.。"

　　批注圈劃:書中有胡適的批注劃綫數十處。

　　夾紙:書中有夾紙1張。

3419 The Rittenhouse Orrery/by Howard C. Rice, Jr.. —Princeton, New Jersey: Princeton University Library, 1954

　　xi, 88 p., xvi plates; 24.1 cm

　　HSMH(HS-N19F4-004)

　　附注:

　　　印章:内封面頁鈐有"胡適的書"朱文方印。

　　　題記:扉頁有作者題贈:"For Hu Shih this little story of stars, wheels and human beings, with respect and best wishes, Howard C. Rice Jr. Princeton, May 20, 1954。"

3420 River Strategy: A Phase of the Taipings' Military Development/by Laai Yi-faai. —[s.l.]:[s.n.],[n.d.]

　　302-329 p.; 25.4cm

　　HSMH(HS-N19F2-052)

　　附注:

　　　其他:抽印本。

3421 The Road to Inner Freedom: The Ethics/by Baruch Spinoza. —New York: Philosophical Library, Inc., 1957

　　215 p.; 20.7 cm

　　HSMH(HS-N04F5-037)

　　附注:

　　　印章:内封面頁鈐有"胡適的書"朱文方印。

　　　夾紙:頁82、83間夾有贈書卡片1張。

3422 The Road to Pearl Harbor: The Coming of the War between the United States and Japan/by Herbert Feis. —Princeton, New Jersey: Princeton

University Press, 1950

xii, 356 p. ; 24.2 cm

HSMH（HS-N04F2-020）

附注：

　　印章：扉頁有胡適簽名"Hu Shih Sept. 1951"，並鈐有"胡適的書"朱文方印。

　　批注圈劃：書中有胡適的批注劃綫數處。

　　夾紙：書中有夾紙3張。

　　與胡適的關係：内容與注釋均提及胡適。

3423 The Road to Serfdom/by Friederich A. Hayek. —Chicago：The University of Chicago Press, 1950

viii, 248 p. ; 17.3 cm

HSMH（HS-N04F1-028）

附注：

　　印章：内封面頁鈐有"胡適的書"朱文方印。

　　題記：扉頁有胡適題記："Hu Shih New York Dec. 8, 1953. — A birthday present to myself。"

　　批注圈劃：書中有胡適的批注劃綫數處。

　　相關記載：胡適對於本書的看法，參見《胡適日記》1953年11月24日條。

3424 The Rockefeller Foundation Annual Report, 1958.—New York：The Rockefeller Foundation, 1958

xxii, 511 p. , illus. , plates, ports. ; 21.7 cm

HSMH（HS-N19F1-032）

附注：

　　印章：内封面頁鈐有"胡適的書"朱文方印。

　　批注圈劃：書中有胡適的劃綫數處。

3425 The Role of Education in American History/by Paul H. Buck, et al. —New York：The Fund for the Advancement of Education, 1957

16 p.；20.9 cm

HSMH（HS-N19F3-021）

附註：

其他：小冊子。

3426 The Role of Nature in Zen Buddhism/by Daisetz Teitaro Suzuki. —Zürich：Rhein-Verlag, 1954

291-321 p.；20.7 cm

Eranos-Jahrbuch, XXII

HSMH（HS-N19F2-064）

附註：

印章：頁 291 鈐有"胡適的書"朱文方印。

題記：封面有作者題贈："胡適先生 惠存 大拙拜。"

其他：(1)作者爲鈴木大拙。(2)抽印本。

3427 Roosevelt and Hopkins：An Intimate History/by Robert E. Sherwood. —New York：Harper & Brothers, 1948

xvii, 979 p.；21.5 cm

HSMH（HS-N04F3-003）

附註：

印章：扉頁有胡適簽名"Hu Shih"；內封面頁鈐有"胡適的書"朱文方印。

批注圈劃：書中有胡適的批注劃綫數十處。

夾紙：書中有夾紙 7 張。

3428 The Roster of the Round Table Dining Club. —New York：Knickerbocker Club, 1951

36 p.；22.3 cm

HSMH（HS-N19F2-057）

附註：

印章：館藏 2 冊,內封面頁均鈐有"胡適的書"朱文方印。

批注圈劃：兩冊書中均有胡適的劃綫數處。

内附文件：其中一冊的扉頁夾有文件 4 種，分別爲"Members of the Round Table Club"、William Church Osborn 致胡適函、1950 年 12 月 8 日的菜單（背後有出席人士的簽名，包括 Hu Shih），以及補充會員名單小紙條；另一冊的封底夾有 Whitney H. Shepardson 致 The Members of the Round Table Dining Club 函 1 張。

與胡適的關係：胡適是 Knickerbocker Club 的圓桌會議俱樂部會員（Members of the Round Table Club）之一。

其他：兩冊的頁 34—36 均有書寫或粘貼補充會員名單資料。

3429 The Russian Revolution/by Alan Moorehead. —New York：Harper & Brothers Publishers，1958

 xiv，301 p.；21.8 cm

 HSMH（HS-N04F1-020）

附注：

 印章：館藏 2 冊，其中一冊的扉頁有美國駐華大使莊萊德的簽名"E. F. Drumright"；內封面頁鈐有"胡適的書"朱文方印。另一冊的扉頁鈐有"胡適的書"朱文方印。

 夾紙：其中一冊夾有感恩節火鷄畫 1 張。

3430 The Sacred Books of China：The Texts of Confucianism，Part I/translated by James Legge. —Oxford：The Clarendon Press，1879

 xxx，492，36 p.；23 cm

 The Sacred Books of The East，Vol. III

 HSMH（HS-N12F4-017）

附注：

 印章：內封面頁鈐有"胡適"紫色戳印。

 批注圈劃：書中有胡適的批注劃綫數十處。

 夾紙：書中有夾紙 3 張。

3431 The Sacred Books of China：The Saddharma-Pundarîka or the Lotus of the True Law/translated by H. Kern. —Oxford：The Clarendon Press，1884 xlii, 454, 8 p. ; 23 cm

The Sacred Books of The East, Vol. XXI

HSMH（HS-N12F4-019）

附註：

　　印章：内封面頁鈐有"胡適"紫色戳印。

　　批注圈劃：書中有胡適的紅筆劃綫數處。

　　夾紙：書中有夾紙2張。

　　其他：封面扉頁似有撕頁痕迹。

3432 The Sacred Books of China：The Texts of Tâoism, Part I/translated by James Legge. —Oxford：The Clarendon Press, 1891

　　xxii, 396, 8 p. ; 22.7 cm

The Sacred Books of The East, Vol. XXXIX

HSMH（HS-N12F4-020）

附註：

　　印章：内封面頁鈐有"胡適"紫色戳印。

　　批注圈劃：書末有鉛筆打叉數處。

　　夾紙：書中有夾紙2張。

3433 The Sacred Books of China：The Texts of Tâoism, Part II/translated by James Legge. —Oxford：The Clarendon Press, 1891

　　viii, 340, 8 p. ; 23 cm

The Sacred Books of The East, Vol. XL

HSMH（HS-N12F4-018）

附註：

　　印章：内封面頁鈐有"胡適"紫色戳印。

　　批注圈劃：書末有鉛筆打叉注記數處。

　　夾紙：書中有夾紙4張。

3434 Sacred Writings, Vol. I：Confucian, Hebrew, Christian, Part I/edited by Charles W. Eliot. —New York：P. F. Collier & Son Corporation, 1910

486 p., [1] plate; 21 cm

Harvard Classics: The Five-Foot Shelf of Books, Vol. 44

HSMH（HS-N12F5-014）

附注：

　　印章：内封面頁鈐有"胡適的書"朱文方印。

　　批注圈劃：版權頁及頁5各有胡適的批注一處。

3435　**Sacred Writings, Vol. II: Christian, Part II, Buddhist, Hindu, Mohammedan**/edited by Charles W. Eliot. ——New York: P. F. Collier & Son Corporation, 1910

491-1007 p., [1] plate; 21 cm

Harvard Classics: The Five-Foot Shelf of Books, Vol. 45

HSMH（HS-N12F5-015）

附注：

　　印章：内封面頁鈐有"胡適的書"朱文方印。

　　批注圈劃：版權頁及頁573各有胡適的批注一處，其中頁573記"These are taken from Warren's 'Buddhism in Translation' (1896). Warren was already dead when 'The Harvard Classics' were first published in 1910. Hu Shih"。

3436　**Sailors' Knots**/by W. W. Jacobs. ——London: Methuen & Co., 1909

vii, 302, 47p., illus.; 19.5 cm

HSMH（HS-N19F5-072）

附注：

　　印章：内封面頁鈐有"胡適的書"朱文方印。

　　題記：扉頁有贈書者題贈："To Dr. Hu Shih my favorite author from his friend Eugene L. Delafield Mar. 15, 1958."

3437　**San Min Chu I: The Three Principles of the People**/by Sun Yat-sen; translated into English by Frank W. Price（畢範宇）; edited by L. T. Chen（陳立廷）. ——Chungking, China: Ministry of Information of the Republic of China,

1943

xvii, 514 p. ; 20.5 cm

HSMH（HS-N20F1-006）

附注：

印章：内封面頁鈐有"胡適的書"朱文方印。

3438　Satan in the Suburbs and Other Stories/by Bertrand Russell. —New York：Simon and Schuster, 1953

viii, 148 p. ; 21.9 cm

HSMH（HS-N04F5-022）

附注：

印章：内封面頁鈐有"胡適的書"朱文方印。

夾紙：頁100、101間有夾紙1張。

3439　Satanism and Witchcraft：A Study in Medieval Superstition/by Jules Michelet；translated by A. R. Allinson. —New York：The Citadel Press, 1939

xx, 332 p. ; 21 cm

HSMH（HS-N19F6-021）

附注：

印章：内封面頁鈐有"胡適的書"朱文方印。

批注圈劃：書中有胡適的批注劃綫數十處。

3440　The Sayings of Confucius：The Teachings of China's Greatest Sage/translated by James R. Ware. —New York：The New American Library, 1955

125,［3］p. ; 18.1 cm

HSMH（HS-N03F5-002）

附注：

印章：内封面頁鈐有"胡適的書"朱文方印。

3441　The Sayings of Lao-Tzǔ/translated by Lionel Giles. —London：John Murray, 1937

53，[5] p.；17 cm

The Wisdom of the East Series

HSMH（HS-N03F5-009）

附注：

印章：扉頁有胡適簽名"Hu Shih New York City Dec. 3, 1942"；內封面頁鈐有"胡適的書"朱文方印。

批注圈劃：書中有胡適的批注圈劃數處。

3442 Scandinavian Journey：Norway/by Prem Chaya. —Bangkok：Chatra Books，1956

161 p., illus.；19.7 cm

HSMH（HS-N19F2-050）

3443 Science & Civilisation in China, Vol. I：Introductory Orientations/by Joseph Needham. —Cambridge：Cambridge University Press，1954

318 p.；25.7 cm

HSMH（HS-N03F1-018）

附注：

印章：內封面頁鈐有"胡適的書"朱文方印。

批注圈劃：書中有胡適的批注劃綫數十處。

夾紙：書中有夾紙8張。

與胡適的關係：內文提及胡適，參考書目則引用胡適的《胡適文存》以及 *Chinese Renaissance*。

相關記載：胡適與楊聯陞往來函，見館藏號：HS-LS01-005-022～024。

其他：內封面頁前有冀朝鼎題籤："李約瑟著 中國科學技術史 冀朝鼎。"

3444 Science & Civilisation in China, Vol. II：History of Scientific Thought/by Joseph Needham. —Cambridge：Cambridge University Press，1956

xxii, 696 p.；25.6 cm

HSMH（HS-N03F1-019）

附注：

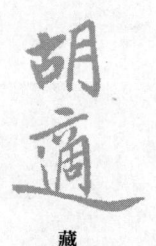

印章：館藏 2 冊，內封面頁均鈐有"胡適的書"朱文方印。

批注圈劃：其中一冊有胡適的批注劃綫數十處，如頁 390 記"此言是值得我們考慮的，如皮錫瑞諸人的經學史，都不夠用。應有一部經學史從方法的演進入手。適之"；另一冊有胡適的批注劃綫數處。

夾紙：其中一冊的目次頁夾有卡片 1 張，印有"To the Book Review Editor：We take Pleasure in sending for review：Science & Civilisation in China, V. II By Joseph Needham Publication date：July, 1956 Price ＄ 14.50"；頁 128、129 間夾一份 Science & Civilisation in China, Vol. 1：Introductory Orientation 的書評（刊載在 *American Journal of Archaeology* 的頁 211—215）；書中另有夾紙 22 張。另一冊書中有夾紙 5 張。

與胡適的關係：內文提到胡適。

相關記載：1956 年 8 月 10 日楊聯陞致胡適函，館藏號：HS-LS01-006-029。

其他：內封面頁前有冀朝鼎題籤："李約瑟著 中國科學技術史 冀朝鼎。"

3445 Science & Civilisation in China, Vol. III：Mathematics and the Sciences of the Heavens and the Earth/by Joseph Needham. —Cambridge：Cambridge University Press, 1959

　　xlvii, 877 p.；25.6 cm

　　HSMH（HS-N03F1-020）

　　附注：

　　　印章：內封面頁鈐有"胡適的書"朱文方印。

　　　與胡適的關係：內文提及胡適。

　　　其他：內封面頁前有冀朝鼎題籤："李約瑟著 中國科學技術史 冀朝鼎。"

3446 Science and the Moral Life/selected Writings by Max C. Otto；preface by Eduard C. Lindeman. —New York：The New American Library, 1952

　　192 p.；18 cm

　　HSMH（HS-N19F4-021）

　　附注：

　　　印章：扉頁有胡適簽名"Hu Shih"；內封面頁鈐有"胡適的書"朱文方印。

其他:此書爲第 2 次印刷。

3447 Science and the Moral Life/selected Writings by Max C. Otto; preface by Eduard C. Lindeman. —New York: The New American Library, 1953

  192 p. ; 18 cm

  HSMH (HS-N19F4-020)

  附注:

    印章:内封面頁鈐有"胡適的書"朱文方印。

    其他:此書爲第 3 次印刷。

3448 Scientific Papers: Physics, Chemistry, Astronomy, Geology/edited by Charles W. Eliot. —New York: P. F. Collier & Son Corporation, 1910

  351 p. , [1] plate; 21 cm

  Harvard Classics: The Five-Foot Shelf of Books, Vol. 30

  HSMH (HS-N12F6-030)

  附注:

    印章:内封面頁鈐有"胡適的書"朱文方印。

3449 Scientific Papers: Physiology, Medicine, Surgery, Geology/edited by Charles W. Eliot. —New York: P. F. Collier & Son Corporation, 1910

  418 p. , [1] plate; 21 cm

  Harvard Classics: The Five-Foot Shelf of Books, Vol. 38

  HSMH (HS-N12F5-008)

  附注:

    印章:内封面頁鈐有"胡適的書"朱文方印。

3450 The Scientific Revolution, 1500-1800: The Formation of the Modern Scientific Attitude/by A. R. Hall. —Boston: The Beacon Press, 1954

  xvii, 390 p. ; 20.3 cm

  HSMH (HS-N19F4-027)

  附注:

印章：内封面頁鈐有"胡適的書"朱文方印。

3451 Second Asian Influenza Epidemics Occurring in Vaccinated Men Aboard U. S. Navy Vessels/by Walter E. Beam Jr., J. Thomas Grayston and Raymond H. Watten. —Taipei, Taiwan：United States Naval Medical Research No. 2, 1959

15 p.；26.5 cm

NAMRU TWO, January 6, 1959（NM 52 05 02. 4. 2）

HSMH（HS-N19F5-007）

附注：

其他：釘書針裝訂。

3452 Second Presentation of the Charles Lang Freer Medal. —Washington, D. C.：Freer Gallery of Art, Smithsonian Institution, 1960

v, 35 p., plates；24.8 cm

HSMH（HS-N19F2-027）

附注：

印章：内封面頁鈐有"胡適的書"朱文方印。

批注圈劃：書中有胡適的劃綫數處。

夾紙：扉頁有夾紙1張。

3453 The Second United Nations Regional Cartographic Conference：The Figure of the Earth from the Measurement in the South-Western part of China/by M. Tsao. —Taipei, Taiwan, 1958

1 p.；26.4 cm

HSMH（HS-N19F2-021）

附注：

題記：封面有作者題贈："適之老先生指正 曹謨敬贈。"

其他：此爲1958年10月20日至11月1日在東京舉行的學術會議資料。

3454 The Secret History of Stalin's Crimes/by Alexander Orlov. —New York：Random House, 1953 xvi, 366 p. ; 21.5 cm

HSMH（HS-N04F1-019）

附注：

印章：扉頁有胡適簽名"Hu Shih 胡適 New York, Dec. 8, 1953"；內封面頁鈐有"胡適的書"朱文方印。

批注圈劃：書中有胡適的批注劃綫數十處。

相關記載：胡適曾爲預備演講，用本書撰寫"杜威在墨西哥"之筆記一條，參見《胡適日記》1959年10月20日條。

3455 A Selected and Annotated Bibliography of the Republic of China 1958-1959/edited by Paul T. H. Chen. —Taipei, Taiwan：" National Central Library", 1960

127 p. ; 20.9 cm

HSMH（HS-N03F3-030）

附注：

批注圈劃：書中有胡適的劃綫打叉數處。

夾紙：書中有夾紙1張。

與胡適的關係：內容有評介胡適著《新校定的敦煌寫本神會和尚遺著兩種》（收入《"中央研究院"史語所集刊》）。

3456 Selected Chinese Texts in the Classical and Colloquial Styles/compiled by Lien-sheng Yang. —Cambridge, Mass. : Published for the Harvard-Yenching Institute by Harvard University Press, 1953

192, xviii p. ; 23 cm

HSMH（HS-N03F1-024）

附注：

印章：內封面頁鈐有"胡適的書"朱文方印。

與胡適的關係：收錄胡適的文章《介紹我自己的思想(胡適文選自序)》。

其他：(1)編者爲楊聯陞。(2)本書爲中文內容。

3457 Selected Short Stories of John O'Hara/by John O'Hara；with an introduction by Lionel Trilling. —New York: The Modern Library, 1956

xiii, 303 p. ; 18.4 cm

HSMH（HS-N19F5-063）

附註：

印章：扉頁鈐有"胡適的書"朱文方印。

題記：扉頁有胡適題記："Gift of Prof. and Mrs. R. C. Rudolph。"

批注圈劃：目錄頁有胡適的紅筆打勾數處。

3458 Serge Eliss éeff/by Edwin O. Reischauer. —Cambridge, Mass. : Harvard-Yenching Institute, 1957

35 p. ; 25.3 cm

Harvard Journal of Asiatic Studies, Vol. 20, Nos. 1 & 2, June 1957

HSMH（HS-N19F3-001）

附註：

印章：內封面頁鈐有"胡適的書"朱文方印。

其他：(1) 抽印本。(2) 中文篇名"英利世夫先生小傳"。（按：Serge Eliss éeff 的中文名爲"葉理綏"。)

3459 Seven Famous Greek Plays/edited with introductions by Whitney J. Oates and Eugene O'Neill, Jr. . —New York: Random House, 1950

xxv, 446 p. ; 18.4 cm

HSMH（HS-N04F6-033）

附註：

印章：內封面頁鈐有"胡適的書"朱文方印。

3460 The Seventeenth Century Background: Studies in the Thought of the Age in Relation to Poetry and Religion/by Basil Willey. —Garden City, New York: Doubleday & Company, Inc. , 1953

316 p. ; 18 cm

Doubleday Anchor Books

HSMH（HS-N19F6-019）

附注：

印章：內封面頁鈐有"胡適的書"朱文方印。

3461 Shakespeare's Sonnets/by William Shakespeare. —Garden City, New York： Doubleday & Company, Inc., [n.d.]

159 p.；18.2 cm

HSMH（HS-N04F6-001）

附注：

印章：內封面頁鈐有"胡適的書"朱文方印。

其他：胡適曾在日記中贊許此書收錄許多百讀不厭的好詩，並略記友人摘錄文句，參見《胡適日記》1951年6月13日條。

3462 Shinsho Hanayama Bibliography on Buddhism/edited by the Commemoration Committee for Prof. Shinsho Hanayama's sixty-first birthday. —Tokyo： Hokuseido Press, 1961

xiii, 869 p.；27 cm

HSMH（HS-N06F1-006）

附注：

題記：扉頁有胡適題記："Gift of The Asia Foundation Tokyo, Japan. Hu Shih 胡適 Feb. 18, 1962。"

其他：書末粘貼日文版權頁1張，書名爲"Bibliography on Buddhism 英文仏教文献目録"；著者爲花山信勝。

3463 A Short History of Chinese Philosophy/by Fung Yu-lan；edited and translated by Derk Bodde. —New York：The MacMillan Company, 1948

xx, 368 p.；21.8 cm

HSMH（HS-N03F5-022）

附注：

印章：內封面頁鈐有"胡適的書"朱文方印。

批注圈劃：書中有胡適的批注劃綫數十處。

夾紙：書中有夾紙1張。

與胡適的關係：內容提及胡適。

相關記載：胡適閱讀此書之心得，可參考《胡適日記》1950年1月5日條。

其他：內封面頁左側印有"中國哲學小史 馮友蘭著 [The Chinese title by Mrs. Fang Chao-ying]"。

3464 A Short History of Confucian Philosophy/by Liu Wu-chi. —Harmondsworth, Middlesex: Penguin Books, 1955

229 p.; 18.1 cm

HSMH（HS-N03F4-039）

附注：

印章：內封面頁鈐有"胡適的書"朱文方印。

與胡適的關係：內容提及胡適。

其他：作者爲柳無忌。

3465 A Short History of Science: Origins and Results of the Scientific Revolution/by Herbert Butterfield, et al. —New York: Doubleday & Company, Inc., 1959

xi, 138 p.; 18.1 cm

HSMH（HS-N19F4-030）

附注：

印章：扉頁鈐有"胡適的書"朱文方印。

批注圈劃：書中有胡適的劃綫數十處。

3466 Siegfried: A Music Drama in Three Acts/by Richard Wagner. —New York: Fred Rullman Inc., [n.d.]

64 p.; 25.4 cm

Metropolitan Opera House Grand Opera

HSMH（HS-N19F5-044）

附注：

印章：內封面頁鈐有"胡適的書"朱文方印。

3467 The Similarity of the Ancient Chinese Kinship Terminology to the Omaha

Type(中國古代親屬稱謂與奧麻哈型的相似)/by Yih-fu Ruey(芮逸夫). — Taipei, Taiwan: "National Taiwan University", 1958

18 p.; 26 cm

The Bulletin of the Department of Archaeology and Anthropology, No. 12, November, 1958

HSMH (HS-N19F5-033)

附註:

 題記:封面有作者題贈:"適之師教正 生 芮逸夫謹呈。"
 其他:《"國立臺灣大學"考古人類學刊》第12期抽印本。

3468 Sino-American Conference on Intellectual Cooperation: Report and Proceedings, Held at the University of Washington, July 10-15, 1960/by George E. Taylor, et al. —Seattle: University of Washington, [n.d.]

321 p.; 22.9 cm

HSMH (HS-N03F6-018)

附註:

 印章:內封面頁鈐有"胡適的書"朱文方印。
 與胡適的關係:收錄胡適的文章"The Chinese Tradition and the Future"。
 相關記載:館藏有多件1960年"中美學術合作會議"("Sino-American Conference on Intellectual Cooperation")相關資料。

3469 Six Keys to the Soviet System/by Bertram D. Wolfe. —Boston: The Beacon Press, 1956

xv, 258 p.; 21.5 cm

HSMH (HS-N04F1-016)

附註:

 印章:內封面頁鈐有"胡適的書"朱文方印。
 夾紙:書中有夾紙4張。

3470 Sketches of a Cottager = 雅舍小品/by Liang Shih-chiu(梁實秋); translated by Shih Chao-ying(時昭瀛). —Taipei, Taiwan: Far East Book Company, 1960

219 p. ; 18.8 cm

HSMH（HS-N03F3-005）

附注：

印章：内封面頁鈐有"胡適的書"朱文方印。

3471 Slavery and Freedom/by Nicolas Berdyaev. —New York：Charles Scribner's Sons, 1944

271 p. ; 22.2 cm

HSMH（HS-N19F3-035）

附注：

印章：内封面頁鈐有"胡適的書"朱文方印。

批注圈劃：書中有注記劃綫兩處。

3472 Snow Country/by Yasunari Kawabata. —New York：Alfred A. Knopf, Inc., 1956

x, 175 p. ; 18.7 cm

HSMH（HS-N04F5-008）

附注：

印章：内封面頁鈐有"胡適的書"朱文方印。

3473 Society and Knowledge：The growth of Human Traditions/by V. G. Childe. —New York：Harper & Brothers Publishers, 1956

xvii, 131 p. ; 19.5 cm

World Perspectivers, Vol. 6

HSMH（HS-N19F3-017）

附注：

印章：扉頁鈐有"胡適的書"朱文方印。

夾紙：頁98、99間夾有本書的購書收據1張。

3474 Some Remarks on the Structure of the Verb Complex in Standard Chinese/ by H. F. Simon. —［s.l.］：［s.n.］, ［n.d.］

553-577 p. ; 24.7 cm

Bulletin of the School of Oriental and African Studies, University of London, Vol. XXI, Part 3, 1958

HSMH（HS-N19F2-019）

附注：

 题记：封面有作者题赠："Dr. Hu Shih With my compliments Henry Simon Taipei February '59。"

 其他：抽印本。

3475 The Song of God：Bhagavad-Gita/translated by Swami Prabhavananda and Christopher Isherwood. —New York：The New American Library, 1954

 143 p. ; 18.1 cm

 HSMH（HS-N03F1-001）

 附注：

  印章：内封面页钤有"胡适的书"朱文方印。

3476 South of Tokyo/by John C. Caldwell. —Chicago：Henry Regnery Company, 1957

 160 p. ; 21.7 cm

 HSMH（HS-N19F6-006）

 附注：

  印章：内封面页钤有"胡适的书"朱文方印。

  夹纸：页68、69间夹有此书的 Review Copy 卡片1张。

3477 Soviet-American Relations, 1917-1920, Vol. 2：The Decision to Intervene/by George F. Kennan. —Princeton, New Jersey：Princeton University Press, 1958

 xii, 513 p. ; 24.1 cm

 HSMH（HS-N04F1-023）

 附注：

  印章：内封面页钤有"胡适的书"朱文方印。

題記：扉頁有贈書者題贈："您還記不記得您的留學日記，您在這本書所記的故事的那個時代，對於一些事情的反應與威爾遜總統同。全是錯的；好人易犯的錯誤。送給 適之先生 之薦於馬克吐溫玩水河畔，一九五八年三月。"

夾紙：內封面頁有夾紙1張。

3478 Soybeans for Health Longevity and Economy/by Philip S. Chen. —South Lancaster, Mass.：The Chemical Elements, 1956

xii, 241 p.；21 cm

HSMH（HS-N19F4-010）

附注：

印章：內封面頁鈐有"胡適的書"朱文方印。

3479 Spanish Stories and Tales：A Collection Designed for Good Reading/edited by Harriet De Onís. —New York：Alfred A. Knopf, 1954

xi, 270 p.；21.5 cm

HSMH（HS-N19F6-002）

附注：

印章：扉頁有胡適簽名"Hu Shih"；內封面頁鈐有"胡適的書"朱文方印。

批注圈劃：目錄頁有胡適紅筆打勾。

3480 Speak Chinese/by M. Gardner Tewksbury. —New Haven：Published for the Institute of Far Eastern Languages by Yale University Press, 1948

xvi, 189 p.；22.4 cm

HSMH（HS-N03F1-030）

附注：

印章：內封面頁鈐有"胡適的書"朱文方印。

3481 Speaking Frankly/by James F. Byrnes. —New York：Harper & Brothers, 1947

xii, 324 p.；21.9 cm

HSMH（HS-N04F2-011）

附注：

　　印章:内封面頁鈐有"胡適的書"朱文方印。

　　批注圈劃:書中有胡適的批注劃綫數處。

3482　Spinoza Dictionary/edited by Dagobert D. Runes. —New York：Philosophical Library, Inc., 1951

　　xiv, 309 p.；22.2 cm

　　HSMH（HS-N04F5-039）

附注：

　　印章:内封面頁鈐有"胡適的書"朱文方印。

　　夾紙:頁140、141間夾有信封地址殘片1張。

3483　The Spirit of Chinese Philosophy/by Fung Yu-lan; translated and edited with an introduction by E. R. Hughes. —London：Kegan Paul, Trench, Trubner & Co., Ltd., 1947

　　xiv, 224 p.；22.3 cm

　　HSMH（HS-N03F5-021）

附注：

　　印章:内封面頁鈐有"胡適的書"朱文方印。

　　題記:内封面頁有胡適的題記:"馮友蘭的《新原道》。"

　　批注圈劃:書中有胡適的批注劃綫數處。

　　其他:(1)扉頁有"Chinese News Service Library"藍色戳印。(2)原作者爲馮友蘭。

3484　The Spirit of Zen：A Way of Life, Work and Art in the Far East/by Alan W. Watts. —Frome and London：Butler & Tanner Ltd., 1948

　　136 p.；18 cm

　　Wisdom of the East Series

　　HSMH（HS-N06F1-014）

附注：

　　印章:鈐有"胡適的書"朱文方印。

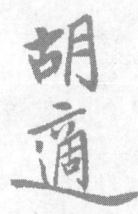

批注圈劃：書中有胡適的鉛筆批注劃綫數處。

其他：再印本。

3485　The Spring of Civilization: Periclean Athens/edited by Charles Alexander Robinson, Jr.. —New York: E. P. Dutton & Co., Inc., 1954

xv, 464 p., 74 plates (incl. ports.), map; 22 cm

HSMH（HS-N19F6-024）

附注：

印章：內封面頁鈐有"胡適的書"朱文方印。

3486　The Statesman's Year-Book: Statistical and Historical Annual of the States of the World for the Year 1950/edited by S. H. Steinberg. —New York: The Macmillan Company, 1950

xxiii, 1594 p.; 19 cm

HSMH（HS-N19F1-030）

附注：

印章：內封面頁鈐有"胡適的書"朱文方印。

3487　Still the Rice Grows Green: Asia in the Aftermath of Geneva and Panmunjom/by John C. Caldwell. —Chicago: Henry Regnery Company, 1955

312 p.; 21.8 cm

HSMH（HS-N03F1-012）

附注：

印章：內封面頁鈐有"胡適的書"朱文方印。

批注圈劃：書中有胡適的批注劃綫數處。

3488　Stories from the Thousand and One Nights (the Arabian Nights' Entertainments)/translated by Edward William Lane. —New York: P. F. Collier & Son Corporation, 1909

441 p., [1] plate; 21 cm

Harvard Classics: The Five-Foot Shelf of Books, Vol. 16

HSMH（HS-N12F6-016）

附注：

印章：內封面頁鈐有"胡適的書"朱文方印。

夾紙：扉頁夾有畫紙1張。

3489 Storm over Laos: A Contemporary History/by Sisouk Na Champassak. ——New York: Frederick A. Praeger, Inc., 1961

x, 202 p.; 21 cm

HSMH（HS-N19F6-004）

附注：

相關記載：1961年6月22日Frederick A. Praeger致胡適函，贈送此書，參見館藏號：HS-NK05-164-030。

3490 The Story of America in Pictures/by Alan C. Collins. ——Garden City, New York: Doubleday & Company, Inc., 1953

xiv, 480 p.; 21.7 cm

HSMH（HS-N04F5-001）

附注：

印章：扉頁鈐有"胡適的書"朱文方印。

題記：扉頁有胡適題記："前天花了一塊三角多，買了三部書，這是其中的一部。今晚翻看一遍，很感覺興趣。胡適 一九五四、九、十一（舊曆中秋）。"

批注圈劃：書中有胡適的批注劃綫數處。

3491 The Story of Khun Chang Khun Phan, Book One/told in English by Prem Chaya; with illustrations by Hem Vejakorn. ——Bangkok: Chatra Books, 1955

97 p., illus.; 19 cm

HSMH（HS-N19F2-047）

3492 The Story of Khun Chang Khun Phan, Book Two/told in English by Prem Chaya; with illustrations by Hem Vejakorn. ——Bangkok: Chatra Books, 1959

12, 197 p., illus.; 18.6 cm

HSMH（HS-N19F2-048）

3493　The Story of Phra Abhai Mani/told in English by Prem Chaya; with illustrations by Hem Vejakorn. —Bangkok: Chatra Books, 1959

[7], 141 p., illus.; 18.9 cm

HSMH（HS-N19F2-046）

附注：

其他：本書爲第2版。

3494　Strange Stories from the Lodge of Leisures/translated from the Chinese by George Soulié. —Boston and New York: Houghton Mifflin Company, 1913

xi, 166 p.; 17.8 cm

HSMH（HS-N03F4-016）

附注：

印章：封面裏有簽名"Phila Pu June 1920"；內封面頁鈐有"胡適的書"朱文方印。

批注圈劃：書中有胡適的批注數處。

其他：封面裏粘貼小紙片1張，印有"Property of George Abbott 'Tide-Mill Farm' Salem, N. J."。

3495　The Struggle for the World/by James Burnham. —New York: The John Day Company, Inc., 1947

248 p.; 21.2 cm

HSMH（HS-N04F2-024）

附注：

印章：內封面頁鈐有"胡適的書"朱文方印。

其他：此書爲第3次印刷。

3496　Studies in Chinese Institutional History/by Lien-sheng Yang. —Cambridge, Mass.: Harvard University Press, 1961

229 p. ; 25.4 cm

Harvard-Yenching Institute Studies, XX

HSMH（HS-N19F1-001）

附注：

 印章：內封面鈐有"胡適的書"朱文方印。

 夾紙：扉頁夾有 Harvard-Yenching Institute 的贈書卡 1 張。

 其他：作者爲楊聯陞。

3497 Studies in Chinese Thought/edited by Arthur F. Wright. —Chicago, Illinois：The University of Chicago Press, 1953

 xiv, 317 p. ; 24.1 cm

 The America Anthroplogist, Vol. 55, No. 5, Pt. 2, Memoir No. 75, December 1953

 HSMH（HS-N03F5-019）

附注：

 印章：內封面頁鈐有"胡適的書"朱文方印。

 與胡適的關係：內容與注釋均提及胡適。

 相關記載：1953 年 4 月 10 日 Miriam Brokaw 致胡適函，館藏號：HS-US01-064-034。

3498 Studies on the Population of China, 1368-1953/by Ping-ti Ho. —Cambridge Mass.：Harvard University Press, 1959

 xviii, 341, xxxii p. ; 24.1 cm

 Harvard East Asian Studies 4

 HSMH（HS-N03F5-029）

附注：

 印章：內封面頁鈐有"胡適的書"朱文方印。

 題記：扉頁有作者題贈："適之吾師教正 生炳棣敬呈 一九五九 十月六日。"

 夾紙：頁 66、67 間夾有寄自加拿大 P. T. Ho 的信封地址殘片 1 張。

 其他：作者爲何炳棣。

3499 A Study of Chinese Dependence upon the Soviet Union for Economic Development as a Factor in Communist China's Foreign Policy/by Calvin Suey Keu Chin. —Kowloon, Hong Kong: Union Research Institute, 1959

181 p. ; 25.9 cm

Communist China Problem Research Series

HSMH（HS-N03F2-015）

附注：

印章：内封面頁鈐有"胡適的書"朱文方印。

其他：封面有"Complimentary Copy"的藍色戳印。

3500 The Summing Up/by W. Somerset Maugham. —New York: The New American Library, 1957

191 p. ; 18 cm

HSMH（HS-N19F5-066）

附注：

其他：此書爲第8次印刷。

3501 Sun Yat-Sen/by Stephen Chen and Robert Payne. —New York: The John Day Company, 1946

v, 242 p. ; 20.7 cm

HSMH（HS-N20F1-007）

附注：

印章：内封面頁鈐有"胡適的書"朱文方印。

其他：封面有孫科題字"天下爲公"。

3502 The Sung Wang T'ai and the Location of the Travelling Courts by the Seashore in the Last Days of the Sung=宋王臺與宋季之海上行朝/by Hsiang-lin Lo(羅香林). —Hong Kong: Hong Kong University Press, 1958

185-217 p., xiv plates, fold. maps; 26.6 cm

Journal of Oriental Studies

HSMH（HS-N20F1-041）

附注：

　　印章：内封面頁鈐有"胡適的書"朱文方印。

　　其他：（1）《東方文化》1956年7月第3卷第2期抽印本。（2）内容含中、英文。

3503 A Survey of Chinese Students in American Universities and Colleges in the Past One Hundred Years: In Commemoration of the One Hundredth Anniversary of the Graduation of the First Chinese from an American University, Yung Wing, B. A. Yale 1854. —New York: "National Tsing Hua University Research Fellowship Fund and China Institute in America", 1954

　　68 p. ; 22.9 cm

　　HSMH（HS-N19F2-055）

附注：

　　印章：内封面頁鈐有"胡適的書"朱文方印。

3504 Survey on the Main Trends of Inquiry in the Field of the Natural Sciences, the Dissemination of Scientific Knowledge and the Application of Such Knowledge for Peaceful Ends/by Pierre Auger. —[s. l.]: United Nations Economic and Social Council, 1960

　　xxi, 445 p. ; 27 cm

　　HSMH（HS-N13F1-017）

附注：

　　印章："Preface"鈐有"胡適的書"朱文方印。

　　其他：訂書針裝訂。

3505 The Sutra of Wei Lang (or Hui Neng)/translated from the Chinese by Wong Mon-Lam; new edition by Christmas Humphreys. —London: The Buddhist Society, 1947

　　128 p. ; 17.5 cm

　　HSMH（HS-N19F2-058）

附注：

印章：内封面頁鈐有"胡適的書"朱文方印。

題記：扉頁有胡適題記："A very poor translation, even in this 'new edition'. Hu Shih July 10, 1952。"

批注圈劃：書中有胡適的批注圈劃數十處。

夾紙：頁126、127間夾有胡適筆記紙片1張。

3506 Symposium on Chinese Culture/edited by Sophia H. Chen Zen. —Shanghai：China Institute of Pacific Relations, 1931

316 p. ; 24.2 cm

HSMH（HS-N03F6-027）

附注：

題記：扉頁有胡適題記："Clifford, from H. S. New York, Sept. 1933。"

批注圈劃：書中有胡適的批注劃綫數處。

夾紙：書中有夾紙1張。

與胡適的關係：收錄胡適的文章"Religion and Philosophy in Chinese History"及"The Literary Renaissance"。

其他：（1）中文書名"中國文化討論集"；編者爲陳衡哲。（2）本書爲韋蓮司奉還胡適所贈之書。

3507 Syntans and Newer Methods of Tanning/by Philip S. Chen. —South Lancaster, Mass. : The Chemical Elements, 1950

134 p. ; 21.6 cm

HSMH（HS-N19F4-009）

附注：

印章：内封面頁鈐有"胡適的書"朱文方印。

3508 T'ai-Shang Kan-Ying P'ien = 太上感應篇/translated by Teitaro Suzuki and Paul Carus. —Chicago, Ill. : The Open Court Publishing Co., 1944

139 p. ; 20 cm

HSMH（HS-N03F4-010）

附注:

　　印章:內封面頁鈐有"胡適的書"朱文方印及"胡適"紫色戳印。

　　其他:譯者之一爲鈴木大拙。

3509　Taiwan as Seen by Visitors/by Constantine Brown, et al. —Taipei, Taiwan:
"Free China Review", 1958

　　56 p. ; 18.4 cm

　　HSMH (HS-N03F2-001)

3510　Taiwan's Development as Free China/by Richard L. Walker. —Philadelphia: The American Academy of Political and Social Science, 1959

　　122-135 p. ; 23.5 cm

　　Annals of the American Academy of Political and Social Science, Philadelphia, Vol. 321, January, 1959

　　HSMH (HS-N19F5-034)

　　附注:

　　題記:封面有作者題贈:"For Dr. Hu Shih With respect and best wishes Dick Walker March 1959。"

　　其他:抽印本。

3511　The Taming of the Nations: A Study of the Cultural Bases of International Policy/by F. S. C. Northrop. —New York: The MacMillan Company, 1954

　　xii, 362 p. ; 21.5 cm

　　HSMH (HS-N03F6-007)

　　附注:

　　印章:內封面頁鈐有"胡適的書"朱文方印。

　　批注圈劃:書中有胡適的批注劃綫數處。

3512　Tannhäuser: German and English Text and Music of the Principal Airs/by Richard Wagner. —Philadelphia: Oliver Ditson Company, [n.d.]

　　28 p. ; 24.4 cm

Grand Opera Librettos

HSMH（HS-N19F5-040）

附注：

印章：内封面頁鈐有"胡適的書"朱文方印。

其他：頁 16、17 間夾有 2 月 2 日星期五"Boston Opera House"的節目單 1 張。

3513 Tao Tê Ching/A New translation by Ch'u Ta-Kao. —London：the Buddhist Society, 1945

94 p. ; 19 cm

HSMH（HS-N06F1-015）

附注：

印章：内封面頁鈐有"胡適的書"朱文方印。

批注圈劃：書中有胡適的批注劃綫數處。

其他：封面有中文書名"新意章句老子道德經"，初大告譯注。

3514 Tao Teh King (Nature and Intelligence)/by Lao Tzu；interpreted as Nature and Intelligence by Archie J. Bahm. —New York：Frederick Ungar Publishing Co.，1958

126 p. ; 19.1 cm

HSMH（HS-N03F5-012）

附注：

印章：内封面頁鈐有"胡適的書"朱文方印。

3515 Tellers of Tales：100 Short Stories from the United States，England，France，Russia and Germany/selected and with an introduction by W. Somerset Maugham. —New York：Doubleday, Doran & Company, Inc.，1939

xxxix, 1526 p. ; 23.5 cm

HSMH（HS-N19F5-083）

附注：

印章：内封面頁鈐有"胡適的書"朱文方印。

批注圈劃:書中有胡適的批注劃綫數十處。

夾紙:書中有夾紙 1 張。

摺頁:"Introduction"有摺角。

相關記載:胡適閱讀此《短篇小說百年集》的心得,參考胡適日記 1939 年 7 月 3 日條。

3516 Tensions in the Taiwan Straits/by Hu Shih, et al. —Taiwan:"American University Club Republic of China", 1959

ii, 69 p.;18.7 cm

HSMH(HS-N20F2-068)

附注:

印章:館藏 9 冊,其中一冊的内封面頁與"Preface"頁 1 鈐有"胡適的書"朱文方印。

與胡適的關係:頁 63—69 收録胡適的文章"A Sum-up and A Warning",此書爲留美同學會(American University Club)以"台灣海峽緊張情勢"爲題的六次演講集成的小冊子,胡適的演説是最後一場。

相關記載:(1)館藏有"A Sum-up and A Warning"的胡適手寫稿及打字校稿,參見 HS-NK05-204-007,HS-NK05-204-008。(2)1958 年 11 月 7 日 J. L. Huang 致胡適函,邀請胡適擔任"台灣海峽緊張情勢"系列演講的最後一場演説者,參見館藏號:HS-NK05-152-039。

3517 The Tenth Anniversary Cornell Cosmopolitan Club. —Ithaca, New York:Cornell Cosmopolitan Club, 1915

[7] p.;18 cm

HSMH(HS-N19F2-017)

附注:

批注圈劃:此小冊有鉛筆劃綫一處。

與胡適的關係:(1)胡適是康乃爾世界學生會(Cornell Cosmopolitan Club)的幹事長。(2)此節目單有胡適的祝詩(Foreword)。

相關記載:此爲 1915 年 1 月 9 日至 11 日舉行的康乃爾世界學生會十年祝典節目單,參見館藏號:HS-NK05-288-007,HS-JDSHSE-0499-081。

其他:摺頁小冊。

3518 Thank God for My Heart Attack/by Charles Yale Harrison. —New York: Henry Holt and Company, 1949

144 p. ; 19.4 cm

HSMH（HS-N19F4-008）

附注:

印章:内封面鈐有"胡適的書"朱文方印。

題記:頁 144 有胡適題記:"Read with much enjoyment and with kindest recollections. Hu Shih July 4, 1949。"

3519 The Theban Plays: King Oedipus Oedipus at Colonus Antigone/by Sophocles; translated by E. F. Watling. —Harmondsworth, Middlesex: Penguin Books, 1949

168 p. ; 18.1 cm

The Penguin Classics

HSMH（HS-N04F6-030）

附注:

印章:内封面頁鈐有"胡適的書"朱文方印。

夾紙:内封面頁有夾紙 1 張。

3520 A Theory of Foreign-Exchange Speculation under a Floating Exchange System/by S. C. Tsiang. —Chicago: The University of Chicago, 1958

399-418 p. ; 24.2 cm

The Journal of Political Economy, Vol. LXVI, No. 5, October 1958

HSMH（HS-N19F2-054）

附注:

題記:封面有作者題贈:"適之院長教正 後學 蔣碩傑敬贈。"

其他:抽印本。

3521 The Theory of Forward Exchange and Effects of Government Intervention on the Forward Exchange Market/by S. C. Tsiang. —Washington：International Monetary Fund, 1959

75-106 p. ; 22.9 cm

The April 1959 Issue of the International Monetary Fund Staff Papers

HSMH（HS-N19F5-029）

附注：

　　題記：封面有作者題贈："適之先生教正　後學蔣碩傑敬贈。"

　　相關記載：1959年4月3日Bent Hansen致蔣碩傑函,提及對此文之意見,參見HS-NK05-124-003。

3522　This American People/by Gerald W. Johnson. —New York：Harper and Brothers Publishers, 1951

xii, 205 p. ; 22 cm

HSMH（HS-N04F4-027）

附注：

　　印章：內封面頁鈐有"胡適的書"朱文方印。

3523　Thomas Jefferson：A Biography/by Nathan Schachner. —New York：Appleton-Century-Crofts, Inc., 1951

2 Vols.（xiii, 1070 p.）; 25 cm

HSMH（HS-N04F3-026, HS-N04F3-027）

附注：

　　印章：兩冊內封面頁均鈐有"胡適的書"朱文方印。

　　題記：第1冊扉頁有贈書者題記："The trustees of China Institute in America send Dr. Hu Shih their heartiest congratulations on his sixtieth birthday. They offer him this story of Thomas Jefferson, another university leader, with their admiration and affection. New York December 17, 1951。"

　　其他：兩冊外裝紙匣。

3524　Thomas Paine：Common Sense and Other Political Writings/edited by Nelson F. Adkins. —New York：The Liberal Art Press, 1953 liii, 184 p.; 18.6 cm

HSMH（HS-N04F3-019）

附注：

印章：內封面頁鈐有"胡適的書"朱文方印。

3525 Three Essays on the International Economics of Communist China/edited by C. F. Remer. —Ann Arbor：The University of Michigan Press Published for Center for Japanese Studies and the Department of Economics, 1959

v, 221 p.; 28 cm

HSMH（HS-N13F1-021）

附注：

夾紙：頁108、109間夾有信封地址殘片1張。

3526 Three Times around Earth：A Statement by Lieut. Col. John H. Glenn, Jr., USMC Project Mercury Astronaut, February 23, 1962/by John H. Glenn, Jr.. —United States Information Service, 1962

18 p.; 17.9 cm

United States Policy Statement Series-1962

HSMH（HS-N19F2-014）

3527 Three Ways of Thought in Ancient China/by Arthur Waley. —London：George Allen & Unwin Ltd., 1946

275 p.; 20.2 cm

HSMH（HS-N03F5-013）

附注：

印章：內封面頁鈐有"胡適的書"朱文方印及"胡適"紫色戳印。

批注圈劃：書中有胡適的批注劃綫數十處。

3528 To Thee, Wisconsin, State and University and Other Public Addresses/by William H. Kiekhofer. —New York：Appleton-Century-Crofts, Inc., 1950

121 p.; 21.2 cm

HSMH（HS-N19F3-015）

附注：

印章：感謝頁鈐有"胡適的書"朱文方印。

與胡適的關係：本書第 VIII 章記載威斯康辛大學 1939—1950 年的榮譽博士接受者，其中頁 77、78 報導胡適："Hu Shih: Chinese Ambassador to the United States, LL. D. , 1942。

3529 Together … In Peril and In Hope/by Edwin A. Burtt. —［Ithaca, New York］: Edwin A. Burtt, ［1959］.

　　55 p. ; 22.9 cm

　　HSMH（HS-N19F2-024）

　　附注：

　　　印章：内封面頁鈐有"胡適的書"朱文方印。

　　　題記：内封面頁有作者題贈："To Dr. Hu Shih in respect and esteem E A Burtt。"

　　　批注圈劃：書中有批注劃綫數處。

3530 Tombeau Des Liang, Famille Siao/by Le P. Mathias Tchang. —Chang-Hai: Imprimerie De La Mission Catholique, 1912

　　xiii, 108 p. ; 25.4 cm

　　HSMH（HS-N03F4-023）

　　附注：

　　　印章：内封面頁鈐有"胡適的書"朱文方印。

3531 Toward the Liberally Educated Executive/edited by Robert A. Goldwin. —White Plains, New York: The Fund for Adult Education, 1957

　　ix, 111 p. ; 20.6 cm

　　HSMH（HS-N19F3-022）

　　附注：

　　　印章：内封面頁鈐有"胡適的書"朱文方印。

3532 Transformation: The Story of Modern Puerto Rico/by Earl Parker Hanson; with an introduction by Chester Bowles. —New York: Simon and Schuster, 1955

xxiii, 416 p.; 21.3 cm

HSMH（HS-N19F6-003）

附注：

印章：内封面頁鈐有"胡適的書"朱文方印。

題記：扉頁有題贈："To Doctor Hu Shih: May this book be a source of inspiration and assistance to you in the Herculean task you have imposed upon yourself of saving your beloved nation, China, from Communism. Yours very sincerely Heliodoro Blanco Morales San Juan, P. R., Dec. 21, 1957。"

夾紙：扉頁有夾紙2張，一張是H. Blanco Morales寄給胡適的信封地址殘片；另一張是手寫Heliodoro Blanco Morales地址的紙片。頁118、119間亦有夾紙1張。

3533 The Travels of Lao Ts'an = 老殘遊記/by Liu Tiéh-yün（Liu E）; translated from the Chinese and annotated by Harold Shadick. —Ithaca, New York: Cornell University Press, 1952

xxiii, 277 p.; 23.5 cm

HSMH（HS-N03F4-017）

附注：

印章：内封面頁鈐有"胡適的書"朱文方印。

批注圈劃：書中有胡適的批注圈劃數處。

内附文件：書末粘貼1953年3月1日胡適致康乃爾大學Harold Shadick教授函1張。

其他：作者爲劉鶚。

3534 A Treasury of Modern Asian Stories/edited by Daniel L. Milton and William Clifford. —New York: The New American Library, 1961

237 p.; 18 cm

HSMH（HS-N03F1-010）

附注：

印章：内封面前有"R. M. McCarthy"的簽名；内封面頁鈐有"胡適的書"朱文方印。

   夾紙：書中夾有10月4日Richard M. McCarthy贈書給胡適的便條1張。

3535 A Treasury of Science/edited by Harlow Shapley, Samuel Rapport and Helen Wright; with an Introduction by Dr. Shapley. —New York：Harper & Brothers Publishers, 1958

   xiii, 776 p.；21.8 cm

   HSMH（HS-N19F4-031）

   附注：

   印章：内封面頁鈐有"胡適的書"朱文方印。

   批注圈劃：書中有胡適的批注劃綫數處，其中頁14批注："此文似不如'The Method of Zadig'。"

   其他：本書爲修訂第4版（Fourth Revised Edition）。

3536 Truth and Opinion：Historical Essays/by C. V. Wedgwood. —New York：The MacMillan Company, 1960

   254 p.；21.5 cm

   HSMH（HS-N19F6-034）

   附注：

   印章：扉頁有胡適簽名"Hu Shih August 31, 1960 New York, N. Y."。

3537 Truth and Tradition in Chinese Buddhism：A Study of Chinese Mahayana Buddhism/by Karl Ludvig Reichelt（艾香德）. —Shanghai：The Commercial Press, Limited, 1934

   xii, 415 p.；22.7 cm

   HSMH（HS-N03F4-009）

   附注：

   印章：内封面頁鈐有"胡適的書"朱文方印及"胡適"紫色戳印。

   題記：内封面頁有胡適題記："A worthless book！H. S. 。"

   批注圈劃：内封面頁及頁206有胡適的批注。

其他：封面裏有貼紙1張，印有"Truth and Tradition in Chinese Buddhism Price：＄4.50 中國佛教源流考 上海商務印書館印行"。

3538 Turkish Nationalism and Western Civilization：Selected Essays of Ziya Gökalp/translated and edited with an introduction by Niyazi Berkes. —London：George Allen and Unwin Ltd.，1959

336 p.；22.4 cm

HSMH（HS-N19F6-001）

附注：

印章：內封面頁鈐有"胡適的書"朱文方印。

題記：扉頁有編譯者題贈："With best wishes from Niyazi Berkes Montreal Oct. 30，1959。"

夾紙：扉頁夾有 McGill University 的 N. Berkes 寄給胡適的信封地址殘片1張。

3539 The Twentieth Century：A Mid-way Account of the Western World/by Hans Kohn. —New York：The Macmillan Company，1949

ix，242 p.；21 cm

HSMH（HS-N03F6-005）

附注：

印章：扉頁有胡適簽名"Hu Shih Sept. 20，1949"；內封面頁鈐有"胡適的書"朱文方印。

題記：封底裏有胡適鉛筆題記："Charismatic leaders" p. 46 p. 56。"

批注圈劃：書中有胡適的批注劃綫數十處。

3540 Twilight in the Forbidden City/by Reginald F. Johnston. —New York：D. Appleton-Century Company，1934

486 p.；24 cm

HSMH（HS-N03F3-002）

附注：

印章：扉頁鈐有"胡適"紫色戳印；內封面頁鈐有"胡適的書"朱文方印。

題記:扉頁有贈書者題贈:"To the man of the 20th Century — Dr. Hu Shih A great diplomat, historian and philosopher from an admirer — with the best of good wishes. Alex Faerbery New York, May 1951。"

批注圈劃:頁478 注記:"406。"

夾紙:書中有夾紙4張。

與胡適的關係:(1)另一扉頁有胡適的朱筆題籤:"莊士敦 紫禁城晚霞錄 胡適題。"(2)內文及注釋均提及胡適。

3541 Two Years before the Mast and Twenty-Four Years After/by R. H. Dana. —New York: P. F. Collier & Son Corporation, 1909

405 p., [1] plate; 21 cm

Harvard Classics: The Five-Foot Shelf of Books, Vol. 23

HSMH(HS-N12F6-023)

附注:

印章:內封面頁鈐有"胡適的書"朱文方印。

3542 Ulysses/by James Joyce. —New York: The Modern Library, 1942

xvii, 768 p.; 20.9 cm

HSMH(HS-N04F5-014)

附注:

印章:內封面頁鈐有"胡適的書"朱文方印。

摺頁:頁503 右上有摺角。

3543 The Umbrella Garden: A Picture of Student Life in Red China/by Maria Yen. —Hong Kong: The Union Press, 1957

vi, 339 p.; 18.1 cm

HSMH(HS-N03F2-019)

附注:

印章:內封面頁鈐有"胡適的書"朱文方印。

其他:扉頁有"友聯出版社贈"的藍色戳印。

3544 The Undeclared War, 1940 – 1941/by William L. Langer and S. Everett Gleason. —New York：Harper & Brothers, 1953

xvi, 963 p.；24 cm

HSMH（HS-N04F2-028）

附注：

印章：内封面頁鈐有"胡適的書"朱文方印。

批注圈劃：頁899有胡適的劃綫打叉一處。

與胡適的關係：内容提及胡適。

3545 Understanding Human Nature/by Alfred Adler. —New York：Greenberg & Publisher, 1928

ix, 286 p.；21.2 cm

HSMH（HS-N19F4-046）

附注：

印章：内封面頁鈐有"胡適的書"朱文方印。

3546 UNESCO：Purpose, Progress, Prospects/by Walter H. C. Laves and Charles A. Thomson. —Bloomington：Indiana University Press, 1957

xxiii, 469 p.；23.7 cm

HSMH（HS-N19F4-007）

附注：

印章：内封面頁鈐有"胡適的書"朱文方印。

夾紙：頁178、179間夾有紙張3張，一爲印地安那大學校長辦公室寄給胡適的信封地址殘片1張，上記"President H. B. Wells"；二爲"Herman B. Wells"名片1張，上記"With Best Wishes for the New Year"；三爲名片信封1張。

3547 United States Relations with China：With Special Reference to the Period 1944–1949. —Washington：U. S. Government Printing Office, 1949

xli, 1054 p.；23.6 cm

HSMH（HS-N03F2-035）

附注：

  印章：内封面頁鈐有"胡適的書"朱文方印。

  題記：扉頁有胡適題記："Hu Shih, August 6, 1949, Gift of Dr. Wellington Koo.。"

  批注圈劃：書中有胡適的批注劃綫數百處。

  夾紙：書中夾有《新中華高商統計學（下册）》的版權頁1張及夾紙14張。

  内附文件：(1)封面裏粘貼英詩"Lament in China"剪報一則，上有胡適記"N. Y. Sun—（H. I. Phillips）Aug. 18, 1949"。(2)頁271粘貼打字文件1張，内容爲New York Sun 報導1948年2月22日南京訊息，關於美國大使司徒雷登（J. L. Stuart）對國共内戰的看法。

3548 University of Hawaii General Catalogue 1960–1961. —Hawaii：University of Hawaii Bulletin, June 1960

  198 p.；22.9 cm

  HSMH（HS-N19F2-001）

  附注：

    印章：館藏2册，内封面頁均鈐有"胡適的書"朱文方印。

3549 Unpopular Essays/by Bertrand Russell. —New York：Simon and Schuster, 1950

  175 p.；20.4 cm

  HSMH（HS-N04F5-028）

  附注：

    印章：内封面頁有胡適簽名"Hu Shih Feb. 1951"，並鈐有"胡適的書"朱文方印。

    批注圈劃：書中有胡適的批注劃綫數處。

3550 The Uses of the Past：Profiles of Former Societies/by Herbert J. Muller. —New York：The New American Library, 1954

  384 p.；17.8 cm

  HSMH（HS-N19F6-039）

附注:

印章:內封面頁鈐有"胡適的書"朱文方印。

批注圈劃:書中有胡適的劃綫數處。

與胡適的關係:頁 340 提及胡適。

3551 Values in a Universe of Chance: Selected Writings of Charles S. Peirce (1839 - 1914)/edited by Philip P. Wiener. —Garden City, New York: Doubleday Anchor Books, 1958

xxvi, 446 p. ; 18.2 cm

HSMH (HS-N04F4-004)

附注:

印章:內封面頁鈐有"胡適的書"朱文方印。

3552 Venus, the Lonely Goddess/by John Erskine. —New York: William Morrow & Co. , 1949

155 p. ; 21.8 cm

HSMH (HS-N04F6-035)

附注:

印章:內封面頁鈐有"胡適的書"朱文方印。

題記:扉頁有題記:"For Rily's Homecoming 2. 20. 50。"

3553 Village Life in China: A Study in Sociology/by Arthur H. Smith. —New York: Fleming H. Revell Company, 1899

360 p. , plates; 21.2 cm

HSMH (HS-N03F3-025)

附注:

印章:內封面頁鈐有"胡適的書"朱文方印。

3554 The Vintage Mencken/by H. L. Mencken. —New York: Vintage Books, 1955

xiv, 240 p. ; 18.5 cm

HSMH (HS-N04F3-009)

附注：

 印章：内封面頁鈐有"胡適的書"朱文方印。

3555 Virgil's Æneid/translated by John Dryden. —New York：P. F. Collier & Son Corporation, 1909

 427 p., [1] plate；21 cm

 Harvard Classics：The Five-Foot Shelf of Books, Vol. 13

 HSMH（HS-N12F6-013）

 附注：

  印章：内封面頁鈐有"胡適的書"朱文方印。

3556 Vision & Action：Essays in Honor of Horace M. Kallen on His 70th Birthday/edited by Sidney Ratner. —New Brunswick, New Jersey：Rutgers University Press, 1953

 xvii, 277 p.；21.9 cm

 HSMH（HS-N04F4-001）

 附注：

  印章：内封面頁鈐有"胡適的書"朱文方印。

  夾紙：書中夾有贈書卡片1張及地址殘片1張，上記"Pei Shin Yang 562 West 113 st.（Apt. 4D. 6）New York 25, N. Y."。

3557 The Voyage of the Beagle/by Charles Darwin. —New York：P. F. Collier & Son Corporation, 1909

 524 p., [1] plate；21 cm

 Harvard Classics：The Five-Foot Shelf of Books, Vol. 29

 HSMH（HS-N12F6-029）

 附注：

  印章：内封面頁鈐有"胡適的書"朱文方印。

3558 Voyages and Travels：Ancient and Modern/edited by Charles W. Eliot. —New York：P. F. Collier & Son Corporation, 1910

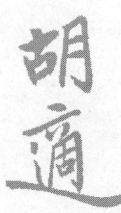

380 p., [1] plate; 21 cm

Harvard Classics: The Five-Foot Shelf of Books, Vol. 33

HSMH (HS-N12F5-003)

附注:

印章:內封面頁鈐有"胡適的書"朱文方印。

3559 Die Walkuere (the walkyr): A Music Drama in Three Acts/by Richard Wagner; English version by Charles Henry Meltzer. —New York: Fred Rullman Inc., [n. d.]

57 p.; 25.4 cm

Metropolitan Opera House Grand Opera

HSMH (HS-N19F5-043)

附注:

印章:內封面頁鈐有"胡適的書"朱文方印。

3560 Wang An Shih = 王安石: A Chinese Statesman and Educationalist of the Sung Dynasty, Vol. 1/by H. R. Williamson. —London: Arthur Probsthain, 1935

x, 388 p.; 19.5 cm

Probsthain's Oriental Series, Vol. XXI

HSMH (HS-N03F4-020)

附注:

印章:內封面頁鈐有"胡適的書"朱文方印。

批注圈劃:目錄頁有胡適的注記數處。

3561 Wang An Shih = 王安石: A Chinese Statesman and Educationalist of the Sung Dynasty, Vol. 2/by H. R. Williamson. —London: Arthur Probsthain, 1937

viii, 424 p.; 19.3 cm

Probsthain's Oriental Series, Vol. XXII

HSMH (HS-N03F4-021)

附注：

　　印章：內封面頁鈐有"胡適的書"朱文方印。

　　批注圈劃：書中有胡適的批注劃綫數十處。

　　與胡適的關係：內容提及胡適。

3562　The War Memoirs of General de Gaulle, Vol. 1：The Call to Honour 1940-1942/by Charles De Gaulle. ——New York：The Viking Press, 1955

　　319 p. ; 21.9 cm

　　HSMH（HS-N04F2-009）

　　附注：

　　　印章：扉頁鈐有"胡適的書"朱文方印。

　　　題記：扉頁有題記："return to Dr. Hu。"

3563　The War We Are In, View 1. ——Hamilton, Ohio：The Champion Paper and Fibre Company, 1960

　　28 p. ; 32.9 cm

　　HSMH（HS-N20F1-106）

　　附注：

　　　夾紙：封面夾有"Marvin Liebman"名片1張。

3564　Water and Electrolyte Balance Studies in Cholera/by Raymond H. Watten, Francis M. Morgan, Yachai na Songkhla, Bunam Vanikiati, Robert A. Phillips. ——Taipei, Taiwan：United States Naval Medical Research No. 2, 1959

　　16 p. ; 26.5 cm

　　NAMRU TWO, March 10, 1959（NM 52 11 02. 3. 2）

　　HSMH（HS-N19F5-011）

　　附注：

　　　其他：（1）釘書針裝訂。（2）館藏2冊。

3565　The Way and Its Power：A Study of the Tao Tê Ching and Its Place in Chinese Thought/by Arthur Waley. ——London：George Allen & Unwin Ltd.,

1949

262 p.；20.8 cm

HSMH（HS-N03F5-006）

附注：

印章：内封面頁鈐有"胡適的書"朱文方印及"胡適"紫色戳印。

批注圈劃：書中有胡適的批注劃綫數十處。

與胡適的關係：注釋提及胡適。

3566 The Way of Life：Lao Tzǔ（a new translation of the Tao Tê Ching）/by R. B. Blakney. —New York：The New American Library，1955

134 p.；18.3 cm

HSMH（HS-N03F5-011）

附注：

印章：内封面頁鈐有"胡適的書"朱文方印。

3567 The Web of Subversion：Underground Networks in the U. S. Government/by James Burnham. —New York：The John Day Company，1954

248 p.；21 cm

HSMH（HS-N04F2-029）

附注：

印章：内封面頁鈐有"胡適的書"朱文方印。

題記：扉頁有胡適題記："Hu Shih July 4, 1954 此書是 July 6 買的，我要紀念這個節日，故寫 July 4。"

批注圈劃：書中有胡適的劃綫數處。

3568 Webster's New Collegiate Dictionary/edited by John P. Bethel. —Springfield, Mass.：G. & C. Merriam Co.，Publishers，1949

xxii，1209 p.；25.3 cm

HSMH（HS-N19F1-046）

附注：

印章：扉頁有胡適簽名"Hu Shih 胡適 March 1951"；内封面頁鈐有"胡適

的書"朱文方印。

3569 Webster's New Vest-Pocket Dictionary of the English Language/compiled by E. T. Roe. —Chicago: Wilcox & Follett Co., 1951

284 p.; 14.5 cm

HSMH (HS-N19F1-044)

附注：

印章：扉頁鈐有"胡適的書"朱文方印。

3570 Wedemeyer Reports! /by Albert C. Wedemeyer. —[s.l.]: [s.n.], [n.d.]

xii, 497 p.; 19.3 cm

HSMH (HS-N03F2-029)

附注：

印章：内封面頁鈐有"胡適的書"朱文方印。

其他：作者譯名"魏德邁"。

3571 The Western Intellectual Tradition: From Leonardo to Hegel/by J. Bronowski and Bruce Mazlish. —New York: Harper & Brothers Publishers, 1960

xviii, 522 p.; 21.4 cm

HSMH (HS-N04F6-036)

附注：

印章：内封面頁鈐有"胡適的書"朱文方印。

3572 What Can I Know: The Prophetic Answer/by Herrymon Maurer. —New York: Harper & Brothers Publishers, 1953

253 p.; 21.2 cm

HSMH (HS-N19F4-043)

附注：

印章：内封面頁鈐有"胡適的書"朱文方印。

與胡適的關係：頁64提及胡適。

3573 What China Policy? /by Vladimir Petrov. —Hamden, Conn.: Shoe String
　　　 Press, 1961
　　　　　x, 141 p.; 21 cm
　　　　　HSMH（HS-N03F2-017）

3574 What Happened in History/by Gordon Childe. —Harmondsworth, Middlesex:
　　　 Penguin Books, 1952
　　　　　288 p.; 18 cm
　　　　　HSMH（HS-N19F6-022）
　　　　　附注：
　　　　　　印章：扉頁鈐有"胡適的書"朱文方印。
　　　　　　夾紙：書中有夾紙1張。

3575 What Is Literature? /by Jean-Paul Sartre. —New York: Philosophical Library,
　　　 1949
　　　　　306 p.; 22 cm
　　　　　HSMH（HS-N04F5-027）
　　　　　附注：
　　　　　　印章：内封面頁鈐有"胡適的書"朱文方印。

3576 What's Happening in China? /by Boyd Orr and Peter Townsend. —Garden
　　　 City, New York: Doubleday & Company, Inc., 1959
　　　　　xii, 159 p.; 20.3 cm
　　　　　HSMH（HS-N03F2-020）
　　　　　附注：
　　　　　　印章：内封面頁鈐有"胡適的書"朱文方印。
　　　　　　批注圈劃：書中有胡適的批注圈劃數處。

3577 Whither Mankind: A Panorama of Modern Civilization/edited by Charles A.
　　　 Beard. —New York: Longmans, Green And Co., 1928
　　　　　vii, 408 p.; 21.8 cm

HSMH（HS-N04F4-021）

附注：

印章：扉頁有胡適簽名"Hu Shih"；內封面頁鈐有"胡適的書"朱文方印。

題記：內封面頁有胡適題記："Eugene Delafield got this copy for me. Nov. 14, 1952 Hu Shih。"

批注圈劃：書中有胡適的批注劃綫數十處。

夾紙：書中有夾紙1張。

與胡適的關係：收錄胡適的文章"The Civilizations of the East and West"。

相關記載：館藏有"The Civilizations of the East and the West"抽印本，參見館藏號：HS-NK05-198-011。

3578 "Whither Must I Fly？"：A Key to Current Plans for a Warless World Order/ by Alexander D. Mebane. —[s. l.]：[s. n.]，[n. d.]

v, 93 p.；28 cm

HSMH（HS-N19F3-005）

3579 Who's Who in America：A Biographical Dictionary of Notable Living Men and Women, Vol. 27：1952-1953 Two Years. —Chicago：The A. N. Marquis Company, 1961

3216 p.；27.9 cm

HSMH（HS-N12F5-027）

附注：

印章：內封面頁鈐有"胡適的書"朱文方印。

夾紙：頁358、359間夾有簡介、廣告單等資料5件；頁1218、1219間夾有訂購單1張；頁1468、1469間夾有簡介殘片1張；其餘尚有夾紙3張。

與胡適的關係：頁1218爲胡適的簡介。

3580 Wiley Books, 1958. —New York：John Wiley & Sons, Inc., 1958

266 p.；20.8 cm

HSMH（HS-N19F1-036）

附注：

其他：內封面頁有"秀鶴行 H. C. Ling Book Store"的戳印。

3581 William James/edited with a commentary by Margaret Knight. —Harmondsworth, Middlesex：Penguin Books, 1950

248 p. ; 18 cm

Pelican Books, A229

HSMH（HS-N04F4-005）

附注：

印章：內封面頁鈐有"胡適的書"朱文方印。

3582 The Wisdom of China and India/edited by Lin Yutang. —New York：Random House, 1942

1104 p. ; 23.4 cm

HSMH（HS-N03F2-041）

附注：

印章：內封面頁鈐有"胡適的書"朱文方印。

批注圈劃：書中有胡適的批注劃綫數處。

夾紙：書中夾有 Mrs. James A. Field 借此書的借書卡 1 張。

其他：作者爲林語堂。

3583 The Wisdom of Confucius/edited and translated by Lin Yutang. —New York：Random House, 1938

xvii, 290 p. ; 18.4 cm

HSMH（HS-N03F5-004）

附注：

批注圈劃：書中有胡適的批注劃綫數處。

其他：編譯者爲林語堂。

3584 The Wit and Wisdom of John Dewey/edited by A. H. Johnson. —Boston：The Beacon Press, 1949

ix, 111 p. ; 24.3 cm

HSMH（HS-N04F4-006）

附注：

印章：内封面頁鈐有"胡適的書"朱文方印。

3585 Woodrow Wilson: A Great Life in Brief/by John A. Garraty. —New York: Alfred A. Knopf, 1956

vi, 206 p.; 19 cm

HSMH（HS-N04F3-002）

附注：

印章：内封面頁鈐有"胡適的書"朱文方印。

題記：扉頁有贈書者題贈："爲適之先生的書架補空 治 焕綬敬送 一九五六 十二、十七 紐約。"

3586 The Woodrow Wilson Reader/Selected and edited by Frances Farmer. —New York: Oceana Publications, 1956

286 p.; 17.6 cm

Docket Series, Vol. 4

HSMH（HS-N19F3-011）

附注：

印章：内封面頁鈐有"胡適的書"朱文方印。

3587 Woodrow Wilson, Wellington Koo and the China Question at the Paris Peace Conference/by Wunsz King. —Leiden, Netherlands: A. W. Sythoff, 1959

32 p.; 23.2 cm

HSMH（HS-N19F5-025）

附注：

印章：内封面頁鈐有"胡適的書"朱文方印。

3588 The World Almanac and Book of Facts, 1960: Seventy-Fifth Year of Issue/edited by Harry Hansen. —New York: New York World-Telegram and the Sun,

A Scripps-Howard Newspaper, 1960

896 p. ; 21 cm

The World Almanac

HSMH（HS-N19F1-019）

3589 The World Almanac and Book of Facts, 1961: Seventy-Sixth Year of Issue/edited by Harry Hansen. —New York: New York World-Telegram and the Sun, A Scripps-Howard Newspaper, 1961

896 p. ; 21.5 cm

The World Almanac

HSMH（HS-N19F1-020）

附註：

印章：內封面頁鈐有"胡適的書"朱文方印。

3590 The World Almanac and Book of Facts, 1962: Seventy-Seventh Year of Issue/edited by Harry Hansen. —New York: New York World-Telegram and the Sun, A Scripps-Howard Newspaper, 1962

896 p. ; 21 cm

The World Almanac

HSMH（HS-N19F1-021）

附註：

印章：內封面頁鈐有"胡適的書"朱文方印。

3591 World Atlas/by Rand McNally. —Chicago: Rand McNally & Company, 1959.

30 p. : maps; 32 cm

HSMH（HS-N13F1-016）

附註：

印章：目錄頁鈐有"胡適的書"朱文方印。

3592 The World of Suzie Wong/by Richard Mason. —Cleveland and New York: The World Publishing Company, 1957

345 p.；19.4 cm

HSMH（HS-N19F5-067）

附注：

其他：此書爲第 5 次印刷。

3593 World Politics Faces Economics：With Special Reference to the Future Relations of the United States and Russia/by Harold D. Lasswell. —New York：McGraw-Hill Book Company, Inc., 1945

x, 108 p.；19.4 cm

HSMH（HS-N04F5-013）

附注：

印章：內封面頁鈐有"胡適的書"朱文方印。

3594 The World We Live In：A New Interpretation of Earth History/by Amadeus W. Grabau. —Taipei, Taiwan：The Geological Society of China, 1961

xxv, 229 p.；23.2 cm

HSMH（HS-N19F4-015）

附注：

相關記載：*The World We Live In* 是北大地質學古生物學教授葛利普（A. W. Grabau）的最後著作，由胡適買下稿本送給中國地質學會，爲葛利普留作紀念，參見《胡適日記》1957 年 1 月 15 日條。此書爲中國地質學會出版的書。

3595 The World's Best/edited by Whit Burnett. —New York：The Dial Press, 1950

xxv, 1186 p.；21.7 cm

HSMH（HS-N04F6-040）

附注：

印章：內封面頁鈐有"胡適的書"朱文方印。

題記：扉頁有胡適題記："Hu Shih See pp. 1066-1078。"

夾紙：頁 1066、1067 間有夾紙 1 張。

與胡適的關係：收錄胡適的文章"The Civilizations of the East and West"。

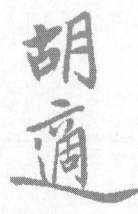

3596 The Year Book of the International Council of Scientific Unions 1960. —London and Colchester, Great Britain: Spottiswoode, Ballantyne & Co., Ltd., 1960

109 p.; 21.5 cm

HSMH（HS-N20F2-076）

3597 The Year Book of the International Council of Scientific Unions 1961. —London: The International Council of Scientific Unions, 1961

110 p.; 21.5 cm

HSMH（HS-N20F1-043）

附注：

印章：內封面頁鈐有"胡適的書"朱文方印。

3598 The Years That Were Fat: Peking, 1933–1940/by George N. Kates. —New York: Harper and Brothers Publishers, 1952

268 p.; 21.6 cm

HSMH（HS-N03F3-001）

附注：

印章：內封面頁鈐有"胡適的書"朱文方印。

3599 The Yellow Wind: An Excursion in and around Red China with a Traveler in the Yellow Wind/by William Stevenson. —Boston: Houghton Mifflin Company, 1959

xv, 424 p.; 22 cm

HSMH（HS-N03F2-028）

附注：

印章：內封面頁鈐有"胡適的書"朱文方印。

夾紙：書中夾有紐約市的 Womrath's Book Shop & Library 寄給胡適的信封地址殘片 1 張。

相關記載：館藏有評論此書的剪報一則："All Must Think as the Leaders

Think and Also Think for Themselves"（載 *The New York Times Book Review*, November 1, 1959），參見館藏號：HS-NK05-335-028。

3600 You and Psychiatry/by William C. Menninger and Munro Leaf. —New York：Charles Scribner's Sons, 1949

　　xi, 175 p.；20.8 cm

　　HSMH（HS-N19F4-036）

　　附註：

　　　印章：內封面頁鈐有"胡適的書"朱文方印。

　　　批注圈劃：書中有鉛筆批注劃綫數十處。

　　　摺頁：頁99有摺角。

3601 The Youth Movement in China/by Tsi C. Wang. —New York：New Republic Inc., 1928

　　xv, 245 p.；18.7 cm

　　HSMH（HS-N03F3-019）

　　附註：

　　　印章：扉頁有胡適簽名"Hu Shih June 1951"；內封面頁鈐有"胡適的書"朱文方印。

　　　批注圈劃：書中有胡適的劃綫數處。

　　　與胡適的關係：(1)內封面頁有胡適題籤："王際昌著 中國的青年運動。"(2)書中"The Literary Renaissance：The Vernacular press"與"The Literary Renaissance：The Literary Revolution"的內容均提及胡適。

　　　相關記載：1927年4月24日胡適致Mrs. Rublee函，建議其閱讀王際昌刊載在 *New Republic Press* 的文章"The Youth movement in China"，參見館藏號：HS-JDSHSE-0108-018。

　　　其他：封面有中文書名"新青年"。

3602 Zen Buddhism/by Christmas Humphreys. —Melbourne；London；Toronto：William Heinemann Ltd., 1949

　　xv, 241 p., plates；22 cm

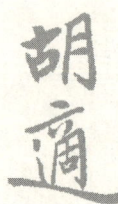

HSMH（HS-N06F1-010）

附注：

印章：內封面後一頁鈐有"胡適的書"朱文方印。

批注圈劃：書中有胡適的鉛筆注記與劃綫數處。

3603 Zen Buddhism：Selected Writings of D. T. Suzuki/edited by William Barrett. —Garden City, New York：Doubleday & Company, Inc., 1956

294 p.；18 cm

Doubleday Anchor books

HSMH（HS-N06F1-012）

附注：

印章：內封面頁鈐有"胡適的書"朱文方印。

題記：內封面頁有胡適題記："今天第二次買此書，還是看不下去！適之 一九五九，九，十。"

3604 Zen Buddhism and Psychoanalysis/by D. T. Suzuki, Erich Fromm, and Richard De Martino. —New York：Harper & Brothers, 1960

viii, 180 p.；22 cm

HSMH（HS-N06F1-011）

附注：

夾紙：內封面頁夾有"Boyd R. Compton"名片1張。

3605 Zen in the Art of Archery/by Eugen Herrigel；with an introduction by Daisetz Teitaro Suzuki. —New York：Pantheon Books, Inc., 1953

109 p.；21 cm

HSMH（HS-N03F4-003）

附注：

印章：內封面頁鈐有"胡適的書"朱文方印。

題記：扉頁粘貼似是贈書者的名片1張，印有"Mr. Charles B. Fahs Director for the Humanities The Rockefeller Foundation 49 West 49th Street New York 20"。

其他：作序者爲鈴木大拙。

3606 The Zen Teaching of Huang Po：On the Transmission of Mind/translated by John Blofeld. —New York：Grove Press, Inc., 1959

　　136 p.；20.4 cm

　　HSMH（HS-N03F4-011）

　　附注：

　　　　印章：扉頁有英文簽名"RMMcC."。

　　　　內附文件：扉頁夾有 1960 年 11 月 14 日美國新聞處（United States Information Service）處長 Richard M. McCarthy 致胡適函 1 張。

　　　　與胡適的關係：內容提及胡適。

期刊目錄

（一）北大圖書館館藏目録

8687 Harvard Journal of Asiatic Studies. —Cambridge, Mass. : Harvard-Yenching Institute

    April 1936: Vol. I, No. 1

    161p. ; 25.4cm

    PKUL（館藏號缺）

  附注：

    印章：封面有胡適鋼筆簽名"Hu Shih"。

8688 The Rotarian/by International Association of Rotary Clubs. —Chicago: International Association of Rotary Clubs

    October, 1948

    64p. ; 29.2cm

    PKUL（館藏號缺）

8689 Time/by Henry R. Luce. —New York: Time Inc.

    August 18; December 15, 1947

    40p. ; 27.8cm

    PKUL（館藏號缺）

8690 Chinese Affairs/by Kan-li Kiang. —Nanking: The International Relations Committee

    Vol. VI, No. 9

    193-216p. ; 29.8cm

    PKUL（館藏號缺）

8691 Botanical Bulletin of Academmia Sinica/by S. C. Tseng. —Shanghai: The Institute of Botany, Academia Sinica

Vol. I, No. 3

173-242p.；25.7cm

PKUL（館藏號缺）

附注：

印章：封面有胡適鋼筆簽名"胡適"。

8692　The Brooklyn Museum Quarterly/by William Henry Fox. —New York：The Brooklyn Musuem

Vol. XIII, No. 1

34p.；24.8cm

PKUL（館藏號缺）

8693　University of Iowa Studies in Character/by Edwin D. Starbuck. —Iowa：The University of Iowa

Vol. II, No. 3

63p.；23.3cm

A Comparative Study of Those Who Report the Experience of the Divine Presence and Those Who Do Not

PKUL（館藏號缺）

附注：

題記：封面有編者題記："To Doctor Hu Shih, with warm appreciation, Edwin D. Starbuck。"

夾紙：書內夾有英文書信一，電報一，日程表一，節目單一，電話記錄一。

8694　Far East Digest/by Institute of Pacific Relations. —New York：Institute of Pacific Relations

June 1947：No. 4

16, 4p.；22.9cm

PKUL（館藏號缺）

8695　Philobiblon：A Quarterly Review of Chinese Publications/by C. S.

Ch'ien. —Nanking: The National Central Library, China

March 1947: No. 4

48p. ; 26cm

PKUL（館藏號缺）

8696 Pacific Digest/编者不詳. —Kweilin: Pacific Digest

Vol. 11, No. 4

110p. ; 19.1cm

PKUL（館藏號缺）

8697 Readers Digest/by DeWitt Wallace. —New York: The Reader's Digest Association

1940: Vol. 37, No. 221

136p. ; 18.3cm

PKUL（館藏號缺）

8698 Journal of the North-China Branch of the Royal Asiatic Society. —Shanghai: A. H. de Carvalho

New Series No. VIII

XII, 187p. ; 21.4cm

PKUL（館藏號缺）

8699 L. R. B. & M. Journal. —[s.l.]: Lybrand, Ross Bros. & Montgomery

Vol. 25, No. 4

24p. ; 23.1cm

PKUL（館藏號缺）

附注：

題記：封面有胡適朱筆題記："See Page 9。"

夾紙：封面夾有卡片1張，上書"Dear Dr. Hu, I think you will be interested in C. H.'s article on page 9, and with hope to see you soon. Kindest regards, Eleann Montgomery"。

（二）胡適紀念館館藏目錄

3607 6500 Paperbound Books in Print/edited by Olga Svatik Weber. —New York：R. R. Bowker Company

Spring 1960：Vol. 5, No. 2

200 p.；21.5 cm

HSMH（HS-N19F1-024）

附註：

印章：內封面頁鈐有"胡適的書"朱文方印。

3608 Amerasia：A Review of America and the Far East/edited by Philip J. Jaffe. —New York：Amerasia, Inc.

July 1938：Vol. 2, No. 5

226-272 p.；22.8 cm

HSMH（HS-N20F1-077）

附註：

題記：封面有胡適題記："Hu Shih July 29, 1995— a gift from Mr. M. Faerber of the Paragon Book Gallery, 857 Lexington Ave, New York。"

批注圈劃：書中有胡適的劃綫數處。

與胡適的關係：頁243—247 收錄胡適的文章"The Westernization of China and Japan"。

相關記載：館藏有"The Westernization of China and Japan"抽印本及郭博信的譯文，參見館藏號：HS-NK05-199-022。

3609 American Journal：A Quarterly Review of Contemporary Thought/by Robert Frost, et al. —Manila：United States Information

June 1961：Vol. 1, No. 1

128 p.；25.5 cm

HSMH（HS-N20F1-034）

3610 American Journal: A Quarterly Review of Contemporary Thought / by George Russell Harrison, et al. —Manila: United States Information

September 1961: Vol. 1, No. 2

128 p. ; 25.5 cm

HSMH（HS-N20F1-033）

3611 The Asia Magazine/edited by Norman Soong. —Hong Kong: Asia Magazines, Ltd.

1961: Vol. 1, No. 1

22 p. ; 34 cm

HSMH（HS-N20F1-097）

附註：

相關記載：1961 年 Adrian Zech 致胡適 2 函，介紹及說明此刊，參見館藏號：HS-NK05-174-001, HS-NK05-174-002。

3612 Asiatic Research Bulletin/by Asiatic Research Center of Korea University. —Seoul, Korea: Korea University

January 1961: Vol. 3, No. 8

16 p. ; 26.5 cm

HSMH（HS-N19F5-001）

附註：

夾紙：頁 1 夾有 The Asiatic Research Center 的回函 1 張。

其他：(1)封面有中文刊名"亞細亞問題研究所月報"。(2)釘書針裝訂。

3613 The Atlantic. p. —Boston, Mass. : The Atlantic Monthly Co.

February 1959: Vol. 203, No. 2

113 p. ; 28 cm

HSMH（HS-N20F2-021）

3614 The Atlantic. —Boston, Mass. : The Atlantic Monthly Co.

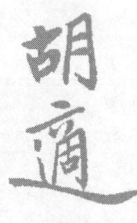

March 1959: Vol. 203, No. 3

110 p. ; 28cm

HSMH（HS-N20F2-022）

3615 The Atlantic. —Boston, Mass. : The Atlantic Monthly Co.

May 1959: Vol. 203, No. 5

107 p. ; 28 cm

HSMH（HS-N20F2-023）

3616 The Atlantic. —Boston, Mass. : The Atlantic Monthly Co.

June 1961: Vol. 207, No. 6

106 p. ; 28 cm

HSMH（HS-N20F2-024）

3617 The Atlantic. —Boston, Mass. : The Atlantic Monthly Co.

July 1961: Vol. 208, No. 1

132 p. ; 28 cm

HSMH（HS-N20F2-025）

3618 The Atlantic. —Boston, Mass. : The Atlantic Monthly Co.

August 1961: Vol. 208, No. 2

99 p. ; 28 cm

HSMH（HS-N20F2-026）

3619 The Atlantic. —Boston, Mass. : The Atlantic Monthly Co.

September 1961: Vol. 208, No. 3

104 p. ; 28 cm

HSMH（HS-N20F2-027）

3620 The Atlantic. —Boston, Mass. : The Atlantic Monthly Co.

October 1961: Vol. 208, No. 4

131 p.；28 cm

HSMH（HS-N20F2-028）

3621 Aux Éditions De La Baconnière Neuchatel（Suisse）. —Paris：Editions Albin Michel

Nouveautés 1960 & 1961

23 p.；21 cm

HSMH（HS-N20F2-075）

附注：

 印章：頁3鈐有"胡適的書"朱文方印。

 其他：法文書。

3622 Books on the Orient/prepared by Max Faerber. —New York：Paragon Book Gallery

Autumn 1960：Catalogue No. 30

192 p.；21.6 cm

HSMH（HS-N19F1-022）

附注：

 印章：館藏2冊，其中一冊目錄頁鈐有"胡適的書"朱文方印。

 夾紙：其中一冊（鈐有"胡適的書"朱文方印）的頁30、31間夾有 *Harem Favorites of an Illustrious Celestial*（by Howard S. Levy）一書的廣告單1張；另一冊（没有胡適鈐印）的頁34、35間夾有 *Harem Favorites of an Illustrious Celestial*（by Howard S. Levy）及 *Christian Missions and Oriental Civilizations*（by Maurice T. Price）的廣告單各1張。

 與胡適的關係：書中頁66第930條目錄列有 *Hu Shih and Lin Yu-tang*（《胡適與林語堂》）一書。

 其他：Max Faerber 中文名"馬松柏"。

3623 Books on the Orient/prepared by Max Faerber. —New York：Paragon Book Gallery

Autumn 1961：Catalogue No. 32

224 p.；21.6 cm

HSMH（HS-N19F1-023）

附注：

其他：Max Faerber 中文名"馬松柏"。

3624 Bulletin of the Chinese Association for the Advancement of Science/edited by Huan-Hsu Li. —Taipei, Taiwan："Chinese Association for the Advancement of Science（CAAS）"

August 1958：Vol. 6, No. 4

23 p.；26.5 cm

HSMH（HS-N20F2-016）

3625 Bulletin of the Institute of Chemistry, Academia Sinica/edited by the Institute of Chemistry, Academia Sinica. —Taipei, Taiwan：Institute of Chemistry, Academia Sinica

June 1961：No. 4

76 p.；23 cm

HSMH（HS-N20F2-010）

附注：

其他：中文刊名是"中央研究院化學研究所集刊"。

3626 Cahiers D'Histoire Mondiale Journal of World History Cuadernos de Historia Mundial/by Antonio Tovar, et al. —Neuchatel：Editions De La Baconniere-Neuchatel

1958：Vol. IV-2

291-496 p.；23.8 cm

HSMH（HS-N04F1-001）

附注：

印章：內封面頁鈐有"胡適的書"朱文方印。

夾紙：書中夾有書籍廣告單 1 張。

3627 Cahiers D'Histoire Mondiale Journal of World History Cuadernos de Historia Mundial/by Denis Sinor, et al. —Neuchatel：Editions De La Baconniere-Neuchatel

 1958：Vol. IV-3

 513-786 p.；23.8 cm

 HSMH（HS-N04F1-002）

 附注：

  印章：内封面頁鈐有"胡適的書"朱文方印。

  夾紙：扉頁夾有廣告單1張。

3628 Cahiers D'Histoire Mondiale Journal of World History Cuadernos de Historia Mundial/by D. G. Reder, et al. —Neuchatel：Editions De La Baconniere-Neuchatel

 1958：Vol. IV-4

 801-1036 p.；23.8 cm

 HSMH（HS-N04F1-003）

 附注：

  印章：内封面頁鈐有"胡適的書"朱文方印。

  夾紙：扉頁夾有"Errata"勘誤表1張，書中夾有 *Haiti：la terre, les hommes et les dieux* 的書訊1張。

3629 Cahiers D'Histoire Mondiale Journal of World History Cuadernos de Historia Mundial/by M. E. Masson, et al. —Neuchatel：Editions De La Baconniere-Neuchatel

 1959：Vol. V-1

 16-277 p.；23.8 cm

 HSMH（HS-N04F1-004）

 附注：

  印章：内封面頁鈐有"胡適的書"朱文方印。

3630 Cahiers D'Histoire Mondiale Journal of World History Cuadernos de Historia

Mundial/by A. G. Spirkin, et al. —Neuchatel：Editions De La Baconniere-Neuchatel

    1959：Vol. V-2

    293-511 p. ; 23.8 cm

    HSMH（HS-N04F1-005）

    附注：

        印章：內封面頁鈐有"胡適的書"朱文方印。

        夾紙：書中夾有訂購單1張及書目單1張。

3631 Cahiers D' Histoire Mondiale Journal of World History Cuadernos de Historia Mundial/by J. Polisensky, et al. —Neuchatel：Editions De La Baconniere-Neuchatel

    1960：Vol. VI-1

    15-198 p. ; 23.8 cm

    HSMH（HS-N04F1-006）

    附注：

        印章：內封面頁鈐有"胡適的書"朱文方印。

        夾紙：扉頁夾有書目單1張。

3632 Cahiers D' Histoire Mondiale Journal of World History Cuadernos de Historia Mundial/by R. C. Majumdar, et al. —Neuchatel：Editions De La Baconniere-Neuchatel

    1960：Vol. VI-2

    215-442 p. ; 23.8 cm

    HSMH（HS-N04F1-007）

    附注：

        印章：內封面頁鈐有"胡適的書"朱文方印。

        夾紙：扉頁夾有訂購單1張。

3633 CAP（Chinese American Progress）/edited by G. H. Wang. —Chicago：Chinese American Civic Council

October 1959：Vol. 9, No. 3

43 p.；21.5 cm

HSMH（HS-N20F2-073）

附注：

其他：中文刊名爲"中美會報"。頁 35—43 是中文内容。

3634 CAP（Chinese American Progress）/edited by G. H. Wang. —Chicago：Chinese American Civic Council

May 1961：Vol. 11, No. 2

47 p.；21.5 cm

HSMH（HS-N20F2-074）

附注：

其他：中文刊名爲"中美會報"。頁 34—47 是中文内容。

3635 The Catholic World/edited by John B. Sheerin. —Mahwah, New Jersey：The Paulist Fathers, 1960

August 1960：Vol. 191, No. 1145

262-324 p.；24 cm

HSMH（HS-N20F1-081）

附注：

印章：目次頁鈐有"胡適的書"朱文方印。

夾紙：頁 266、267 間有夾紙 1 張。

内附文件：封面内頁與目次頁之間夾有 1960 年 8 月 26 日薛光前致胡適函 1 頁，内容提及其"A New Program for the New Situation in Asia"一文刊載於此刊上（參見頁 301—307），故以此寄贈，參見館藏號：HS-NK05-135-005。

3636 China Post. —Taipei, Taiwan："China Post"

1960：April 29 Supplement

19 p.；38 cm

HSMH（HS-N20F1-109）

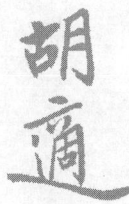

3637 China Post. —Taipei, Taiwan："China Post"

1960：July 4th Supplement

34 p.；38 cm

HSMH（HS-N20F1-107）

附注：

與胡適的關係：頁11有胡適照片1張,圖片說明："Dr. Hu Shih in a VOA interview。"

3638 China Post. —Taipei, Taiwan："China Post"

October 10, 1961

58 p.；38 cm

HSMH（HS-N20F1-108）

3639 China Post：Tourism magazine. —Taipei, Taiwan："China Post"

July 4, 1961

35 p.；38 cm

HSMH（HS-N20F1-098, HS-N20F1-110）

附注：

其他：館藏2冊。

3640 The China Post Sunday Supplement：The Asia Magazine/edited by Norman Soong. —Hong Kong：Asia Magazines, Ltd.

October 8, 1961

22 p.；34 cm

HSMH（HS-N20F1-111）

附注：

其他：中文刊名是"英文中國郵報星期增刊"。

3641 The China Post Sunday Supplement：The Asia Magazine/edited by Norman Soong. —Hong Kong：Asia Magazines, Ltd.

October 22, 1961

22 p. ; 34 cm

HSMH（HS-N20F1-112）

附注：

其他：中文刊名是"英文中國郵報星期增刊"。

3642 The China Post Sunday Supplement：The Asia Magazine/edited by Norman Soong. —Hong Kong：Asia Magazines, Ltd.

October 29, 1961

22 p. ; 34 cm

HSMH（HS-N20F1-113）

附注：

其他：中文刊名是"英文中國郵報星期增刊"。

3643 The China Post Sunday Supplement：The Asia Magazine/edited by Norman Soong. —Hong Kong：Asia Magazines, Ltd.

November 5, 1961

22 p. ; 34 cm

HSMH（HS-N20F1-114）

附注：

其他：中文刊名是"英文中國郵報星期增刊"。

3644 The China Post Sunday Supplement：The Asia Magazine/edited by Norman Soong. —Hong Kong：Asia Magazines, Ltd.

November 12, 1961

22 p. ; 34 cm

HSMH（HS-N20F1-115）

附注：

其他：中文刊名是"英文中國郵報星期增刊"。

3645 The China Post Sunday Supplement：The Asia Magazine/edited by Norman

　　Soong. —Hong Kong：Asia Magazines，Ltd.

　　November 19，1961

　　22 p.；34 cm

　　HSMH（HS-N20F1-116）

　　附注：

　　　　其他：中文刊名是"英文中國郵報星期增刊"。

3646　The China Post Sunday Supplement：The Asia Magazine/edited by Norman Soong. —Hong Kong：Asia Magazines，Ltd.

　　November 26，1961

　　22 p.；34 cm

　　HSMH（HS-N20F1-117）

　　附注：

　　　　其他：中文刊名是"英文中國郵報星期增刊"。

3647　The China Post Sunday Supplement：The Asia Magazine/edited by Norman Soong. —Hong Kong：Asia Magazines，Ltd.

　　December 24，1961

　　22 p.；34 cm

　　HSMH（HS-N20F1-118）

　　附注：

　　　　摺頁：頁18、20的左下均有摺角。

　　　　其他：中文刊名是"英文中國郵報星期增刊"。

3648　The China Post Sunday Supplement：The Asia Magazine/edited by Norman Soong. —Hong Kong：Asia Magazines，Ltd.

　　December 31，1961

　　22 p.；34 cm

　　HSMH（HS-N20F1-119）

　　附注：

　　　　其他：中文刊名是"英文中國郵報星期增刊"。

3649 The China Quarterly/edited by Roderick MacFarquhar. —London：The Congress for Cultural Freedom

　　July–September 1960：No. 3

　　128 p. ; 24 cm

　　HSMH（HS-N20F1-016）

　　附注：

　　　印章：頁1鈐有"胡適的書"朱文方印。

　　　夾紙：扉頁夾有"The China Quarterly"的空白訂購單1張。

3650 The China Quarterly/edited by Roderick MacFarquhar. —London：The Congress for Cultural Freedom

　　January–March 1961：No. 5

　　168 p. ; 24 cm

　　HSMH（HS-N20F1-017）

3651 China Today. —Taipei, Taiwan："The Institute of Chinese Culture"

　　April 1960：Vol. 3, No. 4

　　64 p. ; 25.9 cm

　　HSMH（HS-N19F1-025）

　　附注：

　　　其他：封面有中文刊名"英文今日中國月刊"。

3652 Chinese Culture = 中國文化. —Taipei, Taiwan："Chinese Cultural Research Institute"

　　April 1958：Vol. 1, No. 4

　　199 p. ; 26 cm

　　HSMH（HS-N20F1-042）

　　附注：

　　　印章：內封面頁鈐有"胡適的書"朱文方印。

　　　與胡適的關係：胡適是編輯之一。

3653 The Chinese Magazine/edited by Hengtse Tu（杜蘅之）. —Taipei, Taiwan："The Chinese Magazine"

　　June 1958：Vol. 2, No. 6

　　12 p.；26.5 cm

　　HSMH（HS-N20F2-002）

　　附注：

　　　與胡適的關係：（1）頁 1、2 的社論"Meet the Challenge of Retrogression"（《對抗復古主義》）提及《胡適與國運》一書攻擊胡適的事。（2）頁 4 的"Freedom for Creative Writing"（《創作自由》）提及胡適的話"在共黨統治下是没有創作自由的"，並及胡適對白話文學運動成功的看法、胡適的"争取學術獨立的十年計劃"以及胡適建議"光復大陸設計委員會"擴大對大陸問題的研究。（3）頁 8 的"Chronology：April 16 to May 15, 1958"（1958 年 4 月 16 日至 5 月 15 日大事記），刊載 4 月 19 日"胡適博士説臺灣民營報紙採取一致行動，反對政府修改出版法，是争取新聞自由的最負責，合理及合法的方法"。

　　　其他：中文刊名是"英文中國月報"。

3654 The Chinese Magazine/edited by Hengtse Tu. —Taipei, Taiwan："The Chinese Magazine"

　　August 1959：Vol. 3, No. 8

　　12 p.；26.5 cm

　　HSMH（HS-N20F2-003）

　　附注：

　　　批注圈劃：書中有劃綫數處。

　　　其他：中文刊名是"英文中國月報"。

3655 The Chinese Magazine/edited by Hengtse Tu. —Taipei, Taiwan："The Chinese Magazine"

　　September 1959：Vol. 3, No. 9

　　12 p.；26.5 cm

HSMH（HS-N20F2-004）

附注：

其他:中文刊名是"英文中國月報"。

3656　The Chinese Magazine/edited by Hengtse Tu. ——Taipei, Taiwan："The Chinese Magazine"

October 1959：Vol. 3, No. 10

12 p.；26.5 cm

HSMH（HS-N20F2-005）

附注：

夾紙:頁6、7間有夾紙1張。

其他:中文刊名是"英文中國月報"。

3657　The Chinese Magazine/edited by Hengtse Tu. ——Taipei, Taiwan："The Chinese Magazine"

February 1960：Vol. 4, No. 2

12 p.；26.5 cm

HSMH（HS-N20F2-006）

附注：

批注圈劃:書中有胡適的校改一處。

其他:中文刊名是"英文中國月報"。

3658　Columbia Law Review：Community Security vs. Man's Right to Knowledge/edited by William K. Jones. ——New York：Columbia University

May 1954：Vol. 54, No. 5

667-837 p.；25.4 cm

HSMH（HS-N19F5-021）

附注：

印章:廣告頁鈐有"胡適的書"朱文方印。

批注圈劃:頁784有胡適的校改一處。

夾紙:目次頁有夾紙1張。

與胡適的關係：頁 780—786 收錄胡適的文章"Communist Propaganda and the fall of China"。

3659 Columbia University Forum/edited by Erik Wensberg. —New York：Columbia University Central Records

 Fall 1961：Vol. 4，No. 4

 56 p. ; 28 cm

 HSMH（HS-N20F1-083）

 附注：

  題記：封底有鉛筆題記："China Found. Rm 704 1790 B'way NYC。"

  其他：封面右上角有"OCT 18 1961"戳印。

3660 Confluence：An International Forum/edited by Henry A. Kissinger. —Cambridge，Mass. : Harvard University

 March 1952：Vol. 1，No. 1

 76 p. ; 22.8 cm

 HSMH（HS-N03F6-015）

 附注：

  印章：內封面頁鈐有"胡適的書"朱文方印。

  內附文件：目次頁夾有 1952 年 Henry A. Kissinger 致胡適函 1 張。

3661 Congress News for Cultural Freedom. —Paris：Congress News for Cultural Freedom

 September–October 1960

 16 p. ; 30 cm

 HSMH（HS-N20F1-099）

3662 Congress News for Cultural Freedom. —Paris：Congress News for Cultural Freedom

 January 1961

 12 p. ; 30 cm

HSMH（HS-N20F1-100）

3663 The Current Digest of the Soviet Press/edited by Leo Gruliow. —Michigan：
The Joint Committee on Slavic Studies
1955：Vol. 7, No. 19
30 p.；28 cm
HSMH（HS-N19F2-044）
附注：
批注圈劃：頁10、11 有胡適的校改劃綫數處。
與胡適的關係：頁10、11 收錄"Hu Shih, Hu Feng and the Chinese intellectuals"一文。

3664 Dædalus：Journal of the American Academy of Arts and Sciences/edited by Gerald Holton. —Boston, Mass.：The American Academy of Arts and Sciences
Fall 1958：Vol. 87, No. 4
165 p.；23 cm
HSMH（HS-N04F1-008）
附注：
批注圈劃：書中有胡適的批注劃綫數處。
夾紙：目次頁夾有雜志简介1張。

3665 Dædalus：Journal of the American Academy of Arts and Sciences/edited by Gerald Holton. —Boston, Mass.：The American Academy of Arts and Sciences
Spring 1960：Vol. 89, No. 2
271-431 p.；22.8 cm
HSMH（HS-N04F1-009）
附注：
印章：内封面頁鈐有"胡適的書"朱文方印。

3666 Dædalus：Journal of the American Academy of Arts and Sciences/edited by Gerald Holton. —Boston, Mass.：The American Academy of Arts and Sciences

Summer 1960: Vol. 89, No. 3

438-670 p. ; 22.8 cm

HSMH（HS-N04F1-010）

附注：

批注圈劃：目次頁有劃勾一處。

夾紙：內封面頁有夾紙1張，上印記"With the Compliments of N. C. Nyi Chinese News Service"。

3667 Dædalus: Journal of the American Academy of Arts and Sciences/edited by Gerald Holton. —Boston, Mass. : The American Academy of Arts and Sciences

Fall 1960: Vol. 89, No. 4

674-1075 p. ; 22.8 cm

HSMH（HS-N04F1-011）

附注：

批注圈劃：書中有胡適的批注劃綫數十處。

3668 Dædalus: Journal of the American Academy of Arts and Sciences/edited by Gerald Holton. —Boston, Mass. : The American Academy of Arts and Sciences

Winter 1960: Vol. 89, No. 1

268 p. ; 23 cm

HSMH（HS-N04F1-012）

附注：

其他：本期卷號疑有誤，應為"Vol. 90"。

3669 Dædalus: Journal of the American Academy of Arts and Sciences/edited by Gerald Holton. —Boston, Mass. : The American Academy of Arts and Sciences

Spring 1961: Vol. 90, No. 2

220-401 p. ; 22.9 cm

HSMH（HS-N04F1-013）

附注：

印章：內封面頁鈐有"胡適的書"朱文方印。

3670 Encounter/edited by Stephen Spender and Melvin J. Lasky. —London：Encounter Ltd.

　　November 1960：Vol. 15, No. 5

　　88 p. ; 25.2 cm

　　HSMH（HS-N20F1-078）

3671 Encounter/edited by Stephen Spender and Melvin J. Lasky. —London：Encounter Ltd.

　　April 1961：Vol. 16, No. 4

　　88 p. ; 25.2 cm

　　HSMH（HS-N20F1-079）

　　附註：

　　　　夾紙：(1)頁8、9間夾有讀者回函1張。(2)頁18、19間夾有 Encounter 雜誌訂購單1張。

3672 Encounter/edited by Stephen Spender and Melvin J. Lasky. —London：Encounter Ltd.

　　June 1961：Vol. 16, No. 6

　　96 p. ; 25.2 cm

　　HSMH（HS-N20F1-080）

　　附註：

　　　　夾紙：(1)頁38、39間夾有 Encounter 雜誌訂購單1張。(2)頁46、47間夾有 Chamber's Encyclopedia 書訊1張。(3)頁54、55間夾有 Advisory Centre for Education（ACE）Limited 的簡介暨會員申請表1張。

3673 ETC：A Review of General Semantics/edited by S. I. Hayakawa. —Bloomington, Illinois：International Society for General Semantics

　　1959：Vol. 16, No. 4

　　389-512 p. ; 18.4 cm

　　HSMH（HS-N19F2-059）

附注：

印章：扉頁鈐有"胡適的書"朱文方印。

3674 Exide Topics and Storage Battery Power/edited by Arthur J. Hedges. —Philadelphia：The Electric Storage Battery Co.

Spring Edition-1961

16 p. ; 27.8 cm

HSMH（HS-N20F1-086）

3675 The Far Eastern Magazine/edited by Man-kuei Li. —New York：Chinese Students Association of America

June 1939；Vol. 2, No. 10

467-514 p. ; 22.8 cm

HSMH（HS-N19F2-037）

附注：

印章：頁467鈐有"胡適的書"朱文方印。

與胡適的關係：胡適是顧問編輯委員會（Advisory Editorial Board）成員之一。

3676 Foreign Affairs/by Council on Foreign Relations, Inc. —New York：Council on Foreign Relations, Inc.

October 1950；Vol. 29, No. 1

170 p. ; 26 cm

HSMH（HS-N19F5-050）

附注：

印章：封面有胡適簽名"Hu Shih"。

批注圈劃：書中有鉛筆打勾數處。

與胡適的關係：頁11—40收錄胡適的文章"China in Stalin's Grand Strategy"。

3677 Forum and Century：The Magazine of Controversy/edited by Henry Goddard

Leach. —New York: Forum Publishing Company, Inc.

February 1931: Vol. 85, No. 2

65-128, xl p.; 29.2 cm

HSMH（HS-N20F2-007）

附註：

與胡適的關係：（1）頁 iii—iv 的"Editorial Foreword"提及胡適。（2）頁 114—122 收錄胡適的文章"What I Believe"。

3678 Free China Review. —Taipei, Taiwan："Free China Review"

January 1958: Vol. 8, No. 1

58 p.; 25.8 cm

HSMH（HS-N20F2-030）

3679 Free China Review. —Taipei, Taiwan："Free China Review"

February 1958: Vol. 8, No. 2

50 p.; 25.8 cm

HSMH（HS-N20F2-031）

3680 Free China Review. —Taipei, Taiwan："Free China Review"

March 1958: Vol. 8, No. 3

56 p.; 25.8 cm

HSMH（HS-N20F2-032）

3681 Free China Review. —Taipei, Taiwan："Free China Review"

April 1958: Vol. 8, No. 4

68 p.; 25.8 cm

HSMH（HS-N20F2-033）

附註：

其他：Special Chinese Opera Number。

3682 Free China Review. —Taipei, Taiwan："Free China Review"

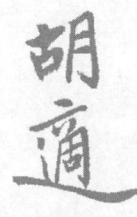

May 1958：Vol. 8, No. 5

58 p. ; 25.8 cm

HSMH（HS-N20F2-034）

3683 Free China Review. —Taipei, Taiwan："Free China Review"

June 1958：Vol. 8, No. 6

54 p. ; 25.8 cm

HSMH（HS-N20F2-035）

3684 Free China Review. —Taipei, Taiwan："Free China Review"

July 1958：Vol. 8, No. 7

60 p. ; 25.8 cm

HSMH（HS-N20F2-036）

3685 Free China Review. —Taipei, Taiwan："Free China Review"

August 1958：Vol. 8, No. 8

62 p. ; 25.8 cm

HSMH（HS-N20F2-037）

3686 Free China Review. —Taipei, Taiwan："Free China Review"

September 1958：Vol. 8, No. 9

58 p. ; 25.8 cm

HSMH（HS-N20F2-038）

3687 Free China Review. —Taipei, Taiwan："Free China Review"

October 1958：Vol. 8, No. 10

57 p. ; 25.8 cm

HSMH（HS-N20F2-039）

3688 Free China Review. —Taipei, Taiwan："Free China Review"

November 1958：Vol. 8, No. 11

62 p.；25.8 cm

HSMH（HS-N20F2-040）

3689 Free China Review/edited by I-cheng Loh. —Taipei, Taiwan："Free China Review"

March 1962：Vol. 12, No. 3

88 p.；25.8 cm

HSMH（HS-N20F1-082）

附注：

夾紙：頁84、85 間夾有"*Free China Review*"訂購單1張。

與胡適的關係：(1)封面人物爲胡適；頁7—14 刊有胡適的照片。(2)有多篇紀念胡適的文章：頁7—14 的"Hu Shih and His Times"；頁23—28 的"Hu Shih：Intellectual Rebel"；頁29—31 的"What Hu Shih Means To Me"（by Tingfu F. Tsiang,蔣廷黻）、"Enduring Impact on Chinese Thought"（by Mao Tse-shui,毛子水）；頁36—38 的"Blueprint for Science Education"（by Hsu Kao-yuan,徐高阮）；頁53、54 的"Chinese Press Opinion：Death of Dr. Hu Shih"；頁65—84 的"Documents—Selected Bibliography of Dr. Hu Shih's Writings"。(3)頁39—41 收錄胡適的演講"Social Changes and Science"。

相關記載：(1)館藏有胡適1961年11月6日在"亞東區科學教育會議"（The Four-nation Science Education Conference）開幕的演講"Social Changes and Science"資料,參見館藏號：HS-NK04-004-007。(2)紀念文章亦可參見胡適紀念館胡適檔案檢索系統。

其他：胡適先生過世後出版的期刊。館藏2冊。

3690 Harvard Journal of Asiatic Studies/edited by Serge Elisséeff. —Cambridge, Mass.：Harvard-Yenching Institute

June 1955：Vol. 18, Nos. 1 & 2

ix, 1-299 p., iv plates；25.4 cm

HSMH（HS-N19F2-002）

附注：

印章：致謝頁鈐有"胡適的書"朱文方印。

其他：編者中文名爲"葉理綏"。

3691 Harvard Journal of Asiatic Studies/edited by Serge Elisséeff. —Cambridge, Mass. : Harvard-Yenching Institute

December 1955：Vol. 18, Nos. 3 & 4

301–508 p. , 1 plate；25.4 cm

HSMH（HS-N19F2-003）

附注：

印章：頁 301 鈐有"胡適的書"朱文方印。

批注圈劃：頁 425、444 有胡適的紅筆劃綫及所打問號。

夾紙：頁 454、455 間夾有破損信封 1 張；封底夾有第 18 卷的總目次 1 份。

與胡適的關係：頁 454、455 的 Kenneth Ch'en 評 Daisetz Teitaro Suzuki, *Studies in Zen*，提及《胡適文存》三集、《胡適論學近著》。

其他：編者中文名爲"葉理綏"。

3692 The Humanist/edited by Gerald Wendt. —Buffalo, N. Y. : The American Humanist Association & the American Ethical Union

September–October 1959：Vol. 19, No. 5

259–320 p. ; 25.3 cm

HSMH（HS-N20F2-014）

附注：

夾紙：頁 296、297 間夾有此期刊的訂購單 1 張。

其他：頁 259—266 收錄杜威百年紀念文章"The Centennial of John Dewey"。

3693 International Conciliation/edited by Anne Winslow. —New York：Carnegie Endowment for International Peace

January 1959：No. 521

259–336 p. ; 19.8 cm

HSMH（HS-N20F2-071）

附注:

　　其他:本期編輯説明頁有"Presented United States Information Service Taipei 台北美國大使館新聞處敬贈"的藍色戳印。

3694　International Press Correspondence. —New York: American China Policy Association, Inc.

　　1928: Vol. 8, No. 88

　　1659-1676 p.; 27.9 cm

　　HSMH（HS-N19F5-020）

　　附注:

　　　批注圈劃:書中有劃綫一處。

　　　其他:（1）封面有"American China Policy Association, Inc. 1 West 37th Street New York 18, New York"紅色戳印。（2）釘書針裝訂。

3695　Journal Asiatique. —Paris: Société asiatique

　　1951: Vol. 239, No. 1

　　107 p.; 22.3 cm

　　HSMH（HS-N20F1-028）

　　附注:

　　　印章:頁1鈐有"胡適的書"朱文方印。

　　　題記:封面有贈刊者題贈:"To my revered teacher Dr. Hu Shih Richard J. DeMartino。"

　　　其他:法文期刊。

3696　Journal of Oriental Studies/edited by F. S. Drake. —Hong Kong: University of Hong Kong, 1961

　　1957&1958: Vol. 4, Nos. 1 & 2

　　477p.; 26.7 cm

　　HSMH（HS-N03F1-008）

　　附注:

　　　印章:内封面頁鈐有"胡適的書"朱文方印。

夾紙：頁44、45 間夾有卡片1 張。

其他：(1)封面有中文刊名"東方文化"。(2)刊內夾有2 本小冊子，一冊是"Institute of Oriental Studies, University of Hong Kong：Publications"簡介目錄；另一冊是"Hong Kong University Publications—Journals and Books 1953–1961"簡介目錄。

3697 Journal of the American Oriental Society/edited by Edward H. Schafer. — New Haven：American Oriental Society
July–September 1958：Vol. 78, No. 3
141–235 p. ; 25.6 cm
HSMH（HS-N19F2-004）

3698 Journal of the American Oriental Society/edited by Edward H. Schafer. — New Haven：American Oriental Society
October–December 1958：Vol. 78, No. 4
237–336 p. ; 25.6 cm
HSMH（HS-N19F2-005）
附注：
其他：刊末附有第78 卷的目錄、索引表。

3699 Journal of the American Oriental Society/edited by Edward H. Schafer. — New Haven：American Oriental Society
January–March 1959：Vol. 79, No. 1
1–72 p. , 1 plate; 25.6 cm
HSMH（HS-N19F2-006）
附注：
印章：封面有胡適簽名"Hu Shih"。

3700 Journal of the American Oriental Society/edited by Edward H. Schafer. — New Haven：American Oriental Society
July–September 1959：Vol. 79, No. 3

169-223 p.；25.8 cm

HSMH（HS-N19F2-007）

3701 Journal of the American Oriental Society/edited by Edward H. Schafer. — New Haven：American Oriental Society

October-December 1959：Vol. 79, No. 4

225-348 p.；25.7 cm

HSMH（HS-N19F2-008）

附注：

  其他：刊末附有第 79 卷的目錄、索引表。

3702 Journal of the North-China Branch of the Royal Asiatic Society for the Year 1929/edited by Arthur De C. Sowerby. —Shanghai：Kelly & Walsh, Limited

1929：Vol. 60

xix, 178 p.；24.1 cm

HSMH（HS-N19F5-052）

附注：

  批注圈劃：書中有胡適的劃綫數處。

  與胡適的關係：(1) 頁 20—41 刊載胡適的文章"The Establishment of Confucianism as a State Religion During the Han Dynasty"。(2) 胡適是 1929—1930 年的 Councilors 之一。(3) 頁 169 刊載 1929 年的會員名單，記胡適是在 1928 年獲選爲 North-China Branch of the Royal Asiatic Society 會員。

  相關記載：館藏有"The Establishment of Confucianism as a State Religion during the Han Dynasty"的抽印本，參見館藏號：HS-NK05-198-016。

3703 Life. —Chicago, Ill.：Time Inc.

1961：Vol. 51, No. 13

146 p.；35.8 cm

HSMH（HS- N20F1-120）

3704 Life International.—Chicago, Ill.：Time Inc.

1959：Vol. 26, No. 3

84 p.；35.8 cm

HSMH（HS-N20F1-121）

3705 The Lion/edited by J. R. K..—Mount Morris, Illinois：Lions International

October 1958：Vol. 41, No. 4

56 p.；28.2 cm

HSMH（HS-N20F1-085）

3706 The Mankind Quarterly/edited by R. Gayre.—Edinburgh, Scotland：The Mankind Quarterly

July 1960：Vol. 1, No. 1

1-72 p.；22 cm

HSMH（HS-N20F1-030）

附注：

印章：頁1鈐有"胡適的書"朱文方印。

夾紙：頁26、27間有夾紙1張；頁36、37間夾有本期簡介及訂購單1張。

3707 The Mankind Quarterly/edited by R. Gayre.—Edinburgh, Scotland：The Mankind Quarterly

October 1960：Vol. 1, No. 2

77-152 p.；22 cm

HSMH（HS-N20F1-031）

附注：

印章：頁77鈐有"胡適的書"朱文方印。

夾紙：頁86、87間夾有贈書單及訂購單各1張。

3708 Mark Twain Journal/edited by Cyril Clemens.—Missouri：The Mark Twain Journal

Summer 1960：Vol. 11, No. 2

25 p. ; 26.7 cm

HSMH（HS-N19F1-018）

附注：

 題記：封面有編者題贈："To the Academia Sinica Library with Editor's Cordial Greetings, Cyril Clemens。"

 相關記載：1960 年 3 月 21 日 Cyril Clemens 致胡適函，告知其被選爲 Xnight of Mark Twain。

3709 The Metropolitan Museum of Art Bulletin/edited by Marshall B. Davidson. — New York: The Metropolitan Museum of Art

 1953：Vol. 11, No. 8

 201-240 p. ; 25.5 cm

 HSMH（HS-N20F1-013）

附注：

 印章：頁 201 鈐有"胡適的書"朱文方印。

3710 The Museum Journal. —Philadelphia: The Museum of the University of Pennsylvania

 December 1926：Vol. 17, No. 4

 325-446 p. ; 25.4 cm

 HSMH（HS-N19F4-003）

附注：

 印章：封面與内封面頁均有胡適簽名"Hu Shih"；内封面頁鈐有"胡適的書"朱文方印。

3711 Museum News/edited by Erwin O. Christensen. —Washington: American Association of Museums

 Summer 1961：Vol. 39, No. 10

 48 p., illus. ; 27.8 cm

 HSMH（HS-N20F2-009）

3712 The New York Times (Advertisement). —New York: The New York Times Co.
　　May 8, 1960
　　15 p.；33 cm
　　HSMH（HS-N20F1-094）
　　附注：
　　　夾紙:封面夾有"Marvin Liebman"的名片1張。

3713 The New York Times (Advertisement). —New York: The New York Times Co.
　　June 24, 1961
　　15 p.；33 cm
　　HSMH（HS-N20F1-095）
　　附注：
　　　其他:此爲國際版。

3714 The New York Times (Advertisement). —New York: The New York Times Co.
　　November 6, 1961
　　15 p.；33 cm
　　HSMH（HS-N20F1-096）
　　附注：
　　　其他:此爲國際版。

3715 Newsweek: Civil War in the Congo? /edited by Osborn Elliott. —Tokyo, Japan: Newsweek Inc.
　　1961：Vol. 57, No. 9
　　60 p.；27 cm
　　HSMH（HS-N20F2-041）
　　附注：
　　　其他:太平洋版(Pacific Edition)。

3716 Newsweek/edited by Osborn Elliott. —Tokyo, Japan: Newsweek Inc.
　　1961：Vol. 58, No. 1

60 p. ; 27 cm

HSMH（HS-N20F2-042）

附注：

其他:太平洋版。

3717 Newsweek/edited by Osborn Elliott. —Tokyo, Japan: Newsweek Inc.

1961: Vol. 58, No. 2

64 p. ; 27 cm

HSMH（HS-N20F2-043）

附注：

其他:太平洋版。

3718 Newsweek: War over Berlin: The Brutal Question/edited by Osborn Elliott.
—Tokyo, Japan: Newsweek Inc.

1961: Vol. 58, No. 3

64 p. ; 27 cm

HSMH（HS-N20F2-044）

附注：

其他:太平洋版。

3719 Newsweek: A New Arms Race? /edited by Osborn Elliott. —Tokyo, Japan:
Newsweek Inc.

1961: Vol. 58, No. 4

68 p. ; 27 cm

HSMH（HS-N20F2-045）

附注：

其他:太平洋版。

3720 Newsweek: Escape to Freedom: Berlin's Refugees/edited by Osborn
Elliott. —Tokyo, Japan: Newsweek Inc.

1961: Vol. 58, No. 5

64 p. ; 27 cm

HSMH（HS-N20F2-046）

附注：

其他：太平洋版。

3721 Newsweek/edited by Osborn Elliott. —Tokyo, Japan：Newsweek Inc.

1961：Vol. 58, No. 6

60 p. ; 27 cm

HSMH（HS-N20F2-047）

附注：

其他：太平洋版。

3722 Newsweek/edited by Osborn Elliott. —Tokyo, Japan：Newsweek Inc.

1961：Vol. 58, No. 7

68 p. ; 27 cm

HSMH（HS-N20F2-048）

附注：

其他：太平洋版。

3723 Newsweek/edited by Osborn Elliott. —Tokyo, Japan：Newsweek Inc.

1961：Vol. 58, No. 8

72 p. ; 27 cm

HSMH（HS-N20F2-049）

附注：

其他：太平洋版。

3724 Newsweek/edited by Osborn Elliott. —Tokyo, Japan：Newsweek Inc.

1961：Vol. 58, No. 9

68 p. ; 27 cm

HSMH（HS-N20F2-050）

附注：

其他:太平洋版。

3725 Newsweek/edited by Osborn Elliott. —Tokyo, Japan: Newsweek Inc.

1961: Vol. 58, No. 10

64 p. ; 27 cm

HSMH(HS-N20F2-051)

附注:

其他:太平洋版。

3726 Newsweek/edited by Osborn Elliott. —Tokyo, Japan: Newsweek Inc.

1961: Vol. 58, No. 11

68 p. ; 27 cm

HSMH(HS-N20F2-052)

附注:

其他:太平洋版。

3727 Newsweek/edited by Osborn Elliott. —Tokyo, Japan: Newsweek Inc.

1961: Vol. 58, No. 12

76 p. ; 27 cm

HSMH(HS-N20F2-053)

附注:

其他:太平洋版。

3728 Newsweek/edited by Osborn Elliott. —Tokyo, Japan: Newsweek Inc.

1961: Vol. 58, No. 13

68 p. ; 27 cm

HSMH(HS-N20F2-054)

附注:

其他:太平洋版。

3729 Newsweek/edited by Osborn Elliott. —Tokyo, Japan: Newsweek Inc.

1961：Vol. 58，No. 14

64 p.；27 cm

HSMH（HS-N20F2-055）

附注：

其他：太平洋版。

3730 Newsweek/edited by Osborn Elliott. —Tokyo, Japan：Newsweek Inc.

1961：Vol. 58，No. 15

60 p.；27 cm

HSMH（HS-N20F2-056）

附注：

其他：太平洋版。

3731 Newsweek/edited by Osborn Elliott. —Tokyo, Japan：Newsweek Inc.

1961：Vol. 58，No. 16

68 p.；27 cm

HSMH（HS-N20F2-057）

附注：

其他：太平洋版。

3732 Newsweek/edited by Osborn Elliott. —Tokyo, Japan：Newsweek Inc.

1961：Vol. 58，No. 17

68 p.；27 cm

HSMH（HS-N20F2-058）

附注：

其他：太平洋版。

3733 Newsweek/edited by Osborn Elliott. —Tokyo, Japan：Newsweek Inc.

1961：Vol. 58，No. 18

88 p.；27 cm

HSMH（HS-N20F2-059）

附注：

其他：(1)太平洋版。(2)頁37周恩來的照片(Chou：He took exception)鈐有"匪"字藍文方印。

3734 Newsweek/edited by Osborn Elliott. —Tokyo, Japan：Newsweek Inc.

1961：Vol. 58, No. 19

68 p. ; 27 cm

HSMH（HS-N20F2-060）

附注：

其他：(1)太平洋版。(2)頁30周恩來的照片(China's Chou) 鈐有"匪"字藍文方印。

3735 Newsweek：New York, N. Y.：Can Anyone Run It? /edited by Osborn Elliott. —Tokyo, Japan：Newsweek Inc.

1961：Vol. 58, No. 20

72 p. ; 27 cm

HSMH（HS-N20F2-061）

附注：

其他：太平洋版。

3736 Newsweek/edited by Osborn Elliott. —Tokyo, Japan：Newsweek Inc.

1961：Vol. 58, No. 21

70 p. ; 27 cm

HSMH（HS-N20F2-062）

附注：

其他：太平洋版。

3737 Newsweek：Common Market at the Crossroads/edited by Osborn Elliott. —Tokyo, Japan：Newsweek Inc.

1961：Vol. 58, No. 22

76 p. ; 27 cm

HSMH（HS-N20F2-063）

附註：

批注圈劃：頁 32 有胡適的紅筆劃綫。

其他：太平洋版。

3738 Newsweek/edited by Osborn Elliott. —Tokyo, Japan：Newsweek Inc.

1961：Vol. 58, No. 23

72 p.；27 cm

HSMH（HS-N20F2-064）

附註：

其他：太平洋版。

3739 Newsweek：Those Washington Columnists/edited by Osborn Elliott. —Tokyo, Japan：Newsweek Inc.

1961：Vol. 58, No. 25

74 p.；27 cm

HSMH（HS-N20F2-065）

附註：

其他：太平洋版。

3740 Newsweek：Big Questions of '62/edited by Osborn Elliott. —Tokyo, Japan：Newsweek Inc.

1961：Vol. 58, No. 26

68 p.；27 cm

HSMH（HS-N20F2-066）

附註：

其他：太平洋版。

3741 Pennsylvania History/edited by Paul A. W. Wallace. —Gettysburg, Pennsylvania：The Pennsylvania Historical Association

October 1952：Vol. 19, No. 4

391-526, viii p. ; 23 cm

HSMH（HS-N04F1-014）

附注：

　　印章：內封面頁鈐有"胡適的書"朱文方印。

　　夾紙：書中夾有名片 1 張,印有"With Best Wishes of W. Reginald Wheeler 114 East 84th Street・New York 28, N. Y."。

3742 People's China/edited by Tsun-chi Liu. —Peking, China: The Foreign Languages Press

1955：No. 14

42 p. ; 26 cm

HSMH（HS-N19F1-026）

附注：

　　批注圈劃：頁 15 有胡適注記"何家槐"。

　　其他：頁 15—19 收錄何家槐（Ho Chia-huai）的"Exposure of the Hu Feng Counter-Revolutionary Clique"一文,亦參見館藏號：HS-US01-110-015。

3743 The Personalist: An International Review of Philosophy, Religion, and Literature/edited by Florence H. Smith. —Los Angeles: School of Philosophy, University of Southern California

Summer, July 1959：Vol. 40, No. 3

226-336 p. ; 26 cm

HSMH（HS-N20F1-032）

附注：

　　批注圈劃：書中有胡適的批注劃綫數處。

3744 Philosophy East and West: A Quarterly Journal of Oriental and Comparative Thought/edited by Charles A. Moore. —Honolulu, Hawaii: The University of Hawaii Press

April, July 1957：Vol. 7, Nos. 1 & 2

88 p. ; 25.5 cm

HSMH（HS-N20F1-038）

附注：

　　印章：目次頁鈐有"胡適的書"朱文方印。

　　與胡適的關係：胡適是顧問編輯（Advisory Editors）之一。

3745 Philosophy East and West：A Quarterly Journal of Oriental and Comparative Thought/edited by Charles A. Moore. —Honolulu, Hawaii：The University of Hawaii Press

　　October 1958, January 1959：Vol. 8, Nos. 3 & 4

　　99-186 p. ; 25.5 cm

　　HSMH（HS-N20F1-039）

　　附注：

　　　　題記：封面有胡適題記："April 14, 1960 寄出。May 22 到。"

　　　　與胡適的關係：胡適是顧問編輯之一。

3746 Philosophy East and West：A Quarterly Journal of Oriental and Comparative Thought/edited by Charles A. Moore. —Honolulu, Hawaii：The University of Hawaii Press

　　October 1960, January 1961：Vol. 10, Nos. 3 & 4

　　99-190 p. ; 25.3 cm

　　HSMH（HS-N20F1-040）

　　附注：

　　　　與胡適的關係：胡適是顧問編輯之一。

3747 Phronesis：A Journal for Ancient Philosophy/edited by D. J. Allan. —Assen, Netherlands：Royal VanGorcum Ltd.

　　1961：Vol. 6, No. 1

　　82 p. ; 23.8 cm

　　HSMH（HS-N20F2-012）

　　附注：

　　　　題記：頁53有陳忠寰（陳康）題贈："適之先生教正 後學陳康敬乞。"

批注圈劃：書中有胡適的校改一處。

其他：頁53—58 收錄陳忠寰(Chung-hwan Chen)文章。

3748 Princeton Alumni Weekly. —Princeton, New Jersey: Princeton University Press

1952: Vol. 52, No. 19

34 p. ; 27.8 cm

HSMH（HS-N19F1-027, HS-N20F2-078）

附注：

題記：館藏2冊，其中一冊封面有鉛筆注記："p. 9--"，正文前一頁亦有鉛筆注記："See P.9 #131。"

與胡適的關係：頁9、10 收錄胡適的文章"The Gest Oriental Library: The Eye Trouble of an Engineering Contractor Leads to a Rare Collection of 100,000 Volumes"，並有胡適與童世綱(Shih-kang Tung)的合照1張。

相關記載：館藏亦有"The Gest Oriental Library: The Eye Trouble of an Engineering Contractor Leads to a Rare Collection of 100,000 Volumes"抽印本，參見館藏號：HS-US01-041-021。

3749 The Princeton University Library Chronicle/edited by Alexander D. Wainwright.
—Princeton: The Princeton University Press

Spring 1954: Vol. 15, No. 3

113-167 p., plates; 24 cm

HSMH（HS-N19F2-029）

附注：

與胡適的關係：頁113—141 收錄胡適的文章"The Gest Oriental Library at Princeton University"；頁137 有胡適與童世綱的合照1張。

3750 The Princeton University Library Chronicle/edited by Alexander D. Wainwright.
—Princeton: Friends of the Princeton University Library

Autumn 1958: Vol. 20, No. 1

62 p. ; 24.1 cm

HSMH（HS-N20F1-018）

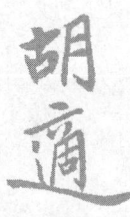

3751 The Princeton University Library Chronicle/edited by Alexander D. Wainwright.
　　—Princeton：Friends of the Princeton University Library
　　Winter 1959：Vol. 20，No. 2
　　63-126 p.，illus.；24.1 cm
　　HSMH（HS-N20F1-020）
　　附注：
　　　　與胡適的關係：頁118—122 的"An Important Addition to the Gest Library's Buddhist Collection"一文提及胡適。
　　　　其他：此期年份，疑將1958 誤植爲1959。

3752 The Princeton University Library Chronicle/edited by Alexander D. Wainwright.
　　—Princeton：Princeton University Library
　　Summer 1959：Vol. 20，No. 4
　　165-210 p.，illus.；24.1 cm
　　HSMH（HS-N19F2-025，HS-N20F1-019）
　　附注：
　　　　印章：本期有2 冊，其中一冊頁165 鈐有"胡適的書"朱文方印。
　　　　夾紙：其中一冊封面裏有夾紙1 張；兩冊封面裏均夾有第20 卷總目錄摺頁1 張。

3753 The Princeton University Library Chronicle/edited by Alexander D. Wainwright.
　　—Princeton：Princeton University Library
　　Summer 1960：Vol. 21，No. 4
　　187-257 p.，illus.；24.1 cm
　　HSMH（HS-N20F1-022）
　　附注：
　　　　夾紙：封面裏夾有第21 卷總目錄摺頁1 張。

3754 The Princeton University Library Chronicle/edited by Alexander D. Wainwright.
　　—Princeton：Princeton University Library

Autumn 1959 & Winter 1960：Vol. 21, Nos. 1 & 2

103 p., 16 plates；24.1 cm

HSMH（HS-N20F1-021）

附注：

其他：疑將 Winter 1959 誤植爲 Winter 1960。

3755 The Princeton University Library Chronicle/edited by Alexander D. Wainwright. —Princeton：Princeton University Library

Spring 1961：Vol. 22, No. 3

105-155 p.；24 cm

HSMH（HS-N20F2-019）

3756 Proceedings of the American Academy of Arts and Sciences：Records of the Academy 1957-1958.—Boston, Mass.：American Academy of Arts and Sciences

1958：Vol. 85, No. 4

248-362 p.；23 cm

HSMH（HS-N20F1-027）

附注：

與胡適的關係：頁 286 的 " Class III, Section 5—Administration and Affairs—11" 提及胡適。

3757 Proceedings of the American Philosophical Society：Benjamin Franklin, 1706-1956/edited by Luther P. Eisenhart. —Philadelphia：The American Philosophical Society

1956：Vol. 100, No. 4

283-416 p., illus., ports.；26.8 cm

HSMH（HS-N19F1-004）

3758 Proceedings of the American Philosophical Society/edited by Luther P. Eisenhart. —Philadelphia：The American Philosophical Society

1957：Vol. 101, No. 3

245-315 p. , illus. , tables；26.8 cm

HSMH（HS-N19F1-005）

附注：

　　印章：頁245鈐有"胡適的書"朱文方印。

3759 Proceedings of the American Philosophical Society/edited by Luther P. Eisenhart. —Philadelphia：The American Philosophical Society

1958：Vol. 102, No. 5

413-546 p. , illus. ；26.8 cm

HSMH（HS-N19F1-006）

附注：

　　印章：頁413鈐有"胡適的書"朱文方印。

　　批注圈劃：書中有批注勾劃數處。

3760 Proceedings of the American Philosophical Society：Studies of Historical Documents in the Library of the American Philosophical Society/edited by Luther P. Eisenhart. —Philadelphia：The American Philosophical Society

1958：Vol. 102, No. 6

547-623 p. , illus. , ports. ；26.8 cm

HSMH（HS-N19F1-007）

3761 Proceedings of the American Philosophical Society/edited by Luther P. Eisenhart. —Philadelphia：The American Philosophical Society

1959：Vol. 103, No. 1

1-158 p. , illus. , tables；26.8 cm

HSMH（HS-N19F1-008）

3762 Proceedings of the American Philosophical Society：Commemoration of the Centennial of the Publication of the Origin Species by Charles Darwin, Annual General Meeting, April, 1959/edited by Luther P. Eisenhart. —

Philadelphia: The American Philosophical Society

1959: Vol. 103, No. 2

159-319 p., illus., tables; 26.8 cm

HSMH (HS-N19F1-009)

3763 Proceedings of the American Philosophical Society/edited by William J. Robbins. —Philadelphia: The American Philosophical Society

1959: Vol. 103, No. 3

321-529 p., illus., tables; 26.8 cm

HSMH (HS-N19F1-010)

附注：

印章:頁321鈐有"胡適的書"朱文方印。

3764 Proceedings of the American Philosophical Society/edited by William J. Robbins. —Philadelphia: The American Philosophical Society

1959: Vol. 103, No. 4

531-608 p., illus.; 26.6 cm

HSMH (HS-N19F1-011)

3765 Proceedings of the American Philosophical Society/edited by William J. Robbins. —Philadelphia: The American Philosophical Society

1959: Vol. 103, No. 5

609-725 p., illus.; 26.7 cm

HSMH (HS-N19F1-012)

附注：

其他:封面粘貼地址變更啓事紙片1張。

3766 Proceedings of the American Philosophical Society: Studies of Historical Documents in the Library of the American Philosophical Society/edited by William J. Robbins. —Philadelphia: The American Philosophical Society

1959: Vol. 103, No. 6

727-821 p. , illus. ; 26.8 cm

HSMH（HS-N19F1-013）

附注：

夾紙：封面粘貼變更啓事紙片 1 張。

3767 Proceedings of the American Philosophical Society/edited by William J. Robbins. —Philadelphia：The American Philosophical Society

1960：Vol. 104, No. 1

1-112 p. , illus. ; 26.8 cm

HSMH（HS-N19F1-014）

3768 Proceedings of the American Philosophical Society/edited by William J. Robbins. —Philadelphia：The American Philosophical Society

1960：Vol. 104, No. 3

249-347 p. , illus. ; 26.7 cm

HSMH（HS-N19F1-015）

3769 Proceedings of the American Philosophical Society：Dedication of Library Hall of the American Philosophical Society, Autumn General Meeting, November, 1959/edited by William J. Robbins. —Philadelphia：The American Philosophical Society

1960：Vol. 104, No. 4

349-418 p. , illus. ; 26.8 cm

HSMH（HS-N19F1-016）

3770 Proceedings of the American Philosophical Society/edited by George W. Corner. —Philadelphia：The American Philosophical Society

1960：Vol. 104, No. 5

419-547 p. , illus. ; 26.7 cm

HSMH（HS-N19F1-017）

附注：

印章：頁419鈐有"胡適的書"朱文方印。

3771 Proceedings of the American Philosophical Society：The Influence of Science upon Modern Culture：Conference Commemorating the 400th Anniversary of the Birth of Francis Bacon/edited by George W. Corner. —Philadelphia：The American Philosophical Society

1961：Vol. 105, No. 5

459-512 p. ; 26.5 cm

HSMH（HS-N20F2-017）

3772 Proceedings of the American Philosophical Society：Studies on Benjamin Franklin, the Two Hundred and Fiftieth Anniversary of His Birth, January 17, 1956/edited by Luther P. Eisenhart. —Philadelphia：The American Philosophical Society

1955：Vol. 99, No. 6

359-476 p., illus., ports. ; 26.8 cm

HSMH（HS-N19F1-003）

附注：

印章：內封面頁鈐有"胡適的書"朱文方印。

3773 Quarterly Journal of the Taiwan Museum. —Taipei, Taiwan：The Taiwan Museum

June 1958：Vol. 11, Nos. 1 & 2

145 p., plates；26.3 cm

HSMH（HS-N20F1-035）

附注：

印章：目次頁鈐有"胡適的書"朱文方印。

夾紙：目次頁夾有此刊第10卷的總目次。

其他：中文封底，刊名為"臺灣省立博物館季刊"。

3774 Reader's Digest/edited by DeWitt Wallace and Lila Acheson Wallace. —

Pleasantville, N. Y. : The Reader's Digest Association, Inc.

October 1960: Vol. 77, No. 462

304 p. ; 18.8 cm

HSMH（HS-N20F2-069）

附注：

印章：廣告頁鈐有"胡適的書"朱文方印。

3775 Reader's Digest/edited by DeWitt Wallace and Lila Acheson Wallace. —Pleasantville, N. Y. : The Reader's Digest Association, Inc.

November 1961: Vol. 79, No. 475

336 p. ; 18.8 cm

HSMH（HS-N20F2-070）

附注：

摺頁：頁137右下有摺角，標題是"Communists From the Congo"。

3776 The Reporter: A Neutralized Middle East? /edited by Max Ascoli. —New York: The Reporter Magazine Company

1956: Vol. 15, No. 4

48 p. ; 28.8 cm

HSMH（HS-N19F1-028）

3777 Saturday Review. —New York: Saturday Review, Inc.

November 8, 1958

45-58 p. ; 27.8 cm

HSMH（HS-N20F1-103）

附注：

其他：特別推薦文章"A Visit to Red China's Hidden Capital of Science"，by J. Tuzo Wilson。

3778 Saturday Review: John Dewey Centennial. —New York: Saturday Review, Inc.

November 21, 1959

60 p. ; 27.8 cm

HSMH（HS-N20F1-102）

附注：

    批注圈劃：書中有胡適的紅筆批注劃綫數處。

    其他：此期爲杜威先生百年紀念專刊。

3779 Science and Freedom/edited by George Polanyi. —Manchester, England：The Committee on Science and Freedom

June 1960：No. 15

40 p. ; 23 cm

HSMH（HS-N19F2-031）

附注：

    夾紙：頁11夾有捐款單1張。

3780 Science and Freedom/edited by George Polanyi. —Manchester, England：The Committee on Science and Freedom

December 1960：No. 17

31 p. ; 22.7 cm

HSMH（HS-N20F2-018）

附注：

    夾紙：目次頁夾有地址變更紙條1張。

3781 Soviet Survey：A Quarterly Review of Cultural Trends/edited by Walter Z. Laqueur. —London：Congress for Cultural Freedom

January-March 1961：No. 35

119 p. ; 24.9 cm

HSMH（HS-N19F3-002）

3782 Taiwan/edited by King Ko. —Taipei, Taiwan：Taiwan Pictorial Society

November 1961

32 p.；28.7 cm

HSMH（HS-N20F1-084）

附注：

內附文件:頁5、6間夾有1961年11月25日臺灣省政府新聞處吳紹璲致胡適函。

其他:此爲"臺灣畫刊海外版"（"*Taiwan Pictorial English Edition*"）。

3783 TIME/edited by Henry R. Luce. ——New York：Time Inc.

1959：Vol. 73，No. 17

68 p.；28.4 cm

HSMH（HS-N20F1-052）

附注：

其他:此爲太平洋版。

3784 TIME/edited by Henry R. Luce. ——New York：Time Inc.

1961：Vol. 77，No. 27

64 p.；28.4 cm

HSMH（HS-N20F1-053）

附注：

其他:此爲亞洲版（Asia Edition）。

3785 TIME/edited by Henry R. Luce. ——New York：Time Inc.

1961：Vol. 78，No. 1

64 p.；28.4 cm

HSMH（HS-N20F1-054）

附注：

其他:此爲亞洲版。

3786 TIME/edited by Henry R. Luce. ——New York：Time Inc.

1961：Vol. 78，No. 2

74 p.；28.4 cm

HSMH（HS-N20F1-055）

附注：

其他：此爲亞洲版。

3787 TIME/edited by Henry R. Luce. —New York：Time Inc.

1961：Vol. 78, No. 3

60 p. ; 28.4 cm

HSMH（HS-N20F1-056）

附注：

其他：此爲亞洲版。

3788 TIME/edited by Henry R. Luce. —New York：Time Inc.

1961：Vol. 78, No. 4

68 p. ; 28.4 cm

HSMH（HS-N20F1-057）

附注：

其他：此爲亞洲版。

3789 TIME/edited by Henry R. Luce. —New York：Time Inc.

1961：Vol. 78, No. 5

64 p. ; 28.4 cm

HSMH（HS-N20F1-058）

附注：

其他：此爲亞洲版。

3790 TIME/edited by Henry R. Luce. —New York：Time Inc.

1961：Vol. 78, No. 6

68 p. ; 28.4 cm

HSMH（HS-N20F1-059）

附注：

其他：此爲亞洲版。

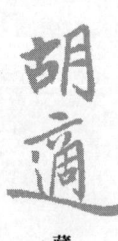

3791 TIME/edited by Henry R. Luce. —New York: Time Inc.

　　1961: Vol. 78, No. 7

　　68 p. ; 28.4 cm

　　HSMH（HS-N20F1-060）

　　附注：

　　　　其他:此爲亞洲版。

3792 TIME/edited by Henry R. Luce. —New York: Time Inc.

　　1961: Vol. 78, No. 8

　　72 p. ; 28.4 cm

　　HSMH（HS-N20F1-061）

　　附注：

　　　　其他:此爲亞洲版。

3793 TIME/edited by Henry R. Luce. —New York: Time Inc.

　　1961: Vol. 78, No. 9

　　64 p. ; 28.4 cm

　　HSMH（HS-N20F1-062）

　　附注：

　　　　批注圈劃:書中有胡適的劃綫數處。

　　　　其他:此爲亞洲版。

3794 TIME/edited by Henry R. Luce. —New York: Time Inc.

　　1961: Vol. 78, No. 10

　　68 p. ; 28.4 cm

　　HSMH（HS-N20F1-063）

　　附注：

　　　　其他:此爲亞洲版。

3795 TIME/edited by Henry R. Luce. —New York: Time Inc.

1961：Vol. 78, No. 11

72 p.；28.4 cm

HSMH（HS-N20F1-064）

附注：

　　摺頁：頁 23 右下有摺角。

　　其他：此爲亞洲版。

3796　TIME/edited by Henry R. Luce. —New York：Time Inc.

1961：Vol. 78, No. 12

80 p.；28.4 cm

HSMH（HS-N20F1-065）

附注：

　　其他：此為亞洲版。

3797　TIME/edited by Henry R. Luce. —New York：Time Inc.

1961：Vol. 78, No. 13

60 p.；28.4 cm

HSMH（HS-N20F1-066）

附注：

　　其他：此爲亞洲版。

3798　TIME/edited by Henry R. Luce. —New York：Time Inc.

1961：Vol. 78, No. 14

68 p.；28.4 cm

HSMH（HS-N20F1-067）

附注：

　　摺頁：頁 15—17 右下有摺角。

　　其他：此爲亞洲版。

3799　TIME/edited by Henry R. Luce. —New York：Time Inc.

1961：Vol. 78, No. 15

71 p.;28.4 cm

HSMH（HS-N20F1-068）

附注：

其他:此爲亞洲版。

3800 TIME/edited by Henry R. Luce. —New York：Time Inc.

1961：Vol. 78，No. 16

76 p.;28.4 cm

HSMH（HS-N20F1-069）

附注：

其他:此爲亞洲版。

3801 TIME/edited by Henry R. Luce. —New York：Time Inc.

1961：Vol. 78，No. 17

72 p.;28.4 cm

HSMH（HS-N20F1-070）

附注：

其他:此爲亞洲版。

3802 TIME/edited by Henry R. Luce. —New York：Time Inc.

1961：Vol. 78，No. 18

68 p.;28.4 cm

HSMH（HS-N20F1-071）

附注：

其他:此爲亞洲版。

3803 TIME/edited by Henry R. Luce. —New York：Time Inc.

1961：Vol. 78，No. 19

72 p.;28.4 cm

HSMH（HS-N20F1-072）

附注：

其他:此爲亞洲版。

3804 TIME/edited by Henry R. Luce. —New York: Time Inc.
  1961: Vol. 78, No. 20
  72 p.; 28.4 cm
  HSMH(HS-N20F1-073)
  附注:
    批注圈劃:書中有胡適的注記一處。
    其他:此爲亞洲版。

3805 TIME/edited by Henry R. Luce. —New York: Time Inc.
  1961: Vol. 78, No. 21
  76 p.; 28.4 cm
  HSMH(HS-N20F1-074)
  附注:
    其他:此爲亞洲版。

3806 TIME/edited by Henry R. Luce. —New York: Time Inc.
  1961: Vol. 78, No. 23
  72 p.; 28.4 cm
  HSMH(HS-N20F1-075)
  附注:
    其他:此爲亞洲版。

3807 TIME/edited by Henry R. Luce. —New York: Time Inc.
  1961: Vol. 78, No. 24
  74 p.; 28.4 cm
  HSMH(HS-N20F1-076)
  附注:
    其他:此爲亞洲版。

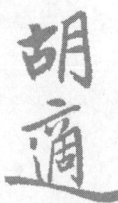

3808 U. S. News & World Report/edited by David Lawrence. —Washington D. C. : The United States News Pub.

January 19, 1951

56 p. ; 28.5 cm

HSMH（HS-N20F1-101）

附注：

題記：館藏2冊,其中一冊的封面有胡適題記："Hu Shih's Interview pp. 34-37";封底有鉛筆注記："Dr. Hu Shih 104-81-54。"

內附文件：其中一冊的頁34、35間夾有剪報一則：《胡適博士答問"主戰場在亞洲"》（"中央日報",1951年1月29日）。

與胡適的關係：頁34—37收錄胡適的訪談"Why the Main War Will be Fought in Asia—Not Europe：An Interview with Hu Shih";頁35有胡適照片1張。

3809 Unesco Features/by Pierre de Latil, et al. —Paris：United Nations Educational, Scientific and Cultural Organization

1958：Nos. 305,306

15 p. ; 27.5 cm

HSMH（HS-N19F5-002）

附注：

其他：封面有"Dr. Dan Saint-Rossy UNESCO Expert Chinese Ministry of Education 教育部 Taipei, Taiwan"藍色戳印。

3810 Unesco Features/by Pierre Vernier, et al. —Paris：United Nations Educational, Scientific and Cultural Organization

1958：Nos. 307,308

15 p. ; 27.5 cm

HSMH（HS-N19F5-003）

附注：

其他：封面有"Dr. Dan Saint-Rossy UNESCO Expert Chinese Ministry of Education 教育部 Taipei, Taiwan"藍色戳印。

3811 Unesco Features/by E. G. Schwimmer, et al. —Paris: United Nations Educational, Scientific and Cultural Organization

1958: No. 313

11 p.; 27.5 cm

HSMH (HS-N19F5-004)

附註:

其他:封面有"Dr. Dan Saint-Rossy UNESCO Expert Chinese Ministry of Education 教育部 Taipei, Taiwan"藍色戳印。

3812 World Affairs/edited by Margaret Allison Billings. —Washington, D. C.: American Peace Society

Winter 1958: Vol. 121, No. 4

99-132 p.; 28 cm

HSMH (HS-N20F1-104)

附註:

印章:目次頁鈐有"胡適的書"朱文方印。

夾紙:封面夾有 SKH(Stanley K. Hornbeck)贈書卡片 1 張。

3813 The Yale Review/edited Paul Pickrei. —New Haven: Yale University Press, 1951

Winter 1952: Vol. 41, No. 2

xxxii, 161-320 p.; 23.9 cm

HSMH (HS-N19F5-048)

附註:

印章:廣告頁鈐有"胡適的書"朱文方印。

題記:封面有贈者題贈:"For Dr. Hu。"

附　錄　一

1963年北京大學圖書館移交現國家圖書館胡適古籍、拓本目錄

　　按：胡適1948年底留在北平的藏書，後寄存北大圖書館。1957年，胡適在紐約立下遺囑，將"102箱書籍和書信文件集全部捐贈給北京大學"。1962年，當時的文化部決定將一部分善本古籍移交北京圖書館，也就是現在的國家圖書館，此事具體操作完成應該是在1963年。關於此事的討論文獻，主要有北大圖書館沈乃文教授的《關於〈岳飛傳〉與胡適藏書——没有實現鄧先生心願的兩件事》，臺灣東海大學陳以愛教授的《1960年代北大圖書館移交胡適藏書的曲折原委》兩篇文字。兩文關於當年移交的數量有很大的不同，沈乃文教授根據《北京圖書館選留胡適藏書清單》，認爲是105種，陳以愛教授根據2006年到國家圖書館和北大圖書館瞭解雙方相關檔案和藏書情況，推斷上述書單上的105種藏書，"1963年只由北大圖書館移交了10種（外加《四松堂集》兩種，合計12種）給北京圖書館，其餘都留存北大了"。我們後來調出北大檔案館所藏《北京圖書館1964年選留胡適藏書清單》，檢索北大圖書館"古文獻資源庫"，目前爲止查到確爲胡適所藏的圖書47種。考慮到北大圖書館尚有十餘萬冊未編綫裝書，以往新編綫裝書時有胡適藏書發現；以及此次檢索過程中發現清單所列書名與實際編目後的書名存在不一致的情況，在"古文獻資源庫"中的查找可能會因此有所遺漏等因素，我們認爲陳以愛教授的推斷更爲合理可信。

感謝陳以愛教授慷慨提供她當年調查這 12 種古籍、拓本的兩個文檔:《中國國家圖書館善本特藏部收藏的胡適藏書》、《2006 中國國家圖書館所見胡適藏書題跋》。我們依照本書綫裝書部分的著録體例,結合國家圖書館相關目録,整理成書目如下。索書號前收藏單位國家圖書館,用 NLC 指代。

1. 大般涅槃經四十卷（北涼）釋曇無讖譯 宋元間(960—1368)平江路磧沙延聖院刻大藏本

    1 冊

    NLC(18239)

2. 大智度論一百卷（後秦）釋鳩摩羅什譯 宋元間(960—1368)平江路磧沙延聖院刻大藏本

    2 冊

    NLC(18240)

3. 績溪縣志十二卷（明）陳嘉策修（明）何棠纂 明萬曆(1573—1620)刻本

    3 冊

    NLC(18234)

4. 高夢旦墓碑 胡適撰 民國二十六年(1937)拓本

    1 張

    NLC(索書號不詳)

5. 水經（漢）桑欽撰 明正德十三年(1518)盛燮刻本

    2 冊

    NLC(18236)

    附注:

      印章:兩冊扉頁均鈐有"沅叔持贈"印章;第 2 冊末鈐有胡適之印。

      題記:第 2 冊末有胡適題記:"盛燮寫刻楊慎校定《水經》三卷,傅沅叔先生贈送給我的。盛跋題正德戊寅(十三年,一五一八),在黃省曾刻本之前十六年。胡適,一九四七,五,十五。"

6. 水經考次（清）戴震撰 清鈔本

1冊

NLC（18235）

附注：

印章：目録末鈐有胡適之印章；頁33鈐有胡適印章。

題記：目録末有胡適題記："民國卅五年八月我才看見北京大學圖書館藏的李木齋舊藏的戴東原自定《水經》一卷。我在八月裏寫了兩篇文字，指出這稿本的重要。卅六年一月十夜周一良先生來看我，把他家叔弢先生收藏的一本東原自定《水經》一卷帶來給我研究。我今年才得空寫成兩篇文字，其中一篇是比較這兩個本子的。簡單説來，周本是從東原在乾隆三十年寫定本抄出的精抄本。李本的底子也是三十年本抄出的，後來又用硃筆加上了東原乾隆三十七年的修改本。例如周本河水第三行'河水冒以西南流'七字，李本全刪了；又'南出葱嶺山'，李本改'出'為'入'，山字下增'又從葱嶺出而東北流'九字。周本表示東原在乾隆三十年的見解，李本則是他在金華書院欲刻《水經注》時全部修改本，故與他後來自刻《水經注》最接近。其時他還没有見到《永樂大典》的《水經注》，故附考中渭水中篇的脱葉還只補得一百多字，穎水篇的錯簡也還有大錯的改訂。周本抄寫最精緻可愛。今年一良奉叔弢先生命，把這本子贈送給我，我寫此跋，敬記謝意。胡適，卅七、八、十二。"另頁33下有胡適的校記："這個周叔弢先生藏本也有特別勝處，李本所不及。如《水經》上欄的附録有兩種，一為酈注考訂經文者，一為東原自己的考訂，李本不加區別，周本于後者每條各有硃筆小圈。又自記上欄有注文二條，又增文二十一字，李本皆無。胡適又記。"

內附文件：扉頁貼有周一良手札：

上礼拜回天津，家父説那本戴東原《水經》的鈔本他没有什麼用。您既有興趣，便送給您留供參考吧。但他頗想知道那本和李木齋藏的關係如何，希望您能便中見示！

連日閲攷卷，恐怕要看到下礼拜，所以没工夫進城奉□。拙作讀完請寄下，或交羨林兄都可以。謝謝！敬祝

安好！　晚一良謹上　八月五日

書内另夾有胡適校記便條。

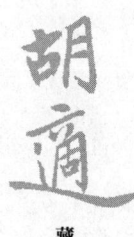

7. 水經注四十卷（北魏）酈道元撰 明嘉靖十三年（1534）黃省曾刻本

12 冊。

NLC（18231）

附注：

印章：第 1—10,12 冊首頁，《刻水經序》後頁，卷 40 末均鈐有胡適印章。

題記：《刻水經序》後頁有胡適的題記："民國三十六年三月，我在上海，來薰閣主人陳濟川先生把這部黃省曾刻本給我看。我托魏建功先生對他說明我買不起貴書。陳君說，'別人買，須出六十萬元；胡先生買，我只要三十萬'。所以我用膨脹的法幣三十萬元買了這部四百多年前的刻本。胡適，卅六，三，廿七夜。"

8. 水經注釋四十卷首一卷附錄二卷水經注箋刊誤十二卷（清）趙一清撰 清乾隆五十一年（1786）趙氏小山堂刻本

20 冊

NLC（18237）

附注：

印章：卷首有胡適印章。

題記：卷末有 1947-01-16 胡適的題記："民國卅六年一月得此本，定為趙東潛書刻本的最初刻本的初印本，毫無可疑。試舉一證：此本卷三十八葉二'故昭陵也'下趙注'洛陵漢表作洛陽'，與四庫本及吳騫家寫本及其他寫本相同。此第一刻本原狀也。海源閣藏刻本（今歸于我）與芝城大學北京大學藏刻本，此注'漢表'二字剜改作'一本'，此初次剜改本也。我藏的修改重刻本，此注改作'洛陵漢表作路陵'，此句以下又剜改了廿四個字。此二字大剜改本也。（參看卷一葉一上'山三成'句我的校記。）此本與王先謙所見本，及張壽榮父子所見本，完全相同。三十六年一月十六日，胡適記。"

9. 四松堂集不分卷雜誌一卷鷦鷯庵筆麈一卷（清）敦誠撰 稿本

6 冊

NLC（18229）

附注：

印章：扉頁鈐有胡適之印章；《鷦□庵筆塵》一卷，首頁鈐有胡適印章；《鷦□庵雜志》一卷，首頁鈐有胡適印章；書中鈐有"北大圖書館註銷圖書"章。

題記：扉頁有胡適題記："《四松堂集》四冊，《鷦□庵筆塵》一冊，《雜志》一冊，民國十一年四月買的，價叁拾圓。我訪求此書，已近一年，竟不能得。去年夏間在上海，我曾寫信去問楊鍾羲先生借此書，他回信說辛亥亂後失落了。今年四月十九日，松筠閣書店在一個旗人延某家尋着這一部稿本。我仔細翻看，見集中凡已刻的詩文，題上都有'刻'字的戳字；凡未收入刻本的，題上的都貼小紅箋。我就知道此本雖爲當日付刻的底本，但此本的内容多有爲刻本所未收的，故更可寶貴。即如第一冊《贈曹芹圃》一首，不但《熙朝雅頌集》、《雪橋詩話》都不曾收，我可以推測《四松堂集》刻本也不曾收。又如同冊《輓曹雪芹》一首，不但題上貼有紅箋而無'刻'字可證其爲刻本所不曾收，並且題下注'甲申'二字，貼有白箋，明是編者所删。此詩即便收入刻本而删此'甲申'二字，便減少多少考證的價值了。我的狂喜還不曾歇，忽然四月二十一日蔡元培先生向晚晴□遺詩社裏借來《四松堂集》的刻本五卷，計卷一，詩一百三十七首；卷二，詩一百四十四首；卷三，文三十四首；卷四，六十九首；卷五，《筆塵》八十一則。卷首止刻紀昀一序，和敦敏的小傳；凡此本不曾打'刻'字戳字的，果然都不曾收入。三日之中，刻本與稿本一齊到我手裏，豈非大奇！況且世間只有此一個底本，居然到我手裏，這也是我近年表章曹雪芹的一點苦心的很大酬報了。今天買成此書。我先已把書中的重要材料都考證過了，本無出重價買此書的必要；但書店的人爲我訪求此書，功勞不少，故讓他賺幾個錢去。十一，四，二五，胡適。"另《鷦□庵雜志》卷末有胡適題記："今天重翻這部《四松堂集》，覺得敬亭的遊記同筆記都還可讀。胡適，卅七，六，廿八。"

批注圈劃：書中多處有胡適的年份注記及校記。

與胡適的關係：《鷦□庵筆塵》一卷，封面爲胡適的題字；《鷦□庵雜志》一卷，封面爲胡適的題字。

10. 四松堂集（清）敦誠撰 清刻本

1 冊

NLC（索書號不詳）

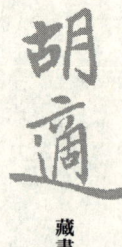

11. 章實齋手劄不分卷 （清）章學誠撰 稿本

　　1 冊

　　NLC（18242）

12. 中華民國華北軍第七軍團第五十九軍抗日戰死將士公墓碑 胡適撰 錢玄同書 劉明堂刻 民國二十二年（1933）拓本

　　1 張

　　NLC（索書號不詳）

附 錄 二

胡適贈給北大圖書館圖書目録

　　按:此處收録胡適贈給北大圖書館的圖書6種,其中綫裝書2種,普通書4種,分別按照各類書的著録體例著録。

1. 墨子經説解二卷 (周)墨翟撰 (清)張惠言述 清宣統元年(1909)上海國學保存會影印本

　　1函1册;18厘米

　　PKUL(X/111.1312/1150/C4)

　　附注:

　　　題記:書衣有胡適題記:"今天我出城就医,正值神州國光社大减价之期,此書每部只售一角二分大洋,故我買了幾部同來,把一部送給北京大學圖書館。胡適。九,十一,廿六。"

2. 文木山房集四卷 (清)吴敬梓撰 民國二十年(1931)上海亞東圖書館刻本

　　1函2册;16.7厘米

　　PKUL(X/811.07/2644)

　　附注:

題記：書衣有題記："此書係胡適之先生贈與北京大學圖書館。二十，九，四。"

3. **胡思永的遺詩**/胡思永著. ——上海：亞東圖書館，1924

6，14，123，14 頁；18.1 厘米

PKUL（811.2/4763）

附注：

題記：扉頁有胡適題記："送給北大圖書館，胡適贈。"

4. **西遊記考證**/胡適著. ——出版地不詳：出版者不詳，出版年不詳

64 頁；18.3 厘米

PKUL（813.384/2616a）

附注：

題記：封面有胡適題記："敬贈北京大學圖書館，胡適。"

5. **哲學的改造**/杜威著；胡適，唐擘黃譯. ——上海：商務印書館，1934

1，1，3，201 頁；21.1 厘米

PKUL（126.7/2743）

附注：

題記：扉頁有題記："胡適之先生贈。"

6. **The Chinese Renaissance: The Haskell Lectures, 1933**/by Hu Shih. —Chicago: The University of Chicago Press, 1934

XI, 110p.；21.8cm

PKUL（O/323.51/H85）

附注：

題記：扉頁有胡適題記："送給北大圖書館，胡適，一九三四，七，十。"

索 引

編輯説明

一、本索引爲著者索引。中文部分按照漢語拼音順序排列，日文部分按照日文五十音圖順序排列，西文部分按照英文字母順序排列。

二、本索引詞條基本照録正文著者項。僅對西文作者確定爲同一作者而縮寫、全稱不同者進行合併，合併後采用全稱形式。

三、中文著者中涉及同一單位而表述不同者，如"國立北京大學"、"北京大學"、"北大"等，依據正文相關内容編排，不統一合併。

四、同一中文著者，在不同著作中有不同寫法，如"譚介甫"、"譚戒甫"等，依據正文相關内容編排，不統一合併。

五、同一中文著者的名、字、號、室名、別名、避諱改字等不同稱謂，如"章學誠"、"章實齋"等，依據正文相關内容編排，不統一合併。

六、同一日本著者，表述有不同者，如"今関天彭"、"今關天彭"等，依據正文相關内容編排，不統一合併。

七、外國著者的不同譯名，如"斯大林"、"斯塔林"等，依據正文相關内容編排，不統一合併。

一、著者索引中文部分

A

阿諦思 / 598

阿格 / 466

阿英 / 10（2），33，243，244，247，373，390，411，477

哀利斯 / 231

埃爾巴德 / 278

靄理斯 / 4，47，141，223

靄沈都夫 / 162

艾迪 / 393，566

艾倫 / 855

艾儒略 / 1117，1162

艾山 / 803

艾思奇 / 718，830

艾香德 / 2921

艾約瑟 / 1549

愛德華 / 94

愛絲女士 / 104

愛停頓 / 462

愛新覺羅·焕明 / 901

安岡正篤 / 2085

安和 / 1325（2）

安徽叢書編審會 / 1103（2）

安徽省立圖書館 / 5

安井衡 / 1234

安樂山樵 / 1671

安納 / 403

安藤文英 / 2077

安文溥 / 210

安志敏 / 461

奧斯丁 / 180

奧斯基 / 1805

B

巴德 / 203

巴金 / 410，472

白滁洲 / 20，114，115

白居易 / 576，577，1622

白駒 / 826

白鳥庫吉 / 65，764

白壽彝 / 44，351，457，538，559（2）

白胤昌 / 1461

白雲霽 / 1168

白占友 / 249，535

白志謙 / 49

柏烈偉 / 249

拜倫 / 968

拜蘋女士 / 36

班固 / 300，1106

班玆 / 436

坂本安吉 / 2114

半軒主人 / 1220

半月論壇編輯委員會／1902

包資／232

包世傑／87

包司／94

包遵彭／140,515,1074

保爾巴西／22

保羅梵樂希／1525

寶存我／562

抱恨生／198

抱經堂書局／1822

鮑彪／487,1024

鮑鰲人／553

鮑明鈴／387,484

鮑士鎏／1033

鮑照／580

北大學生會三十五週年紀念籌備會出版委員會／15

北大研究所國學門歌謠研究會／1925(2)

北大醫療隊／338

北京大學國學季刊編輯委員會／1927(2),1928(3),1929(3),1930(4)

北京大學歷史系／1055(2)

北京大學民國九年畢業同學會／122

北京大學農學院中國農村經濟研究所／2068

北京大學潛社／343

北京大學圖書館／581

北京大學文科研究所／815

北京大學文學研究所／939(2)

北京大學研究所國學門／1903(4),1904(3),1905(2),1906(4),1907(3)

北京大學研究所國學門歌謠研究會／1888(2)

北京大學哲學會／492

北京大學中國語文學系／14(2),581

北京述學社／1933

北京述學社編輯部／1933(2),1934(4),1935

北平北海圖書館編目科／136

北平方濟堂聖經學會／499

北平故宮博物院／16,1334

北平國立第一助産學校編輯委員會／1901

北平市政府／19

北平市政府社會局／117

北平市政府統計處／1886

北平市政府統計室／18,1886

北平協和醫院／19

北浦藤郎／584

北社／435

貝爾德／806

貝爾納斯／247

貝瓊／845

倍根／431

本村泰賢／1693

本間立也／2060

本田成之／518

畢慶昌／974

畢沅／981,1147,1406(3)

畢雲程／254

"邊疆政教制度研究會"／843

邊壽民／1592

邊孫／282

卞之琳／314(2)

遍照金剛／395

彬敬齋／498

濱田耕作／107

波多野重太郎／2065,2068,2085

伯格森／39

伯杭／1578

伯希和／497

伯英／291

柏拉圖／777
博洽德／197
卜凱／526

布那柯夫／5
布渥爾／279
步月主人／1706

C

財政部甘末爾設計委員會／544
財政部公債司／486
蔡觀明／28
蔡金重／289
蔡謙／194
蔡清／1125
蔡上翔／1587,1856
蔡尚思／210
蔡沈／1038,1510
蔡升元／1420
蔡世遠／1195
蔡樞衡／506
蔡斯／563
蔡松筠／565
蔡雪村／521
蔡邕／586,1124,1181
蔡有鷖／1124
蔡元培／490,943,1007,1049
蔡雲／1124
蔡運辰／1832
蔡楨／1153
蔡正中／187
參與國際聯合會調查委員會中國代表處／544
參與國聯東案調查委員會中國代表處／30(2)
曹葆華／170,226,241
曹本榮／1706
曹秉仁／825
曹誠英／448

曹端／1128
曹冠／1672
曹國鋒／675
曹經沅／1241(2)
曹聚仁／135
曹丕／1173
曹紹濂／753
曹師式／826
曹廷杰／1179
曹未風／13,316(5),317(4)
曹雪芹／593,672,707,711,712(3),838,1036,1771(2),1785,1792,1793,1819,1875
曹耀湘／1407
曹寅／1274,1355
曹穎甫／1126
曹禺／214
曹元忠／1350
曹載奎／1281
曹霑／1267(2),1715,1741
岑學呂／976(2)
岑仲勉／90(2),661
查浦曼／185
柴田鍊三郎／736
昌彼得／908
昌德／403
長善／1763
長澤規矩也／2111
常風／212,285

常乃悳 / 328,531,550

常盤大定 / 2070,2071,2116

常璩 / 728(2),1276

常燕生 / 121,313,864,865,866,871,940,951

晁補之 / 738

晁公武 / 1878

晁説之 / 1405

車垓 / 1516

車若水 / 1304

辰伯 / 224

陈嘉策 / 3002

陳阿平 / 1134

陳百藥 / 371

陳邦泰 / 1635,1636

陳寶泉 / 250

陳豹隱 / 439

陳壁 / 1590

陳彬龢 / 313,523(2)

陳璸 / 592

陳柄德 / 1320

陳伯陶 / 1331,1487,1542

陳伯莊 / 425,858(2),2010(2),2011

陳布雷 / 811

陳長蘅 / 1425

陳琛 / 1766

陳承澤 / 135

陳誠 / 6,573,913

陳澄之 / 455

陳鏦 / 1383

陳達 / 296

陳大齊 / 250,340,460,491

陳大猷 / 1510

陳大章 / 1490

陳岱孫 / 383

陳德榮 / 441

陳登原 / 143,190,351

陳第 / 1388,1809,1826,1835

陳鼎 / 1701

陳定山 / 1862

陳東原 / 497,507,514,519

陳獨秀 / 69(2),591

陳鐸 / 1345,1447

陳凡 / 836

陳方之 / 393

陳澧 / 1179,1759,1781,1782

陳傅良 / 1037,1134

陳高林 / 14

陳庚仝 / 1617

陳功甫 / 306,459

陳恭禄 / 304,485,516

陳顧遠 / 507

陳光垚 / 172,251,257,408,429

陳國符 / 631

陳果夫 / 61,76,148,166,217,393,402,428,456,463,513(2)

陳寒光 / 225

陳翰笙 / 87,148

陳沆 / 869

陳豪 / 1175

陳鎬基 / 346

陳澔 / 1349

陳和銑 / 29,131,345

陳鶴琴 / 393

陳恒壽 / 970

陳衡恪 / 1747

陳衡哲 / 435

陳鴻璧 / 472

陳瑚 / 1454(2)

陳夬 / 1490
陳暉 / 530
陳紀瀅 / 827,868
陳繼儒 / 387,1134
陳家瓚 / 385
陳嘉謨 / 1590
陳建 / 1417,1658(2),1745
陳建民 / 97,465
陳健夫 / 686
陳介白 / 976
陳介祺 / 1212(2)
陳瑾昆 / 253(3),440(2)
陳藎民 / 84
陳荊和 / 871
陳克疇 / 726
陳揆 / 1291
陳蘭瑞 / 1232
陳朗 / 1662
陳樂素 / 359
陳立夫 / 332,391
陳櫟 / 1133,1510
陳璉 / 1437
陳亮 / 789,1368,1369
陳烈 / 81
陳琳 / 1134
陳履 / 1657
陳茂源 / 854
陳懋烈 / 570
陳眉公 / 10
陳夢家 / 107,248(3),382,438,567,1001
陳綿 / 5,416
陳銘珪 / 1130,1210,1350
陳乃乾 / 475,1414,1450,1505,1773,1935(3)
陳槃 / 41,74,101(2),102,488,601,956,
1770(2)
陳培根 / 726
陳培源 / 368
陳彭年 / 683,1237
陳聘之 / 189,500
陳溥 / 1102
陳其志 / 1299
陳啓天 / 73,121,143
陳啓雲 / 784
陳樵 / 1374
陳青之 / 514
陳清華 / 198
陳清泉 / 560
陳去病 / 1258
陳銓 / 94
陳人重 / 1249
陳榮捷 / 2858
陳瑞祺 / 54
陳三立 / 1471
陳善 / 1391(2)
陳石孚 / 1900
陳實 / 1165
陳士珂 / 1338
陳士元 / 810,1300,1377,1394,1399,1647
陳氏尺蠖齋 / 1639
陳世崇 / 1554(2)
陳世鎔 / 1187
陳世熙 / 1564
陳世驤 / 1805
陳世箴 / 1397
陳受頤 / 261
陳壽 / 859,860
陳壽卿 / 69
陳壽僧 / 433

陳壽嵩／1468
陳述／3
陳漱琴／334
陳樹桓／757
陳樹人／487
陳所聞／1635,1636
陳田／1403
陳田夫／1415
陳鐵凡／646,1783
陳廷瑤／346
陳廷耿／182
陳廷傑／1493
陳萬里／108,256,259,287,413
陳維崧／592
陳文達／660,913,914
陳文述／1115,1165
陳文緯／1791
陳文燭／1195
陳熙晉／1460
陳錫康／489
陳錫璋／899
陳習庭／352
陳獻章／1106
陳祥春／23
陳小蝶／60
陳孝威／164
陳嘯江／52
陳修堂／1452
陳洵／1250
陳巖肖／1219
陳衍／912,1499
陳倚興／156
陳益／562
陳翊林／489

陳寅恪／800,902(2),919,1011
陳應燿／576
陳應莊／1473
陳誤／861
陳映璜／297
陳永齡／451
陳用光／1561,1616(2)
陳有豐／302
陳禹謨／1562
陳與義／1023
陳裕菁／283
陳淵／1815
陳元德／511
陳元龍／1219
陳垣／43,269,289,341,383(2),404(2),
468,473,475,476,823,873,1022,1045,1189,
1404,1440,1484,1500,1710,1749,1784
陳允／240
陳增榮／358
陳鱣／1298
陳占甲／496
陳振孫／1741
陳正謨／402
陳正祥／907
陳之邁／448
陳埴／1430
陳植／484
陳志豪／689
陳鐘凡／1511
陳仲濤／268
陳洙／1200
陳柱／290,1815
陳著／1115
陳瑑／1531

3015

陳倬 / 1335
陳子昂 / 591
陳子楷 / 1765
陳子展 / 516
陳宗蕃 / 450,1590
陳遵嫣 / 254
陳作樑 / 66
陳作霖 / 1242,1243
諶克終 / 140
成都各界救國聯合會 / 34
成仿吾 / 55
成瓘 / 1293
成玄英 / 1168
承齡 / 1162
程本 / 1884
程秉釗 / 1447
程大城 / 999
程大中 / 1538
程端禮 / 593,1135,1774
程瀚章 / 99
程顥 / 1193(2)
程會昌 / 71,325
程際盛 / 1752
程嘉燧 / 1541
程晉芳 / 1395
程霖生 / 1505
程敏政 / 732
程樹德 / 200(2),1255
程天放 / 807,1033
程鉄華 / 164
程廷祚 / 1438(3),1825
程偉元 / 1771(2),1785,1792,1793
程硯秋 / 35

程艷秋 / 1339
程頤 / 997(2),1193(2)
程瀛章 / 405
程振甲 / 1408
冲霄漢閣主 / 11
重光葵 / 855
崇文書局 / 1738
廚川白村 / 222
褚鳳儀 / 384
褚人穫 / 1297,1539(2)
儲安平 / 1889
儲光羲 / 1146
儲仁 / 478
儲嗣宗 / 1146
儲皖峰 / 533,1146(2),1570
川島 / 470
川口長孺 / 907,914
創元社辞典編集部 / 2102
春飛 / 247
春雨樓 / 731
崔豹 / 1223
崔東壁 / 45
崔敬伯 / 489,502(2)
崔榮秀 / 533
崔寔 / 1536
崔適 / 1501
崔述 / 45,585,659(2),765(2),923,955,1085,1087,1122,1155(2),1182,1205,1225,1321,1335(3),1378,1394,1465(2),1474,1568,1605,1606,1619,1685,1759(2)
崔曉岑 / 555
崔致遠 / 685
寸草 / 289

D

達爾波／62
達鑑三／819
達尼爾·笛福／230
大阪每日新聞社／2074,2095
大村西崖／523(2),1747,1786
大島五郎／2122(3)
大道弘雄／2084
大東書局編審處／92
大公報社／423
大華晚報社／913
大陸雜誌編輯委員會／1909(3),1910(3),1911(4),1912(4),1913(3),1914(3),1915(4),1916
大陸雜誌社／607
大同大學數理研究會／151
大窪行／1848
大衛·埃文／840
大西齋／2093
大學生活編輯委員會／1916
大野法道／1473
大隱翁／1328
大仲馬／954,980
戴表元／991,1670
戴德／607
戴德發／1851
戴楫／1657
戴季陶／366,563
戴濟／67
戴堅／25
戴良／761,1327,1328
戴璐／1128,1571
戴名世／629,1799

戴望／989,1233,1667,1668,1735(3)
戴渭清／138
戴錫章／1613
戴銑／1882
戴雪／467
戴嶽／522
戴震／51(2),629,850,978,1147,1166(2),1167,1486,1517,1778(2),1811,1839,3003
丹羽正義／2097
但燾／1787
但丁／973
但明倫／1805
澹慧居士／1206
島木赤彦／2096
道安法師／1066
道端良秀／2105
道字總社／54
德禄／219
鄧邦述／1420
鄧傳安／778
鄧高鏡／1405,1408
鄧廣銘／171,361,431,479
鄧嘉純／1336
鄧嘉縝／1446
鄧啓／257
鄧嗣禹／371
鄧廷楨／1517(2)
鄧文儀／1006
鄧析／56,632,1170,1779
鄧熙／860
鄧之誠／268,545,861,1228,1585
狄亞／81

狄雲鼎／1228
荻岸散人／1638
荻原雲來／2095
笛卡兒／83
第·博雅／164
第一屆"國民大會代表全國聯誼會"／633
第一綫雜誌社編輯委員會／1887
殿春生／1403
刁包／838,1430
刁敏謙／511
丁寶書／1717
丁賓／1370
丁伯恆／202
丁傳靖／1515
丁春膏／495
丁福保／850,1208,1529,1570
丁格蘭／529(2)
丁念先／843,1812(2)
丁謙／1421
丁芮樸／1203
丁山／220,469,565,1529
丁紹儀／639
丁聲樹／237,349
丁韙良／1572,1708
丁文江／444,445,783
丁燮林／93
丁緒賢／160(2)
丁彥臣／1390
丁晏／1114,1134,1145,1390
丁以此／1389
丁卓／881
丁作韶／1888
定生／499
東北社／64

東北問題研究會／66,134,201,303,304,506
東北物資調節委員會／64
東北物資調節委員會研究組／190,274,276, 354,419,499,564
東璧山房主人／1641
東方圖書館復興委員會／65
東方文化學院京都研究所／2106
東方文化研究所／2121
東方問題研究會／369
東方學會／2123(2),2124
東方與西方雜誌社／1887
東方雜誌社／346
東海學報編輯委員會／1917(2)
東京帝室博物館／2098
東京日日新聞社／2074,2095
東京市役所／2082
東南大學南京高師國學研究會／137
東亞病夫／90,232,278
東亞同文書院／2079
東亞語學研究會／2061
東洋文庫／2106
東陽無疑／1428
董德芳／303
董鼎／1509
董誥／841,1434
董解元／640,950,1180
董金榜／1557
董康／1509,1549
董孟汾／1662
董其昌／1180
董說／952,1180,1860
董思靖／917
董天工／906
董同龢／665

董威／1659
董文／545
董洗凡／168
董暘／1365
董兆熊／1412
董之學／436
董仲篯／180
董仲舒／600,1149(3),1181
董遵／1459(3)
董作賓／171,741,933,964,965,966,1022,1634,1870
竇克勤／1349
都穆／1575
獨立評論社／1917
獨逸窩退士／1630
讀書雜誌社／1918(2),1919(6),1920(6)
堵允錫／1188
杜長之／487
杜呈祥／768
杜聰明／910
杜大爲／182
杜而未／1047
杜甫／657,1188,1819
杜綱／1114,1411
杜光庭／1235
杜光塤／959
杜蘅之／2958

杜俊東／197,367
杜濬／1117
杜聯喆／1023
杜魯門／246
杜牧／652
杜若／929
杜威／252,262,1029,1095,3008
杜亞泉／298,331
杜預／41,582,601
杜增瑞／297
杜旃／1421
杜佐周／185
渡邊格司／2067
渡邊秀方／2069
渡部溫／636
端木埰／1116
段朝端／1601,1733
段成己／1194
段成式／470,1006
段克己／1194
段玉裁／887,1151,1166,1226,1323(2),1388,1528,1752
段仔文／1137
敦誠／1847,3004,3005
敦煌文獻研究聯絡委員會／2107
敦敏／1809

E

鄂爾泰／1759
鄂裕綿／193
恩格斯／565,669
恩澤／1320

兒島獻吉郎／560,1059
爾㮈／138
二十五史刊行委員會／78(2),79,648(2)

F

筏提摩多 / 1507

法國新聞處 / 80

法式善 / 1280, 1443

帆足理一郎 / 2083

樊弘 / 60, 98, 282, 326(2), 420

樊明茂 / 120

樊兆庚 / 386

樊仲雲 / 344

樊宗師 / 1302

范成大 / 872, 1496

范耕研 / 264

范浚 / 1622

范鍇 / 1198, 1275

范寧同 / 582

范梈 / 652

范錡 / 492

范鄅鼎 / 1235

范欽 / 755

范攄 / 1019

范望 / 915

范文瀾 / 294, 398(2)

范希曾 / 746

范咸 / 597

范祥雍 / 802

范祥雲 / 512

范辛來 / 1290

范揚 / 170, 442

范曄 / 1270(2)

范寅 / 1719

范祖述 / 1257

范祖禹 / 1564

方柏容 / 245

方苞 / 653

方賓觀 / 527

方昌翰 / 1580

方潮聲 / 134

方大鎮 / 1419(3)

方東樹 / 1105, 1683, 1790

方鳳 / 1156, 1608, 1678

方光燾 / 398

方豪 / 83, 242, 992, 1791, 1855

方湖 / 1900

方濟堂聖經學會 / 867, 1040

方繼仁 / 811

方俊 / 31

方濬師 / 1303, 1581, 1582

方孔炤 / 1144, 1211(2), 1451, 1611, 1741, 1742

方瀾 / 1199

方霖 / 804

方若 / 1798

方勺 / 1119, 1438

方樞 / 1546

方甦生 / 1443

方瑋德 / 62

方文正 / 221

方顯廷 / 379, 380, 1892

方孝孺 / 986, 1663

方學漸 / 1179, 1647, 1697

方以智 / 1290, 1578, 1607, 1617, 1624, 1856

方毅 / 10, 357, 605

方勇 / 42

方玉潤／870,1492
方張登／1146
方正瑗／1199(2),1231
方中履／1254
方壯猷／46,65,348
方宗誠／1110
房玄齡／680,754,755,1233,1318
房兆楹／1023
費爾樸／452
費賴之／857
費密／1265,1282,1671
費孝通／37
廢名／264
廢止內戰大同盟總會／317
奮鬥日報／402
封溎川／242
封演／659,1202
馮百川／482
馮辰／1347
馮承鈞／75,140,219(2),412,414(3),439,468,474,497,525,560,607,627,650,661,759,814,818,857,1012,1032,1054
馮從吾／1206
馮登府／1496
馮恩榮／293
馮國瑞／1733
馮家昇／71,165
馮金伯／1405
馮夢龍／674,749,759,1472,1786
馮乃超／399
馮雄／345
馮友蘭／434,476,477(2),542(2),559,1067
馮沅君／41,103(2),186,202,271,528,534,1060

馮雲濠／1547
馮澤芳／448
馮贊／1723
馮作民／1052
奉寬／252,1824
奉天商工公會／2094
鳳岡及門弟子／315(2)
佛教研究會／2121
佛書刊行會／2081,2082
佛陀多羅／1776
敷之／82
弗蘭柔／178
伏爾佛遜／24
伏勝／1477(2),1478
伏無忌／1209
服部孝／1825
服部宇之吉／2058
服虔／1577
符定一／782
符樹勳／40
福爾區／422
福格／928
福建省研究院／90
福建省研究院社會科學研究所／90
福井康順／2105,2106
福開森／1354
福康安藏／927
福田德三／2063,2095
福田千代／2094
福原隆成／2065
輔仁大學輔仁學誌編輯會／1922,1923(3),1924(3),1925
傅東華／22,91,135,806
傅汎際／1398(3)

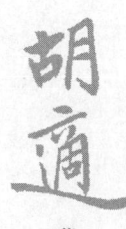

傅霖 / 1155,1644
傅孟真先生遺著編輯委員會 / 664
傅佩青 / 429,557
傅勤家 / 764
傅山 / 1303,1515
傅斯年 / 21,48,64,177,237,432,456,1646
傅統先 / 512
傅惜華 / 812,813,1012

傅習 / 732
傅熊湘 / 1191
傅以漸 / 1706
傅寅 / 1704
傅沅叔 / 470
傅芸子 / 8
傅增湘 / 1127(3),1516,1542
富察明義 / 1807

G

干寶 / 1549,1550,1637
甘師禹 / 472
甘熙 / 1107
岡島冠山 / 2082,2083
岡實 / 2096
岡田家武 / 2072
岡野一朗 / 2096
鋼和泰 / 47,463
高拜石 / 673
高本漢 / 145,539,571
高步瀛 / 921
高島平三郎 / 2096
高道素 / 1411
高等考試典試委員會 / 253
高鶚 / 1771(2),1785,1792,1793
高方 / 469
高拱 / 583
高亨 / 774,818,1764
高犖 / 1401
高覺敷 / 76
高瀨武次郎 / 2096,2097
高良佐 / 410
高魯 / 424

高夢旦 / 338
高名凱 / 145
高明 / 1134,1290
高楠順次郎 / 627,649,1778,2080(5),2081(4)
高攀龍 / 1217,1218
高平子 / 1065
高岐 / 1785
高啟 / 665,1215(2)
高橋健 / 2084
高橋昇造 / 2078
高橋吾良 / 2093
高山 / 368
高士奇 / 1300
高叔康 / 757
高似孫 / 1671
高天成 / 654
高田儀光 / 2078
高田真治 / 2065
高魏 / 1214
高希聖 / 563
高孝本 / 1295
高亞偉 / 454,876
高陽 / 727

高一涵 / 279,496,525,541	龔開 / 1238
高蔭祖 / 1072	龔明之 / 1880
高誘 / 729,793(2),991,1278(3),1279,1729	龔慶宣 / 1364
高毓華 / 1756	龔翃 / 1221
高元 / 94	龔學遂 / 541
高正臣 / 1216	龔鉞 / 211
高仲武 / 1077	龔自珍 / 100,637,1174
高崟 / 1177	共田浩 / 2093
戈公振 / 502	苟宗道 / 1654
哥德 / 839	孤獨及 / 831
歌德 / 55	辜懷 / 463
歌底斯英 / 986	古柏遜 / 119
葛秉仁 / 340	古川喜九郎 / 2074
葛長庚 / 1249	古狂生 / 1768
葛定華 / 342,411	古朗士 / 953
葛洪 / 579,1481(2)	古楳 / 309
葛雷德 / 430	古物保管委員會 / 107
葛又華 / 425	古應芬 / 255
葛祖蘭 / 305,307,565	古澤廣樹 / 2077
庚桑楚 / 1787	谷春帆 / 461,462
耿定向 / 1220	谷萬川 / 48
耿文光 / 1551	谷鍾秀 / 547
工商部工商訪問局 / 509	故宮博物院 / 1191
公孫龍 / 1779	故宮博物院圖書館掌故部 / 1734
公孫嬿 / 697	故宮博物院文獻館 / 1140,1485(2),1877
公田連太郎 / 1190(2),1647	顧藹吉 / 1354
宮內省圖書寮 / 2078,2083	顧炳 / 1786
宮原虎 / 35	顧敦鍒 / 215
恭阿拉 / 1436	顧觀光 / 1276,1287,1328(2),1366,1475, 1483,1553,1604,1607,1751,1794
龔橙 / 1490	顧廣圻 / 728
龔鼎臣 / 1179	顧季高 / 197
龔紱 / 1221	
龔古愚 / 2877	顧頡剛 / 45(2),93,101,103,105(2),106, 250,252,321,325,333,336,342,351,356,
龔景瀚 / 1345	

3023

364,390,406,437,488,556,560,571,606,878,890,1899
顧藎丞／937
顧康樂／101,199
顧琅／528
顧柟／439
顧謙吉／300
顧青海／412
顧實／144
顧樞／1229
顧隨／1282,1339,1363,1593,1604
顧太清／1574
顧廷龍／944,1224,1811
顧睎元／1433
顧憲成／1167,1177(2),1229,1248,1320,1323,1415,1459,1629,1703,1740,1744,1766
顧湘／1628
顧燮光／1262
顧修／1288
顧炎武／382,814,872,927,1013,1129,1229(2),1314,1327,1332,1461,1472,1497(2),1573,1576(3),1724(2),1769,1855
顧野王／1009
顧一樵／196,401,412,479(2),700
顧翊羣／775
顧有孝／1403
顧與沐／1229
顧毓琇／96,307,344,519
顧雲臣／580
顧允成／1625
顧貞觀／1229
顧震福／769
顧之義／1530
顧祖禹／1184

官道尊／1610
關漢卿／1014,1782
關琪桐／7,26,34,56,431,493
關稅特別會議／1231
關文瑛／1578
關野貞／2070,2071
關一／97
關源吉／2112
觀禮堂／1232
管公度／942
管庭芬／1544
管仲／1233
貫酸齋／1863
灌園耐得翁／1181
"光復大陸設計研究委員會"／593(3),780(2),1922(2),2000
"光復大陸設計研究委員會"秘書處／671,672(2),680,681
光明甫／173
光明日報編輯所／888,889(2)
廣東建設廳蠶絲改良局／113
廣東建設廳順德縣蠶業改良實施區總區／113
廣東省堤工委員會秘書室／113
廣瀨熹六／2075
廣西省立醫學院／113
廣西省通志館第一組／1889
廣西省政府秘書處編譯室／114
廣西統計局／103
廣智報局／1234
廣州市牙科學術進修班／116
歸玄恭／117
歸有光／1032
歸莊／1305
鬼谷子／1779

桂馥／1583
桂裕／654
貴泰修／1103,1104
貴州省政府統計室／117
郭靄春／990
郭昇／1789
郭伯恭／166,357,468
郭步陶／694
郭達德／320(2)
郭大力／197
郭德坤／416
郭鼎堂／417
郭鈇／1495
郭輝／855
郭沫若／55,220,224,421,1316
郭璞／862(2),1410,1472
郭其炳／1402
郭紹儀／58
郭紹虞／377,395,532(2)
郭壽華／299
郭嗣汾／795
郭廷以／916
郭希仁／424
郭顯德／1487
郭象／1090,1138,1411,1763
郭孝先／323
郭休／1679
郭翼／1360
郭有守／78,402
郭玉堂／1428
郭元鎬／1615
郭湛波／24,194
郭志嵩／801
郭智石／282

郭忠恕／1420
郭鐘岳／1260(2)
郭子雄／454,503
"國防部"情報局／1922
國防部史政局／58(2),118(2),306
國防研究院編譯組／218,277
國防月刊社／1889
國風社／27,28(3)
"國魂編輯委員會"／1926
國際聯合會／119
國際聯盟秘書處／96
國際文化振興會／300
國立北京大學／581
國立北京大學教務處／122
國立北京大學課業處／123
國立北京大學南京同學會／122
國立北京大學史學會／1900
國立北京大學史學社／1895
國立北京大學臺灣同學會／947
國立北京大學研究所國學門／1902(3)
國立北京大學研究院文史部／1140,1202,1265
國立北平故宮博物院／1246
國立北平故宮博物院文獻館／124,272,397
國立北平師範大學圖書館／125(6),126(5)
國立北平圖書館／127(2),1356
國立北平圖書館館刊編輯委員會／1890
國立北平圖書館索引組／289,381
國立北平圖書館圖書季刊編輯部／1897
國立北平研究院／127
國立北平研究院總辦事處／127
國立編譯館／37(2),128,160,183,451
"國立故宮博物院"／1785
國立故宮博物院文獻館編輯會／397

"國立故宮中央博物館"聯合管理處／677
"國立故宮中央博物院"／1789
"國立故宮中央博物院"聯合管理處／677
國立湖北師範學院史地學系／1894
國立南洋大學南洋文化事業部／497
國立清華大學農業研究所蟲害組病害組／129
國立清華大學清華學報編輯部／1893
國立清華大學土木工程系／318
國立山東大學勵學社／1893
國立上海商學院出版組／1890
國立社會教育學院／129
國立西北大學／130
國立西北大學出版組／1890
國立西南聯合大學南京校友會／222
"國立政治大學出版委員會"／1932(2), 1933
國立中山大學廣西猺山採集隊／28
國立中山大學圖書館／1246
國立中山大學研究院文科研究所歷史學部／1891
國立中山大學語言歷史學研究所／255
"國立中央博物院"／1785
國立中央大學商學院圖書館／130
"國立中央圖書館"／690, 691(4), 753, 908, 1071(3)
國立中央圖書館／1891
"國立中央研究院"傅故所長紀念會籌備委員會／692
國立中央研究院歷史語言研究所／342, 847, 1401(3), 1416(2), 1440, 1816
國立中央研究院歷史語言研究所集刊編輯委員會／693
國立中央研究院天文研究所／1246
"國民參政會史料編纂委員會"／693
國民大會代表立法院立法委員選舉總事務所／132
"國民大會"秘書處／605, 633, 694, 960, 1005, 1073(2)
國民大會秘書處／61, 131, 132(4), 133, 256, 378
國民新聞社／135
國民政府法制局／485
國民政府立法院編譯處／96
國木田獨步／864
國史館／1246
國史研究會／2108
果戈理／387

H

哈代／162
哈爾／562
哈爾司特／85
哈佛燕京學社引得編纂處／225, 239, 311, 557, 606
海本／1458
海潮音編委會／1936
海瑞／1250(2)
海天出版社／983
"海外出版社"／960
海外留學咨詢委員會／227
"海外論壇編輯委員會"／1937
邗上蒙人／1204
韓邦奇／1716
韓邦慶／699(2)
韓非／56

韓靜齋／39
韓亮儼／196
韓祿卿／1540
韓儒林／384
韓信／1254
韓嬰／1253(2)
韓愈／1085,1252
韓組康／448
漢白納／299
杭立武／502
杭世駿／1169(2),1256,1257,1271,1318,1462,1497,1498,1598,1653,1655,1760
杭州市參議會秘書處／146
郝經／1258,1654
郝敬／1150,1389,1477,1685
郝立權／1372,1484
郝懿辰／1133
郝懿行／862,1471,1472(2),1739
郝浴／704
合信／1452
何炳松／383,435,493
何炳賢／1893
何焯／1259,1687,1688
何春蓀／368
何德明／443
何福同／802
何浩若／812
何會源／99
何基／1259,1310
何健／1104
何健民／649
何潔／1403
何進善／1388
何廉／522

何林華／467
何其鞏／71
何錡章／862
何去非／1259
何容森／182
何士驥／495,1221
何棠／3002
何天行／39,416,599
何蓮／1152(3)
何文煥／1353
何心／883
何休／600
何煜／1415
何兆瀛／1631
何肇菁／82
何植三／275
何兹全／65
何作霖／112
河北省教育廳／146
河東碧梧桐／2096
河南省立輝縣百泉鄉村師範學校／147
河上公／772
河田嗣郎／385
核子科學季刊社／1937
賀昌群／48,226,415,541
賀川豐彥／2073
賀光中／798,1916
賀麟／53,54,396
賀龍驤／1168
賀生樂／416
賀聖鼐／569
賀嗣章／910
賀揚靈／105
赫勒斯／95

赫胥黎 / 898, 1574(2)
黑屋政彥 / 2072
亨利德蒙 / 7
亨利詹姆士 / 632
橫井時冬 / 2089
蘅塘退士 / 1566
弘曆（清高宗）/ 1434(2), 1612(2)
洪北平 / 8
洪承疇 / 1322
洪鈞 / 1713
洪亮吉 / 149, 602, 707, 1212, 1320
洪邁 / 1566, 1680, 1830(3), 1831(3)
洪楩 / 845, 1824
洪朴 / 1194
洪棄父 / 1558, 1746
洪緝 / 1294(2)
洪汝奎 / 1534
洪昇 / 1650
洪式閭 / 25, 282
洪适 / 828, 1803
洪煨蓮 / 72
洪興祖 / 598(2)
洪炎秋 / 301, 855, 1020
洪業 / 44, 343, 462
洪飴孫 / 1467
洪頤煊 / 642, 1233, 1333, 1339
洪正治 / 1293
洪咨夔 / 1423
洪遵 / 1425
侯岱麟 / 950
侯峒曾 / 1269
侯健 / 2009(2)
侯銓 / 1541
侯失勒 / 1562(2)

侯毅 / 203
侯哲葊 / 221
忽滑谷快天 / 2077, 2102
忽思慧 / 1773
胡安國 / 1776
胡秉虔 / 703, 1227, 1527, 1528(3)
胡不歸 / 727
胡長清 / 523(3), 524
胡超伍 / 207
胡承諾 / 642, 1000, 1185, 1690(2)
胡傳 / 1271, 1852(2)
胡道靜 / 322(2), 324(2)
胡定安 / 277
胡爾霖 / 278
胡鳳丹 / 1205, 1309, 1310, 1369, 1381, 1512, 1564, 1750
胡廣 / 1646
胡漢民 / 313
胡翰 / 1272
胡浩川 / 503
胡恒錦 / 110
胡宏 / 1272
胡厚宣 / 25, 26
胡懷琛 / 9, 111, 323, 674, 1055
胡惠天 / 482
胡紀常 / 120
胡寄南 / 206
胡繼瑗 / 141
胡家鈺 / 1456
胡建偉 / 829
胡居仁 / 1272
胡君復 / 167
胡濬濟 / 495
胡匡衷 / 1683

胡爌／1499

胡蘭成／863

胡林翼／641,642

胡鳴盛／4,1535

胡培翬／1665,1793,1865

胡培系／1295,1793

胡樸安／941

胡秋原／987

胡三省／1091,1092

胡善恆／27,92,99

胡紹勳／1538

胡適／9(4),30,32(3),42,43,50(2),72(2),73,138,151,152(3),153(5),154(5),155(3),161(2),188,230,250,272,282,297(2),329,352,358(2),407(2),448,454,458,490(2),491(2),534,542(2),543,572,575(3),587,589(3),590,593,603(2),604,627,628(2),635,636(2),643,644(2),646,696,715,716(3),717,721(3),722(3),723(5),724(3),725(2),729,730,739,810,817,823,824(2),835(2),852(2),865(2),884,885,891(2),892(3),893,904,942,943(2),956,971,995,998,1028(2),1029,1039,1047,1061(2),1064,1067,1068,1070,1090,1710,1852(2),1878,1879,2067,2069,2091,2097,2100,2101,3002,3006,3008(2)

胡叔仁／647,840

胡叔異／133

胡述兆／574

胡澍／1285

胡思敬／1599,1708

胡思永／156,3008

胡渭／998

胡錫侯／1220

胡曦／1729

胡先驌／497

胡祥翰／1313,1610

胡敩／336

胡行之／545

胡宣明／170,509

胡學古／1004

胡延／1115

胡毅／554

胡寅／1141

胡應麟／356,890,1479(2),1493

胡永齡／7

胡永祥／2045,2046(2)

胡垣／1223

胡遠濬／1343

胡雲翼／212,216,277,350,411,604,1044,1059

胡韞玉／1935(3)

胡澤／198,352

胡肇昕／1728

胡哲敷／231

胡直／1272

胡鍾吾／1797(2),1848

胡助／1153

胡仔／1338

胡宗楙／1654

胡宗憲／1141

湖南地質調查所／157(2)

湖南省憲法審查會／157

花菴詞客／921

花下解人／1475

華北農業合作事業委員會／159

華北水利委員工會／505

華北政務委員會政務廳情報局／83

華北政務委員會總務廳情報局／466
華長忠／1724
華超／183，386
華德生／442
華林／8，291
華林一／1049
華生／839，968
華學潤／430
華嚴／1039，1040
畫川逸叟／1622
懷德／530
桓寬／991，1669
桓譚／1282
幻影禪師／1767
荒村曉月／413
皇都風月主人／795
皇甫謐／1216
皇甫湜／232
黃安綏／1243
黃寶熙／1441（2）
黃超曾／1579
黃朝琴／47，114
黃承增／1237
黃淬伯／1289
黃大輿／1391
黃澹哉／563
黃道讓／1662
黃道周／1286，1462，1463
黃典權／906，911，1035，1991（2），1992
黃定宜／1338
黃奮生／23
黃奉西／251
黃郛／489
黃榦／733

黃公覺／544
黃海化學工業研究社／163
黃煥文／875
黃暉／236，797
黃機／1762
黃汲清／314
黃嘉謨／741
黃建中／22
黃杰／700
黃節／579，587，936，969，1298
黃溍／751
黃景仁／1357
黃凱鈞／1715
黃廬隱／230
黃耐庵／1362
黃彭年／1772
黃丕烈／1503（4）
黃潛／1286，1310，1460
黃強／408
黃慶瀾／3
黃群／1325
黃裳／1017
黃晟／1839
黃勝白／291
黃石／1633
黃石公／1796
黃士恆／273
黃奭／1285
黃綬／374
黃叔璥／906，1244
黃叔琳／1597，1598
黃嗣東／1170
黃素封／206，271，295，320（2），337
黃滔／734

黃庭堅／1011
黃文弼／104,1214
黃文昌／1777
黃文山／396
黃興中／164
黃醒初／568
黃省曾／1482
黃學周／1886
黃巽／292
黃葯眠／40
黃貽楫／1346
黃貽清／142
黃以周／1285
黃毅民／135
黃蔭萊／511

黃元吉／554
黃元生／139
黃月淡／553
黃雲眉／1223,1480
黃肇年／100
黃正銘／1058
黃子通／308
黃宗羲／816,821,897,1404,1547（2）,1800,1813
黃尊生／70,535
黃遵憲／480,1457
惠迪人／94,118,288,440,441
惠棟／761,1255,1328,1540,1739
慧遠／945
伙夫／226

J

姬佛陀／1235（2）
姬清波／1130
嵇康／1488
嵇文甫／39,571
嵇永仁／1515,1672
箕作元八／2057,2066
吉川幸次郎／1015,1773,1782,1802,1804,1806,1818,1866,2097,2099,2100,2123
吉天保／903
吉田靜致／2077
吉田松陰／1700
戢翼翬／67
紀德／926
紀曉嵐／480
紀映鍾／1764
紀昀／841,1018,1597,1665,1721,1797,1820

計六奇／1400
暨南大學商學院南洋商業調查部／271
繼昌／1644
加賀美嘉富／2104
加藤繁／2100
加藤熊一郎／2073
加藤武雄／367
迦納／495
賈昌朝／1454
賈島／248
賈凫西／1409
賈景德／1570
賈豐臻／521
賈思勰／836,1427
賈仙洲／378
賈誼／1640,1798

監谷温／1673
簡朝亮／1184,1186
簡野道明／2110(2),2111
簡又文／191,371
建設社／559
建文書局編輯部／861
江標／1267,1286,1361,1435,1547,1714,1733
江藩／1118
江公正／256
江瀚／1131,1337,1484,1485,1491(2),1499
江流／748
江琮／1187
江紹原／422,1207
江蘇第一圖書館／1302
江蘇省衛生處秘書室／174,175
江田益英／1854
江西省電務局統計室／176
江西省公路局編纂股／176(2)
江西省農業院／177
江西省政府經濟委員會／177(2)
江西省政府統計處／199
江俠菴／417,956
江洵／1170
江庸／368,1449
江永／1301,1317(2),1338,1385,1691(2)
江有誥／1227,1301,1302,1417,1464,1568
姜貴／597,750,982
姜夔／577
姜琦／421
姜尚賢／602
姜紹書／1446
姜文佐／422
姜蘊剛／1893

姜忠奎／1367,1532,1663
蔣百里／304
蔣伯潛／1874
蔣超伯／1298
蔣重光／1734
蔣春華／1239
蔣方震／27
蔣鳳藻／1575
蔣復璁／901,929
蔣光慈／36,168
蔣光煦／1544
蔣國祚／1357
蔣和／701
蔣衡／1764
蔣經國／934,941
蔣夢麟／852
蔣瑞藻／426,427(2)
蔣善國／72,102,309,528,534
蔣師轍／844,915
蔣石洲／465
蔣士銓／1750(2)
蔣廷黻／567,569
蔣廷黼／165
蔣唯心／191
蔣維喬／233,237,1747
蔣一安／1784
蔣逸雪／490
蔣鏞／829
蔣攸銛／1579
蔣元卿／181
蔣中正／666
蔣拙誠／53
交通部國際電台／178
交通銀行／178,179(2),180

焦贛 / 1303
焦竑 / 1344
焦奴士威爾士 / 162
焦廷琥 / 1396,1465,1478
焦循 / 1173,1274,1378
焦延壽 / 180,745(2)
焦易堂 / 111
焦袁熹 / 856
膠澳商埠觀象臺 / 180
教育編譯館 / 182
"教育部" / 747
教育部 / 60,488,701
教育部參事室 / 184
教育部讀音統一會 / 747
"教育部"高等教育司 / 668
教育部國際文化教育事業處 / 503
教育部國語統一籌備委員會 / 182
教育供應社有限公司編輯委員會 / 1060
教育通訊社 / 1891
教育與文化週刊社 / 1938(3)
教育總署教育局普遍教育科 / 158
揭傒斯 / 1206
結城令聞 / 2074
今関天彭 / 2113
今關壽麿 / 361
今關天彭 / 2062,2069,2090
今日婦女編輯委員會 / 1939
金榜 / 1756
金葆光 / 131
金步瀛 / 44,1746
金長佑 / 305
金烽 / 134
金公亮 / 870
金國寶 / 465

金國珍 / 347
金和 / 1448
金檜門 / 1289
金江 / 331,1688
金九經 / 1304,1799
金涓 / 1437
金俊 / 195
金梁 / 1230(2),1534
金陵大學農林科 / 274
金履祥 / 800,854,1163,1355,1376,1377,1386,1393(2),1459(3),1477(2),1543(2),1765(2)
金滿成 / 468
金尼閣 / 1612
金鵬 / 566
金擎宇 / 507
金人瑞 / 33,1172
金山縣政府 / 190
金聲 / 1316
金聖嘆 / 590,1864
金吳瀾 / 1238
金武祥 / 1552(2),1553(3)
金祥恆 / 1865
金冶井谷 / 301
金岳霖 / 240
金雲銘 / 34
金鍾華 / 4
金子馬治 / 1030
津田左右吉 / 2075,2085
近藤萬太郎 / 277
近衛家熙 / 1776
進步書局 / 1115
靳志 / 1115
京都大學人文科學研究所 / 1875

3033

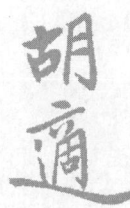

京都國立博物館／2099
京漢鐵路管理局／1671
京滬週刊社／1892
旌德縣政府／196
經利彬／52
井出季和太／855,2066(2)
井上勤／162
井上圓三／2090
景洪／199
景學鈐／250,449(2)
境野黄洋／2071
靜嘉堂文庫／760,2076(2)

靜恬主人／1315
競業學會／1941(3),1942(2)
鳩摩羅什／751
九龍真逸／1542
九容樓主人／1694
久保得二／1359,1447
久保天隨／2074
鶯尾順敬／2109
菊池寬／483
橘道人／1703
橘惠勝／2058
軍訓部軍學編譯處／58(2)

K

開濟／778
開灤礦務總局／203
闞鐸／150,1267,1334
康白情／148
康繼祥／182
康梁／881
康琴／796
康有爲／49,110,114,1148,1149,1241,1338,1641,1760,1810,1858
考茨基／328,563
考夫卡／76
考試院秘書處／205
考試院秘書處文書科／205,485
柯璜／298,1337
柯培元／666
柯紹忞／974
柯巖舊樵／1566
科學教育編輯部／1943(4)
克伯屈／184

克拉勃／191
克洛特／346
孔晁／737
孔次／185
孔繁霖／408
孔鮒／766,1337(2),1803
孔廣林／1576
孔廣牧／1349
孔廣森／1663,1684
孔繼涵／1519,1553,1578
孔孟學會／1944(2)
孔平仲／980,1264
孔穎達／1476,1757
孔昭聲／1322
堀籠美善／2079
蒯德模／1166,1604
蒯光典／1315
況周儀／1720
況周頤／1196,1289,1641,1739

鄺震鳴 / 543

昆明廣播電臺 / 446

L

來集之 / 1569

來裕恂 / 144

來知德 / 1355

萊蒙托夫 / 187

萊維 / 607

賴山陽 / 181

藍鼎元 / 640,832

藍夢九 / 385

藍斯堡洛 / 97

蘭陵笑笑生 / 672

蘭茂 / 1724

郎靜山 / 200

郎曄 / 757,1264

郎依山 / 246

勞榦 / 235,762,763(2),1330,1802(2)

勞格 / 1186,1566,1568

勞乃宣 / 1222(2),1460(2),1580

老聃 / 773

樂觀法師 / 831(2)

樂嘉藻 / 1747

雷賓南 / 467

雷潔瓊 / 281

雷通羣 / 184,413

雷維不魯爾 / 81

雷香庭 / 217,454

雷學淇 / 1088

雷延壽 / 1445

雷震 / 1041

狸弔疋 / 166

黎東方 / 210,417,521,541,638,954,957,973

(2),1053

黎錦暉 / 283,312

黎錦明 / 459

黎錦熙 / 7,22,88(2),137,138,139(2),172,309(2),330,361,413,439,541,545,561,696

黎靖德 / 1883

黎烈文 / 926

黎明 / 574

黎仁 / 911

黎庶昌 / 1151,1227,1653

黎崱 / 573

李安宅 / 178,247,457,459,473

李昂 / 713

李翱 / 216,776,1348

李白英 / 174,255

李百強 / 363

李百藥 / 582

李柏朝 / 188

李葆恂 / 1605

李寶嘉 / 110

李寶洤 / 1760

李壁 / 1857

李步青 / 428

李材 / 1299

李長傅 / 271

李辰冬 / 150,311,711,924,938,939,940,1898

李春芳 / 1636

李春坪 / 1479

李淳風 / 1081

李慈銘 / 480,1719	李孤帆 / 491
李次民 / 570	李光地 / 1707,1708
李從周 / 1884	李光濤 / 815
李達 / 385,715	李光廷 / 1237,1257
李道平 / 1685,1755	李光庭 / 1292
李燾 / 981	李光炘 / 1369
李德淦 / 1320	李圭 / 1663
李德啓 / 3,126	李軌 / 1673(2)
李德裕 / 217,776	李貴良 / 866
李滌生 / 985	李國祁 / 1067
李鼎祚 / 1084,1347	李瀚章 / 1726(2)
李定 / 202	李浩培 / 409
李定國 / 522	李賀 / 248
李定一 / 1074	李珩 / 207
李東陽 / 1417	李鴻章 / 776
李侗 / 776	李華民 / 1457
李敦化 / 227	李焕燊 / 727
李耳 / 772(2)	李璜 / 643,780
李發全 / 554	李滉 / 930
李方晨 / 1050	李輝英 / 775
李方桂 / 286,539,2804	李吉甫 / 1711
李昉 / 916,917,1558	李集 / 1263
李鳳苞 / 1502	李季 / 77,401
李富孫 / 1262,1263	李季開 / 1891
李復言 / 1656	李濟 / 518,966,2021
李綱 / 1356	李霽野 / 20,192
李根源 / 1400	李家瑞 / 18,362
李庚桐 / 307	李甲孚 / 1982
李塨 / 775,866,880,968,983,989,1018, 1141,1147,1148,1163(2),1347,1375,1376, 1417,1423,1424,1487,1491(2),1492,1513, 1514(2),1535,1548,1572,1629,1659(2), 1661,1666(2),1668(2),1720,1749,1755	李建興 / 857,1833
	李健吾 / 91,332,437
	李劍農 / 517,1049
	李嶠 / 1346
	李進之 / 94
李覯 / 1037	李京生 / 234

李景漢／63(2),339

李景均／898

李璟／1412

李鏡池／557

李鍇／1307

李魁春／1514

李栗谷／781

李笠／1174,1500

李廉方／1640

李良／440

李林甫／1565,1776

李霖燦／795

李綠園／284

李洛之／379

李曼瑰／40,380

李培／1287

李朋／1888

李樸生／271,734,941,942

李喬苹／406,471

李翹／1343

李青崖／494

李清照／1157

李清植／1599

李榮陞／1722

李榮達／500

李汝珍／200,759,1096,1347

李善／228,789

李善蘭／1562

李商隱／1198,1348

李紹唐／857,994,1040

李慎溶／1275

李聖五／118,120

李石岑／952,1068

李石曾／585,588(3),672,742,805,876(3),877(2)

李書華／1037,1038(2)

李述禮／32,589

李樹青／381

李樹桐／1896

李素同／1244

李泰／1341

李泰棻／528,1309,1615,1616

李棠階／1348

李天夢／209

李田意／674,759

李威／1362

李未農／465,466

李蔚堂／275

李文邦／281

李文漢／1674

李文林／1674

李文田／1260,1526,1532,1614

李文藻／1363

李文仲／1766

李錫麟／1244

李仙舟／570

李相顯／53,222,240,298,418,492,560

李相勛／447

李絜非／489

李心傳／630

李醒愚／277

李旭／407,496

李續祖／405

李玄伯／1047

李延壽／583,822

李儼／1057

李冶／1326

李翊灼／89

李逸民 / 1590
李寅賓 / 1443
李寅恭 / 1443
李邕 / 1854
李顒 / 1195
李永富 / 676
李攸 / 894
李漁 / 419,1332,1333,1345(2),1620
李遇孫 / 1263,1461
李煜 / 1412
李毓澍 / 931
李元 / 1464
李元春 / 1205,1580
李元度 / 1574
李岳瑞 / 40
李則綱 / 343,344
李澤仁 / 1372
李杖原 / 486
李兆洛 / 1346
李兆垣 / 365
李振翻 / 524
李之純 / 1812
李之鼎 / 1511(2)
李之藻 / 1398(3),1817
李直夫 / 1773
李執中 / 305
李植泉 / 99
李贄 / 587,979,1125,1172,1346,1370,1636,1639
李鍾漢 / 1218
李鍾珏 / 1634
李仲三 / 378
李周望 / 1243(2)
李紫乾 / 287

李宗侗 / 953,1092
李宗昉 / 1431
李宗黃 / 57
李宗吾 / 327,566
李宗禕 / 1517
李祖韓 / 60
李祖望 / 1630
李佐賢 / 1498
里嘉圖 / 197
里盛翻而特 / 405
理約翰 / 1549
立法院編譯處 / 40,219,547
"立法院"秘書處 / 778(2),961
立法院憲法初稿審查委員會 / 423
利類思 / 1132
栗永錄 / 1660
笠間龍跳 / 1112
厲鼎煃 / 285
厲鶚 / 83,653,1332,1412,1448
歷史研究編輯委員會 / 1944
歷史語言研究所研究員外國通信員編輯員助理員 / 291
酈道元 / 353,883,884(2),1518(2),1519(3),1520(3),1521(3),1522(2),1698(2),1827,1837,1838,1839(2),1840,1841(2),1842,1843,1845,3004
連橫 / 743
連雅堂 / 370
廉布 / 1446
聯共(布)中央特設委員會 / 899
梁冰弦 / 405
梁川孟緯 / 1644
梁方仲 / 421
梁恭辰 / 1453

梁光復／155

梁濟／1118,1209,1214,1241,1505,1632,1682

梁嘉彬／681

梁晉竹／223

梁敬錞／959

梁龍／1817

梁品如／1131,1374

梁啓超／75,89,223,265(3),266,279,290,377,418,463,510,521,564,629,661,674,680,694,695,754,768,771,797,818,819,844,856,924,929,932,933,957,970,1002,1050,1052,1058,1059,1065,1066,1069(2),1070,1085,1087,1094,2075

梁啓雄／447

梁容若／1058

梁紹壬／1356(2)

梁升俊／744

梁實秋／6,51,215,241,297(2),308,391,478,1017,2901

梁漱溟／66,392,424,464(2)

梁思成／19,67,95,227,291,294,339,368,468,561

梁廷燦／779

梁廷枏／996,1178

梁學昌／1576

梁逸／1268

梁玉繩／1422

梁遇春／167

梁章鉅／860,1512,1581,1598,1745,1808

梁子青／364

梁宗岱／1525

廖白泉／43

廖碧虛／484

廖漢臣／911

廖平／107,1308(2)

廖燕／1195

列寧／669

列禦寇／1137

林伯修／378

林逋／787

林超真／24,565

林朝榮／910

林春溥／1761

林岱雲／2108

林庚／533,1174

林光／1410

林豪／639

林和成／340

林和民／527

林惠祥／396

林佶／993,1007

林繼庸／208

林潔娘／320(2)

林焜熿／752

林籟餘／494

林培廬／33,255

林賽／195

林紓／230

林四郎／2118(4),2119(6),2120(5),2121(4)

林頌河／60,376

林天蔚／894

林同濟／301

林維源／1771

林熊祥／907,927,1034,2005,2006(3)

林耀南／914

林疑今／469

林以亮／1095
林義光／1492
林應翔／1826
林勇／906
林語堂／431,473,1257
林兆恩／1538
林致平／942
林紫貴／930
"臨時行政改革委員會"／975,1095
凌純聲／358,753
凌叔華／158,425
凌雪／823,1412
凌竹銘／891
凌昌焕／331
凌曙／600,1149(2),1150,1201,1220,1221,1350,1536
凌望超／82
凌宴池／1671
鈴木大拙／1833,1862,2070
鈴木貞太郎／1190(2),1647,1783
嶺南大學／116,355,356
令狐德棻／1083
留菴／505
留雲居士／1400
劉安／729,730,1278(3),1279(2)
劉安世／1319
劉百閔／308
劉半農／12
劉寶楠／800
劉秉麟／27
劉昒／1458
劉伯生／1365
劉昌／1749
劉昶／203

劉敞／668
劉超然／1140
劉辰／1399
劉成禺／1266(2)
劉成忠／1261
劉承幹／754,1318,1731
劉崇倫／91,92,258,303
劉傳瑩／1394
劉大白／11,577,578(2),761,923,961,1006,1107
劉大杰／163,212,224,394,446,498,531
劉大鈞／514
劉大櫆／1248
劉道元／799
劉東生／1633
劉鶚／213,771(2),927,1575,1745
劉逢禄／571,1364
劉斧／1437
劉復／12,22,243,362,380,410,432,530
劉光第／1751
劉海粟／1747
劉和／385
劉鴻略／1139,1140
劉厚滋／16,376
劉豁軒／13,262
劉基／594,1559
劉基磐／58
劉璣／1033
劉濟民／1984,1985
劉家立／1279(2)
劉家謀／1127,1790
劉階平／1818
劉節／145,514,1145
劉經菴／503

劉鈞 / 378
劉鈞仁 / 504
劉開 / 1393
劉克莊 / 713,1202,1269(2)
劉焜 / 1219
劉立夫 / 1125
劉良璧 / 596
劉麟生 / 1060
劉冕執 / 273
劉盼遂 / 73,216(2),228,390,449,797,1188(2),1217,1323,1587(2)
劉鵬九 / 649
劉乾初 / 212
劉汝霖 / 45
劉若愚 / 1765
劉邵 / 300,853,1458
劉師培 / 42,773,803,819,984(2),1090,1365,1769
劉世珩 / 1331
劉壽曾 / 1361
劉恕 / 1094
劉台拱 / 1364,1461,1462
劉體智 / 1474
劉鉄孫 / 323
劉廷蔚 / 318
劉萬章 / 6,38,115(2),350,364
劉文典 / 161,303,1278(3)
劉文輅 / 6
劉文興 / 13,228,578
劉西渭 / 202
劉熙 / 1506(3)
劉熙載 / 1527,1539,1689
劉錫鴻 / 1694
劉錫五 / 1073

劉喜海 / 1130,1297
劉仙洲 / 196
劉獻廷 / 683,1237
劉向 / 887,1144(2),1360,1532,1633,1640(2)
劉孝標 / 878,1504(3),1505
劉勰 / 938,1597,1598
劉心學 / 890
劉心源 / 1226
劉歆 / 949,1610,1611
劉行驥 / 508
劉修業 / 136(2),673,944
劉昫 / 761
劉壎 / 1002
劉荀 / 1399
劉雅農 / 604,834,981,1056
劉弇 / 1370
劉衍淮 / 380
劉儼然 / 281
劉燕谷 / 308
劉以祥 / 195
劉義慶 / 878,1504(3),1505
劉因 / 760,1326
劉蔭仁 / 1531
劉應秋 / 1364
劉禹錫 / 788,1000,1363
劉玉麐 / 1193
劉馭萬 / 569
劉毓盤 / 42
劉沅 / 1280
劉源淥 / 1185,1318
劉雲份 / 46
劉載賡 / 980
劉兆霖 / 340

劉振東／502
劉枝萬／823
劉知幾／874,1501
劉芷汀／240
劉致平／67,95,227,294,339,368,561
劉摯／1081
劉晝／1638,1806
劉肅和／1635
劉子任／285,409
劉子亞／409
劉宗周／1293,1365
柳成龍／950
柳存仁／863
柳大綱／160
柳貫／788,1366
柳開／705
柳榮宗／1531
柳田聖山／2099
柳僖／1305,1366
柳詒徵／531
柳子光／1722
六十七／651,875
龍倦飛／807
龍啟瑞／1227,1767
龍文彬／814,1400
瀧川龜太郎／873,2068
瀧精一／2084
婁貽哲／1095
婁子匡／326
樓桐孫／197
樓鑰／668
樓穎／1474
盧弼／860
盧辯／1158

盧德嘉／660
盧冀野／267,476
盧見曾／1244,1664
盧柟／1396
盧前／1693,1712
盧仝／1009
盧文弨／13,579,989,1455,1511,1667,1829
盧錫榮／69,71
盧于道／206,329
廬隱／828
鸕鶿子／483
魯大東／1405
魯迅／76,79,84,86,107,109,145,158,159(2),166,167(2),211,223,268(2),269,286,287(2),295,312,376,392,426(2),452,491,536,537,563,964,1063
魯一同／1105
陸次雲／1181
陸德明／756,1411,1686,1753,1763
陸佃／924,1570,1791
陸費墀／1171
陸費逵／545
陸龜蒙／1804
陸翽／1679
陸機／791,1372
陸績／755
陸楫／1223
陸賈／1145,1807
陸建三／172
陸九淵／962,1624(2)
陸侃如／80,87,189,271,292,361,479,480,528,534,571
陸隴其／1471,1541
陸世儀／791,1105,1116,1131,1202,1210

(3),1211(2),1280,1296,1297,1370,1372,1375,1471,1537,1551,1646,1651,1717,1740,1744(2),1745

陸小曼／23

陸心源／1456,1567,1682(2),1714,1829,1868

陸秀夫／1372

陸燿／1433

陸耀遹／1314

陸衣言／137,214,545

陸以湉／1344

陸游／758,935,1342

陸志鴻／646

陸志韋／38,72,107,145,168,169(2),188,231,336,354

陸贄／792,920,1565

鹿橋／935

鹿善繼／1374

鹿野忠雄／908

路大荒／225,785

路家榜／365

呂寶榮／37

呂本中／637,1780

呂不韋／241,1382

呂誠／1342

呂澂／415,1208

呂大防／1252

呂大元／112

呂大忠／1383

呂得勝／963

呂光／974,1063

呂皓／1723

呂坤／1238,1482

呂聯珠／1264

呂留良／1383(2),1384(2)

呂美蓀／1583(2)

呂珮芬／1124,1623

呂浦／1761

呂喬年／1354

呂瑞廷／436

呂世宜／1771

呂殊／1397

呂思勉／20,364,524

呂溫／232,792

呂惺吾／1336

呂湛恩／1860

呂振中／233

呂祖謙／162,731,734,864,1161,1176(3),1225,1311,1353,1382,1383,1479,1492,1545,1564,1600,1728,1756,1769,1770

綠牕居主人／1231

綠濤文藝出版社編輯部／1945

綠天館主人／1786

綠漪女士／234

倫敦聖教書類會社／2057

倫偉良／1026

羅本／1097,1125

羅常培／137,286,417,498,539

羅從彥／801

羅大經／1262

羅惇曧／1695

羅爾綱／149,234,333,372,425,867,868(3),917,1852(2)

羅根澤／112,365,387(2),394,506,532,557,562,1233

羅貫中／859,1348,1467,1828,1829

羅光／747,781,977

羅洪先／1379,1418(2)

羅翮雲 / 1336

羅家倫 / 193(2),553,687

羅錦華 / 561

羅錦堂 / 780,958,1053

羅隆基 / 297(2)

羅倫 / 1380

羅懋登 / 1763

羅門 / 880

羅念生 / 229

羅聘 / 1600

羅欽順 / 770

羅撒盧森堡 / 433

羅師楊 / 1616

羅士琳 / 1141,1728

羅素 / 212,471(2),851,878

羅天白 / 726

羅廷光 / 185

羅香林 / 48,209,373,447,833,919(3),961,2910

羅莘田 / 539,879

羅雄飛 / 400

羅燁 / 1099,1100

羅以智 / 1574

羅有高 / 1768

羅虞臣 / 1379

羅玉東 / 520

羅願 / 1632

羅澤南 / 1183,1379,1380,1456,1611,1630,1677,1755

羅振玉 / 1001(2),1022,1125,1189,1190,1217(2),1568,1594(2),1654,1692(2),1712,1734

羅正鈞 / 1770

羅志如 / 331,384

羅仲言 / 196

羅宗洛 / 391

洛里哀 / 22

落華生 / 600,731,802,826,1091

駱賓王 / 1381

M

馬導源 / 854

馬冠群 / 1748

馬國翰 / 630,856,1138,1872(4),1873(2)

馬翮飛 / 1687

馬鶴天 / 273

馬衡 / 1496

馬洪焕 / 304

馬繼楨 / 1247

馬堅 / 164,182

馬建忠 / 242(2),1506

馬克勒蘭 / 193

馬克思 / 268

馬克斯 / 669

馬雷 / 866

馬立勛 / 224

馬廉 / 1387

馬凌甫 / 97

馬念祖 / 885

馬瑞辰 / 804

馬士奇 / 86

馬士圖 / 1404

馬驌 / 1690(2)

馬偕／914
馬敘倫／1343
馬寅初／516,544
馬瀛／357,753
馬永卿／1011,1342
馬裕藻／51
馬鋆／595(2)
馬振圖／176
馬致遠／1818
馬宗霍／518
馬宗榮／327
馬總／999
麥嘉締／1487
麥柯／184
麥耐／1329
麥塔／352
麥耶夫／317
邁格文／1207
曼殊斐爾／777
曼殊逸叟／1456
毛德琦／1371
毛鳳枝／1473
毛晉／1367,1544(2)
毛念恃／1665
毛奇齡／1325,1537,1609(2),1614
毛起／41,561
毛思誠／811
毛祥麟／1189
毛一波／911
毛嶽生／1648
毛澤東／679,798,972
毛子晉／360
毛子水／2013(3),2014(2)
茅乃文／505(2)

茅於美／1678
茆泮林／1209,1226,1279,1293,1504
冒廣生／1145
冒襄／1579
枚乘／1390
梅村野史／792
梅光羲／1108
梅里靄／81
梅文鼎／1077
梅堯臣／932,1582
梅毓／1364
梅原末治／2090
梅曾亮／1110
美國新聞處／246
美濃部達吉／278
妹尾韶夫／2057
蒙文通／35,294
夢麟／1159
孟德斯鳩／1584
孟繁榮英／763
孟郊／248,809
孟洛／347
孟森／7,144,166,225,699,813,844,1440,1814
孟世傑／21,417,515
孟憲承／184
孟心如／405
孟瑤／964
糜文開／676
米国遣傳教使事務局／2114
密立根／62
苗銳羅／266
繆昌期／1155
繆純白／1155

繆敬持 / 1177

繆荃孫 / 1020,1194,1242,1319(2),1359, 1363,1503,1643,1664,1688,1689,1814, 1864,1868

繆天華 / 599

繆天綬 / 334

繆虛白 / 1155

民治週刊社 / 1893

"民主潮編輯委員會" / 1956(3),1957(3)

"民主憲政編輯委員會" / 1958(2)

"民主中國編輯委員會" / 1959(4)

閔爾昌 / 1112,1772

閔孫奭 / 1451(2)

閔泳珪 / 1098

明珊居士 / 1719(2)

明耀五 / 331

摩根 / 551

末松保和 / 2068

莫泊桑 / 494,574,739,846,996,1005,1031

莫東寅 / 227

莫亮 / 568

莫洛托夫 / 392

莫友芝 / 1136,1384(2),1385(2)

墨翟 / 820,1406(3),1815,3007

默鳳道人 / 1003

牟融 / 1408

木村泰賢 / 2059

木村英一 / 2099

木村增太郎 / 503

木爾茲 / 336

木蘇牧 / 1644

木下彪 / 664,2101,2111(2)

木下正中 / 194

牧野二 / 2089,2090

牧野藻洲 / 2094

慕維廉 / 1164

穆超 / 258

穆文富 / 512

穆湘玥 / 280

穆修 / 1261

N

那須皓 / 2073

那志良 / 677

南京市教育局 / 269

南京中央日報 / 975

南京中央日報編輯部 / 148

南開大學社會經濟研究委員會 / 269

南開學校 / 269(2)

南葵文庫 / 2088(2)

南滿洲鐵道株式會社農事試驗場 / 52

南洋學會研究組 / 988

南洋中學復校特刊編輯委員會 / 272

南總宇惠 / 1857

內堀維文 / 307

內藤藤一郎 / 2067

內田繁隆 / 2067

內務府 / 1429,1436

能田忠亮 / 2073

尼登 / 297

倪國璉 / 1434

倪樸 / 1416

倪守約 / 1309

倪維思 / 1502,1657

倪元坦／1187,1195,1288,1296,1342,1463,
1464,1563,1703,1737,1744

倪瓚／825

倪正和／562

聶光甫／357

聶華苓／632,644,654,806

聶其杰／1232,1307

聶士成／1178

聶湯谷／379

聶鈫／1562

聶雲台／299

牛山／94

鈕樹玉／1201,1285

努力週報社／1960(3),1961(3),1962(4),
1963(3),1964(3),1965(3),1966(3),1967
(3),1968(4),1969(3),1970(3),1971(3),
1972(4),1973(3),1974(3),1975(3),1976
(4),1977(4),1978(3),1979(3),1980(4),
1981(4),1982(2)

O

歐蘇／1102

歐陽漸／1725

歐陽蘭／453

歐陽溥存／545

歐陽溱／171

歐陽修／827,921,946,1238,1239,1835

歐陽玄／683

歐陽頤／785

歐陽詹／216

P

帕刻／283

拍琴／471

潘昂霄／1126

潘伯明／189

潘承弼／1811

潘德輿／1676

潘飛聲／1527

潘光旦／70,425,544,564

潘家洵／458

潘浚／701

潘良貴／1408

潘愨／1081

潘慎生／1743

潘文舫／1642

潘文熊／1112

潘希曾／1761

潘賢模／974,1063

潘衍桐／1757

潘一塵／181

潘蔭東／1432

潘欲仁／1348

潘淵／231

潘源來／119

潘肇元／1420

潘殖／1590

潘鐘祥／319

潘梓年／262

潘尊行／25,38

龐元英／1595

培根／828

裴普賢／1080

裴文中／941

裴希度／1652

朋九萬／638

彭百川／62,459

彭楚珩／779

彭大雅／1263

彭定求／1415(2),1563

彭歌／782,1100

彭國棟／682,999,1070,1080,1775

彭基相／80,81(2),83,415

彭家元／85

彭麗天／34

彭鑾／1590

彭紹升／1128,1194(2),1232,1330,1680,1768,1802

彭叔夏／1859

彭崧毓／1396

彭先澤／54

彭曉／1754

彭學沛／277

彭玉麟／1421

彭元瑞／1497

彭兆良／4,47,95,348

彭子明／551

彭遵泗／1513

丕強／430

皮日休／830,1807,1859

皮錫瑞／198,751,758,1308,1322(2),1488,1489,1589

片上伸／2093

朴趾源／1829

品川彌二郎／1700

平步青／955

平岡武夫／2105

平林初之輔／398

平綏鐵路管理局／281,444,482

萍社／1422

蒲分白／467

蒲風／229,330

蒲徠士／420

蒲立德／307

蒲松齡／225,785,786,1358,1359,1805(2),1860

浦起龍／1501

普列寒諾夫／487

Q

戚祚國／1426

祁彪佳／1017

祁承㸁／262,815

祁仍奚／157

祁韻士／1283,1584

祁致賢／742,867,967(2),1021(2),1086

齊白石／834

齊令辰／1833

齊門／454

齊群／245

齊如山／108,689,836,1044,1049,1246,1391
齊思和／415
齊學裘／1299(2)
齊召南／779,1351
齊之鸞／1462
齊周華／1398
啓明書局編輯所／954,980
啓明書局編譯所／574,695,739,781,846,856,996,1005,1029,1031,1054,1056,1061,1065
啓平／471
綺紋／162
千家駒／504
千葉玄之／1138
前田慧雲／1653
乾化市政府／285
錢寶琮／51,372
錢昌照／556
錢澄之／904
錢大昕／285,839,871,1204,1263,1266(2),1297,1372,1417,1430(2),1431,1470(2),1483,1486,1494(2),1543,1577,1670,1682,1713(2),1760
錢大昭／1123,1269,1270,1467,1530
錢稻孫／1154
錢德蒼／1137
錢端升／54,80,255,465
錢枋／1678,1867
錢杲之／1345
錢靜方／426
錢臨照／349
錢穆／38,100,136,164,204,266,418(2),483,516,957,1050,1057,1059
錢南揚／251,362,897

錢謙益／267,268,820,821,1188,1359,1409(2),1819
錢尚濠／243,1388
錢少華／1693
錢泰／1043
錢唐／1500
錢文選／1701
錢文子／1121
錢熙祚／980
錢錫寶／1571
錢星海／471(2)
錢杏邨／399
錢玄同／102,3006
錢伊庵／1767
錢儀吉／1174,1333(2),1595,1772
錢繹／1701
錢泳／1385
錢曾／1409(2)
錢振常／1198
錢振倫／1198
錢鍾書／895
喬孟符／1804
喬衍琯／1783
喬曾劬／1818
樵川樵叟／847,1826
橋本凝胤／2108
橋川時雄／1687,2075,2091
譙周／1432
秦篤輝／1184,1423,1686
秦鳳翔／22
秦更年／1285,1300
秦觀／729,1277
秦九韶／1514
秦越人／821

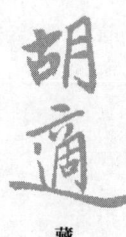

覃子豪 / 799,962
沁園主人 / 1249
青島市港務局統計室 / 548(2)
青浮山人 / 1180
青眉 / 1551
青木正兒 / 510,516,1047,2062
青年協會書報部 / 393,419
青陽旅外學聯會 / 1888
"清華學報社編輯委員會" / 1982,1983(3),1984(2)
清華學校圖書館 / 290
清華學校研究院 / 136
清史編纂委員會 / 845
清史館 / 1444,1445
清室善後委員會 / 109
清水安三 / 2069
清水泰次 / 2070
清水由隆 / 194
慶保胤 / 1460
慶澤彭 / 192,280,501
丘逢甲 / 788
丘光庭 / 742
丘峻 / 291
丘濬 / 1086
丘勤寶 / 482
邱昌渭 / 459
邱濬 / 1447(2)
邱言曦 / 987
邱祖銘 / 553

秋谷老人 / 1249
秋貞理 / 580
裘開明 / 245(2)
裘璉 / 1264
曲瀅生 / 391,483,1254
曲直生 / 146,158,274
屈大均 / 1283,1599
屈復 / 1348
屈勒味林 / 465
屈萬里 / 965
屈燨 / 565
屈原 / 1144(2)
瞿兌之 / 143,224
瞿菊農 / 209
瞿明宙 / 367
瞿同祖 / 1045
瞿宣穎 / 528,1113
瞿中溶 / 1449
全大聲 / 225
全國稻麥改進所 / 292
全國經濟委員會衛生實驗處藥物研究室 / 451
全漢昇 / 270,342,360,501
全增嘏 / 467
全祖望 / 186,187,748,749,1220,1307,1547(2),1656,1783,1816,1827,1870
銓敍部秘書處第三科 / 294
權德輿 / 851
群眾編輯部 / 480

R

饒孟任 / 356

饒旬宣 / 1768

熱希達原 / 1021
人間世社 / 407
人民文學出版社編輯部 / 1048
仁井田陞 / 2088
任白濤 / 222,468
任大椿 / 1629
任二北 / 646
任昉 / 1513
任訪秋 / 534,536,1765
任鴻雋 / 207,337,573
任鴻年 / 1109
任松如 / 353
任溪盧 / 221
任熊 / 1459
任一碧 / 329
任映滄 / 1066
任淵 / 714
任瑗 / 1136
任中敏 / 1712
任卓宣 / 667,668
日本大正一切經刊行會 / 609,610(3),611(3),612(3),613(4),614(3),615(2),616(4),617(4),618(4),619(3),620(4),621(3),622(4),623(3),624(2),625(2),626(3)
日本京都大學人文科學研究所 / 1875
容庚 / 274,287,1224,1316,1436,1474
容媛 / 1314
容肇祖 / 8,71,74,169,209,217,232,250,261,280,394,445,478,487,533,706,777,813,1252
蓉子 / 842
阮大鋮 / 1421,1699(4),1700
阮福 / 779,1351
阮葵生 / 588,1128
阮維周 / 634(2)
阮逸 / 1599
阮毅成 / 98,838
阮元 / 681,732,988,1004,1141,1174,1284(2),1291,1321,1350,1795
阮閱 / 1024
芮逸夫 / 2901
瑞士國防軍總司令部 / 58

S

薩都剌 / 858
薩爾地 / 62,459
薩君陸 / 273
薩孟武 / 98,1033,1053
塞力格曼 / 567
賽昂里 / 80
三家村學究 / 742,1298
"三軍大學中國歷代戰爭史編纂委員會" / 1051
三聯書局 / 784(2)
三民主義青年團中央團部 / 313
三民主義研究所 / 947
三浦周行 / 2092
三通書局編輯部 / 1084
三餘氏 / 822
桑戴克 / 345,346
桑木嚴翼 / 204,2083
桑欽 / 884,1518(2),1519(3),1837,1840,1841(2),1842,3002

3051

桑原隲蔵 / 2078, 2095
澁江全善 / 1801
森金五郎 / 2078
森立之 / 1801
僧佑 / 149
沙不列 / 814
沙多維奴 / 782
沙耳非米尼 / 343
沙畹 / 412, 818
沙文淵 / 994
沙志培 / 160
莎士比亞 / 13, 203, 861
莎彝尊 / 1738
山川均 / 24, 420, 563
山東大學 / 129
山東鄉村建設研究院 / 318
山口察常 / 484, 2065
山崎百治 / 2072
山崎弓束 / 2079
山崎宏 / 2104
山崎精華 / 2064
山謙之 / 1602
山西省長公署 / 319
山西省經濟管理局 / 319(2)
杉森孝次郎 / 2067, 2071(2), 2085
珊山散人 / 485
善後救濟總署臺灣分署經濟技正室 / 370(2)
善後事業委員會保管委員會秘書處 / 31
單寵乾 / 447
單士釐 / 1442(2)
單晏一 / 562
商承祚 / 1692(2)
商盤 / 1745
商企翁 / 1395

商務印書館 / 49, 321(2), 903, 1653
商務印書館編審委員會 / 50
商務印書館編譯所 / 162, 411
商務印書館善後辦事處 / 323
商鞅 / 56, 1474
商章孫 / 205
上海法學編譯社 / 323
上海廉美書社 / 412
上海市公用局統計室 / 324
上海市政府社會局 / 324
上海圖書館 / 1044
上海戲劇協社 / 763(2)
上海信托股份有限公司編輯部 / 323
上海醫學書局 / 36(2)
上海銀行週報社 / 548
上海證券交易所 / 325
上田恭輔 / 2098
尚秉和 / 1352(2)
少年中國學會 / 121
邵伯溫 / 706, 1262
邵博 / 705, 1480
邵蕙西 / 1258
邵晉涵 / 1535
邵瑞彭 / 1511, 1561
邵嗣堯 / 1137
邵松年 / 1656
邵廷采 / 638
邵洵美 / 334, 453
邵循正 / 996
邵懿辰 / 1401
邵雍 / 995
邵友保 / 855
邵元冲 / 113, 202
邵遠平 / 1654

社會部統計處／326(2)
社會調查所／59
申丙／733
神保如天／2077
神田喜一郎／646,2106
沈葆楨／1484
沈步洲／448
沈赤然／1252
沈初／1736
沈從文／68,168,329(2),425
沈達夫／658
沈大成／983
沈德符／583,1678,1867
沈度／1815
沈復／662
沈遘／1834
沈家本／1484,1737
沈兼士／73,115,471
沈近思／1351
沈覲鼎／302
沈涇河工局文牘科／190
沈璟／1139,1727
沈君實／363
沈括／809,1395(2)
沈鯉／1685
沈麟趾／1310
沈熳若／337
沈夢麟／1603
沈瓶庵／150
沈起／1728
沈啓無／192,296
沈欽韓／1183
沈泰／1834
沈濤／1302,1494

沈威恆／799
沈性仁／243
沈璿／67,639
沈亞之／248
沈延國／233
沈亦雲／1286
沈尹默／1449
沈英名／837
沈鎣／1363
沈瑜慶／1569
沈豫／1183,1184,1187,1192,1200,1209(2),1284(2),1449,1455(2),1714,1752,1769
沈元起／574
沈約／896,1088,1484
沈雲龍／960,1046
沈之繒／1751
沈知方／1874
沈仲緯／1645
沈宗瀚／766(2),1049,1075,1076,2688
沈宗畸／1135
沈奏廷／382
沈祖憲／1462
瀋陽製材廠／178
慎到／1485,1779
慎懋賞／1485
生活讀書新知三聯書店／718(2),719(3),720(3)
生田長江／2062
盛成／401
盛俊／324
盛清沂／905(2),1851
盛熙明／1197
聖多瑪斯／1132

3053

失野仁一／2089
施邦曜／1489
施補華／1725
施伏量／24
施國祁／1315
施化遠／1382
施括乾／1457,1573,1650,1743
施琅／759
施夢龍／1646
施密特／23
施耐庵／352,882,995,1348,1518
施閏章／1489
施肇基／869
施蟄存／46,189,321,360,387
十字論壇編輯委員會／1991
石嫯／1749
石沖白／330
石川六郎／2084
石村貞一／1802
石廣權／1125
石介／872,1634
石井光雄／1189
石梁／587,1128
石山福治／2065
石田幹之助／2086(6),2087(6),2088(3),2107
石英／275
石永楸／1378
石玉崑／1470
石原皋／52
石璋如／964
石芝／1496
拾穗月刊社／1989
時報館／1500

時報雜誌編輯委員會／1987
時代批評編輯委員會／1988(4),1989(5)
時瀾／1728
時與潮編輯委員會／1990(2),1991
時昭瀛／2901
時子周／695,696
蒔園居士／309
實業部全國度量衡局／48,555
實業部中央農業實驗所／339(2)
實業部中央農業實驗所農業經濟科／253
史恩緜／1531
史國綱／120
史密斯普萊德富／807
史念祖／1702
史諾／804
史盤／198
史善長／1670
史特林堡／572
史虛白／1173
史一如／1693
史游／1285
史玉涵／93
史炤／1093
史震林／159,412,1611
矢吹慶輝／2067
矢内原忠雄／854
世界科學社青年輔導部／1898
世界科學社藝術部／940,1854
世界書局編輯部／1031
世界文化合作中國協會籌備委員會／96
市川白弦／1907,1908
市民治促進會／347
市隱／165
事業部中央農業實驗所農業經濟科／275

侍桁／29	釋慧寶／1114
室伏高信／2091	釋慧超／1796
釋白延／1208	釋慧皎／1215
釋般刺密帝／1159	釋慧立／1158,1161,1777
釋寶雲／1206	釋慧然／1777
釋辯機／1162（2）	釋慧訓／1468
釋波羅末陀／1507	釋吉藏／1108,1469
釋不染居士／1274	釋際界／1613
釋乘恩／1325	釋畺良耶舍／1473
釋道誠／1507	釋皎然／746
釋道謙／1160	釋净覺／1344
釋道世／82,650	釋鳩摩羅什／1494（2），1533,1591,3002
釋道宣／682,1216	釋瞿曇悉達／1162
釋道原／1324,1801	釋窺基／1119,1591,1691
釋德洪／873,1360	釋禮言／1199
釋德清／1735,1790	釋良定／1571
釋闍那崛多／1196	釋良山／1143
釋法藏／1119	釋亮典／1526
釋法海／1367,1368（3）	釋妙明／1468
釋法顯／1207	釋普濟／1605
釋法穎／1206	釋齊己／576
釋法雲／651,1198	釋契嵩／1853
釋飛錫／1418	釋慶老／1129
釋佛陀跋陀羅／1156,1159	釋求那毗地／1109
釋佛陀多羅／1159	釋如惺／1216
釋高泉／1175	釋僧祐／1265,1793
釋貫休／1129	釋僧肇／578,1112,1734,1735
釋灌頂／1157	釋善導／1473
釋廣賓／1613	釋神會／1483
釋寒山／702	釋神清／1114
釋恒演／415	釋施護／1292
釋懷海／1109	釋師鍊／1711
釋惠洪／1129	釋太虛／1169,1207,1418
釋慧能／1368（2），1806,1833	釋曇無讖／3002

釋通炯／1790
釋維祇難／1197
釋祥邁／1117
釋信行／1832
釋行深／1621
釋續法／1197,1621
釋玄應／1680
釋玄奘／608,1135,1157,1162（2）,1201,1307,1591,1686,1687,1703
釋延壽／1767
釋彥悰／1158,1161,1777
釋一然／1467
釋義淨／1198,1514
釋圓覺／1276
釋雲峯／1591
釋贊寧／1216
釋真諦／1157,1158
釋真界／1158
釋真源／1199
釋智達／1239
釋智旭／1621,1720
釋智儼／1207
釋智顗／1196,1366,1534,1648
釋智者／1309
釋袾宏／1129
釋竺法／1425
釋袾宏／1723
釋宗杲／1737
釋宗密／1159,1276
釋祖雍／1215
首都警察廳編譯室／350
首都普通考試典試委員會／254
狩野壽信／2114
狩野直喜／1802

狩野直禎／1802
壽鵬飛／149
叔衡／563
舒夢蘭／1107
舒位／1424
舒新城／193,299,514
雙修主人／40
水谷真成／2098(2),2110
水世嫦／2102
水野梅曉／2070,2071,2076,2088
説劍樓主／161
"司法行政部"／666,667
司法行政部／489
"司法行政部"調查局／655(4),656(3),657(2),669(2),670(4),671(3),934(2),948,960,1926(2)
司空圖／877,1533
司馬承禎／926
司馬光／395,564,735,840,888,936,998,1091(2),1092(2),1093(2),1224,1296(2),1433,1580
司馬璐／640
司馬遷／342,874
司甯春／1847
司香舊尉／1475
私立福建協和學院秘書處／355
思高聖經學會／663,762,805,957,1095
思想與時代社／1897
斯賓塞爾／356
斯大林／235,798
斯塔斯／280
斯偉夫特／95
斯文赫定／32,401,589
寺西秀武／2064

松本龜次郎／2061(2),2064(2),2082,2096
松本文三郎／2093,2110
松菁／665
松平圓次郎／2079
松崎鶴雄／2068
松下大三郎／2061
淞滬警備司令部／453
嵩山／1175
宋邦綏／1123
宋曹／1510
宋長白／228
宋鴻年／281
宋繼澄／1584
宋介／347
宋經畬／1763
宋克／1548
宋孔顯／553
宋濂／560,790,896,1014,1266,1369,1425,1546
宋犖／1608
宋綿初／1253
宋敏求／918,1130
宋佩韋／65,390
宋若瑜／168
宋史研究會／895,896
宋文薰／908
宋咸／766
宋翔鳳／1247,1377(2),1378,1626
宋應星／924,1573,1854
宋育仁／1124
宋衷／1504
甦庵道人／1143
酥醪洞主／1210
蘇伯衡／900,1551

蘇德宏／204
蘇繼廎／1887
蘇甲榮／1764
蘇晉仁／224
蘇聯大使館新聞處／363(2),364
蘇時學／1407,1815
蘇軾／900,1178(3),1470,1550,1848
蘇舜欽／364,900
蘇天爵／686,1713
蘇同炳／836
蘇雪林／925
蘇洵／740,1470
蘇演存／518
蘇興／1149,1774
蘇澤東／1545
蘇轍／796,1470,1550(2)
蘇州中華基督教青年會／92
蘇籀記／1374
蘇祖斐／77
素庵主人／1317
隋樹森／591,971
綏遠省政府／365
隨園主人／1649
孫本文／156,168,192,327(3),328(2),422,1894
孫傳鳳／1625
孫次舟／358
孫道昇／215,451
孫德謙／1312,1560,1608,1760
孫德中／585,586(2)
孫殿起／652
孫馮翼／1282
孫復／1557
孫光憲／1113

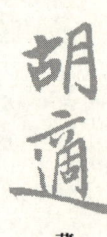

孫海波／740	孫席珍／67,158,286
孫寒冰／414,495	孫星衍／903,1338,1341,1593,1607,1654,1795
孫會源／366	
孫景烈／1619	孫雄／1221
孫毅／675	孫學顏／1386(2)
孫楷第／33,111,187,215,223,315,428,769,801,1013,1057	孫洵侯／853
	孫詒讓／746,819,1082,1083,1158,1228(2),1407,1478,1594,1753(2)
孫奎／1147	
孫連仲／902	孫應鰲／1122,1278,1306,1537,1557,1658,1700
孫俍工／399(3),518,532,540(2)	
孫梅／1536	孫毓棠／140,510
孫奇逢／1558,1589,1619	孫毓秀／1251
孫仁和／1375	孫豫壽／471
孫榮彬／499	孫元衡／596
孫紹遠／1486	孫雲鑄／481,502
孫奭／1786	孫澤英／68
孫樹馨／1797	孫拯／462
孫蓀意／1669	孫中山／312(2),313,366,552
孫彤／1231	孫仲寬／401
孫桐生／1819	孫作雲／354
孫望／294	梭羅文／55
孫文／172,366	索予明／678
孫武／1558(2)	

T

台灣大學文學院古文字學研究室／1062	印小組／663
台灣省氣象所／926	臺灣大學考古人類學刊編輯委員會／1931(2)
台灣省政府教育廳／934	臺灣大學文史哲學報編輯委員會／1931,1932
台灣銀行經濟研究室／840,977	臺灣風物編輯委員會／1993(2)
臺北縣文獻委員會／904	臺灣省接收委員會日產處理委員會／369
臺靜農／57,173	臺灣省立岡山中學校慶特刊編輯委員會／332
臺糖農業工程處／608	臺灣省立師範大學／909(3),910,1987(3)
臺灣大學紀念傅故校長籌備委員會哀輓錄編	臺灣省立師範大學人事室／910

臺灣省立臺北圖書館／913
臺灣省通志館／1994(2)
臺灣省文獻委員會／2004(4),2005(3)
臺灣省文獻委員會編纂組／1995(4),1996(5),1998(7),1999(4),2000(2)
臺灣省行政長官公署統計室／370(2)
臺灣省政府交通處／368
臺灣省政府教育廳／369(2)
臺灣省政府民政廳／368
臺灣鐵路局運務處餐旅服務所／912
臺灣銀行經濟研究室／572,662,829,832,841,888,907,908,912(3),914,974
臺灣"中華書局編輯部"／1071
太平洋雜誌編輯部／1897
太田孝太郎／1225
太虛大師／47
太虛法師／88,372
太虛上人／298
泰戈爾／970
檀萃／1172
譚炳訓／424
譚旦冏／1075,1077
譚健常／279
譚介甫／265
譚戒甫／77,321
譚丕模／844
譚峭／1276
譚勤餘／471
譚嗣同／1562
譚希思／1400
譚熙鴻／337
譚獻／1111,1136,1200,1213,1259,1433
譚延闓／1563,1776
譚儀／1255

譚元春／373,1838
譚貞默／1563
譚振歐／75
湯斌／1381,1563,1743
湯賓尹／1525(2)
湯爾和／4,35,52,66,194(2)
湯垕／1277
湯晉／373
湯茂如／63
湯鵬／1210
湯顯祖／1364
湯象龍／515
湯一雯／1890
湯用彤／69,70,464,561,703
唐寶鍔／67
唐秉鈞／1456
唐擘黃／491,3008
唐圭璋／293,1451
唐海／520
唐鴻烈／419
唐鴻學／1283,1536,1681
唐紀翔／511
唐鑑／1658
唐景崧／1446
唐敬杲／436
唐君毅／299,1030
唐蘭／26,29,104,110,213,235,237,380
唐龍／1704
唐慶增／517
唐慎微／597
唐士恥／1362
唐世隆／1397
唐守曾／50
唐順之／755

唐太宗／632
唐天成／355
唐玄度／970
唐玄宗／1565
唐壎／1552,1577
唐彥謙／1373
唐晏／1357,1373,1381
唐鉞／118,444,688,1054
唐允／64
唐甄／838
唐仲友／1171,1311,1327,1371,1490,1704,1718
唐柱國／582(2)
唐祖命／1572
韜園／449
陶百川／775
陶保廉／1632
陶葆楷／96
陶弼／1695
陶成章／181
陶德怡／414
陶弘景／1031,1083
陶鴻慶／641(4),1187
陶桓萊／348
陶樂勤／397
陶樑／1242
陶孟和／17,327,328,515,520
陶潛／1549(2),1570(2)
陶然／1593
陶汝鼐／1463
陶望齡／1379,1631
陶希聖／374
陶錫祈／1218,1503
陶先畹／1650

陶湘／1543
陶潯霍／1589
陶毓英／1505
陶淵明／1854
陶元珍／311
陶雲逵／111
陶貞白／1812
陶知行／250
陶宗儀／1153,1526,1816
滕固／165,374
滕元發／1557
藤島達朗／2105
藤岡啓／66
藤卷良知／2059
藤田豐八／359,1288,1289(2),1796
惕莊主人／1268
天花才子／1340(2)
天津新學書院書館／484
天理教海外傳道部／380
天台宗宗典刊行會／600,2092
田村德治／2066
田村羊三／2096
田繼綜／7
田崎仁義／2060,2069
田雯／1131,1392
田肇麗／1392
田中耕太郎／2094
田中修／472
田中智學／2096
鉄道部統計處／545
鐵保／1435,1856
鐵道部財務司調查科／12
同學會八屆幹事會／690
桐廬／889

童漢章 / 1332
童璜 / 1436
童冀 / 1476
童品 / 1150
童士愷 / 244
童世亨 / 346
童書業 / 77,139
童永慶 / 62
童宗說 / 1089
涂天相 / 1326
涂序瑄 / 851

屠格涅夫 / 224
屠繼善 / 1791
屠景山 / 504
屠隆 / 1700
土肥慶藏 / 2077
土屋詮教 / 2074
推士 / 207
托洛斯基 / 508
脫察安 / 1709(2)
脫脫 / 752,785,896,1882
陀思妥夫斯基 / 20

W

"外交部"情報司 / 741
外交部統計科 / 1582
宛敏灝 / 79
萬德固 / 85
萬福 / 1138
萬光泰 / 1606
萬國鼎 / 199
萬經 / 1256
萬斯年 / 374
萬斯同 / 1353,1455,1463,1642(2)
萬蔚亭 / 770
萬衣 / 1585
萬異 / 430
萬兆芝 / 550
萬宗一 / 155,265
汪北平 / 928
汪辟疆 / 920
汪長祿 / 545
汪大捷 / 24,306
汪大鈞 / 1499

汪大義 / 389
汪德餘 / 422
汪奠基 / 420
汪端 / 1402
汪馥泉 / 341,534
汪輝祖 / 1501(2),1585,1712
汪繼培 / 1430,1489,1712
汪縉 / 1586
汪景祺 / 1186
汪敬熙 / 206,441
汪靜之 / 11,164,169,571
汪厥明 / 2853
汪康年 / 1586
汪黎慶 / 1629
汪懋祖 / 38,246
汪孟慈 / 1478
汪乃剛 / 749
汪榮寶 / 650
汪少倫 / 234
汪士鐸 / 1524,1585,1586,1846

汪士鍾／1689

汪廷儒／1236

汪琬／993

汪文臺／1279,1426

汪喜孫／1586

汪協如／110

汪怡／137,389

汪吟龍／400

汪應辰／937

汪由敦／1195

汪佑／1606

汪淵／1592(2)

汪原放／110,141,200,230,311(2),647,699(2),771,882,883

汪遠孫／1307,1308

汪藻／662

汪澤／1295

汪兆銘／1837

汪蟄庵／810

汪震／49,138,210,283,499

汪正／1620

汪之昌／1439

汪之選／1277

汪中／880,1247,1461,1462,1513,1836

王安國／1588

王安石／1082,1857

王柏／336,791,987,1311,1371(2),1493,1512,1544,1665

王柏心／1168,1512

王必昌／597

王弼／737,1083,1857

王冰／733,1123

王秉恩／1497,1731

王昶／1242,1271,1313,1399

王琛／1277

王承烈／1284

王城／1439

王墀／1728

王充／235,796,797,1375

王崇炳／1312

王崇慶／1011

王崇武／87,259,260,261

王崇植／288

王大同／1899

王得臣／1762

王德昭／951

王定安／1623

王定保／1742

王端履／1139(2)

王莪孫／530

王斐烈／237,434

王夫之／642,744

王符／837,1430

王福民／986

王撫洲／97

王復／1120,1196,1428,1736,1739

王艮／1402,1857

王構／1648

王古魯／516,568,975

王官壽／1542

王官獻／756

王光祈／246,310

王國維／296(2),362,673,679,798,849,897,1130,1157,1192,1222,1223,1232,1254,1256,1263,1308,1326,1358,1363,1380,1388,1392,1445,1450,1458,1488,1502,1507,1545,1560,1567,1568,1594,1618,1691(2),1693,1697,1722,1725,1754,1789

王鴻霖／67,428

王鴻緒／1435

王鸑／1637

王懷琛／61,562

王會釐／1599

王畿／1370,1587

王輯五／302,400,444,452,527

王季烈／1716

王季同／88,460

王驥德／1450

王家棟／323

王檢／191

王介忱／481

王瑾／207

王晶心／987

王靜如／89,148,201,236,285,349,384,413

王靜齋／104

王鏡清／1900

王俊瑜／510

王凱泰／1695

王闓運／1477

王克家／222

王肯堂／1708

王況裴／1807

王藍／771,867,969

王力／43,214(2),322,530,531,536,539,540

王立中／400

王亮／1442(3),1445,1614

王了一／540

王齡／1459,1702

王鏐／1258

王茂材／1107

王懋竑／1107,1757,1881,1882

王夢阮／150

王名元／417

王明／916

王明清／1581(2),1706

王明仲／1547

王謨／1727

王木岡／186

王南屏／393

王念孫／1236(2),1506,1529,1587

王攀／1244

王鵬運／1111,1539,1540,1751

王闢之／1487

王平陵／284,333,398,572,634

王溥／920,946,1564

王青芳／378

王清彬／60

王慶雲／1498,1617

王仁俊／1190(2),1218

王日蔚／455

王榮商／1256

王汝南／979

王瑞嫻／73

王若虛／715,1271

王森然／191

王善治／297

王紹蘭／1233

王紳／1295

王繩祖／279

王十朋／737,805

王石安／735,853

王時槐／1569

王時潤／1753

王實甫／1613,1614

王士達／193

3063

王士點／1318,1395

王士禎／1566

王士禛／35,1589,1623

王士正／1805

王世棟／436

王世杰／22,501,526,1785

王世憲／806,807

王世穎／768

王世貞／1670

王守仁／933,1588

王叔和／803

王叔岷／1798,1807

王書林／202,430

王樹枏／69,1635(2)

王樹勲／60

王思任／390

王斯睿／330

王松闓／1456

王肅／210,768

王韜／1569,1600,1694

王廷紹／1416,1417

王廷相／1333,1663

王同春／1461

王同祖／1659

王桐齡／301,524,2069

王稌／1242

王維／933

王維誠／213

王維克／315

王維亮／1165

王偉俠／284

王文禄／1088

王文濡／1583,1847

王文山／752

王汶／1427

王惜時／707

王熙／1630

王羲之／1848

王錫榮／1657

王先謙／562,702(2),714,984,985,1176,1270(2),1506,1588,1651(3),1837

王先慎／701

王顯恩／247

王襄／1212

王祥輝／240

王象之／1512,1704

王小航／1627(2),1727

王信忠／551(2)

王星拱／206

王星賢／890

王頊齡／1435

王宣忱／438

王學理／714

王迅中／303

王亞南／197

王言／1313

王彦威／1442,1445,1614

王一仁／300

王揖唐／347,1476

王禕／1275,1439,1589

王奕／1705

王益之／1609,1742

王逸／598,1144(2)

王憶菴／352

王翼之／403

王懿榮／1573

王寅生／148

王引之／758,1321,1323,1587,1588

王應麟／1341(2),1705,1739,1803,1833
王應山／1397
王應偉／340
王庸／505(2)
王永祥／180,1146,1303,1343
王禹偁／963
王與／1605
王愈擴／1465
王鈺／176
王毓霖／197
王毓銓／389
王元啓／1183
王元增／1620
王源／1331
王越／1203
王芸生／229,481
王筠／940,1305,1373,1389(2)
王雲五／57,388,490
王惲／849
王再勵／1892
王造時／120
王曾善／654
王贈芳／1293
王昭然／687
王照圓／1359,1360,1395
王肇晉／1377
王哲甫／537
王真／1268
王鎮／500
王之春／842
王之鈞／458
王植／1294(2)
王芷章／1431
王志堅／1117

王治心／103,166
王銍／1408,1814
王鍾麒／195,311
王重民／30,74(3),190,371,688,1105(2),1111
王竹泉／158,281,318,319
王竹亭／382
王助／146
王灼／1684
王緇塵／695
王子建／305
王梓材／1547
微明學社／211,474
韋叢蕪／95
韋爾斯／345
韋穀／1123
韋宏岐／202
韋縠／585
韋鏡權／160
韋廉臣／1218,1290,1716
韋羅貝／550
韋羅璧／550
韋述／1357
韋漱園／387
韋休／529
韋昭／925
韋志彪／683
韋莊／1871
惟白／1165
維拉・凱瑟／806
尾崎金右衛門／2073
偉烈亞力／1562
衛布夫婦／465
衛爾德／429

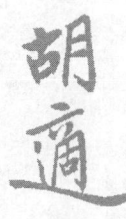

衛聚賢 / 106(2),143,519
衛中 / 182
魏建功 / 30,33,108,206,231,350,376,461,511
魏了翁 / 707
魏茂林 / 1422
魏收 / 935
魏崧 / 1680
魏特 / 918
魏熙元 / 1464
魏錫曾 / 1295
魏象樞 / 1251
魏野 / 1331
魏易 / 230,474
魏裔介 / 1300
魏應麒 / 23
魏源 / 772(2),1392
魏肇基 / 321
魏徵 / 294,852
魏重慶 / 359
温公頤 / 53,492
温吉 / 907
温汝能 / 1178
文公直 / 569
文化財保護委員會 / 2100
文康 / 647,1192(2)
文聯季刊編輯委員會 / 2002
文史薈刊編輯小組 / 2002
文史雜誌社 / 1897
文天祥 / 397,937,1743
文廷式 / 1723
文同 / 630,1227
文物編輯委員會 / 2002(2),2003
文物參考資料編輯委員會 / 2003(4)

文獻編纂委員會 / 948(2)
文星雜誌編輯委員會 / 2006,2007(4),2008
文訊月刊社 / 1897
文藝家協會 / 2094
文藝列車編輯委員會 / 2010
文徵明 / 940,1424
聞華英 / 117
聞齊 / 445
聞一多 / 93,335,356
聞亦博 / 522
聞宥 / 239
翁白 / 1391
翁大年 / 1329
翁方綱 / 929,1213(2),1255,1572
翁輝東 / 1290
翁同龢 / 1424,1600
翁萬達 / 1290
翁文灝 / 520
翁之潤 / 1426
翁之鏞 / 174,495
翁洲老民 / 697
巫寶三 / 197,276,521
烏梁諾夫 / 310
鄔孟暉 / 330
吳藹宸 / 266,432
吳半農 / 146,381
吳博 / 200
吳昌齡 / 1673
吳長元 / 1133
吳承恩 / 944,952,1097,1098(2),1481(2)
吳承洛 / 188
吳承仕 / 1321
吳承禧 / 504
吳楚材 / 486,665,675

3066

吳處厚／1439(2)
吳大澂／1263,1336,1452,1527,1827
吳德功／1027
吳調侯／486
吳鼎昌／728
吳恩裕／258,392,496
吳豐本／1249
吳貫因／134,344
吳光祖／1287
吳廣成／1613
吳桂華／1660
吳晗／110,156(2),220,260(2),263,337,475(2)
吳瀚濤／65
吳懷珍／1165
吳趼人／1600
吳金鼎／481
吳盡我／348
吳經熊／544,549
吳景超／56,351,410,516
吳景奎／1677
吳敬敷／276
吳敬模／365
吳敬所／1637,1638
吳敬軒／259,272
吳敬梓／308,1096(2),1463,1858,3007
吳靜山／322,403
吳覺農／387,388,494,503
吳均／1602,1655
吳俊升／36,333
吳濬／1201
吳闓生／1462
吳康／894
吳寬／828

吳昆吾／381
吳萊／1709(2)
吳立行／1043
吳歷／1855
吳陵／866
吳魯芹／736
吳梅／292,1012,1222,1480,1481
吳宓／403
吳勉學／1765
吳佩孚先生集編輯委員會／945
吳平齋／69
吳其昌／460
吳其濬／1742(2)
吳其玉／310
吳綺／1689
吳仁德／347
吳榮光／1352
吳汝綸／1580
吳尚鷹／385
吳師道／1024,1326,1601(2)
吳士鑑／754,1318
吳世昌／251,335(2),349,394
吳守禮／1790
吳壽暘／1110
吳曙天／203
吳頌皋／386,499
吳所敬／1124
吳唐林／1268
吳天任／1028
吳廷燮／1351
吳惟平／241
吳偉業／804
吳渭／1717
吳文溥／1174

吳文藻 / 249, 1045
吳相湘 / 844, 1062(2), 1063, 1074
吳省蘭 / 1689
吳修 / 1734
吳秀峯 / 120
吳學周 / 207
吳延環 / 764
吳燕生 / 176
吳蔭培 / 1259
吳應箕 / 1356
吳瀛 / 512
吳映奎 / 1230
吳永 / 1219
吳有訓 / 62
吳虞 / 404
吳玉搢 / 1495, 1531
吳育 / 1601
吳棫 / 1724
吳元泰 / 1636
吳雲 / 1358(2)
吳藻 / 1431
吳曾祺 / 141, 142(3), 1341
吳縝 / 1863
吳振棫 / 1604, 1676
吳正 / 388
吳之器 / 1608

吳直 / 1324
吳志青 / 371
吳稚暉 / 404(2), 405(3)
吳濁流 / 659
吳子通 / 945
吳自牧 / 1810
吳宗濂 / 1104
吳宗信 / 1869
五來欣造 / 308
五五旅行團 / 117
伍非百 / 259, 264, 266(2)
伍光建 / 201, 336, 412, 782, 839
伍蠡甫 / 414
伍受真 / 870
伍廷芳 / 408
伍憲子 / 131
伍友書 / 307
伍遵契 / 1239
武昌書局 / 1881
武穆淳 / 1103, 1104, 1213
武陽漢各界慶祝第二十五屆國際合作節紀念大會 / 59
武億 / 1182, 1315, 1321, 1454, 1468, 1508(4)
武則天 / 1722
物茂卿 / 1782

X

西北實業公司總管理處 / 410
西林 / 455
西田幾多郎 / 321
西周生 / 1098, 1645(2)
希特勒 / 55

希元 / 1320
席存泰 / 1295
席勒 / 55
席鳴九 / 384
席世臣 / 1175

下中邦彥 / 2109
夏承燾 / 1101
夏德儀 / 1092
夏敦復 / 1619
夏濟安 / 644,2008(2),2009(4)
夏堅白 / 451,467
夏菁 / 829
夏敬渠 / 1031
夏康農 / 236
夏琳 / 812
夏鼐 / 371
夏勤埔 / 1294
夏荃 / 1248
夏仁虎 / 1631(2)
夏壽田 / 1558
夏燮 / 1750
夏心客 / 598,783
夏炘 / 1324
夏育民 / 1748
夏元鼎 / 824
夏元瑮 / 5,462,1103
夏允彝 / 1645,1646
夏曾佑 / 510
夏志清 / 2792
夏忠道 / 143
纖雲女士 / 243
冼榮熙 / 424
現代評論社 / 2010
現代知識半月刊社編輯委員會 / 1898
現行法規大全編纂委員會 / 1073
憲政實施促進委員會 / 44
香港佛教編輯委員會 / 2011
香月居主人 / 1561
鄉村衛生研究會 / 338

向達 / 345,356,478
向乃祺 / 385
向培根 / 280
向夏 / 704
向真 / 188
蕭純錦 / 495
蕭恩承 / 76,185(2),1192
蕭而化 / 706
蕭繼宗 / 809
蕭君絳 / 294
蕭克木 / 567
蕭令裕 / 1294
蕭師毅 / 23
蕭士贇 / 657
蕭舜華 / 231,242(2),309
蕭統 / 228
蕭望卿 / 377
蕭文業 / 1697
蕭文哲 / 284
蕭孝嶸 / 444,446
蕭雄 / 1575
蕭一山 / 289,290,1317
蕭繹 / 1313
蕭正誼 / 412
蕭子顯 / 822
小倉正恆 / 1552
小川晴暘 / 2084
小柳司氣太 / 2078,2090,2093,2098
小泉郁子 / 2082,2096
小山左文二 / 2094
小田內通敏 / 2083
小野藤太 / 2065
小野秀雄 / 2089
小野玄妙 / 2092

小雲石海崖 / 1863
小仲馬 / 189(2)
笑笑生 / 189
歇浦學人 / 1324
謝愛群 / 246
謝翱 / 1631
謝彬 / 527
謝冰瑩 / 802,944
謝朝徵 / 1107
謝鼎卿 / 1651
謝恩增 / 438
謝枋得 / 1780
謝扶雅 / 112
謝觀 / 20,538
謝國文 / 1834
謝國楨 / 109,261,262(2),678,1440,1583
謝家榮 / 386,529
謝靈運 / 1470
謝六逸 / 901,951
謝蒙 / 89
謝乃壬 / 1410
謝清高 / 140
謝汝川 / 1834
謝聲溢 / 365
謝頌羔 / 389,395
謝無量 / 43,281,559
謝香開 / 1175
謝興堯 / 1559
謝循初 / 441
謝詒徵 / 362
謝義偉 / 497
謝瀛洲 / 543
謝雲聲 / 258,369
謝祖源 / 1234

心理學系研究報告編輯委員會 / 1931
心鐵道人 / 1259
辛笛 / 350
辛克萊 / 317
辛啓泰 / 171
辛未白 / 228
辛文 / 1293
辛鈃 / 1577,1859
新潮社 / 29
新潮雜誌社 / 2011,2012
新城新藏 / 67,408,639
新路周刊編輯部 / 1898
新時代編輯委員會 / 2012
新聞天地社 / 2014,2015(3)
新運婦女指導委員會 / 98
"新中國評論社編輯委員會" / 2016(2)
新自由社 / 1898
信士哈巴 / 1488
信天翁 / 1173
行政院農村復興委員會 / 114,147(2),175,274,302,320,482,493,526(2)
"行政院"主計處 / 1072
邢昉 / 1564
邢契莘 / 376
邢澍 / 1795
幸德秋水 / 166
熊賜履 / 1659
熊飛 / 1649(2)
熊鈇 / 975
熊會貞 / 1845
熊崎武良溫 / 2085
熊十力 / 283
熊野與 / 1218
熊毅 / 385

熊之孚 / 422
虚心 / 566
徐本僡 / 1229
徐斌 / 948
徐炳昶 / 445
徐炳堃 / 471
徐滄水 / 272
徐昌霖 / 338
徐沉泗 / 1084
徐承禮 / 1628
徐大椿 / 1721
徐道 / 1352
徐道鄰 / 842
徐調孚 / 958
徐定文 / 1584
徐敦璋 / 119,120
徐復觀 / 1057
徐幹 / 1652
徐高阮 / 1774
徐誥 / 545
徐光啓 / 486,1419,1652
徐吉 / 1652
徐嘉瑞 / 194,203,287,501,1043
徐建寅 / 1170,1562
徐鉴 / 1548
徐居敬 / 1125
徐鈞 / 1502
徐鍇 / 886
徐康 / 1429
徐珂 / 1334
徐孔僧 / 304
徐孔生 / 56
徐昆 / 1366
徐禮輔 / 1374

徐良董 / 47
徐陵 / 978,1009
徐靈府 / 1577
徐鹿卿 / 1548
徐夢麟 / 482
徐乃昌 / 1238,1280,1291,1411,1554,1628,1849
徐袍 / 1544
徐浦 / 1150
徐乾學 / 1167
徐慶卿 / 1411
徐慶譽 / 337,446,525
徐聲越 / 1486
徐時棟 / 1664(2)
徐世昌 / 1161(2),1666(2),1667
徐淑希 / 64
徐松 / 1543,1615,1643
徐天祐 / 1603,1604
徐天麟 / 637,948,1175,1609
徐廷瑚 / 1017
徐廷榮 / 433
徐庭瑤 / 167
徐霆 / 1263
徐渭 / 1536,1650,1652
徐蔚南 / 324
徐文靖 / 1761
徐文珊 / 342
徐燨 / 1327
徐訏 / 743(3)
徐緒昌 / 373
徐鉉 / 977,1291
徐養原 / 1386
徐業 / 273
徐義宗 / 855

3071

徐盈／14
徐永棠／109
徐友蘭／1454,1480
徐淵若／276(2),305
徐元夢／1398
徐則敏／38
徐兆搽／299
徐照／314,772
徐照英／751
徐志摩／4,7,23,60,85,235,243,249,777,970,978,1039
徐中舒／52,102,191,458,483
徐仲白／537
徐仲航／258
徐肅／1186,1628(2)
徐子明／726
徐子室／1288
徐宗幹／889,890
徐宗澤／486,816
許寶善／1114
許炳漢／27,198,567
許超／1780
許承堯／1682
許崇清／493
許丹／392
許道齡／17
許德鄰／86
許地山／46,54,464
許公武／469
許冠三／875
許廣平／791
許渾／635
許乃昌／1554
許南英／1340

許謙／1108(2),1185,1186,1490,1864
許善長／1116(2)
許慎／354,730,887,1528
許世英／163,1837
許仕廉／396
許同莘／490
許晚成／725
許維遹／1382
許文玉／335,375
許希哲／786,931
許錫五／443
許嘯天／213
許有壬／1744
許玉瑑／1181
許元淮／1546
許雲樵／823
許贊堃／1340
許正綬／1102
許之衡／1450,1486,1507
許仲琳／1638,1649
續可／1896
玄奘／608
薛典曾／503
薛福成／1142(4),1143(2),1250,1597,1598,1695,1696(5),1736
薛恨生／223
薛鴻志／184
薛蕙／773,1717
薛居正／762
薛賚時／27
薛蕾／234
薛尚功／1354
薛紹元／844
薛舜華／566

薛濤 / 1265
薛熙 / 1403
薛瑄 / 982,1185,1657
薛以恆 / 223
薛元植 / 445
薛允升 / 1183,1565
薛仲三 / 785

學粹雜誌編輯委員會 / 2017(2)
學原社 / 1899
雪林女士 / 217
薰風月刊編輯委員會 / 2018(4),2019
荀況 / 985,1662(2)
荀悦 / 1429,1482,1807
循環日報社 / 447

Y

押尾乾夫 / 2072
雅曼 / 654
瘂弦 / 789
亞當士 / 27
亞東圖書館 / 207
亞歷山大・勃洛克 / 336
亞汀 / 962
岩井大慧 / 2108
岩田大慧 / 2086(6),2087(6),2088(3)
研石山樵 / 1636
閻焕文 / 220
閻簡弼 / 116,270,452
閻若璩 / 1389
閻錫山 / 24
閻幼甫 / 1891
顔滄波 / 368
顔綸澤 / 351
顔師古 / 1340
顔元 / 606,890,954,1350,1534,1538,1618,1666(2),1758
顔元孫 / 665
顔真卿 / 988
顔之推 / 300,989,1667(2),1866
嚴賓杜 / 602

嚴長明 / 1669,1705
嚴從簡 / 1509
嚴恩椿 / 170
嚴復 / 150,833,1574(2)
嚴耕望 / 920
嚴觀 / 1301
嚴鴻瑤 / 207
嚴可均 / 850,1488,1567,1630
嚴靈峯 / 197,774,787,923,1076,1077
嚴懋功 / 1821(2),1822,1823(2),1824
嚴如熤 / 1469
嚴樹森 / 1283
嚴嵩 / 1429
嚴一萍 / 740,980,1870,1879
嚴虞惇 / 1533
嚴楨 / 240
嚴莊 / 201
巖崎胖 / 1880
鹽谷温 / 532
晏端書 / 1657
晏嬰 / 991,1670,1874
燕夫 / 1046
燕京大學歷史學會 / 1895(2),1896
燕京大學新聞學系 / 436

燕京大學宗教學院／3
揚雄／653,915,1673(2)
楊丙辰／121,918
楊炳南／140
楊伯愷／55
楊朝英／590,591,971,1133,1721
楊晨／859
楊成志／257,465,481
楊冲嶼／420
楊椿／1392
楊大膺／444
楊殿珣／127
楊調元／252(2)
楊東澤／1231
楊鳳藻／1643
楊光先／1123
楊漢輝／91
楊禾／1686
楊鴻烈／48,341,506(2),1015
楊虎嘯／4,141
楊輝／1624,1674
楊晦／13,20
楊基／1390
楊繼盛／993
楊家駱／604,645,834,850,981,1056,1070,1097(2),1098
楊家瑜／97
楊簡／1154(2),1836
楊捷／832
楊景仁／1142
楊倞／985,1662(2)
楊敬修／141
楊静／443
楊炯／992

楊筠松／1369
楊開渠／277
楊克毅／31
楊寬／233
楊堃／81,170
楊立誠／1596,1746
楊廉／699
楊漣／1673
楊聯陞／2936
楊鍊／107
楊亮功／184
楊懋建／1319
楊沒累／264
楊念先／1136
楊齊賢／657
楊清磬／60
楊泉／1607
楊人梗／80
楊仁愷／786
楊榮國／767
楊鋭／1675
楊慎／629,918,1089,1560,1674
楊時／648,992,1673,1674,1787
楊士奇／1177
楊士琦／1540
楊適生／401
楊守敬／353,879,1287,1353,1361,1458,1524(2),1610,1845
楊樹／1283
楊樹達／42,106,143,144,233,442,602,674,1182,1224,1343,1387,1755
楊萬里／35,594,1135,1675(2)
楊維新／223
楊維楨／639,927

楊西孟／498,512	姚紹華／44
楊希閔／1541,1704	姚思廉／592,783
楊顯之／1806	姚燧／820,1409
楊祥蔭／2067	姚文爕／1856
楊向奎／239,1609	姚燮／1309
楊笑湛／508	姚鉉／922
楊杏佛／450	姚彥渠／601
楊秀鶴／660	姚瑩／637,1042
楊衒之／802,1381(2),1774,1808,1809	姚元之／1762
楊一峯／995	姚振宗／1339
楊億／949,1607,1611	耶律楚材／1025,1614
楊吟秋／409	野上俊静／2105
楊英／1665	葉秉敬／1826
楊永泰／420	葉昌熾／1126(2),1705,1716
楊玉清／422	葉崇勛／530
楊毓健／1139,1140	葉春墀／288
楊雲萍／781	葉德輝／1354,1532,1617,1618
楊載／701,1676	葉德祿／257,357,360,374,375,476
楊增新／1120(2),1121(4)	葉兌／1536
楊哲夫／26	葉爾愷／1171
楊振鍔／992	葉法無／396
楊鍾羲／1106,1488,1661(3),1662	葉公回／1881
楊仲明／451	葉恭綽／219,1603,1822
姚從吾／354	葉古紅／440
姚大榮／1387	葉圭綬／1655
姚範／1715	葉華／1559
姚合／993	葉季紅／440
姚際恆／103	葉景葵／278,494,552
姚江濱／174	葉良／307
姚名達／267,325,491,558,1028(2)	葉夢草／1275
姚鼐／953,1616(2)	葉夢得／584,1498(2)
姚枬／337	葉青／152,717
姚蓬子／830	葉秋原／33
姚淇清／1004	葉紹鈞／437,871

葉紹翁 / 1533
葉紹袁 / 1679(2)
葉時 / 1546
葉適 / 886,1525,1618
葉忘憂 / 1084
葉爲耽 / 15
葉維庚 / 1294
葉夏聲 / 686
葉星 / 328
葉衍蘭 / 1250,1448
葉英華 / 1275
葉穎林 / 116
葉顒 / 1432
葉玉麟 / 10
葉裕仁 / 1210,1211,1454(2)
葉志詵 / 1422
葉醉白 / 1868
葉作舟 / 367
一個退避三舍者 / 550
一粟 / 708
伊本納茲 / 783
伊達龍城 / 82
醫界春秋社編輯委員會 / 2019
易白沙 / 57
易本烺 / 1148,1482,1647,1722
易卜生 / 458
易培基 / 859
易順豫 / 1437
易宗夔 / 1639
逸見梅榮 / 2058
藝文印書館 / 841
因格拉門 / 198
殷海光 / 1021(2)
殷勤道 / 546

殷元勳 / 1123
陰少曾 / 14
尹會一 / 794,1381,1693
尹靜夫 / 488
尹彭壽 / 1473
尹壽松 / 551(2),552
尹焞 / 1002
尹文 / 1002,1779
尹文敬 / 27
尹喜 / 1787
尹哲生 / 187
尹仲容 / 793,794(2)
尹洙 / 706
引得編纂處 / 8,41,45,88,144,218,229,243,244,289,293,358,361,372,375,398,476,558
胤禛(清世宗) / 1706,1718
英傑修 / 1657
應成一 / 98
應劭 / 658,1203,1204(2)
應時 / 240
應廷育 / 1311
盈昂 / 102
雍家源 / 543
永惠 / 1483
游春楙 / 1003
游國恩 / 292
有本邦太郎 / 2059
于道泉 / 126
于敏中 / 1702,1873
于能模 / 553
于石 / 1766
于式玉 / 304
于熙儉 / 212,297,806
于省吾 / 238,701,731,774,794,819,863,881

(2),882(3),985,1090,1516(3)

于右任／1871

于在春／167

于藻／1607

于振翮／206

于準／1619

余昌之／200,311

余光中／2845

余祐／1595

余懷／1110,1706

余嘉錫／195,267,372,450,890,1535

余堅／749,750,807

余金／1617

余精一／199,527,554

余崑／500

余龍光／1515

余明德／245

余楠秋／55

余鵬／808

余青松／254

余上沅／208(2),325,416

余邵魚／1637

余紹宋／1510

余天休／498

余又蓀／204

余元遜／1697

余雲岫／162,455,456(2)

余允文／1100

余治／1514

余仲奎／561

俞成／1694

俞德浚／297

俞鳳賓／393

俞銘傳／335

俞平伯／63,150,707,711,1036,1672

俞慶棠／184

俞松笠／346

俞萬春／1290

俞棪／117

俞樾／1087,1152

俞正燮／684(2),1240(4)

俞仲久／423

俞子夷／283

魚豢／1593

魚玄機／1566(2)

瑜亮／767

虞集／631

漁業生物試驗所／1940

餘不釣徒／1403

宇井伯壽／2058,2103(2),2104

宇文懋昭／1160

羽田亨／952,1078,2069

羽溪了諦／415

郁達夫／46,664,790,864

郁松年／1681

郁永河／1791

尉遲偓／1746

喻良能／1621

喻亮／543

喻謙／1641

喻震孟／1379

鷲熊／1874

元好問／457,997,1080

元結／1434

元稹／1015

原頌周／545

原田康子／932

原田淑人／1154

原子彈防禦問題研究學會 / 477

袁昌英 / 316, 318

袁方 / 739

袁宏 / 713, 1269

袁宏道 / 478(2), 1016(4), 1017, 1652, 1715

袁凫若 / 817

袁黄 / 1324, 1727

袁桷 / 845, 1444

袁康 / 1527, 1718

袁枚 / 1182, 1555(4), 1556(2), 1625, 1626(4), 1639, 1655(2), 1714, 1772, 1792(2), 1806, 1817, 1849(2), 1850(3), 1851(2), 1861(3), 1862, 1863, 1867, 1870, 1875, 1876, 1883, 1884

袁仁林 / 676

袁殊 / 436

袁樞 / 928

袁樹 / 1792(2), 1883

袁帥南 / 846

袁同禮 / 688, 2714

袁燮 / 969

袁儼 / 1727

袁衣萍 / 39

袁逸塵 / 215

袁振英 / 328

袁中道 / 477

袁宗道 / 10

袁祖志 / 1851

圓正造 / 294

約法會議秘書廳 / 1716

約翰·狄恩 / 215

約瑟夫 / 225

月華報社 / 1899

岳浚 / 1621

岳珂 / 764, 769, 1315

岳騫 / 936

雲林縣政府 / 1019

允祿 / 1476, 1707(2), 1708

惲格 / 1413

惲敬 / 609

惲樹玨 / 426

蘊雯 / 403

Z

臧晉叔 / 1013, 1014

臧克家 / 214, 570

臧勵龢 / 511, 1048, 1052

臧懋循 / 1712

臧啓芳 / 128

臧亦蘧 / 365

臧庸 / 1110, 1253, 1577

臧玉淦 / 441, 442

曾炳鈞 / 119

曾鞏 / 1012, 1710

曾廣勛 / 345

曾國藩 / 336, 485, 1022, 1726(5)

曾后希 / 1021

曾幾 / 1128

曾傑 / 296

曾克耑 / 1385

曾樸 / 485, 1122

曾問吾 / 518

曾悟生 / 738

曾虛白 / 1010

曾仰豐 / 294,495
曾燠 / 1475
曾昭掄 / 486,1893
曾昭然 / 916
曾昭燏 / 481(2)
曾珠森 / 2868
曾資生 / 535,544
查鐸 / 1688
查繼佐 / 790
查慎行 / 760,1456
查爲仁 / 1332
查燕緒 / 1355
翟顥 / 928
翟灝 / 1577
詹體仁 / 1729
詹耀謙 / 855
展望雜誌編輯委員會 / 2020
展望雜誌社 / 2020
張安世 / 96
張寶樂 / 833
張秉鐸 / 104
張秉潔 / 414
張秉權 / 965,966(2)
張伯行 / 682,754,770,782,967,979,1738(2),1878
張伯楨 / 1410
張采田 / 1501
張寀臣 / 745
張昌圻 / 560
張長昌 / 466
張弨 / 1293
張潮 / 1703
張承華 / 1660
張純明 / 1896

張鴬鷗 / 489
張大成 / 1281
張大復 / 244
張岱 / 212,1465
張道 / 1329,1361,1452
張燾 / 1316
張德昌 / 52,260
張東蓀 / 39,208,392,439
張度 / 1529
張爾岐 / 1203,1258(2)
張鈁 / 1323
張芬 / 1367
張鳳 / 489
張福僖 / 1234
張富歲 / 461
張公輝 / 139,535
張穀若 / 162
張觀光 / 1423
張國忱 / 1551
張國維 / 431
張含英 / 353
張漢賢 / 763
張漢裕 / 950
張鶴 / 1821
張宏英 / 1078
張鴻來 / 37
張鴻翔 / 31,259,263(3)
張鴻藻 / 552
張華 / 1119
張化工 / 333
張惠言 / 817,1407,1683,1815,3007
張機 / 1089,1474
張籍 / 232
張堅 / 1281

3079

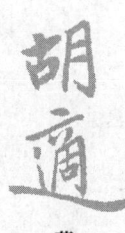

張謇 / 1732(2)
張鑑 / 1344,1390,1613
張江裁 / 16,17,18,264,1113,1441
張金鑑 / 442
張蓋 / 1310
張敬 / 815
張敬原 / 1052
張静廬 / 35,159,376,412,419,643
張鏡予 / 15
張競生 / 4,47,141,223,245,443
張九成 / 1264,1877,1880
張九齡 / 849
張九如 / 84
張九韶 / 1349
張居正 / 1301,1404
張君房 / 1019
張君俊 / 525
張君勱 / 134
張可久 / 1550
張可治 / 97
張耒 / 1027
張櫟任 / 539
張履鸞 / 526
張懋賞 / 1137
張孟兼 / 1106
張銘 / 244
張鳴珂 / 1251(2)
張默 / 789
張默生 / 458
張目寒 / 984
張穆 / 1230(2),1666
張培仁 / 1396
張培濚 / 62,459
張佩芳 / 1565

張佩綸 / 1299,1300
張鵬一 / 1560,1593
張溥 / 1256
張其柯 / 288
張其昀 / 233,296,525,550,571,687,694,812,937,1060,1074,1075,1076
張起鈞 / 774
張契靈 / 60(2)
張慶泰 / 279
張如心 / 830
張瑞機 / 1237
張埏 / 1616
張申府 / 439
張繩祖 / 429
張世禄 / 145
張世文 / 62,63
張栻 / 684,1025,1413(4)
張壽鏞 / 1836,1876,1880
張澍 / 1203,1466(3),1469,1676
張樹棻 / 490
張説 / 1733
張説之 / 1025
張思孝 / 1694
張天麟 / 525
張天翼 / 457
張廷濟 / 1445
張廷玉 / 816
張為綱 / 19
張唯中 / 98
張維屏 / 1244,1275
張瑋 / 1160
張蔚瑜 / 137
張文成 / 470
張文虎 / 1305

3080

張文穆／50,53,424,440

張西曼／414

張西堂／107,375

張希哲／667,808

張奚若／430

張憲秋／811

張相／869

張相文／1135,1172,1191,1208,1252,1414(3),1584,1677,1701,1729,1746

張祥河／1538

張祥齡／1261

張小柳／649

張孝若／270(2)

張孝祥／1007

張心泰／1567

張心一／348

張信民／1732

張星烺／553

張興唐／808

張玄之／1602

張學翰／34

張雪門／76(2),472

張洵如／19

張炎／1153,1721

張野青／1123

張一麐／1632

張宜泉／1775

張怡祖／1732

張易／878

張蔭麟／171,1026,1055

張印堂／57

張映南／442

張永懋／95

張永善／315,427

張友松／460

張玉書／636

張裕釗／1355

張鈺哲／112

張元濟／549,1799

張岳／1627

張樾丞／1495

張雲伏／75,120,466

張載／1025,1734,1877

張澤垚／62

張湛／786,1137,1360

張兆璿／574

張振鏞／533

張振之／267

張政烺／1789

張之洞／1026,1453(3),1511,1605

張志和／1714,1796

張中川／556

張忠紱／253,256,547,548

張資平／222,244,295,322,493,564

張紫林／86

張自英／931,955

張宗櫨／1153

張宗泰／1193,1394,1752

張宗祥／1120,1809

張宗子／376,411

張祖同／1623,1624

張作梅／775

張作楠／1122

章炳麟／837,915,1027,1090,1151(2),1168,1225,1234,1236,1245(2),1298,1362,1365,1427,1560,1561,1572,1597(2),1628,1633,1634,1730(2),1763

章鴻釗／339,460,1048

章嘉胡土克圖 / 1435,1579

章懋 / 1205(2),1312

章樵 / 675,1226(2)

章紹烈 / 465

章實齋 / 397

章太炎 / 135

章希呂 / 200(2),311,883

章學誠 / 1118(2),1199,1200,1261,1273(4),1304(2),1582(2),1595(2),1596(3),1643(2),1684(2),1685,1698(2),1720(2),1730(2),1731(2),1740,1741,3006

章衣萍 / 203,273

章友江 / 73

章徵言 / 116

章之汶 / 277

章宗源 / 1432,1554

長孫無忌 / 901,1565,1786

招子庸 / 1018

昭明太子 / 789,938

趙秉文 / 958

趙承信 / 474

趙誠之 / 284

趙澂璧 / 436

趙崇祚 / 727,894

趙傳雲 / 382

趙聰 / 712(2),859,952

趙鼎 / 1750

趙盾 / 766

趙爾巽 / 846

趙藩 / 1172

趙鳳喈 / 218,252,275,508

趙蝦 / 1593

趙廣志 / 134

趙鶴 / 1310

趙吉士 / 790,1585

趙家璧 / 537,1064(2)

趙經達 / 1239,1586

趙景深 / 5,70,426,459,475

趙君才 / 215

趙均 / 1251

趙康節 / 11

趙連芳 / 959

趙璘 / 1000

趙孟頫 / 893

趙敏恒 / 386

趙明誠 / 1314,1800

趙木森 / 105

趙南星 / 1592,1660

趙岐 / 810,1466

趙清身 / 339

趙慶熺 / 1622(2)

趙仁舉 / 1302

趙汝适 / 1087

趙善詒 / 233

趙尚輔 / 1272

趙苕狂 / 785

趙少侯 / 251

趙士麟 / 1185

趙士煒 / 1542

趙宋岑 / 874

趙廷為 / 1891

趙萬里 / 1113,1304

趙魏 / 1762

趙希弁 / 1878

趙曦明 / 989,1667(2)

趙憲卿 / 181

趙演 / 185

趙彥衛 / 1019

趙彥修／1277
趙曄／945,1603,1604
趙一清／1522(2),1523,1524,1781,1844,1845,3004
趙詒琛／1702
趙詒璹／1679
趙翼／664,825,1214,1420
趙蔭棠／555
趙友欽／1139
趙元任／421,432,435,539,568,1008,2736
趙元益／1104
趙鉞／1566,1568
趙昀／1556
趙蘊琦／247
趙曾儔／205
趙曾玨／205
趙貞信／147,238(3),659,1202
趙之遠／82,1197,1379
趙志新／445
趙紫宸／47,332,452
趙尊嶽／1260
浙江省立西湖博物館出版股／493
浙江省文物管理委員會／752
真德秀／950,1163,1376,1393,1612,1749
真山民／1736
正論社／1899
正文編輯委員會／877
"政治導論編輯委員會"／2020
"政治評論編輯委員會"／2020,2021
鄭柏／1312
鄭伯謙／1559
鄭成功／988
鄭次川／185
鄭達三／1337

鄭德坤／886
鄭端／1086,1758
鄭方坤／1244
鄭豐稔／284
鄭剛中／1114,1615(2),1756
鄭辜生／524
鄭國勳／1370
鄭鶴聲／11,220,355,477
鄭經／988
鄭康明／341
鄭克／1030
鄭蘭華／339
鄭烺／1156
鄭良／908
鄭廖／773
鄭謐／1171
鄭啓愚／483
鄭騫／605,1855
鄭樵／333
鄭清茂／932,1015
鄭汝諧／800
鄭壽麟／55
鄭濤／1320
鄭天挺／75,290
鄭俠／1860
鄭小同／1739
鄭曉／676,1034(2)
鄭孝胥／1248(2),1341
鄭燮／1739
鄭玄／996,999,1082,1099,1120,1196,1377,1378,1428,1477(2),1478,1630,1736,1739,1753,1756
鄭學稼／1094
鄭業斅／69

鄭倚虹 / 114
鄭毅堅 / 187
鄭泳 / 1688
鄭毓旒 / 119
鄭元芳 / 952
鄭元慶 / 1602
鄭元勳 / 247
鄭肇經 / 147
鄭珍 / 1132(3),1133,1683
鄭貞文 / 569
鄭振鐸 / 31,84,201,312,360,365,398,529,748,1443,1444
鄭知同 / 1449
鄭作新 / 332
支那內學院 / 273
支那駐屯軍司令部 / 301
支偉成 / 213,450
知識與生活社 / 1900
知堂 / 647,944
織田得能 / 2092
植野武雄 / 2095
志賀潔 / 194
志銳 / 1732
智顗 / 968
摯虞 / 1466
中川忠順 / 2084
中村久四郎 / 2064
中村康一 / 2072(2)
中島半次郎 / 185
中島連城 / 1812
中德文化協會 / 394
中等算學社 / 500
中法漢學研究所 / 41,87,233,236,730
中谷武世 / 94

"中國邊疆歷史語文學會" / 953
中國地學會 / 1171
"中國工程師學會刊物出版委員會" / 1993
中國工程學會貴陽分會 / 455
中國公學 / 403
中國公學大學部己巳級畢業紀念刊編輯委員會 / 509
中國公學大學部民國廿二年畢業同學會 / 509
中國國民黨廣東省執行委員會 / 567
中國國民黨河北省黨部 / 549
中國華洋義賑救災總會 / 172
中國化學會成都分會 / 188
中國教育電影協會總務組 / 513(3)
中國經濟學社 / 517
中國科學促進會 / 519
中國科學社 / 79,519,1892
中國科學院歷史所第一、二所 / 1055
中國科學院歷史研究所第一、二所 / 1055
中國科學院哲學研究所中國哲學史組 / 1068,1069
"中國勞工運動史編纂委員會" / 1051
中國南洋義賑救災總會 / 526
"中國農村復興聯合委員會" / 826
"中國農業推廣學會" / 826
"中國青年黨中央黨部" / 2016
中國史地圖表編纂社 / 507
中國太平洋國際學會 / 59,64,146,301,386,387,484,520
"中國圖書館學會會報編輯委員會" / 2021(2)
"中國土木工程學會出版委員會" / 2001(2)
"中國文藝協會" / 2022
中國物理學會 / 536
中國西部博物館 / 536

"中國憲法學會年刊編輯委員會" / 2022
中國學會 / 1170
中國學術討論社 / 538
"中國一周編輯委員會" / 1065
"中國語文學會" / 2022, 2023
中國哲學會 / 1899
"中國自然科學促進會編輯委員會" / 1943(4)
中華教育文化基金董事會 / 546, 547
"中華科學協進會" / 1942
中華民國國民政府外交部 / 119
"中華民國外交部禮賓司" / 931
中華年鑑社 / 566
"中華農學會" / 2023
中華全國美術協會北平分會 / 1898
中華全國文藝作家協會北平分會 / 1898
"中華圖書館協會" / 2001
"中華文化出版事業委員會" / 2738
中華職業教育社 / 551
中南人民出版社 / 747
中山和夫 / 2101
中山時子 / 2102
中尾万三 / 2072(3)
中央大學經濟資料室 / 381
中央黨史史料編纂委員會 / 567
"中央故宮博物院"聯合管理處出版委員會 / 1078
中央廣播事業管理處中央電波研究所 / 508
中央通訊社總社編譯部 / 247
"中央研究院"近代史研究所 / 697, 698(4), 769, 1041(3), 1042(2)
"中央研究院"歷史語言研究所 / 1813(2)
中央研究院歷史語言研究所 / 692(2), 1078, 1079
"中央研究院"歷史語言研究所集刊編輯委員會 / 847, 848(2), 1079(3)
"中央研究院"院刊編輯委員會 / 635
"中央研究院"植物研究所 / 2024(2)
"中央研究院"總辦事處 / 1078(2)
中野達慧 / 1653
中澤臨川 / 2062
忠孝學識編纂社 / 302
終南山人 / 77
鍾伯毅 / 973, 1794
鍾鳳年 / 46, 487
鍾間 / 62
鍾敬文 / 209, 212, 231, 256, 465, 504, 556
鍾駿聲 / 1676
鍾錂 / 990, 1668, 1669
鍾魯齋 / 21, 186, 428
鍾嶸 / 1493
鍾嗣成 / 1633
鍾泰 / 446
鍾天心 / 470, 563
鍾心煊 / 525
鍾惺 / 1500, 1638, 1649
鍾勳 / 2018
鍾作猷 / 93
塚本善隆 / 2085, 2101, 2107, 2109, 2124
仲子 / 739
周藹聯 / 1762
周必大 / 648, 1423, 1757
周辨明 / 6, 12
周策縱 / 700, 2831
周春 / 1206, 1876
周法高 / 1866
周佛海 / 198, 1081
周馥 / 1754
周鯁生 / 118, 129

周谷城 / 331

周濟 / 1545

周家祿 / 1509

周金聲 / 1051

周鯨文 / 658

周駿章 / 466

周凱 / 955

周昆田 / 1043

周亮工 / 35,879,1869

周履靖 / 595

周論編輯委員會 / 1901

周夢顏 / 1040

周密 / 1332,1427(2),1607

周明泰 / 68,1169,1444,1779,1782,1796,1811,1824

周銘 / 1360

周乃昌 / 963

周其勛 / 466

周謙冲 / 343

周慶雲 / 1351

周日用 / 1119

周容 / 1147

周汝昌 / 710

周汝登 / 1180

周瑞庭 / 12

周若漁 / 925

周紹良 / 645

周世南 / 1603

周壽昌 / 1533

周叔迦 / 1408,1747

周叔嬪 / 558

周樹人 / 473

周樹聲 / 1779

周頌久 / 409

周威 / 25

周希武 / 473

周先庚 / 290,429

周祥光 / 1003

周學普 / 666

周易藻 / 1625

周因夢 / 14

周嬰 / 1035

周永年 / 1620

周游 / 1637

周育和 / 883

周元文 / 596

周雲青 / 404

周貞亮 / 1511(2)

周振鶴 / 365

周之鳴 / 898(2),899

周之琦 / 1268,1281(2),1312,1313,1581

周止菴 / 584

周志輔 / 980,997,1031

周中孚 / 1035

周子義 / 1884

周祖謨 / 151,357,359,361,449

周作人 / 25,61,87,109,140,204,211(2),305,373(2),451,453,469,473,918,994(2),1008,1020,1035,1084(2),1094

朱安 / 1008(2)

朱長文 / 1436

朱定鈞 / 429

朱敦儒 / 1432(2),1820

朱方 / 504

朱福榮 / 1119

朱肱 / 1826

朱古微 / 1542

朱光潛 / 24,96,334,400,1897

朱珪／1282
朱浩懷／901
朱和羲／1639
朱河／1144
朱胡彬夏／526
朱基俊／193
朱記榮／1644
朱進／234
朱經農／262
朱景英／697，1281
朱君毅／430，521
朱駿聲／1530（2）
朱孟實／36
朱敏章／386
朱謀㙔／1838，1843（2）
朱謀㙔／1422
朱睦／1508
朱琦／1681（2）
朱企霞／173
朱起鳳／605
朱啟鈐／1156
朱謙之／86，406，420，531，558
朱尚文／813
朱少軒／241
朱師轍／19，863
朱士嘉／226，261，688，1045，1746
朱仕玠／963
朱書／1701
朱松／1858
朱天民／96
朱庭祜／176
朱維魚／1261
朱文長／342
朱文鑫／780

朱希祖／151
朱溪／378
朱熹／310，558，598，705，734，754，799，859，870，946，1085，1144，1245（2），1287，1317（2），1376（2），1393，1493，1595，1606，1664，1680，1686，1708，1725，1754，1757，1758（2），1788（2），1800，1808，1810，1835，1836，1866，1869（2），1879，1880，1882，1883
朱襄廷／562
朱孝臧／1340
朱嘯秋／2002
朱偰／982
朱虛白／708
朱學勤／1288，1306（2）
朱琰／1402
朱一新／1319，1605，1859
朱彝尊／834，1154，1322，1426（2），1429
朱有燉／1725
朱有璲／1887
朱右曾／1000，1222
朱筠／1540
朱震亨／1167，1219，1331
朱之瑜／1103，1214，1526，1672
朱執信／559
朱子素／1297
朱自清／377，756，1045，1086
朱祖謀／1274
珠海夢餘生／1642
諸橋轍次／2065，2103（2）
諸青來／172，313，314
竹添光鴻／1151
竺可楨／206，421
竺沙雅章／2101
祝昌泰／1425

3087

祝慶祺／1644,1656

祝實明／26,209

祝廷錫／1137

祝秀俠／846

祝淵／1137

祝允明／1678,1740

莊綽／1292（3）

莊鼎彝／223

莊季裕／736

莊繼曾／348

莊景琦／463

莊述祖／1495

莊爲璣／195

莊文亞／293

莊有可／1752

莊俞／569

莊元臣／878

莊澤宣／467

莊周／1411

卓定謀／1730,1766

卓宏謀／554

濯纓／437（2）

資源委員會／91

自由批判社編輯委員會／1901

"自由太平洋編輯委員會"／2026

"自由太平洋月刊社"／2026

"自由談雜誌社"／2026

"自由亞洲編輯委員會"／2026

自由與進步社編輯委員會／1901

"自由中國編輯委員會"／750,2028,2029（4）,2030（4）,2031（4）,2032（3）,2033（4）,2034（4）,2035（4）,2036（3）,2037（4）,2038（2）,2039（3）,2040（2）,2041（3）,2042（3）,2043（3）,2044（2）,2045（2）

"自由中國社"／725,726

宗白華／227,239

宗華／192

宗澤／1750

鄒柏森／1342

鄒恩潤／252

鄒魯／164

鄒森／679

鄒漪／814

鄒元標／1768

足立喜六／649

祖國周刊編輯委員會／2046（2）,2047（4）,2048（4）,2049（5）

祖國周刊社／1042

祖珽／1648

醉園狂客／1362

左輔／1418

左圭／1108

左舜生／515（2）

左文質／1603

左宗棠／1101

佐倉孫三／905

作家出版社編輯部／709（3）,857

二、著者索引日文部分

エス・ジ・マクラレン / 2062
オースチン・フリーマン / 2057
シルレル / 2067

ネイサン・ブラウ / 2076
T・チェルナアヴィン / 2060

三、著者索引西文部分

A

Abbott, James Francis / 2393
Abbott, Lyman / 2372
Abend, Hallett / 2185,2391,2465,2547,2841
Acton, Lord / 2768
Acworth, W. M. / 2267
Adamic, Louis / 2312
Adams, Brooks / 2814
Adams, Francis Ottiwell / 2352
Adams, Henry / 2754
Adams, James Truslow / 2693
Adams, John / 2289
Adams, Lady / 2623
Adcock, F. E. / 2185
Addams, Jane / 2671
Addison, Joseph / 2603
Ade, George / 2460
Adeney, Walter F. / 2168
Adkins, Nelson F. / 2917
Adler, Alfred / 2924
Aeschylus / 20,2848

Agar, Herbert / 2405
Agger, Eugene E. / 2490
Ahleers, John / 2390
Aiken, Conrad / 2453
Akagi, Roy Hidemichi / 2396
Aksakov, Sergei / 2568
Albee, Ernest / 2511
Alcock, Rutherford / 2399
Aldanov, Mark / 2297
Aldington, Richard / 2242
Alexander, F. Matthias / 2437,2649
Alexander, Franz / 2494
Alexander, S. / 2426
Alighieri, Dante / 2252(2)
Allan, D. J. / 2982
Allan, J. / 2185
Allen, Clement Francis Romilly / 2173
Allen, F. Sturges / 2660
Allen, Frederick Lewis / 2704,2856
Allen, G. C. / 2392

3089

Allen, George E. / 2874

Allen, Grant / 2289

Allen, Hervey / 2149

Allinson, A. R. / 2892

Aly, Bower / 2689

Ambrois / 2236

The American Philosophical Society / 2142(4)

American Society of Newspaper Editors / 2538

TheAmerican University Club Shanghai / 2143

Ames, Van Meter / 2704

Andersen, Robert / 2223

Anderson, Adelaide Mary / 2671

Anderson, B. M., Jr. / 2264

Anderson, Bert G. / 2400

Anderson, Elam Jonathan / 2275

Anderson, Melville B. / 2252

Andersson, J. Gunnar / 2195

Andrews, C. F. / 2620

Anesaki Masaharu / 2554

Angell, James Rowland / 2191

Angell, Norman / 2238, 2303, 2312, 2327, 2413, 2505, 2526, 2538, 2607

Angoff, Charles / 2785

Anshen, Ruth Nanda / 2310, 2778, 2838

Appel, John W. / 2251

Appel, Kenneth E. / 2251

Arberry, A. J. / 2179

Archer, Laird / 2160

Archer, William / 2326

Aristophanes / 2130, 2848

Arlen, Michael / 2329

Armstrong, Hamilton Fish / 2665

Arnold, Edwin / 2422

Arnold, Matthew / 2524, 2525

Arnold, Sarah Louise / 2438, 2580

Arnold, Thurman W. / 2618

Arnow, Harriette / 2796

Aron, Raymond / 2854

Asbury, Herbert / 2161

Asch, Sholem / 2151, 2470

Ascoli, Max / 2990

Ashley, W. J. / 2347

Asiatic Research Center of Korea University / 2947

Aston, W. G. / 2325, 2352, 2586

Asvaghosha Bodhisattva / 2774

Atwood, Nora / 472

Auerbach, Joseph S. / 2161

Auger, Pierre / 2911

Aurelius, Marcus / 2151

Austen, Jane / 2480

Austin, Walter F. / 2602

Autry, Gene / 2662

Ayres, C. E. / 2578

Ayscough, Florence / 2299

B

Baedeker, Karl / 2427, 2618

Bagchi, Prabodh Chandra / 2803

Bahm, Archie J. / 2914

Bain, Alexander / 2344

Baker, Dorothy / 2682
Baker, Franklin T. / 2287(3)
Baker, Newton Diehl / 2143
Baker, Ray Stannard / 2672,2673(5),2674
Bakewell, Charles M. / 2602
Balázs, Stefan / 2166
Balch, Emily G. / 2671
Baldwin, Hanson W. / 2784,2873
Baldwin, James / 2297
Balfour, Frederic Henry / 2409,2655
Balfour, Marshall C. / 2876
Ball, Arthur E. / 2635
Ball, J. Dyer / 2628
Ball, W. MacMahon / 2529
Ballou, Robert O. / 2169
Balzac, Honoré de / 2230,2319
Banno Masataka / 2810
Barbour, Thomas / 2469
Barker, Ernest / 2552
Barlow, Nora / 2192
Barnes, Harry Elmer / 2356
Barnhart, Clarence L. / 2691
Barrett, John / 2501
Barrett, William / 2940
Barrie, J. M. / 208(2),2439
Barrows, David P. / 2873
Barth, Alan / 2826
Bartlett, John / 2293
Baruch, Bernard M. / 2865
Barzun, Jacques / 2748
Basil, George C. / 2626
Basler, Roy P. / 2129
Bates, H. E. / 2293
Bau, Mingchien Joshua / 2455,2489

Bauer, Raymond A. / 2795
Baur, John I. H. / 2845
Bawden, Arthur T. / 2303
Baynes, Cary F. / 2797,2798
Beal, S. / 2180
Beal, Samuel / 2181(2),2189,2626,2774
Beam, Walter E., Jr. / 2896
Beard, Charles A. / 297,806,2534,2692,2932
Beatty, Richmond Croom / 2428
Becker, Carl L. / 2230,2341,2741,2778
Beddie, James Stuart / 2844
Bedier, F. / 36
Beer, Thomas / 2338
Begbie, Harold / 2421,2585
Bellows, John / 2248
Belshaw, H. / 2552
Bemelmans, Ludwig / 2483
Benda, Julien / 2703
Benét, Stephen Vincent / 2583,2662
Bennett, Arnold / 2268,2345,2434
Bennett, Charles E. / 2306
Bennett, W. H. / 2168
Benson, Sally / 2400
Benson, Stella / 2294
Bentham, Jeremy / 2308
Bentley, Arthur F. / 2820
Benton, Charles W. / 2260
Berdyaev, Nicolas / 2902
Berger, Meyer / 2446
Bergler, Edmund / 2737
Bergson, Henri / 2232,2441,2633
Berkeley, G. / 7
Berkes, Niyazi / 2922
Berkov, Robert / 2611

Berlin, Isaiah / 2687

Berlitz, M. D. / 2448

Berry, T. Sterling / 2210

Bertram, James M. / 2300

Bethel, John P. / 2930

Bhikshu Wai-Tao / 2407

Bialoguski, Michael / 2863

Biddle, George / 2848

Billingham, Anthony J. / 2185

Billings, Margaret Allison / 2999

Binder, Rudolph M. / 2473

Bingham, Alfred M. / 2646

Bird, Isabella L. / 2644

Bishop, Morris / 2190,2711

Bisson, T. A. / 2142,2390

Blachly, Frederick F. / 2296

Black, Davidson / 2500

Black, Ebenezer Charlton / 2636

Blackie, John Stuart / 2430

Blackwell, Basil H. / 2174

Blake, W. H. / 2440

Blake, William / 2252

Blakeslee, George H. / 2499

Blakney, R. B. / 2930

Bliss, Paul Southworth / 2568

Bliss, William D. P. / 2473

Blofeld, John / 2941

Boas, Franz / 2150

Boccaccio, Giovanni / 2242,2243

Bodde, Derk / 2790,2791,2899

Bodman, Nicholas Cleaveland / 2816

Boehme, Jacob / 2591

Bogen, JulesI. / 2381

Bolton, Theodore / 2675

Bond, Earl D. / 2856

Bone, Edith / 2685

Bonney, Elizabeth C. / 2438,2580

Boodin, John Elof / 2641

Booker, Edna Lee / 2477

Boorman, Howard L. / 2739

Booth, M. L. / 2705

Boothe, Clare / 2285

Borchardt / 341

Borel, Henry / 2407

Borgese, G. A. / 2322

Bosanquet, B. / 2535,2649

Bosanquet, Bernard / 2281,2426

Bosworth, Joseph / 2324

Bourne, Randolph S. / 2635

Bouyssy, Savinien / 2347

Bowen, Francis / 2744

Bowen, Ralph H. / 2748

Bowers, Claude G. / 2682

Bowles, Chester / 2920

Bradford, Gamaliel / 2670

Bradley, Edward Sculley / 2342

Bradley, James / 2533

Bradley, Phillips / 2744

Bradshaw, Marion J. / 2628

Brailsford, Mabel R. / 2720

Braithwaite, William Stanley / 2149

Bramah, Ernest / 2655

Brandt, J. J. / 2456

Breal, Michel / 2584

Breasted, James Henry / 2146,2491

Bredon, Juliet / 2364

Bridges, B. C. / 2530

Bridgman, Percy Williams / 2880

Briere, O. / 2771

Brill, E. J. / 2707

Brinton, Crane / 951

the British Government / 2311

British Museum / 2329,2330(2)

Britton, Karl / 2811

Britton, Roswell S. / 2298

Broad, C. D. / 192

Brockman, Fletcher S. / 2365

Brogan, D. W. / 2308

Bronowski, J. / 2931

Bronson, Walter C. / 2274

Brontë, Charlotte / 2390

Brontë, Emily / 2680(2)

Brooks, Van Wyck / 2473,2490

Broun, Heywood / 2149

Browder, Earl / 2830

Brown, Constantine / 2913

Brown, Horatio F. / 2397

Brown, Margaret H. / 2341

Brown, Marshall Stewart / 2276

Brown, S. R. / 2217,2533

Brownell, W. C. / 2650

Browning, Robert / 2523,2562

Bruce, J. Percy / 2211

Bryce, James / 2138(2),2382,2455

Buck, Paul H. / 2887

Buck, Pearl S. / 2255,2323(2),2504,2609, 2689,2781

Buckle, Henry Thomas / 2350

Budd, Lillian / 2696

Budenz, Louis Francis / 2629

Buell, Raymond Leslie / 2228,2388

Bulfinch, Thomas / 2182

Bullett, Gerald / 2322,2781

Bullitt, William C. / 2783

Bundy, McGeorge / 2486,2852

Burbank, Luther / 2666

Burder, Samuel / 2491

Burgess, John W. / 2550,2571

Burke, Edmund / 2488

Burne, Charlotte Sophia / 257

Burnet, John / 2258

Burnett, Whit / 2937

Burnham, James / 2908,2930

Burns, C. Delisle / 2375

Burns, James MacGregor / 2811

Burns, Robert / 2222,2523

Burton, Richard F. / 2300

Burtt, Edwin A. / 2757,2919

Bury, J. B. / 2185,2351,2791

Busch, Marie / 2581

Bushell, S. W. / 522

Butcher, S. H. / 2483,2850

Butler, Bishop / 2144

Butler, Nicholas Murray / 2138, 2168, 2182, 2218,2294,2382,2427,2504,2666,2677

Butler, Samuel / 2276

Butterfield, Herbert / 2805,2900

Byas, Hugh / 2392

Bynner, Witter / 2659

Byrnes, James F. / 2603,2904

C

Cairns, Huntington / 2627
Caldwell, John C. / 2732,2903,2906
Calkins, Earnest Elmo / 2183
Calvin, John / 2804
Campbell, C. Samuel / 2361
Campbell, Joseph / 2864
Campbell, Thomas J. / 2397
Canby, Henry Seidel / 2176
Candlin, Clara M. / 2343,2789
Cardozo, Benjamin N. / 2469
Cargill, Oscar / 2788
Carlson, Evans Fordyce / 2642
Carlyle, Thomas / 2234,2311,2572
Carman, H. J. / 807
Carnegie Endowment for International Peace, Division of International Law / 2298(2),2332(3),2333(3),2334(3),2335(2),2336(3)
Carnegie Endowment for International Peace, Division of Intercourse and Education/ 2557
Carnegie, Dale / 2422
Carpenter, Frances / 2621
Carrel, Alexis / 2434(2)
Carroll, Gordon / 2790
Carroll, Lewis / 2264
Carter, Thomas Francis / 2386,2808(2)
Carus, Paul / 2186,2407,2620,2682,2709,2912
Carver, Thomas Nixon / 2533
Cary, Henry F. / 2749
Cary, Joyce / 2698
Casanova, Jacques / 2445
Case, Leland D. / 2678

Casse, Gustav / 2314
Cassirer, Ernst / 2882
Caswell, H. L. / 2625(2)
Cather, Willa / 2241,2572
Catlin, George E. G. / 2147,2373,2610,2614
Cattell, Jaques / 2748
Cecil, Robert / 2250
Ch'en Kung-po / 2734
Ch'ien, C. S. / 2944
Ch'u Ta-Kao / 2914
Cha, Lincoln H. / 2417
Chabrié, Robert / 814
Chalmers, John / 2130,2493,2604
Chamberlain, Basil Hall / 2214,2628
Chamberlain, Joseph P. / 2268
Chamberlin, William Henry / 2705
Champassak, Sisouk Na / 2907
Chan Wing-tsit / 2513,2844,2858,2882
Chaney, Ralph W. / 2452
Chang Chen-chi / 2873
Chang Chi-Hsien / 2207
Chang Chi-Yun / 2215,2723
Chang Chung-Fu / 2147
Chang Hsin-Chang / 2689
Chang Kia-Ngau / 2202
Chang Tso-Shuen / 2349
Chang Yin-T'ang / 2191,2260
Chang, C. C. / 2201
Chang, Eileen / 2885
Chang, W. S. / 2246
Chang, Y. Z. / 2854
Chang, F. H. / 2779

Chao Buwei Yang / 2158

Chao Liang Chi / 2200

Chao Nai-Tuan / 2561

Chao Tze-chiang / 2724

Chao Yuen-ren / 2712,2736,2830

Chao, Samuel M. / 2199

Chao, T. C. / 2198

Chapman, Guy / 2751

Charles, R. H. / 2554

Charlton, Ebenezer / 2218

Charques, Richard D. / 647

Chase, D. P. / 2479

Chase, Ilka / 2777

Chase, Lewis / 2235,2380

Chavannes, Edouard / 650, 818

Chaya, Prem / 2828,2893,2907(2),2908

Chekhov, Anton Pavlovich / 2871

Chen Chi-ying / 2775

Ch'en Meng-Chia / 2614

Chen Shih-Hsiang / 2761

Ch'ên Shou-yi / 2238, 2398, 2592, 2600, 2630,2724

Chen Su Ching / 2550

Chen, Gideon / 2641

Chen, L. T. / 2571,2891

Chen, Philip S. / 2904,2912

Chen, Sophia H. / 2206

Chen, Stephen / 2910

Chen, Paul T. H. / 2897

Cheng Che-yu / 2491

Cheng Ching Yi / 2198

Cheng Chun-hao / 2288

Cheng Chu-yuan / 2862

Cheng Shou-Lin / 2207

Cheng Tien-fong / 2793

Cheng, Andrew C. Y. / 2501

Cheng, F. T. / 2751,2840

Cheng, Hawthorne / 2199

Chesterton, G. K. / 2192,2521

Chevalier, Haakon M. / 2437

Cheyney, Edward Potts / 2356,2385

Chiang Kai-Shek / 2316,2559,2874

Chiang Yee / 2725

Chikashige, Masumi / 2856

Childe, V. Gordon / 2802,2902,2932

Childs, Marquis W. / 2768

Chin Szu-k'ai, / 2732

Chin Ti / 2732

Chin, Calvin Suey Keu / 2910

Chin, Grace / 2317

theChina Council for East Asian Studies / 2884

"China Culture Publishing Foundation" / 2738

theChina Yearbook Editorial Board / 2716(2), 2717(2)

Chinese Ministry of Information / 2216

Ching Ren-Chang / 2367,2368

Chisholm, Brock / 2709

Chisholm, Hugh / 2270

Chiu Kwong Ki / 2059(2)

Chou Yi-Liang / 2622

Chow Tse-tsung / 2831

Chow, S. R. / 2669

Christensen, Erwin O. / 2973

Christian, John Leroy / 2454

Christie, Agatha / 2463

Ch'u Chai / 2724

Chu Kwang-Tsien / 2542

Chu Shih-Chia / 2190

Ch'u Ta-Kao / 2914

Chu, T. H. / 2623

Ch'u, T. K. / 2607

Chun Woon-Young / 2368

Chung Kei-Won / 2620

Chung Tso-You / 2162,2344

Churchill, Winston / 2172, 2234, 2315, 2677

(2)

Clark, Barrett H. / 2286,2327

Clark, Walter Van Tilburg / 2498

Clarke, Comer / 2754

Clarke, G. H. / 2593

Clarke, T. Wood / 2269

Clemens, Cyril / 2972

Clemens, Samuel L. / 2133

Cleveland, Frederick A. / 2457

Clifford, William / 2920

Clifford, William Kingdon / 2410

Clinchy, Everett R. / 2137

Close, Upton / 2561

Clough, Frank C. / 2667

Clyde, Paul Hibbert / 2646

Cobb, Irvin S. / 2290

Coffin, Henry Sloane / 2773

Coffman, Harold Coe / 2140

Coghill, G. E. / 2145

Cohen, Julius Henry / 2408

Cohn, Alfred E. / 2451

Coil, William H. / 2884

Cole, G. D. H. / 2597

Colegrove, Kenneth W. / 2380,2744

Coleridge, Samuel Taylor / 2827

Collier, John / 2635

Collingwood, R. G. / 2799

Collins, Alan C. / 2907

Collis, Maurice / 2405

Commager, Henry Steele / 2253,2521,2693

the Commemoration Committee for Prof. Shinsho Hanayama's sixty – first birthday / 2899

Commission of Financial Experts / 2540

Committee on Un-American Activities / 2769

Conant, James Bryant / 766,2834,2837,2854

Condliffe, J. B. / 2136,2197

The Conference on Science / 2577,2578

Conrad, Joseph / 26, 167, 2137, 2190, 2427, 2580,2617,2642

Conway, Thomas / 2490

Conybeare, Fred. Cornwallis / 2468

Conze, Edward / 2708

Cook, S. A. / 2185

Copeland, Melvin T. / 2183

Copleston, Reginald Stephen / 2180

Corder, F. / 2860

Cordier, Henri / 2249

Corliss, John B., Jr. / 2328

Corneille, P. / 416

Cornell University / 2741,2749

Corner, George W. / 2988,2989

Corson, Hiram / 2806

Corwin, Edward S. / 2738

Cosmos / 2163

The Cosmos Club / 2641

Cotton, T. Henry / 2322

Coulson, J. / 2591

Council on Foreign Relations / 2964

Couturat, Louis / 2136

Cowley, Patrick / 2309

Cozzens, James Gould / 2400

Crabb, Alfred Leland / 2250

Craigie, W. A. / 2275

Crankshaw, Edward / 2742

Cranmer-Byng, L. / 2430

Cravath, Paul D. / 2414(2)

Crawford, M. D. C. / 2376

Creel, George / 2878

Creel, Herrlee Glessner / 2171, 2612, 2720, 2728, 2738

Creighton, James Edwin / 2386(2)

Crew, Joseph C. / 2625

Crombie, A. C. / 2833

Cronin, A. J. / 2402

Crookshank, F. G. / 2460

Cross, E. A. / 2424(2), 2624

Cross, Wilbur L. / 465, 466

Crossman, Richard / 2780

Crow, Carl / 2197, 2304, 2307, 2367, 2440

Cumston, Charles Greene / 2385

Cunningham, Clarice / 2165, 2167

Curie, Eve / 2398

Curry, W. B. / 2187

Curtis, Lionel / 2213

Cushing, Richard J. / 2714

Cushman, Herbert Ernest / 2164

Czarnomska, Elizabeth / 2156

D

D'Ohsson, C. / 75

Dampier-Whetham, W. C. D. / 207

Dana, R. H. / 2923

Dana, R. H., Jr. / 2643

Dark, Eleanor / 2633

Darrow, Clarence / 2152, 2242, 2292, 2378, 2549, 2770

Darwin, Charles / 2245, 2493, 2654, 2857(2), 2927

Darwin, Francis / 2418

Das, Santosh Kumar / 2260

Datta, S. K. / 2155

Daudet, Alphonse / 2572

David, Alexandra / 2512

Davids, C. A. F. Rhys / 2181

Davidson, Frank P. / 2164

Davidson, Marshall B. / 2973

Davies, Joseph E. / 2453

Davis, Elmer / 2319

Davis, J. Merle / 2379

Davis, John Francis / 2207

Dawson, Miles Menander / 2284(2)

Dawson-Scott, C. A. / 2168, 2172

De Bary, Wm. Theodore / 2696

De Cervantes, Miguel / 2301, 2772

De Chambrun, Marquis Adolphe / 2800

De Coulanges, Fustel / 2694

De Gaulle, Charles / 2929

De la Mare, Walter / 2445

De Latil, Pierre / 2998

De Martino, Richard / 2940

De Mattos, Alexander Teixeira / 2421

De Maupassant, Guy / 2249, 2429, 2431, 2582, 2650, 2706

De Montesquieu, Baron / 2606

De Morgan, Jacques / 2533

De Onís, Harriet / 2904
De Roussy de Sales, Raoul / 2432
De SaintExupéry, Antoine / 2668
De Selincourt, Aubrey / 2790
De Sismondi, J. C. L. / 2355
De Spinoza, Benedictus / 2535
De St. Aulaire, R. J. / 2438
De Tocqueville, Alexis / 2744
De Unamuno, Miguel / 2637
De Vargas / 2599
De Voltaire, M. / 2794
Deacon, William Arthur / 2467
Dean, Leon W. / 2133
Deffendall, P. H. / 2400
Defoe, Daniel / 2134
Delafield, Eugene / 2688
Demiéville, Paul / 2616
Department of External Affairs, United States of America / 2559
The Department of Philosophy of Columbia University / 2613
Department of State, United States of America / 2504
Descartes, René / 34, 493, 2443
Deschler, Lewis / 2226
Deutsch, Monroe E. / 2413
Devine, Edward T. / 2250
Dewey, Alice Chipman / 2413
Dewey, Evelyn / 2476, 2575
Dewey, John / 491, 493, 1095, 2154, 2191, 2220, 2232, 2244(2), 2263, 2279, 2283, 2290(2), 2318(2), 2363, 2375, 2376, 2413, 2417, 2426, 2427, 2513, 2543, 2545, 2551(2), 2574, 2575, 2713, 2766, 2778, 2818, 2820, 2826, 2852, 2879
Dharmaraksha / 2774
Di Donato, Pietro / 2209
Diamant, Gertrude / 2241
Dibner, Bern / 2822, 2839
Dickens, Charles / 2418
Dickins, Frederick V. / 2208
Dickinson, G. Lowes / 415, 2135
Dickson, Carter / 2399
Dickson, W. P. / 2353
Dietzgen, Joseph / 2529
Dilliard, Irving / 2462, 2708
Din, Sa'd-ud / 182
Dinesen, Isak / 2669
Disraeli, Benjamin / 2225
Dixon, W. Macneile / 2364
Dixon, William Gray / 2405
Dodds, Harold W. / 2496
Dodds, John W. / 2846
Dodwell, H. H. / 2185
Donne, John / 2523
Doolittle, Justus / 2596, 2652
Dorf, Philip / 2731
Dorian, Sylvestre / 2494
Dostoyevsky, Fyodor M. / 2233, 2750
Douglas, Robert K. / 2224, 2406
Dowlin, Cornell M. / 2648
Dowson, Ernest / 2319
Doyle, A. Conan / 2467
Drake, F. S. / 2969
Draper, John William / 2354(2)
Dreier, Katherine S. / 2454
Dressler, Helmut / 2661
Drummond, Henry / 2368

Dryden, John / 2927

Du Bois, Gaylord / 2311, 2521

Du Bois, W. E. Burghardt / 2134

Du Ponceau, Peter S. / 2251

Duboscq, André / 2203

Dubs, Homer H. / 2355, 2449, 2793(3), 2795

Duff, F. D. / 2568

Duffy, Richard / 2660

Duggar, Benjamin M. / 2519

Dumas, Alexandre / 2233, 2631, 2641, 2650

Dumas, Alexandre, fils / 2237

Dumbauld, Edward / 2871

Dumond, Dwight L. / 2876

Dumoulin, Heinrich / 2745

Duncan, Robert Moore / 2507

Dunning, William Archibald / 497

Dunsany, Lord / 2302

Durant, Will / 2152, 2184, 2420, 2437, 2609, 2687, 2880

Dutt, Romesh C. / 2546

Duyvendak, J. J. L. / 2369, 2723

Dwight, Timothy / 2569

Dwyer, Sheila Maureen / 2458

Dyson, Verne / 2405

E

Early, Eleanor / 2146

Eastman, Max / 2592, 2869, 2880

Easton, H. T. / 2272

Eberhard, W. / 2211

Ecke, Gustav / 2611

Eckermann, J. P. / 666

Eddy, Sherwood / 419

Edgerton, Franklin / 2501

the editors of Life / 2690, 2824

Edkins, Joseph / 2202, 2203, 2385, 2553

Edman, Irwin / 2186, 2307, 2511

Edward, William / 704, 2785

Edwards, I. E. S. / 2877

Edwards, Newton / 2613

Efremoff, Jean / 2507

Ehrlich, Leonard / 2320

Einstein, Albert / 2425, 2857

Eisenhart, Luther P. / 2985(2), 2986(4), 2989

Eldridge, Paul / 2215

Eliot, Charles / 2346, 2789

Eliot, Charles W. / 2141, 2158, 2211, 2221, 2224, 2228, 2261, 2267(2), 2272, 2274, 2275, 2278, 2303, 2416, 2422, 2455, 2518, 2532, 2535, 2569, 2578, 2579, 2651, 2655, 2692, 2696, 2701, 2705, 2729, 2735, 2736, 2740, 2752, 2753, 2755(2), 2757, 2758(4), 2760, 2765, 2766(2), 2770(2), 2775, 2779, 2812, 2822, 2824, 2837, 2866, 2868, 2869, 2873, 2875, 2890, 2891, 2895(2), 2927

Eliot, George / 2450

Elisséeff, Serge / 2967, 2968

Elizabeth / 2463

Elliot, Hugh S. R. / 2415

Elliott, Osborn / 2974(2), 2975(4), 2976(4), 2977(5), 2978(4), 2979(4), 2980(3)

Ellis, Clifford / 2453

Ellis, H. F. / 2595

3099

Ellis, Havelock / 348, 2670
Ellis, Rosemary / 2453
Ely, Richard T. / 2265, 2498
Embree, Edwin R. / 2179, 2388
Emerson, Ralph Waldo / 2277(2), 2765, 2768
Emery, Richard W. / 2767
Engle, Robert H. / 2140
English, E. Schuyler / 2184
Epictetus / 2151
Epstein, M. / 2607
Erkes, Eduard / 2208

Erskine, John / 2744, 2926
Espey, John J. / 2452
Esslemont, J. E. / 2160
Eucken, Rudolf / 2538
Euripides / 2848
Eustis, Dorothy Harrison / 2254
Evans, Bergen / 2843
Evans, Roger F. / 2876
The Executive Yuan of The Republic of China / 2821
Exner, M. J. / 2547

F

Faber, Ernst / 2384, 2620
Fabre, J. Henri / 2421
Fadiman, Clifton / 2540
Faerber, Max / 2949(2)
Fairbank, John King / 2718, 2728, 2810
Fairbank, Wilma / 2611
Falubert, Gustave / 2632
Fang, Thomé H. / 2729
Farley, James A. / 2810
Farmer, Frances / 2935
Farquhar, J. N. / 2457, 2497, 2534, 2859
Farrell, James T. / 2879
Faulds, Henry / 2479
Faulkner, William / 994
Fei Hsiao-Tung / 2195
Feibleman, James / 2528
Feis, Herbert / 2191, 2704, 2716, 2729, 2886
Feldman, W. T. / 2515
Fenn, Courtenay H. / 2302, 2773
Ferber, Edna / 2595

Ferm, Vergilius / 2695
Ferrero, Guglielmo / 2536
Ferril, Thomas Hornsby / 2661
Field, Walter Taylor / 2548
Fielding, William J. / 2173
Finch, George A. / 2639
Finger, Charles J. / 2508
Finkelstein, Louis / 2136, 2510
Finlay, George / 2328
Firth, Moray / 2268
Fischer, Louis / 2270, 2446
Fish, George W. / 2458
Fishbein, Morris / 2456
Fisher, Dorothy Canfield / 2419
Fiske, Bradley A. / 2387
Fiske, John / 2278
Fitch, Robert E. / 2189
Fitzgerald, C. P. / 2199
Fitzgerald, Edward / 2567(3)
Fitzhugh, Harriet Lloyd / 2223, 2736

Fitzhugh, Percy K. / 2736
Fitzpatrick, D. R. / 2772
Flaubert, Gustave / 332
Fleddérus, M. L. / 2382
Fleisher, Wilfrid / 2494,2654
Fleming, Berry / 2218
Fleming, Peter / 2489
Fleure, Herbert John / 2150,2365,2507,2534,2607
Flewelling, Ralph Tyler / 2737,2862
Flexner, James Thomas / 2667
Flexner, Simon / 2667
Flournoy, Th. / 2517
Flynn, John T. / 2231,2821
Foley, Martha / 2167
Fontaine, C. / 2308
Forbes, Esther / 2504
Forbes, Robert B. / 2508
Forbes, William Cameron / 2313
Ford, Henry / 2466
Ford, Julia Ellsworth / 2370,2595
Ford, Paul Leicester / 2327,2532
Forke, Alfred / 2677,2826,2827
Forster, Lancelot / 2273
Fosdick, Emerson / 2436
Fosdick, Harry Emerson / 2442,2829
Foster, John / 2243
Foster, John W. / 2140
Fowler, F. G. / 2223,2522
Fowler, H. W. / 2223,2248,2522,2591
Fox, William Henry / 2944
Fraenkel, Michael / 2163
Francois, Victor E. / 2470

Frank, Bruno / 2241
Frank, Glenn / 2606
Frank, Judge Jerome / 2849
Frank, Leonard / 2186
Frank, Pat / 2776
Franke, Wolfgang / 2503,2683
Frankfurter, Felix / 2543
Franks, Augustus W. / 2394
Fraser, W. H. / 2221,2591
Frazer, James George / 2135,2321(2)
Freeman, Mansfield / 2208,2516,2681
Freeman, R. Austin / 2431,2592
French, Joseph Lewis / 2326
Frenz, Horst / 2698
Frere, J. Hookham / 2130
Freud, Sigmund / 2244
Freyn, Hubert / 2309
Friedrich, Carl J. / 2471,2779
the Friends of the Library / 2710
Frierson, William C. / 2273
Fries, Hoarace S. / 2283
Fromm, Erich / 2940
Frost, Robert / 2946
Fry, Roger / 2154
Fryer, Eliza Nelson / 2164
Fryke / 337
Ftizhugh, Percy K. / 2223
Fu Mao-lan / 2614(2)
Fuchs, Walter / 2459
Fuçi, Utato / 2365
Fuller, Richard E. / 2809
Fulton, John F. / 2338
Fung Yu-lan / 2790,2791,2899,2905

G

Gabriel, Ralph Henry / 2268, 2786
Gaffey, Margaret Y. / 2674
Gailey, Robert R. / 2674
Galantière, Lewis / 2668
Gale, Henry Gordon / 2530
Gale, Zona / 2453
Gallagher, Louis J. / 2714
Galli, Enrique V. / 2144
Gallie, W. B. / 2861
Galsworthy, John / 2455, 2461
Gamow, George / 2742
Gardiner, A. G. / 2420
Gardiner, Samuel Rawson / 2226
Gardner, Edmund G. / 2239
Gardner, Erle Stanley / 2188
Gardner, Martin / 2783
Garfield, Harry Augustus / 2428
Garnett, Constance / 2148, 2209, 2229, 2233, 2358, 2404, 2502, 2574, 2575
Garraty, John A. / 2935
Garrett, Garet / 2496
Garside, B. A. / 2855
Garwood, Darrell / 2154
Gasquet, Cardinal / 2286
Gaus, John Merriman / 2787
Gayre, R. / 2972(2)
Gee, N. Gist / 467
Geiger, John L. / 2840
George, David Lloyd / 2656, 2657(5)
George, H. B. / 2348
George, Henry / 2540
Gernet, Jacques / 2759

Gesellschaft, Telefunken / 2129
Gibbon, Edward / 2354
Gibson, Charles R. / 2565
Gibson, Hugh / 2532
Gide, Charles / 197
Gideonse, Harry D. / 2345
Giles, F. T. / 2743
Giles, Herbert A. / 2189, 2207, 2212, 2315, 2349, 2719
Giles, Lionel / 2174, 2669, 2694, 2705, 2840, 2892
Ginn, Edwin / 2520
Giovannitti, Arturo / 2697
Gissing, George / 2537
Gleason, S. Everett / 2924
Glenn, John H., Jr. / 2918
Glick, Carl / 2255
Goddard, Dwight / 2407
Goddard, W. G. / 2776
Godkin, John David / 2326
Goette, John / 2390
Goetz, Delia / 2199
Goldberg, Isaac / 2388, 2671
Golden, Harry / 2710
Goldring, Douglas / 2256
Goldwin, Robert A. / 2919
Gooch, G. P. / 2527
Goodman, Jack / 2300
Goodman, Paul / 2734
Goodman, Percival / 2734
Goodrich, Edwin S. / 2289
Goodrich, L. Carrington / 2588, 2808

3102

Goodspeed, Edgar J. / 2221, 2324
Gordon, A. / 2471
Gordon, Arthur / 2884
Goris, Jan-Albert / 2166
Gorki, Maxim / 2175
Gould, Randall / 2196
Gowen, Herbert H. / 2496, 2497
Grabau, Amadeus W. / 2632, 2937
Grace, J. H. / 2229
Grad, Richard A. / 2828
Graham, Frank / 2441
Graham, Harvey / 2609
Gramling, Oliver / 2150
Granet, Marcel / 2720
Graves, Robert / 2548
Gray, A. Herbert / 2299
Grayston, J. Thomas / 2686, 2699, 2760 (2), 2761, 2780, 2863, 2896
Green, Elizabeth / 2553
Green, Gretchen / 2666
Green, H. P. / 2518
Green, John Richard / 2589
Green, Thomas Hill / 2540
Greenbie, Sydney / 2263
Greene, Evarts Boutell / 2473
Greene, Joseph I. / 2817
Greene, Theodore M. / 2417

Greenlaw, Edwin / 2327, 2328
Greenslet, Ferris / 2530
Gregg, Richard B. / 2530
Gregory, J. W. / 2317
Grenard, Fernand / 2161
Grew, Joseph C. / 2559
Grey, Viscount / 2641
Grierson, H. J. C. / 2160
Griffin, Eldon / 2215
Griffis, William Elliot / 2230, 2449
Griffith, V. A. / 1004
Grinko, G. / 363
Groat, George Gorham / 2386
Groeneveldt, W. P. / 2438
Grote, George / 2351
Gruliow, Leo / 2961
Guerrin, M. / 2647
Guffey, Joseph F. / 2566
Guillemin, Ernst A. / 2807
Gulick, Sidney L. / 2210, 2669
Gumpert, Martin / 2682
Gundry, R. S. / 2196
Gunn, John W. / 2419
Gunther, John / 2378, 2379
Gutzlaff, Charles / 2594
Gwatkin, H. M. / 2185

H

H. P. B. / 2653
Haan, M. R. De / 2819
Habe, Hans / 2631
Hackworth, Green Haywood / 2249

Hadamard, Jacques / 2876
Haddon, Alfred C. / 2431
Haeckel, Ernst / 2562
Haensel, Pane / 363

Hahn, Emily / 2462
Haig, T. Wolseley / 2185
Haines, Anna J. / 2339
Halasz, Nicholas / 2710
Haldeman-Julius, E. / 2156,2441,2666
Halevy, Elie / 2785
Hall, A. R. / 2895
Hall, D. G. E. / 638
Hall, James Norman / 2428
Hall, Josef Washington / 2496
Hall, Radclyffe / 2660
Hall, Sidney B. / 2625(2)
Hallgren, Mauritz A. / 2636
Halsey, Frank D. / 2833
Halsey, Margaret / 2670
Hamilton, Alexander / 2296(2)
Hamilton, Alice / 2671
Hamilton, Clarence H. / 2660
Hamilton, J. W. / 2677
Hammond, M. B. / 2179
Hammond, William A. / 2511
Han Jen / 2482
Han, S. T. / 2538
Hanbury, Daniel / 2482
Handlin, Oscar / 2810
Handy, Craighill / 2553
Hanford, James Holly / 2327,2328
Hankin, Hanbury / 2220
Hanna, Paul L. / 2179
Hannover, Ingehr O. Franzius / 161
Hansen, Alvin H. / 2381
Hansen, Harry / 2735,2935,2936(2)
Hanson, Earl Parker / 2920
Hardy, Daphne / 2239

Hardy, H. Reginald / 2828
Hardy, R. Spence / 2259,2438
Hardy, Thomas / 2363,2560,2640,2644
Hargrove, Marion / 2580
Harnack, Adolf / 2859
Harris, Charles / 2321
Harris, Frank / 2339
Harris, W. T. / 2660
Harrison, Austin / 2309
Harrison, Charles Yale / 2916
Harrison, George Russell / 2947
Harrow, Benjamin / 2228
Hart, Albert Bushnell / 2237
Hart, Henry H. / 2365
Hart, James / 2280
Hart, Joseph K. / 2378
Hart, Moss / 2854
Harte, Bret / 2589
Harte, Geoffrey Bret / 2414
Harvey, James / 2509
Haskin, Frederic J. / 2140
Haskins, George L. / 2811
Hatfield, H. Stafford / 2286
Hatings, James / 2270
Hattori Unokichi / 146
Hausman, Leon Augustus / 2370
Hawks, Ellison / 2527
Hayakawa, S. I. / 2406,2963
Haydon, A. Eustace / 2170,2546
Hayek, Friederich A. / 2887
Hayes, Carlton J. H. / 567,2143
Hayes, L. Newton / 467
Hayward, F. H. / 2283
Healy, Raymond J. / 2687

Heard, John / 2373

Hearn, Lafcadio / 2320,2391,2565

Hearnshaw, F. J. C. / 2246

Hecht, Ben / 2375,2526

Heckscher Art Museum / 2426

Hedges, Arthur J. / 2964

Hedin, Sven / 2192,2444,2592

Heiden, Konrad / 2313

Heisenberg, Werner / 2866

Hemingway, Ernest / 2303,2615

Hémon, Louis / 2440

Henderson, Helen Ruth / 2625

Henderson, Nevile / 2293

Henke, Frederick Goodrich / 2516,2865

Henry, O. / 2490,2564,2593,2653(2),2665, 2735

Hepburn, J. C. / 2395,2477

Hermans, Mabel C. / 2612,2626

Hernan, W. J. / 2664

Herodotus / 2790

Herrigel, Eugen / 2940

Herriot, Edouard / 2660

Hibben, Paxton / 2342

Hibschman, Harry / 2668

Hill, Adams Sherman / 2537

Hilton, James / 2428

Hinshaw, David / 2358

Hinton, Harold B. / 2137,2230

Hirschfeld, Magnus / 2446

Hitchcock, Alfred M. / 2343,2399,2476,2561

Hitler, Adolf / 2444

Hitti, Philip K. / 2697

Ho Ju / 2680

Ho Ping-ti / 2909

Hoang, Peter / 2850

Hobbes, Thomas / 2357,2416

Hockett, Homer Carey / 2870

Hocking, William Ernest / 2212,2560,2644

Hodge, Alan / 2548

Hodous, Lewis / 2747

Hoe Yung Chi / 2492

Hoey, William / 2180

Hoffman, Barbara Frank Harold M. / 2849

Hoffman, Paul G. / 2861

Hogendorp, Gijsbert Karel van / 2730

Hogg, George / 2366

Holcombe, A. N. / 2142

Holderness, T. W. / 2507

Holland, W. L. / 2539

Holmes, John Haynes / 2242

Holt, Edwin B. / 2144,2312,2476

Holt, Rackham / 2317

Holton, Gerald / 2961(3),2962(3)

Hook, Sidney / 2397,2870

Hoover, Herbert / 2532

Hope, E. R. / 2813

Horan, Ellamay / 2169

Horden, Heinz / 2800

Hornbeck, Stanley K. / 2707

Horne, Charles F. / 2602

Horose, S. / 2619

Horton, Mildred McAfee / 2837

Hoshino, Ken / 2659

Hosie, Lady / 2528

Hou Te-Pang / 2438

Hourticq, Louis / 2330

House, Edward H. / 2392

Hoving, Walter / 2683

3105

How, Julie Lien-ying / 2750

Howard, William Lee / 2361

Howe, E. W. / 2531

Howe, George Frederick / 2692

Howells, William Dean / 2563

Howey, Walter / 2771

Howley, Frank L. / 2862

Hoyt, Florence Stevens / 2325

Hoyt, Mary Wilkins / 2325

Hsia Hsiao / 2713

Hsia, C. T. / 2792

Hsiao Ch'ien, / 2255, 2338, 2604

Hsiao Kung-Chuan / 2225

Hsiao Tso-liang / 2799

Hsiung, S. I. / 2404, 2565

Hsü Shuhsi / 2160, 2396, 2436

Hsu, Francis L. K. / 2195

Hsu, Immanuel C. Y. / 2718

Hsu, L. C. / 2779

Hsu, P. C. / 2198

Hsüeh, Chün-tu / 2795

Hu Chang-tu / 2713

Hu Hsen-Hsu / 2368, 2452

Hu Schï / 2648

Hu Shih / 2132, 2181, 2198, 2206(2), 2222, 2235, 2247(2), 2282, 2306, 2374, 2396, 2423, 2464, 2466, 2480, 2613, 2643, 2671, 2714, 2726, 2734, 2746, 2755, 2842, 2915, 3008

Hu Suh / 2206, 2387, 2439, 2746

Huang Jolin / 2586

Huang Siu-Chi / 2429

Hubbard, Elbert / 2424

Hudson, Alec / 2556

Hudson, G. F. / 2822

Hudson, Henry Norman / 2585, 2636

Hudson, Manley O. / 2264

Hughes, E. R. / 2205, 2698, 2726, 2905

Hughes, H. Stuart / 2761

Hugo, Victor / 2452

Hulen, Bertram D. / 2379

Hull, Cordell / 148, 2132, 2834

Hulme, Edward Maslin / 2448

Hulsewé, A. F. P. / 2882

Hume, David / 2639

Hume, Edward H. / 2750

Hummel, Arthur W. / 2158, 2269, 2756

Humphreys, Christmas / 2617, 2707, 2807, 2830, 2911, 2939

Hundhausen, Vincenz / 2485

Hung, William / 2357

Hunt, Frazier / 2430, 2489

Hunt, Robert / 2582

Hunter, Dard / 2860

Hunter, Edward / 2706

Hunter, Evan / 2838

Huntington, Charles White / 2270

Hurst, Fannie / 2367

Hutchins, Robert M. / 2381

Hutchins, Robert Maynard / 2344

Huxley, Aldous / 2150, 2177, 2271, 2463, 2526

Huxley, Julian / 2280, 2818, 2845

Huxley, Leonard / 2418

Huxley, Thomas Henry / 2239, 2250, 2288, 2364, 2410, 2437, 2447, 2575, 2576(2), 2762(2), 2763(3), 2764(2), 2765(2)

I

Ibsen, Henrik / 2217,2341

Imbrie, William / 2337

Ingersoll, Robert G. / 2320,2377,2410,2599

Inglis, J. W. / 2501

Innes, Kathleen E. / 2720

Innis, Harold A. / 2558

TheInstitute of Pacific Relations / 2379,2944,2529

The Institute of Chemistry, Academia Sinica / 2950

International Association of Rotary Clubs / 2943

International Monetary Fund / 2382

Irvine, E. Eastman / 2676(2)

Isherwood, Christopher / 2903

Itani, Zenichi / 2292

I-Tsing / 2551

Iturralde, Augusto / 2826

Ives, Mabel Lorenz / 2725

Iwadô, Z. Tamotsu / 2480

J

J. G. Bourinot, / 2129

J. R. K. / 2972

Jackson, Henry E. / 2221,2412

Jacobs, W. W. / 2156, 2186, 2243, 2479, 2483,2570,2579,2587,2699,2848,2850,2891

Jacoby, Catherine Murray / 2488

Jaffe, Bernard / 2447

Jaffe, Philip J. / 2946

Jagendorf, M. / 2372

James, Edmund J. / 2411(3)

James, Henry / 2192

James, Marquis / 2815

James, William / 2280, 2362, 2445, 2517, 2520,2531,2536,2582

Jay, John / 2296(2)

Jeans, J. H. / 2266

Jefferson, Thomas / 2419,2630,2815

Jen T'ai / 2793(2)

Jenks, J. W. P. / 2527

Jespersen, Otto / 2784,2785

Jessup, Alexander / 2176

Jessup, Philip C. / 2141,2267

John, J. A. St. / 2512

Johnson, A. H. / 2934

Johnson, Alvin Saunders / 2219,2270

Johnson, Bolingbroke / 2667

Johnson, Chalmers A. / 2734

Johnson, E. A. J. / 2531

Johnson, Gerald W. / 2616,2819,2917

Johnson, Henry / 2624

Johnson, Kinchen / 466

Johnson, Osa / 2366

Johnson, Samuel / 2491,2492

Johnston, Alexander S. / 2558

Johnston, Paul B. / 2686,2699,2760,2863

Johnston, Reginald F. / 2416,2922

Johnstone, William C. / 2646

The Joint Educational Committee / 2398

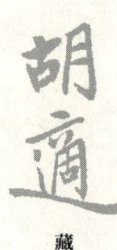

Jonas, Carl / 2810
Jones, Adam Leroy / 2426
Jones, E. Stanley / 2210
Jones, Guy Pearce / 2642
Jones, Howard Mumford / 2855
Jones, John Harry / 2558
Jones, Joseph M., Jr. / 2623
Jones, S. Shepard / 2253

Jones, William K. / 2959
Josephson, Matthew / 2650
Jourdain, Philip E. B. / 2469, 2515
Joyce, James / 2923
Joynes, Edward S. / 2318
Juan Vei Chow / 2450, 2615, 2779, 2797
Julien, Stanislas / 2448, 2560, 2619
Jung, C. G. / 2797, 2798, 2807

K

Kabir, Humayun / 2495
Kaempffert, Waldemar / 2458
Kallen, Horace M. / 2861
Kane, Harnett T. / 2429
Kant, Immanuel / 2371
Kao Hao-jan / 2799
Kao Ping-shu / 2305
Kaplan, J. D. / 2747
Karlgren, Bernhard / 541, 2145, 2157, 2259, 2510, 2599, 2601, 2674, 2706, 2782
Karski, Jan / 2608
Kates, George N. / 2472, 2938
Kaufman, George S. / 2854
Kaufman, Theodore N. / 2319
Kawabata Yasunari / 2902
Keeton, George W. / 2432
Keith, A. Berriedale / 2180
Keith, Arthur / 2222
Keith, Arthur Berriedale / 2604
Kelchner, Warren H. / 2407
Keller, James / 2446
Kellock, Harold / 2359
Keltie, John Scott / 2607

Kemler, Edgar / 2808
Kemmerer, Edwin W. / 2381
Kendall, Carlton / 2431
Kennan, George F. / 2903
Kennedy, Robert F. / 2749
Kent, Frank R. / 2616
Kern, H. / 2889
Kerner, Robert Joseph / 2160, 2173, 2568
Kettridge, J. O. / 2786
Keynes, John Maynard / 2278
Keyte, J. C. / 2372
Keyworth, J. S. / 2311
Khayyám, Omar / 2567(3)
Khrushchev, Nikita S. / 2742
Kiang Wen-han / 2727
Kiang Kang-hu / 2407
Kiang Kan-li / 2943
Kiekhofer, William H. / 2918
Kimbrough, Emily / 2495
Kin Huie / 2555
King Kien-Kün / 2212
King Wunsz / 2935
King, F. H. / 2295

3108

Kingsley, Charles / 2137

Kinney, Henry W. / 2456

Kiong, Le P. Simon / 2877

Kipling, Rudyard / 2330, 2450, 2509, 2518, 2580, 2585

Kiplinger, W. M. / 2658

Kirby, E. Stuart / 2739

Kirby, Rollin / 2345

Kirkpatrick, J. E. / 2138

Kissinger, Henry A. / 2960

Klaproth, J. / 2571

Klingsor, Tristan-L. / 2190

Knight, C. E. / 2843

Knight, Margaret / 2934

Knox, Howard V. / 2517

Knutson, Jeanne Nickell / 2858

Ko King / 2991

Ko Liang-Shi / 2760

Ko, L. S. / 2863

Koestler, Arthur / 2239, 2579

Kogan, Herman / 2783

Kohn, Hans / 2304, 2678, 2875, 2922

Komroff, Manuel / 2151, 2227

Koo, T. Z. / 2198

Korzybski, Alfred / 2436(2)

Kossak, Zofia / 2172

Kotschnig, Walter M. / 2594

Koyas, T. / 2272

Kraus, René / 2446

Kridl, Manfred / 2303

Kristeller, Paul Oskar / 2882

Kruif, Paul de / 2448

Krutch, Joseph Wood / 2457

Ku Hung Ming / 2224, 2606

Kubn, Franz / 2249

Kuhn, Irene / 2155

Kulp, Daniel Harrison / 2231

Kung Tai / 2585

Kung, I. G. / 346

Kuno, Yoshi S. / 2393

Kuntz, Robert E. / 2805, 2862, 2884

Kuo, Helena / 2389

Kwan, Kikuchi / 2634

Kwei, Chih-Ber / 2169

L

La Fargue, Thomas E. / 2718

La Motte, Ellen N. / 2284

La Piere, Richard / 2600

Laai Yi-faai / 2886

Labiche, E. M. / 251

Labiche, Eugène / 2654

Labriola, Antonio / 2277

Laidlay, W. / 2517

Laing, Samuel / 2363, 2457

Lamb, Charles / 2281, 2851

Lamb, Harold / 2439

Lamb, Jefferson D. H. / 2247

Lamont, Corliss / 2747, 2799

Lancaster, Samuel Christopher / 2218

Lane, Edward William / 2152, 2608, 2906

Lang, Andrew / 2483, 2850, 2369

Lang, Olga / 2204

Lange, Franz / 2317

Langer, William L. / 2756,2924

Lankester, E. Ray / 2403

Lao Tzu / 2914

Laqueur, Walter Z. / 2991

Lasker, Bruno / 2538,2539,2541

Lasker, Edward / 2686

Laski, H. J. / 100

Laski, Harold F. / 2665

Lasky, Melvin J. / 2963(3)

Lasswell, Harold D. / 2937

Latourette, Kenneth Scott / 2246,2349,2745,2792

Lattimore, Owen / 2377

Laves, Walter H. C. / 2924

Law Revision Planning Group CUSA / 2821

Lawrence, David / 2998

Lawson, McEwan / 2681

Lawson, Ted W. / 2629

Lay, Charles Downing / 2675

Le Corbeau, Adrien / 2305

Le Motteux, Peter / 2424

Lea, Henry Charles / 2803

Lea, Homer / 2649

Leach, Henry Goddard / 2772,2964

Leacock, Stephen / 2178

Leaf, Munro / 2939

Leaf, Walter / 2369

Leahy, William D. / 2798

Lecky, Elisabeth / 2834

Lecky, William Edward Hartpole / 2351,2356

Lee, Andrew / 2806

Lee, C. H. / 2686

Lee, C. Y. / 2863

Lee, Gerald Stanley / 2235,2236

Lee, Orient / 2219,2856

Lee, Robert E. / 2550

Lee, Vernon / 2359

Leech, Margaret / 2149,2561

Legge, James / 2204,2551,2553,2568,2623,2720,2721(2),2722(3),2777,2889,2890(2)

Lehman, Irving / 2376

Lehman, Linwood / 2231

Leigh, Robert D. / 2508

Leith, C. K. / 2266

Lemenceau, George / 2373

Lengyel, E. / 86

Lenin, N. / 2371

Lenin, V. I. / 2583

Leo Shoo-Tze / 2216,2243,2265(2),2545

Leon, Philip / 2513

Lessing, Ferdinand Diederich / 2683

Lessing, Gotthold Ephraim / 2451

Leung, George Kin / 2603

Lévi, Sylvain / 607,627,650,1032

Levy, Howard S. / 2787

Levy, Isaac D. / 2741

Lew, Daniel H. / 2435

Lew, T. T. / 2198(2)

Lewicki, James / 2824

Lewis, Arthur M. / 2612

Lewis, C. Day / 2687

Lewis, Elizabeth Foreman / 2197

Lewis, Hodous / 704

Lewis, Lloyd / 2468

Lewis, Oscar / 2169

Lewisohn, Ludwig / 2601

Li Fang-kuei / 2146,2804

Li Ch'iao-p'ing / 2712

Li Chi / 2434, 2702

Li Choh-ming / 2752

Li Fang-kuei / 2146

Li Huan-Hsu / 2950

Li Man-kuei / 2964

Li Tchang-Chain / 2260

Li Tien-yi / 2878

Li Ung Bing / 2329

Li, C. C. / 2779

Li, K. C. / 2139(3)

Liang Shih-chiu / 2901

Liang Yuen-Li / 2499

Lieberman, Henry R. / 2715

Lieu, D. K. / 2200, 2201

Lillie, Frank R. / 2514(2)

Lillienthal, D. E. / 258

Lin Chi-Kai / 2493

Lin K'i Kai / 2285

Lin Mousheng / 2445, 2835

Lin Shao-Yang / 2203

Lin Tung Chi / 2204, 2675

Lin Yutang / 2355, 2409, 2414, 2463, 2651, 2689, 2934(2)

Lin, T. C. / 2416, 2435

Lin, W. Y. / 2474

Lindeman, Eduard C. / 2659, 2744, 2894, 2895

Lindsay, A. D. / 2514

Lindsey, Ben B. / 2132

Linebarger, Paul / 2615

Linebarger, Paul Myron Anthony / 2196, 2324(2), 2526

Linen Trade Association / 2148

Ling Ch'i / 2733

Ling, Timothy H. / 2264

Linton, Ralph / 2130

Liou Kin-Ling / 2656

Lippmann, Walter / 2644(2), 2730

Litch, J. E. Crawford / 2637

Little, William / 2591

Liu Gjuen / 2170

Liu Chai-Lien / 2152

Liu E / 2920

Liu Fu / 2284, 2461

Liu Hsieh / 2824

Liu Shaw-tong / 2858

Liu·Shih-chao / 2853

Liu Ta-Chung / 2201

Liu Tiéh-yün / 2920

Liu Tsun-chi / 2981

Liu Wu-chi / 2737, 2878, 2900

Liu, William Tien-Chen / 2613

Livingstone, R. W. / 2500

Lo Ch'ang-P'ei / 2316

Lo Hsiang-lin / 2910

Lo, R. Y. / 2202

Locke, John / 2484, 2512, 2643, 2851

Lockhart, L. W. / 2162, 2186

Lodge, Henry Cabot / 2584

Lodge, Oliver / 2133, 2576, 2617

Logan, Edward B. / 2142

Loh I-cheng / 2967

Lombard, Frank Alanson / 2402

Lombard, Helen / 2658

TheLondon Geographical Institute / 2155

Lord Allen of Hurtwood / 2178

Lorwin, Lewis L. / 2470

Lotze, Hermann / 2426

Lou Kan-Jou / 2347

Lou Kao / 2502

Lourié, Ossip / 2367

Lowe Chuan-Hua / 2395

Lowell, A. Lawrence / 2534

Lowell, D. O. S. / 2276

Lowenthal, Marvin / 2701

Lu Tze-Wei / 2485

Luce, Henry R. / 2943,2992(4),2993(4),2994(5),2995(4),2996(4),2997(4)

Ludendorff, Erieh / 2467

Ludwig, Emil / 853,2171,2600

Lugard, F. D. / 2257

Luh, C. W. / 2486

Lunn, Arnold / 2275

Lunt, W. E. / 2791

Luther, Martin / 2875

Lyall, Leonard A. / 2212,2573

Lyman, Robert Hunt / 2676

Lynch, A. J. / 2563

Lyon, F. H. / 2592

Lyons, Eugene / 2552

M

M., Arthur R. / 2709

MA Ting Ying H. / 2711,2740,2746,2754,2780,2881

Macaraig, Serafin E. / 2596

MaCaulay, Lord / 2348,2408

Macaulay, Rose / 2238

Macaulay, Thomas B. / 2234,2350

MacCurdy, George Grant / 2259

MacDonald, Betty / 2867

MacDonell, Arthur A. / 2354

MacFarquhar, Roderick / 2796,2957(2)

Macgowan, J. / 2204

Macgowan, Kenneth / 2817

Machiavelli, Niccolo / 2703,2874

Mackinder, Halford J. / 2244

MacLeish, Archibald / 2408,2478,2525

MacIver, Robert M. / 2823

MacMechan, Archibald / 2187

MacMurray, John V. A. / 2638

MacNair, Harley Farnsworth / 2194

Macnicol, Margaret / 463

Madelin, Louis / 2561

Madison, Charles A. / 2743

Madison, James / 2296(2)

Maeterlinck, Maurice / 2648

Magee, David / 2389

Maine, Henry Summer / 2146

Majumdar, R. C. / 2952

Makower, Stanley V. / 2174

Malinowski, Wladyslaw / 2303

Malone, Dumas / 2231

Malraux, André / 2437

Mangan, Thomas J. / 2801

Manly, John Matthews / 2274,2603

Mann, Martin / 2861

Mann, Thomas / 2398

Mannheim, Karl / 2433

Manzoni, Alessandro / 2366,2798

Mao Tse-tung / 2822

Margaret, Queen of Navarre / 2342

Margouliès, Georges / 2288,2403

Marke, Julius J. / 2812

Marlio, Louis / 2228

Marquand, John P. / 2331,2595,2666,2869

Marshall, Henry / 2183

Marshall, Henry Rutgers / 2656

Marshall, James / 2310

Martin, Édouard / 2654

Martin, Everett Dean / 2542,2832

Martin, W. A. P. / 2207

Marvin, Walter T. / 2476

Masefield, John / 2587

Mason, C. P. / 2273

Mason, J. W. T. / 2232

Mason, John / 2288

Mason, John Alden / 2694

Mason, Richard / 2936

Massey, Vincent / 2852

Masson, Louis T. / 2316

Masson, M. E. / 2951

Mathews, John Mabry / 2280

Mathews, R. H. / 2757,2831

Mathiez, Albert / 80

Matthews, Brander / 2193

Maugham, W. Somerset / 2910,2914

Maurer, Herrymon / 2270, 2485, 2730, 2776, 2931

Maverick, Lewis A. / 2713

Mawson, C. O. Sylvester / 2564(2)

Mayer, J. P. / 2136

Mayers, Lewis / 2296

Mayo, Katherine / 2594

Mazlish, Bruce / 2931

Mazzini, Joseph / 2258

McAdoo, Eleanor Wilson / 2674

McCabe, Joseph / 2129, 2156, 2161, 2166, 2245,2252(2),2474,2493,2542,2562,2640, 2672

McCarthy, Joseph R. / 2691

McCloskey, Robert G. / 2779

McComas, J. Francis / 2687

McDonald, James G. / 2841

McIlwain, Charles Howard / 2227

McLaughlin, Andrew C. / 2237

McNally, Rand / 2936

McNeile, A. H. / 2374

McNichols, Charles L. / 2232

McReynolds, George E. / 2390

McVey, Frank L. / 2299

Mead, Edwin D. / 2376

Meade, Robert Douthat / 2399

Meadows, Thomas Taylor / 2719

Mearns, David C. / 2823

Mebane, Alexander D. / 2933

Medhurst, W. H. / 2200

Meeker, Arthur, Jr. / 2389

Mei Yi–Pao / 2282,2461

Meiklejohn, Alexander / 2261

Mellor, J. W. / 2345

Melnitz, William / 2817

Meltzer, Charles Henry / 2885,2928

Melville, Herman / 2170

Members of the Revision Committee / 2385

Members of the Faculty of theSouth Philadelphia High School for Girls / 2262

Mencken, H. L. / 2141, 2478, 2616, 2835, 2846,2860,2926

Mennie, D. / 2196

3113

Menninger, Flo V. / 2241
Menninger, Karl A. / 2363
Menninger, William C. / 2939
Merivale, Charles / 2354
Merriam, C. Edward / 2349
Merriam, Charles E. / 2488
Merrill, Arch / 2813
Methuen, A. / 2149
Michelet, Jules / 2892
Michelson, A. A. / 112
Micklem, Nathaniel / 2314
Milbank Memorial Fund / 2244
Milburn, George / 2547
Mill, John Stuart / 801, 1094, 2157, 2487, 2649
Millard, Thomas F. / 2271
Millay, Edna St. Vincent / 2556
Miller, Dickinson S. / 2668
Miller, Herbert Adolphus / 2165
Millikan, Robert Andrews / 2530, 2577
Millis, Walter / 2563, 2776
Milne, A. A. / 568, 2668
Milton, Daniel L. / 2920
Minor, Henry / 2610
Les Missionaires de Corée / 2248
Mitchell, Arthur / 2232
Mitchell, Edwin Knox / 2859
Mitford, A. B. / 2622
Mitsubishi Economic Research Bureau / 2394
Miyamori Asatarō / 2148, 2441
Miyaoka Tsunejiro / 2639
Moffatt, W. C. / 2176
Mogi, Sobei / 2537
Moley, Raymond / 2135
Molnar, George / 2700

Mommsen, Theodor / 2353
Moncrieff, C. K. Scott / 2329, 2555, 2670
Monier-Williams, Monier / 2345, 2374
Monroe, Paul / 2199, 2237, 2307
Montague, William Pepperrell / 2476, 2659
Montgomery, Charles F. / 2690
Montgomery, D. H. / 2167
Montgomery, George R. / 2412
Montgomery, Robert H. / 2298
Moorad, George / 2819
Moore, Addison W. / 2232
Moore, Benjamin / 2492
Moore, Charles A. / 2513, 2766, 2864 (2), 2981, 2982 (2)
Moore, Ernest Carroll / 2610
Moore, Frederick / 2669
Moore, George / 2287, 2404, 2503
Moore, J. Howard / 2573
Moorehead, Alan / 2889
Moorman, Frederic W. / 2300
Mora, José Ferrater / 2866
Moraes, Frank / 2883
More, Sir Thomas / 2874
Morgan, Evan / 2474
Morgan, Francis M. / 2929
Morgan, James Henry / 2247
Morgan, L. G. / 2624
Morgenthau, Henry / 2136
Morison, Samuel Eliot / 2246
Morley, Christopher / 2632
Morley, Felix / 2597
Morley, John / 2487
Morris, Earl H. / 2624
Morris, Richard B. / 2756

Morris, William / 2524

Morrison, Arthur / 2622

Morrison, G. H. / 2558

Morrison, R. / 2248

Morshead, E. D. A. / 2848

Mosher, Arthur T. / 2695

Moule, A. C. / 2620

Moulton, Harold G. / 2228

Moulton, Richard G. / 2456, 2457

Mounsey, H. / 2573

Mowrer, Edgar Ansel / 2319

Moy, Ernest K. / 2444

Muhlen, Norbert / 2884

Mui King-Chau / 2148

Muirhead, Findlay / 2618

Muirhead, J. H. / 2227, 2266

Müller, F. Max / 2156, 2569

Muller, Herbert J. / 2809, 2925

Müller, Max / 2593

Müller-Freienfels, Richard / 2318

Mumford, Lewis / 2446

Mumford, W. Bryant / 2388

Mundy, John H. / 2767

Munro, Thomas / 2578

Munro, William Bennett / 246

Münsterberg, Hugo / 2144

Murasaki, Lady / 2679

Murphy, Gardner / 2801

Murphy, Raymond E. / 2468

Murray, Alexander S. / 2438

Murray, Gilbert / 2387, 2640, 2848

Murry, J. Middleton / 2415

Myers, Denys P. / 2253, 2337, 2492

Myers, Ernest / 2369

Myers, Philip Van Ness / 2316

Myres, J. L. / 2240

N

Nakosteen, Mehdi / 2257

Nariman, G. K. / 2423

Nash, Ogden / 2323

Nash, Philip Curtis / 2134

The National Assembly / 2739

National Education Association of the United States / 2261, 2262, 2544, 2611, 2645

National Government of the Republic of China / 2540

The National Library of Peiping / 2215

Nearing, Scott / 2320

Needham, Joseph / 2893(2), 2894

Nehru, Jawaharlal / 2647

Neil, A. S. / 2254

Neilson, William Allan / 2193, 2539, 2821

Nelson, Benjamin N. / 2767

Nevins, Allan / 2415

Nevinson, Henry W. / 2294

Newbigin, Marion I. / 2456

Newcomer, Alphonso G. / 2141

Newton, William I. / 2169

Nicolaevsky, Boris I. / 2742

Nicolson, Harold / 2250, 2543

Nietzsche, Friedrich / 2515

Nikhilananda, Swami / 2789

Nitobé, Inazo / 2183, 2391, 2396, 2411, 2555

3115

Noback, Gustav Joseph / 2257

Norbelie, Bernard / 2192

Nordemann, Edmond / 2509

North, Eric M. / 2173

Northrop, F. S. C. / 2735, 2834, 2913

Notestein, Frank W. / 2876

Nourse, Mary A. / 2199

Nugent, Thomas / 2606

Nukariya, Kaiten / 2881

O

O. M. / 402

O'Hara, Albert Richard / 2528, 2873

O'Hara, John / 2709, 2897

O'Hara, Mary / 2465, 2632

O'Neill, Eugene / 2461

O'Neill, Eugene, Jr. / 2898

Oates, Whitney J. / 2898

Oatman, Miriam E. / 2296

Obata, Shigeyoshi / 2675

O'Brien, George / 276

O'Brien, Justin / 2812

Oeser, Oscar / 2605

Ogden, C. K. / 2242, 2620

Ogg, Frederic Austin / 2325

Okakura Kakuzo / 2175

Oldenberg, Hermann / 2179

Olschki, Leonardo / 1805

Onions, C. T. / 2591

Oppenheim, James / 2361

Oppert, Ernest / 2304

Orlov, Alexander / 2896

Orr, Boyd / 2932

Orwell, George / 2685, 2730

Osborn, Henry Fairfield / 2372

Osborn, Sherard / 2503

Osler, William / 2535

Otto, Emil / 2317

Otto, Max C. / 2668, 2894, 2895

Ou Itaï / 2564

Ou Tsuin-Chen / 2254

Overstreet, H. A. / 2783

Ozaki, Madame Yukio / 2565

P

P. Y. / 78

Pacific Council / 2499

Paetow, Louis John / 2330

Page, Curtis Hidden / 2310, 2393, 2458

Pagés, Léon / 2347

Paine, Thomas / 2562

Pairs, John / 2392

Palmer, L. R. / 2383

Palmer, W. Scott / 2441

Pan Chia-Lin / 2746

Pan Ku / 2355, 2793(3)

P'an Lo-chi / 2793(3)

Pan Yuan-King / 2626

Panikkar, K. M. / 2346,2617,2642

Papini, Giovanni / 2419

Pareto, Vilfredo / 2450

Paris, John / 2402

Park No-Yong / 2200,2560

Park, Helen / 2263

Parker, DeWitt H. / 2291

Parker, James / 2710

Parker, Willis L. / 2292

Parkhurst, Helen / 2769

Parrington, Vernon Louis / 2432

Parsons, Eugene / 2869

Pascal, Blaise / 2631

Passos, John Dos / 2818

Pater, Walter / 2440

Paton, Stewart / 2362

Patten, William / 2589,2590(3)

Patterson, Ernest M. / 2490

Paul, Cedar / 2171,2459

Paul, Eden / 2171,2459

Paul, Herbert / 2415

Paul, Nancy Margaret / 2441

Paulsen, Friedrich / 2383

Payne, Robert / 2305,2910

Peake, Harold / 2150,2365,2507,2534,2607

Pearson, Henry Carr / 2281

Pearson, Hesketh / 2314

Peattie, Donald Culross / 2690

Peek, George A. / 2871

Peffer, Nathaniel / 2163,2200

Pelo, W. J. / 2522

Penn, William / 2701

Penniston, John Benjamin / 2466

Périgord, Paul / 2381

Perrin, Marshall Livingston / 2256

Perry, Ralph Barton / 2630

Perry, W. J. / 2492

Petech, L. / 2849

Peters, D. W. / 2625(2)

Peters, Harry T. / 2236

Petrov, Vladimir / 2932

Pfister, Aloys / 857

Pfoundes, C. / 2313

Phelps, William Lyon / 2159

Phillips, Robert A. / 2929

Piave, F. M. / 2820

Pick, Otto / 2581

Pickrei, Paul / 2999

Pierson, Eleanor / 2323

Pillsbury, W. B. / 2353,2542

Pirenne, Henri / 2833

Pittenger, L. A. / 2217

Plato / 2151,2301,2597(2)

Plehn, Carl C. / 2384

Plumptre, E. H. / 2848

Poe, Edgar Allan / 2621

Pogson, F. L. / 2633

Polanyi, George / 2991(2)

Polisensky, J. / 2952

Pollack, Martyn P. / 2654

Pompe, W. P. J. / 2373

Pope, Alexander / 2369

Pope, John A. / 2194

Pott, F. L. Hawks / 2413

Potulicki, Michel / 2131

Pound, Roscoe C. / 2408

Power, Eileen / 2443,2559

3117

Prabhavananda, Swami / 2903

Pratt, Fletcher / 2470

Pratt, James Bissett / 2441

Prawdin, Michael / 2459

The President / 2292,2482

Presidents and Fellows ofHarvard College / 2157,2292,2374,2482,2625

Price, Don K. / 2212

Price, Frank W. / 2571(2),2891

Prichard, E. F. Prichard, Jr. / 2408

Priestley, J. B. / 2147,2546

Priestley, K. E. / 2753

Pringle, Henry F. / 2419

Pringle, John Douglas / 2700

Proudhon, P. J. / 2541

Proust, Marcel / 2329,2555,2618,2670(2)

Przyluski, M. / 661

Puleston, W. D. / 2153

Pumpelly, Raphael / 2131

Putnam, Samuel / 2871

Pyle, Ernie / 469

Pyle, Wiliard R. / 2530

Q

Quan Lau-King / 2202

Queen, Ellery / 2205,2452,2471

Quiller-Couch, Arthur / 2498

R

R., Theodore M. / 2281

Rabelais, François / 2424,2676,2872

Racine, J. B. / 5

Radin, Paul / 2406

Raleigh, John Henry / 2788

Raman, Sir C. V. / 2847

Raman, T. A. / 2558,2662

Ramstedt, G. J. / 2554

Ran In-Ting / 2877

Rand, Benjamin / 2454

Randall, John Herman / 2882

Randall, John Herman, Jr. / 2432

Rapport, Samuel / 2638,2921

Rashid, P. A. / 2380

Rathenau, Walther / 2476

Ratner, Joseph / 2380,2514,2804

Ratner, Sidney / 2863,2927

Rauschning, Hermann / 2561

Raushenbush, Stephen & Joan / 2298

Rawlings, Majorie Kinnan / 2235

Rawlinson, H. G. / 2802

Reder, D. G. / 2951

Redman, Ben Ray / 2872

Reed, Edward J. / 2391

Reeve, Henry / 2744

Rehman, Irving / 2257

Reichelt, Karl Ludvig / 2921

Reid, Gilbert / 2198,2210

Reinhard, John Revell / 2442

Reinsch, Paul S. / 2543

Reischauer, Edwin O. / 2759(2),2898

Reitzel, William / 2646

Remer, C. F. / 2918

Remington, Woodbern E. / 2235

Rémusat, Abel / 2483

Renan, Ernest / 2420,2816

Renn, Ludwig / 2656

Reves, Emery / 2145

Reynolds, Quentin / 2742

Rhys, Ernest / 2473

Ricardo, David / 2301

Rice, Edward P. / 2352

Rice, Howard C. / 2730

Rice, Howard C., Jr. / 2839,2886

Richards, I. A. / 2162,2299

Richardson, Henry Handel / 2306

Richthofen, Baron / 2413

Rickaby, Joseph / 2574

Rieff, Philip / 2859

Riegelman, Harold / 2628,2657,2711

Rippmann, Walter / 2267

Rivers, W. H. R. / 2443,2596

Robbins, William J. / 2987(4),2988(3)

Robert, Henry M. / 2521

Roberts, Owen D. / 2741

Robertson, E. Arnot / 2591

Robertson, John M. / 2276,2587,2588

Robey, Ralph / 2459

Robinson, Boardman / 2848

Robinson, Charles Alexander, Jr. / 2906

Robinson, J. H. / 435

Robinson, Victor / 2504

Robinson, William J. / 469

Robson, John / 2346

Rockhill, W. Woodville / 2633

Roe, E. T. / 2931

Roelker, William G. / 2184

Rogers, B. B. / 2848

Roland, Joseph M. / 2468

Rolfe, William J. / 2585

Roll, Eric / 2350

Roman, Agnes / 2541

Roosevelt, Eleanor / 2629

Roosevelt, Elliott / 2292

Roosevelt, Franklin D. / 2544,2566

Roscoe, William / 2420

Rose, H. J. / 2786

Rose-Innes, Arthur / 2165,2275,2394

Rosenberg, F. / 2229

Rosinger, Lawrence K. / 2203

Ross, Gordon / 2825

Ross, John / 2350,2436

Rossiter, Clinton / 2738

Rostow, W. W. / 2751

Rouse, Mary / 2842

Rousseau, J. J. / 2228,2269

Rowbotham, A. H. / 2177

Rowe, David Nelson / 2836

Rowntree, Arnold S. / 2672

Rowse, A. L. / 2605

Roy, Dhirendra Nath / 2612

Ruck, Berta / 2403

Rudolph, Richard C. / 2726

Ruey Yih-fu / 2901

Runes, Dagobert D. / 2748,2851,2854,2905

Runyon, Damon / 2237,2238,2567,2703,2800

Rusk, Dean / 2826

Russell, Bertrand / 2467, 2487, 2495, 2537, 2663, 2700, 2731, 2794, 2800, 2892, 2925

Russell, Oland D. / 2359

Ryan, Thomas F. / 2197

S

Sabatini, Rafael / 2348

Saito, H. / 2570

Sakatani, Y. / 2435

Salt, Henry S. / 2358

Salter, Arthur / 2308

Salter, J. T. / 2142

Sampson, Martin W. / 2583

Samuel, Horace B. / 2458

Samuel, Maurice / 2151

Sandburg, Carl / 2130, 2690

Sanders, Frank Knight / 2794

Sanger, Margaret / 2439, 2474, 2475, 2518, 2663

Sangermano, Rev. Father / 2245

Sansom, G. B. / 2809

Santayana, George / 2407, 2509

Sarkar, Bejoy Kumar / 2377

Saroyan, William / 2466

Sarton, George / 2792

Sartre, Jean-Paul / 2932

Sato Yasunosuke / 2593

Satow, Ernest / 2403

Saunders, Dero A. / 2872

Saunders, K. J. / 2340

Saunders, Kenneth / 2500, 2665, 2789

Saurat, Denis / 2271

Sawyer, W. W. / 2830

Schachner, Nathan / 2917

Schafer, Edward H. / 2970(4), 2971

Schapiro, J. Salwyn / 2453

Scheinfeld, Amram / 2683

Scherman, Harry / 2541

Schiller, F. C. S. / 2612

Schilpp, Paul Arthur / 2515

Schlegel, Gustave / 1054

Schlesinger, Arthur M., Jr. / 2135

Schlesinger, Arthur Meier / 2870

Schmitt, Gladys / 2315

Schneider, Herbert W. / 2307, 2703

Schneider, Isidor / 2812

Schumpeter, Joseph A. / 2800

Schuyler, George S. / 2546

Schwartz, Benjamin I. / 2723

Schwarzenberger, George / 2432

Schweitzer / 337

Schweitzer, Morton D. / 2683

Schwimmer, E. G. / 2999

Scot, Walter / 2621

Scott, Geoffrey / 2697

Scott, James Brown / 2594

Scott, Joanna / 2286

Scott, John A. / 2659

Scott, Walter / 2148, 2231, 2331, 2340, 2388, 2401, 2564

Scroggs, William O. / 2646

Seabury, Ruth Isabel / 2774

Seagrave, Gordon S. / 2182(2)

Seal, Brajendranath / 2529

Sear, R. E. De / 2484

Sears, Paul B. / 2629

Secretariat of the Institute of Pacific Relations / 2380

The Secretaries to the Conference / 2539

Secrist, Horace / 2384

Sedgwick, A. G. / 14,2129

Seeger, Elizabeth / 2500

Seidel, Heinrich / 2410

Self, J. Teague / 2862

Seligman, Edwin R. A. / 367,2270

Seligman, Hilda / 2664

The Senate Committee on Rules Seventy-Fifth Congress / 2584

Seton-Watson, R. W. / 2178

Seymour, Charles / 2383,2691

Sforza, Carlo / 2549

Shadick, Harold / 2920

Shakespeare, William / 6,51,215,241,308, 391,2342,2601,2636(2),2899

Shann, George / 2289

Shapley, Dr. / 2921

Shapley, Harlow / 2638,2921

Sharp, Margery / 2215

Sharp, Thomas / 2245

Shaw Tsen-Hwang / 2171

Shaw, Bernard / 2147,2151,2188,2253,2319, 2341,2397,2433,2452,2631,2632

Shaw, Glenn W. / 2634

Shaw, T. E. / 2851

Shebbeare, C. J. / 2245

Sheerin, John B. / 2953

Shen Tsing-Nang / 2243,2265(2),2545

Shen, Sampson C. / 2225

Shen, T. H. / 2688(2)

Sheng Cheng / 2600

Shepardson, Whitney H. / 2646

Shepherd, Charles R. / 2187,2608

Sheridan, R. B. / 2255

Sheridan, Richard Brinsley / 2520

Sherrod, Julian / 2573

Sherwood, Robert E. / 2888

Shiah, Tsoming N. / 2240

Shibata, M. / 2272

Shih Chao-Ying / 2207,2901

Shih Kuo-Heng / 2195

Shih, Vincent Yu-chung / 2824

Shipley, Arthur E. / 2421

Shipley, Maynard / 2387

Shirasaki Kyoichi / 2480

Sholokhov, Mikhail / 2695

Shotwell, James T. / 2156,2325,2351,2489, 2663

Shridharani / 2658

Shridharani, Krishnalal / 2465

Shu Chiung / 2362

Shu Seyuan / 2306

Shute, Henry A. / 2549

Shute, Nevil / 2503

Siddhichai, Pradith / 2761

Siegmeister, Elie / 2840

Sienkiewicz, Henryk / 2546,2621

Sigerist, Henry E. / 2433(2)

Sigerist, Henry S. / 300

Sih, Paul K. T. / 2795,2820

Simon, H. F. / 2902

Simon, Margaret Sargent / 2388
Simon, Walter / 2684
Simonds, Frank H. / 2185
Simpson, George Gaylord / 2833
Sinclair, May / 2473
Sinclair, Upton / 2177, 2484
Singer, Isidor / 2554
Sinnott, Edmund W. / 2831
Sinor, Denis / 2951
Sirén, Osvald / 2205
Sisam, C. H. / 2145
Sitwell, Osbert / 2164
Skinner, Cornelia Otis / 2495
Slaten, Arthur Wakefield / 2254
Sleeman, John H. C. / 2665
Sloman, H. N. P. / 2706
Smalley, H. R. / 2140
Smedley, Agnes / 2204
Smith, Adam / 2378, 2803
Smith, Albert W. / 2523
Smith, Alexander / 2256
Smith, Arthur D. Howden / 2462
Smith, Arthur H. / 2719, 2926
Smith, Bradford / 807
Smith, David Eugene / 2519
Smith, Florence H. / 2981
Smith, George / 2421
Smith, Huston / 2685
Smith, J. M. Powis / 2221
Smith, J. Russell / 2376
Smith, Lillian / 2610
Smith, Lloyd E. / 2599, 2604
Smith, Logan Pearsall / 2273
Smith, T. V. / 2412, 2699, 2744, 2825

Smith, Thomas Vernor / 2279
Smith, Vincent A. / 2258
Smolens, Bernard J. / 2741
Snell, Lord / 2282
Snow, Edgar / 2163, 2294, 2879
Snyder, Louis L. / 2771
Snyder, Virgil / 2145
Sofio, A. A. / 211, 474
Sokolsky, George E. / 2143, 2498, 2609, 2634
Songkhla, Yachai na / 2929
Sontag, Ramond James / 2844
Soong, Norman / 2947, 2954(2), 2955(4), 2956(3)
Soothill / 704
Soothill, William Edward / 2194, 2612, 2747, 2785
Sophocles / 2848, 2916
Soulié, George / 2908
South Manchuria Railway Company / 2148, 2297, 2435
Southworth, E. F. / 2438, 2580
Sowerby, Arthur De C. / 2971
Spahr, Margaret / 2548
Spalding, W. F. / 462
Sparks, John B. / 2347(2)
Spaulding, Thomas M. / 2423
Speare, M. E. / 2678
Spencer, Herbert / 2157, 2536(2), 2614
Spender, Stephen / 2963(3)
Speyer, J. S. / 2315
Spinoza / 2605
Spirkin, A. G. / 2951
Sprout, Harold & Margaret / 2563
Spurr, Russell / 2715

Squair, J. / 2221,2591

Staël-Holstein, A. von / 2219,2269,2486(2)

The staff of the Union Research Institute / 2802

Starbuck, Edwin D. / 2944

Starbuck, Edwin Diller / 2131,2344,2549

Starrett, Vincent / 2271

Stedgwick, W. T. / 2588

Steele, Esther Baker / 2178

Steele, Joel Dorman / 2178,2527

Steele, Richard / 2603

Steffens, Lincoln / 2159(2)

Steichen, Edward / 2769

Steiger, G. Nye / 2355

Stein, Gertrude / 2700

Stein, Sir Aurel / 356

Steinbeck, John / 2460

Steinberg, S. H. / 2906

Steincrohn, Peter J. / 2305,2340

Steiner, Rudolf / 2321

Stevens, Francis B. / 2468

Stevens, Frank / 2607

Stevenson / 2522

Stevenson, Robert Louis / 2134,2638(2)

Stevenson, William / 2938

Stewart, George R. / 2177,2608

Stimson, Henry L. / 2294,2486,2852

Stinnes, Edmund H. / 2552

Stoddard, Lothrop / 2214,2606

Stone, Grace Zaring / 2216

Stone, Harold A. / 2212

Stone, Irving / 2213,2429

Stone, Kathryn H. / 2212

Strachey, G. L. / 2405

Strachey, John / 2219

Strachey, Lytton / 2528

Straus, Roger Williams / 2143

Strayer, George D. / 2558

Strecker, Edward A. / 2251

Streeter, Burnett Hillman / 2307

Streit, Clarence K. / 2644

Strode, Muriel / 2601

Strong, Anna Louise / 2201

Struther, Jan / 2463

Stuart, Jesse / 2623

Sullivan, Gilbert / 2221

Sullivan, J. W. N. / 2425

Sullivan, Mark / 2262,2496

Sun Yat-sen / 2380,2571(2),2805,2891

Sun, S. S. / 2797

Sundt, Einar / 2371

Sung, Z. D. / 2619,2626

Sûra, Ârya / 2315

Suranyi-Unger, Theo / 757

Sutherland, Louis / 2176

Suzuki, Daisetz Teitaro / 2178, 2280, 2281, 2406,2620,2682,2684,2702,2767(2),2807, 2813,2817,2830,2836,2842,2888,2912,2940 (2)

Suzzallo, Henry / 2281

Swancara, Frank / 2339

Swann, Nancy Lee / 2775

Sweet, Henry / 2534

Sweetser, Arthur / 2301,2531

Sweezy, Paul M. / 2800

Swift, Jonathan / 2526

Symonds, John Addington / 2556,2701

Syrett, H. C. / 807

Sze, Sao-Ke Alfred / 2133

T

Tabouis, G. R. / 2470

Taeuber, Irene B. / 2876

Tagore, Rabindranath / 84, 2233, 2320, 2487, 2555, 2570, 2622

Tai, F. H. / 2686

Taine, H. A. / 2346, 2351, 2512

Taire, Lucian / 2715

Takakusu, J. / 2551

Takenobu Yoshitaro / 2401

Takeuchi, Tatsuji / 2656

Tan Shih-Hua / 2206

Tan Yun-Shan / 2199

Tandy, William / 2245

T'ang Leang-li / 2195, 2202, 2307, 2377, 2878

T'ang Yung-T'ung / 2261

Tang, E. H. / 2166

Tanner, William M. / 2222

Tanshowa / 2396

Tao Loo Yü / 2304

Tao Yü / 2304

Tao, L. K. / 2424

Tawney, R. H. / 2131, 2404

Taylor, A. E. / 2153, 2266, 2630

Taylor, Bayard / 2295

Taylor, G. R. Stirling / 2455

Taylor, George E. / 2901

Taylor, Henry Osborn / 2214, 2309, 2442, 2631

Taylor, Mary / 2415

Tchang Tien-Ya / 2209(2), 2639

Tchang, Le P. Mathias / 2919

Tchehov, Anton / 2209, 2229, 2358, 2404, 2502, 2574, 2575

Tchou, M. T. / 2198

Tchou-Kia-Kien / 2627

Teasdale, Sara / 2216

Teggart, Frederick J. / 2566, 2627

Teng Ssu-yü / 2718

Têng Ssŭ-yü / 2190

Tennyson, Alfred / 2525, 2869

Terman, Lewis M. / 386

Tetens, T. H. / 2403

Tewksbury, M. Gardner / 2904

Thackeray, William Makepeace / 2650

Thatcher, Oliver J. / 2368

Thilly, Frank / 2511

Thomas, Dana Lee / 2825

Thomas, Elbert Duncan / 2205, 2630

Thomas, Henry / 2825

Thompson, Charles Miner / 2373

Thompson, Edward K. / 2784

Thompson, Holland / 2174, 2678

Thomson, Charles A. / 2924

Thomson, J. / 2370

Thomson, J. Arthur / 207, 2577

Thorndike, Ashley H. / 2287(3)

Thorndike, Edward L. / 2263

Thorndike, Lynn / 2587

Thurber, Samuel / 2531

Thyssen, Fritz / 2366

Tichenor, H. M. / 2233

Tieh, T. Min / 2598

Tileston, Mary W. / 2237

Timperley, H. J. / 2165,2391,2598,2663

Ting, V. K. / 2317

Tingley, Katherine / 2627

Tinker, Edward Larocque / 2850

Tirpitz / 2466

Titchener, Edward Bradford / 2291

Titsingh, Isaac / 2480

Tjan, Tjoe-som / 2868

Tobar, Le P. J'erome / 2804

Tokutomi Iichiro / 2394

Tolischus, Otto D. / 2628

Tolstoy, Leo / 386,2148,2193

Tomson, Graham R. / 2583

Tong Lee Chen / 2285

Tong, Hollington K. / 2192

Tovar, Antonio / 2950

Townsend, Peter / 2932

Toynbee, Arnold J. / 2399

Train, Arthur / 2463,2465,2544

Train, Arthur C. / 2681

Trautmann, Oskar P. / 121

Tregaskis, Richard / 2329

Trilling, Lionel / 2898

Trivers, Howard / 2468

Trotsky, Leon / 2625,2825

Trotter, W. F. / 2705

Trustees at Woodbridge / 2710

Tsang Chiu-Sam / 2468

Tsao Mo / 2772

Tsao, M. / 2896

Tsen Tsonming / 2276

Tseng Chin Hsien / 2773

Tseng, S. C. / 2943

Tsiang, S. C. / 2774,2916,2917

Tsing Hua College Library / 2214

Tsu, Y. Y. / 2198

Tsui Chi / 2322,2587

Tu Hengtse / 2958(3),2959(2)

Tufts, James H. / 2283

Tulachandra / 2875

Tumulty, Joseph P. / 2673

Tung Shih-kang / 2755

Tung, L. / 2194

Tupper, Eleanor / 2390

Turgenev, Ivan S. / 2295,2651

Turkington, A. / 2464

Turner, Ralph / 2782(2)

Twain, Mark / 2295

Two Wayfarers / 2210

Tyau, Min-chi'ien T. Z. / 2411

Tyler, H. W. / 2588

Tyndall, John / 2410

U

Ueberweg, F. / 414

Uhlenbeck, C. C. / 2272

Ulianov, N. I. / 275

The Union Hymnal Committee / 283

Union Research Institute / 2732

United States Atomic Energy Commission / 2740

University of London / 2316

Urquhart, Thomas / 2424

Utley, Freda / 2256,2715

V

Valentine, Alan / 2257
Valentine, C. W. / 2384
Valéry, Paul / 2287
Vallery-Radot, René / 2420
Van Dine, S. S. / 2171
Van Doren, Carl / 2166, 2167, 2814
Van Doren, Mark / 2474
Van Gulik, R. H. / 2272, 2648
Van Loon, Hendrik Willem / 2418, 2434, 2494, 2609
Van Paassen, Pierre / 2633
Vanikiati, Bunam / 2929
Vasubandhu / 2660
Veblen, Thorstein / 2344, 2378, 2627
Veith, Ilza / 2796
Vejakorn, Hem / 2907(2), 2908
Vendryes, J. / 2406
Verdi, Giuseppe / 2820
Vernier, Pierre / 2998
Vespa, Amleto / 2570
Veynbaum, M. / 2776
Viereck, George S., Jr. / 2164
Viereck, George Sylvester / 2339
Viner, Jacob / 2381
Vinogradoff, Paul / 2220
Vlasto, Peter / 2328
Voltaire / 2591, 2654
Von Clausewitz, Carl / 2875
Von den Steinen, Diether / 2524
Von der Gabelentz, George / 2147
Von Goethe, Johann Wolfgang / 2229, 2295
Von Moellendorff, P. G. / 2620
Von Schiller, Friedrich / 461
Von Suttner, The Baroness Bertha / 2250
Vossler, Karl / 2605

W

Waddell, Helen / 2430
Wade, Thomas Francis / 2661
Wagner, Richard / 2781, 2860, 2885, 2900, 2913, 2928
Wainwright, Alexander D. / 2983(2), 2984(4), 2985
Wakefield, Eva Ingersoll / 2815
Wakefield, Harold / 2475
Waley, A. / 2481
Waley, Arthur / 2175, 2176, 2364, 2365, 2460(2), 2569, 2624, 2637, 2658, 2694, 2918, 2929
Walker, Hugh / 2581
Walker, Richard Louis / 2733(2), 2839, 2913
Wallace, DeWitt / 2945, 2989, 2990
Wallace, Henry A. / 2532
Wallace, Lila Acheson / 2989, 2990
Wallace, Paul A. W. / 2980
Waln, Nora / 2359

Walpole, Hugh / 2580

Walworth, Arthur / 2574

Wan, Charles C. H. / 2226

Wang Chi-Chen / 2481, 2548, 2549

Wang Ching-Chun / 2395

Wang Ching-ju / 2153

Wang Ching-Wei / 2202, 2205

Wang Chueh-ming / 2853

Wang FungChiai / 2291

Wang Ging-Hsi / 2481, 2485

Wang Hsi / 2514

Wang San-Pin / 2699, 2780, 2839

Wang Tsun-Sheng / 2510

Wang, C. C. / 2488

Wang, G. H. / 2952, 2953

Wang, King KY, S. E. / 2653

Wang, Tsi C. / 2939

Wang, Y. / 2797

Ward, Humphrey / 2144

Ward, Lynd / 2690

Ward, Percy / 2339

Ward, Stephen / 2284

Ward, Wilfrid / 2499

Ware, James R. / 2892

Warhaftig, Zorach / 2553

Warren, Henry Clarke / 2708

Watling, E. F. / 2916

Watson, David Lindsay / 2579

Watson, J. A. S. / 2343

Watson, J. B. / 441

Watson, James E. / 2154

Watson, John B. / 441

Watten, Raymond H. / 2760, 2896, 2929

Watts, Alan W. / 2905

Watts, Charles A. / 2548

Weaver, Henry Grady / 2828, 2829

Weaver, Warren / 2874

Webb, Clement C. J. / 2353

Weber, Olga Svatik / 2946

Wechsler, Herman J. / 2868

Wedemeyer, Albert C. / 2931

Wedgwood, C. V. / 2921

Wei, F. C. M. / 2198

Wei, Wilson S. / 2336

Weigle, Luther A. / 2385

Weiner, J. S. / 2866

Weintz, H. J. / 2359, 2401

Welch, Robert H. W., Jr. / 2816

Welles, Summer / 2532, 2633

Wells, H. G. / 331, 2150, 2163, 2211, 2236, 2291, 2352, 2462, 2483, 2519, 2586, 2662, 2664, 2671

Wen Hsi-Shan / 2839

Wendt, Gerald / 2968

Wenley, A. G. / 2194

Wensberg, Erik / 2960

Wentworth, George / 2519

Werfel, Franz / 2268, 2601

Werner, E. T. C. / 2701

Werner, M. R. / 2162

Werth, Alexander / 2461

Wessely, J. E. / 2475

Westcott, Edward Noyes / 2240

Westerfield, Ray B. / 2381

Wharton, Grace / 2545

Wharton, Philip / 2545

Wheeler, W. Reginald / 2195, 2743, 2773, 2867

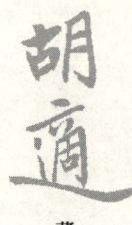

Whitaker, C. W. / 2143

White, Andrew Dickson / 2158, 2356

White, E. B. / 2494, 2615

White, J. H. / 295

White, Katharine S. / 2615

White, Leonard D. / 2314

White, Llewellyn / 2508

White, Newman Ivey / 2586

White, W. L. / 2558

Whiteford, Robert N. / 2322

Whitehead, Alfred North / 2383, 2576

Whitehead, Don / 2770

Whitman, Walt / 2409

Whitney, J. P. / 2185

Whitney, William Dwight / 2418, 2572

Whyte, Lancelot Law / 2152, 2478, 2685, 2847

Wichmann, K. / 2787

Wicker, George Ray / 2265

Wiener, Philip P. / 2769, 2926

Wiggam, Albert Edward / 2472

Wight, O. W. / 2705

Wilbour, Charles E. / 2452

Wilbur, C. Martin / 2734, 2750

Wilde, Oscar / 328, 2241, 2360(2), 2368

Wilder, George D. / 2773

Wilder, Thornton / 2788

Wile, Frederic William / 2477

Wilhelm, Richard / 2208, 2407, 2459

Willcox, Walter F. / 2527

Willett, Herbert / 2140

Willey, Basil / 2898

William, Maurice / 2596, 2616

Williams, Blanche Colton / 2175, 2495

Williams, Henry Smith / 2326, 2348

Williams, J. Wells / 2277

Williams, John H. / 2381

Williams, S. Wells / 2449

Williams, Valentine / 2678

Williamson, H. R. / 2928(2)

Willkie, Wendell L. / 2532

Willoughby, Westel W. / 2282, 2313, 2593

Wilson, Edith Bolling / 2465

Wilson, Edmund / 2634

Wilson, Hardy / 2682

Wilson, Philip Whitwell / 2317

Wilson, Richard A. / 2836

Wilson, Woodrow / 2227

Wimsatt, Genevieve / 2151

Windelband, Wilhelm / 2353, 2519

Windolph, F. Lyman / 2823

Winslow, Anne / 2968

Winter, H. J. J. / 2751

Wittfogel, Karl August / 2447, 2857

WittlinJózef, Józef / 2303

Wolf, A. / 2289

Wolfe, Bertram D. / 2901

Wölfflin, Heinrich / 2729

Wollheim, Donald A. / 2521

Wong Mon-Lam / 2617, 2911

Wong, Y. W. / 2672

Wood, Clement / 2187, 2329

Wood, H. G. / 2425, 2635

Woodbridge, Frederick J. E. / 2277, 2469, 2550, 2843

Woodhead, H. G. W. / 2198

Woodruff, Douglas / 2768

Woodward, Marcus / 2360

Woodworth, Robert Sessions / 2258

Woody, Thomas / 2259,2545

Wooley, Edwin C. / 2337,2679(2)

Woolf, Virginia / 2220,2634

Woolridge, R. L. / 2686

Wordsworth, William / 2827

Wormser, René / 2843

Wreden, Nicholas / 2297

Wright, Arthur F. / 2909

Wright, Benjamin Fletcher, Jr. / 2602

Wright, Helen / 2638,2921

Wright, Philip G. / 2635

Wright, Richard / 2469

Wright, William Kelley / 2279

Wrong, E. M. / 2233

Wu Lien-Teh / 2680,2867

Wu, Alfred Chi-tai / 2853

Wu, Eugene / 2814

Wu, John C. H. / 2400,2577,2820

Wu, K. T. / 2176,2451

Wu, Lucian / 2845

Wu, T. J. / 2686

Wulf, Maurice De / 501

Wylie, A. / 2482

X

Xenophon / 2597(2)

Y

Yang Ching-Kun / 2443

Yang Lien-sheng / 2655, 2736, 2837, 2897, 2908

Yang Pao-San / 2541

Yang Yen-Fei / 2760

Yang, Y. F. / 2863

Yangiwara, Sukeshige / 2394

Yano Tsuneta / 2480

Yen En Tsung / 2490

Yen Hsi-Shan / 2540

Yen, Maria / 2923

Yen, W. Y. / 2229

Yetts, W. Perceval / 2236,2251

Yin, H. C. / 2540

Young Chung-Chien / 2432

Young, A. Morgan / 2371,2563

Young, Arthur A. / 2195

Young, C. Walter / 2382

Young, E. H. / 2667

Young, Ella Flagg / 2600

Young, James R. / 2494

Yu Da-yuen / 2398

Yu Kwang-chung / 2845

YuanTung-li / 2714

Yui, D. Z. T. / 2198

Z

Zacharoff, Lucien / 2653
Zan Tseu Yih / 2608
Zeiger, Henry A. / 2710
Zeller, Edward / 2497
Zelomek, A. Wilbert / 739
Zen, Sophia H. Chen / 2619, 2912
Zetland, The Marquis of / 2415

Zhao Yang Buwei / 2360
Ziff, William B. / 2219
Zimmer, Heinrich / 2864
Zinsser, Hans / 2154
Zucker, A. E. / 2661, 2662, 2727
Zung, Cecilia Sieu-Ling / 2643
Zweig, Stefan / 2761, 2885

後　記

　　經過兩館三年有餘的協作努力，《胡適藏書目録》終于要面世了。作爲北京大學圖書館胡適藏書的主要整理者和本書的主編,此乃本人虛度四十五載中最有意義、最感榮幸的一件事情。

　　如果從 2000 年暑假我開始整理胡適藏書算起,已經有十幾個年頭了,個中感受可謂五味雜陳。我願意借此機會回顧胡適藏書整理以及兩館合作的點點滴滴,既是對將來對此事有興趣者的一種交待,也算作與十餘年爲此事付出辛苦的友朋、同仁、同好者分享當年不該忘却的記憶。

　　北大圖書館胡適藏書的整理,始于上世紀 60 年代,那時候有一些胡適的普通藏書被分類編目上架。上世紀 80 年代,胡適所藏綫裝書被集中整理,可惜的是,没有集中存放,而是被分散到各個分類號下。我接受整理胡適藏書的任務,是在 2000 年。那一年的暑假,當時我還在北大圖書館辦公室工作,在通往辦公室的走廊遇到戴龍基前館長,他叫住我,問我是否有興趣整理胡適的藏書,我頗有些驚喜,雖然知道會有很多困難,還是很痛快地答應下來。時隔十二年之後,我依然清楚地記得當年的情形,那天的天氣也非常好,也許是因爲這件事情對我的影響太大之故吧。

　　那個暑假我就在臨時存放胡適藏書的一間閲覽室開始整理胡適藏書,雖然一捆捆藏書積滿了四十多年甚至更多年的塵土,但整理的過程就像充滿驚喜的探寶之旅,不斷有令我興奮的發現,周作人、徐志摩、趙元任、傅斯年、顧頡剛、錢穆、沈從文……,這些民國時期大名鼎鼎的人物,他們的簽名題贈本不斷出現在我眼前,恰如璀璨的群星,令我心馳神往。而帶有胡適漂亮題記、簽名的藏書,則讓我有一種難以言说的感慨,當年如日中天的胡適之先生研讀過的這些圖書,竟然會被我這樣一個無名小輩翻閱整理,此情此景,恍然如夢。最令我激動的當屬胡適澄衷學堂日記和一批中、英文書信的發現,前者是迄今爲止發現的最早的胡適日記。胡適研究者都知道,胡適的書信和日記現主要由社科院近代史所收藏,北大圖書館所藏胡適資料主要是藏書,能從這批藏書中發現胡適重要的書信日記,的確讓人驚喜。

此後,我因爲工作的安排,整理胡適藏書時斷時續。而我當時還不知道,在胡適藏書的另一主要收藏機構——胡適紀念館,胡適藏書的整理也在進行之中。主要負責此事的,是後來在臺灣東海大學任教的陳以愛教授。以愛教授當時在臺灣"中央研究院"近代史研究所做博士後研究。2003年3月,她應當時紀念館主任楊翠華女士的邀請,負責該館胡適藏書的整理工作。到2006年夏,初步完成胡適紀念館三千餘種中、日文胡適藏書的整理著錄工作。以愛教授不僅對胡適紀念館的胡適藏書整理貢獻頗多,而且在推動北大圖書館與胡適紀念館的合作上功不可没。

2005年,北大圖書館成立特藏部,胡適藏書的普通書部分正式劃歸特藏部下我負責的北大文庫,這部分胡適藏書的整理才算走上正軌。2004—2006年,已到東海大學任教的陳以愛教授連續三年暑假到北大圖書館查閱胡適藏書。也就是在2005年夏,經北大圖書館王世儒老師介紹,我初識陳以愛教授,因之前恰好曾拜讀過她的大作《中國現代學術研究機構的興起——以北京大學研究所國學門爲中心的探討》,對以愛教授很是欽佩,因此相談融洽,並得到她的很多指教。以愛教授關於兩館在胡適藏書整理方面加強合作的建議,我也心有戚戚焉。以愛教授還有一個書面的關於兩館合作的建議書,除了整理藏書之外,還有兩館《水經注》聯展的建議,都頗具眼光。我很快向北大館前任館長戴龍基先生彙報了此事,並得到他的支持和肯定。以愛教授回臺之後,也向新任胡適紀念館主任黄克武先生報告了此事,黄主任也深表贊同。不久,黄克武主任到北大館訪問,參觀瞭解北大館胡適藏書情況,並與戴龍基館長商談兩館合作事宜。也是在此前後我與胡適紀念館彭靖媛小姐建立郵件聯繫,溝通兩館合作進展情況。2007年4月,我和特藏部主任張紅揚應邀到胡適紀念館訪問,並商談具體合作事宜,雙方商談愉快,並達成共識。值得一提的是,4月5日,陰雨綿綿的清明節,我和張紅揚到胡適墓園祭拜了胡適之先生,心中不免感慨繫之。

我和張紅揚主任回北京後,將臺灣之行商談的結果向戴龍基館長作了彙報,得到館方的肯定和支持。大約2008年下半年,胡適紀念館的鄭鳳鳳小姐開始與我郵件聯繫,告知潘光哲先生新任胡適紀念館主任,希望進一步商談促成合作之事。直到最近我才知道,以愛教授在這一年的11月初曾在"中央研究院"近代史所作"兩岸胡適藏書的整理與胡適研究前景"的報告。我想這個報告對於推動胡適紀念館與北大圖書館的合作應該是起到很大作用的。12月，潘主任曾在北京與張紅揚主任和我面談。12月中旬，我和朱強館長參加在胡適先生家鄉績溪舉辦的會議，其間潘主任與朱強館長首次見面，並就交流合作達成一致意見。2009年4月，北大圖書館與胡適紀念館正式簽署"胡適藏書目録整理合作協議"，四年多的聯繫終于有了一個圓滿的結局。

被打散的胡適綫裝書是北大館胡適藏書整理的難點，北大館有綫裝古籍150萬冊，要從中逐本查找胡適藏書，以"大海撈針"、"望洋興嘆"形容，庶幾近之。據陳以愛教授的調查，北大圖書館曾有一本書本式胡適藏書目録——《胡適原藏書目録》，但現在已無從查找其下落。所幸的是，本館還存有一套胡適綫裝書的目録卡片，而有意思的是，此目録是以愛教授的先生臺灣"暨南大學"歷史系李廣健教授偶然發現，後由以愛教授告訴我的。借助這套卡片目録，胡適綫裝書的整理才理出個頭緒來。需要指出的是，北大館至今仍有十餘萬冊綫裝書沒有編目，在新編的綫裝書中，時有胡適藏書發現。也正因爲如此，卡片目録中3100餘種胡適綫裝書中還有一部分沒有找到。我們後來整理的胡適藏書有近3100種，但因爲存在叢書子目分別著録爲一種的問題，估計還有數百種胡適藏書尚未落實。胡適綫裝書整理的另外一個問題是，這部分圖書屬於古籍部，與我所屬的特藏部是兩個部門，我到古籍部查找3000餘種古籍，有諸多不便，且此事牽涉到部門協作的問題。好在此事得到朱強館長的大力支持，在我和張紅揚主任的積極爭取下，古籍部沈乃文主任同意委派該部丁世良老師負責胡適綫裝書的查找核對。

另一件值得一提的事情是，我偶然發現了一張可能是松公府北大圖書館的四層書庫架位圖，其中明確標注了胡適藏書存放在第54—55排書架和第53排書架一部分，這讓我聯想到胡適藏書中都貼有藍色的標籤，其上的號碼是館裏俗稱的"胡同號"，第一排數字就是書架排號，而我們已經確定的胡適藏書，上面的那些藍色標籤第一行數字與架位圖的書架排號完全吻合。由此我推斷，凡是帶有與此相同的藍色標籤，第一行是54、55的圖書肯定是胡適藏書，第一行是53的中文書也是胡適藏書。此條信息成爲我們判斷那些沒有胡適題記、簽名、印章等信息的圖書是否胡適藏書的一個重要依據，對於判斷新編古籍是否胡適藏書也是很好的參考。

此外，比較困難的是，已經被分編的胡適普通書的查找，這些書同樣散在各處，更讓人頭疼的是，沒有一個集中的目録。我們曾試圖在老北大藏民國圖書中查找，但發現甚少。今年暑假前後，北京新文化運動紀念館秦素銀女士偶然提及帶有某具體題記的胡適某本著作，我在整理的胡適藏書中沒有發現，這使我猜想，我所在的北大文庫展示的胡適著作中也許有已編胡適藏書，經過查找，果然發現了5種有胡適題記的胡適藏書。從北大哲學系樓宇烈先生以及一些同事的回憶看，散在本館普通圖書中的胡適藏書應該遠不止此數。

關於1963年北大圖書館移交現國家圖書館的胡適藏書，前不久，我再度與近幾年疏於聯絡的以愛教授郵件聯繫，以愛教授將她2006年調查所得涉及12種移交國圖的胡適藏書目錄的三個檔發給我，不僅包括版本、索書號等信息，而且包括胡適的題跋等重要內容，真令我大喜過望。當我試圖通過同事到國家圖書館進一步核對時，才得知國圖善本部所在館舍正在進行整修，善本圖書已經無法調閱了。以愛教授的這三個文件由此更顯珍貴。以愛教授關於此事的考證文章，讓我想起當年在北大檔案館查過的《北京圖書館1964年選留胡適藏書清單》，於是再度複製一份，並據此檢索本館"古文獻資源庫"，竟然查找到47種我們之前沒有著錄的胡適藏書。考慮到北大館未編古籍中仍時有胡適藏書發現，以及105種清單中存在書名與編目後的書名不完全一致的情況，我更加支持以愛教授關於當年移交國圖胡適藏書只有12種而非105種的判斷。

回顧胡適藏書整理的過程，冥冥之中似有天助，無論是預想的還是意外的困難，均被一一化解，最後的結果可算是水到渠成，而我個人與胡適藏書似乎也有一種注定的緣分。1995年夏，我放棄在某省城某院校的兩居室住房，重新開始讀書生涯，面對茫然未知的將來，激勵我前行的是我抄在自己一張運動會長跑比賽照片上的胡適先生的兩句詩——"做了過河卒子，只能拼命向前。"如果沒有當年的告別以往，如果不是選擇北大圖書館再度從事圖書館工作，我不可能有機會接觸整理胡適藏書。

本書目能夠完成，最應該感謝的是臺灣東海大學的陳以愛教授，如前所述，她在胡適紀念館胡適藏書整理和兩館合作方面的貢獻，令人敬佩。而她對我個人參與胡適藏書整理的支持、幫助與鼓勵，我也銘感於心。

感謝北大圖書館和胡適紀念館幾任主持者的積極支持和促成，感謝胡適紀念館鄭鳳凰、莊茹蘭小姐的幫助，特別是鳳凰小姐，不僅在胡適藏書整理、書目出版方面經年積極協作，且多次在資料查找方面給予我及時的幫助。雖素未謀面，但郵件聯繫頗多，她的勤謹溫和是可以深刻地感受到的。

感謝我所在的北大圖書館特藏部全體同仁給予我的鼎力支持，特別是張紅揚主任，我們多年工作上的彼此瞭解和默契協作，以及由此帶來的愉快的工作環境和心境是我十分珍視和感激的。感謝我的北大文庫工作搭檔吳政同老師，他嚴謹細緻，任勞任怨，心平氣和，在具體整理過程中給了我極大的幫助。特藏部同事周永喜老師主要負責胡適普通圖書的除塵和胡適綫裝書的目錄檢索，同樣對我助益頗多。感謝古籍部李雲主任和古籍部諸多老師的幫助，因前言已經列出，茲不贅述。再次感謝丁世良老師，他的細緻認真，以及在古籍方面的廣博學識，使本館胡適綫裝書得到圓滿整理。感謝北大館分館辦徐韶老師的幫助。

感謝社科院近代史所耿雲志先生、宋廣波先生，以及北大歷史系歐陽哲生教授，他們在有關胡適的學識上給予我很多指教。特別是耿先生，不僅多次鼓勵、肯定我們的努力，而且慨然允諾爲本書題寫序言。

感謝廣西師範大學出版社文獻圖書出版分社雷回興社長和金學勇先生，他們在本書的編輯體例、校對以及出版等具體方面給予了很多幫助和支持。

感謝復旦大學龍向洋老師的鼎力相助，他高超的軟件應用能力和豐富的索引編製經驗，爲本書索引的編製節省了大量時間。

今年是適之先生逝世五十周年，能够以本書作爲一種紀念，是我們的榮幸。

1918年11月，胡適的母親去世，大慟之餘，胡適開始思考關於"不朽"問題，於1919年寫成《不朽——我的宗教》，文章指出了《左傳》著名的"立功"、"立德"、"立言"之"三不朽"的不足，即忽略普通人的貢獻，並提出"社會的不朽論"，大意是説個人的"小我"會消滅，社會的"大我"則不朽，但是"小我"的一切作爲，無論善惡，都留在那個"大我"之中，因此個人應該努力，不辜負"大我"的無窮過去，不貽害"大我"的無窮未來。以胡適的影響和貢獻，"三不朽"足以當之，他的學術思想已經成爲社會這個"大我"的一個重要組成部分。希望今天我們的一點努力，能够不辜負適之先生的輝煌過去，同時使適之先生在社會這個"大我"所留下的影響更加豐富深遠。

北京大學圖書館　鄒新明
2012年11月22日

參考文獻：

1. 樓宇烈：胡適讀禪籍題記、眉批選，收入《胡適研究叢刊》第一輯，北京大學出版社，1995年。
2. 沈乃文：關於《岳飛傳》與胡適藏書——没有實現鄧先生心願的兩件事，收入《仰止集——紀念鄧廣銘先生》，河北教育出版社，1999年。
3. 陳以愛：中國國家圖書館善本特藏部收藏的胡適藏書，未刊稿。
4. 陳以愛：2006中國國家圖書館所見胡適藏書題跋，未刊稿。
5. 陳以愛：北大圖書館移交胡適藏書的曲折，未刊稿。
6. 陳以愛：兩岸胡適藏書與胡適研究前景，未刊稿。
7. 北京圖書館1964年選留胡適藏書清單，北京大學檔案·圖書館檔案，編號：94010。